Jörg Desel   Manuel Silva (Eds.)

Application and Theory of Petri Nets 1998

19th International Conference, ICATPN'98
Lisbon, Portugal, June 22-26, 1998
Proceedings

Springer

Series Editors

Gerhard Goos, Karlsruhe University, Germany
Juris Hartmanis, Cornell University, NY, USA
Jan van Leeuwen, Utrecht University, The Netherlands

Volume Editors

Jörg Desel
Institut AIFB, University of Karlsruhe
D-76128 Karlsruhe, Germany
E-mail: desel@aifb.uni-karlsruhe.de

Manuel Silva
Departamento de Informatica e Ingenieria de Sistemas
Centro Politecnico Superior, Universidad de Zaragoza
c/ Maria de Luna,3, E-50015 Zaragoza, Spain
E-mail: silva@posta.unizar.es

Cataloging-in-Publication data applied for

Die Deutsche Bibliothek - CIP-Einheitsaufnahme

Application and theory of Petri nets 1998 : 19th international conference ;
proceedings / ICATPN '98, Lisbon, Portugal, June 22 - 26, 1998. Jörg Desel ;
Manuel Silva (ed.). - Berlin ; Heidelberg ; New York ; Barcelona ; Budapest ;
Hong Kong ; London ; Milan ; Paris ; Santa Clara ; Singapore ; Tokyo :
Springer, 1998
  (Lecture notes in computer science ; Vol. 1420)
  ISBN 3-540-64677-9

CR Subject Classification (1991): F.1-3, C.1-2, G.2.2, D.4, J.4

ISSN 0302-9743
ISBN 3-540-64677-9 Springer-Verlag Berlin Heidelberg New York

© Springer-Verlag Berlin Heidelberg 1998
Printed in Germany

Typesetting: Camera-ready by author
SPIN 10637435   06/3142 – 5 4 3 2 1 0   Printed on acid-free paper

QA 66.5 LEC1
1420

Lecture Notes in Computer Science

Edited by G. Goos, J. Hartmanis and J. van Leeuwen

DATE DUE FOR RETURN

Springer

Berlin
Heidelberg
New York
Barcelona
Budapest
Hong Kong
London
Milan
Paris
Singapore
Tokyo

Preface

This volume contains the proceedings of the 19th annual International Conference on Application and Theory of Petri Nets. The aim of the Petri net conference is to create a forum for the dissemination of the latest results in the application and theory of Petri nets. It always takes place in the last week of June. Typically there are 150 - 200 participants. About one third of these come from industry while the rest are from universities and research institutions.

The conferences and a number of other activities are coordinated by a steering committee with the following members: G. Balbo (Italy), J. Billington (Australia), G. De Michelis (Italy), C. Girault (France), K. Jensen (Denmark), S. Kumagai (Japan), T. Murata (USA), C.A. Petri (Germany; honorary member), W. Reisig (Germany), G. Roucairol (France), G. Rozenberg (The Netherlands; chairman), M. Silva (Spain).

The 19th conference has been organized for the first time in Portugal, by the Department of Electrical Engineering of the Faculty of Sciences and Technology of the New University of Lisbon, together with the Center for Intelligent Robotics of UNINOVA. It takes place in Lisbon at the same time as EXPO'98, the last world exhibition of the 20th century. Although this exhibition is devoted to the Oceans, this coincidence should not feed the misunderstanding that Petri nets have to do with fishing!

Other activities before and during the conference include: an exhibition and presentation of Petri net tools; introductory tutorials; two advanced tutorials on the state space explosion problem and on Petri nets and production systems; a workshop on net-based concepts, models, techniques, and tools for workflow management; and a workshop on hardware design and Petri nets. The tutorial notes and proceedings of the workshops are not published in these proceedings but copies are available from the organizers.

We received 58 submissions from 18 countries and 17 have been accepted for presentation. Invited lectures are given by A. Arnold (France), G. Chiola (Italy), and R. Valk (Germany). The submitted papers were evaluated by a program committee with the following members: G. Balbo (Italy), D. Buchs (Switzerland), G. Chiola (Italy), D. Ciardo (USA), J. Desel (Germany; co-chair), M. Diaz (France), S. Haddad (France), K. Jensen (Denmark), C. Lakos (Tasmania), M. Koutny (England), S. Kumagai (Japan), G. Nutt (USA), K. Onaga (Japan), W. Penczek (Poland), L. Pomello (Italy), M. Silva (Spain; co-chair), P.S. Thiagarajan (India), W.M.P. van der Aalst (The Netherlands), R. Valk (Germany), and W. Vogler (Germany). The program committee meeting took place at the New University of Lisbon.

We should like to express our gratitude to all authors of submitted papers, to the members of the program committee, and to the referees who assisted them. The names of the referees are listed on the following page. For the local organization of the conference, we greatly appreciate the efforts of all members of the organizing committee: A. Costa, A. Steiger-Garção (co-chair), H. Pinheiro-Pita, J.-P. Barros, J.-P. Pimentão, and Luís Gomes (co-chair). The organizing committee wishes to thank Fundação Calouste Gulbenkian for their sponsoring, which partially supported the publication of these proceedings.

Finally, we should like to acknowledge excellent cooperation with Alfred Hofmann of Springer-Verlag and his colleagues in the preparation of this volume.

April 1998

Jörg Desel
Manuel Silva

List of Referees

K. Ajami
M. Ajmone Marsan
C. Anglano
P. Azéma
C. Balzarotti
S. Barbey
L. Baresi
T. Basten
F. Bause
M. Bernado
L. Bernardinello
E. Best
J. Billington
F. Bobbio
S. Brandt
M. Buffo
N. Busi
J. Campos
L. Capra
S. Christensen
C. Clo
J.M. Colom
J.-P. Courtiat
F. De Cindio
G. De Michelis
A. Diagne
G. Di Marzo
R. Devillers
S. Donatelli
J. Esparza
B. Farwer
G. Ferrari
W. Fraczak
G. Franceschinis
R. Gaeta
H.J. Genrich
P. Godefroid
U. Goltz
R. Gorrieri
A. Griff
N. Guelfi
S. Haar

J.G. Hall
R. Hennicker
K. Hiraishi
J.S. Huang
J.-M. Ilié
R. Janicki
L. Jenner
R.L. Jones
G. Juanole
G. Juhas
N. Kato
K. Keddara
E. Kindler
H. Klaudel
H.C.M. Kleijn
B. Konikowska
L.M. Kristensen
O. Kummer
K. Lautenbach
D.-I. Lee
A. Maggiolo-Schettini
T. Matsumoto
A. Mazurkiewicz
J. McWhirter
A.S. Miner
J. Mirkowski
T. Miyamoto
D. Moldt
D. Montesi
P. Moreaux
K.H. Mortensen
M. Mukund
T. Murata
M. Nakamura
P. Niebert
M. Nielsen
A. Ohta
K. Onogi
A. Pagnoni
E. Paviot-Adet
E. Pelz
C. Péraire

M. Pezzé
G.M. Pinna
D. Poitrenaud
P. Racloz
L. Recalde
H. Reijers
M. Ribaudo
R.-C. Riemann
S. Römer
A. Romanovsky
N. Sabadini
M. Sanders
M. Scarpa
R. Schätzle
K. Schmidt
P. Senac
M. Sereno
C. Simone
E. Smith
L. Somers
M. Srebrny
M.-O. Stehr
T. Suzuki
K. Takahashi
A. Taubin
E. Teruel
R. van de Toorn
N. Uchihira
T. Ushio
J. Vachon
R. Valette
F. Vernadat
I. Vernier
M. Voorhoeve
F. Wallner
R.F.C. Walters
T. Watanabe
W. Weitz
F. Wienberg
J. Winkowski
J. van der Woude
A. Yakovlev

Table of Contents

Petri Nets as Token Objects
An Introduction to Elementary Object Nets

Rüdiger Valk

Universität Hamburg, Fachbereich Informatik
`valk@informatik.uni-hamburg.de`

Abstract. The model of *Elementary Object System* is introduced and motivated by several examples and applications. Object systems support a modeling of systems by Petri nets following the paradigm of Object-Oriented Modeling. They are composed of a *System Net* and one or more *Object Nets* which can be seen as token objects of the system net. By this approach an interesting and challenging two-level system modeling technique is introduced. Similar to the object-oriented approach, complex systems are modeled close to their real appearance in a natural way to promote clear and reliable concepts. Applications in fields like workflow, flexible manufacturing or agent-oriented approaches (mobile agents and/or intelligent agents as in AI research) are feasible. This paper gives an introduction with several examples, but only few definitions and no theorems, which can be found, however, in a more elaborated paper [19].

1 Introduction

1.1 Background

Object-oriented modeling means that software is designed as the interaction of discrete objects, incorporating both data structure and behavior [11]. The notion of *object-oriented modeling* may be understood in (at least) three, somehow different, ways:

- as a *programming style* which is strongly influenced by features and structures of object-oriented programming languages
- as a *modeling concept* leading to system structures that can be easily implemented by object-oriented programming languages
- as a *general modeling principle* producing system models that can be implemented in any language but are in the spirit of the object-oriented paradigm.

This paper intends to contribute to the foundations of object-oriented modeling, in particular with respect to the third of these items within the framework of basic Petri net models. Comparing statements with the goals and advantages of object-oriented modeling on the one hand and Petri net modeling on the other, similar and sometimes identical assertions are found:

- software development by abstraction of objects

- building a language independent design
- better understanding of requirements
- clearer design
- more maintainable systems.

Objects in an object-oriented environment have a dynamical (external) behavior with respect to the basis system and an (internal) behavior, as they change their internal state when interacting with other objects or when being subject of system transactions.

Hence, from a Petri net point of view objects are nets which are token objects in a general system Petri net. We therefore distinguish *Object Nets* from *System Nets*. This paper gives an introduction to some very elementary properties of *Object Systems* composed of a system net and one or more object nets. To keep the model as close as possible to traditional Petri net theory we assume that both system net and object nets are instances of Elementary Net Systems. Therefore this model is called *Elementary Object System (EOS)*. We are not, however, concerned with high level properties of object-oriented modeling and languages, like dynamic instantiation, dynamic binding, inheritance and ploymorphism.

This is in contrast to other approaches within the framework of high level Petri nets ([2], [6], [7], [12]), which introduce object oriented concepts into the Petri net formalism. Our approach has its origins in a work describing the execution of task systems in systems of functional units ([4], [14]). In [16] the formalism is extended in such a way that the objects are allowed to be general EN systems not necessarily restricted to (non-cyclic) causal nets. Further results can be found in [17], [18]. Most results mentioned in this paper are formally elaborated in [19], however, some additional examples are added here.

In the following section we give some examples that will later be used to illustrate the formalism of Elementary Object Systems.

1.2   Examples

Example 1. In the first example task execution by a set of machines is modeled: an object in a production line has to be processed, first by some machine M_1 and then afterwards by machines M_2 or M_3. As it is very natural in the context of manufacturing systems, the process is then reproduced. Besides the machines, operators for the machines are a second type of limited resources: operator O_1 can be working on M_1 or M_2, but not on both at the same time. The same holds for O_2 with respect to M_1 and M_3.

Figure 1 describes this configuration in an intuitive way. Also two of many possible task systems are given. Task system A is composed of four subtasks a_1, a_2, a_3 and a_4 to be sequentially executed on machines M_1, M_2, M_1 and M_3, respectively.

We take an "object-oriented" approach in the sense that the task system is to be modeled as an object that enters machine M_1 and leaves it after execution to be transferred to machine M_2. Attached with the object there is an "execution

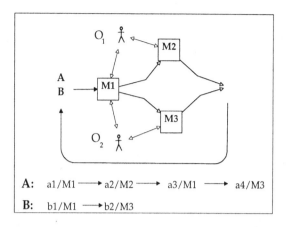

Fig. 1. The example of three machines

plan" specifying the machines to be used and the order for doing so. Also the current "status" of the execution is noted in the execution plan.

Figure 2 gives a Petri net for the machine configuration, which has been used earlier in [8], [9] and [4]. Note that the execution of M_1 is modeled by transitions t_1, t_2 and t_3, t_4 if M_1 is worked by operator O_1 and O_2, respectively. Inscriptions in sharp brackets $<, >$ should be ignored for the moment.

The net is an Elementary Net System (Condition/Event System), with the exception of the objects A and B in place p_1. These are the task systems, as specified in Figure 1. They are represented as Elementary Net System A and B in Figure 3. In the formalism of object nets to be presented here, these nets A and B are considered as token objects. When the subtask a_1 is executed by machine M_1 in a follower marking, net A should be removed from p_1 and appear in the form of A' in place p_6. Hence, both of the following actions are modeled: the task is moved together with its task description *and* the "status" of execution is updated.

Example 2. In the second example we refer to [3], a paper showing a modeling technique for the control of flexible manufacturing systems (*FMS's*) using Petri nets.

In the central example of this paper the manufacturing cell of Figure 4 is studied: "The cell is composed of four machines, *M1*, *M2*, *M3*, and *M4* (each can process two products at a time) and three robots *R1*, *R2*, and *R3* (each one can hold a product at a time). There are three loading buffers (named *I1*, *I2*, *I3*) and three unloading buffers (named *O1*, *O2*, *O3*) for loading and unloading the cell. The action area for robot *R1* is *I1*, *O3*, *M1*, *M3*, for robot *R2* is *I2*, *O2*, *M1*, *M2*, *M3*, *M4* and for robot *R3* is *M2*, *M4*, *I3*, *O1*."

A corresponding P/T-net is shown in Figure 5. When robot *R1* is working, the place *pi_R1* is marked. The capacity restriction for this place is denoted by */1*. This can be seen as a shorthand for an explicit modeling using a complementary place (as done in [3]). The same notation holds for places *pi_R2* and

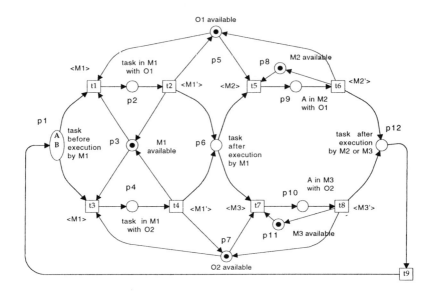

Fig. 2. The three machines' net

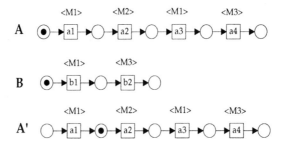

Fig. 3. Task system nets A (A') and B

pi_R3. A transport action from the input buffer *I1* to robot *R1* is denoted by
$< I1 \rightarrow R1 >$ etc. The capacity of *2* for the machines is explicitly modeled by
complementary places. With these explanations the semantics of the net should
be clear; for more details, please refer to [3].

Of particular importance in our context is the observation that usually, in a
FMS, different types of parts must be processed.

We cite from [3]:

> The type of part defines which operations must be made on the raw
> material to get a final product. The type of part is defined by means of
> its *process plan*. For a given architecture, each process plan is defined by
> three components (G, I, O), where
>
> 1. G is a (connected) acyclic graph with dummy root: the *operation
>   graph*. Each path from the root to a leaf represents a possible se-
>   quence of operations to be performed on the part. The dummy node
>   represents the raw state of a part. A node n of this graph $(n \neq root)$
>   will be labeled with pairs (n_r, n_0). n_0 stands for the operation to be
>   made on a part of this type, while n_r represents a resource where
>   the operation must be done.
> 2. I refers to the sites from which the parts of the corresponding type
>   can be introduced into the system.
> 3. O refers to the sites from which the parts of the corresponding type
>   can be unloaded from the system.

Figure 6 represents (in the upper part) three such process plans and
the operation graph $G1$ of $W1$. The type of product characterizes the
process to be made in the cell as follows: 1) a raw product of type $W1$
is taken from $I1$ and, once it has been manufactured, it is moved to $O1$.

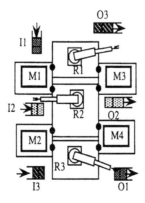

Fig. 4. A flexible manufacturing cell

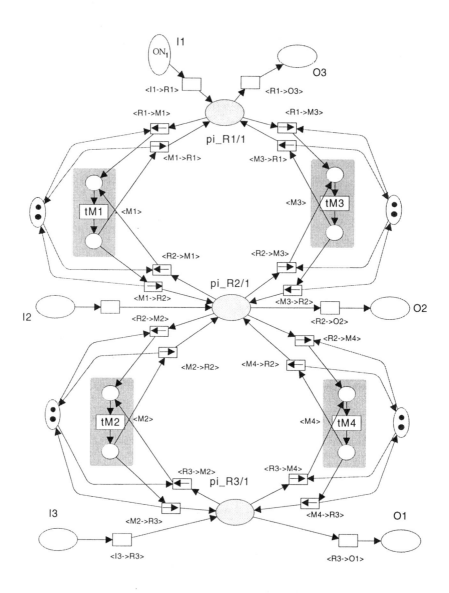

Fig. 5. System net for the FMS cell

In the lower part of Figure 6 an EN system is given, which essentially contains the the same information as $W1$ (by omitting the operations). After the definition of elementary object systems we will use this net as an object net for the example.

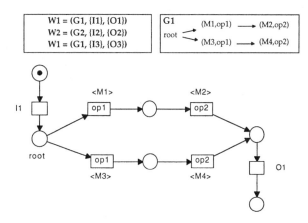

Fig. 6. Task system for the FMS

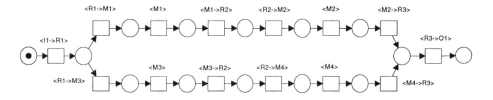

Fig. 7. Refined task system for the FMS

Example 3. In the third example a workflow of the Dutch Justice Department is modeled. It has been used for demonstration of modeling and analysis of workflow applications using Petri nets [1].

The example is introduced in [1] as follows. When a criminal offense has happened and the police has a suspect, a record is made by an official. This is printed and sent to the secretary of the Justice Department. Extra information about the history of the suspect and some data from the local government are supplied and completed by a second official. Meanwhile the information on the official record is verified by a secretary. When these activities are completed, an official examines the case and a prosecutor determines whether the suspect is summoned, charged or that the case is suspended.

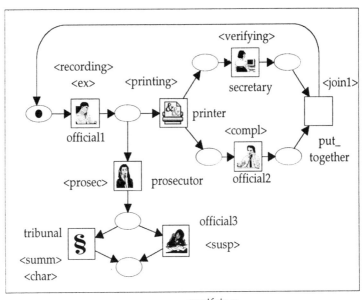

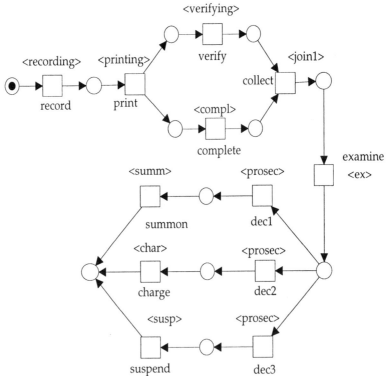

Fig. 8. The work flow example

Originally the case was modeled by a single and "flat" net for the workflow. A slightly modified version is given in the lower part of Figure 8. Observe that verification and completion are concurrent subtasks. The labels in sharp brackets refer to the corresponding functional units (top of Figure 8) executing these subtasks. For instance, "printing" is executed by a printer and "verifying" is executed by the secretary. *Official1* can execute two subtasks ("record" and "examine") for this object net. As there are three possible outcomes of the decision of the prosecutor that are followed by different actions, the decision is modeled by three transitions *dec1*, *dec2* and *dec3*.

Though being more complex than ordinary workflows (where system nets are not considered), the advantage of this kind of modeling lies in the direct representation of functional units. The system net reflects the organizational structure of the system while the object net represents a particular workflow. Obviously there may be different workflows (object nets) for the same system of functional units (system net). The simultaneous simulation of such different executions can be used to determine bottlenecks and execution times.

1.3 Overview

In section 2 *Unary Elementary Object Systems* are introduced. Possible system/object interactions are represented by a relation ρ. The model allows for only one object net which may exist, however, in multiple copies. These copies model a behavior of concurrent execution in a distributed system. The notion of *bi-marking* is shown to be adequate only in special cases. To model a behavior including "fork-" and "join-"control structures, the more general notion of *process-marking* is introduced, which is based on the notion of Petri net processes. The corresponding occurrence rule is discussed and the examples, given in section 1.2, are related to the formal definitions. In section 3.1 elementary object systems are introduced in order to model systems with different object nets. Communication between objects is described in the same way as system/object interaction. For formal reasons a different object/object interaction relation σ is introduced. An EOS is called *separated* if the corresponding graphs of ρ and σ are disjoint. To simplify the formalism the occurrence rule is introduced for *simple* EOS only. By this multiple copies of the same object system are avoided. Using a type classification scheme, a subsystem with respect to a particular object net ON_i (the i-*component*) is defined. A special component (the 0-*component*) is reserved for the object class of indistinguishable tokens. As usual, such tokens are used for synchronization and modeling of resources. For illustration of the model a distributed and object-oriented version of the *five philosophers model* is given.

2 Object Systems

2.1 Unary EOS and Bi-Markings

In this section *Unary Elementary Object Systems* are introduced, consisting of a *system net SN* and an *object net ON*, both being elementary net systems.

10

These are used in their standard form as given in [13]. An *Elementary Net System (EN system)* $N = (B, E, F, C)$ is defined by a finite set of *places* (or conditions) B, a finite set of *transitions* (or events) E, disjoint from B, a flow relation $F \subseteq (B \times E) \cup (E \times B)$ and an *initial marking* (or initial case) $C \subseteq B$. The occurrence relation for markings C_1, C_2 and a transition t is written as $C_1 \to_t C_2$. If t is enabled in C_1 we write $C_1 \to_t$. These notions are extended to words $w \in E^*$, as usual, and written as $C_1 \to_w C_2$. N is called a *structural state machine* if each transition $t \in T$ has exactly one input place ($|{}^\bullet t| = 1$) and exactly one output place ($|t^\bullet| = 1$). N is said to be a *state machine* if it is a structural state machine and C contains exactly one token ($|C| = 1$). $FS(N) := \{w \in E^* | C \to_w\}$ is the set of *firing* or *occurrence sequences* of N, and $R(N) := \{C_1 | \exists w : C \to_w C_1\}$ is the set of reachable markings (or cases), also called the *reachability set* of N (cf. [10]). We will also use *processes* of EN systems in their standard definition [10].

Definition 4. *A* unary elementary object system *is a tuple EOS* $=$ (SN, ON, ρ) *where*

- $SN = (P, T, W, \mathbf{M}_0)$ *is an EN system with* $|\mathbf{M}_0| = 1$, *called* system net *of EOS,*
- $ON = (B, E, F, \mathbf{m}_0)$ *is an EN system, called* object net *of EOS, and*
- $\rho \subseteq T \times E$ *is the* interaction relation.

An elementary object system is called simple *if its system net SN is a state machine.*

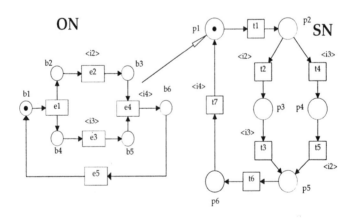

Fig. 9. Elementary object system "ser-task"

Figure 9 gives an example of an elementary object system with the components of an object net ON on the left and a system net SN on the right. The interaction relation ρ is given by labels $< i_n >$ at t and e iff $t\rho e$ ("i_n" stands for interaction number n, which has no other meaning apart from specifying interacting transitions).

Before proceeding to the formalization we describe the intuition behind the occurrence rule to be defined later. The object net ON of Figure 9 should be thought of lying in place p_1 of the system net SN. It is represented by a token in that place. Since there is no label at transition t_1 the object net ON is moved to p_2 by the occurrence of transition t_1. Since it does not change its marking such an occurrence is called a *transport*. In a dual sense also transition e_1 of ON can occur without interacting with the system net. Therefore such an occurrence is called *autonomous*. Now, both nets ON and SN have reached a marking where e_2 and t_2 are activated (as well as e_3 and t_4), when considered as separated EN systems. Since they bear the same label ($< i_2 >$ in this case) they must occur simultaneously in the object system.

In the definitions of the occurrence rule we will use the following well-known notions for a binary relation ρ. For $t \in T$ and $e \in E$ let $t\rho := \{e \in E | (t, e) \in \rho\}$ and $\rho e := \{t \in T | (t, e) \in \rho\}$. Then $t\rho = \emptyset$ means that there is no element in the interaction relation with t.

Definition 5. *A* bi-marking *of an unary elementary object system $EOS = (SN, ON, \rho)$ is a pair $(\mathbf{M}, \mathbf{m})$ where $\mathbf{M}$ is a marking of the system net SN and $\mathbf{m}$ is a marking of the object net ON.*

a) *A transition $t \in T$ is* activated *in a bi-marking $(\mathbf{M}, \mathbf{m})$ of EOS if $t\rho = \emptyset$ and t is activated in $\mathbf{M}$. Then the follower bi-marking $(\mathbf{M}', \mathbf{m}')$ is defined by $\mathbf{M} \rightarrow_t \mathbf{M}'$ (w.r.t. SN) and $\mathbf{m} = \mathbf{m}'$. We write $(\mathbf{M}, \mathbf{m}) \rightarrow_{[t,\lambda]} (\mathbf{M}', \mathbf{m}')$ in this case.*

b) *A pair $[t, e] \in T \times E$ is* activated *in a bi-marking $(\mathbf{M}, \mathbf{m})$ of EOS if $(t, e) \in \rho$ and t and e are activated in $\mathbf{M}$ and $\mathbf{m}$, respectively. Then the follower bi-marking $(\mathbf{M}', \mathbf{m}')$ is defined by $\mathbf{M} \rightarrow_t \mathbf{M}'$ (w.r.t. SN) and $\mathbf{m} \rightarrow_e \mathbf{m}'$ (w.r.t. ON). We write $(\mathbf{M}, \mathbf{m}) \rightarrow_{[t,e]} (\mathbf{M}', \mathbf{m}')$ in this case.*

c) *A transition $e \in E$ is* activated *in a bi-marking $(\mathbf{M}, \mathbf{m})$ of a EOS if $\rho e = \emptyset$ and e is activated in $\mathbf{m}$. Then the follower bi-marking $(\mathbf{M}', \mathbf{m}')$ is defined by $\mathbf{m} \rightarrow_e \mathbf{m}'$ (w.r.t. ON) and $\mathbf{M}' = \mathbf{M}$. We write $(\mathbf{M}, \mathbf{m}) \rightarrow_{[\lambda,e]} (\mathbf{M}', \mathbf{m}')$ in this case.*

In transition occurrences of type b) both the system and the object participate in the same event. Such an occurrence will be called an *interaction*. By an occurrence of type c), however, the object net changes its state without moving to another place of the system net. It is therefore called *object-autonomous* or *autonomous* for short. The symmetric case in a) is called *system-autonomous* or *transport*, since the object net is transported to a different place without performing an action.

By extending this notion to occurrence sequences for the EOS of Figure 9, for example, we obtain the following sequence:

$$[\lambda, e_1], [t_1, \lambda], [t_4, e_3], [t_5, e_2], [t_6, \lambda], [t_7, e_4], [\lambda, e_5].$$

After this sequence, the initial bi-marking is reached again. We call this the *occurrence sequence semantics*. It is possible to characterize the set of all such occurrence sequences of simple EOS by some kind of intersection of the individual occurrence sequences of SN and ON. As simple object systems appear quite frequently in applications, this definition of a bi-marking and transition occurrence semantics is useful. However, the question must be asked whether it is also adequate for general EOS.

The unary EOS "con-task" of Figure 10 has the same object net as "ser-task" of Figure 9 (with the exception of the new label $< i_1 >$), but a different system net. By transition t_1 the object net is duplicated. After this event task execution is concurrently performed on two instances of the same object net. A possible occurrence sequence is:

$$[t_1, e_1], [t_3, e_3], [t_2, e_2], [t_7, e_4], [\lambda, e_5], [t_8, \lambda].$$

The bi-marking reached after the first three steps is $(\{p_3, p_5\}, \{b_3, b_5\})$, which activates the pair of transitions $[t_7, e_4]$.

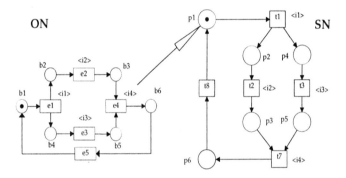

Fig. 10. Elementary object system "con-task"

2.2 Counter Examples

The given occurrence sequence of the EOS "con-task" correctly reflects the intended behavior: subtasks e_2 and e_3 are concurrently executed and the "outcome" of these executions is collected by the "join"-transition t_7. Using bi-markings and the corresponding occurrence sequence semantics may however result in a counter-intuitive behavior. For the EOS "counter1" in Figure 11 the occurrence sequence

$$[t_1, e_1], [t_3, e_3], [t_2, e_6]$$

leads to the bi-marking $(\{p_3, p_5\}, \{b_5, b_6\})$, which activates $[t_7, e_7]$. This somehow "strange" behavior is also due to the fact that not a really distributed

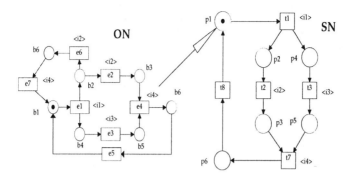

Fig. 11. Elementary object system "counter1"

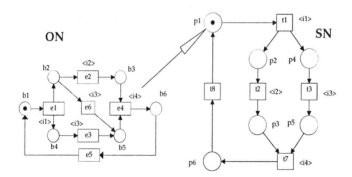

Fig. 12. Elementary object system "counter2"

system is generated. Although transition t_1 should create two independent instances of ON only one instance is referenced. A different choice would be to associate to each instance of ON an individual "local" marking. For the EOS "con-task" the marking activating the pair of transitions $[t_7, e_4]$ would have the form: $((ON, \{b_3, b_4\}); (ON', \{b_2, b_5\}))$, where ON and ON' are copies lying in the places p_3 and p_5. We will refer to markings of this form as *object markings*.

But also this choice of a marking definition is not satisfying. In the EOS "counter2" of Figure 12 the marking $((ON, \{b_3, b_4\}); (ON', \{b_4, b_5\}))$ would be reachable by the occurrence sequence

$$[t_1, e_1], [t_2, e_2], [t_3, e_6].$$

It is obvious that in this case an activation of the pair of transitions $[t_7, e_4]$ is not adequate since the instances in the input places of t_7 result from conflicting executions of the same branch of ON. It is therefore not a suitable formalization of a well-formed "fork/join" control structure.

2.3   Process Markings

As introduced and formalized in [18], [19], a solution to the problems addressed in the previous section is possible by using *Process markings (P-markings)* instead of bi-markings. For a unary EOS, where the referenced object net is unique (modulo the current marking), a P-marking associates to every place of the system net a process of the object net. Processes are represented by causal nets in their standard definition for EN systems (see [10], [19]).

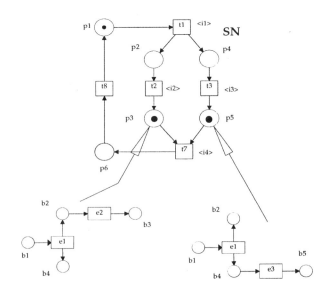

Fig. 13. Elementary object system "con-task" with P-marking

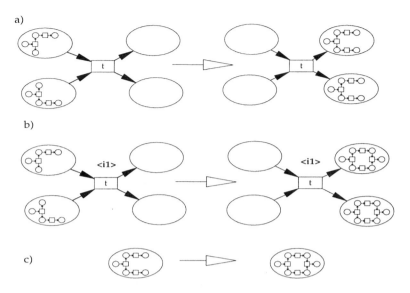

Fig. 14. P-marking occurrence rule

To give an example, in Figure 13 a P-marking for "con-task" is given, corresponding to the marking activating $[t_7, e_4]$, which has been discussed in section 2.2. It shows the (partial) processes of concurrent task execution in the input places of transition t_7. Different to bi-markings, the history of the partial execution is recorded, which allows for a more adequate detection of "fork/join-structures".

Informally the conditions for activation of a transition and the definition of a follower P-marking is described in the following. The cases a), b) and c) are represented graphically in Figure 14. A transition e of an EN system is called *activated* in a process *proc* if the process can be enlarged by this event. The new process is unique and denoted by $proc_e := proc \circ e$. Generally, a process $proc_1$ can be called *smaller* than $proc_2$ if $proc_1$ is an "initial part" of $proc_2$. With respect to this partial ordering on the set of all processes of an EN system, for a subset of such processes a *least upper bound (lub)* may exist. It is constructed by "combining" all the processes in a consistent way.

a) *Transport:* $t \in T$, $t\rho = \emptyset$
   1. Each input place $p_i \in {}^{\bullet}t$ contains a process $proc_i$ of ON.
   2. The set $\{proc_i | p_i \in {}^{\bullet}t\}$ of these processes has a least upper bound $proc_{lub}$.
   3. $[t, \lambda]$ is *activated* if conditions 1. and 2. hold.
   4. The follower P-marking is obtained by removing all processes from the input places of t and by adding the process $proc_{lub}$ to all output places (recall that there are no side conditions in standard EN systems).

b) *Interaction:* $t \in T$, $e \in E$, $(t, e) \in \rho$
   1. Each input place $p_i \in {}^{\bullet}t$ contains a process $proc_i$ of ON.

16

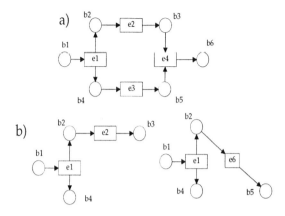

Fig. 15. a) Follower P-marking, b) P-marking for "counter2"

2. The set $\{proc_i|p_i \in {}^\bullet t\}$ of these processes has a least upper bound $proc_{lub}$.
3. e is activated in $proc_{lub}$ i.e. $proc_e := proc_{lub} \circ e$ is defined.
4. $[t, e]$ is *activated* if conditions 1., 2. and 3. hold.
5. The follower P-marking is obtained by removing all processes from the input places of t and by adding the process $proc_e$ to all output places.

c) *Object-autonomous event*: proc in p, $e \in E$, $\rho e = \emptyset$
1. Transition e is activated for $proc$ i.e. $proc_e := proc \circ e$ is defined.
2. $[\lambda, e]$ is *activated* if condition 1. holds.
3. The follower P-marking is obtained by substituting $proc_e$ for $proc$ in the place p.

According to case b) the pair $[t_7, e_4]$ is activated in the P-marking of Figure 13. The follower P-marking is given by the process of Figure 15 a) in the place p_6. A P-marking as in Figure 13 but for the EOS "counter2" is given in Figure 15 b). Now, despite the fact that both input conditions b_3 and b_5 of the ON-transition e_4 are holding, the pair $[t_7, e_4]$ is not activated, since there is no least upper bound for the two processes.

We conclude that bi-markings are sufficient in many cases but not in general. Since they are much simpler to formalize and implement they should be used whenever possible. Notice that P-marking semantics is similar to bi-marking semantics for the example of "counter1", but not for "counter2". The EOS "counter1" was useful to show some counter-intuitive behavior. This is a result of the following property of the EOS "counter1". While the system net transition t_7 requires input from two input places ("input channels of a distributed system") only one of them is effectively used, namely the object system instance from input place p_3. Such a behavior could be excluded by the P-marking semantics by requiring in case b) of the occurrence rule given in this section that process $proc_i$ of each input place p_i contains a precondition of the object net transition $e \in E$ that is indispensable for the activation of e. But this is out of the scope of the present paper. Also for reasons of simplicity, not due to any fundamental problems, in the next chapter we introduce *simple* elementary object systems, where multiple instances of object nets are excluded. The model is extended, however, by allowing more than one *different* object nets that may communicate. Summing up the discussion:

- Bi-markings are references to the marking of a single object net. Different "copies" are nothing but references to the same object. They are preferable due to their simple structure, but have their limit in a distributed environment.
- Object-markings represent copies of objects and not only references. They do not reflect "fork/join"-control structures correctly. This is due to the existence of "superflues" markings in the copies.
- P-markings also represent copies of objects <u>and</u> partially record the past of computations, allowing to merge distributed computations consistently.

There are, however, a lot of formal reasons to prefer P-marking semantics. As shown in [19] a suitable process notion for elementary object systems can be formalized. A theorem is given there, characterizing such a process by a triple $(proc_1, proc_2, \varphi)$, where $proc_1$ and $proc_2$ are processes of the EN systems SN and ON, respectively (in the standard notion of [10]), and φ is a *process morphism* (i.e. a net morphism between causal nets) having particular properties. This theorem strongly relates the theory of object nets to the traditional Petri net theory and therefore proves the compatibility of the concepts.

2.4 Examples

After having introduced unary elementary object systems by formal definitions we take another look at the examples of section 1.2.

Example 1 is modeled by the EN systems in the Figures 2 and 3. If we delete all places containing an indistinguishable token (like p_3) in Figure 2 and replace the letters A and B by a single indistinguishable token, we obtain a system net SN, that - together with the object net A from Figure 3 - represents a unary EOS according to definition 4. The labels in sharp brackets (like $< M1 >$) define the interaction relation ρ. The restricted model does not represent the resources. If these are to be included the EOS is to be interpreted as simple EOS according to definition 8, below. Then the EN systems A and B are interpreted as object nets $ON_1 = A$ and $ON_2 = B$. The object/object interaction relation σ is empty and the arc type function must be defined appropriately (e.g. $type(p_1, t_1) = \{1, 2\}$)

Example 2 has a representation by a simple EOS with the system net SN in Figure 5 and the object net ON_1 in Figure 6. Additional object nets and appropriate arc type functions can easily be added. A closer look, however, shows that the model does not work correctly. This is due to the conflicting granularity of interacting transitions. To solve the problem, all labels different from $< M1 >$, $< M2 >$, $< M3 >$ and $< M4 >$ could be removed from SN. By this deletion the corresponding interacting transitions are transformed into transports. Alternatively, the granularity of the object net could be increased by adding some interacting transitions, as shown in Figure 7. The object net ON plays the role of a process plan as defined in [3] with the additional information on the current state (i.e. the marking of ON).

Example 3 is modeled by the system net SN and the object net ON of Figure 8. It is a unary EOS with concurrent objects where the bi-marking semantics is sufficient. The object net can be seen as a document that can be printed in multiple copies. It contains information how to proceed by the administration and on the current state of this process. Two copies can differ only in the current state (marking).

3   Communicating Objects

3.1   Definitions

In this section unary elementary object systems are extended in such a way that different object nets move through in a system net and interact with both, the system net and with other object nets. As before, the model is kept as simple as possible in order to have a clear formalism.

Definition 6. *An elementary object system is a tuple*
$EOS = (SN, \widehat{ON}, Rho, type, \widehat{M})$ *where*

- $SN = (P, T, W)$ *is a net (i.e. an EN system without initial marking), called* system net *of EOS,*
- $\widehat{ON} = \{ON_1, ..., ON_n\}$ $(n \geq 1)$ *is a finite set of EN systems, called* object systems *of EOS, denoted by* $ON_i = (B_i, E_i, F_i, \mathbf{m}_{0i})$
- $Rho = (\rho, \sigma)$ *is the* interaction relation, *consisting of a system/object inter-action relation* $\rho \subseteq T \times \mathbf{E}$ *where* $\mathbf{E} := \bigcup\{E_i | 1 \leq i \leq n\}$ *and a symmetric object/object interaction relation* $\sigma \subseteq (\mathbf{E} \times \mathbf{E}) \setminus id_E$,
- $type : W \to 2^{\{1,...,n\}} \cup \mathbb{N}$ *is the arc type function, and*
- $\widehat{M}$ *is a marking as defined in definition 7.*

Figure 16 gives a graphical representation of an elementary object system with a system net SN and three object nets ON_i $(1 \leq i \leq 3)$. The value of $type(p_1, t_1) = \{1, 2, 3\}$ is given by a corresponding arc inscription $(1) + (2) + (3)$. Intuitively, an object net ON_i can be moved along an arc (x, y) if $i \in type(x, y)$. Arcs of type $type(x, y) = k \in \mathbb{N}$ are labeled by $k \in \mathbb{N}$. They are used as in the case of P/T-nets. $x \rho y$ holds iff x and y are marked by the same label of the form $< i_1 >$ (e.g. $t_1 \rho e_{1a}$) and $x \sigma y$ is given by a label of the form $[r]$ (e.g. $e_{2a} \sigma e_{2b}$). On the right-hand side the relation $\rho \cup \sigma$ is represented as an undirected digraph. Next, a marking will be defined as an assignment of a subset of the object nets together with a current marking to the places. It is also possible to assign a number k of tokens.

Definition 7. *The set* $\mathbf{Obj} := \{(ON_i, \mathbf{m}_i) | 1 \leq i \leq n, \mathbf{m}_i \in R(ON_i)\}$ *is the set of objects of the EOS. An* object-marking *(O-marking) is a mapping* $\widehat{\mathbf{M}} : P \to 2^{\mathbf{Obj}} \cup \mathbb{N}$ *such that* $\widehat{\mathbf{M}}(p) \cap \mathbf{Obj} \neq \emptyset \Rightarrow \widehat{\mathbf{M}}(p) \cap \mathbb{N} = \emptyset$ *for all* $p \in P$.

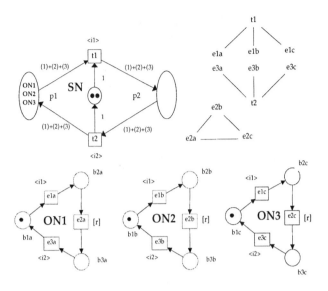

Fig. 16. A simple Elementary object system with 3 objects

A marking of an EOS is a generalization of a bi-marking to more than a single object net. Ordinary tokens easily fit into the concept since they represent a particular object class. The (initial) O-marking of the EOS in Figure 16 is obvious. By restriction to a particular object type from EOS we obtain a unary EOS (i-component, $1 \leq i \leq n$). The 0-component (zero-component) describes the part working like an ordinary P/T-net. This will be used to define simple elementary object systems.

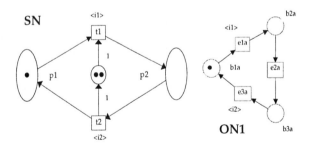

Fig. 17. The 1-component EOS(1) of Figure 16

Definition 8. *Let $EOS = (SN, \widehat{ON}, Rho, type, \widehat{M})$ be an elementary object system as given in definition 6, but in some arbitrary marking $\widehat{M}$.*

- *$Rho = (\rho, \sigma)$ is said to be separated if $i\sigma j \Rightarrow \rho i = \emptyset = \rho j$.*

- *The i-component $(1 \leq i \leq n)$ of EOS is the EN system $SN(i) = (P, T, W(i), \mathbf{M}_{0i})$ defined by $W(i) = \{(x, y) | i \in type(x, y)\}$ and $\mathbf{M}_{0i}(p) = 1$ iff $(ON_i, \mathbf{m}_i) \in \widehat{\mathbf{M}}(p)$. The 0-component (zero-component) is the P/T-net $SN(0) = (P, T, W(0), \mathbf{M}_{00})$ with the arc weight function $W(0)(x, y) = k$ if $type(x, y) = k \in \mathbb{N}$ and $M_{00}(p) = k \in \mathbb{N}$ iff $k \in \widehat{\mathbf{M}}(p)$.*
- *The subnet $SN(1..n) = (P, T, W(1..n), M_{1..n})$, where $W(1..n) = \bigcup\{W(i) \mid 1 \leq i \leq n\}$ and $M_{1..n}(p) = \widehat{\mathbf{M}}(p) \cap \mathbf{Obj}$ is said to be the object-component.*
- *EOS is said to be a simple elementary object system if $SN(1..n)$ is a structural state machine, all i-components of SN are state machines and Rho is separated.*

Remark 9. For each $i \in \{1, ..., n\}$ the i-component $EOS(i) := (SN(i), ON_i, \rho(i))$ is a unary EOS, where $\rho(i) := \rho \cap (T \times E_i)$.

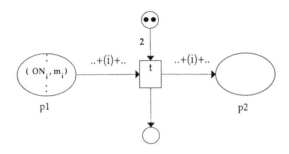

Fig. 18. Occurrence rule for simple EOS

The EOS from Figure 16 is simple since each $SN(i)$ $(1 \leq i \leq 3)$ is a state machine and Rho is separated. The latter property is easily deduced from the depicted graph of $\rho \cup \sigma$. The 1-component is a simple and unary elementary object system (see Figure 17). Dropping the condition that $SN(1..n)$ is a structural state machine would lead to inconsistencies in the definition of the dynamical behavior (definition 10). By the introduction of i-components of EOS we are able to connect the models of unary EOS to general EOS. For instance, the semantical formalization of the behavior of the more complex model of a simple elementary object system can profit from the results obtained earlier in this paper for simple unary elementary object systems. The property of separated interaction relation Rho allows to separate system/object interaction from the new concept of object/object interaction. The latter form of interaction is restricted to the case where the i-components perform autonomous transitions in the same place of the system net. Therefore in the following definition of transition occurrence of simple EOS, system/object interactions are defined using case b) of definition 5 whereas object/object interactions are associated with case c) of this definition.

Definition 10. *Let $EOS = (SN, \widehat{ON}, Rho, type, \widehat{M})$ be an elementary object system as in definition 6 and $\widehat{M} : P \to 2^{\mathbf{Obj}} \cup \mathbb{N}$ an O-marking (definition 7) and $t \in T$, $e_i \in E_i$, $e_j \in E_j$, $i \neq j$*

a) *Transition $t \in T$ is activated in $\widehat{M}$ (denoted $\widehat{M} \to_t$) if $t\rho = \emptyset$ and the following holds:*
   1. *t is activated in the zero-component of SN (definition 8) (i.e. in the P/T-net part)*
   2. *By the state machine property there is at most one type $i \in \{1, \ldots, n\}$ such that $i \in type(p_1, t)$ and $i \in type(t, p_2)$ for some $p_1 \in {}^\bullet t$ and $p_2 \in t^\bullet$. In this case there must be some object $(ON_i, \mathbf{m}_i) \in \widehat{M}(p_1)$.(cf. Figure 18)*

   If t is activated, then t may occur ($\widehat{M} \to_t \widehat{M}'$) and the follower marking $\widehat{M}'$ is defined as follows: with respect to the zero-components tokens are changed according to the ordinary P/T-net occurrence rule. In case of a2) $(ON_i, \mathbf{m}_i)$ is removed from p_1 and added to p_2 (only if $p_1 \neq p_2$).

b) *A pair $[t, e] \in T \times E_i$ with $t\rho e$ is activated in $\widehat{M}$ (denoted $\widehat{M} \to_{[t,e]}$) if in addition to case a) transition e is also activated for ON_i in $\mathbf{m}_i$. Instead of $(ON_i, \mathbf{m}_i)$ the changed object $(ON_i, \mathbf{m}_{i+1})$ where $\mathbf{m}_i \to_e \mathbf{m}_{i+1}$ is added.*

c) *A pair $[e_i, e_j] \in E_i \times E_j$ with $e_i \sigma e_j$ is activated in $\widehat{M}$ (denoted $\widehat{M} \to_{[e_i, e_j]}$) if for some place $p \in P$ two objects $(ON_i, \mathbf{m}_i) \in \widehat{M}(p)$ and $(ON_j, \mathbf{m}_j) \in \widehat{M}(p)$ are in the <u>same</u> place p and $\mathbf{m}_i \to_{e_i} \mathbf{m}_{i+1}$ and $\mathbf{m}_j \to_{e_j} \mathbf{m}_{j+1}$. In the follower marking $\widehat{M}'$ the objects $(ON_i, \mathbf{m}_i)$ and $(ON_j, \mathbf{m}_j)$ in p are replaced by $(ON_i, \mathbf{m}_{i+1})$ and $(ON_j, \mathbf{m}_{j+1})$, respectively.*

d) *A transition $e \in E_i$ with $e\sigma = \sigma e = \emptyset$ is activated in $\widehat{M}$ (denoted $\widehat{M} \to_e$) if for some place $p \in P$ we have $(ON_i, \mathbf{m}_i) \in \widehat{M}(p)$ and $\mathbf{m}_i \to_e \mathbf{m}_{i+1}$. In the follower marking $\widehat{M}'$ the object $(ON_i, \mathbf{m}_i)$ is replaced by $(ON_i, \mathbf{m}_{i+1})$*

3.2   Distributed Philosophers

To apply the definition to a well-known example, we consider the case study of *The hurried Philosophers*. It has been proposed by C. Sibertin-Blanc [12] to test expressive and analytic power of languages merging Petri nets and concepts of the object-oriented approach. We adopt here the distributed character of this extension, but are not concerned with dynamic instantiation, dynamic binding, inheritance and ploymorphism.

Consider the system net SN in Figure 20. There are five object nets $ph_1, \ldots, ph_5$ representing the philosophers. Initially they are in a place "library", but can "go" by interaction $<enter>$ into the dining room. They have their left fork in the hand when entering this room. Two of these object nets, namely ph_i and ph_k are shown in Figures 20 and 19.

In a truly distributed environment the philosophers can only communicate by sending messages. In "his" place p_i philosopher ph_i finds an object net shr_i: *fork*

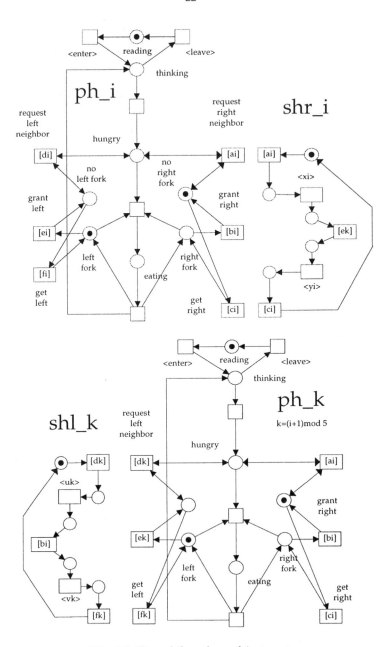

Fig. 19. Five philosophers objects nets

shuttle right, that can be used to send a request to his right neighbor ph_k by the interaction $[a_i]$ (see Figure 19). The shuttle then moves to p_k using interaction $< x_i >$ to take the fork of ph_k using interaction $[e_k]$, provided philosopher ph_k is now at his place and the fork is free. Then it goes back, delivering the fork to ph_i by $[c_i]$. The type of this object net is (s_i) and the corresponding inscriptions are given on the arcs. In a symmetrical way ph_k uses shuttle shl_k (*fork shuttle left*) to obtain the fork back. Note, that by typed arcs a philosopher ph_i can reach his "place" p_i, but none of the others $p_j, (j \neq i)$, at the table.

Many different settings of the distributed philosophers problem could be realized, as well. For instance, a fork shuttle could move around and distribute forks to requesting participants. Also, different approaches for handling forks on leave of the dining room could be realized (e.g.: a philosopher leaves with "his" left fork, as he came in, or he leaves without forks granting the resource to present neighbor.) Such variants of specifications are out of the scope of this paper.

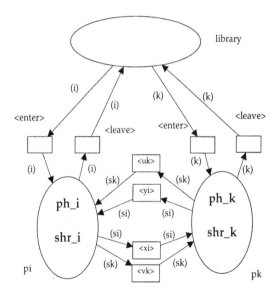

Fig. 20. Five philosophers system net

3.3 Invariants

Since the partners for communication are fixed in this example, by merging communicating transitions, an ordinary net (see [19]) can be constructed, representing the behavior of shuttle exchange. By restriction to only two neighboring philosophers, this net can be seen as a communication protocol for *distributed mutual exclusion*, being similar to the methods of [15] and [5].

It is interesting to compare the different structures of these solutions using P-invariants. While the approach in [15] and [5] reflects a typical *request/grant* scheme, as known in protocol design the object oriented approach presented here contains P-invariants, describing the cyclic behavior of the fork shuttle. By this the difference of *object oriented design* is reflected in the formal structure of of the net graph and the P-invariants. For the proof of properties like mutual exclusion object overlapping P-invariants are need. As a case study has shown, they can be computed from the P-invariants of the individual objects.

4 Conclusion

The increasing importance of the object-oriented modeling paradigm leads to the introduction of object nets. There is, however, a huge number of alternatives for doing so. Up to now no fundamental studies are known as in the case of the basic Petri net model. We introduce such a basic model of object nets using elementary net systems. They are motivated by several examples arising from applications and by the first study of fundamental properties like distributed computations. Unary elementary object nets allow the study of such effects on an elementary level. It is expected that this will give insight to similar properties of high level object nets. Simple elementary object nets include more than one object which may interact. This is illustrated by extending the five philosophers model to a distributed environment.

References

1. W.v.d. Aalst. private communication. 1997.
2. U. Becker and D. Moldt. Object-oriented concepts for coloured petri nets. In *Proc. IEEE Int. Conference on Systems, Man and Cybernetics*, volume 3, pages 279–286, 1993.
3. J. Ezpeleta and J.M. Colom. Automatic synthesis of colored petri nets for the control of fms. *IEEE Transactions on Robotics and Automation*, 13(3):327–337, 1997.
4. E. Jessen and R. Valk. *Rechensysteme – Grundlagen der Modellbildung*. Springer-Verlag, Berlin, 1987.
5. E. Kindler and R. Walter. Message passing mutex. In J. Desel, editor, *Structures in Concurrency Theory*, Berlin, 1995. Springer-Verlag.
6. C.A. Lakos. Object petri nets. Report TR94-3, Computer Science Depart., University of Tasmania, 1994.
7. C.A. Lakos. From coloured petri nets to object petri nets. In M. Diaz G. De Michelis, editor, *Application and Theory of Petri Nets*, number 935 in LNCS, pages 278–297, Berlin, 1995. Springer-Verlag.
8. J.L. Peterson. *Petri Net Theory and the Modeling of Systems*. Prentice Hall, Englewood Cliffs, 1981.
9. W. Reisig. System design using petri nets. *Informatik Fachberichte*, 74:29–41, 1983.

10. G. Rozenberg. Behaviour of elementary net systems. In W. Brauer, W. Reisig, and G. Rozenberg, editors, *Petri Nets: Central Models and their Properties*, number 254 in LNCS, pages 60–94. Springer-Verlag, Berlin, 1987.
11. J. Rumbaugh et al. *Object-Oriented Modeling and Design*. Prentice-Hall, London, 1991.
12. C. Sibertin-Blanc. Cooperative nets. In R. Valette, editor, *Application and Theory of Petri Nets*, number 815 in LNCS, pages 471–490, Berlin, 1994. Springer-Verlag.
13. P.S. Thiagarajan. Elementary net system. In W. Brauer, W. Reisig, and G. Rozeberg, editors, *Petri Nets: Central Models and their Properties*, number 254 in LNCS, pages 26–59. Springer-Verlag, Berlin, 1987.
14. R. Valk. Nets in computer organisation. In W. Brauer, W. Reisig, and G. Rozeberg, editors, *Petri Nets: Central Models and their Properties*, volume 255, pages 218–233. Springer-Verlag, Berlin, 1987.
15. R. Valk. On theory and practice: an exercise in fairness. *Petri Net Newsletter*, 26:4–11, 1987.
16. R. Valk. Modelling concurrency by task/flow EN systems. In *3rd Workshop on Concurrency and Compositionality*, number 191 in GMD-Studien, St. Augustin, Bonn, 1991. Gesellschaft für Mathematik und Datenverarbeitung.
17. R. Valk. Petri nets as dynamical objects. In *Workshop Proc. 16th International Conf. on Application and Theory of Petri Nets, Torino, Italy*, June 1995.
18. R. Valk. On processes of object petri nets. Bericht 185/96, Fachbereich Informatik, Universität Hamburg, 1996.
19. R. Valk. Concurrency in communicating object petri nets. In F. DeCindio G.A. Agha, editor, *to appear in: Advances in Petri Nets*, LNCS. Springer-Verlag, Berlin, 1998.

Synchronized Products of Transition Systems and Their Analysis

André Arnold

LaBRI, Université Bordeaux I and CNRS (UMR 5800)

Petri Nets and the synchronized products of transition systems introduced by Arnold and Nivat are two closely related models of concurrent systems. The second one is used to model finite state systems whose analysis is made on a "behavioural" basis : evaluation of state properties expressed in some temporal logic on the state graph of the system. On the other hand, Petri Nets model infinite state systems, and their analysis is often made on a "structural" basis. But, as soon as the number of states of a finite-state system is so large that it cannot be encoded in the memory of the machine, it is indeed infinite. A way of dealing with such a situation could be to proceed to structural analysis, borrowing concepts from Petri Nets Theory.

Synchronized products of transition systems This model is described in [1]. Several examples are described in this model, and verified with the tool MEC in [2]. We briefly recall the basic definitions.

A *transition system* over a set A of actions is a tuple $A = \langle S, T, \alpha, \beta, \lambda \rangle$ where

- S is a set of *states*,
- T is a set of *transitions*,
- $\alpha, \beta : T \to S$ denote respectively the *source state* and the *target state* of a transition,
- $\lambda : T \to A$ denotes the action responsible for a transition,
- the mapping $\langle \alpha, \lambda, \beta \rangle : T \to S \times A \times S$ is one-to-one so that T is a subset of $S \times A \times S$.

Given n sets of action $A_1, ..., A_n$, a *synchronisation constraint* is a subset I of $A_1 \times ... \times A_n$. If, for $i = 1, ..., n$, $\mathcal{A}_i = \langle S_i, T_i, \alpha_i, \beta_i, \lambda_i \rangle$ is a transition system over A_i, and if $I \subseteq A_i \times ... \times A_n$ is a synchronization constraint, the synchronized product of the $\mathcal{A}_i$'s w.r.t. I is the transition system $\langle S, T, \alpha, \beta, \lambda \rangle$ over the set I defined by

- $S = S_1 \times \cdots \times S_n$,
- $T = \{ \langle t_1, \ldots, t_n \rangle \in T_1 \times \ldots \times T_n \mid \langle \lambda_1(t_1), \ldots, \lambda_n(t_n) \rangle \in I \}$,
- $\alpha(\langle t_1, \ldots, t_n \rangle) = \langle \alpha_i(t_i), \ldots, \alpha_n(t_n) \rangle$,
- $\beta(\langle t_1, \ldots, t_n \rangle) = \langle \beta_1(t_1), \ldots, \beta_n(t_n) \rangle$,
- $\lambda(\langle t_1, \ldots, t_n \rangle) = \langle \lambda_1(t_1), \ldots, \lambda_n(t_n) \rangle$.

Intuitively, when the n systems $\mathcal{A}_i$ are running concurrently, the synchronisation constraint I forces some actions to be performed simultaneously, and many concurrent systems can be defined that way (see [1]).

Petri nets In the previous definition, nothing prevents the $\mathcal{A}_i$ to be infinite, but then their synchronized product could be infinite and not easily constructible. In particular, each $\mathcal{A}_i$ could be the infinite transition system $\mathcal{C}$ over $\{inc, dec, nop\}$ defined by $S = \mathbb{N}, T = \{\langle i, inc, i+1\rangle \mid i \geq 0\} \cup \{\langle i+1, dec, i\rangle \mid i \geq 0\} \cup \{\langle i, nop, i\rangle \mid i \geq 0\}$. Let I be a subset of $\{inc, dec, nop\}^n$. This is nothing but a pure Petri Net with n places and with I as set of transitions. The preset of $\langle a_1, \ldots, a_n\rangle \in I$ is the set $\{i \mid a_i = dec\}$ and its postset is $\{i \mid a_i = inc\}$. It is easy to see that the synchronized product of n $\mathcal{C}$'s w.r.t. I is the marking graph of this Petri net. To get non pure Petri Nets, we have just to consider $\mathcal{C}'$ on the set $\{inc, dec, pos, nop\}$ that is obtained by adding to $\mathcal{C}$ the set of transitions $\{\langle i, pos, i\rangle \mid i > 0\}$.

Traps and deadlocks They are good examples of structural concepts for Petri Net that can be easily extended to synchronized products. Let $\mathcal{A}_1, \ldots, \mathcal{A}_n$ and I that define a synchronized product. A *trap* is a n-uple $\langle Q_1, \ldots, Q_n\rangle$, with $Q_i \subseteq S_i$ such that for any $\langle a_1, \ldots, a_n\rangle$ in I if there is an i and a transition $\langle s, a_i, s'\rangle \in T_i$ such that $s \in Q_i$ and $s' \notin Q_i$, there is a j such that for any $\langle s, a_j, s'\rangle \in T_j, s' \in Q_j$. For instance, if H is a trap in a Petri Net, (seen as a synchronized product of $\mathcal{C}$'s) we take $Q_i = \{n > 0\}$ if i is in H, $\emptyset$ otherwise. Our definition of a trap becomes: for any transition t of the Petri net and for any i in H there is a $j \in H$ such that $i \in pre(t) \Rightarrow j \in post(t)$. The "behavioural" property of the synchronized product associated with a trap is: let Q be the set $\bigcup_{i=1}^{n} S_1 \times \cdots \times S_{i-1} \times Q_i \times S_{i+1} \times \cdots \times S_n$. For every transition t of this product, $\alpha(t) \Rightarrow \beta(t) \in Q$.

The definition of a *deadlock* is quite symmetrical: it is a n-uple $\langle Q_1 \ldots, Q_n\rangle$ such that for any $\langle a_1, \ldots, a_n\rangle$ in I, if there exists $\langle s, a_i, s'\rangle \in T_i$ such that $s \notin Q_i$ and $s' \in Q_i$, then there is a j such that for any $\langle s, a_j, s'\rangle \in T_j, s \in Q_j$. The associated behavioural property is $\forall t, \alpha(t) \notin Q \Rightarrow \beta(t) \notin Q$.

Acknowledgements Thanks to P. Darondeau for discussions on the relationship between Petri Nets and synchronized products, to J.-M. Couvreur and J.-M. Colom for discussions on structural invariants for synchronized products.

References

1. A. Arnold. *Finite transition systems. Semantics of communicating sytems.* Prentice-Hall, 1994.
2. A. Arnold, D. Bégay, P. Crubillé. *Construction and analysis of transition systems with MEC.* World Scientific Pub., 1994.

Manual and Automatic Exploitation of Symmetries in SPN Models

Giovanni Chiola

DISI, Università di Genova,
via Dodecaneso 35, 16146 Genova, Italy
e-mail: chiola@disi.unige.it,
http://www.disi.unige.it/person/ChiolaG/

Abstract. The exploitation of symmetries for the reachability analysis of SPNs was recognized as a necessary step to handle reasonably complex models right from the beginning. Initially this step was performed manually by the modeler, and required a great deal of experience and ingenuity. Subsequently, the research has focused on techniques to automate such symmetries exploitation to simplify the modeler's task and still allow the solution of reasonably complex models. We recall some of the steps of this evolution, that has now simplified the definition of efficiently solvable models. We also attempt to devise some future perspectives to work on.

1 The beginning of GSPNs

The so called Generalized Stochastic Petri Nets (GSPNs) were introduced in the early eighties, the original motivation being the study of multiprocessor computer architectures [3, 2, 5]. The main hope driving this approach was to be able to exploit both the intuitive graphic representation of GSPNs and their simple and rigorous semantics in terms of state transitions so as to allow even unexperienced people to easily define and study accurate performance models of large and complex distributed systems.

Right from the beginning it became clear, however, that due to the size of the reachability graph it would not have been easy to develop models of interesting systems that could be ameanable to numerical Markovian analysis. The practical limitations of the technique could be expressed by the following dicothomy. On the one hand Petri net models were very well suited for the easy development of models of complex distributed systems. On the other hand, such easily contructed models yielded huge state spaces that could not even be generated for system models of reasonable size.

In practice it was usually possible to derive more "compact" (or abstract, or reduced) models that yielded state spaces much more manageable than the original "intuitive" models [2, 5], but the definition of such reduced models in some cases was absolutely non trivial [4]. The underlying idea for the definition of a compact GSPN model was that of reducing the amount of information encoded in the marking of a GSPN model to the bare minimum required to correctly define the transition from a state to the next one. While the concept is very simple, its correct application to a given practical case requires experience, care, and ingenuity by the modeler.

2 Markovian lumping and state space reduction

A formal argument that supports the correctness of the approach to the development of compact models is Markovian lumping [16]. Given a continuous-time Markov chain defined by the pair (S, Q), where S is the set of states and $Q : S \times S \to I\!R^+$ is the infinitesimal generator, and given a partition $\Pi : I\!N \to 2^S$ that identify subsets of states, the partition satisfies the lumpability condition if and only if:

$\forall i, j \in I\!N \ : \ i \neq j, \forall s, s' \in \Pi(i)$

$$\sum_{r \in \Pi(j)} Q(s, r) \ = \ \sum_{r \in \Pi(j)} Q(s', r)$$

If a given partition defined on the state space of a Markov chain satisfies the lumpability condition, then the partition itself defines another Markov chain (S', Q') (the so called lumped Markov chain) such that $S' = \{ i \in I\!N \ : \ \Pi(i) \neq \emptyset \}$, Q' $\forall i, j \in S'$, $\forall s \in \Pi(i)$, $Q'(i, j) = \sum_{r \in \Pi(j)} Q(s, r)$. The lumped Markov chain (that is characterized by fewer states than the original one) is equivalent to the original Markov chain from the point of view of steady-state probability distribution. Indeed, if we indicate with $Pr_{(S,Q)}\{s\}$ the steady-state probability of a generic state s of a Markov chain (S, Q), the following equality holds: $\forall i \in S'$,

$$Pr_{(S', Q')}\{ i \} \ = \ \sum_{s \in \Pi(i)} Pr_{(S,Q)}\{ s \}$$

In principle, Markovian lumping could be exploited in the following straightforward way:

1. define a Markov chain model of the system to be studied in steady-state;
2. look for a partition on the state space that satisfies lumpability condition;
3. ignore the original Markov chain, and substitute it with the lumped one to compute steady-state probability distribution.

The advantage of lumping is to deal with a smaller Markov chain, thus saving computational effort. Still exact probability distributions can be computed on the lumped chain rather than the original chain.

In practice the application of the above procedure to simplify the numerical analysis of a Markovian model is impractical for the following two reasons. First, the original Markov chain (which could be much larger than the lumped one) must be defined (and stored in a computer's memory) anyway. Second, the search for a partition of the state space that satisfies the lumpability condition has NP complexity as a function of the number of states. Hence, in spite of its great potential impact on the complexity of Markovian analysis, the use of the lumpability condition is sporadic in actual performance studies based on Markov chains.

3   Lumping and GSPN symmetries

In the early phases of introduction of the stochastic Petri net modeling approach the PN formalism was intended mainly as a "compact" representation for the state space of the model. The introduction of this compact representation in some cases simplified the identification of the lumpability condition, since this condition became intuitively evident from the net structure.

Consider for example the Markov chain (with 13 states) characterized by the following infinitesimal generator Q:

$$\begin{vmatrix}
-2a & p\,2a & (1-p)2a & 0 & 0 & 0 & 0 & 0 & 0 & 0 & 0 & 0 & 0 \\
0 & -a-b & 0 & b & p\,a & (1-p)a & 0 & 0 & 0 & 0 & 0 & 0 & 0 \\
0 & 0 & -a-b & b & 0 & 0 & p\,a & (1-p)a & 0 & 0 & 0 & 0 & 0 \\
c & 0 & 0 & -a-c & 0 & 0 & 0 & 0 & p\,a & (1-p)a & 0 & 0 & 0 \\
0 & 0 & 0 & 0 & -b & 0 & 0 & 0 & b & 0 & 0 & 0 & 0 \\
0 & 0 & 0 & 0 & 0 & -b & 0 & 0 & b & 0 & 0 & 0 & 0 \\
0 & 0 & 0 & 0 & 0 & 0 & -b & 0 & b & 0 & 0 & 0 & 0 \\
0 & 0 & 0 & 0 & 0 & 0 & 0 & -b & 0 & b & 0 & 0 & 0 \\
0 & c & 0 & 0 & 0 & 0 & 0 & 0 & -a-c & 0 & p\,a & (1-p)a & 0 \\
0 & 0 & c & 0 & 0 & 0 & 0 & 0 & 0 & -a-c & 0 & p\,a & (1-p)a \\
0 & 0 & 0 & c & 0 & 0 & 0 & 0 & 0 & 0 & -c & 0 & 0 \\
0 & 0 & 0 & 0 & 0 & q\,c & (1-q)c & 0 & 0 & 0 & 0 & -c & 0 \\
0 & 0 & 0 & 0 & 0 & 0 & 0 & c & 0 & 0 & 0 & 0 & -c
\end{vmatrix}$$

where a, b, $c > 0$ and p, $q \in (0,1)$ are arbitrary parameters characterizing the speed of the activities carried out in the model.

It might be non trivial to discover that the following partition satisfies the lumpability condition:

$$\begin{aligned}
\Pi(1) &= \{\, s_1 \,\} \\
\Pi(2) &= \{\, s_2, \ s_3 \,\} \\
\Pi(3) &= \{\, s_4 \,\} \\
\Pi(4) &= \{\, s_5, \ s_6, \ s_7, \ s_8 \,\} \\
\Pi(5) &= \{\, s_9, \ s_{10} \,\} \\
\Pi(6) &= \{\, s_{11}, \ s_{12}, \ s_{13} \,\}
\end{aligned}$$

Once we have found this partition we can refer to the 6 state lumped Markov chain characterized by the following infinitesimal generator Q':

$$\begin{vmatrix}
-2a & 2a & 0 & 0 & 0 & 0 \\
0 & -a-b & b & a & 0 & 0 \\
c & 0 & -a-c & 0 & a & 0 \\
0 & 0 & 0 & -b & b & 0 \\
0 & c & 0 & 0 & -a-c & a \\
0 & 0 & 0 & c & 0 & -c
\end{vmatrix}$$

The identification of the lumped Markov chain can be substantially simplified by the examination of the GSPN model in Figure 1, which actually generates the original Markov chain. Indeed the symmetry with respect to the vertical crossing places p_1 and p_{12} is apparent at a first glance. The folding of the two symmetric half nets one over the other yields the GSPN model depicted in Figure 2. This folded GSPN happens to actually generate the lumped Markov chain considered above.

In this particular case the folding performed directly on the net structure is equivalent to the lumping at the Markov chain level. However this is not always

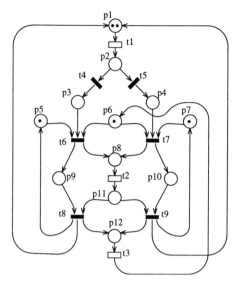

Fig. 1. A GSPN model that generates the original Markov chain considered in our example

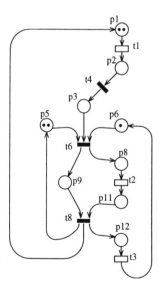

Fig. 2. Folding of the original GSPN model that generates the lumped Markov chain considered in our example

the case (unfortunately). Most of the times such symmetries may arise only in some states and not in other states, so that a trivial folding of the net structure does not produce correct results.

4 Symmetries at state space level versus net level

In general the folding performed at the net level yields a loss of information encoded in the marking of the model that prevents one to identify a partition of the state space for which the lumping condition holds. Consider for example the 10 state Markov chain: whose infinitesimal generator is shown in Figure 3, where a, $b > 0$ are arbitrary parameters characterizing the speed of the activities

$$
\begin{vmatrix}
-3a & 1.5\,a & 1.5\,a & 0 & 0 & 0 & 0 & 0 & 0 & 0 \\
b & -2a-b & 0 & a & a & 0 & 0 & 0 & 0 & 0 \\
b & 0 & -2a-b & 0 & a & a & 0 & 0 & 0 & 0 \\
0 & b & 0 & -a-b & 0 & 0 & 0.5\,a & 0.5\,a & 0 & 0 \\
0 & b & b & 0 & -a-2b & 0 & 0 & 0.5\,a & 0.5\,a & 0 \\
0 & 0 & b & 0 & 0 & -a-b & 0 & 0 & 0.5\,a & 0.5\,a \\
0 & 0 & 0 & b & 0 & 0 & -b & 0 & 0 & 0 \\
0 & 0 & 0 & b & b & 0 & 0 & -2b & 0 & 0 \\
0 & 0 & 0 & 0 & b & b & 0 & 0 & -2b & 0 \\
0 & 0 & 0 & 0 & 0 & b & 0 & 0 & 0 & -b
\end{vmatrix}
$$

Fig. 3. A 10 state Markov chain

carried out in the model. Such a Markov chain is generated, for example, by the GSPN model depicted in Figure 4.

Indeed, the partition reported in Figure 5 is the minimal one that satisfies the lumpability condition for arbitrary values of the parameters a and b.

Notice, however, that the lumped Markov chain identified by this partition and represented by the infinitesimal generator in Figure 6 is not generated by the folding of the two half nets identified by the vertical symmetry line crossing places p_1 and p_10 in the GSPN in Figure 4.

A possible (much more complex) GSPN model generating the lumped Markov chain is, instead, depicted in Figure 7. The problem of this approach was to define a methodology to derive compact GSPN models that yield lumped Markov chains as compared to the "trivial" unfolded GSPN models that everybody is able to draw starting from operational descriptions of the systems under study. The methodology and the related techniques should be reasonably simple so as to allow their application to practical cases.

In the mid eighties the methodology was informally devised and was applied to a number of cases of practical relevance. In most cases its application resulted in a substantial reduction of the size of the (lumped) Markov chain as a function of the size of the problem to be studied. The reduction of the size of the underlying Markov chains allowed the study of systems composed by several tens of components instead of two or three components — as it would have been possible without the exploitation of the lumping technique.

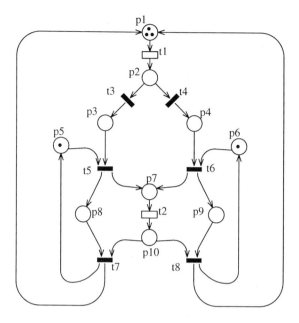

Fig. 4. A GSPN model that generates the given 10-state Markov chain

$$\Pi(1) = \{\ s_1\ \}$$
$$\Pi(2) = \{\ s_2,\ s_3\ \}$$
$$\Pi(3) = \{\ s_4,\ s_6\ \}$$
$$\Pi(4) = \{\ s_5\ \}$$
$$\Pi(5) = \{\ s_7,\ s_{10}\ \}$$
$$\Pi(6) = \{\ s_8,\ s_9\ \}$$

Fig. 5. The partition in 6 subsets that satisfies lumpability

The main idea behind the construction of compact GSPN models was the elimination of the identity of the components making up a system. The typical example was the one of shared memory multiprocessor systems. A typical system was made up of several memory units identified as M1, M2, etc. Clearly the distinction beween a memory module and another was the prime responsible for the explosion of the number of states in the Markov chains describing the dynamic behavior of such systems. A Processor accessing M1 identified a state that was different from the state identified by the same processor accessing M2, even if the behavior of the processor was independent of the actual memory module it made access to.

A first approximation was then to say: "Let us forget about the identity of the memory module, and simply encode that a processor is accessing one of the memory modules." Then the next question was: "If I don't know which one of the memory modules the processor is accessing, am I still able to move to

$$\begin{vmatrix} -3a & 3a & 0 & 0 & 0 & 0 \\ b & -2a-b & a & a & 0 & 0 \\ 0 & b & -a-b & 0 & 0.5\,a & 0.5\,a \\ 0 & 2b & 0 & -a-2b & 0 & a \\ 0 & 0 & b & 0 & -b & 0 \\ 0 & 0 & b & b & 0 & -2b \end{vmatrix}$$

Fig. 6. A 6 state lumped Markov chain

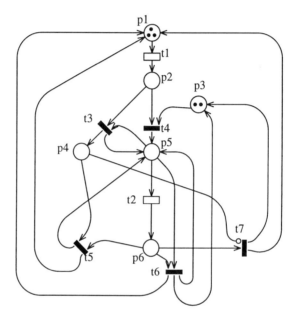

Fig. 7. A GSPN model that generates the lumped 6-state Markov chain

the next state with the same speed parameter that one could measure on the real system in which the identity of the memory module is perfectly defined?" If the answer was "yes", then the GSPN model adopting this abstract view of the system state generated a correctly lumped Markov chain as compared to the one generated by the "detailed" GSPN model. Otherwise the model had to be "refined" in order to encode some additional information in the state of the reduced GSPN so as to make the system Markovian (remember that a stochastic system is Markovian if the information encoded in its current state is sufficient to determine its future behavior, so that a complete knowledge of the history that yielded to the current state is not needed).

For example, let us outline the contruction of the compact GSPN model presented in Figure 7. This can be derived from the folding of the detailed model depicted in Figure 4 by applying the following reasoning. Suppose that transition t_1 fires once from the initial marking. This would determine the arrival of one token in the place resulting from the folding of p_4 and p_5 and of one token in place p_7. Transition t_2 would become enabled once, thus modeling the access of a processor to one of the two memory modules (and by looking at the marking of the GSPN we are not able to tell which one of the two). Therefore the folded model would behave in a way totally consistent with the original unfolded model. On the other hand, if we assume two consecutive firings of transition t_1, in the original model two different situations can occur. The two processor may access two different memory modules, or contend for the access to the same one. In the former case two tokens are deposited in place p_7, while in the latter case only one token is deposited in place p_7 (the other one remains sitting in place p_3 or p_4 due to the lack of enabling of either t_5 or t_6). The folded GSPN, instead, always yields two tokens in place p_7, thus not properly modeling the contention for the same memory module. The solution to this problem is a modification of the folded model with the introduction of transition t_3 and place p_4, as illustrated in Figure 7. Transition t_3 models the "choice of the same memory module already in use" (no matter which one it is), while transition t_4 models the "choice of another free memory module." Place p_4 in Figure 7 collects the marking of places p_3 and p_4 in Figure 4 in case of contention for the same memory module.

Although it is the application of techniques like the one illustrated in the example that made the application of GSPNs so successful for the study of practical cases, the necessity of manually contructing compact models trying to produce lumped Markovian state spaces of small size was also recognized as the main practical limitation ot the GSPN formalism. Producing a correct and effective compact model requires skill and experience from the modeler. This kind of model transformation is certainly not applicable by people that have little or superficial background in performance modeling.

5 Coloured nets and Markovian lumping

The answer that was found to make the lumping technique accessible also to less experienced modelers was the adoption of a coloured net formalism (see, e.g., [19, 17, 18, 7, 12, 15]). Besides several other advantages from the modeling power point of view, the adoption of a coloured formalism allows one to define a detailed model in which potential symmetries are clearly identified. This allows the development of software tools that can automatically check whether a potential model symmetry can be exploited for Markovian lumping or not, and implement the lumping technique in a way that is transparent to the modeler. Indeed the model always defines a detailed coloured GSPN model, and its partial or total folding is performed by the analysis tool in the way that can be automated most efficiently.

The main automatic technique available today for this purpose is the construction of the so called Symbolic Reachability Graph (SRG) in the case of Well-formed nets [8]. The key step in the definition of these automatic techniques aimed at taking advantage of model symmetries was the definition of a restricted syntax for the definition of net inscriptions. A reasonably good trade-off has been consolidated over the years between the necessity of keeping the formalism simple enough for the implementation of efficient analysis algorithms but convenient enough so as to allow the modeler to use it in practical cases.

The SRG may be explained as the application of a folding technique at the state space level. Several states that differ only for a permutation of colours in the marking of some places can be folded into an equivalence class. Considering equivalence classes of states up to a permutation is equivalent to the intuitive idea of forgetting about the colours (identities) of tokens, and taking into account only the total number of tokens contained in the different places. The contruction of these equivalence classes is implemented state by state, so that it is possible to forget about the identity of tokens in one marking and take into account the difference of colour in another marking.

A key issue for the efficient implementation of the SRG generation algorithm is the identification of a unique (canonical) representation for each equivalence class at the state space level. This allows the direct generation of the equivalence classes (i.e., of the lumped Markov chain) without the need of enumerating the individual markings (i.e., constructing the complete Markov chain).

As an example, consider the (well-formed) coloured GSPN model depicted in Figure 8. Assuming that the colour set "m" is defined as a set of two different

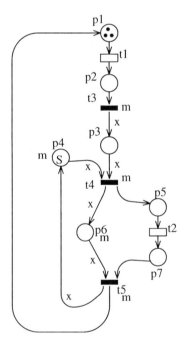

Fig. 8. A (well-formed) coloured version of the GSPN example in Figure 4

elements (say "m1" and "m2"), and assuming that "S" in the initial marking of place "p4" represents the set of the two colours (i.e., $\{m1, m2\}$) and that the symbol "x" labelling some of the arcs denotes the projection function identifying one element in the colour set "m," then this model is perfectly equivalent to the one depicted in Figure 4. The Markov chain generated by its reachability graph is thus exactly the complete one whose matrix is depicted in Figure 3. However, the SRG construction algorithm happens to identify equivalence classes of (coloured) markings that are exactly the ones listed in Figure 5. Therefore the Markov chain derived from the SRG of coloured model in Figure 8 is exactly the 6-state lumped one reported in Figure 6.

This trivial example shows the great practical advantage of using the Stochastic Well-formed Net formalism instead of the (non coloured) GSPN formalism. The conceptual effort required to the modeler to assemble the (detailed, coloured) model in Figure 8 is roughly equivalent to the one of deriving the (unfolded) model in Figure 4 (at least once the coloured net formalism has been sufficiently well understood). The effort of deriving equivalence classes of states and verifying the lumpability condition is carried out by the SRG construction algorithm instead of requiring the modeler to derive a GSPN model like the one depicted in Figure 4. The modeler is only requested to follow the restrictions posed by the WN formalism for the definition of colour domains thus implicitly providing useful "hints" to the SRG construction algorithm on which symmetries are to be exploited.

Of course, the SRG construction algorithm is more complex than the regular Reachability Graph construction algorithm, so that it is still useful to try to "fold" the original model whenever the folding effort is not very high. Indeed the RG analysis of the GSPN depicted in Figure 2 is more efficient than the SRG analysis of a coloured model equivalent to the GSPN depicted in Figure 1. This was a good reason to develop the "decolourization" technique described in [13]. Some simple criteria were proposed that could be very easily checked directly on the structure of a SWN model in order to identify "redundant" colour components that could be "decolourized" in order lump equally behaving states.

As an example, the SWN model depicted in Figure 9 is a more detailed description of our reference example, provided that the colour set "p" is defined to contain 3 different elements representing the identity of three processors. The Markov chain generated by this model has more than 10 states because different permutation of processor identities can be found. However, this extended state space can be lumped into the 10-state Markov chain reported in Figure 3 (hence it can also be lumped into the 6-state Markov chain reported in Figure 6). Indeed the SRG construction algorithm yields anyway a Markov chain with 6 states. However the cost of generation of the same reduced state space is higher than the one required for the model in Figure 8. Fortunately the structure of the SWN in Figure 9 allows the application of the decolourization technique, which precisely yields the SWN model in Figure 8. This example shows that a combination of the decolourization technique (that applies at the Petri net structure level) and of the SRG construction technique (that applies at the state space analysis level)

38

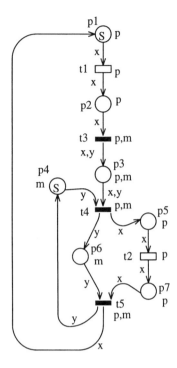

Fig. 9. Another SWN version modeling the same system

can yield the same results that used to be found by experienced modelers in a totally automatic way.

The benefit introduced by these automatic lumping techniques is thus the fact that a larger group of modelers can take advantage of the lumping technique with little conceptual effort (and with much lower chances of introducing erros by manual manipulation of large models). A fair number of case studies reported in the literature (such as, e.g., [1,6]) that were initially proposed in coloured version mainly as a facilitation for the explanation of their inherent symmetries and that were manually reduced, could now be studied in a fully automated way thanks to the application of the SRG construction technique and of the structural decolourization technique [9,10].

6 Dealing with other symmetries

Unfortunately, real life systems are usually much more complex than the motivation examples proposed so far. The idea of taking advantage of symmetries to reduce the size of lumped Markov chains can still apply to real cases, but the type of symmetry to consider is usually more complex than pure permutation.

A classical case of a more complex symmetry that usually arises is rotation. Rotation symmetry can be found, e.g., in ring interconnections. Rotation symmetry is introduced as a primitive feature for the definition of colour domains in SWN models, however the presence of so called ordered classes usually has a strongly negative impact on the efficiency of the SRG construction algorithm.

Other types of symmetry that usually can be found in practical applications such as, e.g., flip around a symmetry center (which arises, e.g., in mesh interconnections) are not allowed as primitive structures for colour clasess in the version of the SWN formalism currently supported by automated software analysis tools.

The problem of extending the SRG technique to other coloured net formalisms besides Well-formed Nets and to other types of symmetry besides permutation and rotation are of a practical nature rather than a theoretical one. Conceptually the extension of the SRG technique to general coloured nets was already done [11]. In practice, however, efficient implementations of the SRG algorithm for arbitrary types of symmetries are difficult to devise.

More general types of symmetry can also be "simulated" in some more or less tricky way, as shown in [14]. The use of such tricks to make the SRG algorithm construct the correctly lumped Markov chain, however, reproduces a very similar situation as the original use of GSPNs to define "compact" models.

As an example, let us consider the interconnection of 36 elements in a 6 × 6 regular grid, as depicted in Figure 10. A quite natural "encoding" of the

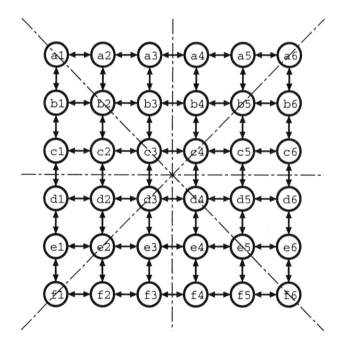

Fig. 10. An example of a 6 × 6 regular grid interconnection

identities of the elements in the grid is the use of a pair of names chosen from two sets of 6 elements. In the example, names are produced as a pair of one letter "a," "b," $\cdots$, "f" and one digit "1," "2," $\cdots$, "6." Clearly such a strucure has several flip-type symmestries highlighted by the dash-dotted lines. However, the "natural" encoding in terms of coloured net markings using a Cartesian product of two basic classes containing 6 elements does not give rise to arbitrary permutation symmetries among the elements of the two basic classes. Hence, the SRG construction algorithm applied to a SWN model containing this kind of colour encoding for the identity of objects is not able to identify any nontrivial partition of the state space.

A trick that was proposed in [14] to derive a SWN model for such a system in which the SRG construction algorithm exploits the available symmetries uses a much more complex encoding for the names of the object. A five-tuple can be used to identify an arbitrary element of the grid according to an encoding schema outlined in Figure 11. The idea is to split the elements in four subsets, as

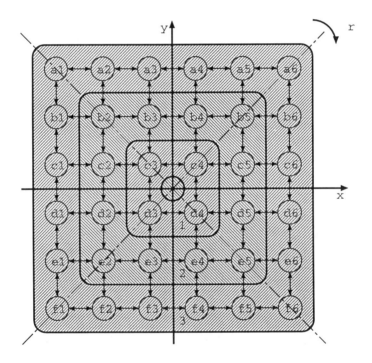

Fig. 11. A schema of encoding in a five-tuple

indicated by the "x" and "y" axes. A two element colour set is used to distinguish between positive and negative coordinates along the "x" or "y" axe (say basic colours "pos" and "neg"). A Cartesian product of two times this basic colour class identifies one among the four subsets of nine elements. For instance, the pair "pos,pos" identifies the nine elements "a4", "a5," "a6,", "b4," $\cdots$, "c6." On the other hand, the pair "pos,neg" identifies the nine elements "d4", "d5," ⋯, "f6," and so on. A third component that can assume values "1," "2," or "3" measures the distance of an element from the center of the structure. Hence the triplet "neg,pos,2" identifies the three elements called "c2," "b2," and "b3" in Figure 10, while the triplet "pos,pos,1" identifies the only element "c4." In the case of the triplet "pos,pos,3" we identify the set of five elements "a4," "a5," "a6," "b6," and "c6."

In order to uniquely identify one element inside a set of one, three, or five elements designated by such a triplet, an additional pair of coordinates is used. The idea is to refer to the diagonal inside the set, that constitutes a center of symmetry. Hence a fourth coordinate is introduced that measures the distance of the element from the diagonal. In our example, elements "a5" and "b6" have both distance "1" from the diagonal, elements "a4" and "c6" have distance "2," and element "a6" has distance "0." The distance of an element from the diagonal is always less than the value of the third coordinate. In case of non-diagonal elements, the distance identifies two element; in order to make a distinction between them we can indicate whether a positive or negative rotation is needed (assuming clockwise rotation as positive). In summary, for instance the 5-tuple <pos,pos,2,1,pos> corresponds to element "c5" and the 5-tuple <pos,pos,3,1,neg> corresponds to element "a5."

All consistent permutations of the first, second and fifth tuple components produce the identity of other elements that are perfectly symmetric. For instance, if we have a state in which "c5" and "a5" are active, while all other nodes are passive (whatever this state could mean), this will belong to the same equivalence class as the states in which only "b4" and "b6" are active, as well as the state in which "a2" and "c2" are active, and so on. Up to eight different states can be grouped into a single equivalence class, exploiting this kind of symmetry. The interest of such a complex encoding of the names of objects is that, once the modeler has accomplished the effort of defining the colour sets the transition predicates and the arc functions according to such a complex encoding, the SRG construction algorithm can automatically and very efficiently construct a lumped Markov chain with a number of states reduced by a factor up to 8 as compared to the complete Markov chain that did not exploit this kind of symmetry.

Admittedly the definition of such SWN models is not an easy task. It becomes a necessity when one is confronted to a practical case to analyze in which the inner system symmetries are not embedded in a primitive way in the formalism and/or the tool used. Indeed the development of such models requires skill, experience and a great deal of effort. An inexperienced or casual user in such a situation would probably give up after a few attempts, thinking that the formalism/tool used is just inadequate for that purpose.

The ideal solution in such cases would definitely be an extension of the modeling formalism and of the associated SRG construction algorithm in order to cover the kind of desired symmetry in a primitive way. However, this ideal solution could be unfeasible in practice due to the difficulty in embedding new algorithms in the solution tools and/or the limited interest of the application at

42

hand, that might make the effort not worthwhile. Hence, it might be the case that in practice the ability and willingness of the modeler to optimize the model representation by manual manipulation will continue to be required in order to solve complex models.

7 Conclusions

The development of performance models based on Petri nets so far has been driven by the hope of providing the modeler a formalism so "natural" and easy to use that even a person with little performance modeling background could use it to set up models that are at the same time meaningful and efficient to analyze. This goal was explicitly stated in the motivations of most of the earlier papers, and is still in the mind of many people working on the subject.

Indeed the idea of identifying symmetries and automatically exploiting them to reduce the Markovian analysis has been a step in this direction. Indeed the adoption of the SWN formalism today allows the efficient analysis of models that at the beginning would have been considered unsuitable to automatic Markovian analysis and that required manual refinements to produce lumped chains.

However we should probably admit that the goal of providing a fool-proof formalism for performance modeling of complex real systems was probably too ambitious, and that most likely it will never be reached. We should probably enjoy the results obtained as a by-product of this "holy graal" research efforts but start considering the use of performance modelling tools as primarily devoted to the use by performance modeling experts.

Also performance modeling experts prefer to limit their personal effort to derive and validate a correct and efficient model. Hence each result that can be exploited to transform a former manual activity into a task automated by a software tool is of great value anyway. However, knowing the difficulties involved in the development of good performance models, an expert modeler can easily accept to provide also his personal contribution to the task, when needed, thus allowing the solution of problems that would definitely be outside the capabilities of a state-of-the-art automatic software tool alone.

References

1. M. Ajmone Marsan, G. Balbo, G. Chiola, and G. Conte. Modeling the software architecture of a prototype parallel machine. In *Proc. 1987 SIGMETRICS Conference*, Banf, Alberta, Canada, May 1987. ACM.
2. M. Ajmone Marsan, G. Balbo, and G. Conte. A class of generalized stochastic Petri nets for the performance analysis of multiprocessor systems. *ACM Transactions on Computer Systems*, 2(1), May 1984.
3. M. Ajmone Marsan, G. Balbo, G. Conte, and F. Gregoretti. Modeling bus contention and memory interference in a multiprocessor system. *IEEE Transactions on Computers*, 32(1):60–72, January 1983.

4. M. Ajmone Marsan and G. Chiola. Construction of generalized stochastic Petri net models of bus oriented multiprocessor systems by stepwise refinements. In *Proc. 2nd Int. Conf. on Modeling Techniques and Tools for Performance Analysis*, Sophia Antipolis, France, June 1985. ACM.

5. M. Ajmone Marsan, G. Chiola, and G. Conte. Performance models of task synchronization in computer systems. In *Proc. 1st Int. Conf. on Computers and Applications*, Beijing, China, June 1984. IEEE.

6. G. Balbo, G. Chiola, S.C. Bruell, and P. Chen. An example of modelling and evaluation of a concurrent program using coloured stochastic Petri nets: Lamport's fast mutual exclusion algorithm. *IEEE Transactions on Parallel and Distributed Systems*, 3(2):221–240, March 1992.

7. G. Chiola, G. Bruno, and T. Demaria. Introducing a color formalism into generalized stochastic Petri nets. In *Proc. 9th Europ. Workshop on Application and Theory of Petri Nets*, Venezia, Italy, June 1988.

8. G. Chiola, C. Dutheillet, G. Franceschinis, and S. Haddad. On well-formed coloured nets and their symbolic reachability graph. In *Proc. 11th International Conference on Application and Theory of Petri Nets*, Paris, France, June 1990. Reprinted in *High-Level Petri Nets. Theory and Application*, K. Jensen and G. Rozenberg (editors), Springer Verlag, 1991.

9. G. Chiola, C. Dutheillet, G. Franceschinis, and S. Haddad. Stochastic well-formed coloured nets and multiprocessor modelling applications. In K. Jensen and G. Rozenberg, editors, *High-Level Petri Nets. Theory and Application*. Springer Verlag, 1991.

10. G. Chiola, C. Dutheillet, G. Franceschinis, and S. Haddad. Stochastic well-formed coloured nets for symmetric modelling applications. *IEEE Transactions on Computers*, 42(11):1343–1360, November 1993.

11. G. Chiola, C. Dutheillet, G. Franceschinis, and S. Haddad. A symbolic reachability graph for coloured Petri nets. *Theoretical Computer Science*, 176:39–65, 1997.

12. G. Chiola and G. Franceschinis. Colored GSPN models and automatic symmetry detection. In *Proc. 3rd Intern. Workshop on Petri Nets and Performance Models*, Kyoto, Japan, December 1989. IEEE-CS Press.

13. G. Chiola and G. Franceschinis. A structural colour simplification in Well-Formed coloured nets. In *Proc. 4th Intern. Workshop on Petri Nets and Performance Models*, pages 144–153, Melbourne, Australia, December 1991. IEEE-CS Press.

14. G. Chiola, G. Franceschinis, and R. Gaeta. Modelling symmetric computer architectures by stochastic well-formed coloured nets. In *15th International Conference on Application and Theory of Petri Nets*, Zaragoza, Spain, June 1994.

15. C. Dutheillet and S. Haddad. Aggregation and disaggregation of states in colored stochastic Petri nets: Application to a multiprocessor architecture. In *Proc. 3rd Intern. Workshop on Petri Nets and Performance Models*, Kyoto, Japan, December 1989. IEEE-CS Press.

16. J.G. Kemeny and J.L. Snell. *Finite Markov Chains*. Van Nostrand, Princeton, NJ, 1960.

17. Chuang Lin and Dan C. Marinescu. On stochastic high level Petri nets. In *Proc. Int. Workshop on Petri Nets and Performance Models*, Madison, WI, USA, August 1987. IEEE-CS Press.

18. Chuang Lin and Dan C. Marinescu. Stochastic high level Petri nets and applications. *IEEE Transactions on Computers*, 37(7):815–825, July 1988.

19. A. Zenie. Colored stochastic Petri nets. In *Proc. Int. Workshop on Timed Petri Nets*, pages 262–271, Torino, Italy, July 1985. IEEE-CS Press.

Dimensioning Handover Buffers in Wireless ATM Networks with GSPN Models*

Marco Ajmone Marsan, Carla-Fabiana Chiasserini, and Andrea Fumagalli**

Dipartimento di Elettronica, Politecnico di Torino,
Corso Duca degli Abruzzi 24, 10129 Torino, Italy,
{ajmone,chiasserini,andreaf}@polito.it

Abstract. Wireless ATM (W–ATM) is an emerging technology for the provision of high-speed data services to mobile users in cellular telecommunication networks. Numerous issues still have to be solved in the design of W–ATM networks. Among those, a relevant problem is the dimensioning of the buffers necessary to guarantee that ATM cells are correctly and sequentially delivered to their destination in spite of the end-user movement. In order to guarantee that the selected buffer sizes are capable of guaranteeing the desired quality of service, accurate performance evaluation models must be provided. This paper presents the first accurate analytical model for buffer sizing in W–ATM networks. The model is based on the Generalized Stochastic Petri Net (GSPN) formalism, and it can be shown to be as accurate as very detailed simulation programs.

1 Introduction

Over the last few years, one of the major commercial successes in the telecommunications world has been the widespread diffusion of cellular mobile telephone services, whose provision relies on sophisticated algorithms implemented by state-of-the-art dedicated computer equipment.

The cellular nature of mobile telephony stems from the subdivision of the serviced area into *cells* that are covered by the electromagnetic signal emitted by the antennas of fixed *base stations* (BSs). The mobility of users implies that it is possible for a terminal to *roam* from one cell to another while a telephone call is in progress. In order for the conversation to continue, it is necessary that the network be capable of transferring the call from the old cell (i.e. from the old BS) to the new one, without interruption. This operation is normally termed call *handover* or *handoff*.

The almost incredible success of mobile telephony is paving the way to the introduction of data communication services for mobile users. Low-speed data services are already available in digital mobile telephony systems as they require minor modification of the existing architecture. Instead, the introduction

---

* This work was supported in part by a contract between CSELT and Politecnico di Torino, and in part by the EC through the Copernicus Project 1463 – ATMIN.
** Presently on leave at the University of Texas, Dallas.

of high-speed data communication services for mobile users poses several technical challenges, mostly related to the poor quality of the mobile radio channel, and the algorithmic complexity of high speed networks.

A natural approach for the introduction of high-speed data communication services for mobile users is to try and adopt also in wireless networks the same techniques developed for the provision of high-speed data communication services in wired networks. This amounts to the exploitation of the Asynchronous Transfer Mode (ATM) in the wireless environment, and results in the so-called Wireless ATM (W–ATM) networks.

Among the numerous critical issues that have to be dealt with in order to design W–ATM networks, mobility management is one of the most challenging. In particular, a great deal of attention must be devoted to handover protocols, since it is necessary to guarantee loss-free and in-sequence delivery of ATM cells to the end users, even if the BS which they are connected to changes. This means that when a user moves from one cell to another, all the ATM connections originating or terminating at the Mobile Terminal (MT) have to be rerouted from the old BS to the new BS.

Several solutions for the handover management in W–ATM networks were proposed in the literature [1–5]. These solutions specifically address the cell buffering requirements originating from the modification of the ATM connection to follow the MT that migrates from one BS to another. This modification implies the establishment of a new radio link between the MT and the new BS and consequently the rerouting of the ATM connection. During this modification phase ATM cells exchanged through the connection may need to be buffered at the MT and in the network to prevent both cell loss and out of order delivery.

Of course, the performance of the various proposed handover algorithms critically depends on the size of the available buffers; however, estimating the impact of the buffer size on the algorithm performance is not easy, because the metrics of interest (specially the cell loss ratio due to buffer overflows during handovers) depend on rare events. In spite of this situation, the performance results reported in the literature were mostly obtained via simulation [3,6] or experimental prototyping [7,8]. Analytical approaches to estimate the effectiveness of the proposed handover solutions in W–ATM networks were not developed so far, or they were based on quite rough approximations that led to poor accuracy of the performance predictions [5].

This paper presents an analytical approach that can be used for the accurate performance analysis of handover protocols for W–ATM networks. The proposed approach is based on Generalized Stochastic Petri Net (GSPN) [9] models of the handover algorithms. Hence, transitions describing time consuming actions are associated with exponentially distributed random firing times, while transitions describing logic actions are associated with null firing times. Due to the isomorphism existing between GSPNs and Continuous-Time Markov Chains, the limiting distribution of the model can then be derived using classical techniques [10], and from it the performance metrics of interest can be computed.

With no loss of generality, the proposed approach is described by applying it to a specific W–ATM handover protocol. The advantage of focusing on a specific protocol is twofold: i) the description of the approach can be based on an example, and ii) the obtained numerical results are directly comparable with the simulation results obtained for the considered protocol, thus providing a convenient means for the validation of the approach and the test of its accuracy. The considered protocol [1, 11] is based on in-band signaling, since specific ATM cells, called MES (Mobile Enhancement Signaling) cells, that contain the protocol messages, are inserted into the data flow. MES cells are exchanged among the network entities directly involved in the handover procedure. The in-band signaling approach does not require any modification of the standard ATM signaling, thus avoiding hybrid solutions that mix signaling and in-band messages [3].

In order to guarantee loss-free and in-sequence delivery of ATM cells, buffering may be necessary for both the upstream and downstream cell flows[1] during the handover procedure, or more precisely during the interruption of the radio link and of the ATM connection. As shown in [1] via simulation results, during handover the buffering of the upstream cells is more critical than the buffering of the downstream cells, in the sense that the former requires larger buffers for a given overflow probability. In this paper we shall validate such conclusions with the GSPN analysis.

The paper is organized as follows: Section 2 very briefly overviews the W–ATM scenario and the considered handover protocol; Section 3 describes the GSPN model in some detail, and defines the performance metrics of interest. Section 4 validates the approach by comparing performance results obtained via simulation with the GSPN predictions, and discusses further GSPN results.

2 Description of the System

In this section we describe the general W–ATM architecture and give a concise overview of the considered handover algorithm, providing the essential elements that allow readers to understand the corresponding GSPN model; more detailed descriptions of the handover algorithm and of the in-band signaling protocol can be found in [1, 11].

2.1 W–ATM Networks

W–ATM networks consist of two components: the fixed network segment and the radio segment. ATM switches and BSs belong to the fixed network segment, whereas MTs communicate with BSs over the radio segment.

As illustrated in Fig. 1, more than one BS can be connected to the same ATM switch, that is termed Local Exchange (LE) with respect to those BSs. Each BS controls a cell, and is the point of access to the fixed network for all MTs roaming in the cell. The radio interface between the MT and the BS has

---

[1] The upstream cell flow goes from the mobile terminal to the remote terminal, through the BS; the downstream cell flow goes from the remote terminal to the mobile terminal.

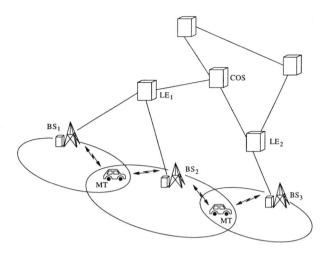

Fig. 1. The W-ATM scenario

the capability to transfer ATM cells in both directions. According to the ATM standard, ATM cells must be transmitted along the connection path established between two end users.

2.2 The Handover Algorithm

The ATM connection rerouting technique adopted by the handover algorithm under consideration is called *incremental re-establishment*, and was originally proposed in [4]. This approach is fast and efficient, since it permits the partial reuse of the connection path used before the handover. According to this technique, during the handover, one ATM switch along the existing ATM connection path is chosen to be the Cross-Over Switch (COS). The portion of the ATM connection path from the remote user to the COS does not change during the handover, while the old path from the COS to the MT performing the handover must be replaced with a newly established path from the COS to the MT via the new BS.

Table 1. MES cells exchanged during the proposed handover protocol

	MES Cells
EDF	End of the Data Flow on the upstream connection through BS_1
HOC	HandOver Confirm (acknowledgment of the handover request)
HOR	HandOver Request (sent by the MT to start a handover)
SDF_{DOWN}	Start Data Flow on the new DOWNstream connection
SDF_{UP}	Start Data Flow on the new UPstream connection
USR	New UpStream connection Ready (through BS_2)

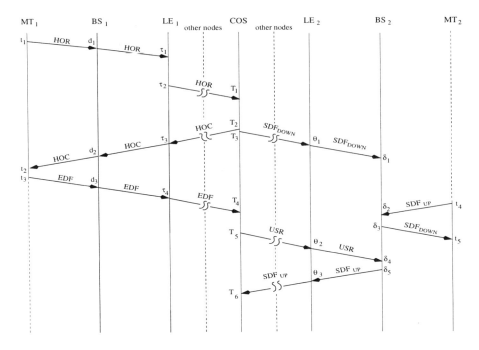

Fig. 2. The considered handover algorithm based on in-band signaling; MT is denoted by MT_1 when connected to BS_1, and MT_2 when connected to BS_2

Fig. 2 shows the flow diagram of the considered handover algorithm, indicating the sequence of control cells (MES cells) exchanged among the network elements involved in the handover. Table 1 contains a succinct explanation of the semantics of the MES cells involved in the algorithm.

The main elements of the handover protocol are the following. When a handover procedure must be initiated, the MT sends a handover request (in the HOR cell) to the BS to which it is connected (BS_1), and waits for the handover acknowledgement while still transmitting and/or receiving ATM cells over the radio link. BS_1 interacts with LE_1, and possibly with the COS in the attempt to create the new connection path through the BS of the cell to which the mobile user is moving (BS_2). In the successful case, the MT receives over the old connection path the HOC cell as acknowledgment, stops using the ATM connection path through BS_1, and holds the cells to be transmitted in its transmission buffer, until the radio link to BS_2 is opened by transmitting the SDF_{UP} cell. The connection from the COS to BS_2 is then opened, and the flow of cells directed to MT is transmitted over this new connection path, and buffered at BS_2 in the *downstream handover buffer* until the radio connection with MT is resumed (the buffering takes place in the period $[\delta_1, \delta_3]$ shown in Fig. 2). However, if the radio connection is resumed before the rerouting of the ATM connection, buffering is not necessary.

Regarding the upstream connection path, if the radio connection between MT and BS_2 is established before the new ATM connection path is opened, then BS_2 has to store the data flow from the MT in the *upstream handover buffer* (the buffering takes place in the period $[\delta_2,\delta_5]$ shown in Fig. 2), in order to guarantee in-sequence cell delivery at the remote terminal. Conversely, if the new ATM connection path is available before the MT connects to BS_2, then buffering is not necessary.

Since the interval $[\delta_2,\delta_5]$ typically is longer than the interval $[\delta_1,\delta_3]$, the occupancy of the upstream handover buffer normally is greater than for the downstream handover buffer.

3   The GSPN Approach to Handover Buffer Dimensioning

The proposed approach for the dimensioning of the upstream and downstream handover buffers requires the following steps:

- identification of the system behaviors that have a significant impact on the handover buffers occupancy;
- choice of the simplifying assumptions to be introduced in the GSPN model;
- construction of the GSPN model;
- solution of the GSPN model and computation of the performance metrics necessary to dimension the handover buffers.

In this section we present the various steps with reference to the considered handover protocol.

3.1   The Handover Buffers Behavior

In order to study the handover buffers behavior, it is important to clearly identify the different phases of the handover procedure that determine a change of the buffer situation. We call *handover cycle* the period starting with the handover request from the MT until the handover buffers are completely emptied.

As shown in Fig. 3, five phases can be identified in the handover cycle, with respect to the handover buffers:

a) MT transmits to BS_1 at the start of the handover algorithm; both handover buffers are bypassed by the cell flows; with reference to Fig. 2 this phase corresponds to the time period $t < t_3$;

b) MT is disconnected from BS_1, but not yet connected to BS_2; the ATM connection is not yet rerouted; upstream cells are stored in the MT transmission buffer; downstream cells are handled by the COS; with reference to Fig. 2 this situation corresponds to $t > t_3$, and $t < \min(\delta_2,\delta_4)$ for the upstream connection, and $t < \min(\delta_1,\delta_2)$ for the downstream connection;

c) MT is disconnected from BS_1, but not yet connected to BS_2; the rerouted ATM connection is available; upstream cells are stored in the MT transmission buffer; downstream cells are stored in the downstream handover buffer of BS_2; this corresponds to the interval $[\delta_4,\delta_2]$ for the upstream connection, and $[\delta_1,\delta_3]$ for the downstream connection;

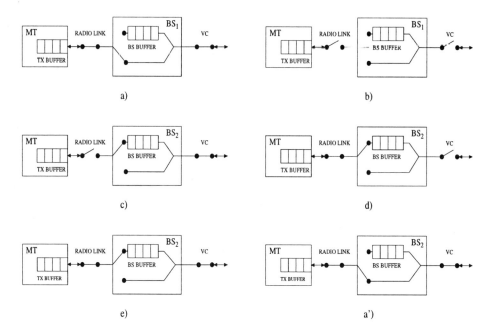

a)

b)

c)

d)

e)

a')

Fig. 3. Sequence of situations of the handover buffers during the execution of the handover algorithm

d) MT transmits to BS_2; the new ATM connection toward COS is not yet available; the upstream cell flow is stored in the upstream handover buffer of BS_2; downstream cells are handled by the COS; this phase corresponds to the interval $[\delta_2, \delta_5]$ for the upstream connection, and $[\delta_2, \delta_1]$ for the downstream connection;

e) MT transmits to BS_2; the upstream ATM connection is rerouted, and BS_2 can empty the handover buffers; this situation corresponds to $t > \max(\delta_2, \delta_4)$ for the upstream connection, and $t > \max(\delta_1, \delta_2)$ for the downstream connection;

a') MT transmits to BS_2; the handover buffers have been emptied, and are bypassed by the cell flows.

Two alternative sequences of phases are possible during the handover cycle, depending on whether the rerouting of the ATM connection is successfully terminated before or after the radio connection between the MT and BS_2 is established. If the ATM connection is rerouted before the radio connection to BS_2, then the sequence of phases is **a, b, c, e, a'**, and buffering is required for the downstream cell flow in the downstream handover buffer in phase **c**. If the ATM connection is rerouted after the radio connection to BS_2, then the sequence of phases is **a, b, d, e, a'**, and buffering is required for the upstream cell flow in the upstream handover buffer in phase **d**.

3.2   The End User Behavior

In order to dimension the handover buffers, it is necessary to know the characteristics of the traffic generated by users. The cell transmission rate on the radio link between a MT and the BS is normally determined by a traffic shaping device based on the GCRA algorithm [12]. This algorithm uses two parameters: the Peak Cell Rate (PCR) and the Sustainable Cell Rate (SCR). A bandwidth equal to PCR is assigned to each ATM connection in the fixed network, but any user transmits cells at an average rate equal to SCR.

According to the chosen handover protocol, cells are put in the upstream handover buffer at rate SCR (phases **d** and **e**) and are removed at rate PCR (phase **e**), and similarly cells arrive at the downstream handover buffer at rate SCR (phases **c** and **e**) and leave at rate PCR (phase **e**).

The average load produced by a MT is denoted by L_o, a variable parameter of the system.

3.3   Assumptions and Modeling Issues

In the case of data communication services, it can be assumed that each MT generates messages formed by a random number of cells that are transmitted at constant rate equal to SCR over the radio link. The number of cells in each message will be assumed to be geometrically distributed with an average that can be derived from the average traffic load generated by the MT.

The time between two handover requests from the same MT is assumed to be much longer than the time required for the completion of the handover algorithm. Thus, we assume that when the MT requests a new handover, the handover buffers involved in the previous handover of the same MT are empty. In other words, we assume that two handover cycles cannot overlap.

We also assume that the propagation delay in the W–ATM network is negligible with respect to the other times involved in the handover.

In the traffic description, we adopt the granularity corresponding to user messages, not to ATM cells, since this approach proved to be sufficiently accurate while producing a smaller number of states.

3.4   The GSPN Model

The GSPN model focuses on the behavior of one ATM connection between a MT and the corresponding remote terminal during the execution of the handover algorithm, with special attention to the buffers storing ATM cells in both the upstream and downstream directions.

Since the behaviors of the upstream and downstream cell flows are at least partially decoupled, two separate but quite similar GSPN models are developed for the dimensioning of the upstream and downstream handover buffers, respectively.

Each model comprises two interacting components, that respectively describe: i) the successive phases of the handover cycle, and ii) the impact of the behavior of the system components on the transmission and handover buffers.

GSPN Model for the Upstream Handover Buffer. In the case of the upstream handover buffer, the model focuses on the flow of messages generated by the MT, and sent toward a remote terminal through BS_1 before the handover, and through BS_2 after the handover. The first GSPN model component is shown

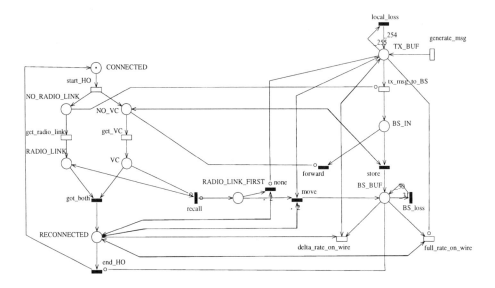

Fig. 4. The GSPN model for the design of the upstream handover buffer

in the left part of Fig. 4. A handover cycle starts when transition *start_HO* removes the token from place CONNECTED. The firing of this transition, with rate μ_{DC}, represents the passage from phase **a** to phase **b** of the handover cycle. The firing of *start_HO* generates a token in two places: NO_VC and NO_RADIO_LINK. The marking of place NO_RADIO_LINK indicates that MT is disconnected from BS_1 and not yet connected to BS_2; the marking of place NO_VC indicates that the ATM connection rerouting has not yet been completed. The marking of these two places enables the two timed transitions *get_radio_link* and *get_VC*, respectively. The former transition has rate μ_{NC}, and its firing models the establishment of the radio link between MT and BS_2; the latter has rate μ_{UT}, and models the rerouting of the ATM connection to BS_2.

If transition *get_radio_link* fires first, a token is generated in place RADIO_LINK, to model the availability of the radio link from MT to BS_2 (the resulting marking is equivalent to phase **d**, when the upstream cell flow is stored into the upstream handover buffer). When transition *get_VC* then fires, the token in place NO_VC is moved into place VC, to model the availability of the ATM connection toward BS_2.

Instead, if transition *get_VC* fires first, a token is generated in place VC, before the marking of place RADIO_LINK (phase **c**), and no message is buffered in the upstream handover buffer because the ATM connection is already open when MT establishes the radio link to BS$_2$.

When a token is present in both places RADIO_LINK and VC, transition *got_both* fires, and a token is generated in place RECONNECTED (phase e).

The token is removed from place RECONNECTED through the firing of transition *end_HO* after the upstream handover buffer has been emptied and the handover has thus been completed.

The second GSPN model component is shown in the right part of Fig. 4. Transition *generate_msg* models the generation of user messages according to a Poisson process with rate μ_{gen}; tokens produced into place TX_BUF model messages stored in the MT transmission buffer, that is assumed to have a capacity equivalent to 254 messages (overflow messages are discarded through the firing of transition *local_loss*). The rate μ_{gen} is computed from the MT average offered load (L$_o$ Mb/s) and the mean number of cells per message (ν_b) by using the relation: $\mu_{gen} = \frac{L_o}{424\,\nu_b}$.

Transition *tx_msg_to_BS* models the continuous transmission of messages from the MT toward the BS to which it is connected (either BS$_1$ or BS$_2$); this transmission is interrupted only in the periods in which no connection is available between the MT and a BS (after disconnecting from BS$_1$ but before connecting to BS$_2$). For this reason an inhibitor arc is necessary from place NO_RADIO_LINK to transition *tx_msg_to_BS*. Since the MT transmits on the radio link at rate SCR, the firing rate of transition *tx_msg_to_BS* is $\mu_r = \frac{SCR}{424\,\nu_b}$.

Tokens produced by the firing of transition *tx_msg_to_BS* are deposited in place BS_IN, that models the input interface of either BS$_1$ or BS$_2$. When a token reaches place BS_IN, if place NO_VC is empty (the ATM connection is available), transition *forward* fires and discards it (the message needs not be stored in the upstream handover buffer since cells can be immediately forwarded onto the fixed network segment). Otherwise (place NO_VC is marked because the ATM connection is not available), transition *store* fires and "moves" the token to place BS_BUF that models the upstream handover buffer where the message is stored. This buffer is assumed to have a capacity equivalent to 30 messages (overflow messages are discarded through the firing of transition *BS_loss*). The transmission of messages out of the upstream handover buffer is jointly modeled by the three transitions *tx_msg_to_BS*, *delta_rate_on_wire*, *full_rate_on_wire*, that are simultaneously enabled when place RECONNECTED is marked (in phase e). When place TX_BUF is empty (the MT transmission buffer contains no message), only transition *full_rate_on_wire* is enabled, and the transmission on the wired network segment proceeds at rate PCR (the transition rate is $\mu_\phi = \frac{PCR}{424\,\nu_b'}$ – for a definition of ν_b' see the next section) emptying the upstream handover buffer of BS$_2$. When place TX_BUF is marked (the MT transmission buffer contains messages), both transitions *tx_msg_to_BS* and *delta_rate_on_wire* are enabled. The two transitions model the fact that the transmission from the MT to the BS proceeds at the usual rate SCR, whereas the transmission on the wired network segment proceeds at rate PCR. The actual flow of messages through the upstream handover buffer is not described in detail in this case. Indeed, tokens generated in place BS_IN are discarded through transition *forward* rather than moved to place BS_BUF (this accounts for the buffer loading rate equal to SCR, and for a portion of the unloading rate that is actually PCR), and the upstream handover buffer content is decreased at rate PCR−SCR (the rate of transition *delta_rate_on_wire* is $\mu_\delta = \frac{\text{PCR}-\text{SCR}}{424\,\nu'_b}$ to model the additional speed at which the buffer is emptied).

Only after place BS_BUF becomes empty the handover terminates, and transition *end_HO* can fire.

Three more transitions are necessary to cope with our choice of modeling the user information with a granularity corresponding to messages rather than cells. If the MT connects to BS_2 before the ATM connection is rerouted, it may happen that at the time the connection is rerouted only a portion of a user message (some cells) is present in the upstream handover buffer. In the real system, the fact that the upstream handover buffer contains some cells, but no whole message, is not relevant, and the handover proceeds as usual. Instead, in our model this means that place BS_BUF is found empty when a token is generated in place RECONNECTED, and this causes the immediate termination of the handover. In order to avoid this behavior, place RADIO_LINK_FIRST is used to record whether the radio link to BS_2 was established before the rerouting of the ATM connection, and the two immediate transitions *none* and *move* are introduced to generate a message into the BS upstream handover buffer, if the MT transmission buffer is not empty (by so doing we actually model with two different tokens two portions of one message; this can be done without much influence on the performance metrics thanks to the geometric characteristics of message lengths). Note that for the model to work properly, transitions *move* and *none* must have higher priority than transition *end_HO*.

The initial marking of the GSPN model comprises just one token in place CONNECTED.

GSPN Model for the Downstream Handover Buffer. In the case of the downstream handover buffer, the model focuses on the flow of messages generated by a remote terminal, and sent to the MT through BS_1 before the handover, and through BS_2 after the handover.

The GSPN model for the determination of the correct size of the downstream handover buffer is shown in Fig. 5. It can be immediately observed that this model is quite similar to the one in Fig. 4. Indeed, the left part of the GSPN remains identical, since it just describes the sequence of handover phases, and the right part of the GSPN still models the message flow and the handover buffer.

However, in this case the generation of user messages takes place at the remote user, that is not performing the handover; thus, transition *tx_msg_to_BS* is not disabled by the presence of a token in place NO_RADIO_LINK, but by the presence of a token in place NO_VC, since now cells cannot reach the base station during the ATM connection rerouting.

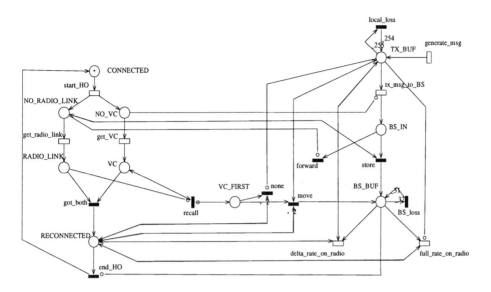

Fig. 5. The GSPN model for the design of the downstream handover buffer

Moreover, transitions *forward* and *store* are now mutually exclusive depending on the marking of place NO_RADIO_LINK, since now cells must be stored at BS_2 in the period of radio link disconnection.

Finally, transition *recall* in this case must fire if the ATM connection rerouting takes place *before* the establishment of the radio link from MT to BS_2.

3.5 Cell Level Performance Indices

The derivation of cell-level performance metrics from the GSPN model requires some work because of the choice of modeling with tokens user messages rather than individual ATM cells.

One token in place TX_BUF models a user message just generated by MT; thus in this case the average number of ATM cells associated with one token is simply ν_b.

Instead, in order to compute the average number of ATM cells represented by tokens marking place BS_BUF, denoted by ν_b', it is necessary to reason about the GSPN behavior.

When transition *get_VC* fires after *get_radio_link*, transitions *tx_msg_to_BS* and *get_VC* are concurrently enabled. Therefore, the average time between two consecutive firings of transition *tx_msg_to_BS* becomes equal to $1/(\mu_r + \mu_{\mathrm{UT}})$. The average number of ATM cells associated with tokens generated in place BS_BUF can thus be derived as the average number of cells transmitted over the radio link during a time lapse equal to $1/(\mu_r + \mu_{\mathrm{UT}})$. Hence, $\nu_b' = \frac{\mathrm{SCR}}{424(\mu_r + \mu_{\mathrm{UT}})}$, where SCR is the cell transmission rate over the radio link.

Moreover, since the time between two consecutive firings of timed transitions is exponentially distributed, the number of ATM cells associated with each token is taken to be geometrically distributed.

Let $e(i)$ denote the probability that one token represents i cells (with $e(0)=0$, i.e., each token models at least one ATM cell). Given $e(i)$, $\forall i \geq 0$, the probability $E_k(i)$ that k tokens model i ATM cells can be derived for $k \geq 0$ as follows:

$$E_0(0) = 1 \tag{1}$$

$$E_1(i) = e(i) \qquad \forall\, i > 0 \tag{2}$$

$$E_k(i) = 0 \qquad \forall\, i, k :\; i < k \tag{3}$$

$$E_k(i) = \sum_{j=1}^{i-1} E_{k-1}(i - j)\, E_1(j) \qquad \forall\, k > 1, i \geq k\,. \tag{4}$$

Given the above expressions, once the GSPN model is solved, and the steady-state probabilities of markings are obtained, the performance metrics of interest can be obtained. We present formulas for the performance metrics referring to the upstream handover buffer, but those referring to the downstream handover buffer can be derived with minor changes.

The probability that during phases **d** and **e** the marking of place BS_BUF is equal to k is written as: $P\{\#\text{BS\_BUF}=k \mid \#\text{RADIO\_LINK}=1\ or\ \#\text{RECONNECTED}=1\}$.

Then, the probability that the upstream handover buffer contains n cells is

$$B(n) = \sum_{k=0}^{n} P\{\#\text{BS\_BUF} = k \mid \#\text{RADIO\_LINK} = 1\ or$$

$$\#\text{RECONNECTED} = 1\}\, E_k(n) \tag{5}$$

$\forall\, n \geq 0$. From these probabilities, given an upstream handover buffer size in cells, it is trivial to compute the cell loss probability due to buffer overflows.

In order to evaluate the average delay affecting the ATM cells stored in the upstream handover buffer, we distinguish between the two phases **d** and **e** of the handover procedure. A cell that is put in the handover buffer during phase **d** leaves the buffer only after the upstream connection is ready and all the cells before the considered one are forwarded toward the fixed network segment. Instead, a cell stored during phase **e** remains in the buffer only for the time necessary to remove the cells before it. Therefore, we need to compute separately for phases **d** and **e** the probabilities that a cell arriving from the MT transmission buffer to the upstream handover buffer finds n cells in the BS buffer as follows:

$$Q_c(n) = \sum_{k=0}^{n} P\{\#\text{BS\_BUF} = k \mid \#\text{RADIO\_LINK} = 1, \#\text{TX\_BUF} > 0\}\, E_k(n) \tag{6}$$

$$Q_d(n) = \sum_{k=0}^{n} P\{\#\text{BS\_BUF} = k \mid \#\text{RECONNECTED} = 1, \#\text{TX\_BUF} > 0\}\, E_k(n)\,. \tag{7}$$

Then, we compute the average delay of ATM cells due to the upstream handover buffer as:

$$M_d = \left[\mu_{\text{UT}} + \left(\sum_n n\, Q_c(n)\right) \tau_{\text{PCR}}\right] \frac{P\{\#\text{RADIO\_LINK} = 1, \#\text{TX\_BUF} > 0\}}{P_T} +$$
$$\left(\sum_n n\, Q_d(n)\right) \tau_{\text{PCR}} \frac{P\{\#\text{RECONNECTED} = 1, \#\text{TX\_BUF} > 0\}}{P_T} \qquad (8)$$

$\forall\, n \geq 0$, being τ_{PCR} the cell transmission time at rate PCR and $P_T = P\{\#\text{RADIO\_LINK} = 1, \#\text{TX\_BUF} > 0\} + P\{\#\text{RECONNECTED}=1, \#\text{TX\_BUF} > 0\}$.

4 Numerical Results

The validation of the GSPN models accuracy was based on the comparison of performance metrics obtained by either numerically solving the Markov chains associated with the GSPN models, or running detailed simulation experiments. The numerical analysis of GSPN models was implemented with the GreatSPN software [13], that is the standard tool for the development and solution of GSPN models. Simulation runs were based on a software tool named CLASS[2] (Cell-Level ATM Services Simulator) [14], that, as the name implies, allows the simulation of ATM networks at the time scale referring to cells and groups of cells; indeed, CLASS simulations implement the movement and handling of ATM cells within the network elements of interest (observe that while GSPN models operate at the message level, CLASS operates at the cell level; the two descriptions of the system dynamics are thus quite different, and could be expected to produce different results). In particular CLASS adopts rather sophisticated statistical techniques for the estimation of the confidence level and accuracy of its performance estimates; all simulation results that will be presented in this secion have 5% accuracy and 99% confidence level.

In our study, for some system parameters we choose specific values, and keep them fixed for all cases; in particular we set $\mu_{\text{DC}}=0.001$ ms^{-1}, $\mu_{\text{NC}}=2.35$ ms^{-1}, and PCR=2.0 Mb/s. This means that we assume that the MT generates a new handover request on the average 1 s after the completion of the previous handover, and that the average time to establish the radio link to BS$_2$ is 425 μs. The time between two successive handover requests is clearly too short if the GSPN model must describe the behavior of just one user, but may be adequate for the description of the collective behavior of a population of MTs. It must be noted however that in this case our model does not capture the effect of simultaneous handovers. Nevertheless, the maximum number of allowed concurrent handovers is a parameter whose value can be fixed by the network manager, and hence can be considered to be known. Once this value is known, the buffer sizing can still

---

[2] CLASS is a general purpose ATM networks simulator developed by Politecnico di Torino, in cooperation with CSELT, the research center of Telecom Italia, and the Technical University of Budapest.

be based on the results obtained with the GSPN model: the result of the buffer sizing with the GSPN model has to be multiplied by the permitted number of concurrent handovers.

Instead, for other system parameters we use variable values in order to produce curves of the system performance as a function of such values. The parameters whose values will be varied are L_o, SCR, and μ_{UT}.

The first validation results concern the probability density function of the number of cells within the upstream handover buffer, that is presented with curves of the probability $B(n)$ that the upstream handover buffer contains n cells. In Fig. 6 the curves of $B(n)$ are presented for L_o=0.5 Mb/s, SCR=1.9 Mb/s, μ_{UT}=0.25 ms^{-1} (the average time to reroute the ATM connection is 4 ms). Fig. 7 presents the same curves with L_o=1.5 Mb/s. Plots on the left use a linear vertical scale, to better show the behavior for large probability values, while plots on the right use a logarithmic vertical scale, to better show the behavior for small probability values. From all plots we can see an extraordinarily good match between simulation results and GSPN predictions. The only significant differences are found for the distribution tails, where the simulation results are based on very small numbers of samples, and are thus unreliable. In Figs. 8

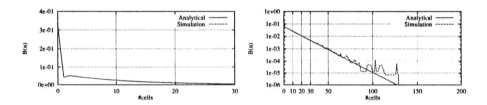

Fig. 6. Probability density function of the number of cells within the upstream handover buffer, for L_o=0.5 Mb/s, SCR=1.9 Mb/s, μ_{UT}=0.25 ms^{-1}

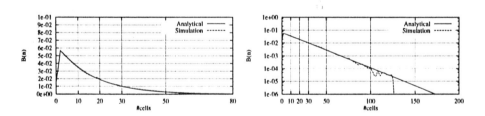

Fig. 7. Probability density function of the number of cells within the upstream handover buffer, for L_o=1.5 Mb/s, SCR=1.9 Mb/s, μ_{UT}=0.25 ms^{-1}

and 9 we again present curves of $B(n)$, for L_o=1.5 Mb/s, SCR=2.0 Mb/s, and μ_{UT}=0.25 ms^{-1} (the average time to reroute the ATM connection is 4 ms) in the first case, and for $L_o=0.5$ Mb/s, SCR$=1.9$ Mb/s, and $\mu_{\mathrm{UT}}=0.1$ ms^{-1} (the average time to reroute the ATM connection is 10 ms) in the second case. Also in these cases significant differences are found only for the distribution tails; otherwise the curves practically overlap. The second set of validation results concerns

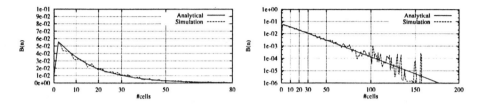

Fig. 8. Probability density function of the number of cells within the upstream handover buffer, for $L_o=1.5$ Mb/s, SCR$=2.0$ Mb/s, $\mu_{\mathrm{UT}}=0.25$ ms^{-1}

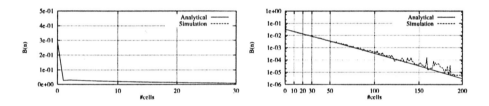

Fig. 9. Probability density function of the number of cells within the upstream handover buffer, for $L_o=0.5$ Mb/s, SCR$=1.9$ Mb/s, $\mu_{\mathrm{UT}}=0.1$ ms^{-1}

the average cell delays in the upstream handover buffer. In Table 2 we present values of M_d, for different values of L_o, SCR, and μ_{UT}. Also for this different performance metrics the accuracy of GSPN predictions is not distinguishable from that of simulation results. Indeed, the GSPN estimates always fall within the confidence interval of the simulator point estimates.

Coming now to the downstream handover buffer, we present in Fig. 10 curves of $B(n)$ for $L_o=0.5$ Mb/s, and SCR$=1.9$ Mb/s, and in Figs. 11 the same curves with $L_o=1.8$ Mb/s. The GSPN results are obtained assuming that transition get_VC in Fig. 5 is immediate, hence supposing that the downstream rerouting of the ATM connection always takes place before the establishment of the radio link between MT and BS$_2$, as normally happens with reasonable system parameters. The match between simulation results and GSPN performance predictions is now less precise, specially as regards the distribution tails. However, it should be noted that the number of cells stored in the downstream handover buffer is quite small, so that the problem of correctly dimensioning this buffer is less critical with respect to the correct sizing of the upstream handover buffer.

Table 2. Average cell delays in the upstream handover buffer for variable values of L_o, SCR, and μ_{UT}

L_o (Mb/s)	SCR (Mb/s)	μ_{UT}(ms^{-1})	M_d (ms) Analys.	Simul.
0.5	1.9	0.25	4.02	4.05
1.5	1.9	0.25	3.97	3.98
1.8	1.9	0.25	4.03	4.09
1.5	2.0	0.25	3.98	4.06
0.5	1.9	0.1	9.69	9.92

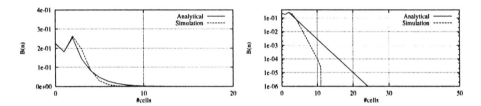

Fig. 10. Probability density function of the number of cells within the downstream handover buffer, for L_o=0.5 Mb/s, SCR=1.9 Mb/s

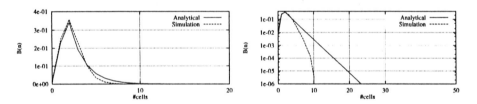

Fig. 11. Probability density function of the number of cells within the downstream handover buffer, for L_o=1.8 Mb/s, SCR=1.9 Mb/s

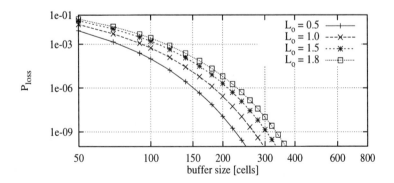

Fig. 12. Cell loss probability versus the upstream handover buffer size, for SCR=1.9 Mb/s, PCR=2.0 Mb/s, μ_{UT}=0.25 ms^{-1}, and variable values of L_o

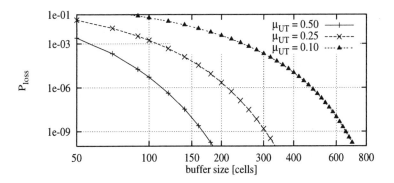

Fig. 13. Cell loss probability versus the upstream handover buffer size for L_o=1.5 Mb/s, SCR=1.9 Mb/s, PCR=2.0 Mb/s, and variable values of μ_{UT}

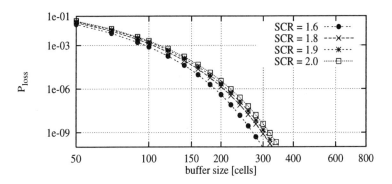

Fig. 14. Cell loss probability versus the upstream handover buffer size for L_o=1.5 Mb/s, PCR=2.0 Mb/s, μ_{UT}=0.25 ms^{-1}, and variable values of SCR

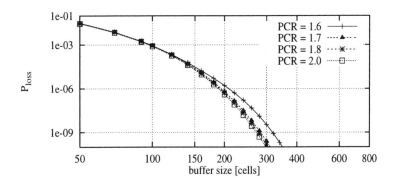

Fig. 15. Cell loss probability versus the upstream handover buffer size for L_o=1.5 Mb/s, SCR=1.6 Mb/s, μ_{UT}=0.25 ms^{-1}, and variable values of PCR

Finally, we present in Fig. 12 the curves of the cell loss probability resulting from a variable upstream handover buffer size (in the abscissa) for SCR=1.9 Mb/s, μ_{UT}=0.25 ms^{-1} (the average time to reroute the ATM connection is 4 ms), and variable L_o. The results are obtained with the GSPN model, and are almost impossible to match with simulation results, due to the excessive amount of CPU time necessary to produce similar curves by simulation (note that loss probabilities become quite small, and thus obtaining accurate estimates by simulation becomes almost impossible). In Fig. 13 we present similar curves for SCR=1.9 Mb/s, L_o=1.5 Mb/s, and variable μ_{UT}. In Fig. 14 we use L_o=1.5 Mb/s, μ_{UT}=0.25 ms^{-1} (the average time to reroute the ATM connection is 4 ms), and variable SCR. In Fig. 15 we use L_o=1.5 Mb/s, μ_{UT}=0.25 ms^{-1} (the average time to reroute the ATM connection is 4 ms), SCR=1.6 Mb/s, and variable PCR (this is the only case in which we vary PCR, contrary to what was said at the beginning of this section). The observation of the curves indicates that the loss probability within the upstream handover buffer is most sensitive to the value of μ_{UT}, hence to the time necessary for the rerouting of the ATM connection. From the observation of the results we may conclude that the sizes of the handover buffers that yield acceptable values of cell loss probabilities are rather small, so that with adequate buffering at the base station it may be possible to permit a significant number of simultaneous handovers without compromising the quality of the services offered to end users.

5   Conclusions

A GSPN model of a specific handover protocol for W-ATM networks was presented, and was shown to be capable of providing accurate estimates on several performance metrics of interest. In particular, the numerical solution of the Markov chain derived from the GSPN model was proved to yield performance predictions as accurate as those generated with detailed and very CPU-intensive simulation runs.

The GSPN model results confirm previous conclusions, reached after observing the outputs of simulation runs, about the greater buffering requirement of the upstream cell flow during handover.

The fact that with the GSPN model it is possible to obtain with little effort accurate estimates about low cell loss probability values (down to 10^{-9}) in the upstream handover buffer, allows its correct dimensioning for predefined quality of service objectives. This same procedure is practically impossible by simulation, due to the excessive CPU requirements for the accurate estimation of such low loss probabilities.

6   Acknowledgments

The authors should like to thank Giuliana Franceschinis, Michela Meo, and Marco Siccardi for their help in the initial phases of this work.

References

1. Ajmone Marsan, M., Chiasserini, C.-F., Fumagalli, A., Lo Cigno, R., Munafò, M.: Local and Global Handovers for Mobility Management in Wireless ATM Networks. IEEE Personal Comm. (1997) 6–15
2. Karol, M.J., Eng, K.Y., Veeraghavan, M., Ayanoglu, E.: BAHAMA: Broadband Ad-Hoc Wireless ATM Local-Area Network. Proc. ICC (1995) 1216–1223
3. Mitts, H., Hansen, H., Immonen, J., Veikkolainen, S.: Lossless Handover for Wireless ATM. ACM/Baltzer MONET Special Issue on Wireless ATM **3** (1996) 299–312
4. Toh, C.-K.: A Hybrid Handover Protocol for Local Area Wireless ATM Networks. ACM/Baltzer MONET Special Issue on Wireless ATM **3** (1996) 313–334
5. Toh, C.-K.: Crossover Switch Discovery for Wireless ATM LANs. Journal on Mobile Networks and Applications **1** (1996) 141–165
6. Yuan, R., Biswas, S.K., French, L.J., Li, J., Raychaudhuri, D.: A Signaling and Control Architecture for Mobility Support in Wireless ATM Networks. ACM/Baltzer MONET Special Issue on Wireless ATM **3** (1996) 287–298
7. Ramjee, R., LaPorta, T., Kurose, J., Towsley, D.,: Performance Evaluation of Connection Rerouting Schemes for ATM-based Wireless Networks. Technical Report UM-CS-1997-038 University of Massachusetts (1997)
8. Porter, J., Hopper, A., Gilmurray, D., Mason, O., Naylon, J.: The ORL Radio ATM System, Architecture and Implementation. Olivetti & Oracle Research Laboratory Technical Report 96-5 (1996)
9. Ajmone Marsan, M., Balbo, G., Conte, G., Donatelli, S., Franceschinis, G.: Modeling with Generalized Stochastic Petri Nets. J. Wiley & Sons (1995)
10. Kleinrock, L.: Queueing Systems. J. Wiley & Sons (1975)
11. Ajmone Marsan, M., Chiasserini, C.-F., Fumagalli, A., Lo Cigno, R., Munafò, M.: Buffer Requirements for Loss-Free Handovers in Wireless ATM Networks. IEEE ATM'97 Workshop (1997)
12. ITU-TSS Study Group 13: Recommendation I.371 Traffic Control and Congestion Control in B-ISDN. (1995)
13. Chiola, G., Franceschinis, G., Gaeta, R., Ribaudo, M.: GreatSPN 1.7: Graphical Editor and Analyzer for Timed and Stochastic Petri Nets. Performance Evaluation Special Issue on Performance Modeling Tools **24** (1995) 47–68
14. Ajmone Marsan, M., Lo Cigno, R., Bianco, A., Do, T.V., Jereb, L., Munafò, M.: ATM Simulation with CLASS. Performance Evaluation Special Issue on Performance Modeling Tools **24** (1995) 137–159

A Class of Well Structured Petri Nets for Flexible Manufacturing Systems [*]

J. Ezpeleta, F. García-Vallés and J.M. Colom

Departamento de Informática e Ingeniería de Sistemas
Centro Politécnico Superior de Ingenieros
María de Luna 3. 50015 Zaragoza. Spain

Abstract. This paper is devoted to the synthesis of "well behaved" (live) nets. The work focuses on the synthesis of a subclass of nets that appear in the modeling of a wide set of flexible manufacturing systems (FMS). Basically, these nets are composed of a set of sequential processes that share a set of common resources (with some constraints in their use). Among the set of problems related to FMS, we are going to concentrate on deadlocks. In this paper, we show that for the systems under consideration it is possible to know, from a structural point of view, if a deadlock is reachable. We also show that this knowledge can be obtained in linear time (with respect to the size of the PN model). The result can be used in order to have a quick answer to whether a given configuration is correct or not, to study if such a configuration exists or not and to conclude if some deadlock control policy is needed.
Topics: System design and verification using nets, Analysis and synthesis, Structure and behaviour of nets, Application to flexible manufacturing.

1 Introduction

The present paper focuses on the study of a special class of nets that appear in the modelling of FMS. Roughly speaking, an FMS can be considered as composed of a set of flexible machines (where different operations can be executed), an automatic transport/handling system used for the transport/storage of work-in-process parts and raw materials, and a sophisticated control system. The control system has to ensure that each production order is accomplished [18, 20]. In an FMS different types of parts have to be processed. For each type, the set of different correct processing sequences is specified by means of its "process plan".

Due to the fact that sets of parts are concurrently processed, and that these parts have to share the same set of system resources, theoretical models of the system behaviour are needed. Among other models, Petri nets are widely used [20, 8, 25, 7, 16] in FMS environments. One important desirable property for these systems (in terms of the Petri net model) is the liveness. The non

---

[*] This work has been partially supported by the Spanish research project CICYT TAP 95-0574

liveness of the model implies that the production of some parts, once started, cannot be finished. Deadlock situations are not desirable when a highly automated system is needed. In this paper we concentrate on the study of liveness properties for the considered systems.

The liveness problem can be mainly approached from three different points of view. The first one is the deadlock detection/recovery problem. From this perspective, the model is used in order to detect when the system reaches a deadlock. Then, a deadlock recovery strategy is applied [17, 23]. The second one is the deadlock prevention/avoidance strategy. When adopted, some constraints are imposed on the system evolution so that it is always possible to ensure that the processing of each part (the execution of each process) can be finished. One of the best known deadlock avoidance algorithms is the "banker algorithm" [9]. See [21, 1, 14, 11] for algorithms applied to FMS environments. The third one is the synthesis approach. The aim of this approach is to build models that verify the desired properties. In the model construction process, only specific rules are allowed. The application of these rules ensures that the final model satisfies the desired properties. These techniques are not suitable for general nets, but for special subclasses [22, 10]. For FMS environments, see for instance [3, 26, 15].

In the present work the synthesis strategy is adopted when working with a class of nets. The class of nets considered in this paper ($L - S^3 PR$, a complicated acronym for a class of structurally simple nets) belongs to a more general class of nets ($S^3 PR$) that was studied in [11].

When the engineer is building the model, the following questions often arise: Is it possible, in the current system configuration, to reach a deadlock? Moreover, if in the current well behaved system new types of parts are introduced (a typical consequence of the system "flexibility"), Is the system behaviour still correct? The answers to these questions fall into the synthesis approach. In this paper we provide answers to the previous questions when we are constrained to the class of $L - S^3 PR$ nets. So, a negative answer means that problems can arise, and some strategy must be adopted. In contrast, if the the answer is yes, no control policy is necessary, and so, the system performance is not decreased by the use of unnecessary control.

As stated in [4], there are four necessary conditions in order to have a deadlock in a concurrent system using a set of common resources. These well known conditions are: 1) *mutual exclusion of resources* (this means that each instance of each system resource cannot be used for more than one process simultaneously), 2) *hold and wait condition* (this means that if a process uses some instance of some resource and needs a new resource in order to change its state, this change of state cannot be carried out if the new resource required is not available), 3) *no preemption condition* (this means that a process will free the resources that it is using only in a "voluntary" way), and 4) *circular wait* (this means that a state is reached in which there exists a circular chain of processes so that each process is using some resource that is required by the next one in the chain in order to change its state).

In FMS, the first three necessary conditions are usually true. Therefore, deadlock prevention/avoidance algorithms have tried to invalidate the last condition in different ways. However, an interesting question arises. Let us consider the static structure of the system given by means of the Petri net model. Observing the model, it is possible to "see" that there exist some *potential* circular waits. Let us consider, for instance, the net in Figure 3. If we consider the resources modeled by means of places $M1$ and $R1$, perhaps a system state (modeled by means of a marking M) is reachable such that $M[P1.M1] = 2$ and $M[P2.R1] = 1$, which establishes a circular wait composed of the processes modeled by means of the tokens in places $P1.M1$ and $P2.R1$. Is it possible to reach such a state (marking M)? In this case, the answer is yes. However, this is not always true. Let us consider, for instance, the net in Figure 1. A potential circular wait analogous to the previous one appears if we consider resources $r1$ and $r2$. But in this system no state is reachable in which this potential circular wait is reached (since the Petri net is live).

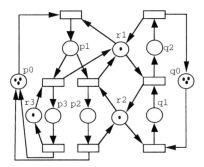

Fig. 1. A potential circular wait that does not generate a deadlock.

In this paper we are going to prove that for the class of systems considered, the existence of a potential circular wait is a necessary and sufficient condition for system deadlocks. As a consequence, we are going to prove that the liveness of a given system (belonging to the class we are working with) can be established in linear time. These results can be used during the system design process in order to find a good system configuration.

The problem of characterizing system deadlocks in this kind of nets has been studied in [24]. The characterization presented in [24] is very different to that developed in this paper, and the proof is wrong, as the reader can easily check with the net depicted in Figure 7.

The rest of the paper is organised as follows: Section 2 introduces, first in an intuitive way and second in a more formal way, the class of nets considered in this paper. The main structural and behavioral properties are also presented. Finally, the close relation between structure and behaviour for this class of nets is also considered. In section 3, a complete characterisation of the liveness property for the class is given. Finally, a linear time characterisation of "well behaved" systems is presented. In Section 4 some conclusions and future work directions are presented.

Through out the paper we are assuming the reader is familiar with the Petri net concepts, terminology and notations. In any case, an Appendix is provided with the main Petri net definitions and notations used in this paper.

2 The class of the $L - S^3PR$

2.1 Definition of the class

Let us now introduce, in an intuitive way, a class of Petri nets that appear in a wide range of FMS. Figure 2 shows the layout of an FMS cell composed of two robots ($R1$ and $R2$) and three machines ($M1$, $M2$ and $M3$). Robot $R1$ can load and unload parts from machines $M1$ and $M2$. Robot $R2$ can load and unload parts from machines $M2$ and $M3$, and also from conveyor $I3$. In this cell, three different types of parts can be processed according to their own process plans. Parts of Type 1 arrive at the system by conveyor $I1$, are processed in $M1$, then in $M2$ and then in $M3$; finally, they leave the system by conveyor $O1/O3$ (process plan WP1). Parts of Type 2 arrive at the system by conveyor $I2$, are processed in machine $M2$ and then in machine $M1$ and leave the system by conveyor $O2$ (process plan WP2). Parts of Type 3 arrive at the system by conveyor $I3$, are processed in $M3$ and leave the system by conveyor $O1/O3$ (process plan WP3). We assume that each machine can process two parts concurrently and that each robot can hold a single part at a time.

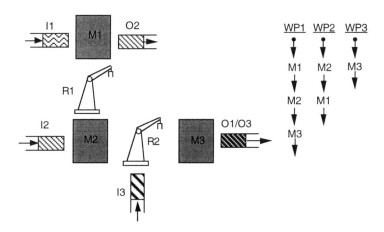

Fig. 2. Layout of an FMS where three types of parts must be processed. Process plans associated with each type of part.

In the Petri net model of the system behaviour (Figure 3), places $R1$, $R2$, $M1$, $M2$, $M3$ model the capacities of the system resources (the two robots R1 and R2, and the three machines M1, M2 and M3). The rest of the places model the different states in which a part, depending on its type and according to its process plan, can stay. Transitions model the changes in the states of parts. For instance, a part of Type 2 can stay, sequentially, in the states modeled by places $P2.M2$, $P2.R1$ and $P2.M1$ that represent the following sequence: when the part arrives at the system, it is loaded into machine $M2$ (the firing of transition $P2toM2$ puts a token in place $P2.M2$); from this state, it has to be picked up by robot $R1$ (the firing of transition $P2toR1$ puts a token in place $P2.R1$); the robot has to load it into machine $M1$ (a token in place $P2.M1$); finally, the part goes to the outside of the cell (firing of transition $P2toO2$).

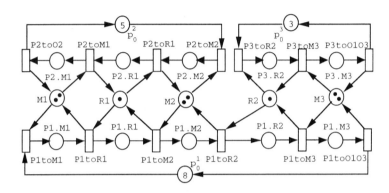

Fig. 3. A Petri net modelling the behaviour of the FMS in Figure 2.

Let us give now a more formal definition of the $L - S^3PR$ class. This class is very similar to that dealt with in [1, 14, 24], only a few modifications have been introduced: 1) The concept of "idle" state place has been added in order to emphasize the cyclic nature of the processing of one type of parts; 2) A type of part can arrive to a given state using different paths. However, as in the nets in [1, 14, 24], no choice, except the resource allocation, is taken in real time during the processing of each part. Then, $L - S^3PR$ is a subclass of the class S^3PR, presented in [11].

A net belonging to this class is formed by a set of state machines (each one modeling the sequences of states in which a part of a given type can stay during its processing in the system) holding and releasing a set of shared resources, each modeled by means of a monitor (whose initial marking models either the number of copies of the resource considered or its capacity). The state machines do not contain choices from internal states (except for the idle state).

Definition 1. *A* Linear S^3PR *($L - S^3PR$) is an ordinary Petri net* $\mathcal{N} = (P, T, F)$ *such that:*

i) $P = P_R \cup P_S \cup P_0$ *is a partition such that:*
   a) $P_0 = \{p_0^1, \ldots, p_0^k\}, k > 0$ *(idle state places).*

b) $P_S = \bigcup_{i=1}^k P_S^i$, *where* $P_S^i \cap P_S^j = \emptyset$, *for all* $i \neq j$.

c) $P_R = \{r_1, \ldots, r_n\}, n > 0$.

ii) $T = \bigcup_{i=1}^k T^i$, *where* $T^i \cap T^j = \emptyset$, *for all* $i \neq j$.

iii) $\forall i \in \{1, \ldots, k\}$ *the subnet* $\mathcal{N}^i$ *generated by* $\{p_0^i\} \cup P_S^i \cup T^i$ *is a strongly connected state machine, such that every cycle contains* $\{p_0^i\}$ *and* $\forall p \in P_S^i$, $| p^\bullet | = 1$.

iv) $\forall i \in \{1, \ldots, k\}$, $\forall p \in P_S^i$, $^{\bullet\bullet}p \cap P_R = p^{\bullet\bullet} \cap P_R$ *and* $| \, ^{\bullet\bullet}p \cap P_R \,| = 1$.

v) $\mathcal{N}$ *is strongly connected.*

Each subnet $\mathcal{N}^i$ in the third point above defines a *Linear Simple Sequential Process* $L - S^2P$. If we consider the subnet generated by a process i and the resources it uses, we have a *Linear Simple Sequential Process with Resources,* $L - S^2PR$. Therefore, an $L - S^2PR$ is an $L - S^2P$ using a single resource for each state other than the process idle state place. The interactions of one process with the rest of processes in the whole system (the System of $L - S^2PR$, $L - S^3PR$) are made by sharing the set of resources. Therefore, it is natural to think that in the idle state there is no interaction and so, in this state no resource is used.

p_0^i is called the idle state place of process i. The fact that each cycle contain the idle state (stated in *iii*) imposes a property of termination on the processing of parts (if a part advances in its processing the idle state is reached, which means that its processing is finished).

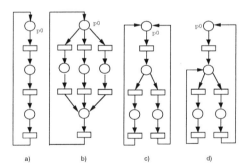

a)   b)   c)   d)

Fig. 4. Some examples of processes (resources are not depicted for the shake of simplicity). In all cases p_0 represents the idle state place: a) and b) represent processes belonging to $L - S^3PR$; c) represents a process belonging to S^3PR but not allowed in $L - S^3PR$; d) represents a process not belonging to the S^3PR class.

The special constraints imposed on the state machines in an $L - S^3PR$ and the way in which they use the set of resources is what give the names *linear* and *simple* to these processes (see examples of allowed and disallowed processes for the class of $L - S^3PR$ in Figure 4).

P_R is called the *set of resources.* We will also use the following terminology:

- for a given $p \in P_S$, ${}^{\bullet \bullet}p \cap P_R = \{r_p\}$. The resource r_p is called the *resource used by* p.
- for a given $r \in P_R$, $H(r) = {}^{\bullet \bullet}r \cap P_S$ $(= r^{\bullet \bullet} \cap P_S)$ is called the *set of holders* of r (states that use r).

Example: Let us consider the $L - S^3PR$ in Figure 3. For this net the elements previously defined are:

1. $P_0 = \{p_0^1, p_0^2, p_0^3\}$
2. $P_R = \{M1, M2, M3, R1, R2\}$
3. $P_S^1 = \{P1.M1, P1.R1, P1.M2, P1.R2, P1.M3\}$,
   $P_S^2 = \{P2.M2, P2.R1, P2.M1\}$, $P_S^3 = \{P3.M3, P3.R2\}$
4. $T^1 = \{P1toM1, P1toR1, P1toM2, P1toR2, P1toM3, P1toO1O3\}$,
   $T^2 = \{P2toM2, P2toR1, P2toM1, P2toO2\}$,
   $T^3 = \{P3toR2, P3toM3, P3toO1O3\}$
5. $H(M1) = \{P1.M1, P2.M1\}$, $H(R1) = \{P1.R1, P2.R1\}$,
   $H(M2) = \{P1.M2, P2.M2\}$, $H(R2) = \{P1.R2, P3.R2\}$,
   $H(M3) = \{P1.M3, P3.M3\}$

From an applied point of view, $L - S^3PR$ models impose that the system controller establishes the production sequence for a part when it arrives to the system. The only decisions to be taken in real time by the FMS refer to the granting of the system resources. Now, a family of initial markings for the $L - S^3PR$ class is introduced.

Definition 2. *Let* $\mathcal{N} = (P_S \cup P_0 \cup P_R, T, F)$ *be an* $L - S^3PR$. *An initial marking* M_0 *is called an* admissible initial marking *for* $\mathcal{N}$ *iff*

i) $M_0[p_0] \geq 1$, $\forall p_0 \in P_0$
ii) $M_0[p] = 0$, $\forall p \in P_S$
iii) $M_0[r] \geq 1$, $\forall r \in P_R$

Figure 3 shows an example of a $L - S^3PR$ with admissible initial marking. Notice that an admissible initial marking puts

- at least one token in each idle state place. This means that processing sequences modeled by means of the associated $L - S^2PR$ can start. The initial marking of one idle state place models the maximum number of copies of this process (parts of the corresponding type) that are allowed to be concurrently executed. In general, this initial marking can be as large as desired since, usually, FMS are open systems and then, the number of parts that can arrive at the system is not ("a priori") bounded. Notice that when this marking is greater or equal than the total number of resources used by the process, the idle place is an implicit place [6](and then it can be withdrawn without producing any changes in the behaviour of the original net system).
- at least one token in every resource. It is clear that if there exists a resource with capacity equal to 0, the system is not well defined (a resource must be used for some production sequence, and it can never be available).

In the rest of the paper, *we assume that initial markings are admissible,* and so, the "admissible" adjective will not appear.

Notation 21 *The following notation will be used in the sequel.*

i) *Given a set $A \subseteq Q$, by means of $e_{A|Q}$, we denote a vector $e_{A|Q} : Q \to \{0,1\}$ such that, $e_{A|Q}[q] = $ if $q \in A$ then 1 else 0.*
ii) *We denote $P_0^i = \{p_0^i\}$.*
iii) *Given an $L - S^3 PR$, $\mathcal{N}$, as in definition 1, we denote $I_{\mathcal{N}} = \{1., ..., k\}$ (the set of indexes denoting the types of processes).*

2.2 Structure and behaviour in $L - S^3 PR$

This section is rather technical, but it is necessary in order to establish how the structural elements relate to the system behaviour. In a first step we present the form of the main structural elements (T-semiflows, P-semiflows and siphons). In a second step we present how these elements relate to the behaviour of the system.

Lemma 1. *[12] Let $\mathcal{N}$ be an $L - S^3 PR$ ($P = P_S \cup P_0 \cup P_R$), $\mathcal{Y}_R = \bigcup_{r \in P_R} \{e_{(H(r) \cup \{r\})|P}\}$, and $\mathcal{Y}_{SM} = \bigcup_{i \in I_{\mathcal{N}}} \{e_{(P_i \cup P_i^0)|P}\}$. The set of minimal P-semiflows of $\mathcal{N}$ is $\mathcal{Y} = \mathcal{Y}_R \cup \mathcal{Y}_{SM}$.*

In the previous result we have characterised a partition of the set of minimal P-semiflows of a given $L - S^3 PR$. The first subset corresponds to the token conservation law associated with each resource. Considering the resource $M2$ in Figure 3, the P-semiflow $Y_{M2} = e_{(H(M2) \cup \{M2\})|P}$ states that for each reachable marking M, the conservation law $M[P1.M2] + M[P2.M2] + M[M2] = 2(= M_0[M2])$ must be respected. This means that the total number of parts using machine $M2$ plus the non-busy positions in that machine must always be equal to 2 (the total capacity of $M2$).

The second subset establishes the conservation law for each state machine (in the sense of process) embedded in an $L - S^3 PR$. Considering once again the same example, and looking at the second process, the P-semiflow $Y_{SM_2} = e_{\{P2.M2, P2.R1, P2.M1, p_0^2\}|P}$ establishes the invariant relation $M[P2.M2] + M[P2.R1] + M[P2.M1] + M[p_0^2] = 5 (= M_0[p_0^2])$ for each reachable marking M. In this case this invariant states that the number of parts of a given type is constant, and equal to maximum imposed by the initial marking.

It is also very easy to see what the minimal T-semiflows are like for these systems. Let us consider an idle state place p_0^i, and let us denote $T_1^i, ..., T_{n_i}^i$ the set of transitions belonging to the different paths joining a transition in $p_0^i{}^{\bullet}$ to a transition in ${}^{\bullet}p_0^i$ and only using transitions of T^i (we only consider the transitions of the path). Then, for all $j \in \{1..n_i\}$, $X_j^i = e_{T_j^i|T}$ is a T-semiflow of the net. In the example in Figure 3, for each T^i we have only one T-semiflow. These T-semiflows are $X_1^1 = e_{\{P1toM1, P1toR1, P1toM2, P1toR2, P1toM3, P1toO1O3\}|T}$, $X_1^2 = e_{\{P2toM2, P2toR1, P2toM1, P2toO2\}|T}$ and $X_1^3 = e_{\{P3toR2, P3toM3, P3toO1O3\}|T}$. Each T-semiflow corresponds to the execution of a different production sequence.

Lemma 2. *[12] Let $\mathcal{N}$ be an $L - S^3PR$, and let $\mathcal{X} = \bigcup_{i\in I_{\mathcal{N}}} \bigcup_{j\in\{1,..,n_i\}}\{X^i_j\}$. $\mathcal{X}$ is the set of minimal T-semiflows of $\mathcal{N}$.*

Notice that an immediate consequence of the previous lemmata is that an $L - S^3PR$ is conservative (all places belong to some P-semiflow) and consistent (all transitions belong to some T-semiflow). The following theorem characterises the form that other structural elements, the siphons, have in these nets.

Theorem 1. *Let $\langle \mathcal{N}, M_0\rangle$ be an $L - S^3PR$ with an admissible initial marking, and let $S \subseteq P_S\cup P_0\cup P_R$. Then, S is a minimal siphon of $\mathcal{N}$ if, and only if, one of the two following statements holds:*

1. *S is the support of a minimal P-semiflow.*
2. *$S = S_S \cup S_R$ where $S_S = S\cap P_S, S_R = S\cap P_R$ so that:*
   a) *$S_S \neq \emptyset, S_R \neq \emptyset$.*
   b) *$S_S = \bigcup_{t\in{}^\bullet S_R}\{p \in P_S \mid p \in {}^\bullet t, {}^\bullet t\cap S_R = \emptyset\}$.*
   c) *The subnet generated by S_R and $S_R{}^\bullet \cap {}^\bullet S_R$ is a strongly connected state machine.*

Proof. The proof is carried out considering the number of resources in the siphon.
$\Longrightarrow$) Let $S = S_S \cup S_R$, where $S_R = S\cap P_R$ and $S_S = S\setminus S_R$.

Case 1: $\mid S_R \mid= 0$. Then $S \subseteq (P_S \cup P_0)$. Since S is minimal, the subnet generated by $S \cup {}^\bullet S$ is strongly connected. So, there exists $i \in I_{\mathcal{N}}$ so that $S \subseteq (P^i_S \cup P^i_0)$. Let us prove, by contradiction, that $S = (P^i_S \cup P^i_0)$. Let $p \in (P^i_S \cup P^i_0)\setminus S$, and let $q \in S$ be a place of the siphon. Since $\mathcal{N}^i$ is a strongly connected state machine, let $p = p_0, t_1, p_1, ..., t_n, p_n = q$ be a path from p to q, where $\{p_{i-1}\} = {}^\bullet t_i, \forall i \in \{1, ..., n\}$ and $t_j{}^\bullet = \{p_j\}, \forall j \in \{1, ..., n\}$ *(pre,post* are restricted to the considered state machine).

Taking into account that ${}^\bullet S \subseteq S^\bullet$, if $p_0 \notin S$, then $p_i \notin S, i \in \{1, ..., n\}$ (since $t_i \in {}^\bullet p_i, \{p_{i-1}\} = {}^\bullet t_i$ and $p_i \notin S$). We can deduce that $q \notin S$, which does not agree with the hypothesis. In consequence, $S = (P^i_S \cup P^i_0)$, and from Lemma 1, S is the support of a minimal P-semiflow.

Case 2: $\mid S_R \mid= 1$. Let us assume that $S_R = \{r\}$. Since S is a siphon, $H(r) = {}^{\bullet\bullet}r\cap P \subseteq S$. Since $\{r\}\cup H(r)$ is a siphon (Lemma 1), we can conclude that $S = \{r\}\cup H(r)$, which is the support of a minimal P-semiflow.

Case 3: $\mid S_R \mid\geq 2$. In this case S cannot be the support of a minimal P-semiflow since S contains at least two resources. On the other hand, S cannot be the support of a non minimal P-semiflow, since in this case S would be non minimal. Then, we have to prove that siphons containing at least two resources have the form stated in the thesis (point 2).

3.1: By contradiction, let us assume the $S_S = \emptyset$. Let $r \in S_R$ and let us consider a process index $i \in I_{\mathcal{N}}$ so that $H(r) \cap P^i_S \neq \emptyset$ (since $S_R \neq \emptyset$ such an index i must exist). Let us now call $\Theta^i_S = P^i_S \cap H(S_R)$. We are going to prove that Θ^i_S is a trap (that is, indeed, contained in P^i_S). Let $t \in T^i \cap \Theta^i_S{}^\bullet$. Notice that $t \in {}^\bullet S_R$; since S is a siphon and $S_S = \emptyset$, we have that ${}^\bullet t\cap P_R \in S_R$, and then, $t^\bullet\cap P^i_S$ is a holder of ${}^\bullet t\cap P_R$, that belongs to P^i_S. So, $t^\bullet\cap P^i_S \in P^i_S\cap H(S_R)$.

This means that $t \in {}^\bullet\Theta_S^i$, and we can conclude that Θ_S^i is trap that, because of its definition, belongs to P_S^i.

But this is not possible since there is no trap contained in P_S^i. In effect, let $\Theta \subseteq P_S^i$ be a trap, and let $p \in \Theta$. Let us consider the place p_0^i, and let assume that $p_0^i \notin \Theta$. Since the state machine is strongly connected, let $p = p_0, t_1, p_1, ..., t_n, p_n = p_0^i$ be a path from p to p_0^i, where $\{p_{k-1}\} = {}^\bullet t_k$, $\forall\, k \in \{1, ..., n\}$ and $t_j{}^\bullet = \{p_j\}$, $\forall\, j \in \{1, ..., n\}$. Taking into account that Θ is a trap, if $p_n \notin \Theta$ then $p_k \notin \Theta$, $k \in \{0, ..., n-1\}$ (since $t_k \in p_k{}^\bullet$, $\{p_{k+1}\} = t_k{}^\bullet$ and $p_{k+1} \notin \Theta$). As a particular case, $p \notin \Theta$, which does not agree with the initial hypothesis. So, each trap contained in P_S^i must contain the place p_0^i. But this is not the case for Θ_S^i. So, a contradiction has been reached, and we can conclude that $S_S \neq \emptyset$.

3.2: Let us take $S_S' = \bigcup_{t \in {}^\bullet S_R} \{p \in P_S \mid p \in {}^\bullet t, {}^\bullet t \cap S_R = \emptyset\}$. We are going to prove that $S_S = S_S'$. In a first step we will see that $S_S' \subseteq S_S$. If there exists $p \in S_S' \setminus S_S$, then there exists $t \in {}^\bullet S_R$ so that $p \in {}^\bullet t, {}^\bullet t \cap S_R = \emptyset$ and ${}^\bullet t \cap S_S = \emptyset$, and so, S is not a siphon, which is not possible. Proving now that $S_R \cup S_S'$ is a siphon, we can conclude that $S_S' = S_S$ (because of the minimality of S). Let ${}^\bullet S_R = T_1 \cup T_2$ where $T_1 = \{t \in {}^\bullet S_R \mid {}^\bullet t \cap S_R \neq \emptyset\}$ and $T_2 = \{t \in {}^\bullet S_R \mid {}^\bullet t \cap S_R = \emptyset\}$. Therefore, $T_1 \subseteq S_R{}^\bullet$ and $T_2 \subseteq S_S'{}^\bullet$. On the other hand, if $p \in S_S'$ and $r \in p^{\bullet\bullet} \cap P_R$ and $r \in S_R$ (by the definition of S_S') we have that ${}^\bullet p \subseteq r^\bullet$, from the definition of $L - S^3 PR$. This means that ${}^\bullet S_S' \subseteq S_R{}^\bullet$, and so, $S_R \cup S_S'$ is a siphon.

3.3: Let us consider the subnet $\mathcal{N}_{S_R} = \langle S_R, T_I, F \cap ((S_R \times T_I) \cup (T_I \times S_R)) \rangle$, where $T_I = S_R{}^\bullet \cap {}^\bullet S_R$. First, we will prove that $T_I \neq \emptyset$. Let $r \in S_R$, and let $t \in {}^\bullet r$ so that ${}^\bullet t \cap S_S = \emptyset$. Notice that this transition has to exist, because otherwise $\{r\} \cup H(r) \subseteq S$, and then (because of the minimality of S) the identity is given, which does not agree with the hypothesis of $\mid S_R \mid \geq 2$. Then, if $\{r'\} = {}^\bullet t \cap P_R$, $r' \in S$. In conclusion, $t \in T_I$. On the other hand, it is straightforward that $\mathcal{N}_{S_R}$ is a state machine since $\forall\, t \in T_I$, $\mid {}^\bullet t \cap S_R \mid = \mid t^\bullet \cap S_R \mid = 1$.

Is this state machine strongly connected? Let $r, r' \in S_R$. We are looking for a path $r = q_0, t_1, q_1, ..., t_n, q_n = r'$ from r to r', where $q_i \in S_R$, $\forall\, i \in \{0, ..., n\}$ and $t_i \in T_I$, $\forall\, i \in \{1, ..., n\}$. We are going to build this path starting in r' and arriving to r. This construction is based on two facts: **1)** since S is a minimal siphon, $\mathcal{N}_{\mid S \cup {}^\bullet S}$ is a strongly connected subnet. **2)** S is not the support of any P-semiflow. Let us consider r', and let $t_1 \in {}^\bullet r'$ so that ${}^\bullet t_1 \cap P_S = \emptyset$ (as previously stated, this transition has to exist). Since S is a siphon, if $\{r_1\} = {}^\bullet t_1 \cap P_R$, it is necessary that $r_1 \in S_R$. Notice that $t_1 \in T_I$. On the other hand, $t_1 \in {}^\bullet S$, and then, ($\mathcal{N}_{\mid S \cup {}^\bullet S}$ is a strongly connected subnet) there is a path from r to t_1. Since $r_1 \in S$, there is a path from r to r_1. In the same way, for r_1, we find a transition $t_2 \in {}^\bullet r_1$ so that ${}^\bullet t_2 \cap S_S = \emptyset$, and so, ${}^\bullet t_2 \cap S_R = \{r_2\} \subset S_R$. Besides, $t_2 \in T_I$. Iterating the reasoning, and taking into account that in the former net there are a finite number of places, we can find a path from r and r', composed of elements in $\mathcal{N}_{S_R}$, and we can conclude.

$\Longleftarrow$) Considering the form of the $L - S^3 PR$, it is obvious that the support of a minimal P-semiflow is a minimal siphon. Let us consider the set of places

$S = S_S \cup S_R$ as stated in the hypothesis. It is straightforward to see that it is a siphon. Let us prove that it is minimal, by contradiction. Let us assume that there exists a siphon S' so that $S' \subset S$. Let $r \in S_R \cap (S \setminus S')$. Let us consider $t \in r^\bullet$ and let $\{r'\} = t^\bullet \cap P_R$. Since $\mathcal{N}_{S_R}$ is a strongly connected state machine, and considering the way in which S_S has been formed, we can ensure that $r' \notin S'$, and, in general, $r'' \notin S \ \forall \ r'' \in r^{\bullet\bullet} \cap S_R$. Given that $\mathcal{N}_{S_R}$ is strongly connected, and iterating the previous reasoning, we can see that $S' \cap S_R = \emptyset$, and so, $S' \subseteq S_S$. Since S' is a minimal siphon, we have that $\exists \ i \in I_N$ so that $S' = P_S^i \cup P_0^i$, and so, $S' \subseteq S_S$. But this is not possible since each element in S_S uses some resource, and this is not true for P_0^i. Considering now $p \in S_S \cap (S \setminus S')$, and taking into account hypothesis b), if $p \in S_S \setminus S'$, then $r_p \notin S'$, and this is the previous case.

The previous characterisation of siphons is important. As we will see later on, empty siphons are the cause of the non-liveness in $L - S^3PR$. The only siphons that can be emptied are those that are not the support of any P-semiflows (taking into account the definition of admissible initial markings, each P-semiflow is initially marked, and by the token conservation law that it induces, these siphons cannot be emptied). Considering now those siphons that are not the support of any P-semiflow, we have the following property: for each resource belonging to a siphon, there exists at least one holder of this resource not belonging to the siphon. In the following, informally speaking, we call "bad" siphons those that do not contain the support of a P-semiflow.

Another interesting feature of the previous characterisation of bad siphons is that they are the manifestation, at the structural level, of the well known necessary condition for the existence of a deadlock related to the existence of a circular wait for the availability of resources. In effect, the existence of bad siphons is necessary for the existence of a deadlock in $L - S^3PR$, and when the deadlock of a transition is reached, we can empty the siphon. So, we obtain a strongly connected state machine formed by resources S_R and $S_R^\bullet \cap {}^\bullet S_R$ containing circuits of resources that represents the circular wait conditions. Notice that these circuits cannot gain tokens because all input transitions to the places belong to the siphon.

Now, using the special structure of an $L - S^3PR$, we present one of its main behavioral properties: if a transition is dead for a reachable marking, then a marking is reachable so that a siphon is empty. These two results have been proved for a larger class of systems, where the $L - S^3PR$ subclass is included (*Systems of Simple Sequential Processes with Resources, S^3PR*) [11].

Theorem 2. *[11] Let $\langle \mathcal{N}, M_0 \rangle$ be a marked $L - S^3PR$, $M \in \mathcal{R}(\mathcal{N}, M_0)$ and $t \in T$ be a dead transition for M. Then, $\exists \ M' \in \mathcal{R}(\mathcal{N}, M)$, and $\exists$ a siphon S such that $M'(S) = 0$.*

The last result is not true in general Petri nets, as shown in Figure 5. Transition t is dead for the shown marking, but the only siphon in the net, $\{p, q, r, s\}$, is always marked. Now, we can characterise the liveness in $L - S^3PR$ models:

75

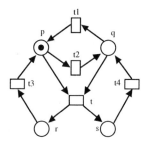

Fig. 5. Transition t is a dead transition for the shown marking, but the only siphon $\{p, q, r, s\}$ is always marked.

Corollary 1. *[11] Let $\langle \mathcal{N}, M_0 \rangle$ be a marked $L - S^3PR$. Then, $\langle \mathcal{N}, M_0 \rangle$ is live if, and only if, $\forall\ M \in \mathcal{R}(\mathcal{N}, M_0),\ \forall$ (minimal) siphon $S,\ M[S] \neq 0$*

3 An efficient liveness characterisation for $L - S^3PR$

In the previous section we have characterised what causes deadlock problems in the $L - S^3PR$ class. Now, we have another important question to answer: If the net contains a "bad" siphon, Is there an initial marking and a firing sequence so that a deadlock can be reached? (i.e., does a bad siphon characterise system liveness for all "admissible" configurations?) As we will see in this section, $L - S^3PR$ class fulfils this property.

In the sequel, we assume an $L - S^3PR$ $\mathcal{N} = \langle P_S \cup P_R \cup P_0, T, F \rangle$ so that: I) $S = S_S \cup S_R$ is a bad siphon ($S_R = \{r_1, ..., r_m\}$) II) The system configuration establishes an initial marking M_0^R for the set of resources. So, we will prove that under these conditions, and if enough clients (new processes requiring the use of computer resources, new parts in the FMS...) arrive at the system, a deadlock can be reached. So, in this section *the input data are the markings of the resource places and the net structure.*

In order to characterise the liveness in an $L - S^3PR$, we will distinguish two cases:

Case A) Each resource is used at most once in each T-semiflow (i.e., no production sequence uses the same resource twice).

Case B) There exists at least one resource that is used more than once in the same T-semiflow (i.e., there exists a production sequence that uses twice the same resource).

In order to construct a bad firing sequence (a firing sequence leading to a deadlock), we establish, first of all, a total order relation in the set of resources of the considered "bad" siphon. This order will take into consideration the structure of the net, and it will be used in order to empty a siphon in an ordered way. The *OrderingSR* algorithm establishes this order (which, indeed, is not unique). In short, the algorithm runs as follows. With each resource in the siphon we associate two things:

1. One of its holders not belonging to the siphon (at least one exists); when the "bad" firing sequence is fired, this holder will contain all initial tokens of the resource (mappings α and β in the following algorithm carry out this correspondence).
2. A T-semiflow. This T-semiflow contains the transition from the resource to the associated holder. The repetitive firing of this transition will empty the considered resource (mapping γ establishes this association).

Algorithm $OrderingSR$
Input: $\mathcal{N}$ (an $L - S^3PR$) and $S = S_S \cup S_R$
Output: α: a total order in S_R
β: associates a holder to each $r \in S_R$
γ: associates a T-semiflow to each $r \in S_R$
Begin
 $\forall\, r \in S_R :\ \alpha(r) := 0$ /* α array indexed by S_R*/
 $\forall\, p \in P_S \cup P_R :\ \beta(p) := 0$ /* β array indexed by $P_S \cup P_R$*/
 $S'_R := S_R;\ l := 0$
 Repeat
  choose $r \in S'_R$
  choose $p \in H(r) \setminus S$
  choose a minimal T-semiflow $TS = t_1 \cdot ... \cdot t_{k+1}$ s.t. $^\bullet p \cap \|TS\| \neq \emptyset$,
  where transitions are ordered following the firing order
  from P_0 in the state machine containing TS
  For $i := 1, ..., k$ **Do**
   If $(t_i{}^\bullet \cap P_S = \{q\}) \wedge (q \in H(r') \setminus S)$
   $\wedge\ (r' \in S'_R) \wedge (\alpha(r') = 0)$ **Then**
    $l := l + 1;\ \alpha(r') := l;\ \beta(q) := l;\ S'_R := S'_R \setminus \{r'\}$
    $\gamma(q) := TS$ /* γ: array of minimal T-semiflows */
  Fi
  Od
 Until $S'_R = \emptyset$
End

If $r \in S_R$, $q \in P_S$ and $\beta(q) = \alpha(r)$, then $q \in H(r)$, $q \notin S$ and q is the holder of r where all tokens of r will remain when the siphon is emptied. Indeed, the repetitive firing of a part of the T-semiflow $\gamma(q)$ will empty r.

Lemma 3. *The* OrderingSR *algorithm verifies:*

1. *It terminates*
2. *α establishes a total order relation in S_R*
3. *Let $T = t_1...t_{k+1}$ be one of the minimal T-semiflows[1] used in the algorithm, and let $\{p\} = t_i{}^\bullet \cap P_S$, $\{q\} = t_j{}^\bullet \cap P_S$ such that $i < j$, $\beta(p) \neq 0$ and $\beta(q) \neq 0$. Then, $\beta(p) < \beta(q)$.*

---

[1] $T = t_1...t_{k+1}$ represents a minimal T-semiflow in one of the state machines where t_1 is the first transition to fire, and then t_2, and so on.

Proof. 1. In each *Repeat* iteration at least one element is removed from S'_R, and since S_R is finite, we can conclude.

2. This can be directly deduced from the fact that α is a $1-1$ mapping from S_R into $\{1, ..., m\}$.

3. Since the numbering of state places using a T-semiflow is made in a correlative way, following the firing "sense" established by the T-semiflow, we can conclude.

Now, using the order given by α (we can see it as a mapping from S_R into $\{1, ..., m\}$) we can construct a firing sequence that empties a siphon in an ordered way: first, we empty resource $\alpha^{-1}(m)$, then resource $\alpha^{-1}(m-1)$, and so on. In the following, and given a reachable marking M and $i \in \{1, ..., m\}$, we say that M satisfies the property $\mathcal{M}(i)$ iff the two following statements are verified:

1. $\forall j \in \{i, ..., m\} : M[\beta^{-1}(j)] = M_0[\alpha^{-1}(j)]$ (that implies $M[\alpha^{-1}(j)] = 0$)
2. $\forall p \notin (\{\alpha^{-1}(j) \mid j \in \{i, ..., m\}\} \cup \{\beta^{-1}(j) \mid j \in \{i, ..., m\}\}) \setminus P_0 : M[p] = M_0[p]$

Notice that if we find a firing sequence σ so that $M = M_0 + C \cdot \bar{\sigma}$, and M satisfies $\mathcal{M}(1)$, then we can deduce that $M[S] = 0$.

Theorem 3. *Let $\mathcal{N}$ be an $L-S^3PR$ containing a "bad" siphon S, and let M_0^R be a given initial marking for the set of resources. Then, there exists: 1) an initial marking M_0 (so that $\forall r \in P_R, M_0[r] = M_0^R[r]$) 2) a firing sequence σ 3) a "bad" siphon S' so that $M_0[\sigma\rangle M$ and $M[S'] = 0$.*

Proof. Let us consider M_0 as follows: 1) $\forall r \in P_R, M_0[r] = M_0^R[r]$ 2) $\forall p \in P_0$, $M_0[p] = \sum_{r \in P_R} M_0^R[r]$ (so, the initial marking of each idle state place is the total system resource capacity. Notice that no more than this number of clients can stay simultaneously in the system).

Case A There is no resource that is used more than once in the same T-semiflow. In this case, we will prove that taking $S' = S$, the siphon can be emptied.

Let us consider the firing sequence $\sigma = \sigma_m \sigma_{m-1} ... \sigma_2 \sigma_1$ where $\sigma_i, i \in \{1, ..., m\}$, is as follows. Let $r = \alpha^{-1}(i)$, $p = \beta^{-1}(i)$, $TS = \gamma^{-1}(i) = t_1 ... t_{k+1}$ so that $\{p\} = t_{i_j} {}^\bullet \cap P_S$, with $1 \le i_j \le k$. Let us consider $\sigma_i = (t_1 ... t_{i_j})^{M_0[r]}$. We prove now, by induction, that σ is a firing sequence and that the reached marking M satisfies $\mathcal{M}[1]$.

Case m: σ_m can be fired, since for all $j < i_m$, ${}^\bullet t_j \cap P_R$ is marked, and each time t_i fires, it takes a token from ${}^\bullet t_i \cap P_R$ that is released when t_{i+1} fires. Moreover, $M_n = M_0 + C \cdot \sigma_n$ satisfies $\mathcal{M}(m)$ (this can be easily seen from the P-semiflow containing the resource $\alpha^{-1}(m)$).

Case i: Let us assume that $M_{i+1} = M_0 + C \cdot \overline{\sigma_{i+1}}$, and M_{i+1} satisfies $\mathcal{M}(i+1)$. From M_{i+1}, σ_i can be fired: Lemma 3 and the fact that *no resource is used twice* in the same T-semiflow allows us to ensure that the marking M_{i+1} of the resources used for the firing of transitions $t_1, ..., t_{i_j}$ has the same value as their initial marking, and that each token of these places used for the firing of

$t_s, 1 \leq s < i_j$ is released when t_{s+1} fires. As in the previous case, it is easy to see that M_i also satisfies $\mathcal{M}(i)$.

Case B In the case that at least a resource is used more than once in the same T-semiflow, a situation as the one shown in Figure 6 appears. Moreover, we can also ensure that no resource in the set $\{r_2, ..., r_i\}$ is used more than once in states $\{p_2, ..., p_i\}$ (it is enough to take p_1 and p_{i+1} as the "first" states in the T-semiflow using the same resource). Now, the resource set $\{r_1, r_2, ..., r_i\}$ can be emptied as in the previous part: first, we empty r_i by firing $(t_1 t_2 ... t_i)^{M_0[r_i]}$, afterward we empty r_{i-1} by firing $(t_1 t_2 ... t_{i-1})^{M_0[r_{i-1}]}$, and so on. Let σ denote to the firing sequence that empties places $\{r_1, r_2, ..., r_i\}$. Now, we are going to build a siphon S' such that $M[S'] = 0$, where $M_0[\sigma\rangle M$. Let $S'' = \bigcup_{\alpha=1}^{i}(H(r_\alpha)) \cup \{r_1, r_2, ..., r_i\}$ (i.e., we complete the resources considered with all their holders). It is very easy to see that $S' = S'' \setminus \{p_1, p_2, ..., p_i\}$ is a siphon and that $M[S'] = 0$.

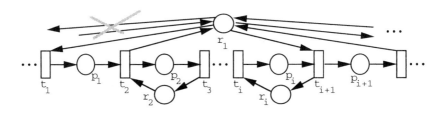

Fig. 6. An structure that arises when a resource is used more than once in the same T-semiflow

In other words, the previous theorem states that when an $L - S^3PR$ contains a bad siphon, and assuming as many clients in the system as necessary (a usual assumption in open systems), there exist at least a firing sequence that yields to a deadlock.

Let us consider the net in Figure 3. It corresponds to the case A in the previous proof. The siphon $S = S_R \cup S_S$, where $S_S = \{P1.M2, P2.M1\}$, $S_R = \{M1, R1, M2\}$ is "bad". Considering $\alpha(M2) = \beta(P2.M2) = 1$, $\alpha(M1) = \beta(P1.M1) = 2$, $\alpha(R1) = \beta(P1.R1) = 3$, $\gamma(P1.R1) = \gamma(P1.M1) = TS$, where $TS = e_{\{P1toM1,P1toR1,P1toM2,P1toR2,P1toM3,P1toO1O3\}|T}$, and $\gamma(P2.M2) = TS'$, where $TS' = e_{\{P2toM2,P2toR1,P2toM1,P2toO2\}|T}$. From these data, $\sigma_3 = P1toM1.P1toR1$, $\sigma_2 = (P1toM1)^2$, $\sigma_1 = (P2toM2)^2$, and then, $\sigma = \sigma_3\sigma_2\sigma_1$.

It is important to note that Theorem 3 does not state that *every* bad siphon can be emptied, but that when a bad siphon exists, some bad siphon can be emptied (perhaps a different one). For example, consider the net in Figure 7. In this system, there are resources that are used more than once by the same process (case B in the proof). The siphon $\{r2, r3, p1, p4, q1, q4\}$ can not be emptied. However, other siphons can be emptied. For example, the siphon $\{r1, r2, p2, p4, q3\}$ is emptied by the firing sequence $t1.s1.s2$.

From the previous theorem, two important corollaries can be deduced.

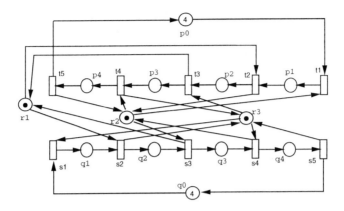

Fig. 7. The siphon {r2,r3,p1,p4,q1,q4} is a "bad siphon", but it cannot be emptied.

Corollary 2. *Let $\mathcal{N}$ be a $L - S^3PR$. $\mathcal{N}$ is live for all (admissible) initial markings M_0 if, and only if, each minimal siphon of $\mathcal{N}$ is the support of a (minimal) P-semiflow.*

Proof. $\Longrightarrow$) Straightforward from Theorems 1 and 3
$\Longleftarrow$) If each minimal siphon is the support of a P-semiflow, and since for each admissible initial marking each P-semiflow is marked, no siphon can be emptied. Therefore, no transition can be dead.

It is well known that for some classes of nets the Commoner's property is strongly related to the liveness properties. The Commoner's theorem was firstly established in [13] for free-choice nets: *a free-choice system is live if and only if every siphon contains a trap marked by the initial marking.* Also, the fact that every siphon contains a marked trap is a sufficient condition to ensure deadlock freeness (but not liveness) for every ordinary Petri net [2]. In the case of *asymmetric systems* (also called *simple systems*) the Commoner's property is sufficient (but no necessary) to ensure the system liveness (see for instance [2]). In the following corollary we prove that the Commoner's structural property (each siphon contains a trap) characterises the liveness of $L - S^3PR$ nets with admissible initial markings. However, one must not think that for $L - S^3PR$ systems deadlock freeness and liveness are equivalent properties (as it occurs for free-choice nets). In the example depicted in Figure 3, the reachable marking m: $m[P1.M1] = 2, m[P1.R1] = 1, m[P2.M2] = 2, m[P_0^1] = 5, m[P_0^2] = 3, m[R2] = 1, m[M3] = 2, m[P_0^3] = 3$, is a deadlock (no transition in T-semiflows X_1^1 or X_1^2 can fire anymore), but it is not a total deadlock (transitions in X_1^3 can be fired infinitely often from m).

Corollary 3. *Let $\mathcal{N}$ be an $L - S^3PR$. $\mathcal{N}$ is live for all admissible initial markings M_0 if, and only if, $\mathcal{N}$ satisfies the structural Commoner's property.*

Proof. ⟹) If $\mathcal{N}$ is live for all (admissible) initial markings M_0, Corollary 2 ensures that each minimal siphon is the support of a (minimal) P-semiflow, which is also a marked trap.
⟸) Every siphon is initially marked because of Theorem 1 and the fact that each resource and each embedded state machine is initially marked. Taking into account that siphon and trap are reverse concepts, and that the reverse net of an $L - S^3PR$ is also an $L - S^3PR$, all traps are initially marked. If each siphon contains a trap, and since each trap is initially marked, no siphon can be emptied (a structural trap remains always marked), no matter which admissible initial marking we consider. So, no reachable markings have dead transitions, and therefore, the net is live.

As we have stated above, if an $L-S^3PR$ is not "well-formed", the system can evolve in order to reach a deadlock. Now, we are interested in $L - S^3PR$ whose structure ensures the liveness. Considering Theorem 3, these systems correspond to nets that do not contain any bad siphons. We are going to show that siphons in this class of nets are strongly related to the concept of circular wait of processes, that is one of the necessary conditions for deadlock in systems of processes sharing resources.

Definition 3. *Let* $\mathcal{N} = \langle P_S \cup P_R \cup P_0, T, F \rangle$ *be an* $L - S^3PR$. *A Circuit of resources is a non-empty path* $t_1, r_1, t_2, r_2, \ldots, t_m, r_m$ *with* $t_i \in T, r_i \in P_R, \forall i \in \{1, \ldots, m\}$, *such that:*

- $\forall i \in \{1, \ldots, m\}, r_i \in t^{\bullet}_i$
- $\forall i \in \{1, \ldots, m-1\}, r_i \in {}^{\bullet}t_{i+1}$
- $r_m \in {}^{\bullet}t_1$

For example $P1toR1.M1.P2toM1.R1$ is a circuit of resources of the $L-S^3PR$ in Figure 3.

Theorem 4. *An* $L - S^3PR$ *is live for all admissible markings if and only if there do not exist any circuits of resources.*

Proof. ⟹) Suppose there exists a circuit of resources, with resources T_c and transitions T_c. Let $S_S = \bigcup_{t \in {}^{\bullet}S_R} \{p \in P_S \mid p \in {}^{\bullet}t, {}^{\bullet}t \cap S_R = \emptyset\}$ and let $S = S_R \cup S_S$. We are going to prove that this circuit of resources generates a bad siphon.
From the circuit of resources, we have that $\forall r \in S_R, \exists t \in T_c$ such that $t \in {}^{\bullet}r$ and ${}^{\bullet}t \cap S_R \neq \emptyset$. Let $p \in {}^{\bullet}t \cap P$. Then $p \notin S_S$ and $p \in H(r)$. Therefore for each resource r in S there exists a holder of r that does not belong to S. Moreover $p_0 \notin S$, and then by Lemma 1, S is not the support of any minimal P-semiflows. Let $T_I = {}^{\bullet}S_R \cap S_R{}^{\bullet}$. Then $\mathcal{N}_{S_R} = \langle S_R, T_I, F \cap ((S_R \times T_I) \cup (T_I \times S_R)) \rangle$ is a strongly connected state machine, and S fulfils condition 2c of Theorem 1. S trivially fulfils the conditions 2a and 2b of Theorem 1, and then the proof follows.

$\Longleftarrow$) Suppose that an $L - S^3 PR$ is not live for a given initial admissible marking. Then there exists a minimal siphon that is not the support of any minimal P-semiflows. By Theorem 1, there exists a strongly connected state machine with places in P_R, and therefore a circuit of resources.

As stated in the introduction, one of the four necessary conditions in order to have a deadlock is that the system reaches a circular wait (the other three necessary conditions are usually satisfied in the class of systems we are dealing with). It is clear that a necessary condition to reach such a situation is the existence of a cycle of resources: If we have a chain of processes, each one of them holding a resource that is needed by the next process in the chain, we can trivially find a cycle of resources in the PN model. But, as shown in Figure 1, the existence of cycle is not a sufficient condition for the general class of systems of processes sharing resources. However, Theorem 4 proves that in the case of $L - S^3 PR$, having a cycle of resources is also a sufficient condition (of course, if no control is added).

As we have reduced the liveness decision problem for $L - S^3 PR$ to the existence of circuits in a directed graph, the problem can be solved in polynomial time: it is sufficient to check if a circuit exists in a directed graph.

Corollary 4. *Deciding if an $L - S^3 PR$ is live for every admissible initial marking can be tested in $\Theta(|\ P_R\ | + |\ P_R{}^\bullet \cap {}^\bullet P_R\ |)$ time.*

Proof. Let us consider the directed graph obtained as follows:

– The set of nodes is P_R
– Let $r, r' \in P_R$. There is an arc from r to r' if and only if $r^\bullet \cap {}^\bullet r' \neq \emptyset$

Finding a circuit of resources in the net is equivalent to finding a cycle in this graph, and this can be done in $\Theta(|\ P_R\ | + |\ P_R{}^\bullet \cap {}^\bullet P_R\ |)$ time (the number of nodes plus the number of edges in the considered graph) [5].

4 Conclusions and future work

The paper has been devoted to the study of a class of Petri nets that appears in FMS environments. A set of structural and structural/behavioral properties have been presented. From these properties, a synthesis problem has been solved by means of a liveness characterisation for a class of initial markings. The main idea behind these systems is that when some processes are in a deadlock, this deadlock is due to the process interactions by means of the shared resources. These situations are related to the notion of circular waits in concurrent systems. These circular waits are due to multi-circuits of resources. This information is captured by means of "bad siphons" of the Petri net model. In a previous work, when bad siphons existed, a control policy for deadlock prevention was established. In the present work we have shown that the existence or not of these potential circular waits characterises, in a structural way, the liveness of an $L - S^3 PR$ net. These nets correspond to the models of a class of FMS where the only decisions to be taken on-line are those corresponding to the granting of resources. We have also proved that for these systems the liveness property can be checked in linear time (linear w.r.t. the size of the Petri net model).

We would like to point out that, even if the results reported here do not solve the deadlock related problems, they can be useful in the system configuration process design: they can be used in order to have a quick answer to whether a given configuration is correct or not, to study if such a configuration exists or not and to conclude if some deadlock control policy is needed.

Another important point is that classical elements used in deadlock related problems (circular waits, ordering of the system resources) have been related to the structure of Petri net models, establishing a closer relation between model structure and system behaviour.

Current/future work must be addressed toward the removal of some of the constrains that appeared in the class of systems studied in this paper. In many applied concurrent systems, the engineer needs to feel free to use multi-sets of resources at some states of a process and also to use other more general processes.

Once this generalisation is achieved, the application domain of the techniques presented here could be extended to other concurrent systems such as database systems, operating systems, parallel processing, etc.

References

1. Z. Banaszak, B. Krogh, Deadlock Avoidance in Flexible Manufacturing Systems with Concurrently Competing Process Flows, *IEEE Transactions on Robotics and Automation, Vol. 6, No. 6*, December 1990, pp. 724-734.

2. E. Best, P.S. Thiagarajan, *Some Classes of Live and Safe Petri Nets*, Concurrency and Nets, K. Voss, H.J. Genrich, G. Rozenberg (Eds.), Advances in Petri NEts, Springer-Verlag, 1987, pp. 71-94

3. D.Y. Chao, M. Zhou, D.T. Wang, Extending Knitting Technique to Petri Net Synthesis of Automated Manufacturing Systems, *Proceedings of the 3th. International Conference on Computer Integrated Manufacturing*, Rensselaer Polytechnic Institute, Troy (New York), 1992, pp. 56-63.

4. E.G. Coffman, M.J. Elphick, A. Shoshani, System Deadlocks, *ACM Computer Surveys, Vol. 3, No. 2*, 1971, pp. 67-78.

5. T.H. Cormen, C.E. Leiserson, R.L. Rivest, *Introduction to Algorithms*, The MIT Press/MacGraw-Hill Book Company, 1992.

6. J.M. Colom, M. Silva, Improving the linearly based characterization of P/T nets, G. Rozenberg Editor, *Advances in Petri Nets 1990, LNCS 483*, Springer Verlag 1991, pp. 113-145.

7. A.A. Desrochers and R.Y. Al-Jaar, *Application of Petri Nets in Manufacturing Systems: Modeling, Control and Performance Analysis*, IEEE Press, 1995

8. F. Dicesare, G. Harhalakis, J.M. Proth, M. Silva, *Practice of Petri Nets in Manufacturing*, Chapman & Hall, 1993.

9. E.W.Dijsktra, Co-operating Sequential Processes, *Programming Languages*, F. Genuys (Ed.), Academic Press, 1965.

10. J. Esparza, M. Silva, Compositional Synthesis of Live and Bounded Free Choice Nets, *CONCUR'91, LNCS vol.527*, Springer-Verlag 1991.

11. J. Ezpeleta, J.M. Colom, J. Martínez, A Petri Net Based Deadlock Prevention Policy for Flexible Manufacturing Systems, *IEEE Transactions on Robotics and Automation, Vol. 11, No. 2*, April 1995, pp. 173-184.

12. J. Ezpeleta, *Analysis and Synthesis of Deadlock Free Models for Concurrent Systems*, Ph. D. thesis, Dpt. de Ingeniería Eléctrica e Informática, University of Zaragoza (Spain), June 1993 (in Spanish).

13. M.H.T. Hack, *Analysis of Production Schemata by Petri Nets*, Cambridge, Maa.: MIT, Dept. of Electrical Engineering, M.S. Thesis, 1972

14. F. Hsieh, S. Chang, Dispatching-Driven Deadlock Avoidance Controller Synthesis for Flexible Manufacturing Systems, *IEEE Transactions on Robotics and Automation, Vol. 10, No. 2*, April 1994, pp. 196-209.

15. M.D. Jeng, F. DiCesare, Synthesis Using Resource Control Nets for Modeling Shared-Resource Systems,*IEEE Transactions on Robotics and Automation,Vol. 11,N. 3*, June 1995, pp. 317-327

16. J.M. Proth and X. Xie, *Petri Nets. A Tool for Design and Management of Manufaturing Systems*, John Wiley & Sons,1996

17. M. Singhal, Deadlock Detection in Distributed Systems, *COMPUTER, IEEE*, November 1989, pp. 37-48.

18. M. Silva, R. Valette, Petri Nets and Flexible Manufacturing, *Advances in Petri Nets, LNCS 424*, Springer-Verlag, 1989, pp. 374-417.

19. A.S. Tanenbaum, *Operating Systems. Design and Implementation*, Prentice-Hall International Editions, 1987.

20. N. Viswanadham, Y. Narahari, *Performance Modeling of Automated Manufacturing Systems*, Prentice-Hall, 1992.

21. N. Viswanadham, Y. Narahari, T. Johnson, Deadlock Prevention and Deadlock Avoidance in Flexible Manufacturing Systems Using Petri Net Models, *IEEE Transactions on Robotics and Automation, Vol. 6, No. 6*, December, 1990, pp. 713-723.

22. W. Vogler, Behavior Preserving Refinements of Petri Nets, *Graph Theoretic Concepts in Computer Science, LNCS, N. 246*, Springer Verlag, 1986, pp. 82-93.

23. R.A. Wysk, N.S. Yang, S. Joshi, Detection of Deadlocks in Flexible Manufacturing Cells, *IEEE Transactions on Robotics and Automation, Vol. 7, No. 6*, December 1991, pp. 853-859.

24. K.Y. Xing, B.S. Hu, H.X. Chen, Deadlock Avoidance Policy for Petri-net Modeling of Flexible Manufacturing Systems with Shared Resources, *IEEE Transactions on Automatic Control, Vol. 41, No. 2*, February 1996, pp. 289-295.

25. M. Zhou, F. Dicesare, *Petri Net Synthesis for Discrete Event Control of Manufacturing Systems*, Kluwer Academic Publishers, 1993.

26. M. Zhou, K. McDermott, P. Patel, Petri Net Synthesis and Analysis of a Flexible Manufacturing System Cell, *IEEE Transactions on Systems, Man and Cybernetics, Vol. 23, No. 2*, March 1993, pp. 523-531.

Modelling and Model Checking
a Distributed Shared Memory Consistency Protocol

Kathi Fisler[1] and Claude Girault[1][2]

[1] Department of Computer Science, Rice University,
6100 Main Street, Houston, TX 77005-1892
[2] University Paris 6, Laboratory of Computer Science LIP6,
4 Place Jussieu, 75252 Paris Cedex 05

Abstract: Distributed Shared Memory (DSM) systems provide the abstraction of a common virtual address space across a network of processors. Such systems employ a variety of protocols to maintain a consistent view of data across all local memories. Li and Hudak proposed several of the pioneering protocols for DSM [LH 89]. We have used both Petri net modelling and model checking to explore some of their protocols. Our work has detected inefficiencies, unstated assumptions, and errors in the original protocol descriptions. This paper presents Petri net models for one protocol at two layers of abstraction. For each model, we describe corresponding specifications for model checking and provide verification statistics. This combination of models and specifications gives different views of the protocol, inspiring greater confidence in the correctness of our analysis than if we had used only one approach.

Keywords: Protocol design and verification, distributed shared memory, memory consistency, model checking, high level Petri nets.

1 Introduction

Processors in a distributed environment can utilize each other's local memories. From a programmer's perspective, however, managing data across shared memory is a complicated and distracting task. Distributed Shared Memory (DSM) systems provide a viable alternative: the abstraction of a common virtual address space for a network of processors (Fig. 1). Based on access requests, DSM systems replicate or migrate data between processors, thus relieving programmers from managing data location. As memory coherence is important for the correct execution of programs, DSM protocols are strong candidates for formal analysis.

Sequential consistency is one of the strongest and most commonly used memory consistency models [AG 96]. It guarantees that all processors see all the data accesses in the same sequential order and also preserves the order of each processor's accesses. Weaker models, such as release consistency or causal consistency, achieve better performance by exploiting synchronization within the program to increase parallelism and reduce network traffic at the price of more elaborate protocols [KCZ 92, CBZ 95].

Li and Hudak proposed several pioneering and widely quoted protocols to achieve sequential consistency in software for DSM systems [LH 89]. We have explored two of them using formal modelling and model checking. This paper presents our work on

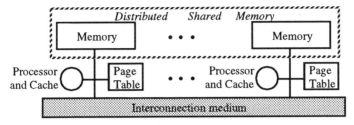

Fig. 1. Distributed Memory Architecture

one of them. Our models follow Li and Hudak's original pseudocode descriptions, adding assumptions only when they are underspecified. We present models at two levels of abstraction. The first considers only data management; the second considers both data and message management. For each level, we provide a high level Petri net description and a series of specifications suitable for model checking. Formal analysis of these identifies unspecified assumptions and errors. The paper demonstrates the relative roles of Petri nets and model checking in locating these problems. It further shows the benefits to using several model checkers (Cospan, Murφ and Spin) for the analysis, due to differences in specification language and underlying semantic models.

Other verification efforts have addressed sequential consistency and similar protocols; Pong and Dubois provide a survey [PD 97]. Our work differs in both the protocols analyzed and the combination of Petri net modelling and model checking. Lindemann and Schön use Petri net modelling for performance analysis of several DSM memory consistency protocols [LS 95]. Gopalakrishnan *et al.* applied model checking to some of Li and Hudak's DSM protocols [GKKR 94]; for the one presented here, we have verified configurations with up to eight processors while their work covered only two processors. Petri net modelling [BG 85] and verification [CGH+ 93] have also been applied independently to cache coherence protocols, which are similar to memory coherence protocols. Blondel *et al.* implemented the protocol discussed here and located several errors [BRRS 98] using distributed debugging tools. Petri net tools such as PEP [G 97], PROD [VHL 97], and Design/CPN [J 95] support model checking. We performed our verifications independently of such tools. Separately developed specifications serve as sanity checks on one another and allow us to investigate what types of errors are easily found with each type of model.

Sect. 2 presents an overview of the Li/Hudak protocol. Sect. 3 presents the Petri net description of the first, more abstract, protocol model. Sect. 4 discusses the formal analysis of this model. Sect. 5 introduces the second model as a refinement of the first and Sect. 6 discusses its formal analysis.

2 Protocol Overview

Li and Hudak's protocol specifies how processors request and receive data. Data are organized into blocks of memory called *pages*. The DSM architecture (Fig. 1) maintains a *page table* on each processor, giving the status of each page relative to the processor. The status indicates the processor's access to the page (nil, read, or write) and whether the processor owns the page. Access is nil if the page is not in local memory or if another processor has modified its local copy of the page. Several processors may have read access to a page at once; write access includes read privileges, but is exclusive. This type of protocol is called multiple-reader, single-writer.

The processor last having write access to a page is its *owner*. The owner, which can change over time, sends the page contents to any other processor that requests them. It also tracks which other processors have read access to the page in a *copy-set*. These processors must be told to *invalidate* their copies before a write to the page occurs.

When a processor wants access privileges that it does not have, it *faults* and invokes a *handler* to request the page. Requests are made via broadcasts to all other processors; accordingly, Li/Hudak call this the *Broadcast Distributed Manager* (BDM) protocol. Processors respond to requests using a *server*. A handler and a server on the same processor may try to access a page simultaneously. To ensure exclusive access, each page table entry also maintains a *lock* which is obtained through a test-and-set technique. Fig. 2 gives the pseudocode for the handlers and servers [LH 89, p. 351] and the invalidation protocol [LH 89, p. 328]. The handler and server definitions are parameterized by the page for which the fault or service request occurred. In addition, the read and write servers take a parameter indicating the processor making the request.

Read fault handler (p)
  Lock (PTable[p].lock);
  broadcast to get p for read;
  PTable[p].access:=read;
  Unlock (PTable[p].lock);
	Read server (p,i)
	  Lock (PTable[p].lock);
	  IF PTable[p].owner=true THEN BEGIN
	    PTable[p].copy set:=PTable[p].copy set$\cup$\{i\};
	    PTable[p].access:=read; send p to i; END;
	  Unlock (PTable[p].lock);

Write fault handler (p)
  Lock (PTable[p].lock);
  broadcast to get p for write;
  invalidate (p,PTable[p].copy set);
  PTable[p].access:=write;
  PTable[p].copy set:=\{ \};
  PTable[p].owner=self;
  Unlock (PTable[p].lock);
	Write server (p,i)
	  Lock (PTable[p].lock);
	  IF PTable[p].owner=true THEN BEGIN
	    send p and PTable[p].copy set to i;
	    PTable[p].access:=nil;
	    END;
	  Unlock (PTable[p].lock);

Invalidate (p, copy set)
  FOR k in copy set DO
    send invalid request to proc k;
	Invalidate server
	  PTable[p].access:=nil;

Fig. 2. Broadcast Distributed Manager (K. Li and P. Hudak)

Li and Hudak state a few assumptions on message communication and system organization. They explicitly assume atomic broadcast of messages [LH 89, p. 334], which guarantees that a message broadcast by a processor arrives at all others before any other message is sent. Simple examples show that starvation and exclusivity violations may occur without this atomicity. Invalidation replies are also needed [L 88, p. 98] to avoid exclusivity violations (otherwise, a processor granted for write could perform an access before the invalidation completes, conflicting with any readers that have not yet invalidated). However, they state no assumptions on the scheduling of handlers and servers within processors. Processors may contain several threads, but only one thread per processor is capable of faulting (the others are system threads). Each such thread has its own handler and each processor has a single server.

Fig. 3 illustrates a write request by processor P_i for a page owned by processor P_j. Dashed lines indicate page locks. P_i's handler broadcasts requests to all servers (*1*). P_j's server sends a grant, the copy set, and the page contents (*2*). The other servers disregard the request (*3*). P_i's handler multicasts invalidations to all the readers in the copy set (*4*) which update to nil access and send acknowledgments (*5*). When all acknowledgments are received, P_i takes exclusive ownership and write access (*6*).

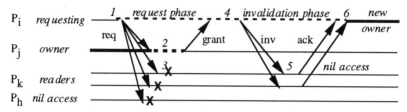

Fig. 3. Protocol Request/Grant Phase and Invalidate/Acknowledgment Phase

The above description suggests three expected safety properties of the BDM protocol:
- **One Owner**: if a processor owns page *p* then no other processor also owns *p*;
- **Exclusive Write**: if a processor has write access to page *p*, then no other processor has either read or write access to *p*;
- **Copy Set Adequacy**: if processor *i* has read access to page *p* but does not own *p*, then *i* is in the copy set for *p* on the processor that owns *p*.

In addition, no processor should deadlock while waiting for a desired access:
- **Request Completion**: if a processor faults for page *p*, it eventually obtains the desired access privileges to *p*.

Request completion is a liveness property. Our analyses explored the above properties, but not sequential consistency. Sequential consistency is irrelevant to the first model because the property relies on the message passing details which only appear in the second model. Sect. 6 discusses sequential consistency in the context of that model.

3. Petri Net Model Without Message Management

Our first model manages locks and page table information as indicated in the pseudocode, but replaces message passing with synchronous rendezvous. Fig. 4 gives a manually developed, colored Petri net [JR 91, J 95] specification of the model. Sect. 3.1 summarizes the notations and describes the places and their initial markings. Sect. 3.2 correlates the places and transitions to the pseudocode in Fig. 3.

3.1 Notations, Initializations, and Places

Let **S** denote the set of processors, **P** the set of pages, and **X** the set of threads on a processor. Elements of these sets are denoted *i*, *p*, and *x* respectively. The model uses several types of tokens, organized around key components of the protocol.

Processors and Threads: A token <i,x> denotes a thread *x* on processor *i*. Place *TR (Thread Ready)* models the set of threads ready to attempt an access. Initially, for each processor *i* it contains the set of tokens denoted by the formal sum $\Sigma_{x \in X}$ <i,x>. Over all the processors, this yields the double sum $\Sigma_{i \in S} \Sigma_{x \in X}$ <i,x>.

Requests and Access Rights: A token <i,x,r,p> models a request by thread *x* on processor *i* for access *r* (either *W* for write or *R* for Read) to page *p*. Place *TW (Thread Waiting)* contains tokens modelling the pending requests. It is initially empty.

Page Table: Place *PT (Page Table)* contains tokens corresponding to the page table entries on all the processors. The page table entry for page *p* on processor *i* is modelled by a token <i,p,li,ai,oi,si> where:

- *li* indicates whether the page is locked on processor *i* (*F* for False, *T* for True);
- *ai* is the access to page *p* of processor *i* (*N* for Nil, *R* for Read, *W* for Write);
- *oi* indicates whether processor *i* is the owner of page *p* (*F* for False, *T* for True);
- *si* is the copy set (the set of processors that have a valid copy of *p*).

We do not model the page contents as they are irrelevant to the control. Li and Hudak do not discuss page table initialization. Any initialization satisfying the desired properties seems reasonable. The Petri net model assumes that each page *p* is owned by some processor *j(p)*. Processor *j(p)* has read access to *p* and all other processors have nil access to *p*. This allows the copy sets to be empty. The initial marking of *PT* therefore consists of the token <j(p),p,R,T,$\varnothing$> for *j(p)* and the formal sum $\Sigma_{i \in S-j(p)}$ <i,p,N,F,$\varnothing$> for all the other processors. The whole set of pages yields the double sum $\Sigma_{p \in P}$ (<j(p),p,R,T,$\varnothing$> + $\Sigma_{i \in S-j(p)}$ <i,p,N,F,$\varnothing$>).

3.2 Transitions

The colored Petri net of Fig. 4 has three parts. The transitions corresponding to data access are towards the left. The transitions for read faults and serves are in the middle. Towards the right are the transitions for write faults, serves, and invalidations.

Data Access Part: Any thread <i,x> available to attempt an access enables transition *trq (thread request)*. Upon firing, *trq* non-deterministically chooses a page *p* and a desired access *r*, placing a token <i,x,p,r> in *TW* to indicate the pending request. If the page table token for *i* and *p* in *PT* shows the desired access and the page is unlocked, the request enables transition *tah (thread access hit)*. When *tah* fires, it returns token <i,x> to ready status in place *TR*. If the page is locked, the request token waits at place *TW*. If it corresponds to a fault, the read management or write management parts handle it, as described below.

Read Management: A read fault is enabled at transition *hrl (handler read lock)* by a request <i,x,r,p> in place *TW* and an unlocked page table token <i,p,F,ai,oi,si> in place *PT* with nil access. After *hrl* fires, the updated page table token shows a locked page and the thread waits for a grant at place *HRP (Handler Read Prepare)*. Processor *j* can serve the request (and enable transition *srlg (server read lock and grant)*) if its page table token for *p* is unlocked and shows ownership. After *srlg* fires, the page table token for *p* on *j* is locked. Tokens also move to places *HRE (Handler Read End)* and *SRM (Server Read Management)* to enable page table updates for processors *i* and *j*.

Transition *sru (server read unlock)* updates the page table to finish a read serve. The page table token becomes <j,p,F,R,oj,sj+i> to unlock the page, set the access to read, and add *i* to the copy set. If the page was in write mode, *sj* now includes only *i*. Transition *hru (handler read unlock)* updates the page table at the end of a read fault. Moving token <i,x> to place *TR* models that the access has been performed. The page table token becomes <i,p,F,R,oi,si> because page *p*, still owned by processor *j*, is unlocked in read mode on processor *i*. Transitions *sru* and *hru* fire asychronously.

Write Management: Write management is similar to read management but includes an invalidation phase. Write faults are enabled at transition *hwl (handler write lock)*. Token <i,x,p> in place *HWP (Handler Write Prepare)* models waiting for the grant.

Transition *swlg (server write lock and grant)* fires when processor *j* can serve a write request for page *p*. The page table token for *p* on *j* is locked and returns to place *PT*. The token in place *SWM (Server Write Management)* enables transition *swu (server write unlock)*, which updates the server's page table entry. Token <i,x,p,sj> in place *HWI (Handler Write Invalidate)* starts the invalidation phase.

Tokens <i,x,p,s> in place *HWI* drive transition *his (handler invalidate server)*; *s* denotes the set of processors yet to invalidate *p*. As the processors *k* in *s* invalidate and acknowledge asynchronously, they are removed from *s*. Transition *hwu (handler write unlock)* may fire when its guard *[s=∅]* indicates completion of the invalidation phase. The new page table token has processor *i* as a write-owner with an empty copy set.

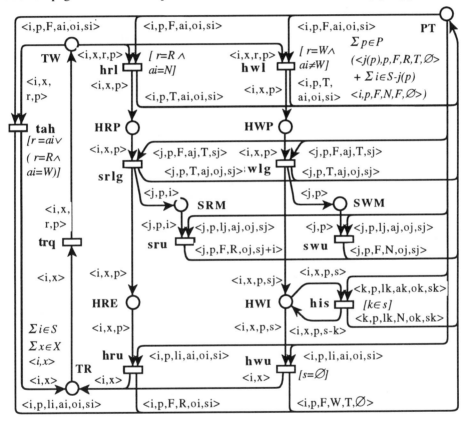

Fig. 4. Original Specification of the First Model

4. Verification of the First Model

This section presents the Petri net analysis and model checking performed on the first model. These analyses located several errors, for which we propose corrections. The discussion refers to *configurations* which indicate the number of processors, threads per processor, and pages in the model being analyzed.

4.1 Petri Net Analysis

P-semi flows allow easy checking of some basic structural invariants and safety properties. They are more general than the safety properties in model checking because they are structural properties of the Petri net, independent of particular configurations. Automatic construction of semi-flows is exponential for non colored Petri nets and still open for general predicate/transition nets [CHP 93, J 95]. If the invariants are known, however, checking is linear in the number of transitions of the net. This section presents flow equations capturing desired invariants for the first model.

Let $(P_1 + ... + P_k)$\<f=x, g=y> denote the total number of tokens in places P_1,..., P_k having the same colors x and y for the fields f and g, respectively, regardless of the other token fields. The first two invariant equations denote that (1) threads are never created or destroyed, and (2) there is exactly one page table token per page per processor.

$$\forall\ i\ \forall\ x\ \ (TR + TW + HRP + HRE + HWP + HWI)\ \backslash<proc=i, thread=x> = 1 \qquad (1)$$

$$\forall\ i\ \forall\ p\ \ PT\ \backslash<proc=i, page=p> = 1 \qquad (2)$$

By equations (3) and (4), each page on each processor is either unlocked or locked but being managed by exactly one handler or server.

$$\forall\ i\ \forall\ p\ \ PT\ \backslash<proc=i, page=p, locked=F> + \qquad (3)$$
$$(HRP + HRE + HWP + HWI + SRM + SWM)\ \backslash<proc=i, page=p> = 1$$

$$\forall\ i\ \forall\ p\ \ PT\ \backslash<proc=i, page=p, locked=T> = \qquad (4)$$
$$(HRP + HRE + HWP + HWI + SRM + SWM)\ \backslash<proc=i, page=p>$$

The next two equations express page ownership invariants. Each unlocked page should have exactly one owner (the One Owner property of Sect. 2.2). For locked pages, there are transient states during which ownership transfers between processors. Equation (5) says that each page either has an owner or is being transferred to a new owner. In the latter case, tokens at place *HWI* indicate that invalidations are in progress for p, while tokens at *SRM* indicate that a processor is about to relinquish ownership.

Equation (6) ensures that all but one processor denies ownership of p. Recall that **S** is defined to be the set of all processors. The second summand requires page table tokens for p with $lock=T$ to correspond to handlers waiting for grants, handlers finishing read requests, or serves about to complete. Handlers finishing write requests are excluded because they result in ownership changes.

$$\forall\ p\ PT\ \backslash<page=p,lock=F,owner=T> +SRM\ \backslash<page=p> +HWI\ \backslash<page=p> = 1 \qquad (5)$$

$$\forall\ p\ PT\ \backslash<page=p,lock=F,owner=F> \qquad (6)$$
$$+ (HRP +HRE +HWP +SWM)\ \backslash<page=p> = |\ S\ | - 1$$

T-semi-flows allow checking of desired stationary sequences. Simple sequences take advantage of symmetries and return to the original symbolic marking under a suitable permutation of node colors [CDFH 97]. Some elementary sequences for the model are:
(1) the hit cycle: *(trq, tah)**,
(2) the transfer of write ownership : *(trq, hwl, swlg, swu, hwu)**,
(3) the ping-pong between a write owner i and a reader j in which i gives j read access, then takes write access and invalidates j.

Manually analyzing the equations and the sequences uncovers some problems in the BDM description. All reported problems reflect underspecifications, omissions, or errors in Li and Hudak's descriptions, not in our models. We suspect most, if not all, of these problems have been corrected by those implementing this protocol (including Li and Hudak). However, corrections to the protocol have never been published. Our analysis therefore reflects problems in the only available protocol description.

Error 1. Multiple processors can claim ownership for the same page because the write servers fail to relinquish ownership when sending grants. From the semi-flow perspective, transitions *swlg*, *swu*, and *hwu* cannot satisfy equations (5) and (6). The corrected model changes transition *swu*, which now puts token <j,p,N,F,Ø> (instead of <j,p,N,oj,sj>) in place *PT*; this indicates *j*'s loss of ownership and resets the copy set.

Error 2. Deadlock occurs if a processor requests write access to a page that it owns with read access. Checking sequence 3 unveiled this error. Transition *swlg*, which needs a processor *j* to serve a request from processor *i*, cannot fire with *j*=*i* because the token <j,p,lj,aj,oj,sj> in place *PT* has lj=T. The handler for *i* has locked the page, waiting for a grant. The server on *i*, meanwhile, waits for the lock to free in order to service the request. Deadlock results. The pseudocode description therefore needs a special case in the write handler for self-requests. Correspondingly, we add transition **hwol** *(handler write owner lock)* to the Petri net (Fig. 5). Firing on tokens from *TW* and *PT* indicating self-ownership, *hwol* locks the page and initiates invalidation by putting a token in place *HWI*. We also add guard oi=F to transition *hwl* to distinguish it from the new transition *hwol*.

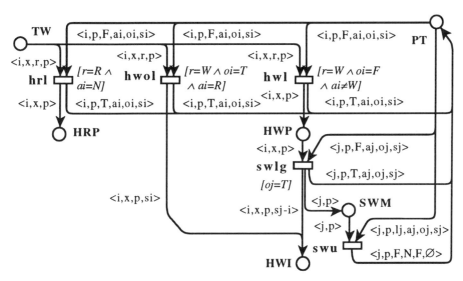

Fig. 5. Corrections for the First Model

Fig. 5 shows the corrections for both errors. It also removes an inefficiency related to invalidations. Consider a processor taking write access to a page for which it had read access. The processor must be in the copy set received from the previous owner. By the pseudocode, the processor therefore sends an (unnecessary) invalidation to itself. Removing the requesting processor from the copy set when the grant is managed avoids the useless invalidation. Fig. 5 adjusts transition *swlg*, putting token <i,x,p,sj-i> (instead of <i,x,p,sj>) in *HWI*. The corrected model satisfies all the desired equations.

4.2 Model Checking

Model checkers vary in numerous dimensions such as semantic models (synchronous or asynchronous), specification languages (hardware oriented or process oriented), property language (temporal logic or automata) and system representation (symbolic or explicit). Different combinations are suited to different problems. Often, the problem to be verified is better suited to a particular semantic model or specification language. The choice between symbolic and explicit system representation is based on both the size of the design and the extent to which variables in the design are mutually dependent. Symbolic representations, such as Binary Decision Diagrams (BDDs), are very compact for many designs. Designs with large degrees of inter-variable dependencies, however, are sometimes more succinct when expressed explicitly as directed graphs.

Most model checkers view systems as sets of simultaneously executing, finite state machines. The full system model is taken to be the cross-product of these machines. As the number of components in a design grows, the number of states in the full model increases exponentially. This situation, known as *state-explosion*, explains the practical upper bound on the sizes of designs amenable to verification. Current model checkers can handle designs with roughly 10^{70} states, sometimes more depending upon the structure of the design in question.

We explored the first model using two model checkers: Cospan [HHK 96] and Murφ [ND 96]. These tools have rather different features and support complementary techniques, as described in the following sections.

Verification with Cospan: We chose the Cospan model checker from Lucent Technologies/Bell Laboratories for several reasons. First, the underlying semantic model is inherently synchronous. This fits our abstraction of messages to synchronous rendezvous between processors. Second, its input language is designed for verification, not synthesis (unlike specification languages such as Verilog, as used in the VIS model checker). The actual connections between the handlers, servers, and page tables may therefore be left implicit, which is consistent with the level of abstraction in the protocol description. Next, Cospan supports symbolic model checking using BDDs, which could be useful for verifying configurations with several processors. Finally, it supports powerful techniques not available in other model checkers, such as the ability to prove whether one machine is a property-preserving refinement of another. Cospan uses LTL properties, though the LTL/CTL distinction is irrelevant for our purposes.

Our specification contains finite-state machines for representing page table entries, threads (with fault handlers), and processors (with request servers). All protocol actions, such as broadcasts, request responses, and page table updates, are performed atomically. While this is a considerable abstraction over the protocol's behavior in practice, it allows us to quickly locate any simple control errors in the model.

Each page table entry machine contains four state variables: *lock_status* (which has values locked or unlocked), *access_right* (read, write, or nil), *owner* (boolean), and *copy_set* (an array of booleans, one for each processor). Each variable is updated according to the protocol description (Fig. 2). Initially, processor zero owns all pages with read access and all other processors have nil access; this is consistent with the initial marking of the Petri net model.

Each thread machine contains three state variables: *status* (one of running, faulted, broadcasting, or invalidating), *faultpage* (any page number), and *faulttype* (read or write). The thread also contains a non-deterministic boolean variable called *fault*. When *fault* is true and the thread status is *running*, the status changes to *faulted* and a particular faultpage and faulttype are selected non-deterministically; these values hold until the fault has been serviced. The model does not consider access hits because the faultpage and faulttype are chosen so as to generate faults only.

Each processor machine maintains a variables corresponding to its server: *serving* (a boolean indicating whether it is serving a request), *serving_to* (a processor number), *serving_type* (read or write), and *serving_page* (a page number). The latter three variables hold their values while *serving* is true and are used for coordination between faulting threads (handlers) and the processors serving their requests.

We do not model messages explicitly. Instead, the machines monitor each other's variables to detect messages. For example, if a thread's status is *broadcasting*, the other processors act as if they had received a request from that thread. As several threads may be broadcasting at once, the servers must uniformly choose one "message" to handle. Given the constructs in Cospan's input language, the only reasonable choice is for each server to see the one broadcast by the lowest numbered thread on the lowest numbered processor (each thread and processor has a unique id).

This modelling decision affects the verification of the liveness property. A thread on processor two may have its broadcast repeatedly ignored if threads on processors zero and one broadcast their own requests at certain times. This problem does not affect processors zero and one. Rather than add a complicated (and potentially expensive) fairness condition, we instead verify the liveness property relative to processors zero and one only. By construction, processors one and two are symmetric. A fair message scheduling protocol should therefore support the liveness property for processor two if it supports it for processor one. The second model (Sect. 5) adds a fair scheduling protocol, so we defer general analysis of the liveness property to that model.

Table 1. Safety and Liveness Checks with Original Information Structures

	one owner				request completion			
u,p,t	reached	BDD nodes	MBytes	CPUsec	reached	BDD nodes	MBytes	CPUsec
2,1,1	1 700	12 165	0.0	16	1 920	11 566	0.0	24
2,1,2	67 957	26 256	2.2	139	105 898	24 650	2.2	74
2,2,1	89 030	31 183	3.2	285	95 901	98 608	13.8	1 033
2,2,2	$2*10^7$	155 076	40.5	3 905				

Errors 1 and 2 (Sect. 4.1) surface almost immediately using a two processor, one thread, two page configuration. The Cospan specification was corrected similarly to the Petri net model. Table 1 shows the verification statistics obtained for various configurations of the corrected model using Cospan version 8.22 on a Silicon Graphics IP19 with 1Gb of memory. As the figures are similar for all the safety properties, we show only those for One Owner. The *u,p,t* column indicates the numbers of units (processors), pages, and threads in the configuration. The *reached* column indicates how many states are actually reachable from the initial state. Model checkers explore only the reachable states (for u,p,t=2,2,2 only $2*10^7$ states of $5*10^{15}$ are reachable). The *BDD nodes* column gives the size of the data structures used in the verification. The *Mbytes* and *CPU sec* columns give memory and time usage statistics.

The table presents only those configurations that were verifiable within the available memory (usually about 500 Mb). Larger configurations face several potential problems with regards to memory usage. First, their state spaces grow rapidly, requiring much more information to be stored. Second, the BDD data structure used for symbolic model checking behaves unpredictably with respect to memory usage. A BDD's size can vary dramatically depending on the order in which it considers design variables. Furthermore, the intermediate computations required in model checking can result in exponential blow-up in the size of the intermediate BDDs. For large designs, this often renders symbolic model checking intractable. From experience, the memory usage leaps in Table 1 are not unusual, nor is the inability to verify larger configurations. The different algorithms needed to verify liveness versus safety properties account for differences in resource usage for properties of the same configuration.

Two optimizations to the Cospan model reduce the number of states and enable us to verify larger configurations. First, a processor only uses the copy sets of pages that it owns. Since a page has at most one owner at a time, we abstract to only one global copy set per page. The copy sets contribute $ProcessorCount^2 \times PageCount$ state bits (ProcessorCount bits for each of ProcessorCount $\times$ PageCount page table entries) in the original specification. Global copy sets reduce this by a factor of ProcessorCount. The statistics in Table 2 show significant savings in the reachable states and resource usage for the larger configurations under the new model. We verified the safety properties simultaneously. We attribute the slight increases in memory usage and time for the safety properties under the smallest configuration to the differences in BDD variable orderings since the numbers of BDD nodes are similar.

Table 2. Safety and Liveness Checks with Global Copy set

u,p,t	one owner & one writer & copy set				request completion			
	reached	BDD nodes	MBytes	CPUsec	reached	BDD nodes	MBytes	CPUsec
2,1,1	937	10 424	0.0	24	1 065	10 458	0.0	23
2,1,2	38 629	23 969	1.1	67	62 626	23 299	2.2	76
2,2,1	27 271	48 586	2.2	131	29 404	55 923	10.6	404
2,2,2	$7*10^6$	504 724	31.0	3 361				
3,2,1	10^7	3764 591	233.0	28 765				

Our second optimization concerns the processor machine variables *serving_to*, *serving_page*, and *serving_type*. Once a server chooses to serve a request from a particular thread, the information kept by these variables can be obtained by looking at the *faultpage* and *faulttype* variables on the thread. The processor number is also accessible through the thread by the structure of the specification. The variables on the server therefore appear to be redundant. We alter the specification slightly, adding a boolean variable *being_served* to each thread machine and removing the *serving_to*, *serving_page*, and *serving_type* variables. Information sharing between thread and server machines is now simple. A server can determine which page it is serving by finding the thread that is being served for a faultpage owned by the server. Since the server can only process one request at a time, only one such thread can exist. Eliminating the server variables makes the specification substantially smaller and allows us to explore larger configurations, as shown in Table 3.

Although this information sharing deviates from real implementations of servers and handlers, such reductions are often necessary to make model checking tractable. This is where the nature of a model checker's specification language becomes important. If the language requires explicit connections between components and the variables they examine (as does a hardware description language like Verilog), making such reductions can require extensive changes to the model. If such connections are left implicit, the variables may be examined without further modification.

Table 3. Safety and Liveness Checks with Global Copy set and Reduced Information

u,p,t	one owner & one writer & copy set				request completion			
	reached	BDD nodes	MBytes	CPUsec	reached	BDD nodes	MBytes	CPUsec
2,1,1	161	13 804	1.1	20	191	14 379	1.1	22
2,1,2	6 103	27 056	2.2	60	15 919	28 089	2.2	75
2,1,3	189 701	52 396	3.5	87	10^6	56 458	3.5	69
2,2,1	3 350	31 183	1.1	51	3 900	31 811	2.1	82
2,2,2	583 969	155 076	9.2	713	10^6	227 582	44.0	1 511
2,2,3	$7*10^7$	288 356	29.8	2 857	$5*10^8$	862 028	181.0	9 759
3,1,1	3 056	30 467	1.1	31	3820	32 819	1.1	46
3,1,2	801 026	60 675	3.7	170	$3*10^6$	80 578	11.0	408
3,1,3	10^8	109 752	8.4	414	$2*10^9$	160 977	23.1	951
3,2,1	368 742	238 346	15.2	1 305	442 999	308 507	25.7	1 956
4,1,1	50 756	72 823	4.5	216	68 423	86 603	6.7	246
4,1,2	$8*10^7$	174 513	13.7	872	$5*10^8$	241 705	44.3	2 712
4,1,3	$8*10^{10}$	231 366	20.2	1 564	$3*10^{12}$	599 200	98.1	7 396
5,1,1	745 296	166 850	20.6	902	10^6	207 370	40.5	1 231

Our Cospan efforts discovered a potential deadlock when multiple threads can fault on a processor. Specifically, a thread t can fault for a page p that its processor comes to own with t's desired access because another thread on the same processor also faulted for p. In this case, t should return to normal operation. Li and Hudak do not handle this situation because they considered only one faulting thread per processor. However, supporting multiple faulting threads is straightforward. Handlers waiting for the lock to begin broadcasting need only monitor the page table and return to ready status if their desired access is obtained. The results in Table 3 are for a model using this revision; all properties verify for the configurations shown.

This deadlock cannot occur in the Petri net model because a thread t waits in place *TW* for its desired access, at which point it enables transition *tah*. This illustrates the advantage to multiple modelling efforts: different modelling decisions elicit different implementation requirements. In this case, threads in the Petri net model resume when their desired accesses appear in the page table. Threads in the Cospan model wait for direct responses to their requests. Either design could arise in practice.

Verification with Murφ: The processors in this protocol are highly symmetric. Given two processors, neither of which has access to a given page, the resulting system runs are similar regardless of which one faults. A model checker need only explore one run from each equivalence class under symmetry. Cospan does not support symmetry reductions; the Murφ verification tool supports user-supplied symmetries [ND 96].

The Murφ specification uses global copy sets and reduced server variables. It differs from the last Cospan model in a few small details due to differences in the tools and their languages. To enable symmetry reduction, Murφ requires the processor initially owning the pages to be chosen non-deterministically; this is more general than in the Cospan model. Also, unlike the Cospan version, the Murφ version is not restricted to responding to the lowest numbered request. Table 4 shows statistics for verifying the safety properties in Murφ (Murφ does not currently support liveness properties under symmetry) under Murφ version 3.0 on an UltraSparc running SunOS 5.1. We do not report memory usage because Murφ does not give accurate memory figures. Instead, it uses as much memory as the user allows. These runs were each allowed 100Mb, though the smaller runs needed as little as 8Mb. General comparisons between the Murφ and Cospan results are not meaningful here because Murφ uses an asynchronous (interleaving) semantic model and explicit-state, rather than symbolic, model checking. These statistics do, however, demonstrate the benefits to exploiting symmetry.

Table 4. Safety Checks with Murφ

u,p,t	With symmetry Reached	CPUsec	Without symm. Reached	CPUsec	u,p,t	With symmetry Reached	CPUsec	Without symm. Reached	CPUsec
2,1,1	66	0.3	131	0.3	4,1,1	2 176	2.5	43 785	42.6
2,1,2	1 423	1.5	5 645	6.0	5,1,1	8 272	15.0		
2,2,1	774	0.8	3 055	4.0	6,1,1	26 479	73.6		
2,2,2	74 832	301.2			7,1,1	74 445	335.1		
3,1,1	451	0.6	2 560	1.3	8,1,1	189 087	1 176.6		
3,1,2	81 878	312.1							
3,2,1	27 356	49.5							

5. Petri Net Model with Message Management

Our second model extends the corrected first model with message management. At the I/O level, queues store messages that cannot be processed immediately either because the handler or server is busy with another task, or because the request concerns a page which is currently locked in the local page table. Several types of messages arise in the BDM protocol: requests, invalidations, grants, and acknowledgments (to invalidations). The first two activate servers, while the latter two awake waiting handler threads. Li and Hudak neither discuss thread scheduling nor specify whether messages are placed on a single or separate queues.

Our Petri net and model checking specifications use slightly different organizational assumptions on queues. The Petri net model uses a distinct queue for each message type, with one queue of each type per page per processor. The model checking specification uses one queue for requests, one for invalidations and another for grants and acknowledgments to make verification more tractable. This optimization is acceptable because a processor can wait either for a grant or for acknowledgments at any given time. The size of the request and acknowledgment queues is bounded by the number of processors. Since a handler may only await one grant at a time, the grant queue needs only one slot. Similarly, the invalidation queue has one slot since a given page can be invalidated by at most one handler at a time.

The Petri net model has six parts: data access, read handler, write handler, read server, write server, and invalidation server. Fig. 6 shows the data access part and the handlers; Fig. 7 contains the server parts. The two figures share the request queue *REQ* and the places *GR (grants)*, *INV (invalidations)*, *ACK (acknowledgments)* and of course the page table place *PT*. Each designator represents a complete array of separate places or queues indexed by the processor numbers.

Data Access Part: This part is similar to that in the first model, except faulted requests are directed into queue *REQ* by transition **tam** *(thread access miss)*. The second field of the request token <i,i,x,r,p> indicates that processor *i* must manage it.

Handler Read Part: Transition *hrl (handler read lock)* is the same as in the first model except the input token <i,i,x,r,p> comes from queue *REQ* instead of place *TW*. Transition *hag (handler already granted)* supports multiple faulting threads; if the requested access has already been obtained, the thread token returns to place *TW*. Firing transition *hrb (handler read broadcast)* broadcasts read requests from handler *i*. It puts a set of tokens <i,j,p,R> in queue *REQ* for each *j* other than *i*. The token moved from place **HRP** *(Handler Read Prepare)* to place **HRW** *(Handler Read Wait)* models waiting for a grant. Grants appear as tokens <j,i,p,g> from place *GR*, where *g* indicates the type of grant. When the grant arrives, transition *hrg (handler read grant)* fires, moving token <i,x,p> from place *HRW* to place *HRE* to update the page table. Finally, transition *hru (handler read unlock)* is the same as in the first model.

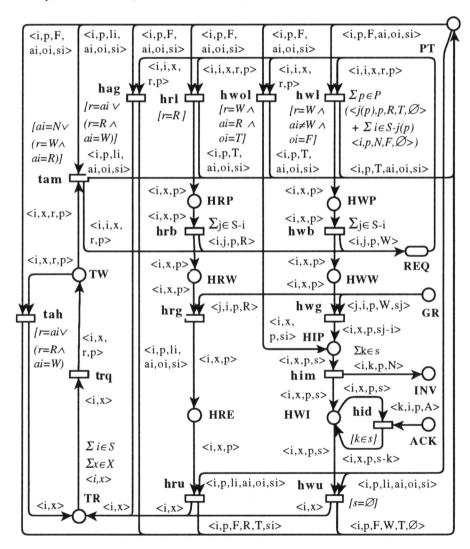

Fig. 6. Communication Refinement. Thread and Handler Parts of the Second Model

Handler Write Part: Transition *hwl (handler write lock)* is similar to *hrl*. Transition *hwol (handler write owner lock)* manages write requests when the faulting processor owns the page for read. For other write faults, firing transition *hwb (handler write broadcast)* broadcasts write requests to other processors through queue *REQ*. The token moved from place *HWP (Handler Write Prepare)* to place *HWW (Handler Write Wait)* awaits a grant token <j,i,p,W,sj> from place *GR*; the *sj* field denotes the sent copy set. When this token arrives, transition *hwg (handler write grant)* fires, moving token <i,x,p,sj-i> to place *HIP (Handler Invalidation Prepare)* to enable the invalidation phase.

Transition *him (handler invalidate multicast)* multicasts invalidation messages by putting one token <i,k,p,N> in place *INV* for each *k* in the copy set. Token <i,x,p,s> moves from place *HIP* to place *HWI (Handler Write Invalidation)* to await the acknowledgments. Transition *hid (handler invalidate done)* receives acknowledgments from place *ACK* as tokens <k,i,p,A> for some *k* ∈ *s* where *s* appears within a token <i,x,p,s> in place *HWI*. The acknowledging processor *k* is removed from *s*. After invalidation, transition *hwu (handler write unlock)* is as in the first model.

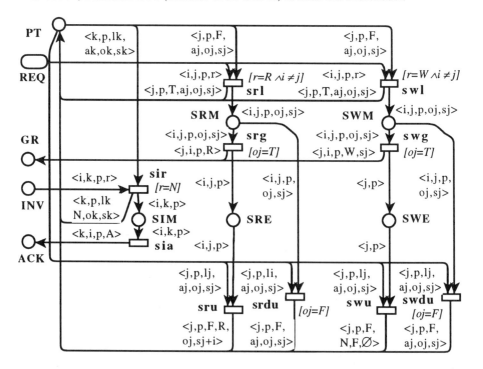

Fig. 7. Communication Refinement. Server Part of Second Model

Server Read Part: Transition *srl (server read lock)* locks a page to analyze a read request from another processor *[i≠j]* by putting a token into place *SRM (Server Read Management)*. If the processor does not own the page, transition *srdu (server read discard unlock)* fires and unlocks the page table entry. If the processor does own the page, transition *srg (server read grant)* fires, putting a grant token in place *GR* and a token <j,p,i> in place *SRE (Server Read End)* to update the copy set. Transition *sru (server read unlock)* updates the page table following a read serve.

Server Write Part: This is similar to the server read part. Transition *swl (server write lock)* puts a request token into place *SWM (Server Write Management)* for analysis. Transition *swdu (server write discard unlock)* fires if the processor does not own the page. If it does, transition *swg (server write grant)* sends a write grant and puts a token in place *SWE (Server Write End)*. This token enables transition *swu (server write unlock)*, which completes the serve.

Server Invalidation Part: Transition *sir (server invalidate reception)* models the atomic updating of the entry for page p by server k when it receives an invalidation request in the place *INV*. Following the pseudocode (Fig. 2), it does not lock the page or check the condition $ak=R$. After firing, it replaces the page table token by <k,p,lk,N,ok,sk> and puts token <i,k,p> into place *SIM (Server Invalidation Management)* to enable the acknowledgment. Transition *sia (server invalidate ack)* sends the acknowledgment by putting a token in place *ACK*.

6. Verification of the Second Model

For verifying the model with message queues, we chose the Spin model checker [H 91] instead of either Cospan or Murφ. Spin provides message queues as a built-in data structure, and is therefore very well-suited to protocols employing message passing. In Cospan or Murφ, we would model a message queue manually using an array of state machines. Each machine would model one position in the queue, and would update its value based on those in adjacent machines whenever elements were added to or deleted from the queue. Spin handles these operations automatically.

Like Murφ, Spin uses explicit-state model checking and an interleaving semantics. However, Spin supports partial-order reductions instead of symmetry. Partial order reductions detect when two transitions can be taken in either order without affecting the truth or falsehood of properties; the model checker explores only one order. They are incomparable to symmetry reductions, but each can yield savings in practice.

Attempting to verify the configuration with two processors, one thread per processor, and one page uncovered a write-exclusivity error. In the following figures, as in earlier figures, thick bars denote ownership and dashed lines indicate page locks.

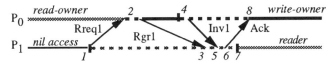

Fig. 8. Dummy Invalidation with Loss of Read-Write Exclusivity

Error 3. A processor may take read access while another processor has write access due to sequencing problems between grants and invalidations. Consider Fig. 8:
- P1 locks and broadcasts read request Rreq1 (*1*).
- P0, the owner, locks the page and returns grant Rgr1 (*2*). P0 unlocks.
- P0 locks to take write access. Since it is the owner, it sends invalidation Inv1 (*4*).
- P1 has both an invalidation (*3*) and a grant (*5*). It looks at the invalidation first and sends an acknowledgment Ack (*6*). Its access does not change.
- P0 receives the acknowledgment and takes write access (*8*).
- P1 sees its grant, takes read access, and unlocks (*7*).

Although this scenario appears to violate assumptions on message ordering, it does not. All message broadcasts were atomic and all access requests were seen in the same order on all processors. The problem arises because P1 had messages waiting in two queues simultaneously. This situation is not unrealistic because processors may run at different rates from one another and from the I/O subsystem. Li and Hudak do not state how to arbitrate such conflicts. The pseudocode in Fig. 2, however, suggests that invalidations should receive immediate attention (invalidations need precedence over requests to avoid deadlock). This example proves such a policy is insufficient.

We tried a modified Spin model, in which grants take priority over invalidations. The safety properties verified for the two processor, one thread, one page configuration (3006 states) in .5 CPU seconds and 4.8 megabytes of memory using Spin version 3.0.0 on an UltraSparc running SunOS 5.1. The number of reachable states for this configuration is higher than for Cospan due to the complexity added by the message queues. Unfortunately, the one owner property fails in a three processor configuration with this modification, so grant priority is also insufficient.

The original Spin model witnesses a separate message-based error, this one affecting the liveness property. We detected Error 4 during manual inspection of the Petri net model given in Fig. 6. As a sanity check, we ran Spin in simulation mode to reproduce the error in the three processors, one thread, one page configuration.

Error 4. Fig. 9 shows a case in which a page becomes permanently unowned by all processors because a requesting processor receives a redundant grant.
- P0 owns the page in write mode. P1 locks and broadcasts a write request Wreq1 (*1*).
- P2 locks for broadcast (*2*) but first receives Wreq1 (*3*) and then broadcasts Wreq2 (*5*).
- P0 receives Wreq1 (*4*) and locks. It queues Wreq2 (*6*) and sends grant Wgr1 to P1 (*8*).
- P0 is no longer the owner, so it discards Wreq2 (X).
- P1 queues Wreq2 (*7*). It receives grant Wgr1 and becomes the owner.
- P1 sends grant Wgr2 to P2 (*9*). P2 receives Wgr2 (*10*) and becomes the owner.
- P2 responds to the queued request Wreq1 by sending a grant Wgr1 to P1.
- P1 receives an unexpected grant (*11*), resulting in no owner.

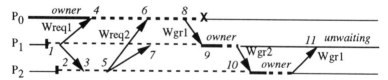

Fig. 9. Redundant Grant with Ownership Loss

Error 4 affects the liveness property because the protocol relies on owners to respond to requests. It provides another example in which message sequencing is insufficient. Clearly, all processors received all messages in the same order, and in the order in which they were sent. However, P2 received Wreq1 after locking to broadcast Wreq2, while P1 received Wreq2 after locking to broadcast Wreq1. Some conditions on locking as well as message sequencing appear necessary.

Unfortunately, we are not aware of any discussions of this protocol that provide a general classification of the necessary message system requirements. Li's IVY prototype for the BDM protocol implements message passing by an I/O sub-system using an Apollo token ring [L 86, L 88]. A token ring contains a slot that circulates to all processors in some fixed order. A processor can send a message if the slot it empty when it passes by. The message circulates to all processors, then back to the original sender, which removes the message from the ring.

Using a token ring could avoid Error 4 in the context of the BDM protocol. As a message passed by in the ring, each processor would either process it or place it in the appropriate queue. Consider processor P2. If it broadcasts a write request on a token ring, it expects to receive that request in its own queue after it has been delivered to all the other processors. Any request P2 sees before seeing its own must have been sent before P2 sent its request. P2 therefore assumes that some prior owner served such a request, and accordingly discards it. This would avoid Error 4.

Using a token ring should satisfy sequential consistency. The token ring guarantees that all processors receive messages from a given processor in the order in which they were sent. It should also guarantee a sequential ordering on all messages sent to all processors. These are the requirements of sequential consistency as stated in Sect. 1. It remains to show in future work, however, that a token ring satisfies the desired properties for the BDM protocol, particularly the liveness property. We have developed a new Petri net model that uses a token ring, but are still analyzing it.

Weaker restrictions than those imposed by a token ring seem plausible for the BDM protocol. Broadcast atomicity is an overly strong assumption for general networks in which mechanisms (such as vector clocks) can be used to insure causal ordering. Furthermore, given the exclusive ownership requirement, classical mechanisms for distributed mutual exclusion may be useful. A system based on time stamps [RA 81], for example, would require all processors to reply to a broadcast and send release messages when leaving their critical sections. Algorithms based on token passing [SK 85] would manage vectors of request counts on all processors and pass these with the grant tokens. Each of these approaches entails more complex management than is suggested in the original protocol description. Refining the necessary assumptions on the I/O system for the BDM protocol requires further experimentation.

7. Conclusion

Modelling and verification have complementary advantages. Modelling develops understanding of a design, while verification increases confidence that it satisfies certain properties. Each is useful for locating errors and uncovering unstated assumptions. This paper illustrates this synergy using one of Li and Hudak's protocols for sequential consistency in a DSM system. We have constructed models of the protocol at two levels of abstraction and in several specification languages. The first level considered page table management; the second also considered the message passing mechanisms.

For the first version, we have presented a compact Petri net model (9 places and 11 transitions) and verified both a Cospan model (340 lines) and a Murφ model (443 lines). These efforts uncovered problems in Li and Hudak's protocol description:
- Two processors may own the same page after a write request.
- A processor deadlocks when requesting write access to a page it owns for read only.
- Two threads on the same processor faulting for the same page can cause deadlock.
The Petri net model also indicated an inefficiency with respect to invalidation requests.

For the second version, we presented an additional Petri net model (19 places and 24 transitions) and discussed verification using a Spin model (262 lines). These efforts show the need for still-unspecified assumptions regarding the message architecture. Underspecification of assumptions was the largest hindrance to analyzing these protocols. General, implementation independent assumptions would be useful.

Analyzing the Petri nets manually locates simple invariant violations. Model checking is better for verifying liveness properties and exploring possible corrections to the original models. The combination of Petri net analysis and model checking is useful because the representations yield models with slightly different semantics. We are therefore more confident that our corrected models and assumptions are sufficient, rather than lucky by-products of modelling decisions in a particular notation.

We have performed similar analyses for Li and Hudak's *Dynamic Distributed Manager* (DDM) protocol, which attempts to reduce the amount of message passing in the BDM protocol. Each processor stores a *probable owner* for each page, to which it sends requests for the page. Servers forward requests for pages they do not own to their stored probable owners. Correctness relies on the chains of probable owners eventually reaching actual owners. We have found no errors in the protocol description, but have identified similar unstated assumptions on message passing that imply correctness.

We plan to explore additional consistency models for DSM systems. In particular, release consistency protocols [AG 96, CBZ 95] and multiple writer protocols [K 92] are distant descendants of the Li/Hudak protocols, sharing many of the same features. We have already begun similar work on the release consistency protocols used in the Munin DSM system [CBZ 91]. Munin also uses probable owners but supports multiple writers with an elaborate page update protocol.

We have also considered writing models for a theorem prover like PVS. This would allow us to explore the protocols over all configurations. More interestingly, however, we could abstract the commonalties in the protocols into libraries and lemmas, hopefully simplifying verification of later extensions to these protocols.

Acknowledgments: The authors thank Willy Zwaenepoel for fruitful comments on DSM, the anonymous reviewers for constructive remarks, and Bob Kurshan and Bell Laboratories for providing access to the latest version of Cospan.

References

[AG 96] Adve, S. V., Gharachorloo, K.: Shared Memory Consistency Models: A Tutorial. In IEEE Computer, 29, 12 (Dec. 1996) 66-76

[BG 85] Baer, J-L., Girault, C.: A Petri net model for a solution to the cache coherence problem. In Proc. First International Conference on Supercomputing Systems, St Petersburg, Florida (1985) 680-689

[BD 91] Barroso, L.A., Dubois, M.: Cache Coherence on a Slotted Ring. In IEEE Trans. on Computers, 44, 7, Berlin, Germany (Sept. 1991)

[BRRS 98] Blondel, X., Rosenfeld, L., Ruget, F., Singhoff, F.: Expériences de Mise au Point d'un Algorithme Réparti. To appear in Technique et Science Informatiques (1998)

[CBZ 91] Carter, J., Bennett, J., Zwaenepoel, W.: Implementation and Performance of Munin. In Proc. 13th ACM Symposium on Operating System Principles (1991) 152-164

[CBZ 95] Carter, J., Bennett, J., Zwaenepoel, W.: Techniques for Reducing Consistency-related Communication in Distributed Shared-memory Systems. ACM Trans. Comput. Syst. 13, 3 (Aug. 1995) 205-243

[CGH 86] Chatelain, C., Girault, C., Haddad, S.: Specification and Properties of a Cache Coherence Protocol Model. In Proc. 7th European Workshop on Application and Theory of Petri nets, Oxford England (June 1986), Advances in Petri nets 87, LNCS., Vol. 266, Springer-Verlag (1987) 1-20

[CDFH 97] Chiola, G., Dutheillet, C., Francheschinis, G., Haddad, S.: A Symbolic Reachability Graph for Coloured Petri Nets, Theoretical Computer Science, Vol. 176 (1997) 39-65

[CGH+ 93] Clarke, E., Grumberg, O., Hiraishi, H., Jha, S., Long, D., McMillan, K., Ness, L.: Verification of the Futurebus+ Cache Coherency Protocol. In Proc. Conf. on Computer Hardware Description Languages and their Application. North-Holland (1993)

[CHP 93] Couvreur, J.M., Haddad, S., Peyre, J.F.: Generative Families of Positive Invariants in Coloured Nets Sub-Classes. In Advances in Petri nets 87, LNCS., Vol. 674, Springer-Verlag (1993) 51-70

[GKKR 94] Golpalakrishnan, G., Khandekar, D., Kuramkote, R., Nalamasu, M.: Case Studies in Symbolic Model Checking: Verification of an Arbiter and DSM Protocols. Tech. Report UUCS-94-009, Dept. of Computer Science, Univ. of Utah (March 1994)

[G 97] Grahlmann, B.: The PEP Tool. In Proc. 9th Int'l. Conf. on Computer-Aided Verification, Haifa, Israel, LNCS., Vol. 1254, Springer-Verlag (1997) 440-443

[HHK 96] Hardin, R. H., Har'El, Z., Kurshan, R.P.: COSPAN. In Proc. Int'l. Conf. on Computer-Aided Verification, LNCS Vol., 1102, Springer-Verlag (1996) 423-427

[H 91] Holzmann, G.: Design and Validation of Computer Protocols, Prentice Hall (1991)

[JR 91] Jensen, K. Rozenberg, G. (eds.): High Level Petri Nets, Theory and Applications, Springer-Verlag (1991)

[J 95] Jensen, K.: Coloured Petri Nets: Basic Concepts, Analysis Methods and Practical Use, Vol. 1, 2 and 3, Springer-Verlag (1995)

[J 96] Jensen, K.: Condensed State Spaces for Symmetrical Coloured Petri Nets, Formal Methods in System Design, Vol. 9, 7 (1996) 7-40

[K 92] Keheler, P. : The Relative Importance of Concurrent Writers and Weak Consistency Models. In Proc. 16th Int'l Conf. on Distributed Computing Systems, IEEE Computer Society Press (May 1992) 91-98

[KCZ 92] Keheler, P., Cox, A.L., Zwaenepoel, W.: Lazy Release Consistency for Software Distributed Shared Memory. In Proc. 19th Annual Int'l Symposium on Computer Architecture (May 1992) 13-21

[L 86] Li, K.: Shared Virtual Memory on Loosely Coupled Multiprocessors. PhD dissertation, Dept. of Computer Science, Yale University, New Haven, Conn., Tech Rep YALEU-RR-492 (May 1992)

[L 88] Li, K.: IVY: A Shared Virtual Memory System for Parallel Computing. In Proc. 1988 Int'l Conf. on Parallel Processing, Vol. II (1988) 94-101

[LH 89] Li, K. Hudak, P: Memory Coherence in Shared Virtual Memory Systems. ACM Trans. on Computer Systems, Vol. 7, 4 (Nov. 1989) 321-359

[LS 95] Lindemann, C., Schön, F.: Modeling Relaxed Memory Consistency Protocols. In Proc. 8th Int'l Conf. on Modelling Techniques and Tools for Computer Systems Performance Evaluation, Heidelberg, Germany (Sept 1995)

[ND 96] Ip, C. N., Dill, D. :Better Verification Through Symmetry. In Formal Methods in System Design, Vol. 9, 1/2 (1996) 41-76

[PD 97] Pong, F. Dubois, M.: Verification Techniques for Cache Coherence Protocols. ACM Computing Surveys, Vol. 29, 1, (March 1997) 82-126

[RA 81] Ricart, G. Agrawala, A.: An Optimal Algorithm for Mutual Exclusion. Comm. ACM, Vol. 24, 1, (Jan. 1981) 9-17

[SK 85] Suzuki, I. Kasami, T.: A Distributed Mutual Exclusion Algorithm. ACM Trans. on Computer Systems, Vol. 3, 4 (Nov 1985) 344-349

[VHL 97] Varpaaniemi, K., Heljanko, K., Lilius, J.: Prod 3.2 - An Advanced Tool for Efficient Reachability Analysis, In Proc. 9th Int'l. Conf. on Computer-Aided Verification, Haifa, Israel, LNCS, Vol. 1254, Springer-Verlag (1997) 472-475

Finding Stubborn Sets of Coloured Petri Nets Without Unfolding

Lars Michael Kristensen[1]* and Antti Valmari[2]**

[1] University of Aarhus, Department of Computer Science
8000 Aarhus C., DENMARK
kris@daimi.aau.dk
[2] Tampere University of Technology, Software Systems Laboratory
PO Box 553, FIN-33101 Tampere, FINLAND
ava@cs.tut.fi

Abstract. In this paper, we address the issue of using the stubborn set method for Coloured Petri Nets (CP-nets) without relying on unfolding to the equivalent Place/Transition Net (PT-net). We give a lower bound result stating that there exist CP-nets for which computing "good" stubborn sets requires time proportional to the size of the equivalent PT-net. We suggest an approximative method for computing stubborn set of process-partitioned CP-nets which does not rely on unfolding. The underlying idea is to add some structure to the CP-net, which can be exploited during the stubborn set construction to avoid the unfolding. We demonstrate the practical applicability of the method with both theoretical and experimental case studies, in which reduction of the state space as well as savings in time are obtained.

Topics: System design and verification using nets, Analysis and synthesis, Higher-level net models, Computer tools for nets.

1 Introduction

State space methods have proven powerful in the analysis and verification of the behaviour of concurrent systems. Unfortunately, the sizes of state spaces of systems tend to grow very rapidly when systems become bigger. This well-known phenomenon is often referred to as *state explosion*, and it is a serious problem for the use of state space methods in the analysis of real-life systems.

Many techniques for alleviating the state explosion problem have been suggested, such as the *stubborn set method* [11, 14]. It is one of a group of rather similar methods first suggested in the late 80's and early 90's [4, 5, 8, 9]. It is based on the fact that the total effect of a set of concurrent transitions is independent of the order in which the transitions are executed. Therefore, it often

---

* The research of the first author was supported by grants from University of Aarhus Research Foundation and the Danish National Science Research Council.

** The research of the second author was a part of the project "Reaktiivisten järjestelmien formaalit menetelmät", Academy of Finland (29110).

suffices to investigate only one or some orderings in order to reason about the behaviour of the system.

In stubborn set state space generation an analysis of the dependencies between transitions is made at each state, and only certain transitions are used to generate immediate successor states. The "stubborn set" is the set of these transitions, together with some disabled transitions. The disabled transitions have no significance, but are included in the stubborn set for technical reasons. The remaining transitions are either taken into account in some subsequent states, or the situation is such that they can be ignored altogether without affecting analysis results. The set of transitions that is investigated in a given state depends on two factors: dependencies between transitions such as conflict (both transitions want to consume the same token), and the properties that are to be checked of the system. In this paper we concentrate on the first factor.

In the field of Petri nets, stubborn sets have been applied mostly to elementary and Place/Transition Nets (PT-nets). This is because a transition of a high-level Petri net such as a *Coloured Petri Net* [6] (*CP-net* or *CPN*), is really a packed representation of several low-level transitions, in CP-net terminology referred to as *binding elements*. The dependency analysis needed by the stubborn set method is difficult with high-level nets, because, for instance, a high-level transition may simultaneously have a binding element that is concurrent and another binding element that is in conflict with a binding element of some other high-level transition. In [13] this problem was avoided by effectively unfolding the CP-net during the construction of stubborn sets. However, the unfolded form of a high-level net may be much bigger than the high-level net itself and may even be infinite. As a consequence, unfolding may be very time-consuming and should be avoided. An algorithm based on constraint systems for alleviating the impact of unfolding has been given for Well Formed Coloured Petri Nets in [2].

An alternative stubborn set construction for high-level net would be to treat each high-level transition as a unit and consider a high-level transition t_2 as dependent on another high-level transition t_1, unless it is certain that no binding element of t_2 depends on any binding element of t_1. In essence, this strategy replaces the detailed low-level dependencies by high-level dependencies that approximate the low-level dependencies from above. Such approximations do not affect the correctness of the results obtained with stubborn sets, but they tend to make the stubborn sets bigger and weaken the reduction results. In our experience, the reduction results obtained with this coarse strategy have usually been very bad.

Efficient construction of "good" stubborn sets of high-level nets seems thus to require more information than can be obtained from the structure of the high-level net without unfolding, but some approximation from above has to be made in order to avoid unfolding too much. In this paper we suggest such a strategy, and demonstrate its power with a couple of examples. The new method is based on adding some structure to the high-level net. The high-level net is divided into disjoint subnets, such that each subnet corresponds either to a set of parallel processes executing the same code or to a variable through which two or more processes communicate (a fifo queue, for instance). Stubborn set construction uses knowledge of this structure in order to prevent the stubborn sets from becoming too big. When dependencies between binding elements have to be analysed, the method approximates from above to avoid unfolding. We will present our method in the framework of CP-nets, but the same ideas should also be applicable to most other high-level net formalisms.

The paper is organised as follows. Section 2 recalls the basic facts of CP-nets and stubborn sets that are needed to understand the rest of this paper. In Sect. 3 we will prove a theorem that, in essence, says that sometimes "good" stubborn sets cannot be constructed without the cost of unfolding. The structure we add to CP-nets is described in Sect. 4. Our new method is given in Sect. 5 and is illustrated with an annotated example in Sect. 6. Section 7 gives some numerical data on the performance of the new method on some case studies. Section 8 contains the conclusions and some directions for future work.

2   Background

This section summarises the basic facts of CP-nets and stubborn sets needed to understand the rest of the paper. The definitions and notation we will use for CP-nets are given in Section 2.1, and they follow closely [6] and [7]. Section 2.1 is not much more than a list of notation, so we assume that the reader is familiar with PT- and CP-nets, their dynamic behaviour, and the unfolding of a CP-net to a PT-net. Section 2.2 introduces the necessary background on stubborn sets.

2.1   Coloured Petri Nets

A **multi-set** ms over a domain X is a function from X into the set of natural numbers. A multi-set ms is written as a formal sum like $\sum_{x \in X} ms(x)'x$, where $ms(x)$ is the number of occurrences of the element x in ms. We assume that addition $(+)$, subtraction $(-)$, multiplication by a scalar, equality $(=)$, and comparison $(\leq)$ are defined on multi-sets in the usual way. $|ms|$ denotes the size of the multi-set ms, i.e., the total number of elements with their multiplicities taken into account. S_{MS} denotes the set of multi-sets over a domain S.

A **CP-net** [6] is a tuple $CPN = (\Sigma, P, T, A, N, C, G, E, I)$ where Σ is a set of **colour sets**, P is a set of **places**, T is a set of **transitions**, and A is a set of **arcs**. N is a **node function** designating for each arc a **source** and **destination**. C is a **colour function** mapping each place p to a colour set $C(p)$ specifying the type of **tokens** which can reside on p. G is a **guard function** mapping each transition t to a boolean expression $G(t)$. E is an **arc expression function** mapping each arc a into an expression $E(a)$. Finally, I is an **initialisation function** mapping each place p to a multi-set $I(p)$ of type $C(p)_{MS}$ specifying the initial marking of the place p.

A **token element** is a pair (p, c) such that $p \in P$ and $c \in C(p)$. For a colour set $S \in \Sigma$, the **base colour sets** of S are the colour sets from which S

was constructed using some structuring mechanism such as cartesian product, record, or union.

For $x \in P \cup T$ the **postset** of x, denoted $Out(x)$, is the set: $\{x' \in P \cup T \mid \exists a \in A : N(a) = (x, x')\}$. Similarly, the **preset** of x denoted $In(x)$ is the set: $\{x' \in P \cup T \mid \exists a \in A : N(a) = (x', x)\}$.

Since it is possible to have several arcs between a place and a transition and vice versa, we denote by $A(x_1, x_2)$ for $(x_1, x_2) \in (P \times T) \cup (T \times P)$ the set of arcs from x_1 to x_2, and define the **expression of** (x_1, x_2) as: $E(x_1, x_2) = \sum_{a \in A(x_1, x_2)} E(a)$.

The set of **variables** of a transition $t \in T$ is denoted $Var(t)$. For a variable $v \in Var(t)$, $Type(v) \in \Sigma$ denotes the **type** of v. A **binding element** (t, b) is a pair consisting of a transition t and a **binding** b of data values to its variables such that $G(t)\langle b \rangle$ evaluates to **true**. For an expression $expr$, $expr\langle b \rangle$ denotes the value obtained by evaluating the expression $expr$ in the binding b. A binding element is written in the form $(t, \langle v_1 = c_1, v_2 = c_2, \ldots, v_n = c_n \rangle)$, where $v_1, \ldots, v_n \in Var(t)$ are the variables of t and $c_1, \ldots, c_n$ are data values such that $c_i \in Type(v_i)$ for $1 \leq i \leq n$. For a binding element (t, b) and a variable v of t, $b(v)$ denotes the value assigned to v in the binding b. $B(t)$ denotes the set of all bindings for t. The set of all binding elements is denoted BE.

In a given **marking** M of a CP-net, the marking of a place p is denoted $M(p)$. M_0 denotes the **initial marking**. If a binding element (t, b) is **enabled** in a marking M_1 (denoted $M_1[(t, b)\rangle$), then (t, b) may **occur** in M_1 yielding some marking M_2. This is written $M_1[(t, b)\rangle M_2$. Extending this notion, an **occurrence sequence** is a sequence consisting of markings M_i and binding elements (t_i, b_i) denoted $M_1[(t_1, b_1)\rangle M_2 \ldots M_{n-1}[(t_{n-1}, b_{n-1})\rangle M_n$ and satisfying $M_i[(t_i, b_i)\rangle M_{i+1}$ for $1 \leq i < n$. A **reachable marking** is a marking which can be obtained (reached) by an occurrence sequence starting in the initial marking. $[M_0\rangle$ denotes the set of reachable markings.

Below we define place weights, place flows and place invariants. The definition is identical to Def. 4.6 in [7] except that we define the weights to map only between multi-sets. This is done for simplicity reasons, since we do not need the more general notion of weighted-sets. For two sets A and B the set of linear functions from A to B is denoted $[A \rightarrow B]_L$.

Definition 1. *([7], Def. 4.6) For a CP-net CPN a* **set of place weights** *with range $A \in \Sigma$ is a set of functions $W = \{W_p\}_{p \in P}$ such that $W_p \in [C(p)_{MS} \rightarrow A_{MS}]_L$ for all $p \in P$.*

1. W is a **place flow** *iff:*

$$\forall (t, b) \in BE : \sum_{p \in P} W_p(E(p, t)\langle b \rangle) = \sum_{p \in P} W_p(E(t, p)\langle b \rangle)$$

2. W determines a **place invariant** *iff:*

$$\forall M \in [M_0\rangle : \sum_{p \in P} W_p(M(p)) = \sum_{p \in P} W_p(M_0(p)) \qquad \square$$

The following theorem is central to place invariant analysis of CP-nets. It states that the static property of Def. 1 (1) is sufficient to guarantee the dynamic property of Def. 1 (2).

Theorem 1. *([7], Theorem 4.7) W is a place flow $\Rightarrow$ W determines a place invariant.* □

2.2 Stubborn Sets

State space construction with stubborn sets follows the same procedure as the construction of the full state space of a Petri net, with one exception. When processing a marking, a set of transitions (or binding elements in the case of a CP-net), the so-called **stubborn set**, is constructed. Only the enabled transitions (binding elements) in it are used to construct new markings. This reduces the number of new markings, and may lead to significant reduction in the size of the state space. To get correct analysis results, stubborn sets should be chosen such that the state space obtained with them (from now on called **SS state space**) preserves certain properties of the full state space. The choice of stubborn sets thus depends on the properties that are being analysed or verified of the system. This has led to the development of several versions of the stubborn set method. However, it is common to almost all of them that the following theorem should hold:

Theorem 2. *Let M be any marking of the net, Stub a stubborn set in M, $n \geq 0$, $t \in Stub$, and $t_1, t_2, \ldots, t_n \notin Stub$.*

1. *If $M [t_1\rangle M_1 [t_2\rangle \ldots [t_{n-1}\rangle M_{n-1} [t_n\rangle M_n [t\rangle M'_n$, then $M [t\rangle$.*
2. *If $M [t_1\rangle M_1 [t_2\rangle \ldots [t_{n-1}\rangle M_{n-1} [t_n\rangle M_n$ and $M [t\rangle M'$, then there are M'_1, $M'_2, \ldots, M'_n$ such that $M' [t_1\rangle M'_1 [t_2\rangle \ldots [t_n\rangle M'_n$, and $M_n [t\rangle M'_n$.* □

It is also required that if M_0 is not a dead marking (a marking without enabled transitions), then *Stub* contains at least one enabled transition (binding element).

From this theorem it is possible to prove that the SS state space contains all the dead markings of the full state space. Furthermore, if the full state space contains an infinite occurrence sequence, then so does the SS state space. By adding extra restrictions to the construction of stubborn sets, the stubborn set method can be made to preserve more properties, but that topic is beyond our present interest. With PT-nets, Theorem 2 holds if stubborn sets are defined as follows:

Definition 2. *Let (P, T, A, W, I) be a PT-net. The set $Stub \subseteq T$ is stubborn in marking M, if the following hold for every $t \in Stub$:*

1. *If $\exists t_1 \in T : M [t_1\rangle$, then $\exists t_2 \in Stub : M [t_2\rangle$.*
2. *If $\neg M [t\rangle$, then $\exists p \in \bullet t : M(p) < W(p, t) \land \bullet p \subseteq Stub$.*
3. *If $M [t\rangle$, then $(\bullet t)\bullet \subseteq Stub$.* □

Because this definition analyses the dependencies between transitions at a rather coarse level, it is not an "optimal" definition in the sense of yielding smallest possible stubborn sets and smallest SS state spaces, but we will use it in the following because of its simplicity. Once the basic ideas of our new CP-net stubborn set construction method are understood, they can be applied to more detailed dependency analysis if required.

Definition 2 gives a condition with which one can check whether a given set of transitions is a stubborn set in a given marking. Part (1) says that unless the marking is a dead marking, the stubborn set should contain at least one enabled transition. Parts (2) and (3) can be thought of as rules that, given a transition t that is intended to be in the stubborn set, produce a set of other transitions that must be included. In the case of (3), the set is just $(\bullet t)\bullet \subseteq \mathit{Stub}$. Part (2) requires the selection of some place $p \in \bullet t$, such that p contains fewer tokens than t wants to consume, and then produces the set $\bullet p$. If there are several such places, most stubborn set algorithms just make an arbitrary choice between them. A somewhat expensive algorithm that investigates all choices for p is explained in [12].

Important for the rest of this paper is that the rules can be thought of as spanning a *dependency graph*: the nodes of the graph are the transitions, and there is an edge from t_1 to t_2 if and only if the above rules (with a fixed arbitrary choice of the p in (2)) demand that if t_1 is in the stubborn set, then also t_2 must be. A stubborn set then corresponds to a set of transitions that contains an enabled transition and that is closed under reachability in the dependency graph. Therefore, to construct a stubborn set, it suffices to know the dependency graph and the set of enabled transitions.

In this paper we will not actually give any concrete algorithm for finding stubborn sets of CP-nets. Instead, we describe a method for obtaining a "good" dependency graph, from which one can construct "good" stubborn sets with the old algorithms that rely on dependency graphs.

3   The Necessity of Unfolding

Because every CP-net can be unfolded to an equivalent PT-net, and because good dependency graphs for PT-nets are known, one can always construct a stubborn set of a CP-net by first unfolding it to a PT-net. Unfolding is, however, often expensive, so one wants to avoid it. We will demonstrate in this section that, unfortunately, there are situations where good stubborn sets cannot be constructed — not even named, as a matter of fact — without unfolding or doing something equally expensive. We will do that by analysing the behaviour of the CP-net in Fig. 1. The CP-net has 9 places, 8 transitions, and all but two of its places have colour set $N = \{1, 2, \ldots, n\}$. The remaining places p_5 and p_8 have a colour set containing only one element (colour) denoted $()$. The variable x is of type N. In the initial marking place p_1 contains the tokens with colour $1 \ldots n$. The remaining places are initially empty.

Let H be any subset of N, and let M_H be the marking where $M(p_1) = M(p_5) = M(p_8) = M(p_9) = \emptyset$, $M(p_2) = M(p_6) = H$, $M(p_3) = M(p_7) = N - H$, and $M(p_4) = N$. This marking can be reached from the initial marking by letting t_1 and t_2 occur with suitable bindings followed by the occurrence of t_7. We will consider the stubborn sets in M_H obtained by unfolding the CP-net to a PT-net, and then using Def. 2.

In M_H, all binding elements of t_5 are enabled, and they are the only enabled binding elements in M_H. Assume that a binding element $(t_5, \langle x = h \rangle)$ where $h \in H$ is in a stubborn set $Stub$. Rule (3) of Def. 2 forces us to include the binding elements $(t_4, \langle x = h \rangle)$ and $(t_6, \langle x = h \rangle)$ into $Stub$. The binding element $(t_6, \langle x = h \rangle)$ is disabled exactly because there is no token of colour h in p_7. So rule (2) forces the inclusion of $(t_2, \langle x = h \rangle)$ into the stubborn set. Rule (2) should then be applied to $(t_2, \langle x = h \rangle)$, but this does not make the stubborn set grow any more, because the only input place of t_2 has no input transitions.

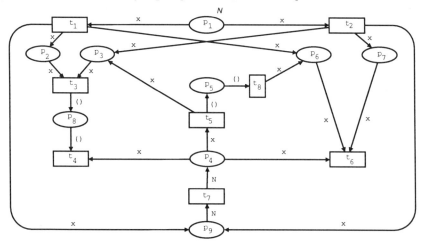

Fig. 1. CP-net demonstrating the necessity of unfolding.

The binding element $(t_4 \langle x = h \rangle)$ is disabled because there is no token on p_8. Rule (2) of Def. 2 forces us to include the binding elements $(t_3, \langle x = k \rangle)$ into $Stub$, where $k \in N$. The binding elements $(t_3, \langle x = k \rangle)$ are disabled because p_2 and p_3 do not contain tokens with the same colour. For those values of k that are not in H, rule (2) takes the analysis through the token element (p_2, k) to t_1 but not to anywhere else. But when the value of k is in H, the analysis proceeds through (p_3, k) to $(t_5, \langle x = k \rangle)$. So we see that $Stub$ must contain all the binding elements $(t_5, \langle x = k \rangle)$ where $k \in H$. On the other hand, the set consisting of those binding elements together with certain disabled binding elements satisfies Def. 2, and is thus stubborn in M_H.

Assume now that $Stub$ contains a binding element $(t_5, \langle x = h \rangle)$ where $h \notin H$. Rule (3) leads to $(t_6, \langle x = h \rangle)$, from which rule (2) takes us through (p_6, h) and further through p_5 to $(t_5, \langle x = k \rangle)$ for every $k \in N$. As a conclusion, $Stub$ must contain all enabled binding elements.

There are thus only two possibilities for the stubborn set in M_H: either the stubborn set consists of the binding elements $(t_5, \langle x = k \rangle)$ where $k \in H$ plus some disabled binding elements, or the stubborn set contains all enabled binding elements. The existence of the above CP-net implies the following lower bound result.

Theorem 3. *The size of the equivalent PT-net PTN is a lower bound on the worst-case time complexity of any algorithm that computes non-trivial stubborn sets (if they exist) according to Def. 2, in all markings encountered during the SS state space construction of a CP-net CPN.*

Proof. The argument preceeding the theorem demonstrated the existence of a CP-net and a marking M_H with two possible stubborn sets: either the stubborn set consists of the binding elements $(t_5, \langle x = k \rangle)$ where $k \in H$ plus some disabled binding elements, or the stubborn set contains all enabled binding elements. The latter is the trivial stubborn set, so the stubborn set construction algorithm should find the former set. But, depending on the history of the CP-net, H may be just any subset of N. Since $|N| = n$, the algorithm has to deliver at least n bits to be able to unambiguously specify its answer. To do that it needs $\Omega(n)$ time. However, the CP-net is of constant size (or of size $\Theta(\log n)$, if you want to charge the bits that are needed to specify n). Since the size of the equivalent PT-net obtained by unfolding the CP-net in Fig. 1 is $\Theta(n)$, constructing a non-trivial stubborn set requires at least time proportional to the unfolding.

We are left with proving that any such algorithm for SS state space construction has to consider the markings M_H for all possible choices of $H \subseteq N$. It suffices to prove that M_H is contained in the SS state space when choosing the stubborn sets with the fewest possible enabled binding elements, since choosing larger stubborn sets will only add markings to the SS state space. Because $(t_1, \langle x = k \rangle)$ and $(t_2, \langle x = k \rangle)$ are in conflict for every $k \in N$ it is relatively straightforward to check that every SS state space of the CP-net relying on Def. 2 contains the markings M_H for all $H \subseteq N$. $\qquad\Box$

It is worth observing that in the above construction it already takes n bits to describe M_H, so the cost of unfolding is not a major factor of the total cost of state space construction for the CP-net in Fig. 1. Even so, the example demonstrates that the construction of non-trivial stubborn sets sometimes requires analysis at the level of unfolding.

4   Process-Partitioned CP-nets

In this section we explain our new method for computing stubborn sets of CP-nets. The method is first explained in an informal way and then followed by the formal definitions. Before that, we introduce an example system used to clarify the definitions.

4.1 The Data Base Example System

The distributed data base system from [6], depicted in Fig. 2, is used as a running example throughout this and subsequent sections.

The CP-net describes the communication between a set of data base managers maintaining consistent copies of a data base in a distributed system. The states of the managers are modelled by the three places *Waiting* (for acknowledgements), *Inactive*, and *Performing* (an update requested by another manager). The managers are modelled by the colour set $DBM = \{d_1, \ldots, d_n\}$ where n is the number of managers. The messages in the system are modelled by the colour set *MES*. A message is a pair consisting of a sender and a receiver. In Fig. 2, the names *DBM*, *E*, and *MES* in italics positioned next to the places denote the colour sets of places. E denotes the colour set consisting of a single element e.

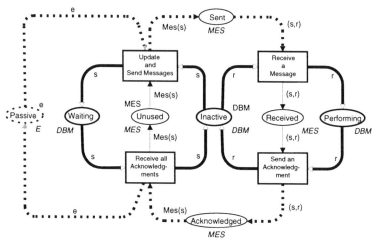

Fig. 2. CPN model of the data base system

The actions of the managers are modelled by the four transitions. *Update and Send Messages (SM)* models a manager updating its copy of the data base and sending a message to every other manager, so that it can perform the same update on its copy. *Receive a Message (RM)* models a manager receiving a request for updating its copy of the data base, and *Send an Acknowledgement (SA)* models the sending of an acknowledgement message after a requested update has been performed. *Receive all Acknowledgements* models the manager receiving the acknowledgements sent back by the other managers. To maintain consistency between the copies of the data base, the place *Passive* ensures mutual exclusion for updating the data base. Initially, all managers are on *Inactive* and all messages are on *Unused*. This is shown by the initial markings MES and DBM positioned next to the places *Unused* and *Inactive*. The initial marking of place *Passive* is the multi-set $1'e$. The initial markings of initially empty places are omitted in the figure.

4.2 Informal Explanation

For the construction of stubborn sets, we will distinguish one or more subnets of the CP-net which we will call **process subnets**. The process subnets may be connected to each other by sharing common **border places**, but are otherwise disjoint. Together the process subnets contain all the transitions and places of the CP-net. A process subnet models the states and actions of one or more processes that run the same program code. The data base system has only one process subnet.

Each transition in the CP-net belongs to some unique process subnet. We require that each transition has a distinct variable, which, when bound in an occurrence of a binding element of that transition, identifies the process executing the action modelled by the transition. We will call this variable the **process variable**. In the data base system, SM and RA have the process variable s, whereas RM and SA have the process variable r. This will allow us to make a disjoint partitioning of the binding elements of a transition according to the following definition.

Definition 3. *Let pv_t be the process variable of a transition $t \in T$, and let $c \in Type(pv_t)$. The c-**binding-class** of **t** denoted $t[pv_t = c]$ is the following set of binding elements: $\{(t, b) \in BE \mid b(pv_t) = c\}$.* □

The term **binding class** will be used when the particular choice of c is not important.

There are three types of places in process subnets: process places, local places and border places.

Process places are used to model the control flow of the processes. In the data base system the places *Waiting*, *Inactive*, and *Performing* are process places. Each token residing on such a place is assumed to have a colour which identifies the corresponding process, and is referred to as a **process token**. When we have a specific process in mind, identified by the colour c, we will talk about the c-**process-token**.

We assume that in any reachable marking there is exactly one c-process-token present in a given process subnet for a given c. This corresponds to a process having only one point of control. Therefore, each transition has at least one input and at least one output process place (process place connected to an incoming / outgoing arc). The arc expressions should ensure that an occurrence of a binding element in the c-binding-class of a transition removes exactly one c-process-token from its input process places, adds exactly one c-process-token to its output process places, and does not affect c'-process-tokens where $c' \neq c$. Because of this, a process token residing on a process place determines one binding class of each of its output transitions, namely the c-binding-class which can remove the process token. We will therefore talk about the **corresponding binding classes** of a process token residing on a process place. For instance, in the initial marking of the data base system, the corresponding binding classes of the d_1-process token on *Inactive* are: the d_1-binding-class of SM, that is, $SM[s = d_1]$; and the d_1-binding-class of RM, that is, $RM[r = d_1]$.

Local places are used to model state information local to a process. Intuitively, a token residing on such a place can only be removed by a specific process, and a token added by one process cannot be removed by another process. In the data base system the local places in the process subnet are: *Unused* (which a data base manager uses to store unused messages) and *Received* (which a data base manager uses to temporarily store a received message).

The **border places** connect the process subnets, and model asynchronous communication between processes, including communication between processes in the same process subnet. There are two kinds of border places: **shared places** and **buffer places**. A token residing on a shared place may be removed by several processes, whereas a token residing on a buffer place may only be removed by a specific process. In the data base system, there are two buffer places: *Sent* and *Acknowledged*, and one shared place: *Passive*.

4.3   Formal Definitions

We now present the formal definitions of the concepts informally introduced in the previous section. First we give the definition of a process subnet of a CP-net. An explanation of the individual parts of the definition is given below.

Definition 4.
A **process subnet** *is a tuple* $(CPN, P_{pr}, P_{loc}, P_{bor}, P_{buf}, \Xi, PV, PrId)$, *where*

1. $CPN = (\Sigma, P, T, A, N, C, G, E, I)$ *is a CP-net.*

2. $P_{pr} \subseteq P$ *is a set of* **process places**, $P_{loc} \subseteq P$ *is a set of* **local places**, *and* $P_{bor} \subseteq P$ *is a set of* **border places** *such that:*

$$P_{pr} \cap P_{loc} = P_{pr} \cap P_{bor} = P_{loc} \cap P_{bor} = \emptyset \text{ and } P = P_{pr} \cup P_{loc} \cup P_{bor}.$$

3. $P_{buf} \subseteq P_{bor}$ *is a set of* **buffer places**.

4. $\Xi \in \Sigma$ *is a common base colour set of* $C(p)$ *for all* $p \in P_{pr} \cup P_{loc} \cup P_{buf}$.

5. PV *is a function associating with each transition* $t \in T$ *a* **process variable** $PV(t) = pv_t \in Var(t)$ *such that* $Type(pv_t) = \Xi$.

6. $PrId = \{PrId_p\}_{p \in P}$ *is a set of place weights with range* Ξ *such that for* $p \in P_{pr} \cup P_{loc} \cup P_{buf}$, $PrId_p$ *projects a multi-set over* $C(p)$ *into a multi-set over the common base colour set* Ξ *(cf. item 4) and maps any multi-set into the empty multi-set on the remaining places in* P. *The colour* $PrId_p(c)$ *is the* **process identity** *of the token element* (p, c).

7. *In the initial marking there is exactly one token with a given colour in* Ξ *on the process places of the process subnet:*

$$\sum_{p \in P_{pr}} PrId_p(M_0(p)) = \Xi \tag{1}$$

8. *The following equations hold for all transitions $t \in T$ and $b \in B(t)$:*

$$\sum_{p \in P_{pr}} PrId_p(E(p,t)\langle b \rangle) = \sum_{p \in P_{pr}} PrId_p(E(t,p)\langle b \rangle) = 1'(b(pv_t)) \qquad (2)$$

$$\forall p \in P_{loc} \cup P_{buf} : PrId_p(E(p,t)\langle b \rangle)(b(pv_t)) = |PrId_p(E(p,t)\langle b \rangle)| \qquad (3)$$

$$\forall p \in P_{loc} : PrId_p(E(t,p)\langle b \rangle)(b(pv_t)) = |PrId_p(E(t,p)\langle b \rangle)| \qquad (4)$$

□

In the definition above, item 1 to item 5 are rather straightforward. Item 6 defines the weights which are used to project out the process identity of tokens on the process, local, and buffer places of the process subnet. In the data base example, the common base colour set used to model the identity of the processes is *DBM*. The weight on the process places *Waiting*, *Inactive*, and *Performing* is the identity function on multi-sets. On the local place *Received* it is the projection into the second component. On the local place *Unused* it is the projection into the first component. This is also the weight on the buffer place *Acknowledged*, because we required in Equation (3) of item 8 that each token in a buffer place has a unique process that may *consume* it, and that process is identified by the first component. On the buffer place *Sent* the weight is the projection into the second component.

Item 7 expresses that a given process has only a single point of control. Notice that the colour set $\varXi$ is interpreted as a multi-set in the equation.

Equation (2) in item 8 expresses that the occurrence of a binding element of a transition in the subnet removes exactly one token from the input process places of the transition, and adds exactly one token to the output process places of the transition. Furthermore, the colour of the tokens removed and added matches the binding of the process variable of the transition. This equation ensures that in any reachable marking, the process places contain exactly one token of each process identity in $\varXi$. Equation (3) in item 8 expresses that a token residing on a local or buffer place of the subnet can only be removed by the occurrence of binding elements belonging to c-binding-classes of transitions in the subnet, where c is the process identity of the token. Similarly, Equation (4) expresses that tokens added to a local place by the occurrence of a binding element get the process identity of the process that added them. Together these imply that tokens in a local place are processed and tokens in a buffer place are consumed by one process only.

We now continue with the definition of corresponding binding classes. By Equation (2) in Def. 4, for a token residing on a process place, they are those binding classes that contain binding elements which can potentially remove the token from the process place.

Definition 5. *Let $(CPN, P_{pr}, P_{loc}, P_{bor}, P_{buf}, \varXi, PV, PrId)$ be a process subnet. Let $p \in P_{pr}$. The **corresponding binding classes** of a token element (p, c) denoted $CB(p,c)$ are $CB(p,c) = \{t[pv_t = PrId_p(c)] \mid t \in Out(p)\}$.* □

We now define process partitioning of a CP-net, which divides a CP-net into a number of process subnets and ensures that these subnets arc only allowed to share border places and are otherwise disjoint.

Definition 6. *A* **process partitioning** *of a CP-net*
$CPN = (\Sigma, P, T, A, N, C, G, E, I)$ *is a set of n process subnets of the CPN:*
$\{(CPN^i, P^i_{pr}, P^i_{loc}, P^i_{bor}, P^i_{buf}, \Xi^i, PV^i, PrId^i)\}_{i \in I=\{1,2,\ldots,n\}}$, *satisfying:*

1. *The set of places of the CP-net is the union of the places in the process subnets: $P = \bigcup_{i \in I} P^i$.*

2. *The set of transitions of the CP-net is a disjoint union of the transitions in the process subnets: $T = \bigcup_{i \in I} T^i$ and $\forall i, j \in I : [i \neq j \Rightarrow T^i \cap T^j = \emptyset]$.*

3. *The set of arcs in the CP-net is a disjoint union of the arcs of the process subnets: $A = \bigcup_{i \in I} A^i$ and $\forall i, j \in I : [i \neq j \Rightarrow A^i \cap A^j = \emptyset]$.*

4. *If two process subnets have common places, then they are border places: $\forall i, j \in I : [i \neq j \Rightarrow P^i \cap P^j \subseteq P^i_{bor}]$.*

5. *If a place is a buffer place of some process subnet, then only that subnet can consume tokens from it: $\forall i \in I : \forall p \in P^i_{buf} : Out(p) \subseteq T^i$.* □

If a border place is not a buffer place of any process subnet, then it is called a **shared place** of the process partitioning.

We can now formulate a proposition stating that the process places of the individual process subnets are related by a place invariant.

Proposition 1. *Let $\{(CPN^i, P^i_{pr}, P^i_{loc}, P^i_{bor}, P^i_{buf}, \Xi^i, PV^i, PrId^i)\}_{i \in I=\{1,2,\ldots,n\}}$ be a process partitioning of a CP-net CPN. For $i \in I$ define the set of place weights $\overline{PrId}^i = \{\overline{PrId}^i_p\}_{p \in P}$ by:*

$$\overline{PrId}^i_p = \begin{cases} PrId^i_p & : \quad p \in P^i_{pr} \\ 0_{MS} & : \quad otherwise \end{cases} \tag{5}$$

where 0_{MS} denotes the function mapping any multi-set into the empty multi-set. Then the following holds:

$$\forall M \in [M_0\rangle : \sum_{p \in P} \overline{PrId}^i_p(M(p)) = \Xi^i \tag{6}$$

Proof. First we prove that $\overline{PrId}^i$ is a place flow. For $t \notin T^i$ the place flow condition in Def. 1 is clearly satisfied since all input and output places of t then have 0_{MS} as weight. For $t \in T^i$ the place flow condition is guaranteed by Equation (2) of Def. 4. Hence, by Theorem 1, $\overline{PrId}^i$ determines a place invariant and the proposition now follows from Equation (1) of Def. 4. □

5 Stubborn Sets of Process-Partitioned CP-nets

In Section 2.2 we pointed out that most stubborn set construction algorithms rely on the notion of *dependency graphs*. In the case of PT-nets, the vertices of a dependency graph are the transitions, and each edge (t_1, t_2) represents a rule of the form "if t_1 is in the stubborn set, then also t_2 must be." To construct a stubborn set it suffices to know the dependency graph and the set of enabled transitions. Several different algorithms for this task have been suggested.

The goal of this section is to define dependency graphs for process-partitioned CP-nets such that their size is proportional to the number of transitions of the CP-net times the number of tokens on process places in the initial marking rather than the size of the equivalent PT-net. To achieve this, vertices of the new dependency graphs will be corresponding binding classes instead of binding elements. Although stubborn sets will eventually be defined as sets of binding elements, the discussion is simplified if we also talk about stubborn sets of binding classes:

Definition 7. *A set Stub of binding classes is stubborn in a marking $M \in [M_0\rangle$, if and only if the following hold for every $t[pv_t = c] \in Stub$:*

1. *If $\exists (t_1, b_1) \in BE : M[(t_1, b_1)\rangle$, then $\exists\ t_2[pv_{t_2} = c'] \in Stub$ and $(t_2, b_2) \in t_2[pv_{t_2} = c'] : M[(t_2, b_2)\rangle$*
2. **Disabled Rule (D-rule):** *assume that $t[pv_t = c]$ may contain disabled binding elements (either it is not known whether $t[pv_t = c]$ contains disabled binding elements, or it is known that it does). For each input border place of t, consider the process subnets containing a transition with this place as an output place. The corresponding binding classes of the process token elements in these process subnets must be in Stub.*
3. **Enabled Rule (E-rule):** *assume that $t[pv_t = c]$ does contain enabled binding elements. For each input shared place of t, consider the process subnets containing a transition with this place as an input place. The corresponding binding classes of the process token elements in these process subnets must be in Stub.*
4. *A process token with process identity c is located on one of the input process places, p, of t in M and $CB(p, c)$ is in Stub.*

A set of binding elements is stubborn, if and only if it is the union of a stubborn set of binding classes. □

The edges of the new dependency graphs are determined according to D- and E-rules in item 2 and 3. Item 4 ensures that only binding classes resulting from the use of the D- and E-rule are included in the stubborn set. The reason for the word "may" in D-rule is that often it is impossible or impractical to decide without unfolding whether a binding class contains disabled binding elements. "Unnecessary" use of D-rule makes the stubborn set larger, but does not endanger correctness, so we may allow it. This is an instance of approximating from above where a precise analysis requires unfolding. On the other hand, any algorithm that constructs the full state space of a CP-net must find all enabled binding elements. Therefore, when formulating E-rule, we assumed that it can be decided whether any given binding class contains enabled binding elements. This is not important, though; also E-rule can be used unnecessarily without affecting correctness. Note that if $t[pv_t = c]$ contains both enabled and disabled binding elements, then both rules must be applied.

Stubborn sets of process-partitioned CP-nets can be constructed from the dependency graphs just as in the case of PT-nets, with the exception that a vertex now represents binding classes that may consist of several binding elements. To start the construction, one can pick a process token in some process subnet such that at least one of the corresponding binding classes contains an enabled binding element. We will illustrate the new dependency graphs and their use in Sect. 6.

To show the correctness of the new method for constructing stubborn sets, we will need an auxiliary notion of **process-closure** $PrCl(t, b)$ of a binding element (t, b). It is defined as the set of binding elements (t', b') such that t' is a transition of the same process subnet as t and $b'(pv_{t'}) = b(pv_t)$. In other words, $PrCl(t, b)$ is the set of those binding elements modelling the actions of the process identified by the binding element (t, b). This notion is extended to sets of binding elements by defining $PrCl(B) = \bigcup_{(t,b) \in B} PrCl(t, b)$.

Theorem 4. *Let PPC be a process-partitioned CP-net, and PTN the PT-net that is obtained by unfolding PPC. Let $Stub_{PPC}$ be a stubborn set of binding elements of PPC in the sense of Def. 7. Then $PrCl(Stub_{PPC})$ is a stubborn set of PTN in the sense of Def. 2.* $\square$

The proof of the theorem is omitted because of lack of space. The theorem says, in essence, that the process closure of the unfolding of any stubborn set obtained with the new dependency graphs is a stubborn set of the unfolded PT-net (albeit not necessarily an optimal one). Therefore, and because a CP-net has exactly the same behaviour as the equivalent PT-net [6], the analysis results obtained with a process-partitioned CP-net and its stubborn sets are the same as what would be obtained with ordinary stubborn sets and the unfolded PT-net. Because PT-net stubborn sets are guaranteed to preserve dead markings and possibility of non-termination, our process-partitioned CP-net stubborn sets also preserve these properties.

6 Stubborn Sets of the Data Base System

We now illustrate the use of D- and E-rule on the data base system for $n = 3$ data base managers in the initial marking M_0, and in two subsequent markings.

Stubborn set in M_0. Assume that we select the d_1-process-token in the only process subnet. Since the d_1-process-token is on *Inactive* we initiate the construction by including $\{SM[s = d_1], RM[r = d_1]\}$ into the stubborn set. We now apply the D- and E-rule recursively.

First we consider $SM[s = d_1]$. Since the transition SM has only one variable, and that variable is the process variable, in this case it is possible to determine that the binding class contains no disabled binding elements. Thus, it suffices to apply only E-rule. SM has the shared place $Passive$ as an input place. There is only one process subnet in the whole system, thus there is only one process subnet with a transition having $Passive$ as an input place. All process tokens of this process subnet are located on $Inactive$ and hence we include the following corresponding binding classes to our stubborn set: $\{SM[s = d_1], RM[r = d_1]\}$ and $\{SM[s = d_2], RM[r = d_2]\}$ and $\{SM[s = d_3], RM[r = d_3]\}$.

We now consider $RM[r = d_1]$. In the initial marking this binding class contains only disabled binding elements, hence (only) D-rule is applied. The transition has one input buffer place: $Sent$. We locate the process tokens in process subnets containing a transition with $Sent$ as an output place, which leads us to include $\{SM[s = d_1], RM[r = d_1]\}$ and $\{SM[s = d_2], RM[r = d_2]\}$ and $\{SM[s = d_3], RM[r = d_3]\}$.

We have now processed the binding classes $SM[s = d_1]$ and $RM[r = d_1]$, and have found out that we also have to investigate the binding classes $\{SM[s = d_2], RM[r = d_2]\}$ and $\{SM[s = d_3], RM[r = d_3]\}$. Because they are symmetric to the first case, their analysis reveals that the inclusion to the stubborn set of $SM[s = d_i]$ and $RM[r = d_i]$ for any $i \in \{1, 2, 3\}$ will force the inclusion of $SM[s = d_i]$ and $RM[r = d_i]$ also with the other two possible values of i. These dependencies between binding classes can be illustrated with the dependency graph depicted on the left hand side of Fig. 3. The dependency graph contains all enabled binding elements and has only one strongly connected component. Hence, any stubborn set must contain all the enabled binding elements in the initial marking.

Stubborn set in M_1. Consider now the marking M_1 reached by the occurrence of the binding element $(SM, \langle s = d_1 \rangle)$ in M_0 (the two other cases corresponding to d_2 and d_3 are similar by symmetry, and we will skip them). Assume that we choose the d_2-process-token located on $Inactive$. Thus we initiate the construction by including $\{SM[s = d_2], RM[r = d_2]\}$ into the stubborn set.

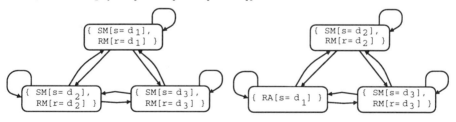

Fig. 3. Computation of the stubborn sets in M_0 (left) and M_1 (right).

Continuing with the application of the rules until all binding classes have been handled yields the dependency graph on the right hand side of Fig. 3. Again, all enabled binding elements must be included into the stubborn set. As a matter of fact, an analysis performed at the unfolded level shows that it is not necessary to take any other enabled binding elements than $(RM, \langle s = d_1, r = d_2 \rangle)$ into the stubborn set, but our method fails to see that this is the case. As was mentioned in the introduction, making the stubborn set analysis at too detailed a level would cause the analysis to collapse to the unfolding of the CP-net, which we want to avoid. It is better to keep the analysis simple and every now and then include more binding classes than absolutely necessary.

Stubborn set in M_2. Consider now the marking M_2 reached by the occurrence of the binding element $(RM, \langle s = d_1, r = d_2 \rangle)$ in M_1. Assume that we pick the d_3-process-token on *Inactive*. Thus, we initiate the construction of the stubborn set by including $\{SM[s = d_3], RM[r = d_3]\}$ into the stubborn set. Continuing with the application of the rules yields the dependency graph in Fig. 4.

An important aspect of the dependency graph is that there are no edges out of $SA[r = d_2]$. The reason is that both D-rule and E-rule look at input border places, but SA has none of them: *Performing* is a process place and *Received* is a local place. Hence we can choose $\{SA[r = d_2]\}$ as the stubborn set in M_2. It contains only one enabled binding element: $(SA, \langle s = d_1, r = d_2 \rangle)$.

It is worth noticing that this result generalises to all data base managers and remains valid even if the total number of the data base managers is not three. That is, independent of the number of the data base managers, the set $\{SA[r = d_j]\}$ is stubborn whenever $(SA, \langle s = d_i, r = d_j \rangle)$ is enabled for some i and j. In the markings reached from now on, there is only a single enabled binding element until the initial marking is reached again.

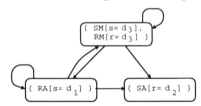

Fig. 4. Computation of the stubborn set in M_2.

The number of markings in the full state space for the data base system is $1 + n3^{n-1} = \Theta(n3^n)$. Observing that the number of tokens on the place *Received* is always at most one with the new method for computing stubborn sets, the number of markings in the SS state space is $1 + n(2^{n-1} + (n-1)2^{n-2}) = \Theta(n^2 2^n)$. With unfolding it is possible to get a reduced state space with as few as $1 + n(1 + 2(n-1)) = \Theta(n^2)$ markings. The reduction given by our new method is thus not as good as what may be obtained if one is willing to do the expensive unfolding.

7 Experiments

To obtain evidence on the practical use and performance with respect to reduction obtained and time used to generate the SS state space, an experimental prototype containing the new method has been implemented on top of the state space tool of Design/CPN [1].

In this prototype, the user supplies the information on process subnets, and specifies which places are process places, local places etc. Once the information has been supplied, the SS state space can be generated fully automatically. The prototype uses a simple heuristic for choosing between the possible stubborn sets. In each marking, one of the stubborn sets containing a minimum number of enabled binding elements is selected as the stubborn set. It is worth noting that in general, this may fail to lead to the best possible reduction of the state space.

Below the prototype is applied to two case studies: the data base system from the previous sections, and to a stop-and-wait protocol. All measures presented in this section were obtained on a Sun Ultra Sparc Enterprise 3000 workstation with 512 MB RAM.

Distributed data base system. First we consider the data base system from the previous sections. Table 1 contains the sizes (nodes and arcs) of the full state space and the SS state space for varying number of data base managers. In addition, the generation times for the state spaces (in CPU seconds) are shown. A careful inspection of Table 1 shows that the experimental sizes fit the theoretical sizes obtained in Sect. 6.

Table 1. Verification statistics for the data base system.

$|DBM|$	Full state space			SS state space		
	Nodes	Arcs	Time	Nodes	Arcs	Time
3	28	42	1	25	30	1
4	109	224	1	81	104	1
5	406	1,090	2	241	330	2
6	1,459	4,872	16	673	972	9
7	5,104	20,426	142	1,793	2,702	40
8	17,497	81,664	1,139	4,609	7,184	157

Stop-and-wait protocol. We now consider a larger example in the form of a stop-and-wait protocol from the datalink control layer of the OSI network architecture. The protocol is taken from [3].

The CP-net of this stop-and-wait protocol is a hierarchical CP-net consisting of five pages. The CP-net has four process subnets modelling the threads in the receiver and sender parts of the protocol. It has six border places. Two border places are used to model the communication between the threads in the receiver and the sender, respectively, and two border places model the communication channels between the sender and the receiver.

Table 2 shows the verification statistics for the stop-and-wait protocol for varying capacities of the data channel (ChanD) and the acknowledgement channel (ChanA), and varying number of packets (Packets) sent from the sender to the receiver. The CP-net of the stop-and-wait protocol uses lists, strings and integers as types of the variables of the transitions, and is therefore an example of a CP-net where the unfolding approach fails to work. As a consequence, we cannot compare the reductions obtained with the new method and the algorithm based on unfolding.

Table 2. Verification statistics for the stop-and-wait protocol.

$ChanD$	ChanA	$Packets$	Full state space			SS state space		
			Nodes	Arcs	Time	Nodes	Arcs	Time
1	1	2	7,929	27,708	44	5,065	9,469	42
1	1	3	12,163	42,652	83	7,775	14,580	76
2	1	2	19,421	70,847	259	12,428	24,268	186
1	2	2	20,303	74,936	291	13,157	25,825	199
2	2	2	49,515	190,383	947	32,145	65,792	579
3	2	2	110,963	433,409	5,618	72,169	150,006	3,812
2	3	2	115,751	453,995	6,157	75,721	157,528	3,991

8 Conclusions and Future Work

We addressed the issue of computing stubborn sets of CP-nets without relying on unfolding to PT-nets. It was shown that the problem is computationally hard in the sense that there are CP-nets for which computing a non-trivial stubborn set requires time proportional to the size of the unfolded CP-net. A method for process-partitioned CP-nets was given which avoids the unfolding by exploiting additional structure on top of the CP-net. The method approximates the unfolded stubborn sets from above, thereby not necessarily yielding the best possible stubborn sets with respect to the reduction obtained.

The practical applicability of the suggested method was assessed by some case studies. A common denominator for the experiments was that the reduction obtained more than cancelled out the overhead involved in computing the stubborn sets. Hence, judging from the experiments, the suggested method seems in practice to give reasonably good stubborn sets, at a very low cost with respect to time. This indicates that the method seems to be a good compromise in the trade-off between not making too detailed an analysis of dependencies and at the same time getting a reasonable reduction. Equally important, unlike the method based on unfolding, the new method does not fail to work when colour sets with an infinite domain are used as types of variables of transitions.

Another interesting aspect arises when combining the stubborn set method with reduction by means of symmetry as suggested in [13]. If the method for computing stubborn sets in this paper is combined with symmetry reduction, then it may result in the same reduction as when the stubborn sets obtained with unfolding is combined with symmetry reduction. This is, for instance, the case with the data base system studied in this paper. Therefore, although the stubborn sets are not as good as the stubborn sets obtained with unfolding, they may still yield equally good results when symmetry is applied on top. This suggests using the symmetry method as a way of further improving the results. Future work will include work in this direction, as well as the application of the new method to more elaborate versions of the stubborn set method that preserve more properties.

Our method requires the user to supply some information regarding the process subnets, process places, local places, border places, etc. It is reasonable to assume that the developer of a CPN model is able to supply such information, as it is similar to declaring types in a programming language. Also, the kind of information which must be supplied seems natural from the point of view of concurrent systems. However, in order to use the method on large examples, the validity of the supplied information must be checked automatically. One possible approach to this would be to exploit the techniques developed in [10] for place invariant analysis of CP-nets.

References

1. S. Christensen, J.B. Jørgensen, & L.M. Kristensen: Design/CPN — A Computer Tool for Coloured Petri Nets. Proceedings of the Third International Workshop on Tools and Algorithms for the Construction and Analysis of Systems, Lecture Notes in Computer Science 1217, Springer-Verlag, 1997. pp 209–223.
2. R. Brgan and D. Poitrenuad An Efficient Algorithm for the Computation of Stubborn Sets of Well Formed Petri Nets. Proceedings of the 16th International Conference on Application and Theory of Petri Nets, Lecture Notes in Computer Science 935, Springer-Verlag, 1995. pp 121–140.
3. D. Bertsekas & R Gallager: *Data Networks (2nd Edition)* Prentice-Hall, 1992.
4. P. Godefroid: Using Partial Orders to Improve Automatic Verification Methods. Proceedings of the 2nd Workshop on Computer-Aided Verification, Lecture Notes in Computer Science 531, Springer-Verlag 1991, pp. 175–186.
5. P. Godefroid: Partial-Order Methods for the Verification of Concurrent Systems, An Approach to the State-Explosion Problem. Lecture Notes in Computer Science 1032, Springer-Verlag 1996, 143 p.
6. K. Jensen: *Coloured Petri Nets — Basic Concepts, Analysis Methods and Practical Use. Vol. 1, Basic Concepts.* Monographs in Theoretical Computer Science. Springer-Verlag, 1991.
7. K. Jensen: *Coloured Petri Nets — Basic Concepts, Analysis Methods and Practical Use. Vol. 2, Analysis Methods.* Monographs in Theoretical Computer Science. Springer-Verlag, 1994.
8. D. Peled: All from One, One for All: On Model Checking Using Representatives. Proceedings of CAV '93, 5th International Conference on Computer-Aided Verification, Lecture Notes in Computer Science 697, Springer-Verlag 1993, pp. 409–423.
9. D. Peled: Combining Partial Order Reductions with On-the-fly Model Checking. Formal Methods in System Design 8 1996, pp. 39–64.
10. J. Toksvig. Design and Implementation of a Place Invariant Tool for Coloured Petri Nets. Master's thesis, Computer Science Department, University of Aarhus, Denmark, 1995.
11. A. Valmari: Error Detection by Reduced Reachability Graph Generation. Proceedings of the 9th European Workshop on Application and Theory of Petri Nets, pp. 95–112.
12. A. Valmari: State Space Generation: Efficiency and Practicality. PhD Thesis, Tampere University of Technology Publications 55, 1988, 169 p.
13. A. Valmari: Stubborn Sets of Coloured Petri Nets. Proceedings of the 12th International Conference on Application and Theory of Petri Nets, Gjern, Denmark 1991, pp. 102–121.
14. A. Valmari: State of the Art Report: Stubborn Sets. Invited article, Petri Net Newsletter 46, April 1994, pp. 6–14.

On Stubborn Sets in the Verification of Linear Time Temporal Properties

Kimmo Varpaaniemi

Helsinki University of Technology, Digital Systems Laboratory
P.O. Box 1100, FIN-02015 HUT, Finland
E-mail: Kimmo.Varpaaniemi@hut.fi

Abstract. The stubborn set method is one of the methods that try to relieve the state space explosion problem that occurs in state space generation. This paper is concentrated on the verification of nexttime-less LTL (linear time temporal logic) formulas with the aid of the stubborn set method. The contribution of the paper is a theorem that gives us a way to utilize the structure of the formula when the stubborn set method is used and there is no fairness assumption. Connections to already known results are drawn by modifying the theorem to concern verification under fairness assumptions.

1 Introduction

Reachability analysis, also known as *exhaustive simulation* or *state space generation*, is a powerful formal method for detecting errors in concurrent and distributed finite state systems. Strictly speaking, infinite state systems can be analyzed, too, but reachability analysis methods are typically such that they cannot process more than a finite set of states. Nevertheless, we can quite well try to find errors even in cases where we do not know if or not the complete state space of the system is finite.

Anyway, reachability analysis suffers from the so called *state space explosion problem*, i.e. the complete state space of a system can be far too large w.r.t. the resources needed to inspect all states in the state space. Fortunately, in a variety of cases we do not have to inspect all reachable states of the system in order to get to know if or not errors of a specified kind exist.

The *stubborn set method* [22–26], and the *sleep set method* [8, 14, 16] are state search techniques that are based on the idea that when two executions of action sequences are sufficiently similar to each other, it is not necessary to investigate both of the executions. *Persistent sets* [8, 9] and *ample sets* [16–18] are strikingly similar to stubborn sets, at least if we consider the actual construction algorithms that have been suggested for stubborn, persistent and ample sets. This similarity is made explicit in [13] where a set is said to be a *stamper set* whenever the set is stubborn or ample or persistent in some way. Other closely related techniques have been presented in e.g. [1, 6, 10, 12, 15, 19, 28, 29]. This paper is concentrated on the theory of the stubborn set method.

Place/transition nets [21] are the formalism to which the stubborn set method is applied in this paper. The main reason for this choice is that there is hardly no simple and well-known formalism where the whole theory of the stubborn set method could be put into practice in a more fine-grained way. (For example, the difference between (general) *dynamic stubbornness* and *strong dynamic stubbornness* [27] is significant in place/transition nets but does not seem to have any useful analogy in the theory of stubborn sets for process algebras [25].)

For historical reasons, "stubbornness" without any preceding attribute is defined in a way that directly indicates how such sets can be computed. When one wants to show results concerning the theoretical properties of the stubborn set method, dynamic stubbornness is a more appropriate notion. When definitions are as they should be, stubbornness implies dynamic stubbornness but not vice versa.

Linear time temporal logics [4] give us a straightforward though of course a limited way to express what should or should not happen in a concurrent or distributed system. Depending on the context, the abbreviation *LTL* refers either to a specific linear time temporal logic or to "a linear time temporal logic in general". In LTL, the satisfaction of a formula is measured w.r.t. an infinite or deadlock-ended execution. A formula is *valid at a state* iff the formula is satisfied by all those infinite and deadlock-ended executions that start from the state. Verifying a formula typically means showing that the formula is valid at the initial state of the system that is under analysis. Validity is sometimes redefined in such a way that the requirement of satisfaction is restricted to paths of a certain kind. *Fairness assumptions* [5] are one form of such a restriction. A definition of fairness expresses some kind of progress that is expected in situations of a certain kind.

On-the-fly verification of a property means that the property is verified during state space generation, in contrary to the traditional approach where properties are verified after state space generation. As soon as it is known whether the property holds, the generation of the state space can be stopped. Since an erroneous system can have much more states than the intended correct system, it is important to find errors as soon as possible. On the other hand, even in the case that all states become generated, the overhead caused by on-the-fly verification, compared to non-on-the-fly verification, is often negligible.

An LTL formula can be verified on-the-fly by means of a *Büchi automaton* [7]. A Büchi automaton that accepts sequences satisfying the negation of the formula can be constructed automatically and intersected with the state space of the modelled system during the construction of the latter. The state space of the system can easily be thought of as a Büchi automaton. The formula is valid in the state space of the system iff the intersection to be computed, also a Büchi automaton, accepts no sequence.

In the fundamental presentation of stubborn sets in the verification of next-time-less LTL-formulas [23], the computation of stubborn sets is directed by atomic formulas only, and the reduced state space can be used for verifying any nexttime-less LTL-formula that is constructible from those atomic formulas.

Unfortunately, the state space generation algorithm in [23] tends to generate the complete state space when verification is done under some of the most typical fairness assumptions. (In [23], all reduction is gained by utilizing transitions that are "sufficiently uninteresting". A typical fairness assumption makes all transitions "too interesting" in this sense.) The approaches [16, 17] improve the approach of [23] by utilizing the structure of the formula and by allowing a fairness assumption. A weakness in [16, 17] is that the structure of the formula is utilized only in cases when fairness is assumed or the formula expresses a safety property. This paper improves the method by utilizing the structure of the formula when fairness is not assumed and the formula is arbitrary. (The expression "fairness is not assumed" should be read to mean "no kind of fairness is assumed" though the latter may sound like "unfairness is assumed".) Though the recently published alternative solution [13] can be considered more goal-oriented, it does not cover our approach.

We also consider the verification of nexttime-less LTL-formulas when fairness is assumed. For convenience, we concentrate on *operation fairness* [16], though we could in principle handle some of the weaker fairness assumptions mentioned by [16] in the same way. The LTL verification approach in [23] can systematically be modified to handle fairness assumptions efficiently, and our approach can be modified quite similarly. It is by no means surprising that we essentially end up in an approach similar to those in [16, 17].

The rest of this paper has been organized as follows. Section 2 presents basic definitions related to place/transition nets. Our version of a linear time temporal logic is presented in Section 3. Section 4 defines *dynamic stubbornness*. Section 5 is devoted to the main preservation theorem of this paper, concerning verification without fairness assumptions. Section 6 extends the results of Section 5 to concern verification with fairness assumptions. Conclusions are then drawn in Section 7.

2   Place/transition nets

This section presents basic definitions related to *place/transition nets with infinite capacities* [21]. (Capacities do not increase expression power and are typically eliminated anyway, so we do not include them in the definitions.) We shall use N to denote the set of non-negative integer numbers, 2^X to denote the set of subsets of the set X, X^* (respectively, X^∞) to denote the set of finite (respectively, infinite) words over the alphabet X, and ε to denote the empty word. For any alphabet X and for any $\rho \in X^\infty$, ρ is thought of as a function from N to X in such a way that $\rho = \rho(0)\rho(1)\rho(2)\ldots$.

Definition 2.1 A *place/transition net* is a quadruple $\langle S, T, W, M_0 \rangle$ such that S is the set of *places*, T is the set of *transitions*, $S \cap T = \emptyset$, W is a function from $(S \times T) \cup (T \times S)$ to N, and M_0 is the *initial marking* (*initial state*), $M_0 \in \mathcal{M}$ where $\mathcal{M}$ is the set of *markings* (*states*), i.e. functions from S to N. The net is *finite* iff $S \cup T$ is finite. If $x \in S \cup T$, then the set of *input elements* of x is

$^\bullet x = \{y \mid W(y,x) > 0\}$, the set of *output elements* of x is $x^\bullet = \{y \mid W(x,y) > 0\}$, and the set of *adjacent elements* of x is $x^\bullet \cup {}^\bullet x$. A transition t *leads (can be fired) from a marking M to a marking M'* ($M[t\rangle M'$ for short) iff

$$\forall s \in S \; M(s) \geq W(s,t) \wedge M'(s) = M(s) - W(s,t) + W(t,s).$$

A transition t is *enabled at a marking M* iff t leads from M to some marking. A marking M is *terminal* iff no transition is enabled at M. □

In our figures, places are circles, transitions are rectangles, and the initial marking is shown by the distribution of tokens, black dots, onto places. A directed arc, i.e. an arrow, is drawn from an element x to an element y iff x is an input element of y. Then $W(x,y)$ is called the *weight* of the arc. As usual, the weight is shown iff it is not equal to 1.

Definition 2.2 Let $\langle S, T, W, M_0 \rangle$ be a place/transition net. The set T^* (respectively, T^∞) is called the *set of finite* (respectively, *infinite*) *transition sequences of the net*. Let f be a function from $\mathcal{M}$ to 2^T. A finite transition sequence σ *f-leads (can be f-fired) from a marking M to a marking M'* iff $M[\sigma\rangle_f M'$, where

$$\forall M \in \mathcal{M} \; M[\varepsilon\rangle_f M, \text{ and}$$

$$\forall M \in \mathcal{M} \; \forall M' \in \mathcal{M} \; \forall \delta \in T^* \; \forall t \in T$$
$$M[\delta t\rangle_f M' \Leftrightarrow (\exists M'' \in \mathcal{M} \; M[\delta\rangle_f M'' \wedge t \in f(M'') \wedge M''[t\rangle M').$$

A finite transition sequence σ is *f-enabled at a marking M* ($M[\sigma\rangle_f$ for short) iff σ f-leads from M to some marking. An infinite transition sequence σ is *f-enabled at a marking M* ($M[\sigma\rangle_f$ for short) iff all finite prefixes of σ are f-enabled at M. A marking M' is *f-reachable from a marking M* iff some finite transition sequence f-leads from M to M'. A marking M' is an *f-reachable marking* iff M' is f-reachable from M_0. The *f-reachability graph* of the net is the pair $\langle V, A \rangle$ such that the set of vertices V is the set of f-reachable markings, and the set of edges A is $\{\langle M, t, M' \rangle \mid M \in V \wedge M' \in V \wedge t \in f(M) \wedge M[t\rangle M'\}$. □

Let Ψ be the function from $\mathcal{M}$ to 2^T such that for each marking M, $\Psi(M) = T$. From now on in this paper, we use a plain ")" instead of ")$_\Psi$", and as far as the notions of Definition 2.2 are concerned, we replace "Ψ-xxx" by "xxx" (where xxx is any word), with the exception that the Ψ-reachability graph of the net is called the *full reachability graph* of the net. When f is clear from the context or is implicitly assumed to exist and be of a kind that is clear from the context, then the f-reachability graph of the net is called the *reduced reachability graph* of the net.

Definition 2.3 Let $\langle S, T, W, M_0 \rangle$ be a place/transition net. Let f be a function from $\mathcal{M}$ to 2^T and let G be the f-reachability graph of the net. For any edge $\langle M, t, M' \rangle$ of G, t is called the *label* of the edge. (The labelling of the paths of G then follows by a natural extension.) A path of G is called a *terminal path* iff the path is finite and no nonempty transition sequence is f-enabled at the last vertex of the path. □

Definition 2.4 Let $\langle S, T, W, M_0 \rangle$ be a place/transition net. Let $T_s \subseteq T$. A finite transition sequence, δ, T_s-*exhausts* a finite transition sequence σ iff for each $t \in T_s$, the number of t's in δ is greater than or equal to the number of t's in σ. The function $\Re$ from $(T^* \cup T^\infty) \times 2^T$ to $T^* \cup T^\infty$ is defined by requiring that for each $Y \in 2^T$, $\Re(\varepsilon, Y) = \varepsilon$, and for each $t_1 \in Y$, for each $t_2 \in T \setminus Y$, for each $\delta \in T^*$ and for each $\rho \in T^\infty$, $\Re(t_1\delta, Y) = t_1\Re(\delta, Y)$, $\Re(t_2\delta, Y) = \Re(\delta, Y)$, and $\Re(\rho, Y) = \Re(\rho(0), Y)\Re(\rho(1), Y)\Re(\rho(2), Y) \ldots$. For any $Y \in 2^T$ and for any $\sigma \in T^* \cup T^\infty$, $\Re(\sigma, Y)$ is called the Y-*restriction* of σ. Let $\Upsilon \subseteq 2^T$. A finite or an infinite transition sequence δ is Υ-*equivalent* to a finite or an infinite transition sequence σ iff for each $Y \in \Upsilon$, $\Re(\delta, Y) = \Re(\sigma, Y)$. Let $\mathcal{T} = \{\{t\} \mid t \in T\}$. A finite or an infinite transition sequence δ is a *permutation of a finite or an infinite transition sequence* σ iff δ is $\mathcal{T}$-equivalent to σ. $\square$

The above Υ can be considered as a set of views to the behaviour of the net. If $T = \{a, b, c, d, e, f, g\}$ and $\Upsilon = \{\{a, b\}, \{c, d\}, \{d, f\}\}$ then $gbdcefa$ is Υ-equivalent to $badfc$ since both of these sequences have the $\{a, b\}$-restriction ba, the $\{c, d\}$-restriction dc, and the $\{d, f\}$-restriction df.

Note that in the case of infinite sequences, the above definition of a permutation does not pay any attention to the possible repeated patterns in the sequences. So, for example the sequence obtained by repeating $bbba$ infinitely many times is a permutation of the sequence obtained by repeating ab infinitely many times.

3 An LTL

This section presents one version of a linear time temporal logic. The presentation assumes that the system to be analyzed has a place/transition net model. Our LTL has effectively the same syntax as the Propositional Linear Temporal Logic (PLTL) in [4]. The semantics are also effectively the same, with the exception that we consider finite executions, too. We make this difference because deadlock-ended executions are important to us whereas the semantic definitions for PLTL assume that every state has a successor.

A formula in our LTL is either atomic or of the form $\bot$, $(A) \Rightarrow (B)$, $\bigcirc(A)$ or $(A)\mathcal{U}(B)$ where A and B are formulas. The following are syntactic abbreviations: $\neg(A)$ means $(A) \Rightarrow (\bot)$, $\top$ means $\neg(\bot)$, $(A)\vee(B)$ means $(\neg(A)) \Rightarrow (B)$, $(A)\wedge(B)$ means $\neg((\neg(A))\vee(\neg(B)))$, $\Diamond(A)$ means $(\top)\mathcal{U}(A)$, and $\square(A)$ means $\neg(\Diamond(\neg(A)))$. An atomic formula is a subset of markings of the net, i.e. a subset of $\mathcal{M}$. In our examples, all atomic formulas are of the form "$M(s)$ op k" where $k \in N$, s is a place in the net, op is a comparison operator and the actual meaning of the formula "$M(s)$ op k" is $\{M \in \mathcal{M} \mid M(s) \text{ op } k\}$.

The operators $\bot$, $\Rightarrow$, $\neg$, $\top$, $\wedge$ and $\vee$ are called *propositional*. The other operators are then called non-propositional or *temporal*. Non-propositional operators have the following names: $\bigcirc$ is "nexttime", $\mathcal{U}$ is "until", $\Diamond$ is "eventually" and $\square$ is "henceforth". A formula is *nexttime-less* iff the formula does not contain any $\bigcirc$. By a *Boolean combination* of formulas from a collection we mean a formula that can be constructed from the formulas of the collection by using propositional operators only. (A single formula can be used several times in the combination whereas it is not necessary to use all formulas of the collection.)

The rules of satisfaction of a formula are given w.r.t. finite and infinite paths in a (reduced or full) reachability graph of the net and are as follows. (We assume that a path always contains at least one vertex and starts with a vertex. Moreover, each finite path ends with a vertex. Also, paths x and y can be concatenated into a path xy iff x is finite and the last vertex of x is the first vertex of y. The path xy is then the path "x continued by y.")

- A path satisfies an atomic formula p iff the first vertex of the path is in p.
- No path satisfies $\bot$.
- A path satisfies $(A) \Rightarrow (B)$ iff the path satisfies B or does not satisfy A.
- A path x satisfies $\bigcirc(A)$ iff there is at least one edge in the path and A is satisfied by the path obtained from x by removing the first vertex and the first edge.
- A path x satisfies $(A)\mathcal{U}(B)$ iff there is a path z and a finite path y such that $x = yz$, z satisfies B, and for any finite paths v and u, $y = uv \neq u$ implies that vz satisfies A.

A formula is *valid at a marking in the graph* iff the formula is satisfied by all those infinite and terminal paths of the graph that start from the marking. (So, a formula $(A) \wedge (B)$ is valid at a marking iff both of A and B are valid at the marking. On the other hand, $(A) \vee (B)$ can be valid at a marking even in the case that neither A nor B is valid at the marking.) *Verifying a formula* means showing that the formula is valid at the initial marking in the full reachability graph of the net.

For convenience, validity is sometimes redefined in such a way that the requirement of satisfaction is restricted to paths of a certain kind. The restriction may or may not be expressible in LTL. *Fairness assumptions* [5] are one form of such a restriction. Fairness is basically an informal concept, and the choice of a formal definition depends much on the context. Anyway, a definition of fairness expresses some kind of progress that is expected in situations of a certain kind. Also, some definitions of fairness have turned out to be of general interest. To this paper, we have chosen one of such definitions, *operation fairness* [16] that is a certain type of *strong fairness* [5].

Definition 3.1 Let $\langle S, T, W, M_0 \rangle$ be a place/transition net. A path in the full reachability graph of the net is *operation fair* iff the following holds for each transition t : if t is enabled infinitely many times on the path, then the path contains infinitely many occurrences of t. (Note that all finite paths are thus operation fair.) □

Operation fairness cannot be expressed in our LTL because our version of LTL has no general way to describe the occurrence of a transition in such a way that the description would match only that transition. On the other hand, as can be seen from [11, 16], operation fairness is easily expressible in action-oriented versions of LTL, at least if the net does not have infinitely many transitions. Though we cannot express operation fairness in our LTL, we can still handle it formally without difficulties, as we shall see in Section 6.

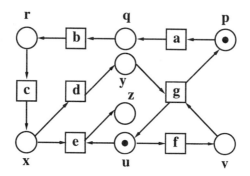

Fig. 1. In the full reachability graph of this net, $(abfcdg)(abfcdg)(abfcdg)\ldots$ labels an operation fair path while $(abcfdg)(abcfdg)(abcfdg)\ldots$ does not.

Operation fairness is not guaranteed to be preserved when the order of firing of transitions is changed in such a way that the resulting path has no suffix that would be a suffix of the original path. In the net in Figure 1, the path starting from the initial marking M_0 and being labelled by $(abcfdg)(abcfdg)(abcfdg)\ldots$ is not operation fair though the path starting from M_0 and being labelled by $(abfcdg)(abfcdg)(abfcdg)\ldots$ is operation fair.

4 Dynamic stubbornness

When one wants to show results concerning the theoretical properties of the stubborn set method, it is often best to use a dynamic definition of stubbornness. The below principles D1 and D2 are the principles 1* and 2* of [20], respectively. Dynamic stubbornness has also been handled in e.g. [24, 27].

Definition 4.1 Let $\langle S, T, W, M_0 \rangle$ be a place/transition net. Let M be a marking of the net. A set $T_s \subseteq T$ *fulfils the first principle of dynamic stubbornness* (*D1* for short) *at* M iff $\forall \sigma \in (T \setminus T_s)^* \ \forall t \in T_s \ M[\sigma t\rangle \Rightarrow M[t\sigma\rangle$. A transition t is a *dynamic key transition of a set* $T_s \subseteq T$ *at* M iff $t \in T_s$ and $\forall \sigma \in (T \setminus T_s)^* \ M[\sigma\rangle \Rightarrow M[\sigma t\rangle$. A set $T_s \subseteq T$ *fulfils the second principle of dynamic stubbornness* (*D2* for short) *at* M iff T_s has a dynamic key transition at M. A set $T_s \subseteq T$ is *dynamically stubborn at* M iff T_s fulfils D1 and D2 at M. A function f from $\mathcal{M}$ to 2^T is a *dynamically stubborn function* iff for each marking M, either $f(M)$ is dynamically stubborn at M or no transition is enabled at M. □

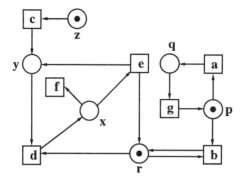

Fig. 2. A net demonstrating dynamic stubbornness.

An interesting thing in Definition 4.1 is that it does not require any true dependency relation between transitions. For example, consider the net in Figure 2. The transition sequences *cdebdf*, *cbdedf* and *bcdedf* all lead from the initial marking M_0 to the same terminal marking, and the only essential difference between the sequences is the position of *b*. Though we can well consider *b* independent of *c*, it is difficult to imagine even any "flexible" dependency relation that would make *b* independent of *d* at all "important" markings. The set $\{a, b\}$ is dynamically stubborn at M_0. If *h* is a dynamically stubborn function and $h(M_0) = \{a, b\}$, the *h*-reachability graph has no path where *c* would be fired at M_0.

5   A preservation theorem

Let us call a formula *directly temporal* iff the outermost operator of the formula is a non-propositional operator. A nexttime-less LTL-formula can be transformed into a nexttime-less LTL-formula where directly temporal subformulas are as short as possible [16]. Then a suitable reduced reachability graph can be generated by using the stubborn set method, provided that the conditions in Proposition 5.1 are satisfied. Note that any formula can be seen as a Boolean combination of directly temporal subformulas. The $\Box(\bigcirc(\top))$ formula occurring in Proposition 5.1 is satisfied by every infinite path whereas no terminal path satisfies it.

Proposition 5.1 *Assumptions:*

(P1) $\langle S, T, W, M_0 \rangle$ *is a place/transition net. (The net and the full reachability graph of the net can be finite or infinite.)*

(P2) Φ *is a collection of nexttime-less LTL-formulas. (Φ can be finite or infinite.)*

(P3) Π *is a function from $2^{\mathcal{M}}$ to 2^S in such a way that whenever we have a subset p of $\mathcal{M}$) and markings M and M' for which $M \in p$ and $M' \notin p$, there exists $s \in \Pi(p)$ for which $M(s) \neq M'(s)$.*

(P4) Ξ *is a function from* Φ *to* 2^T *in such a way that for each* $\phi \in \Phi$ *and for each atomic subformula* p *of* ϕ, $\{t \in T \mid \exists s \in \Pi(p) \ \ W(s,t) \neq W(t,s)\} \subseteq \Xi(\phi)$.

(P5) Υ *is a (finite or an infinite) subset of* 2^T *such that* $\{\Xi(\phi) \mid \phi \in \Phi\} \subseteq \Upsilon$.

(P6) f *is a function from* $\mathcal{M}$ *to* 2^T *in such a way that every terminal path in the* f*-reachability graph of the net is a terminal path of the full reachability graph of the net. (The* f*-reachability graph of the net can be finite or infinite.)*

(P7) *For each terminal path starting from* M_0 *in the full reachability graph, there exists a terminal path starting from* M_0 *in the* f*-reachability graph in such a way that the labels of the paths are* Υ*-equivalent.*

(P8) *For each infinite path starting from* M_0 *in the full reachability graph, there exists an infinite path starting from* M_0 *in the* f*-reachability graph in such a way that the labels of the paths are* Υ*-equivalent.*

Claim: For any boolean combination ϕ *of the formulas in* $\Phi \cup \{\Box(\bigcirc(\top))\}$, ϕ *is valid at* M_0 *in the full reachability graph of the net iff* ϕ *is valid at* M_0 *in the* f*-reachability graph of the net.*

Proof. The "only if" -part of the claim is obvious. The "if" -part can be shown by using a transformation from a path into a *propositional sequence* [13, 17] and by utilizing *equivalence up to stuttering* [13, 17]. □

There is actually nothing new or amazing in Proposition 5.1, and its only purpose is to serve as an interface to Theorem 5.7, i.e. instead of talking about formulas we can talk about Υ-equivalence. Claims of Theorem 5.7 occur as assumptions in Proposition 5.1.

Theorem 5.7, the goal of this section, is a refinement of Theorem 2 of [23] and gives us better chances for reduction. The refinement is strongly inspired by [16, 17]. The new aspect in Theorem 5.7 is that we do not preserve all orders of *visible* transitions. A transition is visible iff at least one member of the above defined Υ contains the transition. Roughly speaking, visible transitions are those transitions that determine the satisfaction of the atomic subformulas of the interesting formulas. In a verification task, if the original formula to be verified is ϕ_0 and an equivalent formula obtained by transformation is ϕ_1, then the collection of interesting formulas consists of directly temporal formulas such that ϕ_1 is a Boolean combination of the formulas in the collection. (If ϕ_1 itself is directly temporal, then the collection is simply $\{\phi_1\}$.)

Let us look at the net in Figure 3. Clearly, the full reachability graph of the net has no terminal path but has exactly two infinite paths that start from the initial marking. Among these two paths, the path labelled by $accc\ldots$ satisfies the formula $\Diamond(M(q) = 0)$ while the path labelled by $baccc\ldots$ does not. However, $\mathcal{M}$ has no markings M_1 and M_2 for which it would be that $M_1[b\rangle M_2$ and either $M_1(q) = 0 \neq M_2(q)$ or $M_2(q) = 0 \neq M_1(q)$. We still consider b as a visible transition w.r.t. the atomic formula "$M(q) = 0$", since in the sequel, transitions like this would anyway be treated like the "pedantically visible" transitions.

The assumptions of Theorem 5.7 are the following.

133

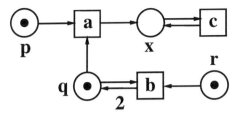

Fig. 3. Both of a and b are visible w.r.t. the atomic formula "$M(q) = 0$".

(A1) $\langle S, T, W, M_0 \rangle$ is a place/transition net, $\Upsilon \subseteq 2^T$, and $J = T \setminus \cup_{Y \in \Upsilon} Y$. (The net, Υ and the full reachability graph of the net can be finite or infinite.)

(A2) f is a dynamically stubborn function from $\mathcal{M}$ to 2^T. (The f-reachability graph of the net can be finite or infinite.)

(A3) For any $Y \in \Upsilon$ and for any marking M, $Y \subseteq f(M)$ or $\{t \in Y \cap f(M) \mid M[t\rangle\} = \emptyset$ (or both).

(A4) For any marking M, if $f(M)$ does not contain all those transitions that are enabled at M, then some transition in J is a dynamic key transition of $f(M)$ at M.

(A5) For any $t \in T \setminus J$, every infinite path (starting from a marking whatsoever) in the f-reachability graph of the net contains at least one marking M such that $t \in f(M)$.

Coarsely speaking, A3 prevents us from changing the order of transitions that are visible w.r.t. a single member of Φ while A4 and A5 prevent us from ignoring any member of Φ. The transitions in J are invisible w.r.t. all members of Φ. There is a following correspondence between A3 – A5 and the assumptions 2 – 4 of Theorem 2 of [23]: if $|\Upsilon| = 1$, n is between 3 and 5 and the f-reachability graph is finite, An becomes assumption $n - 1$ of [23].

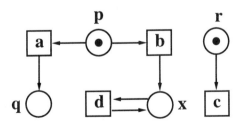

Fig. 4. An example net for verification.

Let us consider an example where we try to verify the formula

$$(\Diamond(M(q) = 1)) \vee (\Diamond(M(r) = 0))$$

about the net in Figure 4. We can let $\Upsilon = \{\{a\}, \{c\}\}$ ($|\Upsilon| = 2$) since the satisfaction of $M(q) = 1$ can be affected by a only whereas the satisfaction of $M(r) = 0$ can be affected by c only. Let us choose $\{a, b\}$ for the dynamically stubborn set at the initial marking. This choice respects all of A1 – A5. (Note that [23] would not accept such a choice but would require us to take all enabled transitions into the set. We have thus gained reduction w.r.t. [23].) At any other encountered nonterminal marking, we let the dynamically stubborn set contain all enabled transitions since A1 – A5 would otherwise be violated. (The same would have to be done if the conditions in [23] would have to be satisfied instead.) The reduced reachability graph has exactly one terminal path that starts from the initial marking, and the label of that path is ac. The labels of the infinite paths starting from the initial marking in the reduced reachability graph are $bddd\ldots$, $bcddd\ldots$, $bdcddd\ldots$, $bddcddd\ldots$, etc. From these paths the path labelled by $bddd\ldots$ invalidates the formula.

Let us then verify the formula

$$(\Diamond(M(x) = 1)) \vee (\Diamond(M(r) = 0)).$$

Using similar reasoning as above, we can let $\Upsilon = \{\{b\}, \{c\}\}$ ($|\Upsilon| = 2$). (Though d is connected to x, d cannot affect the satisfaction of $M(x) = 1$.) Proceeding as above, we actually get exactly the same reduced reachability graph, but that is merely a coincidence. Since there is no counterexample to the formula, we conclude that the formula is valid at the initial marking. (This is indeed an example of a disjunction that is valid despite of the fact that none of the disjuncts is valid.)

Let us also look what would be the consequences if some of A3 – A5 were dropped. Dropping A3 could make us draw a wrong conclusion about

$$\Box(((M(r) = 1) \vee (M(q) = 1)) \vee (\Box(M(q) = 0))).$$

When $\Upsilon = \{\{a, c\}\}$ ($|\Upsilon| = 1$), we could choose $\{a, b\}$ for the dynamically stubborn set at the initial marking. The only counterexample to the formula, i.e. the path starting from the initial marking and being labelled by ca, would then be lost.

Dropping A4 could make us draw a wrong conclusion about $\Diamond(M(r) = 0)$. When $\Upsilon = \{\{c\}\}$, we could choose $\{c\}$ for the dynamically stubborn set at the initial marking. The only counterexample to the formula, i.e. the path starting from the initial marking and being labelled by $bddd\ldots$, would then be lost.

Dropping A5 could make us draw a wrong conclusion about

$$\Box(((M(x) = 0) \vee (M(r) = 0)) \vee (\Box(M(r) = 1))).$$

When $\Upsilon = \{\{b, c\}\}$ ($|\Upsilon| = 1$), we could let $\{a, b, c\}$ be the dynamically stubborn set at the initial marking and choose $\{d\}$ to be the dynamically stubborn set at the marking to which b leads from the initial marking. All the counterexamples to the formula, i.e. the paths where c occurs after b, would then be lost.

In the net in Figure 5, omitting the attribute "dynamic key" in A4 could make us draw a wrong conclusion about

$$(\Diamond(M(q) = 1)) \vee (\Diamond(M(y) = 1)).$$

When $\Upsilon = \{\{a, d\}\}$ ($|\Upsilon| = 1$), we could choose $\{a, b, d\}$ for the dynamically stubborn set at the initial marking. The only counterexample to the formula, i.e. the path starting from the initial marking and being labelled by $ceee\ldots$, would then be lost.

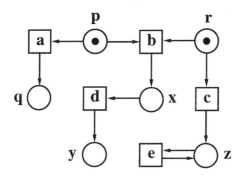

Fig. 5. A net that motivates the assumption A4.

We now start working towards Theorem 5.7. Lemma 5.2 tells us that the used transition selection function respects the important orderings of transitions.

Lemma 5.2 *Assumptions: A1, A2 and A3.*
  Claim: For each nonterminal marking M, for each t in $f(M)$ and for each σ in $(T \setminus f(M))^*$, if $M[\sigma t\rangle$, then $M[t\sigma\rangle$, and $t\sigma$ is Υ-equivalent to σt.

Proof. Let M be a nonterminal marking, $t \in f(M)$ and $\sigma \in (T \setminus f(M))^*$ in such a way that $M[\sigma t\rangle$. From D1 (and, as goes without saying, from A2) it follows that $M[t\sigma\rangle$. Let $Y \in \Upsilon$. If $Y \subseteq f(M)$, then $\sigma \in (T \setminus Y)^*$ and thus $\Re(t\sigma, Y) = t = \Re(\sigma t, Y)$. If $Y \not\subseteq f(M)$, then A3 has the effect that $t \notin Y$, so $\Re(t\sigma, Y) = \Re(\sigma, Y) = \Re(\sigma t, Y)$. □

Lemma 5.3 guarantees that the possible terminal paths of the full reachability graph are sufficiently represented in the reduced reachability graph.

Lemma 5.3 *Assumptions: A1, A2 and A3.*
  Claim: For each finite transition sequence σ'' and for each marking M'', if σ'' leads from M'' to a terminal marking M_d, then there exists a permutation δ'' of σ'' in such a way that $M''[\delta''\rangle_f M_d$ and δ'' is Υ-equivalent to σ''.

Proof. We use induction on the length of σ''. The claim holds trivially when restricted to $\sigma'' = \varepsilon$. Our induction hypothesis is that the claim holds when restricted to any σ'' of length $n \geq 0$.

Let a finite transition sequence σ of length $n + 1$ lead from a marking M to a terminal marking M_d. From D2 it follows that there exist $t \in f(M)$, $\delta \in (T \setminus f(M))^*$ and $\delta' \in T^*$ in such a way that $\sigma = \delta t \delta'$. From Lemma 5.2 it follows that there exists a marking M' in such a way that $M[t\rangle_f M'$, $M'[\delta\delta'\rangle M_d$, and $t\delta\delta'$ is Υ-equivalent to σ.

By the induction hypothesis, there exists a permutation δ'' of $\delta\delta'$ in such a way that $M'[\delta''\rangle_f M_d$ and δ'' is Υ-equivalent to $\delta\delta'$. So, $t\delta''$ is a permutation of σ in such a way that $M[t\delta''\rangle_f M_d$ and $t\delta''$ is Υ-equivalent to σ. □

Lemma 5.4 guarantees that the possible infinite invisible transition sequences are sufficiently represented in the reduced reachability graph.

Lemma 5.4 *Assumptions: A1, A2 and A4.*
Claim: For each $\sigma'' \in J^\infty$ and for each $M'' \in \mathcal{M}$, if $M''[\sigma''\rangle$ then there exists $\delta'' \in J^\infty$ in such a way that $M''[\delta''\rangle_f$.

Proof. Let $\sigma \in J^\infty$ and $M \in \mathcal{M}$ such that $M[\sigma\rangle$. A4 and D1 guarantee that we can define a function τ from N to T, a function μ from N to $\mathcal{M}$ and a function θ from N to J^∞ as follows.

Firstly, $\mu(0) = M$ and $\theta(0) = \sigma$. Let then $k \in N$. If $\theta(k)$ contains a transition from $f(\mu(k))$, we let $t_k \in f(\mu(k))$, $\gamma_k \in (J \setminus f(\mu(k))^*$ and $\zeta_k \in J^\infty$ be such that $\gamma_k t_k \zeta_k = \theta(k)$ and require that $\tau(k) = t_k$, $\mu(k)[\tau(k)\rangle_f \mu(k+1)$ and $\theta(k+1) = \gamma_k \zeta_k$.

In the remaining case, we choose a transition t_k from $f(\mu(k)) \cap J$ in such a way that $\mu(k)[t_k \sigma \theta(k)\rangle$ and require that $\tau(k) = t_k$, $\mu(k)[\tau(k)\rangle_f \mu(k+1)$ and $\theta(k+1) = \theta(k)$.

The function τ represents an infinite transition sequence that is f-enabled at M. □

Lemma 5.5 states that if we have an infinite or a finite sequence in the full reachability graph, we can choose an arbitrary finite prefix of the sequence in such a way that there is a sequence that is Υ-equivalent to the original sequence and has a finite prefix that is f-enabled and covers the prefix we chose. (To remember the meaning of "exhausting", see Definition 2.4.)

Lemma 5.5 *Assumptions: A1, A2, A3, A4 and A5.*
Claim: For each $\sigma'' \in T^*$, for each $\rho' \in T^* \cup T^\infty$ and for each $M' \in \mathcal{M}$, if $M'[\sigma''\rho'\rangle$ and M' is f-reachable from M_0, then there exist $\gamma'' \in T^*$, $\delta_1 \in T^*$, $\delta_2 \in T^*$, $\rho'' \in T^* \cup T^\infty$ and $M'' \in \mathcal{M}$ in such a way that $\gamma''\rho'' = \rho'$, $M'[\delta_1\rangle_f M''$, $M''[\delta_2\rho''\rangle$, δ_1 $(T \setminus J)$-exhausts σ'', and $\delta_1\delta_2$ is Υ-equivalent to $\sigma''\gamma''$.

Proof. We use induction on the length of σ''. The claim holds trivially when restricted to $\sigma'' = \varepsilon$. Our induction hypothesis is that the claim holds when restricted to any σ'' of length $n \geq 0$. The claim holds trivially when restricted to any $\sigma'' \in J^*$ since in that case, ε is Υ-equivalent to σ'' and $(T \setminus J)$-exhausts σ'', so $\gamma'' = \delta_1 = \delta_2 = \varepsilon$, $\rho'' = \rho'$ and $M'' = M'$ are suitable choices for that case. Let then $\sigma \in T^* \setminus J^*$, $\rho \in T^* \cup T^\infty$ and $M \in \mathcal{M}$ be such that $M[\sigma\rho\rangle$, M is f-reachable from M_0 and the length of σ is $n + 1$.

Let L be the set of those transitions that occur in σ. A4 and D1 guarantee that we can define functions ξ, β and η from N to T^*, a function μ from N to $\mathcal{M}$ and a function θ from N to $T^* \cup T^\infty$ as follows. Firstly, $\xi(0) = \varepsilon$, $\beta(0) = \varepsilon$, $\eta(0) = \varepsilon$, $\mu(0) = M$ and $\theta(0) = \rho$. Let then $k \in N$. If there exists $\tau \in L$ such that $\mu(k)[\tau\rangle_f$, then $\xi(k+1) = \xi(k)$, $\beta(k+1) = \beta(k)$, $\eta(k+1) = \eta(k)$, $\mu(k+1) = \mu(k)$ and $\theta(k+1) = \theta(k)$. Otherwise, if $\eta(k)$ contains a transition from $f(\mu(k))$, we let $\tau_k \in f(\mu(k))$, $\gamma_k \in (T \setminus f(\mu(k)))^*$ and $\zeta_k \in T^*$ be such that $\gamma_k \tau_k \zeta_k = \eta(k)$ and require that $\xi(k+1) = \xi(k)$, $\beta(k+1) = \beta(k)\tau_k$, $\eta(k+1) = \gamma_k \zeta_k$, $\mu(k)[\tau_k\rangle_f \mu(k+1)$ and $\theta(k+1) = \theta(k)$. In the remaining case, if $\theta(k)$ contains a transition from $f(\mu(k))$, we let $\tau_k \in f(\mu(k))$, $\gamma_k \in (T \setminus f(\mu(k)))^*$ and $\zeta_k \in T^* \cup T^\infty$ be such that $\gamma_k \tau_k \zeta_k = \theta(k)$ and require that $\xi(k+1) = \xi(k)\gamma_k \tau_k$, $\beta(k+1) = \beta(k)\tau_k$, $\eta(k+1) = \eta(k)\gamma_k$, $\mu(k)[\tau_k\rangle_f \mu(k+1)$ and $\theta(k+1) = \zeta_k$. In the ultimate remaining case, we choose a transition τ_k from $f(\mu(k)) \cap J$ in such a way that $\mu(k)[\tau_k\sigma\eta(k)\theta(k)\rangle$ and require that $\xi(k+1) = \xi(k)$, $\beta(k+1) = \beta(k)\tau_k$, $\eta(k+1) = \eta(k)$, $\mu(k)[\tau_k\rangle_f \mu(k+1)$ and $\theta(k+1) = \theta(k)$.

Clearly, for each $k \in N$, $\xi(k)\theta(k) = \rho$ and $M[\beta(k)\rangle_f \mu(k)$. From Lemma 5.2 it follows that for each $k \in N$, $\mu(k)[\sigma\eta(k)\theta(k)\rangle$, and $\beta(k)\sigma\eta(k)$ is Υ-equivalent to $\sigma\xi(k)$.

Let us first assume that there are no $k' \in N$ and $\tau' \in L$ that would satisfy $\mu(k')[\tau'\rangle_f$. Let us call this assumption B. Since $\sigma \in T^* \setminus J^*$ and L is the set of those transitions that occur in σ, the set $L \setminus J$ is not empty. Let t be any transition in $L \setminus J$. From B and A5 it follows that there exists $k'' \in N$ such that $t \in f(\mu(k''))$. Consequently, there must be some $k_1 \leq k''$, $t' \in L \cap f(\mu(k_1))$, $\gamma \in (L \setminus f(\mu(k_1)))^*$ and $\gamma' \in L^*$ such that $\sigma = \gamma t'\gamma'$. Since $\mu(k_1)[\sigma\rangle$, from D1 it follows that $\mu(k_1)[t'\rangle_f$. We have thus reached a contradiction with B.

So, we can choose $k' \in N$ and $\tau' \in L$ such that $\mu(k')[\tau'\rangle_f$. Since $\mu(k')[\sigma\rangle$, there are some $t_1 \in f(\mu(k'))$, $\delta \in (T \setminus f(\mu(k')))^*$ and $\delta' \in T^*$ such that $\sigma = \delta t_1 \delta'$. Since $\mu(k')[\sigma\eta(k')\theta(k')\rangle$, from Lemma 5.2 it follows that there exists a marking M_1 such that $\mu(k')[t_1\rangle_f M_1$, $M_1[\delta\delta'\eta(k')\theta(k')\rangle$, and $t_1\delta\delta'$ is Υ-equivalent to σ. So, $\beta(k')t_1\delta\delta'\eta(k')$ is Υ-equivalent to $\sigma\xi(k')$ since $\beta(k')\sigma\eta(k')$ is Υ-equivalent to $\sigma\xi(k')$.

By the induction hypothesis, there exists $\gamma'' \in T^*$, $\delta_1 \in T^*$, $\delta_2 \in T^*$, $\rho'' \in T^* \cup T^\infty$ and $M_2 \in \mathcal{M}$ in such a way that $\gamma''\rho'' = \eta(k')\theta(k')$, $M_1[\delta_1\rangle_f M_2$, $M_2[\delta_2\rho''\rangle$, δ_1 $(T \setminus J)$-exhausts $\delta\delta'$, and $\delta_1\delta_2$ is Υ-equivalent to $\delta\delta'\gamma''$. Then $M[\beta(k')t_1\delta_1\rangle_f M_2$ and $\beta(k')t_1\delta_1$ $(T \setminus J)$-exhausts $\delta t_1 \delta' = \sigma$.

Let us first consider the case that γ'' is shorter than $\eta(k')$. Let $\delta_3 \in T^*$ be such that $\gamma''\delta_3 = \eta(k')$. Then $\delta_3\theta(k') = \rho''$. We thus have that $M_2[\delta_2\delta_3\theta(k')\rangle$. On the other hand, $\xi(k')\theta(k') = \rho$. Moreover, $\beta(k')t_1\delta_1\delta_2\delta_3$ is Υ-equivalent to $\sigma\xi(k')$ since $\delta_1\delta_2\delta_3$ is Υ-equivalent to $\delta\delta'\gamma''\delta_3 = \delta\delta'\eta(k')$ whereas $\beta(k')t_1\delta\delta'\eta(k')$ is Υ-equivalent to $\sigma\xi(k')$.

Let us then consider the case that γ'' is at least as long as $\eta(k')$. Let $\delta_4 \in T^*$ be such that $\eta(k')\delta_4 = \gamma''$. Then $\delta_4\rho'' = \theta(k')$. We thus have that $\xi(k')\delta_4\rho'' = \xi(k')\theta(k') = \rho$. On the other hand, $M_2[\delta_1\delta_2\rho''\rangle$. Moreover, $\beta(k')t_1\delta_1\delta_2$ is Υ-equivalent to $\sigma\xi(k')\delta_4$ since $\delta_1\delta_2$ is Υ-equivalent to $\delta\delta'\gamma'' = \delta\delta'\eta(k')\delta_4$ whereas $\beta(k')t_1\delta\delta'\eta(k')$ is Υ-equivalent to $\sigma\xi(k')$. $\qquad\square$

If we have a series of finite prefixes of an infinite sequence in the full reachability graph, Lemma 5.5 gives us a series of finite sequences in the reduced reachability graph, but the series is not necessarily a series of prefixes of any single infinite sequence. There is still one thing we can do: we can move along a path in the reduced reachability graph and apply Lemma 5.5 to any of the markings on the path. Guaranteeing Υ-equivalence is then not difficult at all since for any infinite sequence, Lemma 5.5 just modifies some finite prefix of the sequence and leaves the rest of the infinite sequence untouched. We then just have to make sure that we choose a prefix that includes some of the so far untouched part of the original infinite sequence. This is the idea of the proof of the below Lemma 5.6.

Lemma 5.6 *Assumptions: A1, A2, A3, A4 and A5.*
  Claim: For each $\sigma'' \in T^\infty$ for each $M'' \in \mathcal{M}$, if $M''[\sigma''\rangle$, M'' is f-reachable from M_0 and σ'' contains infinitely many occurrences of transitions from $T \setminus J$, then there exists $\delta'' \in T^\infty$ in such a way that $M''[\delta''\rangle_f$ and δ'' is Υ-equivalent to σ''.

Proof. Let $\sigma \in T^\infty$ and $M \in \mathcal{M}$ be such that $M[\sigma\rangle$, M is f-reachable from M_0 and σ contains infinitely many occurrences of transitions from $T \setminus J$. By Lemma 5.5 we can define functions β, γ, δ, λ, ξ, η and ζ from N to T^*, a function μ from N to $\mathcal{M}$ and functions θ and ρ from N to T^∞ as follows. Firstly, $\beta(0) = \varepsilon$, $\mu(0) = M$, $\gamma(0) = \varepsilon$, $\delta(0) = \varepsilon$, $\lambda(0) = \varepsilon$, $\xi(0) = \varepsilon$, $\eta(0) = \varepsilon$, $\zeta(0) = \varepsilon$, $\theta(0) = \sigma$ and $\rho(0) = \sigma$.

Let then $k \in N$. We choose $\beta(k+1)$, $\mu(k+1)$, $\gamma(k+1)$, $\delta(k+1)$, $\lambda(k+1)$, $\xi(k+1)$, $\eta(k+1)$, $\zeta(k+1)$, $\theta(k+1)$ and $\rho(k+1)$ in such a way that $\xi(k+1)\rho(k+1) = \theta(k)$, $\xi(k+1) \in T^* \setminus J^*$, $\gamma(k+1)\theta(k+1) = \rho(k+1)$, $\beta(k+1) = \beta(k)\delta(k+1)$, $\mu(k)[\delta(k+1)\rangle_f \mu(k+1)$, $\eta(k+1) = \eta(k)\xi(k+1)\gamma(k+1)$, $\zeta(k+1) = \eta(k)\xi(k+1)$, $\mu(k+1)[\lambda(k+1)\theta(k+1)\rangle$, $\delta(k+1)$ $(T \setminus J)$-exhausts $\lambda(k)\xi(k+1)$, and $\delta(k+1)\lambda(k+1)$ is Υ-equivalent to $\lambda(k)\xi(k+1)\gamma(k+1)$.

From this definition it follows that for each $k \in N$, $\eta(k+1)\theta(k+1) = \eta(k)\xi(k+1)\gamma(k+1)\theta(k+1) = \eta(k)\xi(k+1)\rho(k+1) = \eta(k)\theta(k)$, $\beta(k+1) = \beta(k)\delta(k+1)$ $(T \setminus J)$-exhausts $\beta(k)\lambda(k)\xi(k+1)$, and $\beta(k+1)\lambda(k+1) = \beta(k)\delta(k+1)\lambda(k+1)$ is Υ-equivalent to $\beta(k)\lambda(k)\xi(k+1)\gamma(k+1)$. So, if $\beta(k)\lambda(k)$ is Υ-equivalent to $\eta(k)$, then $\beta(k+1)$ $(T \setminus J)$-exhausts $\eta(k)\xi(k+1) = \zeta(k+1)$ and $\beta(k+1)\lambda(k+1)$ is Υ-equivalent to $\eta(k)\xi(k+1)\gamma(k+1) = \eta(k+1)$.

By induction we get that for each $k \in N$, $\eta(k)\theta(k) = \sigma$, $\beta(k)$ $(T \setminus J)$-exhausts $\zeta(k)$ and $\beta(k)\lambda(k)$ is Υ-equivalent to $\eta(k)$. On the other hand, $\eta(k) = \zeta(k)\gamma(k)$, $M[\beta(k)\rangle_f \mu(k)$, $\mu(k)[\lambda(k)\theta(k)\rangle$, and $\zeta(k+1)$ contains more occurrences of transitions from $T \setminus J$ than $\zeta(k)$ contains.

Since for any $k \in N$, $\beta(k+1) = \beta(k)\delta(k+1)$, the function β represents an infinite transition sequence that is f-enabled at M. Let ω be this infinite sequence. From above it follows that for any $Y \in \Upsilon$, every finite prefix of the Y-restriction of ω is a finite prefix of the Y-restriction of σ, and every finite prefix of the Y-restriction of σ is a finite prefix of the Y-restriction of ω. The infinite sequence ω is thus Υ-equivalent to the infinite sequence σ. □

We are now ready to collect together the results we have obtained and prove the desired theorem. The task is simple since all the hard work has been done in proving the lemmas. Note that according to A1 – A5, "everything is possibly infinite".

Theorem 5.7 *Assumptions: A1, A2, A3, A4 and A5.*
    Claims:

    (C1) Every terminal path in the f-reachability graph of the net is a terminal path of the full reachability graph of the net.
    (C2) For each terminal path starting from M_0 in the full reachability graph, there exists a terminal path starting from M_0 in the f-reachability graph in such a way that the labels of the paths are Υ-equivalent.
    (C3) For each finite path starting from M_0 in the full reachability graph, there exists a finite path starting from M_0 in the f-reachability graph in such a way that the labels of the paths are Υ-equivalent.
    (C4) For each infinite path starting from M_0 in the full reachability graph, there exists an infinite path starting from M_0 in the f-reachability graph in such a way that the labels of the paths are Υ-equivalent.

Proof. C1 follows trivially from D2. C2 is an immediate consequence of Lemma 5.3. C3 follows directly from Lemma 5.5, by letting $\rho' = \varepsilon$.

From Lemma 5.5, by letting $\rho' \in J^\infty$, and from Lemma 5.4 it directly follows that C4 holds when restricted to a path where some suffix of the label of the path is in J^∞. From Lemma 5.6 it immediately follows that C4 holds when restricted to a path where no suffix of the label is in J^∞.   □

As we see from Proposition 5.1, C3 is actually not needed in our LTL verification problem. However, C3 is interesting by its own virtue, at least if Υ-equivalence is thought of as a behavioural equivalence.

6   Treating operation fairness

We now consider verification under the assumption of operation fairness. In order to guarantee that operation fair paths are sufficiently retained in a reduction, we extend the assumptions A1–A5 by the following assumption A6 and then drop assumption A4 since A4 and A6 together would simply force us to generate the full reachability graph.

(A6) Let ϖ be a function from T to 2^T such that for each $t \in T$,
    $\{t' \in T \mid \exists s \in {}^\bullet t \;\; W(s,t') \neq W(t',s)\} \subseteq \varpi(t)$. Then $\mathcal{T} \cup \mathcal{Y} \subseteq \Upsilon$ where
$\mathcal{T} = \{\{t\} \mid t \in T\}$ and $\mathcal{Y} = \{\varpi(t) \mid t \in T\}$.

From A6 it follows that all transitions are visible. We observe that if two infinite paths in the full reachability graph start from the same marking and have $(\mathcal{T} \cup \mathcal{Y})$-equivalent labels, then both of the paths are operation fair or neither of them is operation fair. The set $\varpi(t)$ contains at least all those transition that are "visible w.r.t. the enabledness of t", where visibility is understood in the same way as in the discussion after Proposition 5.1. The separation of $\mathcal{T}$ and $\mathcal{Y}$ reflects the fact that the definition of operation fairness does not say anything about what should happen if a transition is enabled at most finitely many times. If we had defined an action-oriented version of LTL [11, 16], operation fairness could have been expressed as an ordinary formula (except possibly in the case that the set of transitions is infinite), and A6 would have been obtained as a side effect of the ordinary construction principles of Υ.

If we return to the example concerning the net in Figure 1, we see that the sequences $(abcfdg)(abcfdg)(abcfdg)\ldots$ and $(abfcdg)(abfcdg)(abfcdg)\ldots$ are not $\mathcal{Y}$-equivalent since both of c and f must be in $\varpi(e)$.

Note that $\mathcal{Y}$-equivalence does not imply $\mathcal{T}$-equivalence. If a net has transitions but no place, we can let $\varpi(t) = \emptyset$ for each transition t, with the consequence that any two transition sequences are $\mathcal{Y}$-equivalent.

Lemma 6.1 is much like Lemma 5.5. The difference is that assumption A4 has been replaced by assumption A6, the sequence to be transformed is definitely infinite and a label of an operation fair path, the result of the transformation is a permutation of the original sequence, and the prefix covering condition has been fixed according to the fact that $J = \emptyset$.

Lemma 6.1   *Assumptions: A1, A2, A3, A5 and A6.*
Claim: For each $\sigma'' \in T^*$, for each $\rho' \in T^\infty$ and for each $M' \in \mathcal{M}$, if $M'[\sigma''\rho'\rangle$, M' is f-reachable from M_0 and the path starting from M' and being labelled by $\sigma''\rho'$ in the full reachability graph is operation fair, then there exist $\gamma'' \in T^*$, $\delta_1 \in T^*$, $\delta_2 \in T^*$, $\rho'' \in T^* \cup T^\infty$ and $M'' \in \mathcal{M}$ in such a way that $\gamma''\rho'' = \rho'$, $M'[\delta_1\rangle_f M''$, $M''[\delta_2\rho''\rangle$, δ_1 T-exhausts σ'', and $\delta_1\delta_2$ is Υ-equivalent to $\sigma''\gamma''$.

Proof. Taking into account that $J = \emptyset$, it suffices to repeat the proof of Lemma 5.5 literally, with the following modifications: the induction hypothesis must refer to the claim of the lemma being proved, a trivial observation concerning operation fairness is needed in the induction step, and the reference to A4 has to be replaced by a reference to D2 and operation fairness. (D2 and operation fairness together guarantee that we never get into a situation where a transition from J would be needed.) $\square$

Lemma 6.2 is a similar continuation to Lemma 6.1 as Lemma 5.6 is to Lemma 5.5.

Lemma 6.2   *Assumptions: A1, A2, A3, A5 and A6.*
Claim: For each $\sigma'' \in T^\infty$ for each $M'' \in \mathcal{M}$, if $M''[\sigma''\rangle$, M'' is f-reachable from M_0, and the path starting from M'' and being labelled by σ'' in the full reachability graph is operation fair, then there exists $\delta'' \in T^\infty$ in such a way that $M''[\delta''\rangle_f$ and δ'' is Υ-equivalent to σ''.

Proof. Taking into account that $J = \emptyset$, it suffices to repeat the proof of Lemma 5.6 literally, with the following modifications: a trivial observation concerning operation fairness is needed before applying any inductive argument, and the reference to Lemma 5.5 must be replaced by a reference to Lemma 6.1. $\square$

We are now ready to present a preservation theorem for operation fair paths.

Theorem 6.3 *Assumptions: A1, A2, A3, A5 and A6.*
Claims: C1 and C2 of Theorem 5.7 and

(C5) For each operation fair infinite path starting from M_0 in the full reachability graph, there exists an operation fair infinite path starting from M_0 in the f-reachability graph in such a way that the labels of the paths are Υ-equivalent.

Proof. Again, C1 follows trivially from D2 and C2 is an immediate consequence of Lemma 5.3. C5 in turn follows directly from A6, Lemma 6.2 and the definition of operation fairness. $\square$

Though $(\mathcal{T} \cup \mathcal{Y})$-equivalence preserves operation fairness and its negation, Theorem 6.3 does not promise anything that would concern the paths that are not operation fair. Let Υ' be an arbitrary subset of 2^T, thus not required to satisfy A6. By substituting Υ' for Υ in Theorem 5.7 and $\Upsilon' \cup \mathcal{T} \cup \mathcal{Y}$ for Υ in Theorem 6.3, one could present a corollary to be applied when operation fair counterexamples are expected but a total absence of operation fair counterexamples makes any counterexample acceptable. However, nothing prevents us from simply verifying a formula first under fairness assumptions and then without fairness assumptions. Such a simple approach is even recommendable since retaining several less than strictly related things during a single state space construction is one of the most typical ways to promote state space explosion.

Theorem 6 is effectively so close to the corresponding theorems in [16, 17] that we have not essentially improved the stubborn set method in verification under fairness assumptions.

7 Conclusions

This paper has considered relieving of the state space explosion problem that occurs in the analysis of concurrent and distributed systems. We have concentrated on one method for that purpose: the stubborn set method. We are fully aware of the fact that the stubborn set method has no special position among verification heuristics. It is also clear that in industrial-size cases, one method alone is typically almost useless. Our motivation is that whenever a method is used, it should be used reasonably.

The contribution of this paper is Theorem 5.7 that gives us a way to utilize the structure of the formula when the stubborn set method is used but fairness is not assumed. Algorithmic implementations can be derived from this theorem in the same way as in [23].

The tester approach in [26] can be considered more goal-oriented than our approach, but so far we have not found any automatic way to construct a useful tester for an arbitrary formula. In [13], a visibility relaxation heuristic for improving the tester technique is presented and the heuristic is shown to apply very well to automatically constructible Büchi automata, too. However, this relaxation technique does not cover our approach. Let us consider a verification task where we need a Büchi automaton that accepts exactly the sequences that satisfy an $n$ary conjunction of formulas. (The formula to be verified then corresponds to an $n$ary disjunction. If an $n$ary conjunction were to be verified, we could verify it simply by verifying its conjuncts separately.) As can be seen from the construction description [7, 13] and from Lemma 6 of [13], all conjuncts become represented in every state of the automaton. Consequently, the visibility relaxation heuristic in [13] does not take any obvious advantage of the fact that the $n$ary conjunction in question is a Boolean combination.

The use of stubborn sets in various formalisms and logics is a fruitful area of future research. On the other hand, we should, by means of large case studies, try to find out what the central problems in the application of the method are and how these problems could be alleviated.

Acknowledgements

This work has been supported by Helsinki Graduate School in Computer Science and Engineering and The Academy of Finland. Discussions with Associate Professor Antti Valmari from Tampere University of Technology have affected the paper in the following things: the assumption A4 (in Section 5) and the idea of intersecting an automatically constructed Büchi automaton with a reduced state space during the construction of the latter.

References

1. Bause, F.: *Analysis of Petri Nets with a Dynamic Priority Method.* Azéma, P., and Balbo, G. (Eds.), Proceedings of PN '97, Toulouse. LNCS 1248, Springer-Verlag 1997, pp. 215–234.
2. Courcoubetis, C. (Ed.): Proceedings of CAV '93, Elounda, Greece. LNCS 697, Springer-Verlag 1993, 504 p.
3. Dembiński, P., and Średniawa, M. (Eds.): Proceedings of PSTV '95, Warsaw. Chapman & Hall 1996, 453 p.
4. Emerson, E.A.: *Temporal and Modal Logic.* van Leeuwen, J. (Ed.), Handbook of Theoretical Computer Science, Vol. B. Elsevier 1990, pp. 995–1072.
5. Francez, N.: *Fairness.* Springer-Verlag 1986, 295 p.
6. Gerth, R., Kuiper, R., Peled, D., and Penczek, W.: *A Partial Order Approach to Branching Time Logic Model Checking.* Proceedings of the 3rd Israel Symposium on Theory of Computing and Systems, Tel Aviv 1995. IEEE Computer Society Press, Los Alamitos CA 1995, pp. 130–140.
7. Gerth, R., Peled, D., Vardi, M.Y., and Wolper, P.: *Simple On-the-Fly Automatic Verification of Linear Temporal Logic.* In [3], pp. 3–18.
8. Godefroid, P.: *Partial-Order Methods for the Verification of Concurrent Systems — An Approach to the State-Explosion Problem.* LNCS 1032, Springer-Verlag 1996, 143 p.

9. Godefroid, P., and Pirottin, D.: *Refining Dependencies Improves Partial-Order Verification Methods.* In [2], pp. 438–449.
10. Janicki, R., and Koutny, M.: *Using Optimal Simulations to Reduce Reachability Graphs.* Clarke, E.M., and Kurshan, R.P. (Eds.), Proceedings of CAV '90, New Brunswick NJ. LNCS 531, Springer-Verlag 1991, pp. 166–175.
11. Kaivola, R.: *Equivalence, Preorders and Compositional Verification for Linear Time Temporal Logic and Concurrent Systems.* Doctoral thesis, University of Helsinki, Department of Computer Science, Report A-1996-1, 1996, 185 p.
12. Katz, S., and Peled, D.: *Verification of Distributed Programs Using Representative Interleaving Sequences.* Distributed Computing 6 (1992) 2, pp. 107–120.
13. Kokkarinen, I., Peled, D., and Valmari, A.: *Relaxed Visibility Enhances Partial Order Reduction.* Grumberg, O. (Ed.), Proceedings of CAV '97, Haifa. LNCS 1254, Springer-Verlag 1997, pp. 328–339.
14. Koutny, M., and Pietkiewicz-Koutny, M.: *On the Sleep Sets Method for Partial Order Verification of Concurrent Systems.* University of Newcastle upon Tyne, Department of Computing Science, Technical Report 495, Newcastle upon Tyne 1994.
15. Overman, W.T.: *Verification of Concurrent Systems: Function and Timing.* PhD thesis, University of California at Los Angeles 1981, 174 p.
16. Peled, D.: *All from One, One for All: on Model Checking Using Representatives.* In [2], pp. 409–423.
17. Peled, D.: *Combining Partial Order Reductions with On-the-Fly Model-Checking.* Formal Methods in System Design 8 (1996) 1, pp. 39–64.
18. Peled, D., and Penczek, W.: *Using Asynchronous Büchi Automata for Efficient Automatic Verification of Concurrent Systems.* In [3], pp. 115–130.
19. Ramakrishna, Y.S., and Smolka, S.A.: *Partial-Order Reduction in the Weak Modal Mu-Calculus.* Mazurkiewicz, A., and Winkowski, J. (Eds.), Proceedings of CON-CUR '97, Warsaw. LNCS 1243, Springer-Verlag 1997, pp. 5–24.
20. Rauhamaa, M.: *A Comparative Study of Methods for Efficient Reachability Analysis.* Helsinki University of Technology, Digital Systems Laboratory Report A 14, 1990, 61 p.
21. Reisig, W.: *Petri Nets: An Introduction.* EATCS Monographs on Theoretical Computer Science 4, Springer-Verlag 1985, 161 p.
22. Sloan, R.H., and Buy, U.: *Stubborn Sets for Real-Time Petri Nets.* Formal Methods in System Design 11 (1997) 1, pp. 23–40.
23. Valmari, A.: *A Stubborn Attack on State Explosion.* Formal Methods in System Design 1 (1992) 4, pp. 297–322.
24. Valmari, A.: *Stubborn Sets of Coloured Petri Nets.* Proceedings of PN '91, Gjern, Denmark, pp. 102–121.
25. Valmari, A.: *Alleviating State Explosion during Verification of Behavioural Equivalence.* University of Helsinki, Department of Computer Science, Report A-1992-4, 1992, 57 p.
26. Valmari, A.: *On-the-Fly Verification with Stubborn Sets.* In [2], pp. 397–408.
27. Varpaaniemi, K.: *On Combining the Stubborn Set Method with the Sleep Set Method.* Valette, R. (Ed.), Proceedings of PN '94, Zaragoza. LNCS 815, Springer-Verlag 1994, pp. 548–567.
28. Vernadat, F., Azéma, P., and Michel, F.: *Covering Step Graph.* Billington, J., and Reisig, W. (Eds.): Proceedings of PN '96, Osaka. LNCS 1091, Springer-Verlag 1996, pp. 516–535.
29. Yoneda, T., Shibayama, A., Schlingloff, B.-H., and Clarke, E.M.: *Efficient Verification of Parallel Real-Time Systems.* In [2], pp. 321–332.

A Compositional Petri Net Semantics for SDL[*]

Hans Fleischhack and Bernd Grahlmann

Fachbereich Informatik, Universität Oldenburg,
Postfach 2503, D-26111 Oldenburg,
fleischhack@informatik.uni-oldenburg.de
grahlmann@informatik.uni-oldenburg.de

Abstract. In this paper a compositional high-level Petri net semantics for SDL (Specification and Description Language) is presented. Emphasis is laid on the modelling of dynamic creation and termination of processes and of procedures – features, which are, for instance, essential for typical client-server systems.

In a preliminary paper we have already shown that we are able to use 'state of the art' verification techniques by basing our approach on M-nets (an algebra of high-level Petri nets). Therefore, this paper concentrates on the details of the semantics.

A distinctive feature of the presented solution is that the 'infinite case' (infinitely many concurrent process and procedure instances as well as unbounded capacities of input queues and channels) is covered.

Keywords: ARQ protocol, Compositionality, Concurrency, Dynamic Processes, Infinity, Petri Net Semantics, Procedures, SDL.

1 Introduction

This paper tackles two problems of the real world formal description technique SDL (Specification and Description Language [6]):

1. *Semantic ambiguities*: A lot of effort has been spent to standardise the language and to specify its semantics in the norm Z100 [6]. Nevertheless, ongoing discussions (e.g., in the SDL mailing list) show that different interpretations of crucial points (such as the atomicity of SDL transitions) still exist. A formal semantics may overcome this problem which is closely related to the large amount of several hundred pages of technical descriptions contained in the Z100 and its appendices.

2. *Lack of verification support*: There is a lack of appropriate tool support for fundamental tasks such as graphical simulation and real verification of SDL properties (such as 'Is it always possible to reach a state of the SDL system in which process π_1 is in state a and the local variable x of process π_2 has the value b and the input queue of process π_3 is empty?').

We suggest to translate SDL specifications into an algebra of high-level (HL) Petri nets to overcome these two problems. We have chosen M-nets (modular

---

[*] This work has been supported by the DFG (German Research Foundation), the HCM (Human Capital and Mobility) Cooperation Network EXPRESS, the Esprit Basic Research Working Group 6067 CALIBAN, and the Procope project POEM. It was carried out while the second author was with the Universität Hildesheim.

multilabelled Petri nets [2]) because their composition and communication operators allow us to define a semantic operator on M-nets for each syntactic operator of the SDL language. Thus, a fully compositional syntax-directed – and hence transparent – semantic mapping is defined. Properties of an SDL system may then be verified in the following five steps (cf. Fig. 1):

1. The M-net semantics of the SDL system is calculated.
2. The M-net is unfolded into a Petri box, a special low-level (LL) net [4].
3. The SDL property is transformed into a net property (similarly to [14]).
4. The net property is checked against the Petri box.
5. The result is transformed back to the SDL level.

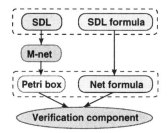

Fig.1. Overview of our approach.

In [10] we have already shown how 'state of the art' verification techniques can be applied. In particular, we have verified a couple of interesting safety, liveness, and progress properties of an ARQ (Automatic Repeat reQuest) communication protocol. We have used the verification component of the PEP tool (Programming Environment based on Petri nets) [5, 13] which presently includes partial order based model checking and algorithms based on linear programming as well as interfaces to other verification packages such as INA, SMV and SPIN providing reduction algorithms based on BDDs, on the stubborn set or sleep set method, and on symmetries. We have also given examples how the compositional nature of our semantics may be used to solve the 'state explosion' problem, and how interactive verification may extend the verification possibilities.

In this paper we focus on the semantics. Our intention is to provide the basis for a complete understanding which is even sufficient for the implementation of a compiler. Due to lack of space, it is not possible to cover full SDL (note that already its syntax hardly fits in 20 pages). Therefore, we have decided to omit parts, such as the abstract data type concept, which are nice but not essential if the main goal is verification. We rather focus on procedures and dynamic creation and termination of processes. These are important features, e.g., for the modelling of client-server systems.

1. Using procedures may enhance the readability of large SDL specifications by structuring the system description and by obeying the rule 'write things only once'.
2. Dynamic creation and termination of processes is even more essential because systems are (typically) not static as, e.g., the number of concurrent

client tasks may change dynamically. Moreover, test scenarios, specifying (or reducing the non-determinism of) the dynamic structure of the system explicitly, may be efficient.

Moreover, we take care that the 'infinite case' (infinitely many concurrent process and procedure instances as well as unbounded capacities of input queues and channels) is covered by the presented semantics. For the time being this is only relevant for simulation, but hopefully appropriate verification algorithms will soon be available.

The paper is organised as follows. The relevant part of SDL is briefly introduced in section 2 by considering our running example, a small client-server system. Section 3 very briefly presents the semantic model of M-nets. The core of the paper is the definition of the M-net semantics of SDL specifications (covering dynamic process creation and – also recursive – procedures) in section 4. After comparing our approach to related work, we conclude in section 6.

2   SDL by an example

SDL is a parallel programming language with a standardised graphical representation (GR) [6]. Especially in the area of telecommunication it is a quasi-standard for the specification of distributed systems. We present the most relevant SDL features very briefly by considering our running example, a simple ARQ (Automatic Repeat reQuest) communication protocol with alternating acknowledgement. We use the GR to enhance readability, although the formal semantics is based on the textual *phrase* representation (PR). This is no restriction because the PR is unique and can be generated automatically from the GR.

An SDL *system* comprises *processes*. The top level of the ARQ specification (cf. Fig. 2) shows two processes, Client (Client (1,2)) and Server (Server (1,1)). Each process declaration is labelled by two parameters (e.g., Client(1,2)) denoting the number of instances created initially and the maximum number of instances that may exist at the same time. A process instance may be created by any other instance of any process type, but can be terminated only by itself.

Fig.2. The ARQ-System.

In SDL communication between processes is established via (asynchronous) FIFO channels with an optional delay and a certain capacity, via (synchronous) signal routes, or combinations of both. In our example the two processes are connected via two signal routes, a and d. Signals of type ack (signal ack ({0,1})) or data with parameter type {0, 1} are transmitted.

For these communication purposes, each process instance owns an (asynchronous) input queue. Different instances of processes can be addressed with unique identifiers of the predefined type Pld of *process identifiers* (including the unique value null which is not used for an existing process). Therefore, each process instance contains four predefined variables of corresponding subtypes of Pld whose values are changed automatically:

- self: the instance itself,
- sender: the sender instance of the most recently consumed signal,
- parent: the instance that created this one, and
- offspring: the most recently created instance.

In Fig. 3 the two processes are specified. While the Server process has no parameter, the Client process has one value parameter (indicated by the keyword fpar). Both processes contain declarations ($\boxed{\text{dcl y \{0,1\};}}$) of local variables. Within this paper we restrict the allowed types to the set of Boolean values, the set of integers (both with the usual operations), and the set Pld. In addition, we allow these types for parameters of processes, procedures, and signals, i.e., for the list of formal parameters of a process declaration and for the list of value parameters (in) as well as for the list of reference parameters (in/out) of a procedure declaration.

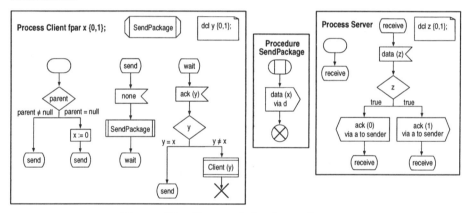

Fig.3. The *Client* and the *Server* Process.

The behaviour of the processes is described by state transitions. They specify the combinations of actions which may be executed if a certain input statement (e.g. $\boxed{\text{ack (y)}}$) is executable in a certain state (e.g. (wait)), and the next state. Examples for actions are process creations $\boxed{\text{Client (y)}}$, procedure invocations $\boxed{\boxed{\text{SendPackage}}}$, outputs $\boxed{\substack{\text{data (x)} \\ \text{via d}}}$, tasks $\boxed{\text{x := 0}}$, or decisions $\langle\text{parent}\rangle$. Initially, each process executes a special transition starting in the initial state ($\bigcirc$).

In this example a sequence of data packages labelled alternately by 0 and 1 should be transmitted. Each Client instance is responsible for the correct transmission of exactly one data package with the label x (which is the formal parameter) via the signal route d to the Server. The Server returns random acknowledgements via the signal route a specifying the receiver (sender) explicitly.

148

The initial instance (parent=null) sets the value of x to 0. The Client instance continues to send x (within the procedure SendPackage) until receipt of the corresponding acknowledgement. Then it creates the next Client instance (passing the next label as parameter) and terminates (✗) afterwards. The Server receives the data packages. Errors are modelled in the Server process by the non-deterministic choice between the answers, 0 and 1.

3 M-nets

This algebra of HL Petri nets has been introduced in [2]. In this paper we use an extension which is well-suited for the purpose of handling dynamic processes and procedures. In order to get an idea of these extensions we briefly characterise the places, transitions and arcs of an M-net. We will focus on the inscriptions because they support composition as well as unfolding (*labels* are used for the compositional construction of complex nets from simple ones while *annotations* drive the unfolding into LL nets).

– A *type* annotates places by a set of allowed tokens including natural numbers, Boolean values, the usual token •, and the special token †, or tuples of these. The label, its *status*, characterises a place as either 'entry' (without incoming arcs), 'exit' (without leaving arcs) or 'internal' (allowing all kinds of arcs). Under the *standard initial marking* each entry place is marked with its type.
– The annotation of a transitions is called *guard* or *value term*. It controls fireability (and thus unfolding). The synchronisation capabilities of a transition are described by its label, a multi set of *action terms*.
– Multisets of *expressions* are allowed as arc annotations. Upon occurrence of the adjacent transition, each expression is evaluated, yielding a token value which has to be removed from or, respectively, put on the adjacent place.

In contrast to [2] we allow entry- and exit-places with complex (i.e. non-singleton) types and tuples. This implies extensions of the composition operators. Moreover, we introduced additional operators, namely transition substitution and a special relabelling operator. Note that all the algebraic and coherence properties are retained [15].

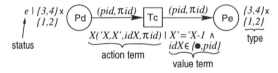

Fig.4. M-net example

We use the slightly simplified[1] part of an M-net (cf. Fig. 4) to explain the *transition rule* for M-nets: Suppose, that the entry place Pd is marked with a pair (3, 2). The variables in the arc inscriptions (*pid* and *πid*) can then only be bound to 3 and 2, respectively. An occurrence of Tc carries the pair (3, 2) from

[1] Brackets around arc annotations and action terms, empty sets and labels of internal places are omitted.

Pd to the internal place Pe. However, Tc can occur in infinitely many modes, because the action term contains variables ($'X$ and X') which are not sufficiently bound (($X'/5, 'X/6$) is a possible binding).

Synchronisation (followed by restriction) with transitions, whose action labels contain an action term of the form $\overline{X}(...)$ may restrict this set of occurrence modes. Upon occurrence, Tc then has to synchronise with such a transition and the variable-bindings of both transitions are unified. Synchronisation of an M-net N w.r.t. a set of action symbols A, followed by restriction is called *scoping* and is denoted as $[A : N]$.

4 Translating SDL specifications into M-nets

In this section, a semantic function ζ is defined which associates to each SDL system S an M-net $\zeta(S)$, the HL net semantics of S. $\zeta(S)$ may be unfolded into a Petri net $U(\zeta(S))$, the LL semantics of S. The semantic function satisfies the property that for each system S the LL semantics $U(\zeta(S))$ is a safe LL Petri net. We explain the definition of ζ by applying it top-down to our running example.

At a first look some of the figures appear complex and too detailed. This comes from the fact that we provide the basis for a complete understanding of the semantics, rather than reducing it to the main ideas. We suggest therefore to look first only at those parts of the figures which are explained in the text.

4.1 General remarks

We explain the translation of procedures and processes by considering the type of the tokens which are passed in the control flow. If neither procedures nor processes (with different instances) are involved, it is sufficient to use black tokens ($\bullet$). If different process instances are involved, process instance identifiers (πids) rather than black tokens are used. If both, procedure and process instances, are involved we use tuples ($pid, \pi id$) containing also a procedure identifier (pid).

Moreover, we use the '$\bullet$' as a pid, in the case of a control flow token outside any procedure, and as a πid, in the case of a control flow token of the net for the global SDL machine (which, e.g., initialises channels and signal routes and creates the initial process instances).

One of the major challenges is to give the complete definition in a coherent way. In order to achieve this, it is necessary to use two additional parameters for the semantic function ζ, namely a set of $pids$ and a set of πids. Moreover, we use some auxiliary functions within the definition of ζ to determine some sets:

- $Q(\Pi)$ contains the states of Π including the internal states $\bullet$ (for the intermediate state) and $\dagger$ (for the dead – i.e., going to terminate – state).
- $\mathcal{ID}(\Pi)$ contains the πids of Π.
- $\mathcal{ID}_s(\Pi)$, $\mathcal{ID}_r(\Pi)$, $\mathcal{ID}_p(\Pi)$, $\mathcal{ID}_o(\Pi)$ contain the πids that can send signals to Π, receive signals from Π, create Π, or be created by Π, respectively. Note that $\bullet$ is contained in these sets in order to represent null.
- $\mathcal{SIG}(\Pi)$ and $\mathcal{SIG}(C)$ contain the signals that can be sent to the process Π or be transmitted via the channel or signal route C, respectively. Note that $\bullet$ is contained in these sets in order to represent empty entries.
- $\mathcal{ID}(P)$ is the set containing the $pids$ of procedure P.

150

In the semantic model of SDL, there are several types of infinite objects. The capacity of a channel $(\mathcal{CAP}(C))$ and the capacity of the input queue of a process $(\mathcal{CAP}(\Pi))$ are unbounded and, the maximal number of instances of a process $(\mathcal{MAX}(\Pi))$ or of a procedure $(\mathcal{MAX}(P))$ may also be unbounded. Even though our semantics is able to handle these infinite objects, we assume that it is possible to limit the number of procedure instances which may be active at the same time and to impose a finite bound on the capacity of channels and input queues. Otherwise, only simulation of the resulting M-nets but not verification would be provided by the currently available tools. Note that these limits may be determined using the model checker by checking with an increasing upper bound until, e.g., the queue cannot be filled completely.

4.2   Semantics of an SDL system

The M-net semantics of an SDL system is the parallel composition of M-nets for its top-level objects. Each process, signal route and channel is translated into an M-net. Moreover, a net for the global control is added. It contains a sequence of initialisation transitions (one for each process, procedure, channel and signal route); one creation transition for each initial instance of each process (in the ARQ example one Client and one Server); exactly one transition for the simultaneous termination of all the processes; and the termination transitions (the same as initialisation).

The upper part of Fig. 5 shows this parallel composition for the ARQ system in an abstract way. It is also depicted that the nets for procedures, variables, formal parameters and the input queue are contained in the nets for the processes (e.g. Client contains SendPackage, y, x, Input queue). The net $\zeta(Global\ control)$ is not shown.

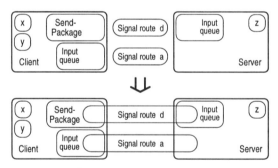

Fig.5. Translation scheme.

The bottom part of Fig. 5 shows that parts of the nets synchronise during the following scoping (e.g., the input queue of Client with the signal route a). The scoping is done w.r.t.:

- the initialisation, creation and termination actions of each process;
- the initialisation and termination actions of each procedure, channel and signal route;

- the input (from outside the process) actions of the input queues of each process denoted, e.g., by *Client!* (scoping w.r.t. output (to the inside of the process) actions is done within the M-net for the process the input queue belongs to); and
- the input (or receive) actions of each signal route and of each channel denoted, e.g., by *a!* (the output or forward actions collapse with input actions of another signal route, channel or input queue of a process).

The semantics for the whole ARQ system is given by the following equation:

$$\zeta(ARQ, \{\bullet\}, \{\bullet\}) = [\{\, Client_{init}, Client_{create}, Client_{term},$$
$$Server_{init}, Server_{create}, Server_{term}, SendPackage_{init}, SendPackage_{term},$$
$$a_{init}, a_{term}, d_{init}, d_{term}, Client!, Server!, a!, d!\} :$$
$$\zeta(Client, \{\bullet\}, \mathcal{ID}(Client)) \,\|\, \zeta(Server, \{\bullet\}, \mathcal{ID}(Server)) \,\|$$
$$\zeta(a, \{\bullet\}, \{\bullet\}) \,\|\, \zeta(d, \{\bullet\}, \{\bullet\}) \,\|\, \zeta(Global\ control, \{\bullet\}, \{\bullet\}) \,]$$

4.3 Semantics of an SDL process

The main part of the semantic function of a single process Π is the process net. Before we go into the details of this net we want to explain its basic structure shown in Fig. 6. The left most part deals with the initialisation and termination of the process net. In particular, a stack for the handling of the πids is initialised and terminated, respectively. This stack is accessed by a creation and a resume part. Besides performing the initialisation (and termination, respectively) of the implicit variables, the parameters, the state, and the input queue for one instance of the process, the body part of this instance is enabled (or disabled, respectively).

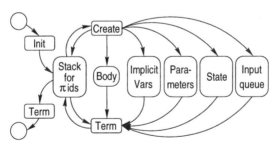

Fig.6. Abstract process net

The process net is constructed w.r.t. the definition of the in-parameters (in SDL processes do not have in/out-parameters) contained in *fpar-list* and the name of the process (further information is retrieved by the auxiliary functions such as $\mathcal{ID}(\Pi)$ or $\mathcal{SIG}(\Pi)$). We show the details of the process net in three steps. First, we explain the main part of the process net; second, the part for the implicit variables, the parameters, and the state; and finally the part for the input queue.

In contrast to earlier approaches (cf., e.g., [8]) we cover the case of infinitely many (simultaneous) process instances. Due to the necessity to avoid infinite arc inscriptions the net becomes more complex. In particular, πids have to be introduced on demand only and have to be removed step by step upon termination (cf. Fig. 7).

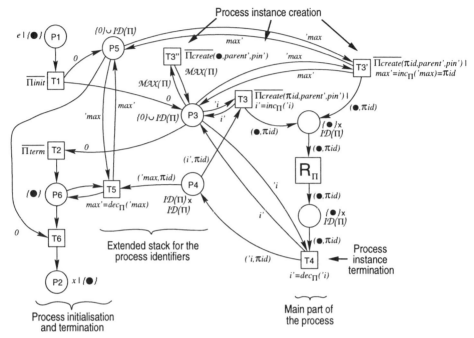

Fig.7. Main part of the SDL process net for a process Π with one parameter pin.

The stack for the handling of the πids is implemented by three places. P4 stores the available (currently not used) πids together with their position in the stack; P3 counts the number of active instances; and P5 counts the number of different πids which have already been used. The initialisation transition T1 (which synchronises with an initialisation transition in the global control net) initialises the two counters (to 0), but does not put a πid-entry on P4.

The stack for the πids is accessed by three different (mutually exclusive) process instance creation transitions:

1. T3 covers the 'normal' case that P4 is non-empty. The number of active instances is incremented $i' = inc_\Pi ('i)$ and the πid which is stored at that position $(i',\pi id)$ is inserted as a control flow token $(\bullet,\pi id)$. For consistency we use $(\bullet,\pi id)$ rather than πid, because for procedures we need tuples $(pid,\pi id)$. Note that the special transition R_Π will be substituted by the M-net $\zeta(body(\Pi))$ for the body of the process Π.

2. T3' is responsible for the introduction of πids if all πids which have been introduced so far are already in use.

3. Finally, T3" deals with the case that the maximum number of process instances is already active (in which case no new instance is created - $\bullet$ represents Null).

There is only one transition for the termination of a process instance. T4 simply pushes the πid to the stack and decrements the counter for the active instances.

The termination is performed stepwise. The 'real' termination transition T2 only removes a 0 from the place counting the active instances and thus prohibits further process instance creations. Afterwards, a sequence of occurrences of T5 step-by-step removes all πid-entries from P4 decrementing the counter for the used instances. Finally, if P4 is empty, T6 terminates the process net removing the last token (a 0) from P5.

Note that we are using process specific incrementation and decrementation functions (inc_{Π} and dec_{Π}, respectively). This is necessary because the πids of the different processes have to be disjoint in order to allow unique communication. Thus, e.g., if $\mathcal{ID}(\Pi) = \{3,6\}$ for a certain process Π, then $inc_{\Pi}(0) = 3$ and $inc_{\Pi}(3) = 6$. We recommend to play the token game to see how the mechanism for the storage of the πids works in practise.

The second part of the process net (cf. Fig. 8) comprises:

1. places for the implicit variables self, parent, offspring and sender (P7, P8, P9, and P10). The action terms of the corresponding transitions (T7, T8, T9, and T10) are used to change their values. The first parameter corresponds to the value before, the second to the value after a change, the third to the pid, and the fourth to the πid.

2. a place for each formal in-parameter in *fpar-list* (in our example *pin* with type *set1*) together with the appropriate transition to change its value (P11 and T11);

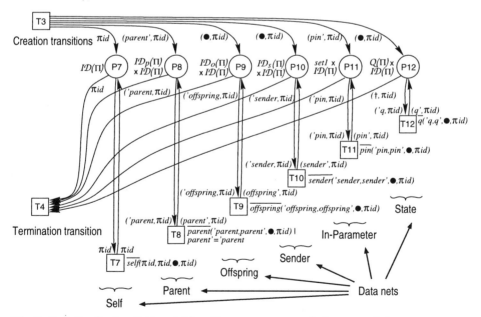

Fig.8. Part for the implicit variables, the parameters, and the state of the process net.

3. a place for the set $Q(\Pi)$ of states of the process together with an appropriate transition for state changes (P12 and T12). Note that in addition to the states defined explicitly in the declaration of the process, $Q(\Pi)$ contains the implicit states • and †, denoting *intermediate state* and *terminating state*, respectively.

The figure also depicts how this part is connected to the first part by the transitions T3 and T4. In fact, T3 abbreviates T3 and T3' which are both connected in the same way.

The part for the input queue with an arbitrary, possibly infinite capacity is also connected via T3, T3', and T4 to the main part of the process net and consists of (cf. Fig. 9):

1. P13 counting (per instance) the number of signals which are contained in the queue;
2. P14 containing (per instance) one entry (consisting of a position in the queue, the signal, and the πids of the sending as well as the receiving instance) for each stored signal and exactly one empty entry;
3. an input (from the outside of an instance) transition (T13). The action term is parameterised with the signal and the πids of the sender and the receiver. An input is always performed at the first position. At this position, an empty entry is replaced by an entry for the received signal and an empty entry is inserted at the first currently unused position.
4. an output (to the inside of the instance) transition (T14), which reads the (non-empty) entry from the last currently used position;
5. a shift transition (T15) which shifts empty entries towards the head of the queue;
6. a part for the stepwise emptying of the queue for the termination of an instance. T16 forwards the number of stored signals to the auxiliary place P15

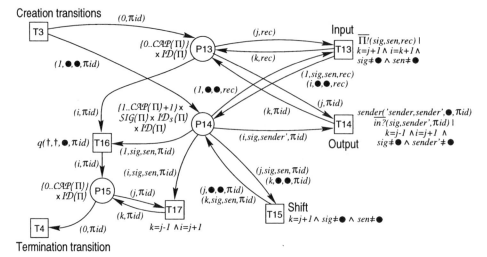

Fig.9. Part for the input queue of the process net.

and thus prohibits further inputs and outputs. The action term $q(\dagger, \dagger, \bullet, \pi id)$ ensures that the instance is going to be terminated. T17 removes step-by-step the entries from the queue.

Nets for all procedures which are declared within Π are put in parallel with the process net. The result is scoped w.r.t. self, parent, offspring, sender, q (for the state), $in?$ (for the output action of the input queue), $call$ and $return$ for each procedure, all relabelled in/out-parameters (of the procedures), all in-parameters of the process and all variables which are declared in the process.

For the Client process of our running example this corresponds to the following equation ($t \leftarrow N$ denotes substitution of (M-net) transition t by the M-net N – cf. [15]):

$$\zeta(Client, \{\bullet\}, \mathcal{ID}(Client)) = [\{\text{self, parent, offspring, sender}, q, in?,$$
$$SendPackage_{call}, SendPackage_{return}, x, y\} :$$
$$N_{Client}(x{:}\{0,1\}) [\text{R}_\Pi \leftarrow (\zeta(body(Client), \{\bullet\}, \mathcal{ID}(Client)))] \|$$
$$\zeta(SendPackage, \mathcal{ID}(SendPackage), \mathcal{ID}(Client))]$$

4.4 Semantics of the body of an SDL process

The M-net $\zeta(body(\Pi), \{\bullet\}, \mathcal{ID}(\Pi))$ for the body of Π, in turn, consists of:

1. a part for each declaration 'dcl $v : set;$' of a variable, given by a special M-net $M_{data}(v, set, \{\bullet\}, \mathcal{ID}(\Pi))$, called *data net* (which is explained later);
2. a sequence of:
   (a) a part for the initialisation of each variable v

$$\gamma^I(v, \{\bullet\}, \mathcal{ID}(\Pi)) = \underset{vinit(\bullet, \pi id)}{\bigcirc \overset{e \,|\, (\bullet) \times \mathit{ID}(\Pi)}{\underset{(\bullet, \pi id)}{\longrightarrow}} \Box \overset{x \,|\, (\bullet) \times \mathit{ID}(\Pi)}{\underset{(\bullet, \pi id)}{\longrightarrow}} \bigcirc});$$

   (b) a part for the control flow of the process ($\zeta(control(\Pi), \{\bullet\}, \mathcal{ID}(\pi))$);
   (c) a part for the termination of each variable v ($\gamma^T(v, \{\bullet\}, \mathcal{ID}(\Pi))$).

These are put in parallel and then scoped w.r.t. the action symbols for the initialisation and termination of the variables declared in Π. For the Client process we get:

$$\zeta(body(Client), \{\bullet\}, \mathcal{ID}(Client)) = [\{y_{init}, y_{term}\} :$$
$$M_{data}(y, \{0, 1\}, \{\bullet\}, \mathcal{ID}(Client)) \|(\gamma^I(y, \{\bullet\}, \mathcal{ID}(Client));$$
$$\zeta(control(Client), \{\bullet\}, \mathcal{ID}(Client)); \gamma^T(y, \{\bullet\}, \mathcal{ID}(Client)))]$$

4.5 Semantics of the control part of an SDL process

The control part of an SDL process consists of an (SDL) start transition and a set of other (SDL) transitions which either terminate the process or yield the next state. This is reflected in the semantics by an iteration construct.

- The (SDL) start transition is translated into the start net of the iteration.
- The main part of the iteration is the choice of the nets for the other (SDL) transitions and for an implicit transition. The net for the implicit transition consists of only one transition which covers the cases for which no SDL transitions are specified, i.e., certain signal consumptions in certain states.

- The exit part is an M-net (N_{exit}^{Π}) which ensures that the iteration is only exited if the state $q = \dagger$ is reached. This state is produced by the (M-net) transition that corresponds to the (SDL) termination.

For the control part of the Client process, which consists of a start transition *start* and two transitions *transition₁* and *transition₂* we have (cf. Fig. 10)[2]:

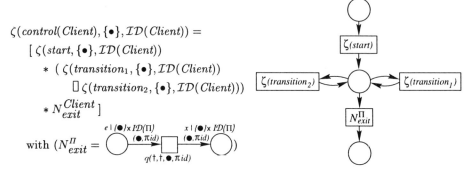

$$\zeta(\mathit{control}(\mathsf{Client}), \{\bullet\}, \mathcal{ID}(\mathsf{Client})) =$$
$$[\ \zeta(\mathit{start}, \{\bullet\}, \mathcal{ID}(\mathsf{Client}))$$
$$*\ (\ \zeta(\mathit{transition_1}, \{\bullet\}, \mathcal{ID}(\mathsf{Client}))$$
$$\square\ \zeta(\mathit{transition_2}, \{\bullet\}, \mathcal{ID}(\mathsf{Client})))$$
$$*\ N_{exit}^{\mathsf{Client}}\ ]$$
$$\text{with } (N_{exit}^{\Pi} =$$

Fig.10. Scheme for the transition loop.

4.6 Semantics of an SDL state transition

We do not describe the compositional derivation of the semantics of a state transition here, but merely explain some interesting points by considering the net semantics of the control part of the Client process (shown in Fig. 11). The part which corresponds to the two branches of the start transition is shown in the upper part (P1, T1, P2, T2, T3, P3, T4, P4, T5 and P5). The first state transition (cf. second transition in the left part of Fig. 3) corresponds to the loop consisting of T6, P6, T7, P7, T8, P8, T9 and P5. Finally, the left part of the net (T10, P9, T11, P10, T12, T13, P11, T14, P12, T15 and P5) corresponds to the second state transition.

We consider the first state transition of the Client process (shown in the middle of the left part of Fig. 3) consisting of three parts which are composed sequentially: Consuming of input none in state send, call of procedure SendPackage, and entering of state wait. These parts are represented in the semantic model by four sequentially connected transitions. The first one (T6) changes the state (currently send) to undefined ($\bullet$). The corresponding action synchronises with the data net for the state. Moreover, the variable for sender is set to πid (which is self) in order to be conform with the SDL specification for an input none. The second one causes a call to the procedure SendPackage, the third one (T8) a resume. Finally, the fourth one (T9) changes the state from undefined to wait.

T4 shows that the semantics of the individual parts of an (SDL) transition (such as a variable access x:=0) is always constructed in the same way, regardless whether they are part of a process or of a procedure. The adjacent arcs are

---

[2] We have omitted the part for the implicit transition because all combinations of possible inputs and states are already covered by the SDL specification.

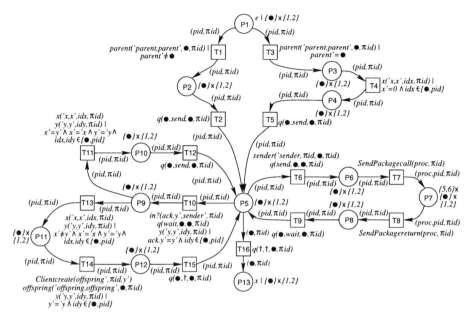

Fig.11. Net for the control part of the *Client* process.

always annotated with $(pid, \pi id)$, but the action term contains idx (instead of pid) together with the condition that idx is either pid (representing access of a local variable) or • (representing global for the process). The order of the scoping during the construction of the overall semantics (first w.r.t to local variables and then w.r.t. global variables) ensures that idx is bound correctly. The types of the adjacent places are determined by the second and the third parameter of the function ζ.

4.7 Semantics of an SDL variable

The semantics of a variable declaration 'dcl X : set;' is given by a special parameterised M-net (cf. Fig. 12). The first parameter of the net is the name of the variable, the second the type, the third the set of $pids$, and the last the set of πids. Thus, the above declaration yields $M_{data}(X, set, \{\bullet\}, \mathcal{ID}(\Pi))$ if X is declared within a process Π itself, and $M_{data}(X, set, \mathcal{ID}(P), \mathcal{ID}(\Pi))$ if X is declared inside a procedure P of a process Π.

The data net consists of four parts. T10 initialises an instance of the variable, and T13 terminates it. P12 stores the values of the variable instances (one for each combination of a pid and a πid). Finally, T12 is the counterpart for the variable access transitions within the control flow (e.g. T4 in Fig. 11).

4.8 Semantics of an SDL procedure

The semantics for the declaration of a procedure P with the formal parameter list *fpar-list* inside a process Π is given by the *procedure net* $N_P^\Pi(\text{fpar-list})$. This net is similar to the main part of the process net (cf. Fig. 7). We use Fig. 13

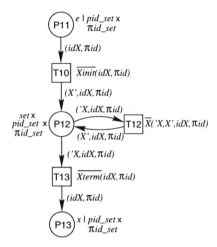

Fig. 12. The parameterised data net $M_{data}(X, set, pid\_set, \pi id\_set)$.

which gives the semantics of a procedure P with one in-parameter (*pin* with type *set1*) and one in/out-parameter (*pinout* with type *set2*) which is declared within the process Π to explain the main differences:

1. The stack handles *pids* instead of πids.
2. *(proc,πid)* instead of *($\bullet$,πid)* is introduced as a control flow token.

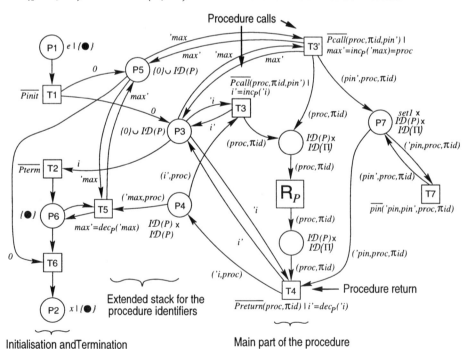

Fig. 13. The parameterised procedure net N_P^{Π} (*fpar-list*).

3. The transition R_P is substituted by the M-net $\zeta(body(P), \mathcal{ID}(P), \mathcal{ID}(\Pi))$ for the body of P which is (in the general case) first relabelled w.r.t. the in/out-parameters.
4. The case in which the maximum number of concurrent instances has been exceeded does not have to be handled explicitly by a transition T3".
5. A subnet which is similar to a data net $M_{data}(pin, set1, \mathcal{ID}(P), \mathcal{ID}(\Pi))$ deals with the formal in-parameter.

The procedure net is then scoped w.r.t. the access actions for the in-parameters. For the general case of a procedure P with the in-parameters $pin_1, ..., pin_n$ with types $set_1, ..., set_n$ (resp.) and the in/out-parameters $pinout_1, ..., pinout_m$ we get the following equation:

$$\zeta(P, \mathcal{ID}(P), \mathcal{ID}(\Pi)) = [\{pin_1, ..., pin_n\} : N_P^\Pi(pin_1 : set_1, ..., pin_n : set_n)[R_P \leftarrow$$
$$\Gamma_{\{pinout_1, ..., pinout_m\}}^P(\zeta(body(P), \mathcal{ID}(P), \mathcal{ID}(\Pi)))]$$

This yields the following for the procedure SendPackage of the Client process:

$$\zeta(SendPackage, \mathcal{ID}(SendPackage), \mathcal{ID}(Client)) = N_{SendPackage}^\Pi()[R_P \leftarrow$$
$$\Gamma_\emptyset^{SendPackage}(\zeta(body(SendPackage), \mathcal{ID}(SendPackage), \mathcal{ID}(Client)))]$$

Note that the construction of the net for the body of the procedure is similar to the the construction of the net for the body of a process.

4.9 Semantics of an SDL procedure call

The semantics of a call to a procedure P which is declared inside a process Π, is given by a special M-net N_{Pcall}. E.g., if the formal parameters of P are given by *fpar-list*, then we have the following equation for a call with actual parameters *actpar-list*: $\zeta(\text{call } P\ (actpar\text{-}list), pid\_set, \pi id\_set) =$
$$N_{Pcall}(fpar\text{-}list, actpar\text{-}list, pid\_set, \pi id\_set).$$
Fig. 14 shows the net (note the distinction between *pid_set* and $\mathcal{ID}(\mathcal{P})$)
$$N_{Pcall}^\Pi((\text{fpar in } pin\ set1, \text{ in/out } pinout\ set2), (X, Z), pid\_set, \pi id\_set)$$
of a call to the procedure P of Fig. 13 with actual parameters X and Z, respectively. This net consists of parts for:

1. *Initialisation:* T7 initiates a call. It synchronises at the same time with the Pcall transition T3 (or T3') of the procedure net (cf. Fig. 13) and with the access transition T12 of the data net (cf. Fig. 12) for the actual in-parameter X. Thus, occurrence of the resulting transition causes the actual value of X to appear on P7 in the procedure net and, in addition, forwards the control flow token, extended by the *pid* (*proc*) of the just created procedure instance, to P8 and P9.
2. *Handling of in/out-parameters:* T8 synchronises with each transition inside the procedure net accessing *pinout* and with the access transition of the data net of Z. Hence, each access to *pinout* causes a corresponding access to the actual parameter Z. Note that this mechanism also works in the case where Z is not a variable, but another – or even the same – in/out-parameter, which might occur with recursive calls or calls within nested procedures.

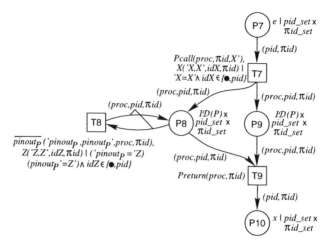

Fig.14. M-net for the call $P(X, Z)$ of procedure P with the reference parameter *pinout*.

Corresponding to the relabelling, which is applied to the procedure net, *pinout* is renamed to *pinout$_P$*. This avoids possible name clashes between the formal in/out-parameter *pinout* and a variable, which might be declared in the environment. Each in/out-parameter has its own subnet (consisting of P8 and T8) within each call net. Otherwise, simultaneous accesses to different in/out-parameters would not be possible.

3. *Termination*: T9 synchronises with the return transition T4 of the procedure net.

4.10 Semantics of an SDL channel

In SDL, communication between processes is modelled by channels and signal routes. Moreover, according to the standard semantics of SDL, each process has an implicit input queue which acts like a channel and which is represented in the M-net semantics of the process (cf. Fig. 9).

A channel may receive input from processes, or another channel, or a signal route. Although there may be multiple input (or *From*) parts, signals are always forwarded to the same output port *To* which may be a process (possibly the same as the sender), or another channel, or a signal route. Signals have a certain type $\mathcal{SIG}(C)$ and the type of a channel is $SIG(C) \times \mathcal{ID}_s(C) \times \mathcal{ID}_r(C)$. ($\mathcal{ID}_s(C)$ denotes the set which contains the πids of all processes whose signals may be transmitted via C, and $\mathcal{ID}_r(C)$ contains the πids of all processes to which signals may be directed via C.) Signals are forwarded after a non-deterministic delay (signal routes cover the case of no-delay channels). The semantics of a channel C is defined by:
$$\zeta(C, \{\bullet\}, \{\bullet\}) = M_{channel}(C, To)$$

The channel net $M_{channel}(C, To)$, (cf. Fig. 15), is parameterised with the name of the channel C and the name of the output side *To*. The mechanism for the modelling of the queue is basically the same as for the input queue (cf. Fig. 9). In particular, the number of tokens (including exactly one empty entry)

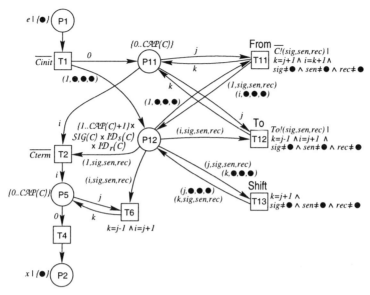

Fig.15. M-net $M_{channel}(C, To)$ for a channel C.

depends on the number of stored signals; input is performed at the first position and output at the last position which is in use; a shift transition shifts the empty entry towards the first position; and termination is done step-by-step. The main difference is that the contents of the queue are not specific for one process instance, i.e., signals with different senders and/or receivers are stored.

4.11 Semantics of an SDL signal route

The semantics of a signal route R is similar to the semantics of a channel:

$$\zeta(R, \{\bullet\}, \{\bullet\}) = M_{route}(R, To)$$

However, the net $M_{route}(R, To)$ for a signal route R is much simpler (cf. Fig. 16). It provides synchronous (no-delay) communication of signals with type $\mathcal{SIG}(R)$ between $\mathcal{ID}_s(R)$ and $\mathcal{ID}_r(R)$. Synchronism is achieved by providing only one transition for both, the *From* part and the *To* part. The type $\{\bullet\}$ is sufficient for P2 because no entries have to be stored.

5 Related work

Following the definition of a formal semantics for SDL in the middle of the eighties, Petri nets became a popular formal model for the analysis of SDL specifications. [12] contains an extensive discussion of the early approaches. As pointed out, in general these were not sufficient, since only control flow was represented in their Petri net models, whereas local data were neglected.

Other Petri net semantics for (parts of) the SDL language have found their way into SDL-tools; some examples are [7, 16]. All of these have their own merits, but, as we claim, none of them at the same time satisfies the requirements

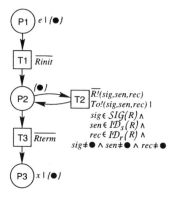

Fig.16. M-net $M_{route}(R, To)$ for a signal route.

of compositionality and transparency and allows the application of the most important 'state of the art' model checking packages.

The Petri net semantics given in this paper can be considered as an extension of the one presented in [1] (where neither dynamic processes, nor procedures, nor the infinite case have been covered). We adapted and extended the techniques developed in [9] for the handling of procedures in the parallel programming language B(PN)^2 in order to be able to handle procedures and dynamic creation and termination of processes in SDL.

An orthogonal extension of [1] (which also does not cover dynamic processes, procedures, and the infinite case, but which may be combined with our approach) is presented in [11]. Real-time requirements are added, and a compositional semantics for the resulting language is given in terms of Time-M-nets, which may be used to check also quantitative temporal properties of SDL-specifications.

In the EMMA (Extendible Multi Method Analyzer) project [16], a tool is constructed for the analysis of TeleNokia SDL (TNSDL), which is a dialect of SDL-88. An SDL system is translated into a formal validation model using high-level Petri nets. This model is analysed with the PROD reachability graph analyser [17]. The aim is to cover full TNSDL, i.e., the tool is planned to manage TeleNokia-specific applications. Hence, in contrast to our approach, not so much emphasis is laid on conformance with the published standard semantics of SDL. E.g., SDL transitions are handled as atomic actions in the EMMA approach and are represented by a single transition at the Petri net level. This is a suitable solution for their special purposes, but not in general. Especially in the area of client-server systems, it is often necessary to build systems whose SDL transitions are not atomic. The non atomicity of a real (executable) implementation should be a good reason for reflecting it in the semantics which is used for the verification. Otherwise, in many cases, errors hidden inside a transition cannot be properly localised in the design phase.

[7] describes the use of Petri nets for analysis and formal verification of SDL specifications within the SITE (SDL Integrated Tools Environment) project. Again, industrial applicability, and not semantic foundation, is the primary goal. For the analysis of SDL specifications, the class of *SDL Time Nets* is introduced,

which extends place/transition nets by guards and time intervals for transitions, and data structures for (special) places. An SDL system is translated into an SDL time net. This covers all features of SDL'92 without any essential restrictions. To yield small net models, also this approach deviates from the standard semantics of SDL at some points. E.g., in the translation of a process declaration, the implicit variables self, sender, parent and offspring are neglected. Also, the guard functions for net transitions and the data structures for process variables and signal parameters have to be coded into C-programs by the user. Thus, the same holds true as for the EMMA approach: it is an appropriate solution for their special purposes, but not a general one.

6 Conclusion and future work

Based on the algebra of M-nets, a flexible and powerful high-level metalanguage, we have presented a fully compositional and transparent semantics of SDL specifications. This Petri net semantics covers dynamic creation and termination of processes as well as (also recursive) procedures, and allows all types of parameters available in SDL. Although we covered the 'infinite case' (infinitely many concurrent process and procedure instances as well as unbounded capacities of input queues and channels), the resulting nets are optimised w.r.t. verification. Moreover, we have followed the standard semantics of SDL as given in Annex F of [6] as closely as possible.

The benefits of our approach are twofold. On the one hand, we have given (the main part of) a completely precise semantic definition avoiding, e.g., ambiguities which are inherent to textual descriptions. On the other hand, our semantics allows verification of SDL specifications. As demonstrated in [10] safety, liveness and progress properties can be checked efficiently[3] using 'state of the art' verification techniques which are already integrated in the PEP tool [3, 5, 13]. Moreover, the compositional nature of the semantics supports compositional and interactive verification methods [10]. This is an important criteria as well as an interesting topic for further research because it is still not realistic to check real world SDL specifications fully automatically.

Acknowledgement: We would like to thank Josef Tapken for his earlier work on the semantics, Eike Best and anonymous referees for comments on the paper, and Stefan Schwoon for the implementation of the semantics which allowed the integration in the PEP tool.

References

1. P. Amthor, H. Fleischhack, and J. Tapken. MOBY – more than a Tool for the Verification of SDL-Specifications. Technical Report, Universität Oldenburg, 1996.

---

[3] The ARQ example yields an M-net with 64 places and 36 transitions. It unfolds to a low-level net with 137 places and 106 transitions for which most of the properties can be checked in less than five seconds.

2. E. Best, H. Fleischhack, W. Frączak, R. P. Hopkins, H. Klaudel, and E. Pelz. A Class of Composable High Level Petri Nets. In G. De Michelis and M. Diaz, editors, *Proc. of ATPN'95 (Application and Theory of Petri Nets), Torino*, volume 935 of *LNCS*, pages 103–118. Springer, June 1995.

3. E. Best. Partial Order Verification with PEP. In G. Holzmann, D. Peled, and V. Pratt, editors, *Proc. of POMIV'96 (Partial Order Methods in Verification.* Am. Math. Soc., 1996.

4. E. Best, R. Devillers, and J. G. Hall. The Box Calculus: a New Causal Algebra with Multi-Label Communication. In G Rozenberg, editor, *Advances in Petri Nets 92*, volume 609 of *LNCS*, pages 21 – 69. Springer-Verlag, 1992.

5. E. Best and B. Grahlmann. PEP: Documentation and User Guide. Universität Oldenburg., 1998. Availabe together with the tool via: http://theoretica.informatik.uni-oldenburg.de/~pep.

6. CCITT. *Specification and Description Language, CCITT Z.100, Geneva.* International Consultative Committee on Telegraphy and Telephony, 1992.

7. J. Fischer, E. Dimitrov, and U. Taubert. Analysis and Formal Verification of SDL'92 Specifications using Extended Petri Nets. Technical report, Humboldt-Universität zu Berlin, 1995.

8. H. Fleischhack and B. Grahlmann. A Compositional Petri Net Semantics for SDL. Technical report, Universität Hildesheim, November 1997.

9. H. Fleischhack and B. Grahlmann. A Petri Net Semantics for B(PN)^2 with Procedures. In *Proc. of PDSE'97 (Parallel and Distributed Software Engineering)*, pages 15 – 27. IEEE Computer Society, May 1997.

10. H. Fleischhack and B. Grahlmann. Towards Compositional Verification of SDL Systems. In *Proc. of 31st HICSS (Hawaii International Conference on System Science) – Software Technology Track*, pages 404 – 414. IEEE Computer Society, January 1998.

11. H. Fleischhack and J. Tapken. An M-Net Semantics for a Real-Time Extension of μSDL. In *Proc. of FME'97*, LNCS. Springer-Verlag, 1997.

12. J. Grabowski. Statische und dynamische Analysen für SDL-Spezifikationen auf der Basis von Petri-Netzen und Sequence-Charts. Diplomarbeit, Universität Hamburg, 1990.

13. B. Grahlmann. The PEP Tool. In Orna Grumberg, editor, *Proc. of CAV'97 (Computer Aided Verification)*, volume 1254 of *LNCS*, pages 440–443. Springer-Verlag, June 1997.

14. B. Grahlmann. The Reference Component of PEP. In Ed Brinksma, editor, *Proc. of TACAS'97 (Tools and Algorithms for the Construction and Analysis of Systems)*, volume 1217 of *LNCS*, pages 65–80. Springer-Verlag, April 1997.

15. B. Grahlmann. *Parallel Programs as Petri Nets.* Ph.D. thesis, Universität Hildesheim, 1998.

16. N. Husberg, M. Malmquist, and T. Jyrinki. Emma: An SDL Analyzer Using High Level Petri Nets. Technical report, Helsinki University of Technology, 1996.

17. K. Varpaaniemi, J Halme, K Hiekkanen, and T Pyssysalo. PROD Reference Manual. Technical report 13, Helsinki University of Technology, August 1995.

An Axiomatisation of Duplication Equivalence in the Petri Box Calculus

Martin Hesketh[1,2] and Maciej Koutny[1]

[1] Department of Computing Science, University of Newcastle, Newcastle upon Tyne
NE1 7RU, U.K.
[2] Nortel PND, Concorde Road, Norreys Drive, Maidenhead, SL6 4AG, U.K.

Abstract. The Petri Box Calculus (PBC) consists of an algebra of box
expressions, and a corresponding algebra of boxes (a class of labelled
Petri nets). A compositional semantics provides a translation from box
expressions to boxes. There are several alternative ways of defining an
equivalence notion for boxes, the strongest one being net isomorphism. In
this paper we consider slightly weaker notion of equivalence, called *duplication equivalence*, which still can be argued to capture a very close structural similarity of concurrent systems represented by boxes. We transfer
the notion of duplication equivalence to the domain of box expressions
and investigate the relationship between duplication equivalent boxes
and box expressions. The main result of this investigation is a sound
and complete axiomatisation of duplication equivalence for a fragment
of recursion-free PBC.
Keywords: Net-based algebra; analysis of structure of nets; verification
using nets; equivalence and axiomatisation.

1   Introduction

Petri nets [20] and process algebras [1, 10, 13, 18] are two widely used and re-
searched models for concurrency. Petri nets have a partial order, or *true concurrency* behaviour, allowing reasoning about causal relationships between events.
In comparison, process algebras are generally based on interleaving behaviours.
The Petri net model, which is graphical in nature, does not readily support the
composition of nets. This makes it more difficult to produce modular designs for
systems than in process algebra based framework.

The Petri Box Calculus (PBC) [2, 3, 5, 6, 8, 16] has been designed to combine
the advantages of both Petri nets and process algebras. The PBC consists of
an algebra of box expressions, and a corresponding algebra of boxes (a class
of labelled Petri nets). A compositional semantics provides a translation from
box expressions to boxes. Earlier approaches to giving a Petri net interpretation
to a process algebra, e.g. [9, 19], have been based on algebras with an existing
semantics in a model other than Petri nets. Note that the design of the PBC does
not preclude a semantics being given in purely process algebraic terms [17, 15].
For example, [15] gives a partial order structural operational semantics for box
expressions which is consistent with the corresponding partial order semantics

of boxes. PBC allows the semantics of high level programming constructs to be simulated, verified and reasoned about at the level of Petri nets. In this respect, the PBC lies midway between Petri nets and high level programming languages such as occam [14] and B(PN)² [4]. The PBC can be considered an extension of CCS [18], providing a more general synchronisation scheme and support for iteration.

One of the main motivations behind the development of the PBC was to make it possible to support in a single framework different verification techniques developed independently for process algebras and Petri nets. An example of the latter is the compositional S-invariant analysis [7]. In this paper we consider one of the standard verification techniques developed for process algebras, namely axiomatisation of behavioural equivalence [18].

There are several alternative ways of defining an equivalence notion for boxes, the strongest one being net isomorphism. In this paper we consider slightly weaker notion of equivalence, called *duplication equivalence* [2], which still can be argued to capture a very close structural similarity of concurrent systems represented by boxes. In essence, duplication equivalent boxes should be equivalent with respect to every reasonable notion of behavioural equivalence. Thus duplication equivalence plays a fundamental role in the PBC approach and deserves a due investigation. In this paper we transfer the notion of duplication equivalence to the domain of box expressions and investigate the relationship between it and the structure of a box expression. The main result of this investigation is a sound and complete axiomatisation of duplication equivalence for a fragment of recursion-free PBC.

The paper is organised as follows. In section 2 we define Petri nets which are used throughout the rest of this paper, and introduce the notion of duplication equivalence. Section 3 discusses the relationship between the operation of synchronisation and duplication equivalence; the remaining operators of the PBC used in this paper are described in the appendix. Section 4 defines box expressions and boxes – a class of Petri nets used in the PBC – and transfers the results on duplication equivalence obtained for boxes to the domain of box expressions. Section 5 contains the proposed axiomatisation of duplication equivalence. It is followed by the discussion of soundness of completeness, in section 6. Finally, we briefly discuss some of the issues related to the proposed axiomatisation. All the proofs can be found in [12].

2 Labelled nets

In what follows, we assume two infinite disjoint sets of elements, called *places* and *transitions* — jointly referred to as *nodes* — and an infinite set of *actions*. Any set of nodes N can be labelled using a *label function* which must return either one of the three special symbols (which are not actions), e, i and x, if applied to a place, or an action if applied to a transition. A *weight function* for N is a mapping from the Cartesian product $N \times N$ to the set of non-negative integers such that it always returns zero for a pair of places or a pair of transitions.

We adopt the standard Petri net way of representing places and transitions as respectively circles and rectangles.

A *net* is a tuple $\mathcal{N} = (S, T, W, \lambda)$ such that S and T are finite sets of respectively places and transitions, and W and λ are respectively a weight and label function for the set of nodes $S \cup T$. A place labelled by e is an *entry* place, by i an *internal* place, and by x an *exit* place. By convention, $^{\circ}\mathcal{N}$ and $\mathcal{N}^{\circ}$ will denote, respectively, the entry and exit places of $\mathcal{N}$. We will later use the entry and exit places to compose nets. For every node n in $\mathcal{N}$, we use $^{\bullet}n$ to denote its *pre-set* which comprises all the nodes m such that $W(m, n) \geq 1$. The *post-set* $n^{\bullet}$ is defined in a similar way. This notation extends in the usual way to sets of nodes. A transition t is *simple* if $W(s, t) \leq 1$ and $W(t, s) \leq 1$, for every place s. The net is *T-restricted* if the pre-set and post-set of every transition are non-empty. An *isolated* place is one whose pre-set and post-set are empty.

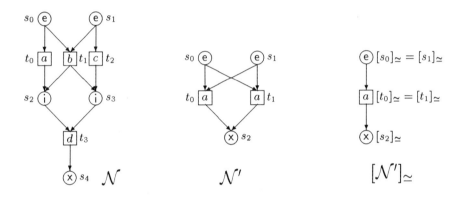

Fig. 1. Two labelled nets and a duplication quotient.

A *labelled net* is a T-restricted net without isolated places. Figure 1 shows a labelled net $\mathcal{N}$ such that

$$S = \{s_0, s_1, s_2, s_3, s_4\}$$
$$T = \{t_0, t_1, t_2, t_3\}$$
$$\lambda = \{(s_0, \mathsf{e}), (s_1, \mathsf{e}), (s_2, \mathsf{i}), (s_3, \mathsf{i}), (s_4, \mathsf{x}), (t_0, a), (t_1, b), (t_2, c), (t_3, d)\}$$

and $W(m, n) = 1$ for $(m, n) \in \{(s_0, t_0), (s_0, t_1), (s_1, t_1), (s_1, t_2), (s_2, t_3), (s_3, t_3),$ $(t_0, s_2), (t_1, s_2), (t_1, s_3), (t_2, s_3), (t_3, s_4)\}$; and $W(m, n) = 0$ otherwise. $\mathcal{N}$ is T-restricted, its entry places are s_0 and s_1, and its only exit place is s_4. We will later see that $\mathcal{N}$ corresponds to the box expression $((a||c) \,\square\, b); d$, where $||$ denotes parallel, $\square$ choice, and the semicolon sequential composition. We will often decorate the different components of a net $\mathcal{N}$ with the index $_{\mathcal{N}}$. The same convention will apply to other notations we subsequently introduce.

We will use the notation $n_1 \ldots n_k \bowtie m_1 \ldots m_l$ to mean that the 'sum' of the weight functions of nodes $n_1, \ldots, n_k$ is the same as the 'sum' of the weight functions of nodes $m_1, \ldots, m_l$. That is, for every node n in $\mathcal{N}$,

$$\sum_{i=1}^{k} W(n_i, n) = \sum_{i=1}^{l} W(m_i, n) \quad \text{and} \quad \sum_{i=1}^{k} W(n, n_i) = \sum_{i=1}^{l} W(n, m_i).$$

We will also say that $n_1, \ldots, n_k$ have the same *connectivity* as $m_1, \ldots, m_l$. For the net of figure 1 we have $t_1 \bowtie_{\mathcal{N}} t_0 t_2$. To simplify some of the definitions we will use δ to denote a 'dummy' simple transition which, if present, would satisfy ${}^\bullet\delta = {}^\circ\mathcal{N}$ and $\delta^\bullet = \mathcal{N}^\circ$. For example, $t \bowtie \delta u$ should be interpreted as signifying that $W(s, t) = W(s, u) + 1$, for all $s \in {}^\circ\mathcal{N}$, and $W(s, t) = W(s, u)$ otherwise; and $W(t, s) = W(u, s) + 1$, for all $s \in \mathcal{N}^\circ$, and $W(t, s) = W(u, s)$ otherwise.

A *duplicate* of a node n of a net $\mathcal{N}$ is a node m which has the same label and connectivity as n, i.e. $\lambda(n) = \lambda(m)$ and $n \bowtie m$. We denote this by $n \simeq m$, and the equivalence class of $\simeq$ containing n will be denoted by $[n]_\simeq$.

An *isomorphism* for two nets, $\mathcal{N}$ and $\mathcal{M}$, is a bijective mapping h from the nodes of $\mathcal{N}$ to the nodes of $\mathcal{M}$ such that for all the nodes n, m in $\mathcal{N}$, $\lambda_{\mathcal{N}}(n) = \lambda_{\mathcal{M}}(h(n))$ and $W_{\mathcal{N}}(n, m) = W_{\mathcal{M}}(h(n), h(m))$. In other words, h is a graph isomorphism for $\mathcal{N}$ and $\mathcal{M}$ which preserves node labelling.

Net union is a partial operation defined only for pairs of *unionable* nets which means that their transition sets are disjoint and their label functions coincide on the common places. The *union* $\mathcal{N} \cup \mathcal{M}$ of two unionable nets, $\mathcal{N}$ and $\mathcal{M}$, is defined as a net with the node set being the union of the nodes of $\mathcal{N}$ and $\mathcal{M}$, and the weight and label functions being inherited from $\mathcal{N}$ and $\mathcal{M}$ (if the value for a weight in the new net cannot be found in the original nets, it is set to zero).

Let $\mathcal{N}$ and $\mathcal{M}$ be unionable nets. Net union will usually be applied when the common places can be partitioned into $\otimes$-sets created by the operation of place multiplication (itself denoted by $\otimes$, see the appendix). A non-empty set of places $P \subseteq S_{\mathcal{N}} \cap S_{\mathcal{M}}$ is a $\otimes$-*set* if for all $s, r \in P$ there is $p \in P$ such that $s \simeq_{\mathcal{N}} p$ and $r \simeq_{\mathcal{M}} p$.

For $\mathcal{N}$ a labelled net, the *duplication quotient* is the labelled net

$$[\mathcal{N}]_\simeq = (\; \{\; [s]_\simeq \mid s \in S \;\} , \; \{\; [t]_\simeq \mid t \in T \;\} , \; W' , \; \lambda' \;)$$

where for all the nodes n and m in $\mathcal{N}$, $W(n, m) = W'([n]_\simeq, [m]_\simeq)$ and $\lambda(n) = \lambda'([n]_\simeq)$. Figure 1 shows a labelled net $\mathcal{N}'$ and its duplication quotient $[\mathcal{N}']_\simeq$. We now can introduce a notion central to this paper.

Labelled nets $\mathcal{N}$ and $\mathcal{M}$ are *duplication equivalent* if their duplication quotients are isomorphic nets. We denote this by $\mathcal{N} \simeq \mathcal{M}$ or $\mathcal{N} \simeq_h \mathcal{M}$, where h is an isomorphism for $[\mathcal{N}]_\simeq$ and $[\mathcal{M}]_\simeq$. As it was shown in [2], $\simeq$ is an equivalence relation. This can be slightly strengthened thus. For all labelled nets $\mathcal{N}, \mathcal{M}$ and $\mathcal{P}$, $\mathcal{N} \simeq_h \mathcal{M}$ and $\mathcal{M} \simeq_g \mathcal{P}$ implies $\mathcal{N} \simeq_{hog} \mathcal{P}$.

Duplication equivalence has been introduced in [2], under the name of *renaming* equivalence, as a structural equivalence relation on Petri nets used in PBC. It preserves both interleaving and partial order semantics of nets, provided we mark them initially by putting exactly one token in each of the entry places and no token on any other place[1]. Duplication equivalence is a congruence with respect to all the net operators considered in [2] and hence also with respect to the net operators used in this paper.

We will often be dealing with labelled nets $\mathcal{N}$ and $\mathcal{M}$ which are *place-sharing*, by which we mean that their place sets and place labellings are exactly the same (no conditions are imposed on the transition sets). In such a case, for all transitions t in $\mathcal{N}$ and u in $\mathcal{M}$, we denote $t \simeq_{\mathcal{N}\mathcal{M}} u$ if $\lambda_{\mathcal{N}}(t) = \lambda_{\mathcal{M}}(u)$ and for every place s in $\mathcal{N}$ (and so in $\mathcal{M}$), $W_{\mathcal{N}}(t,s) = W_{\mathcal{M}}(u,s)$ and $W_{\mathcal{N}}(s,t) = W_{\mathcal{M}}(s,u)$. Intuitively, $t \simeq_{\mathcal{N}\mathcal{M}} u$ means that t and u are 'distant' duplicates since they have the same connectivity if one looks at the places of the two nets.

An isomorphism h for the duplication quotients of $\mathcal{N}$ and $\mathcal{M}$ establishing duplication equivalence of place-sharing nets, $\mathcal{N}$ and $\mathcal{M}$, will be called *place-preserving* if $[h(s)]_{\simeq} = [s]_{\simeq}$, for every place s in the two nets. We will denote this by $\mathcal{N} \cong_h \mathcal{M}$ or $\mathcal{N} \cong \mathcal{M}$. Note that there can be at most one place-preserving isomorphism (between the respective duplication quotients) establishing duplication equivalence of two place-sharing nets.

3 Net Operators

To define a synchronisation operator on nets, we impose a little structure on the set of actions. We assume that it consists of *communication* actions, A, and a distinct *internal* action, $\imath$. There is a bijection $\hat{}: A \rightarrow A$ such that $\hat{a} \neq a$ and $\hat{\hat{a}} = a$, for every a in A. The actions a and $\hat{a}$ will be called *conjugates*. By a *synchronisation set* we will mean a set of communication actions A which contains the conjugates of all its actions, i.e. $\hat{A} = A$. For every communication action a, we will denote by a the synchronisation set $\{a, \hat{a}\}$. As in CCS, it is implicitly assumed that two transitions labelled with conjugate communication actions can be synchronised to yield a new transition labelled with the internal action.[2] Two transitions, t and u, whose labels are conjugates belonging to a synchronisation set A are *A–synchronisable*.

The *synchronisation* of a labelled net $\mathcal{N}$ by a synchronisation set A is a net $\mathcal{N}$ sy A which is defined as $\mathcal{N}$ extended by a set of new transitions. Exactly one new transition, $t \odot u$, is added for every pair of A–synchronisable transitions of $\mathcal{N}$, t and u. The label of $t \odot u$ is $\imath$ and the weight function is extended so that $t \odot u \bowtie_{\mathcal{N} \text{ sy } A} tu$. We also assume that $t \odot u$ is the same as $u \odot t$. Figure 2 shows two consecutive applications of the synchronisation operator. Note that $\mathcal{N}$ sy a and $(\mathcal{N}$ sy a) sy a are duplication equivalent, but not isomorphic. Thus synchronisation is not idempotent with respect to net isomorphism. However,

---

[1] Such markings are the standard initial markings of boxes; we do not represent them explicitly here since we are concerned purely with the structure of the underlying nets.

[2] The synchronisation mechanism used in this paper is basically that of CCS; the original one used in PBC [2] is more general and can also express more complex, multi-way, synchronisation.

it is idempotent with respect to duplication equivalence which was one of the reasons for introducing it in [2].

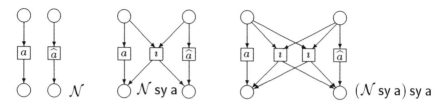

Fig. 2. Synchronisation (place labels omitted).

The following proposition gathers together a number of facts involving synchronisation and duplication equivalence.

Proposition 1. *Let $\mathcal{N}$ be a labelled net, and A and B be synchronisation sets.*

1. $\mathcal{N} \simeq \mathcal{N} \,\mathsf{sy}\, A$ *if and only if* $\mathcal{N} \cong \mathcal{N} \,\mathsf{sy}\, A$.
2. $\mathcal{N} \,\mathsf{sy}\, A \,\mathsf{sy}\, B \cong \mathcal{N} \,\mathsf{sy}\, (A \cup B)$.
3. *If* $\mathcal{N} \,\mathsf{sy}\, A \simeq \mathcal{N} \,\mathsf{sy}\, B$ *then* $\mathcal{N} \,\mathsf{sy}\, A \cong \mathcal{N} \,\mathsf{sy}\, B$.
4. *If* $A \subseteq B$ *and* $\mathcal{N} \simeq \mathcal{N} \,\mathsf{sy}\, B$ *then* $\mathcal{N} \cong \mathcal{N} \,\mathsf{sy}\, A$.
5. *If* $\mathcal{N} \simeq \mathcal{N} \,\mathsf{sy}\, A$ *and* $\mathcal{N} \simeq \mathcal{N} \,\mathsf{sy}\, B$ *then* $\mathcal{N} \cong \mathcal{N} \,\mathsf{sy}\, (A \cup B)$.
6. $(\mathcal{N}_1 \cup \ldots \cup \mathcal{N}_k) \,\mathsf{sy}\, A \cong ((\mathcal{N}_1 \,\mathsf{sy}\, A) \cup \ldots \cup (\mathcal{N}_k \,\mathsf{sy}\, A)) \,\mathsf{sy}\, A$.
7. *If* $\mathcal{M}$ *is a labelled net such that* $\mathcal{N} \simeq \mathcal{M} \,\mathsf{sy}\, A$ *then* $\mathcal{N} \cong \mathcal{N} \,\mathsf{sy}\, A$. $\qquad\square$

The PBC employs net operators which aim at capturing common concurrent programming constructs. We have already introduced synchronisation. The remaining four PBC operators used in this paper are the choice, parallel, sequence and iteration compositions, denoted respectively by $\mathcal{N}_1 \,\square\, \mathcal{N}_2$, $\mathcal{N}_1 \| \mathcal{N}_2$, $\mathcal{N}_1 ; \mathcal{N}_2$ and $[\mathcal{N}_1 * \mathcal{N}_2 * \mathcal{N}_3]$ where the entry and exit places of the component nets $\mathcal{N}_i$ are used to construct a composite net. The detailed definitions of the four operators are given in the appendix, and figure 3 illustrates their use (this example also illustrates the definition of boxes in the next section).

4 Boxes

We now bring to our discussion a class of process expressions. In this paper we will deal with a subset of the Petri Box Calculus [2] assuming the following syntax of *box expressions*:

$$ E \; := \; \beta \; | \; E \,\mathsf{sy}\, A \; | \; E; E \; | \; E \,\square\, E \; | \; E \| E \; | \; [E * E * E] $$

In the above, β is an action in $\mathsf{A} \cup \{\imath\}$ and A is a synchronisation set. The five operators correspond to those introduced for labelled nets. There is a mapping which associates with every box expression, E, a labelled net, $\mathsf{box}(E)$, in

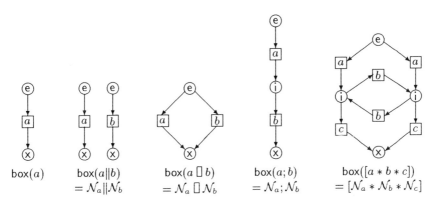

Fig. 3. Examples of boxes where $\mathcal{N}_x = \mathsf{box}(x)$ for $x \in \{a, b, c\}$.

the following way: $\mathsf{box}(\beta)$ is as the leftmost net in figure 3 with a changed to β, $\mathsf{box}(E \,\mathsf{sy}\, A) = \mathsf{box}(E) \,\mathsf{sy}\, A$, $\mathsf{box}(E; F) = \mathsf{box}(E); \mathsf{box}(F)$, $\mathsf{box}(E \,\Box\, F) = \mathsf{box}(E) \,\Box\, \mathsf{box}(F)$, $\mathsf{box}(E\|F) = \mathsf{box}(E)\|\mathsf{box}(F)$ and, finally, $\mathsf{box}([E * F * G]) = [\mathsf{box}(E) * \mathsf{box}(F) * \mathsf{box}(G)]$. In what follows, we will call a *box* a net which can be derived from a box expression through the $\mathsf{box}()$ mapping. In general, isomorphic boxes will be identified. Figures 3 and 4 show examples of different boxes.

A *pre-box* is a labelled net $\mathcal{N}$ such that: (i) $\mathcal{N}^\circ \neq \emptyset \neq {}^\circ\mathcal{N}$; (ii) $(\mathcal{N}^\circ)^\bullet = {}^\bullet({}^\circ\mathcal{N}) = \emptyset$; (iii) all the transitions labelled with communication actions are simple; and (iv) and every ι-labelled transition t satisfies $W(s,t) \leq 2$ and $W(t,s) \leq 2$, for every place s. One can see that each box is a pre-box as well.

4.1 Maximal synchronisation sets

If one looks at proposition 1(1,5) then it is clear that for every net $\mathcal{N}$ there exists the *maximal synchronisation set*[3] A such that $\mathcal{N} \simeq \mathcal{N} \,\mathsf{sy}\, A$. We will denote this set by $\mathsf{max}_\mathcal{N}$. Note that $\mathsf{max}_\mathcal{N} = \bigcup\{A \mid \mathcal{N} \simeq \mathcal{N} \,\mathsf{sy}\, A\}$. Hence, by proposition 1(1,7), if $\mathcal{N} \simeq \mathcal{M}$ then $\mathsf{max}_\mathcal{N} = \mathsf{max}_\mathcal{M}$.

Our first goal – crucial from the point of view of developing an axiomatisation of duplication equivalence of box expressions – is to structurally characterise the maximal synchronisation sets of boxes. To this end we introduce some auxiliary sets of transitions, called *ex-transitions* and *choice context transitions*.

An *ex–transition* of a box $\mathcal{B}$ is a simple transition t such that ${}^\bullet t = {}^\circ\mathcal{B}$ and $t^\bullet = \mathcal{B}^\circ$; we use $\mathsf{ex}_\mathcal{B}$ to denote the set of labels of all *ex*–transitions of $\mathcal{B}$.

Choice context transitions duplicate each other except that they may have different (communication) labels. The terminology is motivated by the fact that such transitions always result from applying the choice composition operator. A set of *choice context* transitions of a box $\mathcal{B}$ is a maximal non-empty set U of transitions labelled with communication actions and all having the same connectivity.

---

[3] Maximal w.r.t. set inclusion.

We also denote $\text{ccall}_{\mathcal{B}} = \{\lambda_{\mathcal{B}}(U) \mid U$ is a set of choice context transitions$\}$. If the transitions in U are not ex-transitions then U is a set of *internal* choice context transitions and we define $\text{ccint}_{\mathcal{B}} = \{\lambda_{\mathcal{B}}(U) \mid U$ is a set of internal choice context transitions$\}$. Note that $\text{ex}_{\mathcal{B}}$ is a set of actions, while $\text{ccall}_{\mathcal{B}}$ and $\text{ccint}_{\mathcal{B}}$ are sets of non-empty sets of communication actions. For the boxes in figure 4, we have $\text{ex}_{\mathcal{B}} = \{a\}$, $\text{ccall}_{\mathcal{B}} = \{\{\widehat{a}, \widehat{b}\}, \{\widehat{c}\}, \{a\}\}$, $\text{ccint}_{\mathcal{B}} = \{\{\widehat{a}, \widehat{b}\}, \{\widehat{c}\}\}$, $\text{ex}_{\mathcal{C}} = \{a, b, c, \imath\}$, $\text{ccall}_{\mathcal{C}} = \{\{a, b, c\}\}$ and $\text{ccint}_{\mathcal{C}} = \emptyset$.

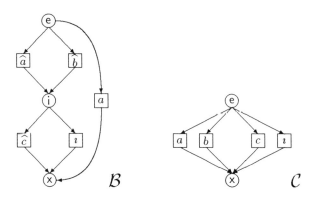

Fig. 4. Boxes generated by $((\widehat{a} \,\square\, \widehat{b}); (\widehat{c} \,\square\, \imath)) \,\square\, a$ and $(a \,\square\, b) \,\square\, (c \,\square\, \imath)$.

The idea behind the structural characterisation of maximal synchronisation sets is that one can apply an a-synchronisation, without losing duplication equivalence, if for every pair of a–synchronisable transitions t and u it is possible to find a duplicate of their synchronisation in at least one of two different ways: as a syntactically generated $\imath$-transition, or as a synchronisation of two transitions with the same connectivity as t and u. To illustrate the latter case, suppose that $(\mathcal{B}\|\mathcal{C})$ sy $A \simeq (\mathcal{B}\|\mathcal{C})$ sy A sy a. Then, if t is a transition in $\mathcal{B}$ and u is a transition in $\mathcal{C}$ then we must be able to find A-synchronisable transitions, t' in $\mathcal{B}$ and u' in $\mathcal{C}$, with the same connectivity as respectively t and u. In other words, a necessary condition for $(\mathcal{B}\|\mathcal{C})$ sy $A \simeq (\mathcal{B}\|\mathcal{C})$ sy A sy a to hold is that for every pair of a–synchronisable transitions t and u from respectively $\mathcal{B}$ and $\mathcal{C}$, there is a pair of A-synchronisable transitions, t' and u', which have the same connectivity as respectively t and u. We can express this rather conveniently using the sets $\text{ccall}_{\mathcal{B}}$ and $\text{ccall}_{\mathcal{C}}$ and some auxiliary notation.

Let $\mathcal{Z}$ and $\mathcal{W}$ be two sets of sets of actions and A be a synchronisation set. Then $\text{cov}^A(\mathcal{Z}, \mathcal{W})$ is the set of all communication actions a such that if $Z \in \mathcal{Z}$ and $W \in \mathcal{W}$ satisfy $a \in Z \wedge \widehat{a} \in W$ or $\widehat{a} \in Z \wedge a \in W$ then there is $c \in A$ such that $c \in Z \wedge \widehat{c} \in W$. Define, for a synchronisation set A and boxes $\mathcal{B}, \mathcal{C}$ and $\mathcal{D}$,

$$\text{covall}_{\mathcal{BC}}^{A} = \text{cov}^A(\text{ccall}_{\mathcal{B}}, \text{ccall}_{\mathcal{C}})$$
$$\text{covall}_{\mathcal{BCD}}^{A} = \bigcap\{\text{covall}_{\mathcal{XY}}^{A} \mid \mathcal{X}, \mathcal{Y} \in \{\mathcal{B}, \mathcal{C}, \mathcal{D}\}\}.$$

We observe that the above necessary condition for $(\mathcal{B}\|\mathcal{C})$ sy $A \simeq (\mathcal{B}\|\mathcal{C})$ sy A sy a simply amounts to saying that a and $\widehat{a}$ belong to $\mathsf{covall}_{\mathcal{B}\mathcal{C}}^{A}$. Note that for the nets in figure 4, $\mathsf{covall}_{\mathcal{B}\mathcal{C}}^{a} = \mathsf{A} - \mathsf{c}$. Characterising maximal synchronisation sets is rather easy in the case of sequential, parallel and iteration composition.

Proposition 2. *Let $\mathcal{B}$, $\mathcal{C}$ and $\mathcal{D}$ be boxes. Then*

$$\mathsf{max}_{(\mathcal{B};\mathcal{C})\,\mathsf{sy}\,A} = \mathsf{covall}_{\mathcal{B}\mathcal{C}}^{A} \quad \cap\, \mathsf{max}_{\mathcal{B}\,\mathsf{sy}\,A} \cap \mathsf{max}_{\mathcal{C}\,\mathsf{sy}\,A}$$
$$\mathsf{max}_{(\mathcal{B}\|\mathcal{C})\,\mathsf{sy}\,A} = \mathsf{covall}_{\mathcal{B}\mathcal{C}}^{A} \quad \cap\, \mathsf{max}_{\mathcal{B}\,\mathsf{sy}\,A} \cap \mathsf{max}_{\mathcal{C}\,\mathsf{sy}\,A}$$
$$\mathsf{max}_{[\mathcal{B}*\mathcal{C}*\mathcal{D}]\,\mathsf{sy}\,A} = \mathsf{covall}_{\mathcal{B}\mathcal{C}\mathcal{D}}^{A} \cap\, \mathsf{max}_{\mathcal{B}\,\mathsf{sy}\,A} \cap \mathsf{max}_{\mathcal{C}\,\mathsf{sy}\,A} \cap \mathsf{max}_{\mathcal{D}\,\mathsf{sy}\,A}$$

for every synchronisation set A. □

Note that by setting $A = \emptyset$ we immediately obtain that, e.g., $\mathsf{max}_{\mathcal{B};\mathcal{C}}$ is the set of all $a \in \mathsf{max}_{\mathcal{B}\,\mathsf{sy}\,A} \cap \mathsf{max}_{\mathcal{C}\,\mathsf{sy}\,A}$ such that if a transition labelled a or $\widehat{a}$ appears in $\mathcal{B}$ then there is no transition with the conjugate label in $\mathcal{C}$. A similarly pleasant characterisation does not hold for the choice composition. One of the reasons is that a synchronised ex–transitions can sometimes be duplication equivalent to a syntactically introduced $\imath$-transition. For example, if $\mathcal{B} = \mathsf{box}(a\|\widehat{a})$ and $\mathcal{C} = \mathsf{box}(\imath)$ then we have $a \in \mathsf{max}_{(\mathcal{B}\square\mathcal{C})\,\mathsf{sy}\,\emptyset}$ but $a \notin \mathsf{max}_{\mathcal{B}\,\mathsf{sy}\,\emptyset}$. Another example is provided by the boxes $\mathcal{B}$ and $\mathcal{C}$ in figure 4 for which we have $a \in \mathsf{max}_{(\mathcal{B}\square\mathcal{C})\,\mathsf{sy}\,b}$ but $a \notin \mathsf{max}_{\mathcal{B}\,\mathsf{sy}\,b} = \mathsf{max}_{\mathcal{B}}$. Note that if we were to repeat our previous discussion for $(\mathcal{B}\,\square\,\mathcal{C})$ sy $A \simeq (\mathcal{B}\,\square\,\mathcal{C})$ sy A sy a then it would no longer be the case that t' and u' had to have the same connectivity as t and u if, e.g., u is an ex–transition in $\mathcal{C}$ since in such a case an ex–transition u' in $\mathcal{B}$ could provide a suitable 'match' for t'.

The characterisation of the maximal synchronisation sets for the choice composition is more complicated. For a box $\mathcal{B}$, let $\mathcal{U}_{\mathcal{B}}$ be the set of all sets of internal choice context transitions U such that if $t \in U$ then there is no transition u in $\mathcal{B}$ satisfying $u \bowtie_{\mathcal{B}} \delta t$. Intuitively, this means that if we were to synchronise t with a conjugate ex-transition coming from the box $\mathcal{C}$ in the context $\mathcal{B}\,\square\,\mathcal{C}$ then the resulting transition would not have the same connectivity as any of the transitions present in $\mathcal{B}$. We then define $\mathsf{ccnoex}_{\mathcal{B}} = \{\lambda_{\mathcal{B}}(U) \mid U \in \mathcal{U}_{\mathcal{B}}\}$ and, for all boxes $\mathcal{B}$ and $\mathcal{C}$ and every synchronisation set A,

$$\mathsf{covnoex}_{\mathcal{B}\mathcal{C}}^{A} = \mathsf{cov}^{A}(\mathsf{ccnoex}_{\mathcal{B}\,\mathsf{sy}\,A}, \{\mathsf{ex}_{\mathcal{C}}\}) \cap \mathsf{cov}^{A}(\mathsf{ccnoex}_{\mathcal{C}\,\mathsf{sy}\,A}, \{\mathsf{ex}_{\mathcal{B}}\})$$
$$\mathsf{covmix}_{\mathcal{B}\mathcal{C}}^{A} = \mathsf{cov}^{A}(\mathsf{ccint}_{\mathcal{B}}, \mathsf{ccall}_{\mathcal{C}}) \qquad \cap \mathsf{cov}^{A}(\mathsf{ccint}_{\mathcal{C}}, \mathsf{ccall}_{\mathcal{B}})$$
$$\mathsf{covint}_{\mathcal{B}\mathcal{C}}^{A} = \mathsf{cov}^{A}(\mathsf{ccint}_{\mathcal{B}}, \mathsf{ccint}_{\mathcal{C}}).$$

The above definitions closely follow that of covall. For the nets in figure 4, we have $\mathsf{ccnoex}_{\mathcal{B}} = \{\{\widehat{a}, \widehat{b}\}, \{\widehat{c}\}\}$, $\mathsf{covnoex}_{\mathcal{B}\mathcal{C}}^{a} = \mathsf{A} - \mathsf{c}$, $\mathsf{covmix}_{\mathcal{B}\mathcal{C}}^{b} = \mathsf{A} - \mathsf{c}$ and $\mathsf{covint}_{\mathcal{B}\mathcal{C}}^{\emptyset} = \mathsf{A}$.

We need a syntactic restriction on the type of expressions used to derive boxes. We will denote by Exp_0 those box expressions E for which there is no subexpression $F \,\square\, G$ and a communication action a such that $a \in \mathsf{ex}_{\mathsf{box}(F)}$ and $\widehat{a} \in \mathsf{ex}_{\mathsf{box}(G)}$. By Box_0 we will denote boxes which can be derived from the box expressions in Exp_0. We then obtain a partial characterisation of the maximal synchronisation sets of boxes involving choice composition.

Proposition 3. *Let $\mathcal{B} = (\mathcal{C} \,[]\, \mathcal{D})\,\mathsf{sy}\,A$ be a box in Box_0. Then*

$$\mathsf{max}_\mathcal{B} = \mathsf{covnoex}^A_{\mathcal{CD}} \cap \mathsf{covint}^A_{\mathcal{CD}} \cap \mathsf{max}_{\mathcal{C}\,\mathsf{sy}\,A} \cap \mathsf{max}_{\mathcal{D}\,\mathsf{sy}\,A}$$

for every A such that $\mathsf{ex}_\mathcal{B} \cap (A \cup \{\imath\}) \subseteq \mathsf{ex}_{\mathcal{C}\,\mathsf{sy}\,A} \cap \mathsf{ex}_{\mathcal{D}\,\mathsf{sy}\,A}$. □

4.2 Duplication equivalent box expressions

We now transfer the notion of duplication equivalence formulated for boxes to the domain of box expressions. Two box expressions, E and F, are *duplication equivalent* if $\mathsf{box}(E) \simeq \mathsf{box}(F)$. We denote this by $E \simeq F$. The maximal synchronisation set of a box expression E is defined as $\mathsf{max}_E = \mathsf{max}_{\mathsf{box}(E)}$. Clearly, many properties of duplication equivalence that hold for boxes can be transferred to box expressions. In particular, we immediately obtain that $\simeq$ is a congruence in the domain of box expressions. Moreover, directly from proposition 1, we have the following.

Proposition 4. *Let E and F be box expressions, and A and B be synchronisation sets.*

1. *$E\,\mathsf{sy}\,A\,\mathsf{sy}\,B \simeq E\,\mathsf{sy}\,(A \cup B)$.*
2. *If $E \simeq E\,\mathsf{sy}\,B$ and $A \subseteq B$ then $E \simeq E\,\mathsf{sy}\,A$.*
3. *If $E \simeq E\,\mathsf{sy}\,A$ and $E \simeq E\,\mathsf{sy}\,B$ then $E \simeq E\,\mathsf{sy}\,(A \cup B)$.*
4. *If $E \simeq F\,\mathsf{sy}\,A$ then $E \simeq E\,\mathsf{sy}\,A$.* □

The main aim of this paper is to axiomatise duplication equivalence of box expressions. When we approached this problem, it soon turned out that a crucial difficulty which had to be solved was the development of a structural characterisation of maximal synchronisation sets, both in order to obtain a set of sound axioms and to define normal form box expressions needed for a completeness proof. Such a characterisation is based on that obtained for boxes, and so we will define the expression counterparts of ex–transitions and choice context transitions as well as other notations introduced in the previous section. However, we will in general have more complicated definitions since in the domain of expressions, we require that all the notions be introduced syntactically, rather than by referring to those defined for the corresponding boxes.

For a box expression E, let ex_E and potex_E be sets of actions defined by induction on the structure of E, thus:

$$\mathsf{ex}_\beta = \{\beta\} \qquad \mathsf{potex}_{E\|F} = (\mathsf{ex}_E \cap \widehat{\mathsf{ex}_F}) \cup (\mathsf{ex}_F \cap \widehat{\mathsf{ex}_E})$$
$$\mathsf{ex}_{E\,[]\,F} = \mathsf{ex}_E \cup \mathsf{ex}_F \qquad \mathsf{potex}_{E\,[]\,F} = \mathsf{potex}_E \cup \mathsf{potex}_F$$
$$\mathsf{potex}_{E\,\mathsf{sy}\,A} = \mathsf{potex}_E$$

$$\mathsf{ex}_{E\,\mathsf{sy}\,A} = \begin{cases} \mathsf{ex}_E \cup \{\imath\} & \text{if } \mathsf{potex}_E \cap A \neq \emptyset \\ \mathsf{ex}_E & \text{otherwise} \end{cases}$$

In all the remaining cases, ex_E and potex_E are defined as empty. The meaning of ex_E is that of $\mathsf{ex}_{\mathsf{box}(E)}$. The auxiliary set potex_E represents *potential* $\imath$-labelled *ex*-transitions which can be generated by applying synchronisation using the actions in potex_E. For example, $\text{potex}_{(a\emptyset b)\|(\widehat{a\emptyset b})} = \text{a} \cup \text{b}$.

We next turn to choice context transitions. For a box expression E, let ccint_E and ccall_E be two sets of sets of communication actions defined by induction on the structure of E, as follows:

$$
\begin{aligned}
\text{ccint}_\beta &= \emptyset & \text{ccint}_{[E*F*G]} &= \text{ccall}_E \cup \text{ccall}_F \cup \text{ccall}_G \\
\text{ccint}_{E\emptyset F} &= \text{ccint}_E \cup \text{ccint}_F & \text{ccint}_{E\|F} &= \text{ccall}_E \cup \text{ccall}_F \\
\text{ccint}_{E;F} &= \text{ccall}_E \cup \text{ccall}_F & \text{ccint}_{E \text{ sy } A} &= \text{ccint}_E
\end{aligned}
$$

$$
\text{ccall}_E = \begin{cases} \text{ccint}_E \cup \{\text{ex}_E \cap \text{A}\} & \text{if } \text{ex}_E \cap \text{A} \neq \emptyset \\ \text{ccint}_E & \text{otherwise.} \end{cases}
$$

Moreover, we define a set of sets of communication actions ccnoex_E, as follows:

$$
\begin{aligned}
\text{ccnoex}_{F\emptyset G} &= \text{ccnoex}_F \cup \text{ccnoex}_G \\
\text{ccnoex}_{F \text{ sy } A} &= \{C \in \text{ccnoex}_F \mid \widehat{C} \cap \text{ex}_F \cap A = \emptyset\}
\end{aligned}
$$

and by setting $\text{ccnoex}_E = \text{ccint}_E$ in all the remaining cases. We then define:

$$
\begin{aligned}
\text{covall}_{EF}^A &= \text{cov}^A(\text{ccall}_E, \text{ccall}_F) \\
\text{covnoex}_{EF}^A &= \text{cov}^A(\text{ccnoex}_{E \text{ sy } A}, \{\text{ex}_F\}) \cap \text{cov}^A(\text{ccnoex}_{F \text{ sy } A}, \{\text{ex}_E\}) \\
\text{covmix}_{EF}^A &= \text{cov}^A(\text{ccint}_E, \text{ccall}_F) \qquad \cap \text{cov}^A(\text{ccint}_F, \text{ccall}_E) \\
\text{covint}_{EF}^A &= \text{cov}^A(\text{ccint}_E, \text{ccint}_F)
\end{aligned}
$$

and $\text{covall}_{EFG}^A = \bigcap\{\text{covall}_{XY}^A \mid X, Y \in \{E, F, G\}\}$. The sets of communication actions we have just defined are direct counterparts of similar notions introduced for boxes.

Proposition 5. *Let E, F and G be expressions and A be a synchronisation set.*

1. $\text{ccall}_E = \text{ccall}_{\text{box}(E)}$, $\text{ccint}_E = \text{ccint}_{\text{box}(E)}$ *and* $\text{ccnoex}_E = \text{ccnoex}_{\text{box}(E)}$.
2. $\text{set}_{EF}^A = \text{set}_{\text{box}(E)\text{box}(F)}^A$, *for* $\text{set} \in \{\text{covall}, \text{covint}, \text{covmix}, \text{covnoex}\}$.
3. $\text{covall}_{EFG}^A = \text{covall}_{\text{box}(E)\text{box}(F)\text{box}(G)}^A$. $\qquad\qquad\qquad\qquad\qquad\qquad\quad\square$

We now can capture the relationship between max_E and the structure of E, using propositions 2, 3 and 5.

Proposition 6. *Let E, F and G be box expressions. Then*

$$
\begin{aligned}
\text{max}_{(E;F) \text{ sy } A} &= \text{covall}_{EF}^A \quad \cap \text{max}_{E \text{ sy } A} \cap \text{max}_{F \text{ sy } A} \\
\text{max}_{(E\|F) \text{ sy } A} &= \text{covall}_{EF}^A \quad \cap \text{max}_{E \text{ sy } A} \cap \text{max}_{F \text{ sy } A} \\
\text{max}_{[E*F*G] \text{ sy } A} &= \text{covall}_{EFG}^A \cap \text{max}_{E \text{ sy } A} \cap \text{max}_{F \text{ sy } A} \cap \text{max}_{G \text{ sy } A} \\
\text{max}_{(E\emptyset F) \text{ sy } A} &= \text{covnoex}_{EF}^A \cap \text{covint}_{EF}^A \cap \text{max}_{E \text{ sy } A} \cap \text{max}_{F \text{ sy } A}.
\end{aligned}
$$

The last case holds assuming $(E \emptyset F) \text{ sy } A \in \text{Exp}_0$ and $A \in \text{simex}_{EF}$, where $A \in \text{simex}_{EF}$ if $\text{ex}_{(E\emptyset F) \text{ sy } A} \cap (A \cup \{\imath\}) \subseteq \text{ex}_{E \text{ sy } A} \cap \text{ex}_{F \text{ sy } A}$. $\qquad\qquad\square$

5 An axiomatisation of duplication equivalence

The axioms for duplication equivalence of box expressions are structured into six groups. Below, β stands for an arbitrary action, A and B for synchronisation sets, and a for a communication action.

Structural Identities. The first group of axioms (STR1-STR5) capture some basic structural identities. The axioms are sound not only with respect to duplication equivalence, but also with respect to net isomorphism. What they express is that the choice, parallel and sequential compositions are associative[4], and that the first two are also commutative operators.

Propagation of synchronisation. The first two of the next group of axioms (PROP1-PROP7) express simple structural facts about synchronisation, namely that applying synchronisation to a single action expression, or using the empty synchronisation set, has no effect at all. The third axiom allows one to collapse consecutive applications of the synchronisation operator. The remaining four axioms amount to saying that synchronisation propagates through the four composition operators.

$$(E;F);G = E;(F;G) \qquad \text{STR1}$$
$$(E \ \square \ F) \ \square \ G = E \ \square \ (F \ \square \ G) \qquad \text{STR2}$$
$$E \ \square \ F = F \ \square \ E \qquad \text{STR3}$$
$$(E\|F)\|G = E\|(F\|G) \qquad \text{STR4}$$
$$E\|F = F\|E \qquad \text{STR5}$$
$$\beta = \beta \,\mathsf{sy}\, A \qquad \text{PROP1}$$
$$E = E \,\mathsf{sy}\, \emptyset \qquad \text{PROP2}$$
$$E \,\mathsf{sy}\, A \,\mathsf{sy}\, B = E \,\mathsf{sy}\, A \cup B \qquad \text{PROP3}$$
$$(E;F) \,\mathsf{sy}\, A = ((E \,\mathsf{sy}\, A);(F \,\mathsf{sy}\, A)) \,\mathsf{sy}\, A \qquad \text{PROP4}$$
$$(E \ \square \ F) \,\mathsf{sy}\, A = ((E \,\mathsf{sy}\, A) \ \square \ (F \,\mathsf{sy}\, A)) \,\mathsf{sy}\, A \qquad \text{PROP5}$$
$$(E\|F) \,\mathsf{sy}\, A = ((E \,\mathsf{sy}\, A)\|(F \,\mathsf{sy}\, A)) \,\mathsf{sy}\, A \qquad \text{PROP6}$$
$$[E * F * G] \,\mathsf{sy}\, A = [(E \,\mathsf{sy}\, A) * (F \,\mathsf{sy}\, A) * (G \,\mathsf{sy}\, A)] \,\mathsf{sy}\, A \qquad \text{PROP7}$$
$$\beta \ \square \ \beta = \beta \qquad \text{DUPL}$$

Duplication. This group comprises only one axiom (DUPL). It captures the essence of duplication equivalence whereby a choice between two copies of the same action is ignored.

ex-actions. The next axiom (EX) is used to deal with *ex*–actions as it allows these to be moved within a box expression. This is necessary, in particular, in

---
[4] We can therefore omit the parentheses in nested applications of sequence, choice and parallel composition operators.

order to make an expression with the main choice composition connective satisfy the first of the premises in the next axiom (LIFT1).

Lifting of synchronisation. The following four axioms (LIFT1-LIFT4) allow one to lift synchronisation sets to a higher level in the syntax tree of a box expression. The main application of these axioms is in the construction of maximal synchronisation sets.

Internal actions. The remaining axioms (INT1-INT2) capture two different ways in which a syntactically generated internal action can find its duplicate generated through synchronisation.

$$\frac{\beta \in A \;\Rightarrow\; \forall B \in \mathsf{ccnoex}_{E\,\mathsf{sy}\,A} : \widehat{\beta} \notin B}{(E\,\mathsf{sy}\,A)\;\square\;\beta = (E\;\square\;\beta)\,\mathsf{sy}\,A} \qquad \text{EX}$$

$$\frac{A \in \mathsf{simex}_{E\,\mathsf{sy}\,a,\,F\,\mathsf{sy}\,a} \text{ and } a \in \mathsf{covint}^{A}_{EF} \cap \mathsf{covnoex}^{A}_{E\,\mathsf{sy}\,a,\,F\,\mathsf{sy}\,a}}{((E\,\mathsf{sy}\,a)\;\square\;(F\,\mathsf{sy}\,a))\,\mathsf{sy}\,A = (E\;\square\;F)\,\mathsf{sy}\,A\,\mathsf{sy}\,a} \qquad \text{LIFT1}$$

$$\frac{a \in \mathsf{covall}^{A}_{EF}}{((E\,\mathsf{sy}\,a);(F\,\mathsf{sy}\,a))\,\mathsf{sy}\,A = (E;F)\,\mathsf{sy}\,A\,\mathsf{sy}\,a} \qquad \text{LIFT2}$$

$$\frac{a \in \mathsf{covall}^{A}_{EF}}{((E\,\mathsf{sy}\,a)\|(F\,\mathsf{sy}\,a))\,\mathsf{sy}\,A = (E\|F)\,\mathsf{sy}\,A\,\mathsf{sy}\,a} \qquad \text{LIFT3}$$

$$\frac{a \in \mathsf{covall}^{A}_{EFG}}{[(E\,\mathsf{sy}\,a)*(F\,\mathsf{sy}\,a)*(G\,\mathsf{sy}\,a)]\,\mathsf{sy}\,A = [E*F*G]\,\mathsf{sy}\,A\,\mathsf{sy}\,a} \qquad \text{LIFT4}$$

$$(((E\;\square\;a)\|(F\;\square\;\widehat{a}))\,\mathsf{sy}\,a)\;\square\;\imath = ((E\;\square\;a)\|(F\;\square\;\widehat{a}))\,\mathsf{sy}\,a \qquad \text{INT1}$$

$$\frac{a \in \mathsf{covmix}^{A}_{E\,\square\,a,\,F\,\square\,\widehat{a}}}{(((E\;\square\;a)\,\mathsf{sy}\,a\|(F\;\square\;\widehat{a})\,\mathsf{sy}\,a)\,\mathsf{sy}\,A)\;\square\;\imath = ((E\;\square\;a)\|(F\;\square\;\widehat{a}))\,\mathsf{sy}\,A\,\mathsf{sy}\,a} \qquad \text{INT2}$$

6 Soundness and completeness of the axiom system

From now on we restrict ourselves to the box expressions which belong to Exp_0. Note that by applying any of the axioms to a box expression in Exp_0 one always produces an expression which also belongs to Exp_0. We will also assume that the set of communication actions A is finite.

Using the results obtained for nets and, in particular, the structural characterisation of the maximal synchronisation sets, it is fairly routine to show that the axiom system is sound. If two box expressions, E and F, can be shown to be equivalent using these axioms, we will write $E = F$.

Theorem 1. *For every box expression E in Exp_0, if $E = F$ then $E \simeq F$.* □

The proof of completeness, structured into two parts, is much more involved. The first part deals with maximal synchronisation sets showing that it is always possible to make the maximal synchronisation set of a box expression the outermost synchronisation. The proof of this result relies on the structural characterisation of the maximal synchronisation sets of box expressions.

Proposition 7. *For every expression E in Exp_0, $E = E \,\mathsf{sy}\, \max_E$.* □

We next develop a normal form for box expressions based on an auxiliary operator on nets which can be thought of as an 'inverse' of the synchronisation operator, or *de-synchronisation*. For a labelled net $\mathcal{N}$ and a synchronisation set A, we denote by $\mathcal{N}\,\mathsf{unsy}\,A$ the net obtained from $\mathcal{N}$ by deleting all the $\imath$–labelled transitions t for which there are A–synchronisable transitions u and w such that $t \bowtie_{\mathcal{N}} uw$.

Proposition 8. *Let $\mathcal{N}$ and $\mathcal{M}$ be labelled nets, and A and B be synchronisation sets.*

1. *$\mathcal{N}\,\mathsf{unsy}\,\emptyset = \mathcal{N}$.*
2. *If $\mathcal{N} \simeq \mathcal{M}$ then $\mathcal{N}\,\mathsf{unsy}\,A \simeq \mathcal{M}\,\mathsf{unsy}\,A$.*
3. *If $A \subseteq \max_{\mathcal{N}}$ then $\mathcal{N} \simeq (\mathcal{N}\,\mathsf{unsy}\,A)\,\mathsf{sy}\,A$.*
4. *If $A \subseteq B$ then $(\mathcal{N}\,\mathsf{sy}\,A)\,\mathsf{unsy}\,B = \mathcal{N}\,\mathsf{unsy}\,B$.* □

De-synchronising a box does not necessarily yield a box. For example, if $E = (((a \,\square\, b); b) \| (\widehat{a} \,\square\, \widehat{b})) \,\mathsf{sy}\, b$ then $\mathsf{box}(E)\,\mathsf{unsy}\,a$ is the leftmost net in figure 5 which, as one can easily see, is neither a box nor is duplication equivalent to any box. But what we can say about a de-synchronised box is that it is a box with some transitions added in a way which resembles 'local' synchronisation.

Proposition 9. *Let $\mathcal{B}$ be a box, A be a synchronisation set and $\mathcal{C} = [\mathcal{B}\,\mathsf{unsy}\,A]_{\simeq}$. Then there is a box $\mathcal{D}$ generated by a synchronisation-free expression and a set of $\imath$-labelled transitions T of $\mathcal{C}$ such that $\mathcal{D}$ is isomorphic to $\mathcal{C}$ with the transitions T deleted. Moreover, for every transition $t \in T$ there are transitions $u, w \in T_{\mathcal{C}} - T$ such that $t \bowtie_{\mathcal{C}} uw$.* □

De-synchronisation distributes over the sequence, parallel and iteration composition. However, this does not extend to the choice operator. For example, if $\mathcal{B} = \mathsf{box}(a \| \widehat{a})$ and $\mathcal{C} = \mathsf{box}(b \| \widehat{b})$ then $((\mathcal{B}\,\mathsf{sy}\,a) \,\square\, (\mathcal{C}\,\mathsf{sy}\,b))\,\mathsf{unsy}\,a = \mathcal{B} \,\square\, \mathcal{C} \not\simeq \mathcal{B} \,\square\, (\mathcal{C}\,\mathsf{sy}\,b) = ((\mathcal{B}\,\mathsf{sy}\,a)\,\mathsf{unsy}\,a) \,\square\, ((\mathcal{C}\,\mathsf{sy}\,b)\,\mathsf{unsy}\,a)$. An important case when de-synchronisation distributes over choice is provided by the next result.

Proposition 10. *Let $\mathcal{B}_1, \ldots, \mathcal{B}_k$ and $\mathcal{B} = \mathcal{B}_1 \,\square\, \ldots \,\square\, \mathcal{B}_k$ be boxes in Box_0. Then*

$$\mathcal{B}\,\mathsf{unsy}\,A = (\mathcal{B}_1\,\mathsf{unsy}\,A) \,\square\, \ldots \,\square\, (\mathcal{B}_k\,\mathsf{unsy}\,A)$$

provided that A is a synchronisation set such that, for every $i \leq k$, $A \subseteq \max_{\mathcal{B}_i}$ and if $\mathsf{ex}_{\mathcal{B}_i} \neq \emptyset$ then $\mathcal{B}_i = \mathsf{box}(\beta)$ for some action β. □

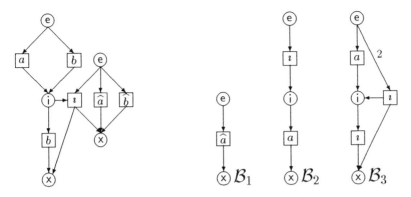

Fig. 5. De-synchronised box may not be a box, and decomposing a de-synchronised box.

The next definition deals with the problem of a unique representation of a net as a composition of other, smaller, nets. Below, a pre-box $\mathcal{B}$ is *c-decomposable* (*s-decomposable*) if there are pre-boxes $\mathcal{D}$ and $\mathcal{H}$ such that $\mathcal{B} \simeq \mathcal{D} \, \Box \, \mathcal{H}$ (resp. $\mathcal{B} \simeq \mathcal{D}; \mathcal{H}$). Note that $\mathsf{box}(\beta)$ is c-decomposable, for every action β. An *i-decomposition* / *p-decomposition* / *s-decomposition* / *c-decomposition* of a pre-box $\mathcal{B}$ is a sequence of pre-boxes $\mathcal{B}_1, \ldots, \mathcal{B}_k$ such that, respectively, the following hold:

- $k = 3$ and $\mathcal{B} \simeq [\mathcal{B}_1 * \mathcal{B}_2 * \mathcal{B}_3]$.
- $k \geq 2$ and $\mathcal{B} \simeq \mathcal{B}_1\|\ldots\|\mathcal{B}_k$ and, for every $i \leq k$, $\mathcal{B}_i$ is connected.
- $k \geq 2$ and $\mathcal{B} \simeq \mathcal{B}_1; \ldots; \mathcal{B}_k$ and, for every $i \leq k$, $\mathcal{B}_i$ is not s-decomposable.
- $k \geq 2$ and $\mathcal{B} \simeq \mathcal{B}_1 \, \Box \, \ldots \, \Box \, \mathcal{B}_k$ and, for every $i \leq k$, if $\mathcal{B}_i$ is c-decomposable then $\mathcal{B}_i \simeq \mathsf{box}(\beta)$ for some action β and $\mathcal{B}_i \not\simeq \mathcal{B}_j$ for all $j \neq i$.

A box expression E in Exp_0 is in *normal form* if it is in one of the following five types. Below, $A = \mathsf{max}_E$ and each E_i is an expression in normal form such that $A \subseteq \mathsf{max}_{E_i}$. Moreover, $\mathcal{B}$ denotes $\mathsf{box}(E)$ unsy A and $\mathcal{B}_i$ denotes $\mathsf{box}(E_i)$ unsy A.

- Type-a $E = \beta$ for some action β.
- Type-i $E = [E_1 * E_2 * E_3]$ sy A.
- Type-p $E = (E_1\|\ldots\|E_k)$ sy A and $\mathcal{B}_1, \ldots, \mathcal{B}_k$ is a p-decomposition of $\mathcal{B}$.
- Type-c $E = (E_1 \, \Box \, \ldots \, \Box \, E_k)$ sy A and $\mathcal{B}_1, \ldots, \mathcal{B}_k$ is a c-decomposition of $\mathcal{B}$.
- Type-s $E = (E_1; \ldots; E_k)$ sy A and $\mathcal{B}_1, \ldots, \mathcal{B}_k$ is an s-decomposition of $\mathcal{B}$.

We now aim at showing that duplication equivalent expressions in normal form are equal up to permutation of subexpressions in choice and parallel composition contexts. The first step is to show that any two duplication equivalent expressions are of the same type. The proof relies on two properties of labelled nets, called internal connectedness and internal interface, introduced in [11].

A pre-box $\mathcal{B}$ is *internally connected* if it is connected after removing all the entry and exit places. It has an *internal interface* if there is a set of internal places P such that if we delete P then $\mathcal{B}$ can be divided into two disjoint subgraphs with the nodes N_1 and N_2 such that: (i) each node in N_1 is connected to an entry place and not connected to any exit place; (ii) each node in N_2 is connected to an exit place and not connected to any entry place; and (iii) if we take $\mathcal{B}_i$ to be $\mathcal{B}$ with the nodes N_i deleted ($i = 1, 2$), then P is a $\otimes$-set for $\mathcal{B}_1$ and $\mathcal{B}_2$. For example, $P = \{s_2, s_3\}$ is the only internal interface of the net in figure 1.

Proposition 11. *Let E be an expression in normal form and m be the number of transitions in $\mathcal{B} = \mathsf{box}(E)\,\mathsf{unsy}\,\mathsf{max}_E$.*

1. *If E is of type-a then $m = 1$.*
2. *If E is of type-p then $m > 1$ and $\mathcal{B}$ is not connected.*
3. *If E is of type-c then $m > 1$ and $\mathcal{B}$ is connected and not internally connected.*
4. *If E is of type-i then $m > 1$ and $\mathcal{B}$ is connected and internally connected and has no internal interface.*
5. *If E is of type-s then $m > 1$ and $\mathcal{B}$ is connected and internally connected and has at least one internal interface.* □

It is then possible to show that duplication equivalent expressions in normal form are equal.

Proposition 12. *If E and F are duplication equivalent expressions in normal form then E is equal to F up to permutation of the components in subexpressions of the form $E_1\|\dots\|E_k$ and $E_1\,\square\,\dots\,\square\,E_k$.* □

Not every expression in Exp_0 can be rewritten into a normal form box expression. For example, if $E = ((a; \imath)\,\square\,\widehat{a})\,\mathsf{sy}\,\mathsf{a}\,\square\,(\imath; a)$ then $\mathsf{max}_E = \mathsf{A} - \mathsf{a}$ and the only decomposition of $\mathsf{box}(E)\,\mathsf{unsy}\,(\mathsf{A} - \mathsf{a}) = \mathsf{box}(E)$ into boxes $\mathcal{B}_i$ which could satisfy one of the parts of the definition of normal form expression are the three nets shown in figure 5 (note that $\mathsf{box}(E)\,\mathsf{unsy}\,(\mathsf{A} - \mathsf{a}) = \mathcal{B}_1\,\square\,\mathcal{B}_2\,\square\,\mathcal{B}_3$). While the first two nets do not create any problems, the third one does, as it is easy to see that there is no box expression E_3 such that $\mathcal{B}_3$ is duplication equivalent to $\mathsf{box}(E_3)\,\mathsf{unsy}\,A$, for any synchronisation set A. Hence E has no normal form in the sense defined above, and we need to restrict the applicability of the choice operator. The definition below is motivated by the way in which the fourth case in the definition of normal form has been formulated (and, indirectly, by the characterisation of the situation when the unsy operator distributes over choice).

A box expression $E \in \mathsf{Exp}_0$ is *choice-restricted* if every subexpression F of E which has choice as the topmost operator is of the form $\beta_1\,\square\,\dots\,\square\,\beta_k\,\square\,H$ and satisfies $\mathsf{ex}_{H\,\mathsf{sy}\,A} = \emptyset$, where A is the union of all the synchronisation sets B such that F lies within the scope of an application of $\mathsf{sy}\,B$ (we allow $k = 0$, and H may be missing if $k > 0$).[5] Then, we denote by Exp_1 the set of all the box expressions $G \in \mathsf{Exp}_0$ such that $G = E$, for some choice-restricted box

---

[5] Note that H can be an expression whose main connective is choice.

expression E. Although the definition of Exp_1 is not fully syntactic, one can give simple syntactic conditions which guarantee that a box expression which is not choice-restricted belongs to Exp_1.

Proposition 13. *If E is an expression in Exp_1 then there is an expression in normal form F such that $E = F$.* □

And, from propositions 12 and 13 we obtain the completeness result.

Theorem 2. *For all box expression E, F in Exp_1, if $E \simeq F$ then $E = F$.* □

7   Concluding remarks

In this paper we have investigated a notion of equivalence within the Petri Box Calculus defined for box expressions and based on the structural similarity of the corresponding boxes (labelled Petri nets). In particular, we have developed a sound and complete axiomatisation of duplication equivalence for a subset of box expressions. In doing so, it turned out that a crucial problem to be solved was that of a structural characterisation of maximal synchronisation sets of box expressions. We have found that such a characterisation is rather complicated for box expressions whose main connective (other than synchronisation) is the choice composition. This has led to a restriction on the set of box expressions for which the soundness and completeness results directly apply. The duplication equivalence is a very strong notion of equivalence which resembles the strong equivalence of CCS [18]. It is therefore natural to envisage that the future research will be concentrated on developing an axiomatisation of a weaker equivalence on box expressions, similar to the observational congruence of CCS. From this point of view the results obtained here should be highly relevant since any axiomatisation of a weaker behavioural equivalence would encompass the axiomatisation of duplication equivalence. Moreover, the restrictions imposed on the type of box expressions for which the soundness and completeness results hold seem to be rather mild when considering a weaker notion of equivalence. Without going into details, if $F_1, \ldots, F_k$ are the subexpressions of a box expression E which cause the latter not to belong to Exp_1 then it should be possible (under any reasonable notion of observational equivalence which ignores internal moves) to replace each F_i by $F_i; \imath$, within E, and the resulting expression, call it $E^{\langle \imath \rangle}$, would now belong to Exp_1. We also conjecture that the same transformation can be used to extend in a somewhat unusual way the completeness result obtained here, in the following way. If E and F are arbitrary box expressions such that $E \simeq F$ then $E^{\langle \imath \rangle} = F^{\langle \imath \rangle}$, where it is assumed that for a box expression E in Exp_1, $E^{\langle \imath \rangle} = E$.

The next remark concerns the non-standard way in which some of the axioms were formulated since they refer to various sets (even sets of sets) of actions, such as covall. The reader might question whether this leads to a significant increase in the algorithmic complexity of the axiomatisation developed here when compared, e.g., with that presented in [18]. The answer is that it does not, as it is not difficult to see that all the sets involved are 'small' which is due to an easy observation that it is always the case that $\sum_{A \in \mathsf{ccall}_E} |A| \leq k$ and $|\mathsf{ex}_E| \leq k$ where k is the number of action occurrences in a box expression E.

Our final explanation is related to the restriction imposed on the basic actions which here are assumed to be very simple, and which, in the full PBC, can be multisets of communication actions. We conjecture that the mechanism for obtaining axiomatisation presented in this paper can be lifted to the general setting for the expressions used to model concurrent programs in PBC which, informally, can be denoted as $(E_{var}||E_{prog})$ sy A rs A where rs A denotes restriction on actions in the set A. Such an expression represents a concurrent program with the 'control part', E_{prog}, and 'variable declarations', E_{var}, satisfying the following: E_{prog} contains only 'non-hatted' versions of communication actions, a, and E_{var} only 'hatted' versions of communication actions, $\hat{a}$ (it is assumed that A is suitably partitioned). Thus we expect that the results obtained here will be of relevance to the arguably most important application of PBC.

Acknowledgments

The first author was supported by an EPSRC Grant No 93314719. The initial stages of work presented here were supported by the Esprit Basic Research Working Group 6067 CALIBAN (Causal Calculi Based on Nets).

References

1. J. Baeten and W.P. Weijland: Process Algebra. Cambridge Tracts in Theoretical Computer Science (1990).
2. E. Best, R. Devillers and J. Hall: The Petri Box Calculus: a New Causal Algebra with Multilabel Communication. Advances in Petri Nets 1992, G. Rozenberg (ed.). Springer-Verlag, Lecture Notes in Computer Science 609, 21-69 (1992).
3. E. Best, R. Devillers and M. Koutny: Petri Nets, Process Algebras and Concurrent Programming Languages. To appear in Advances in Petri Nets (1998).
4. E. Best and R.P. Hopkins: $B(PN)^2$ - a Basic Petri Net Programming Notation. Proc. of PARLE'93, Springer-Verlag, Lecture Notes in Computer Science 694, 379-390 (1993).
5. E. Best and M. Koutny: A Refined View of the Box Algebra. Proc. Petri Net Conference'95, G. De Michelis, M. Diaz (eds). Springer-Verlag, Lecture Notes in Computer Science 935, 1-20 (1995).
6. E. Best and M. Koutny: Solving Recursive Net Equations. Proc. ICALP'95, Z. Fülöp and F. Gécseg (eds). Springer-Verlag, Lecture Notes in Computer Science 944, 605-623 (1995).
7. R. Devillers: S-invariant Analysis of Recursive Petri Boxes. Acta Informatica 32, 313-345 (1995).
8. Devillers, M. Koutny: Recursive Nets in the Box Algebra. To appear in Proc. International Conference on Application of Concurrency to System Design (CSD'98), Fukushima, Japan (1998).
9. U. Goltz: On Representing CCS Programs by Finite Petri Nets. Proc. MFCS'88, Springer-Verlag, Lecture Notes in Computer Science 324, 339-350 (1988).

10. M.B. Hennessy: Algebraic Theory of Processes. The MIT Press (1988).
11. M. Hesketh: On Synthesis of Box Expressions from Petri Boxes. Technical Report TR-552, Department of Computing Science, University of Newcastle upon Tyne (1996).
12. M. Hesketh and M. Koutny: An Axiomatisation of Duplication Equivalence in the Petri Box Calculus. Technical Report TR-585, Department of Computing Science, University of Newcastle upon Tyne (1997).
13. C.A.R. Hoare: Communicating Sequential Processes. Prentice Hall (1985).
14. INMOS: Occam 2 Reference Manual. Prentice-Hall (1988).
15. M. Koutny: Partial Order Semantics of Box Expressions. Proc. Petri Net Conference'94, R. Valette (ed.), Springer-Verlag, Lecture Notes in Computer Science 815, 318-337 (1994).
16. M. Koutny and E. Best: Operational and Denotational Semantics for the Box Algebra. To appear in Theoretical Computer Science (1998).
17. M. Koutny, J. Esparza and E. Best: Operational Semantics for the Petri Box Calculus. Proc. CONCUR'94, B. Jonsson and J.Parrow (eds), Springer-Verlag, Lecture Notes in Computer Science 836, 210-225 (1994).
18. R. Milner: Communication and Concurrency. Prentice Hall (1989).
19. E.R. Olderog: Nets, Terms and Formulas. Cambridge Tracts in Theoretical Computer Science (1991).
20. W. Reisig: Petri Nets. An Introduction. Springer-Verlag, EATCS Monographs on Theoretical Computer Science (1985).

Appendix: PBC composition operators

The definition of parallel, choice, sequence and iteration composition is preceded by three auxiliary notions, viz. place addition, place multiplication and gluing of nets.

We first formalise what it means to replace a place by a set of other places which inherit its connectivity. Let $\mathcal{N}$ be a labelled net and $s_1,\ldots,s_k$ be its places. Moreover, let $S_1,\ldots,S_k$ be disjoint non-empty sets of places not in $\mathcal{N}$ and $l_1,\ldots,l_k \in \{\mathsf{e},\mathsf{i},\mathsf{x}\}$. Then

$$\mathcal{N} \oplus \{(s_1,S_1,l_1),\ldots,(s_k,S_k,l_k)\} = (S',T',W',\lambda')$$

is a net such that $S' = S - \{s_1,\ldots,s_k\} \cup S_1 \cup \ldots \cup S_k$, $T' = T$ and, for all $n,m \in S' \cup T'$,

$$W'(n,m) = \begin{cases} W(n,m) & \text{if } n,m \in S \cup T \\ W(s_i,m) & \text{if } n \in S_i,\ m \in S \cup T \\ W(n,s_j) & \text{if } n \in S \cup T,\ m \in S_j \\ W(s_i,s_j) & \text{if } n \in S_i,\ m \in S_j \end{cases} \qquad \lambda'(n) = \begin{cases} \lambda(n) & \text{if } n \in S \cup T \\ l_i & \text{if } n \in S_i. \end{cases}$$

A *multiplication* of non-empty disjoint sets of places $S_1,\ldots,S_k$ ($k \geq 2$) is a set of places

$$S_1 \otimes \ldots \otimes S_k = \{\{s_1,\ldots,s_k\} \mid s_1 \in S_1 \wedge \ldots \wedge s_k \in S_k\}.$$

In the above, each $\{s_1, \ldots, s_k\}$ is a place which is assumed 'fresh' and hence different from every place in the nets to which places $S_1 \otimes \ldots \otimes S_k$ might be added using the place addition operator, $\oplus$.

Let $\mathcal{N}_1, \ldots, \mathcal{N}_k$ be disjoint labelled nets. Moreover, let Δ be a *gluing set*. The latter is defined by:

$$\Delta = \{(S_1^1, \ldots, S_{r_1}^1, l_1), \ldots, (S_1^m, \ldots, S_{r_m}^1, l_m)\}$$

where $m \geq 1$, $r_1, \ldots, r_m \geq 2$, $l_1, \ldots, l_m \in \{\mathsf{e}, \mathsf{i}, \mathsf{x}\}$, and each S_i^j is the set of entry places or the set of exit places of one of the nets $\mathcal{N}_1, \ldots, \mathcal{N}_k$. It is assumed that, for every $j \leq k$, both $^\circ\mathcal{N}_j$ and $\mathcal{N}_j^\circ$ can appear in Δ at most once and never in the same element of Δ. With such assumptions we define, for $j \leq k$,

$$\mathcal{N}_j : \Delta = \mathcal{N}_j \oplus \{(s, [S_1^i \otimes \ldots \otimes S_{r_i}^i]_s, l_i) \mid s \in {}^\circ\mathcal{N}_j \cup \mathcal{N}_j^\circ \wedge s \in S_1^i \cup \ldots \cup S_{r_i}^i\}$$

where $[S_1^i \otimes \ldots \otimes S_{r_i}^i]_s = \{p \in S_1^i \otimes \ldots \otimes S_{r_i}^i \mid s \in p\}$. Then the net

$$(\mathcal{N}_1, \ldots, \mathcal{N}_k) : \Delta = (\mathcal{N}_1 : \Delta) \cup \ldots \cup (\mathcal{N}_k : \Delta)$$

where $\cup$ denotes the standard net union, is a *glued net* obtained from nets $\mathcal{N}_1, \ldots, \mathcal{N}_k$ using the gluing set Δ.

Let $\mathcal{N}_1$, $\mathcal{N}_2$ and $\mathcal{N}_3$ be disjoint labelled nets such that $^\circ\mathcal{N}_i \neq \emptyset \neq \mathcal{N}_i^\circ$, for $i = 1, 2, 3$. The four composition operators are defined thus.

- Sequential $\mathcal{N}_1; \mathcal{N}_2 = (\mathcal{N}_1, \mathcal{N}_2) : \{(\mathcal{N}_1^\circ, {}^\circ\mathcal{N}_2, \mathsf{i})\}$.
- Choice $\mathcal{N}_1 \,\Box\, \mathcal{N}_2 = (\mathcal{N}_1, \mathcal{N}_2) : \{({}^\circ\mathcal{N}_1, {}^\circ\mathcal{N}_2, \mathsf{e}), (\mathcal{N}_1^\circ, \mathcal{N}_2^\circ, \mathsf{x})\}$.
- Concurrent $\mathcal{N}_1 \| \mathcal{N}_2 = \mathcal{N}_1 \cup \mathcal{N}_2$.
- Iteration $[\mathcal{N}_1 * \mathcal{N}_2 * \mathcal{N}_3] = (\mathcal{N}_1, \mathcal{N}_2, \mathcal{N}_3, \mathcal{M}_1, \mathcal{M}_2, \mathcal{M}_3) : \Delta$

where in the last case $\mathcal{M}_i$ is a disjoint copy of $\mathcal{N}_i$, for $i = 1, 2, 3$, and Δ is a gluing set given by

$$\Delta = \{({}^\circ\mathcal{N}_1, {}^\circ\mathcal{M}_1, \mathsf{e}), (\mathcal{N}_1^\circ, {}^\circ\mathcal{N}_2, \mathcal{M}_2^\circ, {}^\circ\mathcal{N}_3, \mathsf{i}),$$

$$(\mathcal{M}_1^\circ, \mathcal{N}_2^\circ, {}^\circ\mathcal{M}_2, {}^\circ\mathcal{M}_3, \mathsf{i}), (\mathcal{N}_3^\circ, \mathcal{M}_3^\circ, \mathsf{x})\}.$$

Intuitively, sequential composition joins together the exit places of $\mathcal{N}_1$ with the entry places of $\mathcal{N}_2$; choice composition joins together, respectively, the entry and exist places of the two nets; and parallel composition simply places the two nets next to each other. The iteration composition $[\mathcal{N}_1 * \mathcal{N}_2 * \mathcal{N}_3]$ is more complicated and it should be understood as follows. The net $\mathcal{N}_1$ represents the entry part of the iteration construct, after its completion $\mathcal{N}_2$ can be executed zero or more times, and after a successful completion of each execution of $\mathcal{N}_2$ one can pass the control to $\mathcal{N}_3$ which is the exit part of the composite nets (see also figure 3).

Efficiency of Token-Passing MUTEX-Solutions – Some Experiments

Elmar Bihler and Walter Vogler *

Institut für Informatik, Universität Augsburg, Germany

Abstract. A formerly developed approach for comparing the efficiency of asynchronous systems is applied to some token-passing systems (one of them presumably new) that solve the MUTEX-problem. While the original approach compares systems, we also quantify the efficiency by a number and used our tool FastAsy to assess the effects the number of users and the delay in their communication links have. Finally, some new results allowed us to prove correctness of the solutions with FastAsy.

1 Introduction

In [Vog95a,Vog95b,JV96], a faster-than relation for asynchronous systems has been developed in a setting with handshake-communication, where systems communicate by synchronizing on actions, i.e. by performing such an action together. This approach to efficiency was extended to Petri nets with read arcs in [Vog97] in order to compare two solutions of the mutual-exclusion problem (MUTEX-problem). We have built a tool FastAsy that checks whether a net N is faster than some net N'; if this is not the case, a slow behaviour of N is exhibited that N' does not show. This slow behaviour can give good insight into the temporal behaviour of N. Using our tool, we have extended the preliminary results of [Vog97] and, in particular, we have developed a numeric measure of efficiency and shown the correctness of a (presumably) new solution to the MUTEX-problem.

In our action-based setting, a MUTEX-solution is naturally a scheduler, i.e. an independent component the users have to synchronize with when performing the request-, enter- and leave-actions. This view also allows a clean formulation of the correctness requirements: since the users are not part of the scheduler, we make no assumptions what the users do while they are in their noncritical or in their critical sections – which is not so clear in the most common approach. The solutions we study all use a token that allows entry to the critical section and is passed around in a ring; in all such solutions, some independent components are needed to pass the token around the ring while the users are busy, i.e. viewing a MUTEX-solution as an independent scheduler is particularly adequate.

[Vog97] looks at two MUTEX-solutions for two users (recalled in Subsection 5.1); one is (a Petri net implementation of) a solution 2-LL attributed to

---

* Communicating author; this work was partially supported by the DFG-project 'Halbordnungstesten'. email: vogler@informatik.uni-augsburg.de

Le Lann in [Ray86], where the token 'automatically' travels around the ring; the other is a simple version DTR of Dijkstra's Token-Ring [Dij85], where the token has to be ordered in case of need. In our efficiency approach, one system is faster than another if it always serves the environment better than the other, no matter what behaviour pattern this environment shows. This is of course quite strict and, correspondingly, [Vog97] finds that none of the two solutions *always* serves the environment – consisting of both users – better. Interestingly, one can modify the respective nets and then find out that 2-LL is faster from the point of view of *one* user; this is the point of view we will take throughout this paper.

Although this positive faster-than result is plausible, it could depend on some minor details of the two Petri net implementations, and this is the starting point of our studies. In 5.2, we show that the faster solution 2-LL supports the (what we call) *come-back-later strategy* of the user; abstracting from this advantage, we develop a numeric measure for the speed of MUTEX-solutions called *enter-delay*, which is applicable to all the solutions and their variations we study here.

In 5.3, we apply the enter-delay to variations of the above solutions where communication in the token ring takes more time. (This communication covers some distance and is asynchronous, while communication between a user and the respective part of the scheduler is synchronous.) We find evidence that the two solutions are equally fast if only the time taken by the ring communication is relevant. (This was informally conjectured by Ekkart Kindler.) For three and four users, Le Lann's solution is easy to generalize, but Dijkstra's Token-Ring is considerably more difficult for more than two users. Also considering communication delays, we find that the enter-delay for Le Lann roughly corresponds to the worst time it takes a message to travel round the ring once, whereas for Dijkstra's Token-Ring it is twice as long.

An advantage of DTR, which is not taken into account in our temporal efficiency, is that it produces no communication load in the ring if no user wants to enter the critical section – whereas 2-LL does. In 5.4, we try to combine the advantages of the two solutions. In Dijkstra's Token-Ring, the token and orders of the token travel in opposite directions. In our (presumably) new Same-Way solution, they travel in the same direction. The price of this solution is that one has to send the identities of the users who have ordered the token; the advantage is that the enter-delay is roughly the travel time once around the ring, which only has to be unidirectional as in the case of 2-LL, and that communication load is only produced in case of need.

In particular for our new Same-Way solution, correctness is not at all obvious. In Sect. 6, we present results that allowed us to prove all the solutions correct by using FastAsy. Quite surprisingly, it is possible in these correctness proofs to abstract away large parts of the functional behaviour.

To make this paper self-contained, we have to present the concepts and some results of [Vog95b,JV96,Vog97]. Section 2 gives the basic definitions for nets with read arcs. Section 3 describes the approach to compare temporal efficiency, which refines the testing approach of [DNH84]. In the testing approach, a system is an implementation if it performs in all environments, i.e. for all users, at least as well as the specification; in [DNH84], successful performance only depends on the functionality, i.e. which actions are executed, whereas we also consider efficiency. For this, we assume that each transition is fired within one unit of time (or is disabled within this time).

Essential in an asynchronous system is that time cannot help to coordinate the components, i.e. these work with indeterminate relative speeds; even with our unit-time-assumption this is the case, since transitions must fire within time 1 but can also fire arbitrarily fast. Thus, we get a general theory of efficiency for simple nets that have no explicit time bounds attached. (Essentially the same assumption is made e.g. in [Lyn96] in a setting with a different parallel composition, where e.g. the phenomenon of the above mentioned come-back-later strategy cannot occur.) In any case, for the purpose of this paper, it is enough to assume that our systems are built from components with a given guaranteed speed such that indeed each transition fires within time 1; this is certainly a reasonable basis for judging efficiency.

Section 4 presents the fair failure semantics, which is in a sense just right to treat fairness (in the sense of progress) and modular construction of systems; in this section, the upper time bound is *not* assumed. Correctness of a MUTEX-solution is (later) defined in terms of fair failure semantics; we give here a new, more intuitive formulation for this semantics. Section 4 also exhibits the close relation between our efficiency testing and fairness. This is the basis to show correctness of a MUTEX-solution with FastAsy – and it demonstrates that in our approach we indeed deal with the behaviour of general asynchronous systems.

There exist a few approaches to compare the efficiency of asynchronous systems; these are not clearly related to our approach, see [Vog97] for a discussion of this literature. We thank Ekkart Kindler for several motivating discussions.

2 Basic Notions of Petri Nets with Read Arcs

In [Vog97], it is shown that ordinary Petri nets without read arcs cannot solve the MUTEX-problem – whereas Petri nets *with* read arcs can. (See [KW97] for a similar impossibility result; read arcs are also discussed e.g. in [CH93,MR95,JK95].) Thus, read arcs add relevant expressivity and they are included here. We use safe nets whose transitions are labelled with *actions* from some infinite alphabet Σ or with the empty word λ, indicating internal, unobservable actions. Σ contains a special action ω, which we will need in our tests to indicate success.

Thus, a *net* $N = (S, T, F, R, l, M_N)$ consists of finite disjoint sets S of *places* and T of *transitions*, the *flow* $F \subseteq S \times T \cup T \times S$ consisting of (ordinary) *arcs*, the set of *read arcs* $R \subseteq S \times T$, the *labelling* $l : T \to \Sigma \cup \{\lambda\}$, and the *initial marking* $M_N : S \to \{0,1\}$; we always assume $(R \cup R^{-1}) \cap F = \emptyset$. As usual, we draw transitions as boxes, places as circles and arcs as arrows; read arcs are drawn as (sometimes dashed) lines without arrow heads; the label of a transition is written inside the box or the box is empty if the label is λ. The net is called *ordinary*, if $R = \emptyset$.

For each $x \in S \cup T$, the *preset* of x is ${}^\bullet x = \{y \mid (y, x) \in F\}$, the *read set* of x is $\hat{x} = \{y \mid (y, x) \in R \cup R^{-1}\}$, and the *postset* of x is $x^\bullet = \{y \mid (x, y) \in F\}$. If $x \in {}^\bullet y \cap y^\bullet$, then x and y form a *loop*. A *marking* is a function $S \to I\!N_0$. We sometimes regard sets as characteristic functions, which map the elements of the sets to 1 and are 0 everywhere else; hence, we can e.g. add a marking and a postset of a transition or compare them componentwise.

Our basic firing rule extends the firing rule for ordinary nets by regarding the read arcs as loops. A transition t is *enabled* under a marking M, denoted by $M[t\rangle$, if ${}^\bullet t \cup \hat{t} \leq M$. If $M[t\rangle$ and $M' = M + t^\bullet - {}^\bullet t$, then we write $M[t\rangle M'$ and say that t can *occur* or *fire* under M yielding the follower marking M'.

Enabling and occurrence is extended to sequences as usual. If $w \in T^*$ is enabled under M_N, it is called a *firing sequence*. We extend the labelling to sequences of transitions as usual, i.e. homomorphically; thus, internal actions are deleted in this *image* of a sequence. With this, we lift the enabledness and firing definitions to the level of actions: a sequence v of actions is *enabled* under a marking M, denoted by $M[v\rangle\rangle$, if $M[w\rangle$ and $l(w) = v$ for some $w \in T^*$. If $M = M_N$, then v is called a *trace*; the set of traces is the *language* of N.

A marking M is called *reachable* if $M_N[w\rangle M$ for some $w \in T^*$. The net is *safe* if $M(s) \leq 1$ for all places s and reachable markings M.

General assumption: All nets considered in this paper are safe and only have transitions t with ${}^\bullet t \neq \emptyset$. (The latter condition is no serious restriction, since it can be satisfied by adding a loop between t and a new marked place, if ${}^\bullet t$ were empty otherwise; this addition does not change the firing sequences.)

Nets combined with *parallel composition* $\|_A$ run in parallel and have to synchronize on actions from A. To construct $N_1 \|_A N_2$, take the disjoint union of N_1 and N_2, combine each a-labelled transition t_1 of N_1 with each a-labelled transition t_2 from N_2 if $a \in A$ (i.e. introduce a new a-labelled transition (t_1, t_2) that inherits all arcs and read arcs from t_1 and t_2), and delete the original a-labelled transitions in N_1 and N_2 if $a \in A$; e.g. $\|_\emptyset$ denotes disjoint union; the full version of [Vog97] gives a formal definition. We write $\|$ for $\|_{\Sigma - \{\omega\}}$.

3 Timed Behaviour of Asynchronous Systems

We now describe the asynchronous behaviour of a parallel system, taking into account at what times things happen. Components perform each enabled action within at most one unit of time; this upper time bound allows the relative speeds of the components to vary arbitrarily, since we have no positive lower time bound. Thus, the behaviour we define is truly asynchronous. (One can also say that the time we measure is a conceptual time an observer assigns to runs which occur independently of time. The assignment is made such that the assumed time bounds on actions are met.)

For ordinary nets, [JV96] bases a testing preorder on such an asynchronous firing rule using dense time, shows that the preorder is the same when using discrete time, and gives a characterization of this testing preorder. This can be generalized to nets with read arcs, see the full version of [Vog97]; here, we immediately define an asynchronous firing rule using discrete time and present the respective characterization.

Due to the time bound 1, a newly enabled transition fires or is disabled within time 0 – or it becomes *urgent* after one time-unit (denoted by σ), i.e. it has no time left and must fire or must be disabled before the next σ.

The crucial point of read arcs is that they differ from loops w.r.t. disabling. If we have a loop (c, t), (t, c) and an arc or read arc (c, t') for a place c and urgent transitions t and t', then firing t removes the token from c, disables t' momentarily, and t' is not urgent any more. If a read arc (c, t) replaces the loop, t just checks for the token without removing it and, thus, t' is not disabled and remains urgent; hence, t and t' will occur faster since t does not block t'.

Definition 1. An *instantaneous description* $ID = (M, U)$ consists of a marking M and a set U of *urgent* transitions. The *initial ID* is $ID_N = (M_N, U_N)$ with $U_N = \{t \mid M_N[t\rangle\}$. We write $(M, U)[\varepsilon\rangle(M', U')$ in one of the following cases:
1. $\varepsilon = t \in T$, $M[t\rangle M'$, $U' = U - \{t' \mid {}^\bullet t \cap ({}^\bullet t' \cup \hat{t'}) \neq \emptyset\})$
2. $\varepsilon = \sigma$, $M = M'$, $U = \emptyset$, $U' = \{t \mid M[t\rangle\}$

Extending this to sequences and lifting these with l to the level of actions (where $l(\sigma) = \sigma$), we get the set $DL(N) \subseteq (\Sigma \cup \{\sigma\})^*$ of *discrete(ly timed) traces* of N. For $w \in DL(N)$, $\zeta(w)$ is the number of σ's in w.

A net is *testable*, if it has no ω-labelled transitions. A testable net N *satisfies* a timed test (O, D) – where O is a net, the *test net*, and $D \in \mathbb{N}$ –, if each $w \in DL(N \| O)$ with $\zeta(w) \geq D$ contains some ω; we call a net N_1 *faster* than a net N_2, $N_1 \sqsupseteq N_2$, if N_1 satisfies all timed tests that N_2 satisfies. Two nets are *equally fast* if each is faster than the other. $\qquad\qquad\square$

Part 1 allows enabled transitions – urgent or not – to fire; hence, $DL(N)$ includes the language of N and describes an asynchronous behaviour. $U = \emptyset$ in Part 2 requires that no urgent transition is delayed over the following σ. Each enabled transition is urgent after σ. Thus, a discrete trace is any ordinary trace subdivided into rounds by σ's such that no transition enabled at (i.e. immediately before) one σ is continuously enabled until after the next σ.

The testing definitions are standard except for the time bound: here, every run of the system embedded in the test net has to be successful within time D; thus, we only consider traces that last for time D. We call N_1 *faster*, since it might satisfy more tests and, in particular, some test nets within a shorter time.

The test-preorder $\sqsupseteq$ formalizes observable difference in efficiency; refering to all possible tests, it is not easy to work with directly. Thus, we now characterize $\sqsupseteq$ by some sort of refusal traces: we replace the σ's in a discrete trace by sets of actions, indicating the time-steps now. Such a set contains actions that are not urgent, i.e. can be refused when the time-step occurs.

Definition 2. For ID's (M, U) and (M', U') we write $(M, U)[\varepsilon\rangle_r(M', U')$ if one of the following cases applies:
1. $\varepsilon = t \in T$, $M[t\rangle M'$, $U' = U - \{t' \mid {}^\bullet t \cap ({}^\bullet t' \cup \hat{t'}) \neq \emptyset\})$
2. $\varepsilon = X \subseteq \Sigma$, $M = M'$, $U' = \{t \mid M[t\rangle\}$, $l(U) \cap (X \cup \{\lambda\}) = \emptyset$; X is a *refusal set*.

The corresponding *refusal firing sequences* form the set $RFS(N)$. The set of *refusal traces* is $RT(N) = \{l(w) \mid w \in RFS(N)\} \subseteq (\Sigma \cup \mathcal{P}(\Sigma))^*$ where $l(X) = X$. We also call a refusal set a *tick*, since it represents a time-step. The behaviour inbetween two ticks (or before the first one) is called a *round*. □

Occurrence of Σ corresponds to that of σ, hence $RT(N_1) \subseteq RT(N_2)$ implies $DL(N_1) \subseteq DL(N_2)$. To show that RT-semantics induces a congruence for $\|_A$, one defines $\|_A$ for refusal traces: actions from A are merged, while others are interleaved; refusal sets are combined as in ordinary failure semantics:

Definition 3. Let $u, v \in (\Sigma \cup \mathcal{P}(\Sigma))^*$, $A \subseteq \Sigma$. Then $u \|_A v$ is the set of all $w \in (\Sigma \cup \mathcal{P}(\Sigma))^*$ such that for some n we have $u = u_1 \ldots u_n$, $v = v_1 \ldots v_n$, $w = w_1 \ldots w_n$ and for $i = 1, \ldots, n$ one of the following cases applies:
- $u_i = v_i = w_i \in A$
- $u_i = w_i \in (\Sigma - A)$ and $v_i = \lambda$, or $v_i = w_i \in (\Sigma - A)$ and $u_i = \lambda$
- $u_i, v_i, w_i \subseteq \Sigma$ and $w_i \subseteq ((u_i \cup v_i) \cap A) \cup (u_i \cap v_i)$ □

Theorem 4. *For $A \subseteq \Sigma$ and nets N_1 and N_2, we have that $RT(N_1 \|_A N_2) = \bigcup \{u \|_A v \mid u \in RT(N_1),\ v \in RT(N_2)\}$.*

Theorem 5. *For testable nets, $N_1 \sqsupseteq N_2$ if and only if $RT(N_1) \subseteq RT(N_2)$.*

Observe that a faster system has less refusal traces; such a trace witnesses slow behaviour, it is something 'bad' due to the refusal information. If some N has e.g. a refusal trace $r\emptyset\{e\}e$, then we see that e occurs two ticks after r. Possibly, N offers e at the first tick (–it is not refused–) without performing it; such a possibility is relevant, if N has to synchronize e with its environment N' and N' refuses e at this moment – maybe because it is doing something else. Formally, we see in Definition 3 that the combined system can refuse e, if e is in the synchronization set A and just one component like N' refuses it. At the next tick, N refuses e; so even if N' wants to perform e, it has to wait now.

Refusal traces also describe functional behaviour; hence, a faster system N_1 also has 'less behaviour' on this level, it only shows functional behaviour allowed by the specification N_2.

The refusal sets in an refusal trace can be infinite, but in fact one can restrict them to those actions that actually occur in the net. Thus, $RT(N)$ is essentially the language of a finite automaton according to Definition 2: a reachable ID (M, U) consists of a reachable marking M and a set of transitions U, hence there are finitely many ID's. Theorem 5 reduces $\sqsupseteq$ to an inclusion of regular languages, which implies decidability of $\sqsupseteq$. We have built a tool FastAsy that uses PEP [pep] as a graphical interface; it turns a net N into a finite automaton that (essentially) recognizes $RT(N)$, and it makes this automaton deterministic. Then FastAsy checks language inclusion for two of these automata by building a simulation relation, compare e.g. [LV95]; to make this work, the automaton with the larger language has to be deterministic.

FastAsy does not minimize the deterministic automaton, since in our examples the deterministic automaton was much smaller than the nondeterministic automaton anyway. More importantly, FastAsy exhibits a 'responsible' refusal firing sequence, if inclusion fails; such a sequence seems to be difficult to extract after minimization. These 'responsible' sequences are very useful in order to understand the results produced by FastAsy; in particular, they have helped to find one real mistake in our designs (see 5.4), but also 'typos' like forgotten arcs.

FastAsy produces a responsible sequence with a minimal number of visible actions and refusal sets. Such a responsible refusal trace is expanded to a responsible refusal firing sequence by inserting internal transitions from back to front, each time trying to minimize the number of internal transitions. This does neither ensure that the overall number of internal transitions is minimal, nor that the length of the refusal firing sequence is minimal; but it gives a reasonably short reason for FastAsy's result.

4   Efficiency Testing and Fairness

Here, we study compositionality for fair behaviour (in the sense of the progress assumption) and relate it to our notion of asynchronous behaviour. Fairness requires that a continuously enabled activity should eventually occur; in real life, this is automatically true, i.e. it does not have to be implemented. First, we extend some definitions to infinite sequences taking into account that an infinite run should take infinite time.

Definition 6. An infinite sequence is a *(refusal) firing sequence* if all its finite prefixes are (refusal) firing sequences. A *progressing refusal firing sequence* is an infinite refusal firing sequence with infinitely many ticks. The images of these sequences are the *progressing refusal traces*, forming $PRT(N)$. Removing all sets from such a trace v, we get the sequence $\alpha(v)$ of actions in v. □

PRT-semantics extends RT-semantics to infinite runs, required to take infinite time. Using König's Lemma, one can show:

Theorem 7. *For all nets, $RT(N_1) \subseteq RT(N_2)$ iff $PRT(N_1) \subseteq PRT(N_2)$.*

In the following definition, t is continuously enabled during a firing sequence, if it is enabled also *while* each t_i of the sequence is firing. For this, we have to keep in mind that a read arc does not consume a token.

Definition 8. For a transition t, a finite firing sequence $M_N[t_0\rangle M_1[t_1\rangle \ldots M_n$ is *t-fair*, if not $M_n[t\rangle$. An infinite firing sequence $M_N[t_0\rangle M_1[t_1\rangle M_2 \ldots$ is *t-fair*, if we have: if t is enabled under all $M_i - {}^\bullet t_i$ for i greater than some j, then $t = t_i$ for some $i > j$. A finite or infinite firing sequence is *fair*, if it is t-fair for all transitions t. The *fair language* of N is $Fair(N) = \{v \mid v = l(w)$ for some fair firing sequence $w\}$. □

As for ordinary nets, each finite firing sequence can be extended to a fair one.

Assume a net N_2 as component of a parallel composition leads to an acceptable behaviour in the sense of fairness, and further that we want to replace N_2 by a net N_1 that is maybe easier to build; a natural requirement is that the new parallel composition does only show fair behaviour which was possible before. In this sense, N_1 can always replace N_2 if it is a fair implementation as follows.

Definition 9. A net N_1 is a *fair implementation* of a net N_2, if $Fair(N_1\|_A N) \subseteq Fair(N_2\|_A N)$ for all $A \subseteq \Sigma$ and nets N.

For a net N, define the *fair failure semantics* by $\mathcal{FF}(N) = \{(v, X) \mid X \subseteq \Sigma$ and $v = l(w)$ for some, possibly infinite, firing sequence w that is t-fair for all transitions t with $l(t) \in X \cup \{\lambda\}\}$. $\qquad\square$

Intuitively, $(v, X) \in \mathcal{FF}(N)$ if all actions in X can be refused when v is performed – in the sense, that fairness does not force additional performance of these actions. The next theorem shows how $\mathcal{FF}$-semantics supports the modular construction and that it characterizes what a fair implementation is.

Theorem 10. *i) For all nets N, $Fair(N) = \{v \mid (v, \Sigma) \in \mathcal{FF}(N)\}$. In particular, inclusion of $\mathcal{FF}$-semantics implies fair-language inclusion.*

ii) For $A \subseteq \Sigma$ and nets N_1 and N_2, $\mathcal{FF}(N_1\|_A N_2) = \{(w, X) \mid \exists (w_i, X_i) \in \mathcal{FF}(N_i), i = 1, 2 : w \in w_1\|_A w_2$ and $X \subseteq ((X_1 \cup X_2) \cap A) \cup (X_1 \cap X_2)\}$.

iii) N_1 is a fair implementation of N_2 if and only if $\mathcal{FF}(N_1) \subseteq \mathcal{FF}(N_2)$.

The following result establishes a relation to our testing approach.

Theorem 11. *For a net N, $(v, X) \in \mathcal{FF}(N)$ if and only if there is some $w \in PRT(N)$ such that $v = \alpha(w)$ and, for each $x \in X$, there is some suffix of w where x is in all refusal sets.*

A new corollary indicates that proving a faster-than relation (e.g. with a tool) can help to prove correctness based on fair behaviour. This demonstrates that our approach to judging efficiency, which is based on the assumption of an upper time bound for transitions, gives indeed results for general asynchronous systems, since our treatment of fair behaviour does not use this assumption.

Corollary 12. *PRT-inclusion (and thus RT-inclusion) implies $\mathcal{FF}$-inclusion. If N_1 is faster than N_2, then N_1 is a fair implementation of N_2.*

Proof. The first sentence follows from Theorems 7 and 11. The second part now follows with 5 and 10. $\qquad\square$

We close this section by giving a new, alternative formulation for the $\mathcal{FF}$-semantics. $(v, X) \in \mathcal{FF}(N)$ means that N can perform v in such a way that all internal actions and all actions in X are treated fair. Hence, $(v, X) \notin \mathcal{FF}(N)$ means that either N cannot perform v in such a way that all internal actions are treated fair or it can, but which way ever it performs v, it treats some action in X unfair. The latter means that some $x \in X$ is continuously enabled from some point onward. If N is on its own, it certainly performs such an x, but as a component of a larger system, N simply offers such an x. We therefore define:

Definition 13. If for a net N and some $(v, X) \in \Sigma^* \times \mathcal{P}(\Sigma)$ we have $(v, X) \notin \mathcal{FF}(N)$, then we say that N **surely offers** (some action of) X **along** v. $\quad\square$

Similarly, one often says that 'N after v must X', if (v, X) is not in the ordinary failure semantics of N. In our case, if N **surely offers** X **along** v and in a run (i.e. a fair firing sequence) of a composed system, N as a component performs v while the environment offers in this run each action in X, then some action in X will be performed in this run.

5 Efficiency of Some MUTEX-Solutions

5.1 First results from [Vog97]

We start with two MUTEX-solutions for two users and the first results about their efficiency from [Vog97]. As explained in the introduction and in greater detail in [Vog97], we regard such a solution as a scheduler the users have to synchronize with; hence, it is a component of a parallel system and the $\mathcal{FF}$- and RT-semantics are just what we need to study the functional and temporal behaviour of such a component.

All our solutions pass an access-token around which guarantees mutual exclusion. The first solution 2-LL (attributed to Le Lann) is shown in Fig. 1. Clearly, the net has a part for each user (on the left and on the right); in our view, these parts are not the users themselves, but each part communicates with the respective user and handles the access-token for him. In our verbal explanations, we will not always make this distinction.

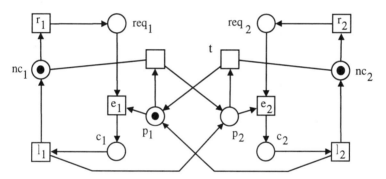

Figure 1

In 2-LL, the first user has priority, i.e. owns the access-token lying on p_1. He can request access with r_1 and enter the critical section with e_1 (marking c_1). When he leaves it with l_1, he passes the token to the other user. If the first user is not interested in entering the critical section, i.e. nc_1 remains marked, the token is passed by an internal transition (to p_2); it is important that this transition checks nc_1 with a read arc, since this way the user is not prevented from requesting, an important requirement for a MUTEX-solution; compare [Vog97], which shows that the MUTEX-problem cannot be solved with ordinary nets without read arcs. It is also important that a user may refuse to request; such a behaviour is allowed in both, the $\mathcal{FF}$- and the RT-semantics: both e.g. contain sequences without any r_1 – but r_1 is also not refused in these cases.

As for any token-passing solution, safety of 2-LL is easy: if one user enters, he must leave before any other enter, since there is always exactly one token on c_1, p_1, p_2 and c_2. (This set is an S-invariant, as also used e.g. in [KW95].)

The second solution DTR, shown in Fig. 2, is a simple version of Dijkstra's Token-Ring [Dij85]. Dijkstra's idea for the case of two users was rediscovered in

[KW95] and modelled as a net with so-called fair arcs; DTR is a modification of this net – using read arcs. In DTR, the user keeps the token when leaving the critical section. The second user misses the access-token (m_2 is marked); if she requests access, she has to order the token by marking o_2; now the first user cannot enter due to the read arc and has to grant the token by marking g_2.

Comparing the efficiency of these two solutions, one sees that both have their advantages: if there is no competition, then moving the access-token to the other part of the net is a useless and time consuming effort; on the other hand, if the competition is strong, ordering the token is an additional overhead. Formally, if in 2-LL the access-token is moved to p_2 immediately before r_1, then t becomes urgent only in the second round, at the end of which e_1 can still be refused; we get $r_1\{e_1\}\{e_1\} \in RT(2\text{-}LL) \setminus RT(DTR)$ showing that sometimes 2-LL is slower – namely if the second user does not want to enter. Vice versa, DTR is sometimes slower as witnessed by $r_2\{e_2\}\{e_2\}\{e_2\} \in RT(DTR) \setminus RT(2\text{-}LL)$, where an additional round is needed to order the token.

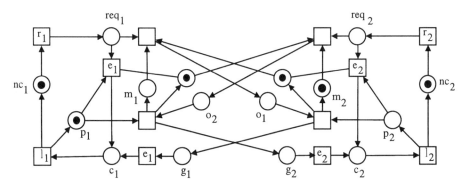

Figure 2

The RT-semantics shows how efficiently the respective MUTEX-solution serves the environment consisting of both users. Interestingly, we can also use our approach to study a different view: how efficiently are the needs of the first user met by the system, which for him consists of a MUTEX-solution and the second user? As second user, we take a standard user who, in the non-critical section, can choose between requesting with r_2 and some other internal activity; if she requests, she is willing to enter the critical section in the next round and to leave it again in the round after. From the point of view of the first user, all activities of the second user are unobservable, i.e. internal transitions. In the present paper, we define more generally:

Definition 14. If a net N satisfies $l(T) \subseteq \{r_i, e_i, l_i \mid i = 1, \ldots, n\} \cup \{\lambda\}$, we call it an n-$MUTEX$ net. The i-th *standard user* SU_i is a net that for $i = 2$ looks like an extension of the right hand side of 2-LL, i.e. it has places nc_i (marked), req_i and c_i and the transitions with labels r_i, e_i and l_i between them *plus* an internal transition on a loop with nc_i.

The *first-user view* $FUV(N)$ of N is obtained by turning all labels from $\{r_i, e_i, l_i \mid i = 2, \ldots, n\}$ into λ in $N\|_{\{r_i,e_i,l_i \mid i=2,\ldots,n\}}(SU_2\|_\emptyset \cdots \|_\emptyset SU_n)$. □

In Fig. 3, $FUV(2\text{-}LL)$ is shown whithout the copies of req_2 and c_2 belonging to the standard user SU_2. It is plausible that $FUV(2\text{-}LL)$ is more efficient than $FUV(DTR)$: we consider worst case efficiency; naturally, for the first user strong competition is the worst case, and in case of strong competition $2\text{-}LL$ is more efficient since it saves the additional effort of ordering the token. Indeed, it is shown in [Vog97] that $FUV(2\text{-}LL)$ is strictly faster than $FUV(DTR)$.

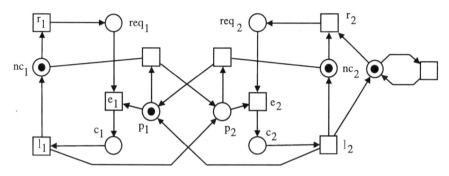

Figure 3

Besides the difference in efficiency, there is also a functional difference between $2\text{-}LL$ and DTR: if in $2\text{-}LL$ e.g. the second user requests, then the first user can enter at most once before the second user enters; in DTR, the first user can enter arbitrarily often (provided he is 'fast'). The first-user view abstracts from such differences; therefore and because of the results in this subsection, we will henceforth *only* compare the efficiency of first-user views.

5.2 Come-back-later strategy and a quantitative measure

Although the above positive faster-than result is plausible, it could depend on some maybe less relevant details of the two Petri net implementations. To study this question, we slow down the net $2\text{-}LL$, and then compare such a slow version with DTR. More precisely, we delay the communication between the parts of $2\text{-}LL$: The *n-delay* of $2\text{-}LL$ is obtained by inserting n internal transitions into each 'link' between the parts, and it is denoted by $2\text{-}LL_n$; in the case of $2\text{-}LL$, these links are the arcs crossing the middle, i.e. the arcs to the places p_1 and p_2. The construction of the 1-delay for one of these arcs is:

Surprisingly, $FUV(DTR)$ is not faster than any $FUV(2\text{-}LL_n)$. The responsible refusal traces produced by FastAsy show $r_1\emptyset^m\{e_1\} \in RT(FUV(DTR))$ for all $m \in \mathbb{N}$, while for any $FUV(2\text{-}LL_n)$ this is not true for all $m \in \mathbb{N}$. In the refusal firing sequence underlying such a refusal trace, the r_1-transition of

196

$FUV(DTR)$ fires; then between any two ticks the internal transition that makes the second user stay noncritical fires, and finally before $\{e_1\}$ the second user requests (internally) and orders. Along this sequence, e_1 is urgent most of the time; only at the end it is prevented by the arrival of an order. This behaviour can occur when the user requests and then does something else before he comes back later and tries to enter. $2\text{-}LL$ and all its n-delays support this *come-back-later strategy*: after r_1, the token might travel round the ring, but eventually it will stay in p_1 and wait for e_1; the time the user spends on something else reduces the waiting time.

Result: $2\text{-}LL$ supports the *come-back-later strategy*, DTR does not: $r_1 \emptyset^m \{e_1\} \in RT(FUV(DTR))$ for all $m \in I\!N$. $FUV(DTR)$ isn't faster than any $FUV(2\text{-}LL_n)$.

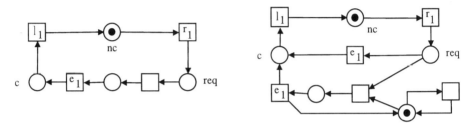

Figure 4

To discuss further consequences of this observation and subsequently to develop a numeric measure of efficiency, we define:

Definition 15. $1\text{-}MTX_n$ is a net consisting of a ring of one r_1-, n internal, one e_1- and one l_1-transition as e.g. $1\text{-}MTX_1$ shown on the left-hand side of Fig. 4.

$1/1\text{-}MTX_1$ is the net shown on the right-hand side; $1/1\text{-}MTX_n$ is obtained from this net by inserting a sequence of $n-1$ further internal transitions before the lower e_1-transition (i.e. 'into' the arc leading to this transition). □

One might expect that the first-user view of a MUTEX-solution simply has the same behaviour as a ring like $1\text{-}MTX_n$ with an r_1-, an e_1- and an l_1-transition and some internal transitions. Indeed, in all our solutions each e_1-transition enables an l_1-transition, which becomes and stays urgent after the next tick; each l_1-transition enables an r_1-transition, which becomes and stays urgent after the next tick – just as in each $1\text{-}MTX_n$. Furthermore, $FUV(2\text{-}LL)$ and $1\text{-}MTX_3$ are equally fast, as are $FUV(2\text{-}LL_1)$ and $1\text{-}MTX_5$ and also $FUV(2\text{-}LL_2)$ and $1\text{-}MTX_7$. So one might even expect that each first-user view is equally fast as some $1\text{-}MTX_n$. As a consequence, one could think of this n as a numeric measure of efficiency for MUTEX-solutions.

The expectation is wrong for at least two reasons: first, in $1\text{-}MTX_n$, the worst-case delay of $n+1$ ticks between r_1 and e_1 can occur every time, but there are MUTEX-solutions where the worst-case delay cannot occur twice in a row. (Our new solution in 5.4 is an example.) Secondly, the behaviour of MUTEX-solutions can be more intricate, as we have seen above: $FUV(DTR)$ is in fact equally fast as $1/1\text{-}MTX_5$.

The behaviour of these nets $1/1$-MTX_n is (compare Fig. 4): initially, r_1 is on offer, so if the user wants to request, r_1 is performed – formally, we can have arbitrarily many ticks as long as r_1 is not refused. After r_1 and a tick, the upper e_1-transition is urgent; the conflicting internal transition is blocked by the loop-transition, and we can have arbitrarily many ticks as long as e_1 is not refused; this behaviour might occur if the user does not want to enter. At any stage, the conflicting internal transition can fire, followed by one of the additional internal transitions after each of the following ticks; in this time, the user might want to enter, but this is not possible. After all in all at most six ticks where e_1 is refused, the lower e_1-transition is urgent and the user can enter whenever he wants to. Next, the user can leave and so on.

Due to the second reason from above, we choose the family of the $1/1$-MTX_n for comparison; due to the first reason from above, we do not insist on equal speed but use a more flexible formulation.

Definition 16. Let N be an n-MUTEX net and m be minimal such that $FUV(N)$ is faster than $1/1$-MTX_m. Then the *enter-delay* of N is m if $FUV(N)$ and $1/1$-MTX_m are in fact equally fast, and it is m^- otherwise. A refusal trace is *responsible* for the enter-delay, if it is in $RT(FUV(N))$ but not in $RT(1/1$-$MTX_{m-1})$. The enter-delay is undefined if $FUV(N)$ is not faster than any $1/1$-MTX_m. □

All the MUTEX-solutions in this paper have an enter-delay – but this is not true in general. Compared to 1-MTX_0, $1/1$-MTX_1 has an additional 'level of complication' formed by the lower three transitions, and this level is in conflict with the upper e_1-transition. Now one could add another 'level of complication' in conflict with the lower e_1-transition and obtain a family $1/2$-MTX_n. We have also checked a variant of Dekker's solution, which does not have an enter-delay in our definition, but could be classified with the nets $1/2$-MTX_n.

5.3 Delays and more than 2 users

Now we will apply our numeric measure: The n-*delay* of DTR is obtained as above by inserting n internal transitions into each 'link' between the parts, and it is denoted by DTR_n. This time, the links are the arcs into g_1 and g_2, which are elongated as above, and the arcs for ordering the access-token. Since each o_i has a marked complement place, these two places have to be treated together, as indicated below for the 1-delay of one of these order-links:

It is not completely evident that these n-delays are correct solutions; but we will see in the next section that this is more or less automatically implied by the following results produced by FastAsy:

Proposition 1. *The enter-delays of 2-LL, 2-LL$_1$ and 2-LL$_2$ are 3^-, 5^- and 7^-. The enter-delays of DTR, DTR$_1$ and DTR$_2$ are 5, 7 and 9.*

For the results on 2-LL recall that this solution supports the come-back-later strategy; hence, it is never equally fast as some $1/1$-MTX_n.

If mainly the communication delay along the token ring is relevant, then this proposition indicates that in the worst case one has to wait roughly twice the time it takes to send a message from one part of the solution to the other. Also the responsible refusal traces show this: in the worst case for 2-LL, the token has just left before the request; it travels to the other part, is used and returns. For DTR, an order arrives just after the request and prevents an entering; while the token travels to the other part and is used by the second user, the order of the first user travels and arrives (this can particularly well be seen in the delayed versions); thus, immediately after the use the token travels back to the first user. Although three messages along the ring are involved, they only take the time of two since two of them happen at the same time.

We call the worst time it takes to send a message from one part of a solution to the other the *message delay*. In 2-LL_n and DTR_n this is $n+1$, and analogously for the solutions below.

Result: If only the communication delay along the token ring is relevant, then 2-LL and DTR are equally efficient: their enter-delays correspond to two message delays.

As a next step, we extend our two solutions to more than two users. This is obvious in the case of 2-LL: in n-LL, we have n parts instead of two parts with arcs from the first part to p_2, from the second to p_3 etc.

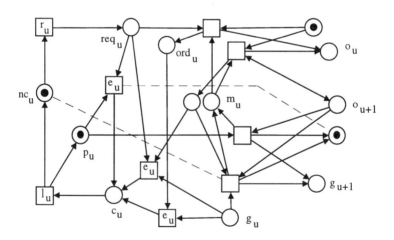

Figure 5

The general version of Dijkstra's Token-Ring is much more complicated than DTR: orders have to be passed on as well as the token, which travels the other way round. Fig. 5 shows the u-th part of n-DTR, which has n such parts – read arcs are dashed to increase readability. The part shown owns the token on p_u; if an order arrives from part $u + 1$, the token is granted to $u + 1$ and now missing (m_u is marked). Now there are two possibilities: either again an order arrives from $u+1$, is sent on to $u-1$ (o_u is marked) and this is recorded in the place next to m_u; or user u requests and the token is ordered, which is recorded in ord_u. Ordering is not necessary if an order was passed on before. When now the token arrives from $u-1$ on g_u, user u can enter with one of the lower e_u-transitions, or he passes the token on if he has no interest (checked by the read arc from nc_u). FastAsy produces the following results:

Proposition 2. *The enter-delays of 2-LL, 3-LL and 4-LL are 3^-, 6^- and 9^-. The enter-delays of 2-DTR, 3-DTR and 4-DTR are 5, 10 and 15.*

When a user is added to 2-LL, the token travels one more link in the ring; when it arrives at a user, the user keeps it for two ticks by requesting and then using it. The results for n-DTR are not so easy to understand, except that each user adds considerable overhead. Delays for the families n-LL and n-DTR are defined as above.

Proposition 3. *The enter-delays of 3-LL, 3-LL$_1$ and 3-LL$_2$ are 6^-, 9^- and 12^-. The enter-delays of 3-DTR, 3-DTR$_1$ and 3-DTR$_2$ are 10, 14 and 18.*

The first sentence is as expected: in the worst case, the token has just left when a request occurs and has to travel round the ring once. For the second senctence, the responsible sequences show this worst case: just after a request, the token is ordered by the next user and stays there; now an order is sent to the previous user and travels almost all around the ring to the next user; then the token travels almost all around the ring and is used on the way by the users it passes. Hence:

Result: If only the communication delay along the token ring is relevant, then the enter-delay of n-LL corresponds to n message delays, that of n-DTR corresponds to $2(n - 1)$ message delays.

5.4 The Same-Way solution

The efficiency problem of n-DTR stems from the fact that orders and tokens travel in opposite directions, which by the way requires bidirectional communication in contrast to n-LL. The idea of our presumably new solution is that they travel the same way; hence, an order travels round the ring until it meets the token, which then travels the rest of the ring. Thus, the enter-delay should correspond to n message delays, only a unidirectional ring is needed, and a communication load on the ring is only created if the token is needed somewhere. We encountered some problems (demonstrating the elegance of n-DTR) and found that we had to attach the user identities to the orders and the travelling token. Consequently, we show our solution n-SW using some high-level-net notation, and we show it in three figures that have to be overlayed.

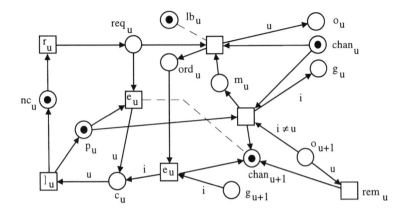

In the first figure above, the owner u of the token can use it as before (inscribing it with u as long as he is in the critical section). If user u misses the token he sends an order u to the previous user on the channel formed by o_u, $chan_u$ and g_u; if subsequently a token inscribed i arrives from the next user, i.e. on g_{u+1}, user u can enter keeping this inscription. The place $chan_u$ is a complement to o_u and g_u; when defining the delays $n\text{-}SW_m$, these places have to be treated together as in $n\text{-}DTR_m$ above. If an order from $i \neq u$ arrives on o_{u+1}, the owner u sends the token inscribed with i to the previous user. Finally, an order from u can travel around the ring after the token without meeting it; hence, if an own order arrives, the token has visited u in the meantime and the order can be removed by rem_u.

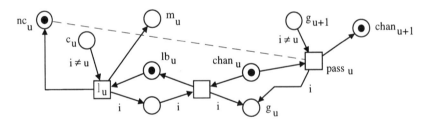

When u uses a token inscribed i, he has to send it on when leaving the critical section, which is shown in the second figure. Since the link to the previous user could be blocked, this could block the leave-action – which is undesirable in our setting (i.e. with our definition of enter-delay). We have therefore introduced a leave-buffer; lb_u is marked if this buffer is empty. The order-transition (in the first figure) checks this place to keep the right order of messages on the link; this is a subtle point that we had overlooked at first; the results and responsible sequences produced by FastAsy were very valuable to detect the mistake. The second figure also shows how a token is passed on if user u is not interested.

The third figure shows how orders are passed on if user u neither owns the token nor has interest in it. If he has ordered the token himself, the order arriving

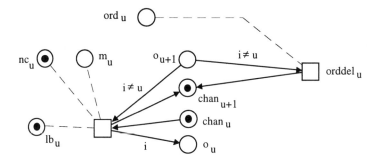

from the next user can be deleted, because it will have been satisfied when the token arrives at u. (The correctness of all this is of course not obvious.)

Proposition 4. *The enter-delays of 3-SW, 3-SW$_1$ and 3-SW$_2$ are 11$^-$, 14$^-$ and 17$^-$.*

These values are quite high; but this result and in particular the responsible sequences show that indeed in the worst case a message has to travel round the ring once. The high values are also caused by some congestion on the links. For this, the hidden users have to show a very particular behaviour pattern, where one user orders twice; now the same pattern cannot be repeated since the user has already ordered, and the enter-delay is 11^- rather than 11 etc. Still, 3-SW is more of the $1/1$-MTX_n type and does not support the come-back-later strategy.

Result: If only the communication delay along the token ring is relevant, then the enter-delay of n-SW corresponds to n message delays.

6   Correctness and Efficiency

To show the correctness of all our solutions, we now formulate a correctness specification based on the $\mathcal{FF}$-semantics, which is a modification and generalization of the specification given in [Vog97].

Definition 17. We call a finite or infinite sequence over $I_n = \{r_i, e_i, l_i \mid i = 1, \ldots, n\}$ *legal* if r_i, e_i and l_i only occur cyclically in this order for each i.   □

In our specification, we will not require that a solution only performs legal sequences: illegal sequences can only occur if the users want to perform them, i.e. make a mistake. But this point is not essential.

Correctness consists of a safety and a liveness requirement. *Safety* requires that never two users are in their critical sections at the same time; if one user enters, then he must leave before another enter is possible. For token-passing solutions this is usually easy to prove with an S-invariant, as demonstrated above for 2-LL. Liveness – i.e. whenever a user wishes to enter he will be able to do so eventually – is more difficult and requires to assume fairness. Our definition of liveness is explained below.

Definition 18. An n-MUTEX net N is a *correct n-MUTEX-solution*, if N satisfies *safety*, i.e. e- and l-transitions only occur alternatingly in a legal trace, and satisfies *liveness* in the following sense. Let $w \in I_n^* \cup I_n^\omega$ be legal and $1 \leq i \leq n$; then:

1. Each e_i in w is followed by an l_i, or N **surely offers** $\{l_i\}$ **along** w.
2. Assume each e_j is followed by l_j in w. Then either each r_i is followed by e_i or N **surely offers** X **along** w where X consists of those e_j where some r_j in w is not followed by e_j.
3. Assume that each r_j is followed by e_j and each e_j is followed by l_j in w. Then we have the following: either r_i occurs and each l_i is followed by another r_i in w, or N **surely offers** $\{r_i\}$ **along** w. $\qquad\square$

Recall that a complete system consists of the scheduler N and its environment comprising the users, and these two components synchronize over I_n. The first part of liveness says that, if user i enters (performs e_i together with the scheduler N), later tries to leave (enables an l_i-transition) and does not withdraw (does not disable the transition again), then he will indeed leave; otherwise l_i would be enabled continuously in the complete system violating fairness. (Technically, recall how the refusal sets of fair refusal pairs are composed according to Theorem 10: the complete system is fair, i.e. Σ is refused, only if one of the components refuses l_i.)

In other words, if user i does not leave again, then he is not willing to leave since l_i is offered to him. This is a user misbehaviour and the behaviour of the scheduler N is correct. As a consequence, we can now assume that each e_j is followed by l_j. Under this assumption, the second part of liveness says that each request of i is satisfied, unless some requesting user is permanently offered to enter. In the latter case, that user is misbehaving by not accepting this offer, and again N is working correctly.

Now we can assume that each request is satisfied. Under this assumption, i requests infinitely often or N at least offers him to request. This is not a user misbehaviour because each user is free to decide whether he wants to request.

The following result shows that the notion of fair implementation makes sense for the MUTEX-problem and it ties together correctness and efficiency.

Theorem 19. *If a net N is a correct n-MUTEX-solution and a net N' is faster than N or a fair implementation of N, then N' is a correct n-MUTEX-solution, too.*

Proof. Safety forbids certain traces. Since each firing sequence can be extended to a fair one, safety in effect forbids certain fair refusal pairs (w, Σ). Also liveness forbids certain fair refusal pairs.

If N' is faster than N, it is also a fair implementation of N, i.e. we have $\mathcal{FF}(N') \subseteq \mathcal{FF}(N)$. Thus, if $\mathcal{FF}(N)$ does not contain a forbidden fair refusal pair, then neither does $\mathcal{FF}(N')$, i.e. N' is a correct n-MUTEX-solution. $\qquad\square$

With this result, we could give correctness proofs using FastAsy, but we would need a correct and slow solution first. Even if we can convince ourselves that e.g. 2-*LL* and maybe also its delays are correct, this does not help for *DTR*: as discussed above, already their functional behaviours are quite different, and on top of this *DTR* will not be faster than any 2-*LL$_n$*, since these support the come-back-later strategy. So it seems that the above theorem is not very useful.

The surprising fact is that, under some symmetry assumptions, it is enough to check the first-user view of a solution; i.e. we can abstract away all visible behaviour of all but one user. As described later, this really allows correctness proofs with FastAsy. It should be remarked that the abstraction does not necessarily reduce the number of reachable ID's, i.e. of states of the nondeterministic automaton generated by FastAsy. E.g. 3-*DTR* has 669 reachable ID's, while *FUV*(3-*DTR*) has 798 – we plan to implement an ad hoc trick to reduce this number. But the deterministic automata used for comparisons have 843 versus 25 states!

Definition 20. A *quasi-automorphism* ϕ of a net N is an isomorphism of the net graph of N onto itself that maps the initial marking to a reachable marking, i.e.: ϕ is a bijection of $S \cup T$ onto itself such that $\phi(S) = S$, $\phi(T) = T$, $(x, y) \in F \Leftrightarrow (\phi(x), \phi(y)) \in F$, $(x, y) \in R \Leftrightarrow (\phi(x), \phi(y)) \in R$, and $\phi(M_N)$ is a reachable marking. (Here, M_N is regarded as a set.) Note that ϕ ignores the labelling.

A quasi-automorphism ϕ of an n-MUTEX net N and a permutation π of $\{1, \ldots, n\}$ form a *user symmetry* (ϕ, π) if, first, $\phi(M_N)$ is reachable with a legal trace where for each i the last i-indexed action (if any) is l_i and, second, for all $i = 1, \ldots, n$ and all $t \in T$ we have $l(t) = r_i \Leftrightarrow l(\phi(t)) = r_{\pi(i)}$, $l(t) = e_i \Leftrightarrow l(\phi(t)) = e_{\pi(i)}$, and $l(t) = l_i \Leftrightarrow l(\phi(t)) = l_{\pi(i)}$.

An n-MUTEX net is *user-symmetric* if, for all $i, j \in \{1, \ldots, n\}$, it has a user symmetry (ϕ, π) with $\pi(i) = j$. □

Similar symmetries can be used to construct reduced reachability graphs, see e.g. [Sta90].

Theorem 21. *Assume an n-MUTEX net N is user-symmetric and satisfies safety. Then, N is a correct n-MUTEX solution if FUV(N) is a correct 1-MUTEX solution.*

Due to lack of space, we omit the proof of this theorem and also do not consider the reverse implication, which is not needed for our application. It should be pointed out that we have modified the correctness definition of [Vog97] to make this theorem work. More precisely, we only require in part 3 that requesting is surely offered *if* the users do not misbehave; it might be preferable that requesting is always offered (at the proper moment), but our specification seems reasonable.

Corollary 22. *If an n-MUTEX net N is user-symmetric, satisfies safety and has an enter-delay, it is a correct n-MUTEX solution.*

Proof. It should be clear that all nets 1/1-*MTX$_n$* are correct. In particular, if in a firing sequence v some r_1 is not followed by e_1, then v is either not fair to the 'upper' e_1-transition, or the internal transition in conflict with it fires; by fairness to internal transitions, the following transitions fire, too, and v is not fair to the 'lower' e_1-transition. Hence, if N has an enter-delay, then by definition and 19, $FUV(N)$ is correct. Now apply 21. □

Theorem 23. *All n-MUTEX solutions treated in this paper – in particular, Dijkstra's Token-Ring and the new Same-Way solution for three users – are correct.*

Proof. As explained, safety can easily be shown with S-invariants; user symmetry follows more or less by construction, and checking one suitable firing sequence. Now 22 implies the theorem with the results of Sect. 5. □

References

[CH93]   S. Christensen, N.D. Hansen. Coloured Petri nets extended with place capacities, test arcs, and inhibitor arcs. In M. Ajmone-Marsan, editor, *Applications and Theory of Petri Nets 1993*, LNCS 691, 186–205. Springer, 1993.

[Dij85]   E.W. Dijkstra. Invariance and non-determinacy. In R. Hoare, C.A and J.C. Sheperdson, editors, *Mathematical Logic and Programming Languages*, 157–165. Prentice-Hall, 1985.

[DNH84] R. De Nicola, M.C.B. Hennessy. Testing equivalence for processes. *Theoret. Comput. Sci.*, 34:83–133, 1984.

[JK95]   R. Janicki, M. Koutny. Semantics of inhibitor nets. *Information and Computation*, 123:1–16, 1995.

[JV96]   L. Jenner, W. Vogler. Fast asynchronous systems in dense time. In F. Meyer auf der Heide and B. Monien, editors, *Automata, Languages and Programming ICALP'96*, Lect. Notes Comp. Sci. 1099, 75–86. Springer, 1996.

[KW95]   E. Kindler, R. Walter. Message passing mutex. In J. Desel, editor, *Structures in Concurrency Theory*, Worksh. in Computing, 205–219. Springer, 1995.

[KW97]   E. Kindler, R. Walter. Mutex needs fairness. *Inf. Proc. Letter*, 62:31–39, 1997.

[LV95]   N. Lynch, F. Vaandrager. Forward and backward simulations I: Untimed systems. *Information and Computation*, 121:214–233, 1995.

[Lyn96]   N. Lynch. *Distributed Algorithms*. Morgan Kaufmann Publishers, San Francisco, 1996.

[MR95]   U. Montanari, F. Rossi. Contextual nets. *Acta Informatica*, 32:545–596, 1995.

[pep]   PEP Homepage. http://www.informatik.uni-hildesheim.de/ pep/.

[Ray86]   M. Raynal. *Algorithms for Mutual Exclusion*. North Oxford Academic, 1986.

[Sta90]   P.H. Starke. *Analyse von Petri-Netz-Modellen*. Teubner, 1990.

[Vog95a] W. Vogler. Timed testing of concurrent systems. *Information and Computation*, 121:149–171, 1995.

[Vog95b] W. Vogler. Faster asynchronous systems. In I. Lee and S. Smolka, editors, *CONCUR 95*, Lect. Notes Comp. Sci. 962, 299–312. Springer, 1995. Full version as Report Nr. 317, Inst. f. Mathematik, Univ. Augsburg, 1995.

[Vog97]   W. Vogler. Efficiency of asynchronous systems and read arcs in Petri nets. In P. Degano, R. Gorrieri, and A. Marchetti-Spaccamela, editors, *ICALP 97*, Lect. Notes Comp. Sci. 1256, 538–548. Springer, 1997. Full version as technical report Nr. 352, Inst. f. Mathematik, Univ. Augsburg, 1996.

Thinking in Cycles

Mark-Oliver Stehr

Universität Hamburg, Fachbereich Informatik
Vogt-Kölln-Straße 30, D-22527 Hamburg
stehr@informatik.uni-hamburg.de

Abstract A new axiomization of the intuitive concept of *partial cyclic orders* is proposed and the appropriateness is motivated from pragmatic as well as mathematical perspectives. There is a close relation to Petri net theory since the set of basic circuits of a safe and live *synchronization graph* naturally gives rise to a cyclic order. As a consequence cyclic orders provide a simple technique for *safety-oriented specification* where safety (in the sense of net theory) is achieved by relying on the fundamental concept of *cyclic causality constraints* avoiding the risk of an immediate and directed causality relation. From a foundational point of view cyclic orders provide a basis for a theory of *nonsequential cyclic processes* and new insights into C.A.Petri's *concurrency theory*. By the slogan *measurement as control* cyclic orders can serve as a tool for the construction of cyclic measurement scales, spatial and temporal knowledge representation and reasoning being only some applications. New results in this article include a characterization of global orientability (implementability) by weak F-density (the existence of a true cut).

Keywords: cyclic orders, causality, concurrency, synchronization graphs

1 Introduction

It was in 1991 on the occasion of the Hamburg colloquium devoted to C.A.Petri's 65th birthday when the author was confronted with the apparently contradictory idea of a cyclic order for the first time. In a meeting with a group of students (the author was among them) C.A.Petri discussed a draft [11] where he proposed new axioms for cyclic orders. The approach to cyclic orders presented here is different[1] but in the spirit of the original ideas [13]. Of equal importance for the present work are some deep insights into synchronization graphs obtained by H.J.Genrich in [3] which have not received much attention until now.

The two figures below convey a first intuition for cyclic orders (*COs*). In Fig. 1 we can see an oriented arrangement of five elements on a closed line. The CO is total since every two elements are ordered. The distinguishing feature of a cyclic order (in contrast to ordinary ones) is its *cyclic symmetry*, i.e. invariance under rotation. Whereas total COs are not really exciting the situation is different with the class of partial COs. A graphical representation of a non-total CO is

---

[1] Our approach is different in one essential and a few superficial aspects, the essential difference being that we consider a cyclic order to be inherently oriented.

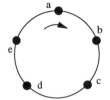

Fig. 1. A total cyclic order

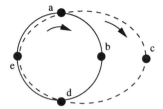

Fig. 2. A (partial) cyclic order

shown in Fig. 2. It specifies the relative positions of elements w.r.t. two different closed oriented lines. It is the fact that the order between elements b and c is not specified which makes this CO non-total.

Trying to describe the structures above by employing an ordinary partial order (i.e. a reflexive, antisymmetric and transitive relation) in the naive way leads inevitably to *a contradiction*: For instance, in both examples we would have $a \leq b$ and $b \leq a$ which violates antisymmetry. An apparent solution is to drop the axiom of antisymmetry. This leads to the well-known notion of quasi-order. However, conceiving the oriented arrangements above as quasi-orders yields trivial quasi-orders (satisfying $x \leq y$ for all elements x and y) and a total *loss of information* in both examples. Quasi-orders abstract from the arrangement of elements on cycles which is just the information we are interested in.[2]

Another obvious idea is the representation of cyclic arrangements by an immediate predecessor relation (which is usually not transitive), for instance $(\lessdot) = \{(a,b), (b,c), (c,d), (d,e), (e,a)\}$ in the first example. However, this deviates completely from the practice of ordinary partial orders and would not be appropriate if the predecessor relation is empty (not informative enough) as it is the case in (partially) dense arrangements. It might be surprising that even for certain finite structures the predecessor relation is not sufficient to distinguish essentially different arrangements, again leading to an undesired *loss of information*.

The solution we favor reflects the structure of cycles exactly and, more surprisingly, this can be achieved by incorporation of cyclic symmetry into an axiomization of ordinary partial orders. It is essential to choose the representation of partial orders appropriately to avoid a contradiction or a loss of information as above. Our choice is based on the key observation that there is no natural binary relation capturing all information we are interested in. So we will resort to more informative relations of higher arity.

The subsequent section will introduce and motivate the axioms of COs in the context of a real world toy example, namely the specification of cyclic schedules. After this intuitive motivation the axioms of COs are formally justified in several steps starting from acyclic orders (AOs) which are not more than a very unusual representation of ordinary partial orders. The problem of global orientability is discussed and it is shown to be equivalent to the existence of a clock representation. To establish a bridge to net theory the notions of concurrency, causality, and basic circuits in synchronization graphs are introduced. The set of basic

---

[2] Quasi-orders are appropriate for many applications where the internal structure of cycles is irrelevant.

circuits gives rise to a CO which has the important property of global orientability. Subsequently, the issue of implementability of COs (which comes in the two flavours of realizability and approximability) by synchronization graphs is made precise and exploited to obtain a characterization of global orientability by weak F-density. The objective of this article is to give an easy introduction to COs and to demonstrate their relevance in the context of net theory. It should be stressed that it is not the intention to present the mathematical theory of COs itself. This has been done in [20] in a formally rigorous way.

2 Motivation

COs are ubiquitous in the real world but one rarely encounters them in their pure form. A well-known example which admits a reasonable abstraction from impurities is the specification of a traffic light controller.

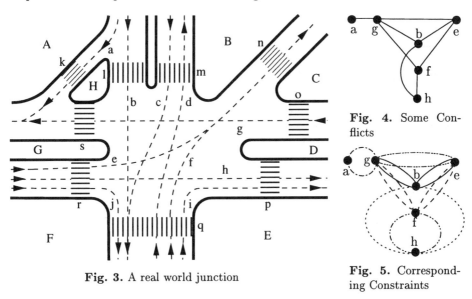

Fig. 3. A real world junction

Fig. 4. Some Conflicts

Fig. 5. Corresponding Constraints

Fig. 3 shows a junction located somewhere in the city of Hamburg. Dashed lines show possible routes for vehicles. Arrows indicate permitted driving directions. Striped areas are pedestrian crossings. Vehicle routes and pedestrian crossings can be considered as spatial resources. Two resources are said to be *mutually exclusive* iff they share some space.[3] The problem is to design a traffic light control policy.

From an abstract point of view we can specify an instance of this problem as a conflict graph (V,E) part of which is shown in Fig. 4. The set of vertices V is given by spatial resources and the set of edges $E \subseteq V \times V$ is a symmetric,

---

[3] There are some exceptions, e.g. the pairs $\{i,p\}$, $\{j,q\}$ and $\{c,b\}$ are not mutually exclusive, because the drivers carry the responsibility of avoiding collisions in these cases.

irreflexive relation holding between every two resources which are mutually exclusive. Observe that we are concerned with an instance of Dijkstra's (general) dining philosophers problem and it is known that every symmetric solution relies on randomness.[4]

Why are solutions of this kind not suited for traffic light control ? One reason is that they involve too much nondeterminism and the degree of fairness provided is not sufficient. For traffic lights nondeterminism should be avoided as far as possible to make them more predictable by humans and thereby eliminating one major source of accidents. Moreover, traffic lights should satisfy very strict fairness conditions to reduce the temporal variance of trips through the city. Another argument against a nondeterministic solution is the desire to realize "green waves" in order to make traffic flow more efficient.

To meet the *requirement of determinism* we impose *strict alternation* for the availability of mutually exclusive resources. As a by-product this rather tight coupling leads to *bounded fairness* if the conflict graph is connected, i.e., the number of other resources made available before the required one is bounded.[5]

From a less detailed point of view we can conceive the two events delimiting beginning and termination of the availability interval of a resource as a single (non-atomic) event. Abusing terminology we will therefore speak of the occurrence of a resource instead of the occurrence of its beginning followed by the occurrence of its termination event.

Consider the set of pairwise mutually exclusive resources $\{b,e,g\}$ in our example. Assume we are just observing the occurrence of b and we ignore all events not contained in $\{b,e,g\}$. Since strict alternation between every pair of $\{b,e,g\}$ was imposed, e or g have to occur before b can occur again. These two possibilities give rise to exactly two possible occurrence sequences, namely $(b\ g\ e\ b\ g\ e\ b\ g\ e\ ...)$ and $(b\ e\ g\ b\ e\ g\ b\ e\ g\ ...)$. Observe that no further sequences are possible: Once two successive elements are fixed, the next element is uniquely determined by the requirement of strict alternation. So once the traffic light controller is running, the order between $\{b,e,g\}$ is specified by the periodic repetition of either $(b\ g\ e)$ or $(b\ e\ g)$ and remains fixed forever. A corresponding statement holds for all finite cliques of pairwise strictly alternating events. In the context of COs this will be formulated as the *axiom of completeness*.[6]

To represent *cyclic causality constraints* of the type described above we employ simple words (i.e. sequences without repetitions) as required by the *axiom of simplicity*. A simple word $w = (w(0)\ w(1)\ ...\ w(n-1))$ specifies that the ele-

---

[4] Unfortunately randomness is not available for free. Arbitration involves confusion (see [16]) and has to cope with a tradeoff between speed and probability of failure (caused by meta-stability).This imposes fundamental limitations on the performance of asynchronous systems and on the reliability of synchronous systems. According to Petri "confusion should be avoided whenever possible" [13].

[5] Bounded fairness has been investigated in [15]. In net theory this strict form of fairness can be measured by means of synchronic distances.

[6] When Petri commented on [11] where a related axiom was proposed, he called it a venturous axiom (ein kühnes Axiom). With the explanation given here it should appear less venturous to the reader.

ments $w(0), w(1), ..., w(n-1)$, which are resources in our example, should always occur exactly in the cyclic succession in which they appear in w.[7] As we are only interested in the cyclic succession, words related by rotation (i.e. cyclic permutation of their elements) describe the same constraint and are said to be (rotation) equivalent. By the assumption of determinism a mutual exclusion constraint such as (b,e) is realized by strict alternation. This makes it appear as a degenerate cyclic constraint $(b\ e)$ which is equivalent to $(e\ b)$.

The specification of a system is given by a set of cyclic constraints with the intended meaning that all constraints should be satisfied. The graphical representation Fig. 5 shows all cyclic constraints that arise from the requirement that pairwise mutually exclusive resources should occur in strict alternation (again restricted to the part shown in Fig. 4). The convention to interpret such diagrams is simple: Every word $w = (w(0)\ w(1)\ ...\ w(n-1))$ is represented by a closed oriented line passing through $w(0)\ w(1)\ ...\ w(n-1)$ in exactly this succession within one round of traversal. Due to the rotation equivalence mentioned above the orientation is irrelevant (and therefore not indicated) for lines with less than three elements.

Clearly, an implementation satisfying a constraint $(c\ d\ m)$ satisfies the constraints $(d\ m\ c)$ and $(m\ c\ d)$ and also $(c\ d)$ and $(d\ c)$. More generally, a specification containing a cyclic constraint w will implicitly or explicitly include all rotations and all (distributed) subwords of w.[8] For mathematical convenience we decided to make them explicit, giving rise to the *axiom of subword closedness* and the *axiom of rotation closedness*.

From the definition of cyclic constraints above it is clear that it is impossible to realize the constraints $(b\ g\ e)$ and $(b\ e\ g)$ simultaneously. So a specification containing both constraints is not *consistent*. Two cyclic constraints are said to be consistent iff they agree on the elements they have in common. For instance $(b\ g\ e)$ and $(e\ b)$ are consistent as they agree on $\{b,e\}$ (the constraints $(b\ e)$ and $(e\ b)$ are equivalent).

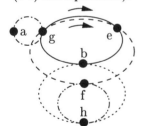
Fig. 6. Cyclic order

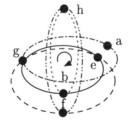
Fig. 7. Clock representation

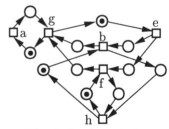
Fig. 8. Implementation

The preliminary specification in Fig. 5 contains the mutual exclusion constraints only. The specification does not satisfy the completeness axiom as no

---

[7] Allowing only simple words is a major restriction on the constraints which can be captured. For instance, we cannot specify the fact that an event a occurs precisely twice between the occurrences of another event b.

[8] In this paper subwords are always distributed subwords, i.e. a subword is obtained from a word by removing any number of arbitrary elements.

cyclic constraint is specified for the clique $\{g,e,b\}$. As the traffic light controller is required to be deterministic the choice, which of the two alternative cyclic constraints $(b\ g\ e)$ or $(b\ e\ g)$ should be realized, has to be decided by the designer of the traffic light schedule. For the following let us choose the cyclic constraint $(b\ g\ e)$. The completeness axiom enforces a decision of the same kind for the clique $\{g,e,f\}$. Depending on whether we add $(g\ e\ f)$ or $(g\ f\ e)$ we obtain completely different solutions. The solution arising from the choice $(g\ e\ f)$ is depicted in Fig. 6. It will turn out later that it is indeed a CO.[9]

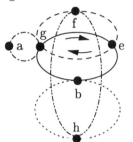 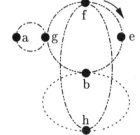 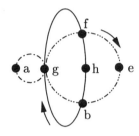

Fig. 9. First design   **Fig. 10.** Second design   **Fig. 11.** Cyclic order

The set of constraints obtained by the choice $(g\ f\ e)$ is shown in Fig. 9. In spite of the fact that the completeness axiom is satisfied, we do not consider it as a CO as the specification is incomplete in a different sense: Consider only the cyclic constraints $(g\ e\ b)$ and $(g\ f\ e)$ we included in our specification. Think of an arbitrary interval delimited by two successive occurrences of g. $(g\ f\ e)$ specifies that f occurs before e and $(g\ e\ b)$ specifies that e occurs before b in this interval. Using (temporal) transitivity we conclude that f occurs before b in this interval which is expressed by the constraint $(g\ f\ b)$. This way to derive cyclic constraints from given ones will be formalized as the *axiom of cyclic transitivity*. Observe that taking into account all elements involved we can even infer the stronger constraint $(g\ f\ e\ b)$ which contains $(g\ f\ e)$, $(g\ e\ b)$ and $(g\ f\ b)$ as subwords. Adding these constraints yields the structure in Fig. 10. Although cyclic transitivity is satisfied, the modification introduced above has destroyed the completeness property: The new clique $\{b,f,h\}$ of pairwise strictly alternating events is not covered by a constraint. Fortunately, a design decision in favor of $(b\ f\ h)$ (the choice $(h\ f\ b)$ would be possible as well) leads to a CO after applying cyclic transitivity once more to $(f\ h\ b)$ and $(f\ b\ g)$. The result is shown in Fig. 11.

Due to their modest size it is obvious that both COs (Fig. 6 and Fig. 11) admit a *clock representation*,[10] where all lines are oriented clockwise around a common center.[11] For the first CO a clock representation is given in Fig. 7. In general the existence of a clock representation is equivalent to *global orientability*, i.e. the

---

[9] In fact an observation of the junction revealed that this CO has been implemented.

[10] The idea of a clock representation has been introduced in [9] in the context of information flow graphs. It has been employed for synchronization graphs [3] and for cycloids [13].

[11] To be more precise we have to add that a radius originating from this center has exactly one point in common with each line.

extensibility to a total CO. It will be proved that this property is a sufficient and necessary condition for the existence of an implementation in terms of a safe and live synchronization graph. A synchronization graph implementation which satisfies exactly the cyclic constraints of our example is shown in Fig. 8. Of course, one might refine each transition by an intermediate state to represent the interval of resource availability.

Another issue is that cyclic constraints can also be used to specify "green waves". Assume for instance that in the evening many people are leaving the shopping center at F to catch a train at the station B. People would be happy if they could join a "green wave" leading them over the pedestrian crossings r, s, l and m. This "green wave" can easily be specified by an additional cyclic constraint $(r\ s\ l\ m)$. Of course, "green waves" for vehicles would make it necessary to take more than one junction into consideration.

In practice cyclic constraints such as "green waves" usually depend on external conditions like inputs from sensors and request buttons, traffic flow, day time and special events. So a real traffic light controller should operate in different modes each of them governed by a deterministic schedule. Depending on external conditions smooth transitions between these modes may be initiated.

3 Acyclic and Cyclic Orders

After advocating a simple framework of generalized relations we apply it to reintroduce the well-known notion of a strict partial order under the name acyclic order (AO). Generalized relations will be useful to present both AOs and COs in a uniform way. Starting from the axioms of AOs we approach the axioms of COs via simple modification and reformulation steps. Proceeding in this way we offer a purely mathematical motivation for the axioms of COs driven by the general idea that cyclic orders can be conceived as an abstraction of AOs.[12]

As usual, a *word* w is a finite sequence. The *length* of w is denoted by $\mathcal{L}(w)$. Its *indices* are $\mathcal{I}(w) := \{0,...,\mathcal{L}(w)-1\}$. The *alphabet* $\mathcal{A}(w)$ is the set of elements occurring in w. Occasionally we conceive w itself as the set $\mathcal{A}(w)$. Usual operations like indexing, written $w(i)$ for $i \in \mathcal{I}(w)$, and concatenation, written $(u\ v\ w\ ...)$, are available. A word of length one is not distinguished by notation from the single element it contains. A word w is *simple* iff $w(i) \neq w(j)$ for all indices $i \neq j$. A word u is a *(distributed) subword* of v $(u \sqsubseteq v)$ iff u is obtained by removing any number of elements from v. The *projection* of a word w on a set X $(w \rhd X)$ yields the subword of w obtained by removing all elements of $\mathcal{A}(w)$ which are not contained in X.

A *generalized relation* is a set of words. If there is no danger of confusion we simply speak of *relations*. They can be seen as mixed arity relations, a generalization of relations with fixed arity. Let R be such a relation. The *alphabet* of R is $\mathcal{A}(R) := \bigcup \{\mathcal{A}(w) : w \in R\}$. R is said to be trivial iff $\mathcal{A}(R) = \emptyset$. Notice that the alphabet is not necessarily finite leading to a proper generalization of formal

---

[12] Proofs of all results in this section can be found in [20].

languages.[13] R is *simple* iff all words $w \in R$ are simple. Simplicity generalizes irreflexivity of binary relations. A relation R is *subword-closed* iff $(\sqsupseteq)[R] = R$. Here $(\sqsupseteq)$ is the inverse of $(\sqsubseteq)$ and $(\sqsupseteq)[R]$ is the *subword closure* of R written as relational image. The *projection* of a relation R on a set X ($R \triangleright X$) is the relation $\{w \triangleright X : w \in R\}$. Two words u and v are *consistent* ($u \sim v$) iff ($u \triangleright \mathcal{A}(v)) = (v \triangleright \mathcal{A}(u))$ (or equivalently $(u \triangleright D) = (v \triangleright D)$ for $D := \mathcal{A}(u) \cap \mathcal{A}(v)$). R is *consistent* iff $u \sim v$ for all $u,v \in R$. R is *transitive* iff $(a\ b) \in R$ and $(b\ c) \in R$ implies $(a\ c) \in R$. The *dependence relation* of R is $(\text{li } R) := \{(x,y) \in \mathcal{A}(R)^2 : (x\ y) \in (\sqsupseteq)[R] \vee (y\ x) \in (\sqsupseteq)[R]\}$. The *independence relation* is $(\text{co } R) := \mathcal{A}(R)^2 - (\text{li } R) - \text{id}(\mathcal{A}(R))$.[14] We will also use their reflexive counterparts $(\underline{\text{li}}\ R) := (\text{li } R) \cup \text{id}(\mathcal{A}(R))$ and $(\underline{\text{co}}\ R) := (\text{co } R) \cup \text{id}(\mathcal{A}(R))$. Kens (i.e. maximal cliques) of $(\underline{\text{li}}\ R)$ and $(\underline{\text{co}}\ R)$ are called *lines* and *cuts* of R, respectively. If we speak of *cliques* and *kens* of R we usually mean cliques and kens of $(\underline{\text{li}}\ R)$. R is *complete* iff for all finite cliques C of R there is a $w \in R$ with $\mathcal{A}(w) = C$.

Definition 1. *R is an* acyclic order (AO) *iff R is simple, subword-closed, transitive and complete. R is* total *iff for all $x,y \in \mathcal{A}(R)$ there is a word $w \in R$ containing x and y.*

The *binary order relation* of R is $(<_R) := \{(x,y) : (x\ y) \in (\sqsupseteq)[R]\}$. The *acyclic predecessor relation* is defined by $x <_R y \Leftrightarrow (x,y) \in (<_R) \wedge \neg \exists z : (x\ z\ y) \in (\sqsupseteq)[R])$. For an AO R the pair $(\mathcal{A}(R),<_R)$ is a strict partial order called the *strict partial order associated to R*. This defines a 1-1 correspondence between the class of AOs and the class of strict partial orders. An AO R is total iff the associated strict partial order $(\mathcal{A}(R),<_R)$ is total. Moreover, for an AO R we have $(\text{li } R) = (<_R) \cup (<_R)^{-1}$.

The following characterization of total AOs does not contain the transitivity axiom but relies on the feature of consistence which is easier to generalize.

Proposition 1. *R is a total AO iff R is simple, subword-closed, consistent, complete and total.*

To incorporate cyclic symmetry we need additional terminology: Two words u and v are *rotation-equivalent* ($u \overset{\text{rot}}{\equiv} v$) iff u can be obtained from v by rotation (i.e. cyclic permutation). A relation R is *rotation-closed* iff $(\overset{\text{rot}}{\equiv})[R] = R$. Here $(\overset{\text{rot}}{\equiv})[R]$ is the *rotation closure* of R. u is a *rotated subword* of v ($u \overset{\text{rot}}{\sqsubseteq} v$) iff $u \sqsubseteq w$ and $w \overset{\text{rot}}{\equiv} v$ for some w. We will also use $(\overset{\text{rot}}{\sqsupseteq})$, the inverse of $(\overset{\text{rot}}{\sqsubseteq})$, and the *rotation subword closure* $(\overset{\text{rot}}{\sqsupseteq})[R]$. Let E be an equivalence on words. Two words u and v are *consistent modulo E* ($u \overset{E}{\sim} v$) iff $(u \triangleright \mathcal{A}(v))\ E\ (v \triangleright \mathcal{A}(u))$ (or equivalently $(u \triangleright D)\ E\ (v \triangleright D)$ for $D := \mathcal{A}(u) \cap \mathcal{A}(v)$). R is *consistent modulo E* iff $u \overset{E}{\sim} v$ for all $u,v \in R$. If we speak of *consistence* in the following we will usually mean *consistence modulo rotation* ($\overset{\text{rot}}{\sim}$) instantiating $(\overset{\text{rot}}{\equiv})$ for E. A relation R is said to be *cyclically transitive* iff $(a\ b\ c) \in R$ and $(a\ c\ d) \in R$ implies $(a\ b\ d) \in R$.

---

[13] As suggested by the traffic light example the major interpretation we favor will be different from the use of formal languages as an *interleaving semantics* of nonsequential processes.

[14] In our application context this definition can be justified by Prop. 4.

Now a definition of total COs can be obtained by a straightforward modification of the preceding characterization of total AOs: To reflect cyclic symmetry we simply add the axiom of rotation closedness. Of course, in order to avoid contradictions in nontrivial cases we have to weaken consistence (modulo identity) to consistence modulo rotation.

Definition 2. *R is a* total cyclic order *(total CO) iff R is simple, subword-closed, rotation-closed, consistent modulo rotation, complete and total.*

Example 1. By the convention introduced in the previous section the COs depicted in Fig. 1 and Fig. 2 are given by $\binom{\text{rot}}{\exists}[\{(a\ b\ c\ d\ e)\}]$ and $\binom{\text{rot}}{\exists}[\{(a\ b\ d\ e),\ (a\ c\ d\ e)\}]$, respectively. Indeed any finite total CO is of the form $\binom{\text{rot}}{\exists}[\{w\}]$.

The magic behind the following step is that cyclic transitivity comes into play only by a reformulation of the previous definition.

Theorem 1. *R is a total CO iff R is simple, subword-closed, rotation-closed, cyclically transitive, complete and total.*

Now the step to (general) COs is obvious: We simply drop the totality axiom. If we do not insist on completeness we obtain the weaker notion of cyclic preorder.

Definition 3. *R is a* cyclic order *(CO) iff R is simple, subword-closed, rotation-closed, cyclically transitive and complete. R is a* cyclic preorder *iff R is simple, subword-closed, rotation-closed and cyclically transitive.*

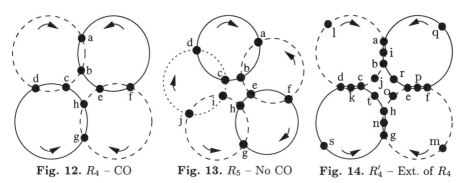

Fig. 12. R_4 – CO   **Fig. 13.** R_5 – No CO   **Fig. 14.** R'_4 – Ext. of R_4

Example 2. The CO of Fig. 6 or Fig. 7 is given by $R_T = \binom{\text{rot}}{\exists}[\{(g\ e\ b),\ (g\ e\ f),\ (a\ g),\ (b\ h),\ (f\ h)\}]$. Another example of a CO is $R_4 = \binom{\text{rot}}{\exists}[\{(a\ b\ c\ d),\ (a\ b\ e\ f),\ (e\ f\ g\ h),\ (c\ d\ g\ h)\}]$ depicted in Fig. 12. In Fig. 13 we see $R_5 = \binom{\text{rot}}{\exists}[\{(a\ b\ c\ d),\ (a\ b\ e\ f),\ (e\ f\ g\ h),\ (i\ j\ g\ h),\ (i\ j\ d\ c)\}]$. It violates cyclic transitivity (since $(c\ j\ d) \in R_5$ and $(c\ d\ a) \in R_5$ but $(c\ j\ a) \notin R_5$) and is therefore not a CO. It can however be extended to a CO by adding $\binom{\text{rot}}{\exists}[\{(i\ j\ d\ a\ b\ c)\}]$.

Every cyclic (pre)order R is consistent modulo rotation. In particular this means that for distinct elements $(a\ b\ c) \in R$ and $(c\ b\ a) \in R$ cannot hold simultaneously. Completeness on the other hand requires that every clique of R

coincides with some word of R. So for a cyclic order R and a clique $\{a,b,c\}$ of distinct elements we have either $(a \; b \; c) \in R$ or $(c \; b \; a) \in R$ but not both.

It is also noteworthy that the class of COs is closed under arbitrary projections, which means that every less detailed view $(R \rhd X)$ of a CO R is again a CO. If R is total then also $(R \rhd X)$ is total. The following proposition justifies the view of a cyclic order as proper composition of its total CO components given by $(R \rhd L)$ for all lines L.

Proposition 2. *R is a CO iff R is $(\sqsupseteq)$ -closed, cyclically transitive and $(R \rhd L)$ is a total CO for all lines L of R. Moreover, a CO R can be written as a union of total COs, namely $R = \bigcup \{R' : L \text{ is a line of } R : R' = (R \rhd L)\}$.*

The *cyclic predecessor relation* is defined by $x \prec_R y \Leftrightarrow (x,y) \in (\underline{\text{li}} \; R) \wedge \neg \exists z : (x \; z \; y) \in (\sqsupseteq)[R]$ for $x \neq y$ and $x \prec_R y \Leftrightarrow (x,y) \in (\underline{\text{li}} \; R) \wedge \neg \exists z : (x \; z) \in (\sqsupseteq)[R] \vee (z \; x) \in (\sqsupseteq)[R]$ for $x = y$. This definition is similar to the acyclic predecessor relation but takes care of self loops. When speaking about *circuits* of a CO R we always refer to circuits of $(\prec_R)$.

Proposition 3. *Let R be a CO. Every nonempty finite line L of R coincides with a circuit $w \in R$ (i.e. $\mathcal{A}(w) = L$).*

Example 3. The predecessor relation of R_4 (Fig. 12) is given by $(\prec_{R_4}) = \{(a,b), (b,c), (c,d), (d,a), (b,e), (e,f), (f,a), (f,g), (g,h), (h,e), (h,c), (d,g)\}$. One might suspect that for finite COs circuits and lines immediately correspond to each other. Notice, however, that R_4 contains a circuit $(a \; b \; c \; d \; g \; h \; e \; f)$ which does not coincide with a line.

Example 4. An extension of R_4 is depicted in Fig. 14. It is given by $R_4' := (\genfrac{}{}{0pt}{}{\text{rot}}{\sqsupseteq})[\{(a \; i \; b \; j \; c \; k \; d \; l), (a \; i \; b \; r \; e \; p \; f \; q), (g \; n \; h \; o \; e \; p \; f \; m), (g \; n \; h \; t \; c \; k \; d \; s)\}]$. Yet another cyclic order R_4'' can be obtained by adding $(\genfrac{}{}{0pt}{}{\text{rot}}{\sqsupseteq})[\{(a \; i \; b \; j \; c \; k \; d \; s \; g \; n \; h \; o \; e \; p \; f \; q)\}]$. Although these two COs are essentially different, both have the same cyclic predecessor relation $(\prec_{R_4'}) = (\prec_{R_4''}) = \{(a,i), (i,b), (b,j), (j,c), (c,k), (k,d), (d,l), (l,a), (e,p), (p,f), (f,q), (q,a), (d,s), (s,g), (g,n), (n,h), (h,t), (t,c), (h,o), (o,e), (f,m), (m,g)\}$.

We conclude that even in finite cases the predecessor relation may not be sufficient to capture all aspects of a CO. As stated by the following theorem it is just the dependence relation which is additionally needed: Every finite cyclic order R can be uniquely specified by two binary relations $(\prec_R)$ and $(\underline{\text{li}} \; R)$.

Theorem 2. *Let R and R' be finite COs.*
Then $(\prec_R) = (\prec_{R'})$ and $(\underline{\text{li}} \; R) = (\underline{\text{li}} \; R')$ implies $R = R'$.

Finally, we turn to the important issue of global orientability. An AO R is said to be *globally orientable* iff there is a total AO R' extending R. Szpilrajn's famous theorem for ordinary partial orders in [23] implies the existence of at least one total order extension. Hence every AO is globally orientable.

A cyclic (pre)order R is said to be *globally orientable* iff there is a total CO R' extending R. It might be surprising that in contrast to the situation for AOs

215

not every cyclic preorder is globally orientable. Indeed this important result has been shown independently by Genrich [3] and Megiddo [8] using finite counterexamples of different kinds. The example of Genrich is of particular interest, since it can be extended to a CO.

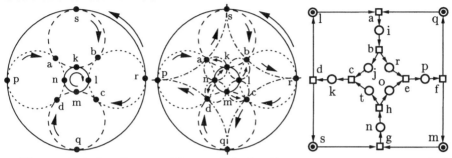

Fig. 15. Relation R_G **Fig. 16.** Relation R_S **Fig. 17.** Realization of R'_4

Example 5. Genrich's counterexample of a cyclic preorder[15] violating global orientability is specified by $R_G := \binom{\text{rot}}{2})[\{(a\ s\ b\ k),\ (b\ r\ c\ l),\ (c\ q\ d\ m),\ (d\ p\ a\ n),\ (p\ q\ r\ s),\ (k\ l\ m\ n)\}]$ depicted in Fig. 15.[16] It is not a CO, as the completeness axiom does not hold (e.g. for the clique $\{a,p,s\}$). However, Genrich's example can be extended to a CO $R_S := R_G \cup \binom{\text{rot}}{2})[\{(p\ a\ s),\ (s\ b\ r),\ (r\ c\ q),\ (q\ d\ p),\ (a\ n\ k),\ (b\ k\ l),\ (c\ l\ m),\ (d\ m\ n)\}]$ depicted in Fig. 16. It is easy to see that R_S is complete and all other axioms are preserved. Clearly, R_S does not admit a total CO extension, otherwise this would also be an extension for R_G which does not exist. So R_S is an example of a CO which is not globally orientable.[17]

For the following theorem and its "proof" we have to rely on an intuitive understanding as we have not formalized the graphical representation of COs here in terms of geometry.

Theorem 3. *For finite COs[18] global orientability is equivalent to the existence of a clock representation.*

Proof. ($\Rightarrow$) Given a globally orientable CO R, draw a clock representation of a total CO extension R' with $\mathcal{A}(R') = \mathcal{A}(R)$ such that the elements of $\mathcal{A}(R)$ are located on a single clockwise oriented circle. Remove the circle without changing the position of the elements. By Prop. 2 R is a union of total COs which are projections of R'. Each of these components of R' is represented by adding an appropriate closed line. As all components are projections of R' all these lines can be oriented clockwise around the original center of R'. In this way a clock

---

[15] To stay in a uniform framework we translate Genrich's result into our terminology.
[16] The violation of global orientability can be proved (see [22]) by exploiting the connection to synchronization graphs which will be stated in Thm. 5.
[17] Recently we discovered a smaller counterexample containing only 9 elements using computer support, but it does not exhibit any symmetry and is more difficult to understand.
[18] This condition can be relaxed if we admit graphical representations of infinite COs.

representation of R is obtained. ($\Leftarrow$) Given a clock representation of the CO R, draw an arbitrary radius originating from the center of the representation. When turning this radius around by 360° in the clockwise direction it touches all elements of the CO. The sequentialized succession w in which the elements occur can be conceived as a total CO $\binom{\text{rot}}{\supseteq}[\{w\}]$. Obviously, this is an extension of R. Hence, R is globally orientable. □

It is easy to obtain a total CO extension from the clock representation in Fig. 7 and vice versa. The reader might convince himself that the counterexamples above do not admit a clock representation. A clock representation is an intuitive way to think about globally orientable COs in geometrical terms. It is however not a normal form in general, since a CO may admit clock representations, which are not geometrically equivalent. Intuitively, two clock representations are *geometrically equivalent* iff one can be continuously transformed into the other in the plane with the center being removed.[19]

4 Synchronization graphs

This section introduces concurrency and causality in safe and live (s&l) T-systems[20] and explains their relationship. Also the central notion of basic circuit and the technical concept of a refined T-net is introduced in preparation of the subsequent sections.

Concerning terminology we exclude nets consisting of single elements and assume that nets are finite, pure and connected. *T-nets* are nets without branching states. A *T-system* $(N,\mathcal{C})$ is a T-net equipped with a case class $\mathcal{C}$.[21]

For a binary relation R and a word w we say w is a *chain* of R iff $w(i)\ R\ w(i+1)$ for all indices i, $i+1$ of w. A chain $w = (w(0)\ ...\ w(n-1))$ of R is a *cycle* of R iff $\mathcal{L}(w) \geq 1$ and $(w(n-1),w(0)) \in R$. A *circuit* of R is a simple cycle of R.

Given a net $N = (S,T,F)$ a *circuit* of N is a circuit of F. A circuit w *carries* $|\mathcal{A}(w) \cap C|$ tokens at a marking C. A circuit of N is a *basic circuit* of $(N,\mathcal{C})$ iff it carries exactly one token at all cases $C \in \mathcal{C}$. The set of basic circuits of $(N,\mathcal{C})$ is denoted by $\mathcal{BC}(N,\mathcal{C})$. We will implicitly use the following folklore result (see e.g. [1] or [3]): A T-system is s&l iff every circuit carries at least one token and every net element is covered by a basic circuit.

For this and the next section we assume that $(N,\mathcal{C})$ is a s&l T-system with $N = (S,T,F)$. For technical convenience we consider also the *transition refined net* $\tilde{N} := (\tilde{S},\tilde{T},\tilde{F})$ obtained by *T-splitting* from N.[22] It is defined by $\tilde{S} := \{\bar{s},\ \bar{t}$

---

[19] Formally we have to ensure a (partial) separation of lines. This can be achieved by employing a multi-layer plane geometry reserving one plane for each line. Of course, some identifications between layers are necessary for points shared by different lines.

[20] We prefer the names "T-system" and "T-net" instead of "synchronization graph" to emphasize the Petri net view including all its aspects, in particular duality and (chrono-)topology.

[21] As a first manifestation of cyclic symmetry we are not interested in the initial marking.

[22] T-splitting has been used in [12] to obtain security from safety.

: $s \in S$, $t \in T\}$, $\tilde{T} := \{\acute{t}, \grave{t} : t \in T\}$ and $\tilde{F}$ being the smallest relation satisfying (a) $\acute{t} \ \tilde{F} \ \bar{t} \ \tilde{F} \ \grave{t}$, (b) $\bar{s} \ \tilde{F} \ \acute{t}$ if $s \ F \ t$, (c) $\grave{t} \ \tilde{F} \ \bar{s}$ if $t \ F \ s$ for $s \in S$ and $t \in T$. This refinement induces a net morphism $\phi : \tilde{N} \to N$ mapping $\acute{x}$, $\bar{x}$, $\grave{x}$ to x for all $x \in S \cup T$. It is lifted to sets and words in the natural way.

Observe that the refinement does not change the behaviour essentially. More precisely, there is a unique s&l case class $\tilde{C}$ of $\tilde{N}$ such that the restriction of $\phi(\tilde{C})$ to markings of N yields the original case class C. $\tilde{C}$ is called the *refined case class* of (N,C). We say that $x \in S \cup T$ is *marked* at a refined case $\tilde{C} \in \tilde{C}$ meaning that $\tilde{C} \cap \phi^{-1}(x) \neq \emptyset$.

Let x and y be different net elements of N. x and y are *causally dependent* ($x \ li \ y$) iff there is a basic circuit in $\mathcal{BC}(N,C)$ containing both x and y. x and y are *concurrent* ($x \ co \ y$) iff there is a refined case in $\tilde{C}$ marking both x and y. In addition to li and co we define their reflexive closures $\underline{li} := li \cup \mathrm{id}(S \cup T)$ and $\underline{co} := co \cup \mathrm{id}(S \cup T)$.

In the traffic light example the original specification is given as a set of binary causality constraints which have to be satisfied by the T-system representing the implementation. A binary causality constraint (x,y) is *satisfied* by a T-system (N,C) iff $x \ li \ y$ holds in (N,C). We do not exclude the possibility that the implementation satisfies more causality constraints than those specified.

For s&l T-systems causality and concurrency are essentially complementary relations as stated by the following proposition.[23]

Proposition 4. *For net elements $x \neq y$ we have $x \ li \ y$ or $x \ co \ y$ but not both.*

A proof of this fundamental property is given in [22]. It is noteworthy that it does not seem to follow immediately from standard results about synchronization graphs as one might expect.

5 The Cyclic Order of Basic Circuits

Partial orders provide a mathematical basis for concurrent processes. So a natural expectation is that COs should provide a similar basis for cyclic processes. In this section the axioms of COs will be derived formally using s&l T-systems which provide a very simple and general representation of cyclic processes.[24]

Considering the CO R_4 in Fig. 12 we might think of the four closed lines as a ring of four coupled gear-wheels and we observe that a cyclic process evolves when all gear-wheels move synchronously in the direction given by the arrows. In such a case we can say that the CO is realized by a cyclic process. On the other hand, we found that the relation R_5 depicted in Fig. 13 is not a cyclic order. This is compatible with the fact that it cannot be realized as a cyclic process: Intuitively, a ring of five coupled gear-wheels will remain stuck.

---

[23] In Petri's concurrency theory this is taken as an axiom.

[24] The use of T-systems can be justified by considering determinism (i.e. absence of conflicts) as the essential feature of a process. However, as explained in Section 2 the axioms can be motivated in a more general setting without relying on nets. More details can be found in [20].

As an ultimate generalization of gear-wheel mechanics we consider T-systems. A T-system implementation of the CO in Fig. 14 is given in Fig. 17. If we ignore states and restrict our interest to transitions only we might also argue that Fig. 17 shows an implementation of the CO in Fig. 12. In the same sense we can say that the T-system in Fig. 8 implements the CO in Fig. 6. In the subsequent section we will make the idea of implementation precise. For this purpose we associate to a s&l T-system a CO which captures the structure of all its basic circuits. As a nice demonstration of the elegance of our framework it turns out that it is essentially the set of basic circuits $\mathcal{BC}(N,\mathcal{C})$ itself (more precisely, its subword closure $(\sqsupseteq)[\mathcal{BC}(N,\mathcal{C})]$) which constitutes a cyclic order.

Theorem 4. $(\sqsupseteq)[\mathcal{BC}(N,\mathcal{C})]$ *is a finite, nontrivial CO.*

That $(\sqsupseteq)[\mathcal{BC}(N,\mathcal{C})]$ is simple, subword-closed and rotation-closed is obvious. Proofs of cyclic transitivity, completenes and also of the following lemma are contained in [22]. Similar results for synchronization graphs (without explicit states) can already be found in [3].

Lemma 1. *There exists a simple word w such that $\mathcal{BC}(N,\mathcal{C}) \subseteq \binom{\text{rot}}{\sqsupseteq}[\{w\}]$.*

Proof. Idea: Consider the refined s&l T-system $(\hat{N},\hat{\mathcal{C}})$ obtained by *S-splitting* (the dual of T-splitting) from $(N,\mathcal{C})$ and apply the fact that $(\hat{N},\hat{\mathcal{C}})$ admits a firing sequence which contains each transition exactly once (cf. [1]).

Corollary 1. *The CO $(\sqsupseteq)[\mathcal{BC}(N,\mathcal{C})]$ is globally orientable.*

We generalize the notion of satisfaction introduced for binary causality constraints: A cyclic causality constraint $w = (w(0) \ldots w(n-1))$ is *satisfied* by a T-system $(N,\mathcal{C})$ iff $w \in (\sqsupseteq)[\mathcal{BC}(N,\mathcal{C})]$. Observe that this is just the notion of satisfaction used in our traffic light example.

A T-net (S,T,F) is *associated* to a CO R iff $S \cup T = \mathcal{A}(R)$ and $F = (\prec_R)$. In this case circuits of (S,T,F) and circuits of R coincide, so we can simply speak of circuits. Notice, that not every finite CO has an associated T-net.

Proposition 5. *The CO $(\sqsupseteq)[\mathcal{BC}(N,\mathcal{C})]$ has N as associated T-net.*

The CO $(\sqsupseteq)[\mathcal{BC}]$ is called the *state transition* order of $(N,\mathcal{C})$. Its projection on transitions only, i.e. $(\sqsupseteq)[\mathcal{BC} \triangleright T]$, is again a CO, the *transition order* of $(N,\mathcal{C})$. Viewing a CO as a cyclic process specification we can distinguish between a *state transition interpretation* and a *transition interpretation* depending on whether elements are intended to represent states and transitions or transitions only. In the traffic light example we used the transition interpretation: The cyclic order in Fig. 6 is the transition order of the T-system in Fig. 8. In the following we will favor the first interpretation making transitions and states explicit in the CO. This choice allows a tight integration with Petri's concurrency theory which heavily relies on the fact that transitions as well as states are first class citizens.

6 Realizability of Cyclic Orders

Based on the state transition interpretation of COs two different notions of implementation arise naturally: For a s&l T-system $(N,\mathcal{C})$ and a CO R we say $(N,\mathcal{C})$ *realizes* R iff $R = (\sqsupseteq)[\mathcal{BC}(N,\mathcal{C})]$ and $(N,\mathcal{C})$ *approximates* R iff $R \subseteq (\sqsupseteq)[\mathcal{BC}(N,\mathcal{C})]$. The following three results can be immediately proved using Cor. 1, Prop. 5 and Prop. 4, respectively.

Corollary 2. *Every approximable or realizable CO is globally orientable.*

Corollary 3. *Let $(N,\mathcal{C})$ be a s&l T-system realizing the CO R. Then N is the T-net associated to R.*

Corollary 4. *Let $(N,\mathcal{C})$ be a s&l T-system realizing the CO R. Then (li R) and (co R) coincide with li and co in $(N,\mathcal{C})$, respectively.*

In view of Cor. 3 we will be mainly interested in COs admitting associated T-nets. Disregarding the finiteness requirement this is only a convenient but not an essential restriction, as it is easy to cast every finite CO (in the transition interpretation) into this form by inserting elements denoting states between every two elements of the CO. This is called *state completion*.

By the following proposition an approximation $(N,\mathcal{C})$ of R implements every line of R as a basic circuit of $(N,\mathcal{C})$, although there may be additional basic circuits in general. Hence, an approximation may exhibit a higher degree of synchronization than required. In contrast, a realization meets the specification exactly in the sense that every line corresponds to a basic circuit and vice versa.

Proposition 6. *Let R be a CO and N be a T-net associated with R. (1) A s&l T-system $(N,\mathcal{C})$ approximates R iff every line coincides with a basic circuit. (2) A s&l T-system $(N,\mathcal{C})$ realizes R iff every line coincides with a basic circuit and vice versa.*

Example 6. By state completion we can cast the CO R_4 in Fig. 12 into the CO R_4' shown in Fig. 14 (cf. Ex. 4), which is realized by the T-system $(N,\mathcal{C})$ in Fig. 17. Notice, however, that the T-net N admits another s&l case class $\mathcal{C}'$ determined by the marking $\{l,m,r,s\}$. The resulting T-system $(N,\mathcal{C}')$ is a realization of R_4'', the extension of R_4' described in Ex. 4. Observe that $(N,\mathcal{C}')$ is also an approximation of R_4'.

The following result could be obtained from a more general theorem in [3]. In [22] we provide an easy proof relying on the use of Prop. 3 and Prop. 6(1).

Theorem 5. *Let R be a globally orientable cyclic order and N an associated T-net. Then there is a s&l T-system $(N,\mathcal{C})$ approximating R.*

Proof. Idea: Starting with the empty marking we fire each transition of N once in the succession specified by a total cyclic order extension of R. During this process tokens are successively added as far as it is necessary to fire a transition. It can be proved that the resulting case generates a s&l case class $\mathcal{C}$ such that $(N,\mathcal{C})$ approximates R. □

Assume we have a cyclic order R with an associated T-net N. In view of Cor. 2 and the previous theorem R is approximable iff $(N,\mathcal{C})$ approximates R for a s&l T-system $(N,\mathcal{C})$.

An example in [22] shows that it is not possible to strengthen the previous theorem to conclude realizability of R. An open problem is the characterization of approximable and realizable COs without relying on the concept of T-system itself.[25] In the following we give a simple solution to the problem of approximability using cuts and finite density requirements which are major ingredients of Petri's concurrency theory.

Let R be a finite CO. In general we have $|C \cap L| \leq 1$ for lines L and cuts C. R is *K-dense* iff for every cut C and every line L of R we have $C \cap L \neq \emptyset$. A slight modification leads to a stronger property: R is *F-dense* iff for every cut C and every circuit w of R we have $C \cap \mathcal{A}(w) \neq \emptyset$. For our purposes a weaker notion of F-density is sufficient: R is *weakly F-dense* iff there is a cut C with $C \cap \mathcal{A}(w) \neq \emptyset$ for every circuit w of R.[26] Such a cut is called a *true cut*. Here, $|C \cap \mathcal{A}(w)| \leq 1$ does not hold in general, the intuitive interpretation being that a circuit may need more than one round w.r.t. a truc cut C.

Lemma 2. *Let R be a CO and N be an associated T-net.*
If R has a true cut then R can be approximated.

Proof. Let $\tilde{C}$ be a true cut of R such that $\tilde{C} \cap \mathcal{A}(w) \neq \emptyset$ for all circuits w of R **(1)**. Let $\tilde{\mathcal{C}}$ be the refined case class generated by $\tilde{C}$. First we prove that every line of R coincides with a basic circuit of $(N,\mathcal{C})$ **(2)**. Let L be a line. By Prop. 3 there is a circuit $w \in R$ such that $\mathcal{A}(w) = L$. We have $|\tilde{C} \cap L| \geq 1$ by (1). It follows that $|\tilde{C} \cap L| = 1$. So w is a basic circuit of $(N,\mathcal{C})$. Now observe that $(N,\mathcal{C})$ is s&l as every circuit is marked at $\tilde{C}$ by (1) and every element can be extended to a line and is covered by a basic circuit using the previous result (2). That $(N,\mathcal{C})$ approximates R follows from Prop. 6(1) using (2) again. □

Lemma 3. *Let R be a CO and N be an associated T-net.*
If R can be approximated then R has a true cut.

Proof. Let $(N,\mathcal{C})$ be a s&l T-system approximating R. Notice that by Prop. 6(1) every line of R coincides with a basic circuit of $(N,\mathcal{C})$. Let $C \in \mathcal{C}$ be an arbitrary case. For different $x,y \in C$ we have $(x,y) \notin (\text{li } R)$: Otherwise x and y would be contained in a basic circuit carrying two tokens because of $R \subseteq (\sqsupseteq)[\mathcal{BC}(N,\mathcal{C})]$. So C is a clique of $(\underline{\text{co}}\ R)$ which can be extended to a cut C' of R. It remains to prove that C' is a true cut. So let w be a circuit. Due to liveness w is marked at C, that is, $C \cap \mathcal{A}(w) \neq \emptyset$. Using $C \subseteq C'$ we obtain $C' \cap \mathcal{A}(w) \neq \emptyset$. □

---

[25] A number of properties which are necessary for realizability are derived from synchronization graphs in [3]. By a counterexample it is shown that these conditions do not guarantee realizability and it is stated as an open problem if they are sufficient for approximability.

[26] F-density has been introduced in the context of concurrency theory in [18] and is related with other axioms in [6]. Motivated by a characterization of global orientability F-density and weak F-density has been defined for COs in [20].

Combining these results we obtain a characterization of global orientability.[27]

Theorem 6. *Let R be a CO and N be an associated T-net. Then the following statements are equivalent: (a) R is globally orientable, (b) R can be approximated, (c) R has a true cut, (d) R is weakly F-dense.*

Proof. (a) implies (b) by Thm. 5. (b) implies (a) by Cor. 2. (b) implies (c) by Lem. 3. (c) implies (b) by Lem. 2. (c) and (d) are trivially equivalent. □

As suggested by our traffic light example the design process can be seen as a decision tree. Every node is an (intermediate) design represented by a generalized relation. We have the initial specification at the root and hopefully some implementations (solutions) at the leaves. Every edge represents a refinement step which formally corresponds to an extension of the relation. To satisfy the precondition of the previous theorem designs should be augmented with explicit states. A design can be successively refined guided by the axioms of cyclic orders. A design which obviously cannot be extended to satisfy these axioms is definitely not implementable by Thm. 4 and need not be persued further. On the other hand a design which is a cyclic order may or may not be implementable. To ensure implementability we can exploit Thm. 6 and try to maintain a (sub)set of true cuts for each single design. By refinement some true cuts may get lost, since they cease to be true cuts in the new design. However, as long as this set is not empty we are sure that the cyclic order is implementable. By Thm. 6 we can alternatively (or in addition) maintain a nonempty (sub)set of total CO extensions. More generally, we may also admit other modification steps during the design phase as long as we maintain extensibility to a cyclic order and existence of at least one true cut or at least one total CO extension.

Given a CO and a realization the CO captures precisely the structure of basic circuits but in general the number of tokens on non-basic circuits remains unspecified leaving some freedom for different realizations.[28] This situation can already be observed in small nets: For instance, the precycloid $(3,2,1,1)$[29] can be equipped with different s&l case classes realizing the same CO. A less degenerate example (even satisfying Petri's axioms of concurrency) is the balanced cycloid $(6,6,2,2)$ which can also be equipped with different s&l case classes realizing the same CO.[30] We conclude that globally orientable COs with associated T-nets are indeed an abstraction of s&l synchronization graphs in the mathematical

---

[27] It might be interesting that a similar characterization of global orientability by the existence of a particular kind of cut has been derived in [20] (Theorem 7169). In contrast to the result presented here it is applicable to arbitrary COs which might be infinite and even (partially) dense. Of course, a new and fundamentally different notion of true cut has to be used which does not depend on a predecessor relation. It might also be of interest here that there is an alternative way to obtain a characterization of global orientability by F-density using the technique of cyclic order quotients [4].

[28] These realizations may differ, for instance, in their slowness, a notion defined in [12].

[29] Cycloids are s&l T-systems with a toroidal structure. See [12] or [7] for a definition.

[30] Cf. the results of a computer analysis in [7].

sense. It is also important to note that the clock representations associated by Cor. 1 to the case classes mentioned above are not geometrically equivalent.

From the viewpoint of a safety-oriented specification technique based on cyclic causality constraints[31] the token-free formalism of COs provides a new level of abstraction. It is the abstraction from cycles which are not causality constraints that allows the designer to defer a decision which is not relevant at the current stage. Applying nets in the usual way this decision may be enforced too early in the design process, e.g. by fixing a particular initial marking. As another fundamental deviation from usual net theory practice the early use of an immediate causality relation is avoided. Instead the safe concept of cyclic causality constraint with built-in feedback is favored as the *atom of specification*.[32] As a by-product the fact that the formalism is not based on immediate causality encourages successive refinement by extension and facilitates abstraction by projection.

On the other hand one has to be aware of the fact that the cyclic order technique is rather specialized, as it can only deal with synchronization aspects of cyclic systems. In practice it is difficult to imagine situations were it can be applied in isolation. Instead it will be necessary to specialize it and to combine it with other techniques, e.g. those which can handle flow and transformation of data. Here the most obvious applications are those involving concurrent but determinitic data flow which does not depend on the concrete data itself.

7 Applications and Related Work

Although applications are many-fold, there are only a few publications dealing with cyclic orders. Cyclic orders based on sets of triples (of distinct elements) enjoying rotation closedness and cyclic transitivity appear in [5], [3], [8], [2] and [14]. The early reference [5] deals only with the less interesting class of total cyclic orders. Except for the fact that cyclic constraints containing less than three elements cannot be captured the remaining approaches are essentially equivalent to our concept of cyclic preorders.[33] The important idea of global orientability (in our terminology) is present in [8], [2] and [3].[34] Genrich and Megiddo found ingenious counterexamples violating global orientability. Unfortunately, the counterexample was taken by Genrich as a reason not to pursue the proposed axiomization based on triples further.[35]

---

[31] The importance to think in causal cycles, as cyclic causality constraints are called in [12], has been repeatedly emphasized by Petri. In fact the axioms of cyclic orders in [11] originated from the motivation to investigate causal cycles in their pure form.

[32] This concept can also be used to specify security and is therefore more flexible than Petri's concurrency theory which has security built in (cf. [18]).

[33] A proof can be found in [20].

[34] The importance of cyclic transitivity and global orientability has been recognized by the author independently. Also it seems that the concept of global orientability was independently discovered by Genrich and Megiddo.

[35] Instead a completely different approach was chosen based on the idea of mutating structures. These are a very interesting generalization of elementary net systems,

The articles [8] and [2] briefly introduce the concept of partial cyclic order and focus on the complexity of global orientation. Using a combination of interacting instances of the counterexample violating global orientability Galil and Megiddo proved in [2] NP-completeness of global orientability for cyclic preorders.

A radically different approach to cyclic orders has been chosen by Petri in [11]. Instead of using (oriented) triples to describe cyclic constraints he employs (unoriented) quads.[36] A quad is of the form $\{\{a,c\},\{b,d\}\}$ where a,b,c,d are distinct elements. It describes the fact that elements a and c separate b and d on a line.[37] As an example, the structure depicted in Fig. 12 would be represented by $\{\{\{a,c\},\{b,d\}\}, \{\{a,e\},\{b,f\}\}, \{\{g,e\},\{h,f\}\}, \{\{g,c\},\{h,d\}\}\}$ which satisfies all of Petri's cyclic order axioms. Notice that due to the symmetry properties of quads the orientation of lines is not taken into account. This makes it difficult to exclude examples like the one in Fig. 13 which does not admit a consistent orientation.[38] As explained in [20] we can elegantly capture Petri's approach by using a more abstract equivalence containing ($\stackrel{\text{rot}}{=}$) and ($\stackrel{\text{rev}}{=}$), where ($\stackrel{\text{rev}}{=}$) is the equivalence induced by reversal of words. Then COs provide just the formal concept of consistent orientability[39] which is needed here to exclude the example.

From a different perspective COs can be seen as an oriented generalization of cyclic concurrency structures. The lack of an adequate concept of cyclic order which has already been pointed out in [10] led to many difficulties with cyclic concurrency structures reported in [7]. Now COs pave the way for an axiomization of cyclic concurrency theory in full analogy to the acyclic case.

Similar to concurrency theory a measurement interpretation for cyclic orders is possible. As explained in [12] measurement can be seen as a form of control. Measurement judgments w.r.t. cyclic scales appear as a particular case of causality constraints. Cyclic orders are collections of judgments underlying some completeness and consistence requirements. The fact that these cyclic orders are usually not total corresponds naturally to the uncertainty of measurement or incompleteness of knowledge. The act of measurement leads to new judgments (containing reference objects from the scale and external objects). For applications like knowledge representation or reasoning a cyclic order may be used as a knowledge base which is successively extended by new (possibly hypothetical) judgments. Axioms of cyclic orders are conceived as inference rules. More details can be found in [14] where so-called CYCORDs serve as a uniform basis integrating different approaches in the field of spatial reasoning.

Another application related to the slogan "Thinking in Cycles" is reported in [17] where the authors present a VLSI design methodology for delay insensitive circuits based on a so-called multi-ring structures which have "some resemblance

---

but the notion of step is inherent in this approach, which is a major restriction and a strong deviation from ordinary partial orders.

[36] Actually the idea to employ quads has already appeared in [10].

[37] This is motivated by the invariant concept of separation in projective geometry.

[38] The essence of a consistent orientation is that it is free of local contradictions.

[39] This property, which is also the essence of the axiom of consistent orientability in concurrency theory, should not be confused with the stronger property of global orientability.

to a mechanical gear-box" as the authors explain without giving a formal model of structure and behaviour. It seems that they are not aware of the fact that the method proposed corresponds closely to the idea of information flow graphs (see [9] and [12]), although it does not aim at reversibility. In any case the abstract data flow is deterministic and can be described by synchronization graphs or more abstractly by cyclic orders.

In the last part of [3] Genrich proves a variety of impressive results about synchronization graphs seen as special mutating structures. Although some of these results became folklore in the meantime, we recently found a number of interesting theorems which have not been published elsewhere. With some surprise we recognized that these theorems are similar to and partly more general than our results Thm. 4, Lem. 1 and Thm. 5. However, the axiomization of cyclic orders we introduced and all other results in the present work are new as far as we know. There is an extended version [22] of this article containing all proofs which could not be included here due to the lack of space and further results including a surprisingly simple sufficient condition for realizability and uniqueness of the clock-representation of cyclic orders which is proved using some almost forgotten results from [1].

8 Conclusions

Similar to the theory of partial orders the theory of COs is intended as a general mathematical theory which is not tailored for specific applications. According to Petri [13] it should be seen as one of those recently emerging foundational theories which can be expected to have applications in different, apparently independent fields. In particular he proposed to study cyclic orders of cycloids and to explore the applications of cyclic orders in asynchronous circuit design, knowledge representation and reasoning. We believe that further applications are possible in design and verification of distributed algorithms. Of course generalizations of cyclic orders to incorporate choice and information are desirable. But even for synchronization graphs it is not an exaggeration to say that their potential has not been fully exploited yet. This is also indicated by connections between cycloids and special relativity theory explained in [12] which provide yet another possible direction for future research.

9 Acknowledgments

We are grateful for Carl Adam Petri's encouraging advice and helpful comments and suggestions of Rüdiger Valk, Berndt Farwer, Ralf Röhrig and members of the General Net Theory Group, in particular Uwe Fenske, Olaf Kummer and Wolfram Roisch.

References

1. F. Commoner et al. *Final Report for the Project "Development of the Theoretical Foundations for Description and Analysis of Discrete Information Systems". Vol. II (Mathematics)*. Wakefield, Mass.: Mass. Computer Associates, Inc., 1974.
2. Z. Galil and N. Megiddo. Cyclic ordering is NP-complete. *TCS*, 5:179–182, 1977.
3. H. J. Genrich. *Einfache nicht-sequentielle Prozesse*. Dissertation, GMD, 1971.
4. S. Haar. *Kausalität, Nebenläufigkeit und Konflikt — Elementare Netzsysteme aus topologisch-relationaler Sicht*. Number 9 in Edition Versal. Beltz Verlag, Berlin, 1998. To appear.
5. E. V. Huntington. A set of independent postulates for cyclic order. volume 2 of *Proc. Nat. Ac. Sc.*, 1919.
6. O. Kummer. *Axiomensysteme für die Theorie der Nebenläufigkeit*. Logos, Berlin, 1996.
7. O. Kummer and M.-O. Stehr. Petri's axioms of concurrency – A selection of recent results. In *Proc. 18th Int. Conf. on Appl. and Theory of Petri Nets*, LNCS 1248. Springer, 1997.
8. N. Megiddo. Partial and complete cyclic orders. *Bulletin of the American Mathematical Society*, 82(2):274–276, 1976.
9. C. A. Petri. Grundsätzliches zur Beschreibung diskreter Prozesse. In *3. Colloquium über Automatentheorie*, pages 121–140. Birkhäuser Verlag, Basel, 1967.
10. C. A. Petri. Concurrency. In *Net Theory and Applications – Proc. Adv. Course on General Net Theory of Processes and Systems*, LNCS 84, pages 251–260. Springer, 1980.
11. C. A. Petri. Zyklische Ordnungen. Unpublished draft, June, 14th 1991.
12. C. A. Petri. Nets, time and space. *TCS*, 153(1–2):3–48, 1996.
13. C. A. Petri. Personal communication, September, 16th 1997.
14. R. Röhrig. Representation and processing of qualitative orientation knowledge. In *KI-97: Advances in Artificial Intelligence*, LNAI 1303. Springer, 1997.
15. M. Silva and T. Murata. B-fairness and structural B-fairness in Petri net models of concurrent systems. *Journal of Computer and System Sciences*, 44, 1992.
16. E. Smith. On the border of causality: Contact and confusion. *TCS*, 153(1–2), 1996.
17. J. Sparsø and J. Staunstrup. Delay-insensitive multi-ring structures. *Integration, the VLSI journal*, 15:313–340, 1993.
18. M.-O. Stehr. Physically Motivated Axiomatic Concurrency Theory – A Posetless Approach. Studienarbeit, Univ. Hamburg, FB Informatik, 1993. Revised version as report [19].
19. M.-O. Stehr. Concurrency Theory of Cyclic and Acyclic Processes. Fachbereichsbericht FBI-HH-B-190/96, Univ. Hamburg, FB Informatik, 1996.
20. M.-O. Stehr. Zyklische Ordnungen – Axiome und einfache Eigenschaften. Diplomarbeit, Univ. Hamburg, FB Informatik, April 1996. Translated and extended version as reports [21].
21. M.-O. Stehr. A Theory of Cyclic Orders, Part I: Generalized Relations and Acyclic Orders, Part II: Total and Partial Cyclic Orders. Fachbereichsberichte FBI-HH-B-206/97 and FBI-HH-B-207/97, Univ. Hamburg, FB Informatik, 1997.
22. M.-O. Stehr. System Specification by Cyclic Causality Contraints. Fachbereichsbericht FBI-HH-B-210/98, Univ. Hamburg, FB Informatik, 1998.
23. E. Szpilrajn. Sur l'extension de l'ordre partial. *Fund. Mathematicae*, 16:386–389, 1930.

[7], [19] and [20] are available via http://www.informatik.uni-hamburg.de/TGI.

Iterative Decomposition and Aggregation of Labeled GSPNs

Peter Buchholz

Informatik IV, Universität Dortmund,
D-44221 Dortmund, Germany

Abstract. The use of Stochastic Petri Nets for performance analysis is limited by the state explosion of the underlying Continuous Time Markov Chain. A class of analysis methods to overcome this limitation are based on repeated decomposition and aggregation. In this paper, we propose a general framework for these kinds of solution methods and extend known techniques by introducing new classes of aggregates to reduce the approximation error. Aggregation relies on a formal definition of equivalence of Stochastic Petri Nets, which allows us to build aggregates at several levels of detail. The approach has been completely automated and allows the analysis of large and complex models with a low effort.

1 Introduction

Stochastic Petri Nets (SPNs) and their extensions are a useful paradigm to analyze the performance and dependability of dynamic systems from different application areas. Usually performance/dependability analysis is based on state space approaches which analyze numerically the Continuous Time Markov Chain (CTMC) underlying a SPN. Although this approach is well established, the major problem is the size of the state space, which can be huge even for harmless looking models. State space explosion limits the size of numerically solvable models to SPNs of a very moderate size which is often not appropriate for the analysis of realistic systems. A common approach to analyze SPNs which are too large to be analyzed at state level is the use of decomposition and aggregation combined with fixed-point computation. This approach has been proposed in different forms by various authors [6, 7, 11, 13–15]. The basic idea of all these approaches is to decompose a SPN into parts and analyze isolated parts in combination with an aggregated representation of their environment. Usually environments are represented by some form of an exponential delay. Analysis of the resulting system yields results which are used to define aggregate parameters for the environment of other parts. This analysis step is iterated until the computed parameters keep constant up to a small value ϵ. Since the models of the isolated parts combined with an aggregated environment can be solved much more efficiently than the complete model, the approach allows the analysis of larger models.

However, although the decomposition approach is conceptually simple, it has some drawbacks. First of all, the decomposition of general SPNs into adequate parts is not easy. There are two general ways of defining parts. The first way is to define parts which communicate via synchronizing transitions yielding superposed SPNs or GSPNs [9, 10]. The second form, which is mainly used in decomposition and aggregation approaches [6, 11, 13, 14], is to define parts with a place input and a transition output. Parts communicate via exchanging tokens. To apply the decomposition and aggregation approach successfully, it has to be assured that the aggregates defined for parts or environments behave in some sense functionally equivalent to the detailed nets they represent. Such an equivalence is hard to assure for general SPNs. Thus the mentioned approaches restrict the net class by considering marked graphs or slightly more general nets where some flow of a token population can be found at the net level. Apart from the problem of defining adequate parts of a net, the decomposition approach may yield other problems. Existence and uniqueness of the fixed-point and convergence of the parameters to the fixed-point cannot be proved. Only first results about the existence of fixed-points are published in [15]. Additionally, even convergence of the method does not guarantee exact results. The assumption of exponential delays for aggregates implies usually an approximation error of an unknown size. Nevertheless, even if the iterative fixed-point approach has some weak points, it is an established approach which often yields accurate results with a very low computational effort.

In this paper, we present also a decomposition approach with fixed-point computation. However, in contrast to the mentioned approaches, we use labeled generalized stochastic Petri nets (LGSPNs) as basic model class. LGSPNs, a net class proposed in [2], are compositional. A model is composed of submodels which communicate via synchronized transitions. This form of composition is common to describe systems of communicating processes, but can also be used to describe asynchronously communicating submodels as common in performance modeling. Based on the compositional description, equivalence of LGSPNs has been defined in [2]. The proposed equivalence for LGSPNs is an extension of bisimulation equivalence and preserves transient and stationary results. In a similar way, bisimulation or other equivalences for untimed nets [18] can be defined for LGSPNs after neglecting timing information. Compositionality and equivalence allow us to develop a formalized approach for decomposition and aggregation, which extends known approaches.

The outline of the paper is as follows. In the subsequent section LGSPNs and the compositional structure of the underlying CTMC are introduced. Equivalence relations for LGSPNs are proposed in Sect. 3. The new fixed-point approach based on decomposition and aggregation is introduced in Sect. 4. The introduction of all steps of the approach is accompanied by a running example describing a manufacturing system with unreliable machines. In Sect. 5 we present a second example from the communication area. The paper ends with the conclusions.

2 Labeled GSPNs

We assume that the reader is familiar with GSPNs [5] and the generation of CTMCs resulting from GSPNs. In the following we introduce LGSPNs as basic model class and composition of LGSPNs.

Definition 1. *A LGSPN is a ten-tuple* $(P, T, \pi, I, O, H, W, L, R, M_0)$ *where*

- P *is the set of places,*
- T *is the set of transitions such that* $T \cap P = \emptyset$,
- $\pi : T \rightarrow \{0, 1\}$ *is the priority function, where transitions with priority 0 are timed and transitions with priority 1 are immediate,*
- $I, O, H : T \rightarrow Bag(P)$, *are the input-, output- and inhibition function, respectively, where* $Bag(P)$ *is a multiset on* P,
- $W : T \times M \rightarrow \mathbb{R}_+$ *is a function that assigns a non-zero weight to each transition depending on the current marking* M *which is a function assigning non-negative integers to places,*
- $L : T \rightarrow Act$ *is a transition labeling function which assigns to each transition a label from a finite set of labels* Act *which includes label* τ, *immediate transitions are by definition labeled with* τ *(i.e.,* $\forall t \in T$ *with* $\pi(t) = 1: L(t) = \tau$ *),*
- $R : Act \rightarrow \mathbb{R}_+$ *is a function assigning basic rates to labels and*
- $M_0 : P \rightarrow \mathbb{N}$ *is the initial marking: a function that assigns a non-negative integer to each place.*

Each LGSPN includes a GSPN which determines the dynamic behavior in isolation. Transition $t \in T$ is enabled in marking M iff $\forall p \in P$: $M(p) \geq I(p,t)$, $M(p) < H(p,t)$ and if $\pi(t) = 0$ and no t with $\pi(t) = 1$ observes the above conditions. Let $M[$ be the set of all transitions enabled in marking M. The actual weight of transition t enabled in marking M is defined as $\mu_t(M) = W(t, M) \cdot R(L(t))$. For notational convenience we define $\mu_t(M) = 0$ for $t \notin M[$. The actual transition weight of enabled transitions is the product of the transition weight and the basic rate depending on the transition label. The distinction between weight and basic rate allows an appropriate definition of the weight of composed transitions as shown below. According to the priority, we distinguish between timed transition with priority 0 and immediate transitions with priority 1. Let T_t the subset of timed transitions and T_i the subset of immediate transitions. If t is a timed transition (i.e., $\pi(t) = 0$), then $\mu_t(M)$ denotes the rate of an exponential distribution associated with transition t in marking M. If t is an immediate transition, then $\mu_t(M)$ describes a relative firing weight. The probability of firing t with $\pi(t) = 1$ in marking M equals $prob(t, M) = \mu_t(M) / \sum_{t' \in M[} \mu_{t'}(M)$ for $t \in M[$ and 0 otherwise. If transition t fires in marking M, then this yields successor marking M' with $M'(p) = M(p) - I(p,t) + O(p,t)$ for all $p \in P$. The set of all markings reachable from the initial marking M_0 is denoted as the reachability set RS. The reachability set contains two different sorts of markings, namely tangible markings where only timed transitions are enabled and vanishing markings where only immediate transitions are enabled. For quantitative analysis vanishing markings are eliminated a-priori. For details about this step we refer to the literature [5]. The resulting set of markings is denoted as the tangible reachability set TRS. The tangible reachability graph TRG includes a node for each marking $M \in TRS$ and an arc from M to M' if M' is reachable from M by firing one timed transition possibly followed by one or several immediate transitions. Arcs in TRG are labeled with the timed transition and a weight which results from the weight of the timed transition multiplied with the probability of reaching the successor via firing immediate transitions (see e.g., [5] for details).

In the sequel we restrict ourselves to LGSPNs with a finite TRS which can be represented by a set of integers $\{0, \ldots, n-1\}$. Integer x belongs to marking M_x. We assume without loss of generality that 0 represents the initial marking and use integer and marking interchangeable. TRG can be characterized by a set of matrices. For each timed transition t we define a $n \times n$ matrix $\mathbf{Q}_t$, where $\mathbf{Q}_t(x, y)$ equals the weight of the arc between M_x and M_y in TRG, if such an arc exists and 0 otherwise. Usually the distinction of specific transitions in TRG is too fine. Labels have been defined to introduce a coarser level. With respect to transition labeling we define for each $a \in Act$ matrices[1] $\mathbf{Q}_a = \sum_{t \in T_t, L(t)=a} \mathbf{Q}_t$. The generator matrix of the CTMC underlying a LGSPN is given by

$$\mathbf{Q} = \sum_{a \in Act} R(a)\mathbf{Q}_a - diag(\sum_{a \in Act} R(a)\mathbf{Q}_a \mathbf{e}^T) , \qquad (1)$$

where $\mathbf{e}$ is a row vector with all elements equal to 1 and $diag(\mathbf{a})$ is a diagonal matrix with $\mathbf{a}(x)$ in position (x, x). The steady state distribution of the CTMC is the solution of $\mathbf{pQ} = \mathbf{0}$ and the additional normalization condition $\sum_{x=0}^{n-1} \mathbf{p}(x) = 1.0$. Knowing $\mathbf{p}$, performance results like the throughput of transitions or the population of places can be determined.

One goal of using labels for transitions is to make GSPNs composable by fusing transitions. In the sequel of this section we introduce the composition of LGSPNs and start with the definition of composition at the net level. In a composition two LGSPNs are composed. We number these LGSPNs using integer numbers i and denote by $LSGPN^i = (P^i, T^i, \pi^i, I^i, O^i, H^i, W^i, L^i, R^i, M_0^i)$ the i-th LGSPN $(i = 1, 2)$.

Definition 2. *The composition of $LGSPN^1$ and $LGSPN^2$ with $R^1(a) = R^2(a)$ for $a \in Act^1 \cap Act^2$ is defined as $LGSPN^0 = LGSPN^1 \|_A LGSPN^2$ where $\mathcal{A} \subseteq (Act^1 \cap Act^2) \setminus \tau$ with*

$- P^0 = P^1 \cup P^2$,
$- T^0 = LT^1 \cup LT^2 \cup ST$, *where* $LT^i = \{t \in T^i | L^i(t) \notin \mathcal{A}\}$, $ST = \cup_{a \in \mathcal{A}} ST_a$ *and ST_a includes for each transition pair $t^1 \in T^1$ and $t^2 \in T^2$ with $L(t^1) = L(t^2) = a$, a transition $t^{1,2}$,*
$- \pi^0(t)$ *equals $\pi^i(t)$ for $t \in LT^i$ and is 1 for $t \in ST$ since all transitions in ST are timed by definition,*
$- I^0(p, t)$ *equals $I^i(p, t)$ for $t \in LT^i$ and $p \in P^i$, it equals 0 for $t \in LT^i$ and $p \notin P^i$ and it equals $I^i(p, t^i)$ for $p \in P^i$ and $t \in ST$ resulting from $t^i \in T^i$,*
$- O^0, H^0$ *are defined similarly,*

---

[1] To be consistent with [4, 12], the notation differs slightly from the notation introduced in [2].

- $W^0(t, M)$ equals $W^i(t, M|_{P^i})$ for $t \in LT^i$ and $W^1(t^1, M|_{P^1}) \cdot W^2(t^2, M|_{P^2})$ for $t \in ST$ resulting from t^1 and t^2, where $M|_P$ is the restriction of marking M to places from set P,
- $L^0(t)$ equals $L^i(t)$ for $t \in LT^i$ and it equals $L^1(t^1) = L^2(t^2)$ for $t \in ST$ resulting from t^1 and t^2,
- $R^0(a) = R^i(a)$ for $a \in Act^i$, by definition $R^1(a) = R^2(a)$ for $a \in Act^1 \cap Act^2$,
- $M_0^0(p) = M_0^i(p)$ for $p \in P^i$.

The above definition looks more complicated than it really is. The idea is to fuse transitions with respect to labels in $\mathcal{A}$ by generating a new transition for each pair of identically labeled transitions in both nets. Weights of transitions resulting from fusion are defined as the product of the weights of the transitions which are fused. Obviously the result of the composition of two LGSPNs is again a LGSPN. Since the composition of LGSPNs is associative, composition of multiple LGSPNs can be defined as repeated composition of two LGSPNs.

Composition can be defined alternatively at the level of the tangible reachability set and graph. This idea, which yields a compositional description of the underlying CTMC, has originally been proposed for networks of stochastic automata [17] and superposed GSPNs [10]. However, in contrast to superposed GSPNs, which result from the decomposition of a GSPN into parts interacting via synchronized timed transitions, LGSPNs are generated by composition. We now show how TRS^0 and TRG^0 can be built by composing tangible reachability sets and graphs. Obviously $TRS^0 \subseteq TRS^1 \times TRS^2$. In a similar way TRG^0 can be characterized by matrices defined via the Kronecker product of the matrices describing TRG^1 and TRG^2.

Definition 3. Let $\mathbf{A}$ and $\mathbf{B}$ two matrices of dimension $n^A \times n^A$ and $n^B \times n^B$, then their Kronecker product $\mathbf{A} \otimes \mathbf{B}$ is defined as a $n^A n^B \times n^A n^B$ matrix

$$\begin{pmatrix} \mathbf{A}(0,0)\mathbf{B} & \cdots & \mathbf{A}(0, n^A - 1)\mathbf{B} \\ \vdots & \ddots & \vdots \\ \mathbf{A}(n^A - 1, 0)\mathbf{B} & \cdots & \mathbf{A}(n^A - 1, n^A - 1)\mathbf{B} \end{pmatrix}$$

The Kronecker sum is defined as $\mathbf{A} \oplus \mathbf{B} = \mathbf{A} \otimes \mathbf{I}_{n^A} + \mathbf{I}_{n^B} \otimes \mathbf{B}$, where $\mathbf{I}_n$ is the identity matrix of dimension n.

By means of Kronecker operations matrices describing TRG^0 can be defined as follows.

$$\mathbf{Q}_a^0 = \begin{cases} \mathbf{Q}_a^1 \oplus \mathbf{Q}_a^2 & \text{for } a \notin \mathcal{A} \\ \mathbf{Q}_a^1 \otimes \mathbf{Q}_a^2 & \text{otherwise} \end{cases} \tag{2}$$

where $\mathbf{Q}_a^i = \mathbf{I}_{n^i}$ for $a \notin Act^i$. The simple idea behind this composition is that synchronization is realized by the Kronecker product of matrices and independent parallel transitions are realized by Kronecker sums. Matrices $\mathbf{Q}_a^0$ describe TRG^0 completely. Each marking from $M^0 \in TRS^0$ can be characterized by $(M^{0,1}, M^{0,2})$, where $M^{0,1} = M^0|_{P^1}$ and $M^{0,2} = M^0|_{P^2}$. TRS^0 contains all markings which are reachable from (M_0^1, M_0^2) in the reachability graph defined by the matrices $\mathbf{Q}_a^0$. Define a generator matrix $\mathbf{Q}^0$ analogously to $\mathbf{Q}$ in (1). Let

$TRS^{0,i}$ be the projection of TRS^0 onto the places of $LGSPN^i$, i.e., $M^i \in TRS^{0,i}$ if a marking $M \in TRS^0$ exists, where the marking of places P^i is given by M^i. Obviously, $TRS^{0,i} \subseteq TRS^i$ holds. In the sequel we assume that $TRS^{0,i} = TRS^i$, which can be easily achieved by eliminating markings from TRS^i.

If $TRS^0 \subset TRS^1 \times TRS^2$, then the compositional description includes some unreachable markings. We assume that TRS^0 contains a single irreducible set of markings. In this case the steady state solution $\mathbf{p}^0 \mathbf{Q}^0 = \mathbf{0}$ can be computed by assigning non-zero probabilities to reachable states/markings only. Other more efficient methods to deal with unreachable states in compositionally generated state spaces have been proposed recently [12, 4]. Consequently we will not consider the problem of unreachable states in compositional descriptions here and refer to the cited literature for methods to handle this problem.

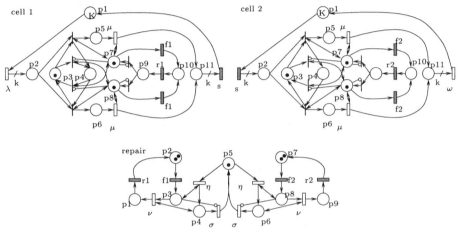

Fig. 1. LGSPN model of an unreliable manufacturing system.

Example: As a running example we take a model of a manufacturing system with unreliable machines. Fig. 1 shows the three components building the complete net. Components are combined by fusing identically labeled grey transitions as described above. The first two components describe two manufacturing cells with two machines each. Cells are arranged in form of a pull production line. K containers including k parts each are attached to a cell. If a container arrives, it is unloaded and the parts are assigned to machines. If both machines in a cell are working (i.e., places $p7$ and $p8$ contain a token), parts are assigned to machines in an alternating sequence. However, whenever a machine is down (i.e., the corresponding place is empty), all arriving parts are assigned to the other machine. If both machines are down, then parts are waiting in place $p2$ until the first machine starts working. Parts which have been assigned to a machine (i.e., tokens at place $p5$ or $p6$) reside in the buffer until they are processed by the machine. Processed parts are collected in place $p11$. If at least k parts are processed in *cell 1*, they move to *cell 2*. From *cell 2* processed parts leave the system in batches of size k. Both cells are coupled via the s labeled transition describing the movements of parts in batches of size k. If machines fail, they have to be repaired by a single repairman. The repairman is described in component *repair*. Due to transitions labeled with fi, failures of machines from cell i are realized. If a machine fails and the repairman is idle (i.e., a token is on place $p5$), then the repairman goes to the corresponding cell. A token on place $p4$ or $p6$ indicates that the repairman repairs machines from *cell 1* or *cell 2*, respectively. The repairman stops repairing machines from one cell, if no more machines from this cell are down. Via ri-labeled transitions repaired machines start working again. It is assumed that the delay of these transitions describes the time a machine needs to go up after being repaired.

For a quantitative analysis we choose the following basic transition rates $R(\tau) = 1.0$, $R(fi) = 1.0e - 6$, $R(ri) = 1.0$ and $R(s) = 10.0$. All transitions which are not labeled with τ have a weight of 1.0, for the remaining transitions the following weight are chosen: $\mu = \sigma = 1.0$, $\lambda = \omega = 10.0$, $\eta = 0.1$ and $\nu = 1.0e - 4$.

Table 1. Size of TRS and TRG for the components and the complete net.

K	k	cell 1/2 $|TRS|$	$|TRG|$	repair $|TRS|$	$|TRG|$	complete net $|TRS|$	$|TRG|$
1	1	26	70	108	324	8748	41688
1	2	44	118	108	324	24300	116712
1	4	86	232	108	324	90828	442392
1	8	206	568	108	324	514188	2562264
2	1	70	216	108	324	67500	353148
2	2	148	462	108	324	292032	1545612
2	4	400	1272	108	324	2086668	11239836
2	8	1288	4164	108	324	21386700	116961612
3	1	150	500	108	324	326700	1809900
3	2	360	1220	108	324	1825200	10232352
3	4	1068	3680	108	324	15759792	89521884

Table 1 includes the size of component transition systems and the transition system of the composed net for different values of K and k. $|TRS|$ describes the number of tangible marking, which includes for the complete net only reachable markings. $|TRG|$ describes the number of transitions in the tangible reachability graph which corresponds to the number of non-zero matrix entries in the generator matrix of the underlying CTMC, excluding the diagonal elements.

3   Equivalence Relations for Labeled GSPNs

Equivalence defines things which are indistinguishable from a certain viewpoint. We will introduce here equivalence relations based on a matrix description. This description has the advantage that several different equivalence relations are covered by a single formula. Before we define equivalence relations, additional matrices are introduced. Matrices $\mathbf{Q}_a$ contain the complete information about the dynamic behavior of a LGSPN. If we are only interested in the functional behavior neglecting timing information, then only the possibility of a transition between two markings is relevant and not its weight. This information can be captured in Boolean matrices $\mathbf{P}_a$ resulting from $\mathbf{Q}_a$ by substituting each non-zero element by a 1 and defining the remaining elements as 0. By using the Boolean *or* as addition and the Boolean *and* as multiplication Kronecker operations for Boolean matrices are well defined. Substitution of the $\mathbf{P}$-matrices for the $\mathbf{Q}$-matrices in equation (2) defines the composition of LGSPNs according to the functional behavior. Summation of all matrices $\mathbf{P}_a$ gives the incidence matrix of the TRG.

Label τ is used for internal transitions which are in some sense not observable from the outside. For the time dependent behavior of a LGSPN, these transitions are important, but if only the functional behavior is considered, then internal transitions are often skipped. This can be done defining the following matrices

$$\mathbf{P}_{\tau*} = \sum_{k=0}^{\infty}(\mathbf{P}_{\tau})^k \text{ and } \mathbf{P}_{a*} = \mathbf{P}_{\tau*}\mathbf{P}_a\mathbf{P}_{\tau*} \text{ for } a \in Act \setminus \tau .$$

$\mathbf{P}_{\tau*}(x,y) = 1$ shows that marking M_y is reachable from M_x by firing only τ-labeled transitions. $\mathbf{P}_{a*}(x,y) = 1$ implies that M_y can be reached from M_x by firing of zero or more τ-labeled transitions, followed by one a-labeled transition, followed by zero or more τ-labeled transitions. Matrices $\mathbf{P}_{\tau*}$ can be generated with a reflexive and transitive closure algorithm with an effort cubic in the number of markings in TRS [8].

As the last set of matrices we consider matrices resulting from rounding transition weights. The reason for this operation is to make similar weights equal. This allows us to define some form of approximate quantitative equivalence. Thus, we define matrices $\mathbf{Q}_{a,\epsilon}$ elementwise as

$$\mathbf{Q}_{a,\epsilon}(x,y) = \epsilon \cdot \lfloor \mathbf{Q}_a(x,y)/\epsilon \rfloor$$

for $\epsilon > 0$, where $\lfloor x \rfloor$ for $x \in \mathbb{R}$ denotes the largest integer equal to or smaller than x.

All presented matrices can be used in one definition of equivalence and yield different equivalence relations. We first have to introduce a matrix representation of equivalence relations. Let $\mathcal{R}$ be an equivalence relation on TRS. $(x,y) \in \mathcal{R}$ describes that x and y are in relation $\mathcal{R}$, i.e., belong to the same equivalence class. Equivalence classes of $\mathcal{R}$ are numbered consecutively 0 through $\tilde{n} - 1$ and $\mathcal{R}[\tilde{x}]$ is the $\tilde{x}$-th equivalence class. For an equivalence relation $\mathcal{R}$ we define a $n \times \tilde{n}$ collector matrix $\mathbf{V}$ with $\mathbf{V}(x,\tilde{x}) = 1$ if x belongs to equivalence class $\mathcal{R}[\tilde{x}]$ and 0 otherwise. Elements of $\mathbf{V}$ can be interpreted as Boolean or real values depending on the context.

Definition 4. *An equivalence relation $\mathcal{R}$ is a bisimulation for a set of LGSPN matrices $\mathbf{A}_a$, iff for all equivalence classes $\tilde{x}, \tilde{y}$ and all $x, y \in \mathcal{R}[\tilde{x}]$, the relation $\sum_{z \in \mathcal{R}[\tilde{y}]} \mathbf{A}_a(x,z) = \sum_{z \in \mathcal{R}[\tilde{y}]} \mathbf{A}_a(y,z)$ holds.*

Depending on the type of matrices used in the above definition, different forms of bisimulation are defined. Matrices $\mathbf{P}_a$ yield strong bisimulation [16], matrices $\mathbf{P}_{a*}$ weak bisimulation [16], matrices $\mathbf{Q}_a$ strong performance bisimulation [2] and matrices $\mathbf{Q}_{a,\epsilon}$ approximate performance bisimulation. Observe that each strong performance bisimulation is also a strong bisimulation and an approximate performance bisimulation, each strong bisimulation is also a weak bisimulation.

To define an aggregated component with respect to an equivalence relation, equivalence classes are represented by single states. To do so, weights among the states in one equivalence class have to be defined. In some cases, the choice of the weight vector does not influence the resulting aggregate, because all weight vectors produce the same aggregate. However, if aggregation is approximative, as described below, the definition of a weight vector is a crucial point which may influence approximation errors significantly. Weight vectors define the relative contribution of states in an equivalence class to aggregated transition rates between equivalence classes. According to an equivalence relation $\mathcal{R}$ and a n-dimensional weight vector $\mathbf{w} \geq \mathbf{0}$ with $\sum_{x \in \mathcal{R}[\tilde{x}]} \mathbf{w}(x) > 0.0$ for all equivalence classes $\tilde{x}$, an aggregated transition system is generated by defining a $\tilde{n} \times n$ distributor matrix $\mathbf{W}$ elementwise as

$$\mathbf{W}(\tilde{x}, x) = \mathbf{w}(x) / \sum_{y \in \mathcal{R}[\tilde{x}]} \mathbf{w}(y) \text{ for } x \in \mathcal{R}[\tilde{x}] \text{ and } 0 \text{ otherwise.}$$

The aggregated transition system is defined on state space $\{0, \ldots, \tilde{n} - 1\}$ with the matrices

$$\tilde{\mathbf{A}}_a = \mathbf{W} \mathbf{A}_a \mathbf{V} . \tag{3}$$

The $\mathbf{A}$-matrices are of one of the matrix types defined above. If Boolean matrices are used, then the elements of $\mathbf{W}$ and $\mathbf{V}$ are interpreted as Boolean values too. Matrices $\tilde{\mathbf{A}}_a$ characterize a TRS with $\tilde{n}$ states.

Definition 5. $LGSPN^1$ *and* $LGSPN^2$ *are bisimulation equivalent if bisimulation relations* $\mathcal{R}^1$ *and* $\mathcal{R}^2$ *exists such that the corresponding aggregated transition systems are identical up to the ordering of states.*

The above definition can be used for all forms of bisimulation equivalence. It is well known that the bisimulation relation with the least number of equivalence classes can be computed for finite systems as the fixed-point of a partition refinement. Let $\mathcal{R}_0 = TRS \times TRS$ and define the following refinement to compute relation $\mathcal{R}_k$ from $\mathcal{R}_{k-1}$.

$$\mathcal{R}_k = \{x, y | (x, y) \in \mathcal{R}_{k-1} \wedge \forall \tilde{z} : \sum_{z \in \mathcal{R}_{k-1}[\tilde{z}]} \mathbf{A}_a(x, z) = \sum_{z \in \mathcal{R}_{k-1}[\tilde{z}]} \mathbf{A}_a(y, z)\} \tag{4}$$

It is easy to show that $\mathcal{R}_k \subseteq \mathcal{R}_{k-1}$ and $\mathcal{R}_k = \mathcal{R}_{k+1}$ implies $\mathcal{R}_k = \mathcal{R}_{k+l}$ for all $l \geq 0$ such that the fixed-point is reached. In the sequel we use the notation $\mathcal{R}$ for the fixed-point. Algorithms to compute $\mathcal{R}$ are known for the functional case [8], extensions for matrices with real values have been developed recently [1, 3]. $\mathcal{R}$ is the largest bisimulation relation, i.e., the relation with the least number of equivalence classes. Since $\mathcal{R}$ is efficiently computable, a minimal equivalent representation can be computed at the state transition level. Observe that this representation generally does not correspond to reductions at the net level. However, since the labeled transition system and also the rate matrices of a composed LGSPN can be generated compositionally using component matrices, it is possible to first compute equivalent aggregates at the state level and compose the resulting matrices afterwards. To distinguish between the different bisimulation equivalence relations $\mathcal{R}$, we use $\mathcal{R}_f$ for strong equivalence, $\mathcal{R}_{f*}$ for weak equivalence, $\mathcal{R}_p$ for strong performance equivalence and $\mathcal{R}_{p,\epsilon}$ for ϵ-approximate performance equivalence whenever a distinction is necessary. We follow Milner [16] and use the term strong/weak equivalence for the largest strong/weak bisimulation. An equivalence relation $\mathcal{R}$ implies an equivalence relation $\mathcal{R}'$, if $(x,y) \in \mathcal{R}'$ for all $(x,y) \in \mathcal{R}$. Observe that $\mathcal{R}_p$ implies $\mathcal{R}_{p,\epsilon}$ and $\mathcal{R}_f$. Additionally $\mathcal{R}_{f*}$ implies $\mathcal{R}_f$. It is possible to compute equivalence relations as refinements of other equivalence relations. If $\mathcal{R}$ is computed as the refinement of $\mathcal{R}'$, then $\mathcal{R}_0$, the initial equivalence relation for the computation of $\mathcal{R}$, is set to $\mathcal{R}'$ in (4). We use this concept for the computation of $\mathcal{R}_{p,\epsilon}$ by starting the refinement with $\mathcal{R}_{f*}$ to assure functional equivalence of states which are potentially aggregated. The resulting equivalence relation will be denoted as $\mathcal{R}_{p*,\epsilon}$.

Theorem 1. *Strong bisimulation, weak bisimulation and strong performance bisimulation relations are congruence relations according to the composition of LGSPNs, i.e., if $LGSPN^1$ and $LGSPN^{1'}$ are equivalent according to one of these bisimulations, then $LGSPN^1\|_A LGSPN^2$ and $LGSPN^{1'}\|_A LGSPN^2$ are also equivalent according to the same type of bisimulation. An ϵ-approximate performance bisimulation is a congruence relation if the row sums of all matrices $\mathbf{Q}_a^2$ for $a \in \mathcal{A}$ are less or equal to 1.0.*

Proof. Proofs for the functional cases are established [16], the proof for performance bisimulation is given in [2]. The results for ϵ-approximate performance bisimulation follow from the proof for strong performance bisimulation. □

Theorem 2. *If $LGSPN^1$ and $LGSPN^2$ are strong performance bisimulation equivalent, then the throughput of a-labeled transitions ($a \in Act^i \cup Act^3$, $i = 1,2$) in $LGSPN^1\|_A LGSPN^3$ equals the throughput of a-labeled transitions in $LGSPN^2\|_A LGSPN^3$ for arbitrary $\mathcal{A} \subseteq Act^i \cap Act^3$ ($i = 1,2$) and arbitrary $LGSPN^3$.*

Proof. The proof can be found in [2]. □

Observe that the aggregated matrices generated via (3) are independent of the weight vector, if the same matrices are used for the computation of $\mathcal{R}$ and the aggregate description. For a strong performance bisimulation all weight vectors yield the same matrices $\tilde{\mathbf{Q}}_a$, for strong bisimulation all weight vectors yield the same matrices $\tilde{\mathbf{P}}_a$. However, if relation $\mathcal{R}_f$, $\mathcal{R}_{f*}$ or $\mathcal{R}_{p,\epsilon}$ are used to generate aggregated matrices $\tilde{\mathbf{Q}}_a$, the matrix entries may depend on the weight vector. For relation $\mathcal{R}_{p,\epsilon}$, the values in $\tilde{\mathbf{Q}}_a$ can vary by at most ϵ for different weight vectors. In this way we can generate aggregates which are functionally equivalent, but have a different quantitative behavior. Using relation $\mathcal{R}_{p*,\epsilon}$ with a small ϵ implies functional equivalence, since $\mathcal{R}_{p*,\epsilon}$ is computed by refining $\mathcal{R}_f$, and approximate quantitative equivalence.

Table 2. Size of TRS and TRG for aggregates of the *repair* component.

original		$\mathcal{R}_{f*}$		$\mathcal{R}_{p,1.0}$		$\mathcal{R}_p$	
$|TRS|$	$|TRG|$	$|TRS|$	$|TRG|$	$|TRS|$	$|TRG|$	$|TRS|$	$|TRG|$
108	324	9	24	72	228	108	324

Example: The sizes of TRS and TRG for the component transition systems and aggregates computed with respect to different equivalence relations are shown in the Tables 2, 3 and 4. Both cells can be aggregated with respect to relation

Table 3. Size of TRS and TRG for aggregates of *cell 1*.

		original		$\mathcal{R}_{f*}$		$\mathcal{R}_{p,1.0}$		$\mathcal{R}_p$	
K	k	TRS	TRG	TRS	TRG	TRS	TRG	TRS	TRG
1	1	26	70	11	25	11	25	11	25
1	2	44	118	14	31	17	41	18	41
1	4	86	232	14	31	30	79	33	79
1	8	206	568	14	31	65	191	75	191
2	1	70	216	31	87	30	86	31	87
2	2	148	462	52	148	53	156	56	158
2	4	400	1272	118	361	120	417	142	427
2	8	1288	4164	328	1063	355	1359	440	1385
3	1	150	500	64	201	62	199	64	201
3	2	360	1220	126	400	119	398	130	410
3	4	1068	3680	342	1152	301	1155	366	1218

$\mathcal{R}_p$ which means that exact aggregates can be built for these components. Component *repair* cannot be reduced with respect to $\mathcal{R}_p$, but the use of $\mathcal{R}_{f*}$ and $\mathcal{R}_{p,1.0}$ allows to build aggregates with smaller state spaces. The use of relations $\mathcal{R}_{f*}$ and $\mathcal{R}_{p,1.0}$ allows us to further reduce the aggregates for *cell 1/2*. However, as mentioned the use of the corresponding aggregates will usually introduce an approximation error.

Table 4. Size of TRS and TRG for aggregates of *cell 2*.

		original		$\mathcal{R}_{f*}$		$\mathcal{R}_{p,1.0}$		$\mathcal{R}_p$	
K	k	TRS	TRG	TRS	TRG	TRS	TRG	TRS	TRG
1	1	26	70	8	18	11	25	11	25
1	2	44	118	11	24	17	41	18	41
1	4	86	232	11	24	30	79	33	79
1	8	206	568	11	24	65	191	75	191
2	1	70	216	19	50	30	86	31	87
2	2	148	462	34	92	53	156	56	158
2	4	400	1272	81	236	121	418	142	427
2	8	1288	4164	229	704	356	1360	440	1385
3	1	150	500	33	95	62	199	64	201
3	2	360	1220	70	204	117	394	130	410
3	4	1068	3680	200	620	302	1155	366	1218

4 Approximate Fixed-Point Computations Using Aggregated Representations

In the previous section, several equivalence relations and the aggregation of transition systems with respect to an equivalence relation have been introduced. These concepts are used to develop an efficient and well formalized approach for the quantitative analysis of LGSPN models composed of several components. We assume that the LGSPN is composed of J components numbered 1 through J. Let n^i be the number of states/tangible markings of the i-th component and assume that all component state spaces are finite. Let $\mathbf{p}$ be the stationary solution vector of the LGSPN and define $\mathbf{p}^i$ as the mapping of $\mathbf{p}$ on the state space of the i-th component LGSPN. Formally $\mathbf{p}^i$ can be computed from $\mathbf{p}$ via

$$\mathbf{p}^i = \mathbf{p}((\bigotimes_{j=1}^{i-1}(\mathbf{e}_{n^j})^T) \bigotimes \mathbf{I}_{n^i} \bigotimes (\bigotimes_{j=i+1}^{J}(\mathbf{e}_{n^j})^T))$$

where $\mathbf{e}_n$ is a vector with n elements which are all equal to 1. $\mathbf{p}^i(x)$ is the stationary probability that component i is in marking M_x. We implicitly assume that $\mathbf{p}^i(x) > 0$ for all $M^i \in TRS^i$. This implies that the irreducible subset of TRS^0 contains for each component i and each $M^i \in TRS^i$ a marking M such that $M|_{P^i} = M^i$. Relevant measures are computed from the vectors $\mathbf{p}^i$. This restriction allows the computation of measures based on the population of places and the throughput of local transitions. Throughputs of synchronized transitions will be computed from aggregated models as introduced below.

If $\mathbf{p}$ is known, then all $\mathbf{p}^i$ can be computed easily. However, the problem is that for many realistic models the size of the state space is so large that the analysis of the complete CTMC is impossible or very time consuming. Thus, it is important to compute $\mathbf{p}^i$ without knowing $\mathbf{p}$. Usually this means that an approximation $\mathbf{x}^i$ of $\mathbf{p}^i$ is computed.

The environment of component i is given by the composition of all components $\{1, \ldots, J\} \setminus i$. The following matrices characterize the environment with respect to component i.

$$
\mathbf{Q}_\tau^{\bar{i}} = \bigoplus_{j=1; j \neq i}^{J} \mathbf{Q}_\tau^j + \sum_{a \in \cup_{j=1}^{J} Act^j \setminus \{\mathcal{A} \cup \{\tau\}\}} \frac{R(a)}{R(\tau)} \bigoplus_{j=1; j \neq i}^{J} \mathbf{Q}_a^j + \sum_{a \in \mathcal{A} \setminus Act^i} \frac{R(a)}{R(\tau)} \bigotimes_{j=1; j \neq i}^{J} \mathbf{Q}_a^j
$$

$$
\mathbf{Q}_a^{\bar{i}} = \bigotimes_{j=1; j \neq i}^{J} \mathbf{Q}_a^j \quad \text{for } a \in \mathcal{A} \cap Act^i
$$

(5)

Matrices $\mathbf{Q}_a^{\bar{i}}$ include weights for transitions which are used for synchronization between component i and its environment. Since the matrices describe synchronization, they are constructed using Kronecker products. Matrix $\mathbf{Q}_\tau^{\bar{i}}$ captures the weights of all transitions which are local in the environment of i. Observe that the normalization $R[\tau]/R[a]$ is necessary to obtain correct weights for transitions which are relabeled from a to τ. The transition rate before relabeling is given by $R[a]\mathbf{Q}_a(x,y)$ which equals $R[\tau]R[a]/R[\tau]\mathbf{Q}_a(x,y)$ after relabeling. Component i can be composed with its environment using the following equations.

$$
\mathbf{Q}_\tau = \mathbf{Q}_\tau^i \oplus \mathbf{Q}_\tau^{\bar{i}}, \quad \mathbf{Q}_a = \mathbf{Q}_a^i \otimes \mathbf{I}_{n/n^i} \text{ for } a \in Act^i \setminus (\mathcal{A} \cup \{\tau\})
$$
$$
\mathbf{Q}_a = \mathbf{Q}_a^i \otimes \mathbf{Q}_a^{\bar{i}} \text{ for } a \in \mathcal{A} \cap Act^i.
$$

In a similar way, an untimed transition system using $\mathbf{P}$ instead of $\mathbf{Q}$ matrices can be built. The resulting matrices still describe a transition system or CTMC with $n = \prod_{j=1}^{J} n^j$ states. To reduce the number of states, we have to generate an aggregated environment representation. Thus, let $\tilde{\mathbf{Q}}^{\bar{i}}$ resulting from an aggregation of the matrices $\mathbf{Q}^{\bar{i}}$. In principle the aggregated matrices can be built by computing one of the equivalence relations defined above on the matrices defined in (5) and then aggregating with respect to these matrices. The problem is that the dimension of these matrices is n/n^i which is usually very large such that equivalence relations often cannot be computed directly. However, since the equivalence relations are congruence relations with respect to composition, it is possible to interleave aggregation and composition. Thus, in a first step, matrices $\tilde{\mathbf{Q}}_a^j$ are built with respect to some equivalence relation computed for component j and some weight vector $\mathbf{x}^{(j)}$. The weight vector $\mathbf{x}^{(j)}$ is chosen as an approximation of the steady state distribution $\mathbf{p}^j$ of component j. Computation of appropriate approximations will be considered below. To generate aggregated matrices $\tilde{\mathbf{Q}}_\tau^{\bar{i}}$, we use the aggregated matrices $\tilde{\mathbf{Q}}_a^j$ instead of the original matrices $\mathbf{Q}_a^j$ in (5). Observe that this aggregated environment can be described as a sum of Kronecker products of smaller matrices which characterize aggregates for the components $j \neq i$. Alternatively, one can built the matrices $\tilde{\mathbf{Q}}_a^{\bar{i}}$ and try to compute an equivalence relation on these matrices to allow further reduction of the state space. Such a reduction is potentially possible, if components in the environment of i synchronize via transitions which are not part of component i. These transitions become internal in the environment of i and may result in an equivalence relation with a reduced number of equivalence classes. If we compose the aggregated environment and component i, we obtain the following generator matrix for the resulting model.

$$
\begin{aligned}
\bar{\mathbf{Q}}^i &= R(\tau)(\mathbf{Q}_\tau^i \oplus \tilde{\mathbf{Q}}_\tau^{\bar{i}}) + (\sum_{a \in \mathcal{A}} R(a)(\mathbf{Q}_a^i \otimes \tilde{\mathbf{Q}}_a^{\bar{i}})) - \bar{\mathbf{D}}^i, \\
\text{where } \bar{\mathbf{D}}^i &= diag(R(\tau)(\mathbf{Q}_\tau^i \oplus \tilde{\mathbf{Q}}_\tau^{\bar{i}})\mathbf{e}^T + (\sum_{a \in \mathcal{A}} R(a)(\mathbf{Q}_a^i \otimes \tilde{\mathbf{Q}}_a^{\bar{i}})\mathbf{e}^T)
\end{aligned} \tag{6}
$$

The stationary distribution of component i embedded in the aggregated environment is computed as

$$
\bar{\mathbf{x}}^i \bar{\mathbf{Q}}^i = \mathbf{0} \text{ and } \bar{\mathbf{x}}^i \mathbf{e}^T = 1.0 \tag{7}
$$

Let $\tilde{n}^{\bar{i}}$ be the number of states in the aggregated environment of component i (i.e., the dimension of $\tilde{\mathbf{Q}}_a^{\bar{i}}$). Then an approximation of the stationary distribution of component i can be computed

$$
\mathbf{x}^i = \bar{\mathbf{x}}^i (\mathbf{I}_{n^i} \bigotimes (\mathbf{e}_{\tilde{n}^{\bar{i}}})^T) \tag{8}
$$

This transformation assures that values for the first $\tilde{n}^{\bar{i}}$ elements in $\bar{\mathbf{x}}^i$ are added to form the probability of state zero in component i, the second $\tilde{n}^{\bar{i}}$ elements belong to state 1 and so on.

Theorem 3. *If the aggregates for the components $j \neq i$ are built using relation $\mathcal{R}_p$, then $\mathbf{x}^i = \mathbf{p}^i$.*

Proof. The proof follows from the congruence property of $\mathcal{R}_p$ and from the preservation of results by performance bisimulation as given in [2]. □

An exact analysis approach computes relations $\mathcal{R}_p$ for all components, generates the corresponding aggregates, which are independent of the weight vector, and solves (7) for all components. The drawback of this approach is that $\mathcal{R}_p$ is a very strong equivalence relation which often yields a large number of equivalence classes such that (7) is still too complex to be solved. Thus, weaker equivalence relations are required to obtain smaller aggregated systems. The price for this reduction in complexity is usually the introduction of an approximation error.

To define the approximation approach, we can in principle use the steps described for the exact case. However, there is one difference, namely the dependency of the aggregate parameters on the weight vector in the approximative case. We obtain a better approximation if the weight vector used for aggregation of a component is similar to the components steady state distribution. Unfortunately, the goal of the analysis is the computation of the steady state distribution. So we have to use an iterative approach starting with initial guesses for the steady state distributions, building aggregates using these vectors and improving the vectors by performing the analysis of the aggregated systems.

Below we summarize the corresponding analysis algorithm. We use $\mathbf{x}^{i,(k)}$ for the vector $\mathbf{x}^i$ in the k-th iteration step of the algorithm. The equivalence relations which are used to build aggregates are not further determined. Usually $\mathcal{R}_{f*}$ is used to preserve the functional behavior of a component or $\mathcal{R}_{p,\epsilon}$ is used to get approximately the same timed behavior. However, we may even use different equivalence relations for different components.

```
for j = 1 to J do
        initialize x^{j,(0)} ;
        compute equivalence relation R^j for aggregation ;
        build Q̃^j_a using R^j and weight vector x^{j,(0)} via (3)
done
k = 0 ;
repeat
        for i = 1 to J do
                generate Q̃^i_a via (5) using matrices Q̃^j_a for j ≠ i
                solve (7) to obtain x^{i,(k+1)} via (8)
                build Q̃^i_a using R^i and weight vector x^{i,(k+1)} via (3)
        done
        k = k + 1 ;
until ‖x^{i,(k)} − x^{i,(k−1)}‖ ≤ ε for all i ∈ {1,...J}
```

Remarks: The above algorithm is one concrete realization of the iterative decomposition and aggregation approach. Solution of (7) can be performed with an arbitrary solution technique, including simulation. We applied iterative numerical techniques. In this case, $\bar{\mathbf{x}}^{i,(k)}$ is used as initial vector for the computation of $\bar{\mathbf{x}}^{i,(k+1)}$, which usually reduces the required number of iterations. Additionally, iterative techniques allow us to compute $\bar{\mathbf{x}}^{i,(k+1)}$ with a varying level of accuracy. At the beginning of the solution process it is usually not necessary to compute the solution of (7) with a high accuracy, since the environment parameters change in every step. After some iterations, the required accuracy for the solution of (7) can be increased to obtain better results. In principle, vectors $\bar{\mathbf{x}}^{i,(k+1)}$ can be computed in parallel for all i. However, in this case, environments are built using weight vectors $\mathbf{x}^{i,(k)}$. In the above algorithm, vectors $\bar{\mathbf{x}}^{j,(k+1)}$ ($j < i$) are used for the generation of the aggregated environment for component i. The outer iteration stops when the normalized difference of component steady state vectors varies by less than a constant ϵ for all components. This is only one stopping criterion. Alternatively one may consider the throughput of synchronized transitions

$$\lambda_a^{(k)} = R(a) \prod_{j\in\{1,...,J\},a\in Act^j} \mathbf{x}^{j,(k)} \mathbf{Q}_a^j \mathbf{e}^T$$

and stop the iteration if $|\lambda_a^{(k)} - \lambda_a^{(k-1)}| < \epsilon'$ for all $a \in \mathcal{A}$. Performance quantities related to components, like throughputs of local transitions or token populations of places, can be computed from $\mathbf{x}^{j,(k)}$ as an approximation for $\mathbf{p}^i$. It is obviously possible to define more sophisticated procedures for the analysis, e.g., in [6, 11] an additional scaling of the rates of aggregated transitions is introduced to improve results. This and similar extensions can be integrated in the algorithm and it is an interesting research topic to figure out which extensions improve the results for which nets.

Example: We apply the proposed fixed-point approach for our example model using different aggregates. Table 5 includes the size of the resulting systems of equations which have to be solved. Columns for $\mathcal{R}_p$ include the size of the transition system when all component are substituted by aggregates computed with respect to equivalence relation $\mathcal{R}_p$. Observe that this is an exact aggregation. Thus, the resulting system has to be solved once to give exact results for the throughput of synchronized transitions (cf. Theorem 2, see also [2]). $|TRS|$ describes the number of states and $|TRG|$ the number of non-zero off-diagonal elements in the generator matrix. Compared to the sizes of the original transition systems shown in Table 1 we obtain a significant reduction without introducing an approximation. The use of aggregates computed with respect to equivalence relations $\mathcal{R}_{f*}$ and $\mathcal{R}_{p,1.0}$ yields a further state space reduction but introduces an approximation error. Consequently we use these aggregates in combination with the fixed-point approach. The corresponding columns in Table 5 include the number of states in the largest set of equations which has to be solved in the fixed-point approach. The last column includes the same value when a standard exponential aggregation approach is used. For this case aggregates for the components consider only the number of machines which are in repair or working (i.e., aggregates for the cells have 3 states and the aggregate for the repair facility has 6 states).

Table 5. Largest TRS to be solved in the fixed-point approach.

		$\mathcal{R}_p$		$\mathcal{R}_{f*}$	$\mathcal{R}_{p,1.0}$	exp. Agg.
K	k	$|TRS|$	$|TRG|$	$|TRS|$	$|TRS|$	$|TRS|$
1	1	1587	6584	1173	1587	72
1	2	4107	17350	2001	3468	108
1	4	13467	60274	2001	10092	108
1	8	68403	325966	2001	43923	225
2	1	11907	57546	7371	10800	108
2	2	41772	205179	24090	35643	168
2	4	261075	1366205	127452	159384	426
2	8	2467947	13511565	991716	1281180	1320
3	1	52272	276171	27324	47628	192
3	2	235200	1256972	125664	178581	390
3	4	1815852	10211695	952650	1024914	1098

The use of aggregates computed with respect to $\mathcal{R}_{p,1.0}$ and $\mathcal{R}_{f*}$ reduce state spaces only slightly compared to the exact aggregates. Since the fixed-point approach requires the solution of several systems of equation, the effort is usually not or only slightly reduced compared to the analysis of the exactly aggregated system resulting from $\mathcal{R}_p$. If we compare the solution effort with the effort for the original system, all aggregated systems allow a much faster analysis and allow the analysis of larger configurations. The use of exponential aggregates obviously yields the smallest systems to be solved in the fixed-point approach.

Table 6. Throughput of the different configurations and approximation errors.

K k	exact Tput.	$\mathcal{R}_{f*}$ rel. err.	$\mathcal{R}_{p,1.0}$ rel. err.	exp. Agg. rel. err.
1 1	$5.80e-1$	+1.2%	±0.0%	+15.0%
1 2	$4.28e-1$	+1.2%	±0.0%	+12.4%
1 4	$2.60e-1$	−3.5%	±0.0%	+10.8%
1 8	$1.52e-1$	−5.9%	±0.0%	+9.2%
2 1	$1.10e+0$	+0.9%	±0.0%	+22.7%
2 2	$7.08e-1$	+0.4%	±0.0%	+16.8%
2 4	$4.02e-1$	+0.2%	±0.0%	+9.0%
2 8	$2.20e-1$	±0.0%	±0.0%	+5.5%
3 1	$1.31e+0$	+0.8%	±0.0%	+13.0%
3 2	$7.93e-1$	+0.1%	±0.0%	+9.5%
3 4	$4.37e-1$	±0.0%	±0.0%	+6.2%

Table 6 contains results for the different configurations. We choose as result measure the throughput of containers. The throughput of parts equals k-times the container throughput. Exact results are computed from the exactly aggregated system using relation $\mathcal{R}_p$. The resulting sets of equations are small enough to be analyzed with a Kronecker based analysis approach after generating an appropriate structure (see [4] for further details). Approximate results are computed from the fixed-point approach using different aggregates. Aggregated systems are solved by Kronecker based numerical techniques. We used $\epsilon' = 0.001$ with respect to the throughput of synchronized transitions as a stopping criterion for the fixed-point approach. Results of the fixed-point approach are shown as relative errors with respect to the exact results. Using aggregates computed with respect to relation $\mathcal{R}_{p,1.0}$ gives excellent results. In all cases, relative errors are smaller than 0.1%. However, as mentioned above, the size of the aggregated systems to be solved is nearly as large as the size of the exactly aggregated system. Even if the required number of iterations of the fixed-point approach is only 3 or 4 for this aggregate, the solution effort is not reduced. Using aggregates computed with respect to $\mathcal{R}_{f*}$ reduces the solution effort for some configurations. For this aggregate the number of iterations in the fixed-point approach lies between 3 and 6. However, for this aggregates the approximation error is also larger. Errors go up to 5.9%, but are often in the range of 1% or below, which is a good value. Using the exponential aggregate, the fixed-point approach requires a larger number of iterations, namely between 10 and 25. Nevertheless, the solution effort is significantly reduced compared to the other aggregate types since the resulting sets of equations are much smaller. However, the exponential aggregates also yield the largest approximation errors. For all configurations the error is larger than 5% and goes up to 22.7%. This clearly shows the limits of the exponential aggregates, in particular, since the throughput is usually a measure which is relatively robust with respect to approximations. Reduction of the approximation error by using more complex aggregates also implies that the solution effort is increased since state spaces of aggregated systems become larger.

5 A Second Example

As a second example we consider a polling system from the computer communication area. Similar models have been analyzed successfully with a fixed-point
approach in [7,14]. Here we show that the fixed-point approach has its limitations for this kind of models, especially if too simple aggregates are used. The
quality of the results depends heavily on the measures and the structure of the
system. A polling system consists of a number of queues which are visited by one
or several severs. Specifically we consider here a system with 6 finite capacity
queues visited by a single server in cyclic order. Queues are numbered consecutively 1 through 6. Request arrive to a queue according to a Poisson process. The
capacity of queue i equals K_i. If a queue is full an arriving requests gets lost (i.e.,
an error is transmitted to the higher levels of the protocol which are not modeled
here). A server arriving at a queue serves all requests which are waiting or arriving during its stay at the queue. Service times are exponentially distributed.
After serving all requests, the server travels to the next queue, traveling times
are also exponentially distributed.

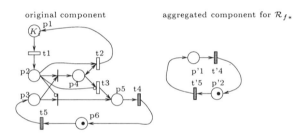

Fig. 2. LGSPN model of the original queue and of two aggregated representations.

Fig. 2 shows on the left side a GSPN component model of a queue. The initial markings of the components $2,\ldots,6$ is as in the picture. For component 1
place $p6$ is initially empty and place $p5$ is marked with a single token. All timed
transitions that are not filled, are labeled with τ. For component i, $L(t4) = a_i$
and $L(t5) = a_{i+1}$ for $i < 6$ and a_1 for $i = 6$. A complete model is generated by
composing identically labeled transitions. The following parameters are used for
our examples: $R(a_i) = 1$, $W(t1) = 0.01$ in components $2,\ldots,6$ and 0.02 in component 1, $W(t2) = W(t3) = 0.1$ and $W(t4) = W(t5) = 1.0$. Buffer capacities K_i
are equal for all queues and are varied in the examples. Aggregates are computed
using $\mathcal{R}_{f*}$ and $\mathcal{R}_{p*,0.5}$. For this example, the aggregated systems have a nice net
level representation which is also shown in Fig. 2. The aggregate computed from
$\mathcal{R}_{f*}$ describes an exponential delay and corresponds to the standard aggregate
type used in other fixed-point approaches [7,14]. The aggregate computed from
$\mathcal{R}_{p*,0.5}$ distinguishes whether customers are waiting at a queue or not. However,
in contrast to the original component, the number of waiting customers is not
distinguished. Thus we obtain a net level representation for this aggregate by
setting K_i to 1 in the net for the original component. Transition rates/weights
for the aggregates are computed from the analysis of the detailed component

embedded in the aggregated environment, i.e., the environment where all other components are represented by the corresponding aggregates.

Table 7. Size of TRS and TRG for the original component, the complete system and the aggregated systems.

K_i	original comp. $|TRS|$	$|TRG|$	original system $|TRS|$	$|TRG|$	system for V1 $|TRS|$	$|TRG|$	system for V2 $|TRS|$	$|TRG|$	system for V3 $|TRS|$	$|TRG|$
1	5	7	576	2208	13	19	60	144	576	2208
2	8	13	7290	35964	20	33	92	238	880	3536
3	11	19	43008	235008	27	47	124	332	1184	4864
4	14	25	168750	975000	34	61	156	426	1488	6192
5	17	31	513216	3071520	41	75	188	520	1792	7520

We use three different version of the fixed point approach. In $V1$, component i is analyzed in an environment, where all other components are substituted by aggregates computed with respect to $\mathcal{R}_{f*}$. In $V2$, the adjacent components $i-1$ and $i+1$ are substituted by aggregates computed with for $\mathcal{R}_{p*,0.5}$, the remaining components are substituted by aggregates computed for $\mathcal{R}_{f*}$. In $V3$, all other components are substituted by aggregates computed for $\mathcal{R}_{p*,0.5}$. Table 7 includes the sizes of TRS and TRG for one original component, the complete system and for the aggregated systems. Observe that in each iteration of the fixed-point approach 6 systems of equations of the same size have to be solved. Relation $\mathcal{R}_p$ allows no reduction of the components since each equivalence class contains only a single marking. Apart from V3 for the case $K_i = 1$, which is an exact representation, the systems to be analyzed in the fixed-point approach are much smaller than the original system. Thus, we can expect to solve larger configurations much faster with the fixed-point approach and we can solve much larger configurations.

Table 8. Exact and approximate results.

measure	K_i	original exact	V1 approx.	rel. err.	V2 approx.	rel. err.	V3 approx.	rel. err.
server tput.	1	$7.58e-2$	$7.11e-2$	-6.2%	$7.26e-2$	-4.3%	$7.58e-2$	$\pm0.0\%$
	2	$5.84e-2$	$5.40e-2$	-7.6%	$5.51e-2$	-5.8%	$5.80e-2$	-0.8%
	3	$5.32e-2$	$5.07e-2$	-4.7%	$5.12e-2$	-3.9%	$5.27e-2$	-1.1%
	4	$5.13e-2$	$5.01e-2$	-2.4%	$5.04e-2$	-1.9%	$5.11e-2$	-0.5%
	5	$5.06e-2$	$5.00e-2$	-1.1%	$5.00e-2$	-1.1%	$5.05e-2$	-0.1%
server pop. 1	1	$2.15e-1$	$2.20e-1$	$+2.3\%$	$2.18e-1$	$+1.5\%$	$2.15e-1$	$\pm0.0\%$
	2	$2.34e-1$	$2.41e-1$	$+3.0\%$	$2.39e-1$	$+2.3\%$	$2.35e-1$	$+0.4\%$
	3	$2.42e-1$	$2.48e-1$	$+2.3\%$	$2.47e-1$	$+1.9\%$	$2.44e-1$	$+0.8\%$
	4	$2.46e-1$	$2.50e-1$	$+1.3\%$	$2.49e-1$	$+1.2\%$	$2.48e-1$	$+0.8\%$
	5	$2.29e-1$	$2.50e-1$	$+0.7\%$	$2.50e-1$	$+0.7\%$	$2.50e-1$	$+0.7\%$
p1 empty in 6	1	$1.57e-1$	$1.51e-1$	-4.1%	$1.64e-1$	$+4.4\%$	$1.57e-1$	$\pm0.0\%$
	2	$5.25e-2$	$2.20e-2$	-58.2%	$3.00e-2$	-42.7%	$4.77e-2$	-9.1%
	3	$1.74e-2$	$2.71e-3$	-84.4%	$5.11e-3$	-70.6%	$1.19e-2$	-31.4%
	4	$6.20e-3$	$3.01e-4$	-95.1%	$8.15e-4$	-86.9%	$2.76e-3$	-55.6%
	5	$2.29e-3$	$3.18e-5$	-98.6%	$1.25e-4$	-94.5%	$5.98e-4$	-73.9%

As results we consider the throughput of synchronized transitions which is identical for all synchronized transitions and corresponds to the server throughput, the mean population of $p3 + p4 + p5$ in component 1, which corresponds to the mean number of servers in component 1, and the probability that the buffer of component 6 is filled, which can be used to compute the loss probability for this component under Poisson arrivals. Table 8 includes exact results and approximation results computed with different versions of the fixed-point approach. For all examples V2 yields smaller approximation errors than V1 and V3 yields significantly smaller errors than V2. Thus, the additional effort due to the more complex aggregates is justified. For larger values of K_i, all fixed-point approaches require significantly less solution time than an exact analysis, if an exact analysis is possible at all. Results related to the server, namely throughput and population in component 1, are acceptable. Relative errors for V1 and V2 are smaller than 10% and most times smaller than 5%. For V3 errors for server related measures are smaller than 1%. The errors of V1 are of the same size than errors reported for mean response times in [7]. Errors reported in [14] are smaller than the errors of V1. But in [14] random polling, several servers and a single buffer per queue are used. Our own experiments indicate that random polling yields significantly smaller errors than cyclic polling. The reason for this behavior is that server interarrival times for a component become more random than in the cyclic case.

Both cited papers consider only server related measures in their analysis. For a user, measures related to the behavior of a buffer are often more important. These measures answer questions how long it takes to transmit a packet or how many packets get lost due to buffer overflow. In particular buffer overflows, which usually have a small probability, are important from a user perspective. Unfortunately, our results indicate that the fixed-point approach fails to compute buffer overflow with a sufficient accuracy. Relative errors are large in all cases and increase for larger buffer capacities. However, the large relative errors hide a little bit that there are big differences between the different versions of the fixed point approach. V3 computes loss probabilities which are about 19 times larger than loss probabilities computed via V1. Unfortunately, the real loss probability is still nearly 4 times larger than the result of V3. The reason for this bad behavior of the fixed-point approach is the high variability of server interarrival times in the original system.

6 Conclusions

We have introduced a new decomposition and aggregation based approach for the quantitative analysis of labeled GSPNs, a class of nets allowing the compositional description of complex models. The new approach relies on the compositional structure of labeled GSPNs and on equivalence relations defined for labeled GSPNs. Different equivalence relations define different aggregate types which are used in the analysis approach. It is possible to define aggregates at several levels of detail, i.e., aggregates preserving only the functional behavior, aggregates preserving approximately or exactly the quantitative behavior. Usually a stronger equivalence relation implies a larger state space for the aggregate and better approximation results. In this way it is possible to find a compromise between an efficient analysis and low approximation errors.

However, the main drawback of decomposition and aggregation based approaches is the unknown size of the approximation error. Errors depend on the model structure and on the required performance measures. We have shown in our second example that in particular detailed measures like the distribution of the token population on a place are very sensitive according to the behavior of the embedding environment. Unfortunately those measures are often very important. This shows that are is still a lot of research to do to estimate or bound approximation errors.

References

1. C. Baier, H. Hermanns; Weak bisimulation for fully probabilistic processes; In: *Proc. CAV'97, Springer LNCS 1254 (1997)*.
2. P. Buchholz; A notion of equivalence for stochastic Petri nets; In: *G. De Michelis, M. Diaz (eds.); 16th Int. Conference on Application and Theory of Petri Nets, Springer LNCS 935 (1995) 161-180.*
3. P. Buchholz; Efficient computation of equivalent and reduced representations for stochastic automata; *to appear in Int. Journ. of Comp. Sys. Sci. & Eng.*
4. P. Buchholz; Hierarchical Structuring of superposed GSPNs; In: *Proc. of the 7th Int. Work. on Petri Nets and Performance Models, IEEE CS-Press (1997) 81-90.*
5. G. Chiola, M. Ajmone Marsan, G. Balbo, G. Conte; Generalized stochastic Petri nets: a definition at the net level and its implications; *IEEE Trans. on Softw. Eng. 19 (1993) 89-107.*
6. J. Campos, J. M. Colom, H. Jungnitz, M. Silva; A general iterative technique for approximate throughput computation of stochastic marked graphs; In: *Proc. of the 5th Int. Work. on Petri Nets and Performance Models, IEEE CS-Press (1993) 138-147.*
7. H. Choi, K. Trivedi; Approximate performance models of polling systems using stochastic Petri nets; In: *Proc. of the Infocom 92, IEEE CS-Press (1992) 2306-2314.*
8. R. Cleaveland, J. Parrow, B. Steffen; The concurrency workbench: a semantics based tool for the verification of concurrent systems; *ACM Trans. on Prog. Lang. and Sys. 15 (1993) 36-72.*
9. S. Donatelli; Superposed stochastic automata: a class of stochastic Petri nets amenable to parallel solution; *Performance Evaluation 18 (1993) 21-36.*
10. S. Donatelli; Superposed generalized stochastic Petri nets: definition and efficient solution; In: *R. Valette (ed.), Application and Theory of Petri Nets 1994, Springer LNCS 815 (1994) 258-277.*
11. H. Jungnitz, B. Sanchez, M. Silva; Approximate throughput computation of stochastic marked graphs; *Journ. of Parallel and Distributed Computing 15 (1992) 282-295.*
12. P. Kemper; Numerical analysis of superposed GSPNs; *IEEE Trans. on Softw. Eng. 22 (1996) 615-628.*
13. Y. Li, C. M. Woodside; Iterative decomposition of stochastic marked graph Petri nets; In: *Proc. of the 12th Int. Conf. on Theory and Appl. of Petri Nets (1991) 257-275.*
14. Y. Li, C. M. Woodside; Complete decomposition of stochastic Petri nets representing generalized service networks; *IEEE Trans. on Comp. 44 (1995) 577-592.*
15. V. Mainkar, K. S. Trivedi; Fixed point iteration using stochastic reward nets; *IEEE Trans. on Softw. Eng. 22 (1996).*
16. R. Milner; Communication and concurrency; *Prentice Hall 1989.*
17. B. Plateau; On the stochastic structure of parallelism and synchronisation models for distributed algorithms; *Performance Evaluation Review 13 (1985) 142-154.*
18. L. Pomello, G. Rozenberg, C. Simone; A survey of equivalence relations for net based systems; In: *G. Rozenberg (ed.); Advances in Petri Nets 1992; Springer LNCS 609 (1992) 410-472.*

On the Use of Structural Petri Net Analysis
for Studying Product Form Equilibrium Distributions
of Queueing Networks with Blocking

Marco Gribaudo and Matteo Sereno

Dipartimento di Informatica, Università di Torino,
corso Svizzera 185, 10149 Torino, Italy

Abstract. In this paper we investigate some relations between the Petri
net formalism and the queueing networks with blocking. This type of
queueing network models are used to represent systems with finite capacity resource constraints, such as production, communication and computer systems. Various blocking mechanisms have been defined in the
literature to represent the different behaviours of real systems with limited resources.
We show that the representation of these queueing networks by means
of Generalized Stochastic Petri Nets offers the possibility of using results
developed within the Petri net framework. In particular, we investigate
product form equilibrium distributions for queueing networks with blocking by means of structural Petri net results. More precisely, we use the
notion of implicit places. With this concept we characterise a class of
queueing networks with blocking having interesting properties. For each
queueing network of this class there exists another model with the same
performance measures and exhibiting product form equilibrium distribution.

1   Introduction

Queueing networks and Stochastic Petri nets are well known formalisms used
to represent and analyse production, communication and computer systems and
have been proved to be powerful tools for performance analysis and prediction.
These formalisms have been developed with different purposes. Historically the
queueing networks represent one of the first modeling paradigms proposed for
performance analysis. The literature on this topic is full of results that allow
to define the queueing network formalism one of the most used performance
analysis tool.

One of the most important analytical results developed for calculating the
equilibrium distribution describing the number of items at nodes in a performance model is the so called *product form* equilibrium distribution, introduced
by Jackson [10], and nowadays found for a rather wide class of queueing models
(see for instance [4] and other extensions). The main advantage of these product
form distributions is their simplicity which makes them easy to use for computational issues as well as for theoretical reflections on performance models involving

congestion as a consequence of queueing. However, practical performance models seldom satisfy the product form conditions. Nevertheless, results obtained via the theoretical product form distributions are used for practical applications since these results are found to be robust, that is models that violate the product form conditions are often found to behave in a way that is "qualitatively similar" to a product form counterpart. Also, various approximation and bounding techniques are based on product form results.

On the other hand the Stochastic Petri nets have been developed starting from the untimed Petri net formalism. A Stochastic Petri net is a Petri net in which a random variable, characterised by a negative exponential distribution function, is associated to any transition of the net. In this paper we consider the *Generalized Stochastic Petri nets (GSPN)* [1]. GSPNs are obtained by allowing transitions to belong to two different classes: immediate transitions and timed transitions.

In the literature there are many effort for the investigation of the relations between queueing networks and stochastic Petri nets. In several cases results developed within the framework of the queueing networks have been imported into the field of the stochastic Petri nets. Examples of this cross-fertilisation are, for instance, the product form solution, the approximate methods, the bounding techniques, and so on. In any of these techniques a result originally developed for queueing networks has been adapted for stochastic Petri nets. In all the cases the features of the Petri net formalism have been used for the exploitation of the potentialities of the methods.

In this paper we propose a different approach. We will use results developed in the framework of untimed Petri net formalism for the investigation of queueing network properties. We focus our attention on queueing networks with blocking. Queueing networks with limited capacity queues (FC-QNs) are used to represent systems with finite capacity resources and with resource constraints. Various blocking mechanisms have been defined in the literature to represent the different behaviours of real systems with limited resources (see [2,3,14,15] for details on these mechanisms).

In [9], a technique that allows to represent FC-QNs by means of GSPNs has been proposed. In this paper we use the Petri net representation of FC-QNs to derive new results for this class of queueing networks.

We investigate the utilisation of the *implicit places* theory for studying product form equilibrium distributions of FC-QNs. In particular using this notion we characterise a class of FC-QNs such that for each element of this class there exists a model with the same performance measures and with product form equilibrium distributions. For some of these FC-QNs the result that will presented in this paper are novel, in the sense that with the proposed method we characterise new product form cases.

These new results are also important because product form equilibrium distributions represent the starting points for studying non-product form models. Many "ad hoc" techniques have appeared in the literature in which the non-product form model is "transformed" into a product form one.

The balance of the paper is as follows. Section 2 provides some basic concepts of the FC-QNs and of the GSPNs. Section 3 reviews the definitions of the pertinent blocking mechanisms and their descriptions by means of GSPNs. Section 4 contains the main contribution of this paper. In this section we describe the utilisation of implicit places for studying product form distributions of FC-QNs. Finally, Section 5 presents some concluding remarks and direction for future work.

2   Queueing Networks with Finite Capacity and Generalized Stochastic Petri Nets : Definitions and Notation

Consider a closed queueing network with M finite capacity service centers (or nodes), and N customers in the network. The customers behaviour between nodes of the network is described by the routing matrix $P = ||p_{ij}||$ $(1 \leq i,j \leq M)$, where p_{ij} denotes the probability that a job leaving node i tries to enter node j. In FC-QNs additional constrains on the number of customers are included to represent different types of resource constrains in real systems. This can be represented in the network by a maximum queue length constraint for a single node. We denote with b_i the maximum queue length admitted at node i (i.e., the buffer size).

Generalized Stochastic Petri Notation. We recall the basic notation on timed and untimed Petri nets that we are using in the paper. More comprehensive presentations of these concepts can be found in [1, 13, 18].

A *Generalized Stochastic Petri net* is a five-tuple $\mathcal{N} = \langle \mathcal{P}, \mathcal{T}, W, Q, m_0 \rangle$, where

$\mathcal{P}$	is the set of places;
$\mathcal{T}$	is the set of transitions;
$W : (\mathcal{P} \times \mathcal{T}) \cup (\mathcal{T} \times \mathcal{P}) \to \mathbb{N}$	defines the weighted flow relation;
$Q : \mathcal{T} \to \mathbb{R}^+$	is a function that associates rates of negative exponential distribution to timed transitions and weights to immediate transitions;
m_0	is the initial marking of the GSPN.

With $\boldsymbol{Pre}$ and $\boldsymbol{C}$ we denote respectively the precondition and the incidence matrices. The row of $\boldsymbol{C}$ corresponding to place p_i is denoted by $\boldsymbol{C}[p_i, \cdot]$, while the column corresponding to transition t_j is denoted by $\boldsymbol{C}[\cdot, t_j]$.

3   Blocking Mechanisms and their GSPN Interpretation

In [9], a technique that allows to represent FC-QNs by means of GSPNs has been proposed. In this section we review the definitions only of the blocking mechanisms that will be used in this paper and their descriptions by means of GSPNs, in particular we only consider the following blocking mechanisms: *Blocking After Service*, and *Blocking Before Service*. Interested readers can find the description of other blocking mechanisms in [2, 3, 14].

For each node i we use PREV(i) to denote the set of nodes j such that $p_{ji} > 0$.

Blocking Before Service (BBS). In this blocking mechanism a customer at node i declares its destination node j before it starts receiving its service. If node j is full, node i becomes blocked. When a departure occurs from the destination node j, node i is unblocked and its server starts serving the customer. If the destination node j becomes full during the service of a customer at node i, the service is interrupted and node i is blocked. The service is resumed from the interruption point as soon as a space becomes available at the destination node. As discussed in [14], two different subcategories can be introduced depending on whether the server can be used to hold a customer when the node is blocked:
Blocking Before Service - Server Occupied (BBS-SO). In this case the server of a blocked node is used to hold a customer.
Blocking Before Service - Server Not Occupied (BBS-SNO). A server of a blocked node cannot be used to hold a customer. In this blocking mechanism, if a node i has a buffer capacity b_i, when it becomes blocked, its capacity must be decrease to $b_i - 1$. This type of blocking can only be implemented in some special topology network. In particular it cannot be implemented in a position in which its upstreams nodes may become full due to an arrival of a customer from a different node.

The distinction between BBS-SO and BBS-SNO blocking mechanisms is meaningful when modeling different types of systems. For example, in communication networks, a server corresponds to a communication channel. If there is no space in the downstream node, then the message cannot be transmitted. Furthermore, the channel itself cannot be used to store messages due to physical constraints of the channel. On the other hand, BBS-SO blocking arises if the service facility can be used to hold the blocked customer. BBS-SO blocking has been used to model manufacturing systems, terminal concentrators, mass storage systems, disk-to-tape backup systems, window flow control mechanisms, and communication systems (for further details see [14] and the references therein).

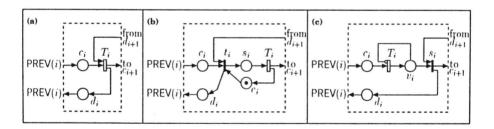

Fig. 1. GSPN subnets representing nodes with BBS-SO (a), BBS-SNO (b), and BAS (c) blocking mechanisms.

GSPN Subnets of a BBS-SO Node. In Figure 1(a) we present the GSPN subnets modeling a node with BBS-SO mechanism that has only one destination node. If the buffer of the destination node is full, transition T_i is blocked. When a departure occurs from the destination node, transition T_i is unblocked and starts serving the customers. The number of tokens in place c_i represents the number of customers in the node i, while the buffer capacity is given by the sum of tokens in place c_i and place d_i. The throughput of the node is given by the throughput of transition T_i.

GSPN Subnets of a BBS-SNO Node. Figure 1(b) shows a BBS-SNO node having one possible destination node. In this GSPN subnet place s_i represents the position in front of the server and hence it can be used as storage room only if the node is not blocked. When the buffer of the destination node is full the immediate transition t_i cannot be enabled because place d_{i+1} is empty. When a departure occurs from the destination node transition t_i can be enabled and hence the position in front of the server becomes again available. The actual capacity of node i is represented by the number of tokens in places c_i, d_i, e_i, and s_i. In the initial marking we must have that $b_i = \boldsymbol{m}[c_i] + \boldsymbol{m}[d_i] + \boldsymbol{m}[e_i] + \boldsymbol{m}[s_i]$ and $\boldsymbol{m}[s_i] + \boldsymbol{m}[e_i] = 1$. The average number of customers in the node is given by the sum of the average number of tokens in place c_i and in place s_i.

Blocking After Service (BAS). This blocking mechanism works as follows: if a customer attempts to enter a full capacity node j upon completion of service at node i, it is forced to wait in node i, until it is allowed to enter destination node j. The server node i stops servicing customers (it is blocked) until destination node j releases a customer. The node i service will be resumed as soon as a departure occurs from node j. At that time the customer waiting in node i immediately moves to node j.

GSPN Subnet of a BAS Node. Figure 1(c) shows a BAS node having one possible destination node. The place c_i represents the queue while transition T_i represents the server of node i. A customer receives its service and reaches place v_i, if the buffer of the destination (place d_{i+1}) is full the customer waits in place v_i. In this case the transition T_i is blocked (inhibitor arc from place v_i to transition T_i). When a position in the buffer of the node $i+1$ is available the customer moves immediately towards its destination and the service of transition T_i is resumed. The place d_i records the free positions in the buffer of node i. The capacity of node i is given by $\boldsymbol{m}[c_i] + \boldsymbol{m}[v_i] + \boldsymbol{m}[d_i]$.

4   Structural Petri Net Results for Product Form Analysis

In this section we present the main contribution of this paper: we show that the structural analysis can be useful for the study of the product form solution of FC-QNs. In the following we first give an interpretation of a known result for FC-QNs and then we discuss some new product form cases using the same arguments.

Theorem 1. (From [3]) *A homogeneous closed cyclic queueing network with exponential service centers, load independent service rates, and with*

$$N \geq \sum_{i=1}^{M} b_i - \min_{j=1}^{M} b_j \tag{1}$$

has product form equilibrium distribution under BBS-SO blocking mechanism.

The proof of the previous theorem has been obtained using the concept of *holes* that has been introduced by Gordon and Newell [8]. Since the capacity of node i is b_i, let us assume that this node consists of b_i cells. If there are n_i customer at node i, then n_i cells are occupied and $b_i - n_i$ are empty. We may say that these empty cells are occupied by holes. Then the total number of holes in the network is equal to $\sum_{i=1}^{M} b_i - N$. As the customers move sequentially through the cyclic network, the holes execute a counter sequential motion since each movement of customer from the i-th node to the $(i+1)$-th node corresponds to the movement of a hole in the opposite direction (from the $(i+1)$-th node to the the i-th node). It is then shown that these two networks are *dual*. That is, if a customer (hole) at node i is blocked in one system, then node $i+1$ has no holes (customers) in its dual. Let (b_i, μ_i) be the capacity and the service rate of node i and $\{(b_1, \mu_1), \ldots, (b_M, \mu_M)\}$ be a cyclic network with N customers. Then its dual is $\{(b_1, \mu_M), (b_M, \mu_{M-1}), \ldots, (b_2, \mu_1)\}$ with $\sum_{i=1}^{M} b_i - N$ customers. Let $\pi(\boldsymbol{n})$ and $\pi^D(\boldsymbol{n})$ be the steady state equilibrium probabilities of the cyclic network and its dual, respectively, where $\boldsymbol{n} = [n_1, n_2, \ldots, n_M]$ is the state of the network with n_i being the number of customers at node i. Then for all the feasible states, we have $\pi([n_1, n_2, \ldots, n_M]) = \pi^D([b_1 - n_1, b_M - n_M, \ldots, b_2 - n_2])$. We note that if the number of customers in the network is such that no node can be empty, then the dual network is a non-blocking network, i.e., the number of holes is less than or equal to the minimum node capacity, and hence the network has product form equilibrium distribution. Inequality (1) ensures exactly this condition, i.e., in a cyclic FC-QN satisfying this inequality no node can be empty.

If we consider the GSPN representation of a closed cyclic queueing network with BBS-SO blocking mechanisms, we can say that Inequality (1) ensures the places corresponding to the queues (the c_i-s of the GSPN of Figure 2) are always marked and hence they cannot block the movement of the holes, i.e., these places never restrict the firing of their output transitions and then they can be removed without affecting the behaviour of the GSPN. In the Petri net literature places that behave in this manner are called *implicit places*.

Definition 1. (From [18]) *Let $\mathcal{S} = \langle \mathcal{P}, \mathcal{T}, W, \boldsymbol{m_0} \rangle$ a Petri net and $\mathcal{S}' = \langle \mathcal{P}', \mathcal{T}, W' \boldsymbol{m_0'} \rangle$ the net resulting from removing place p from $\mathcal{S}$. The place p is an* implicit place *if the removing of p preserves all the firing sequences of the original Petri net. The Petri net $\mathcal{S}'$ is obtained from $\mathcal{S}$ by removing place p.*

A place is implicit depending on the initial marking of the Petri net. Places which can be implicit for any initial marking are said to be *structurally implicit places*.

Definition 2. (From [7]) *Given a Petri net $\mathcal{N}_p = \langle \mathcal{P}, \mathcal{T}, W \rangle$, the place p (with $p \in \mathcal{P}$) is structurally implicit iff $\forall \, \boldsymbol{m_0'}$ of $\mathcal{N}'$ (the net without place p), there exists an $\boldsymbol{m_0}[p]$ such that p is an implicit place in $\langle \mathcal{N}, \boldsymbol{m_0} \rangle$.*

A structurally implicit place p may become implicit for any initial marking of the places $\mathcal{P} \setminus \{p\}$ if we have the freedom to select an adequate initial marking for it.

The following result allows to recognise whether a place is structurally implicit.

Theorem 2. (From [7]) *Let $\mathcal{N} = \langle \mathcal{P}, \mathcal{T}, W \rangle$ be a Petri net. A place $p \in \mathcal{P}$ is structurally implicit iff there exists a subset $\mathcal{I}_p \subseteq \mathcal{P} \backslash \{p\}$ such that $C[p, \cdot] \geq \sum_{q \in \mathcal{I}_p} y_q \cdot C[q, \cdot]$, where y_q is a nonnegative rational number (i.e., $\exists\, y \geq 0$, $y[p] = 0$ such that $y \cdot C \leq C[p, \cdot]$ and $\mathcal{I}_p = \{q \;: q \in \mathcal{P}$ such that $y[q] > 0\}$).*

Next result allows to compute the initial marking such that the structurally implicit place becomes implicit. This result is obtained using the Linear Programming technique.

Theorem 3. (From [7]) *Let $\mathcal{N} = \langle \mathcal{P}, \mathcal{T}, W \rangle$ with initial marking m_0. A structurally implicit place p of $\mathcal{N}$, with initial marking $m_0[p]$, is an implicit place if $m_0[p] \geq z$, where z is the optimal value of the following linear programming problem:*

$$z = \min\; y \cdot m_0 + h \qquad (2)$$
$$s.\ t.\ y \cdot C \leq C[p, \cdot]$$
$$y \cdot Pre[\cdot, t] + h \geq Pre[p, t] \quad \forall\, t \in p^{\bullet}$$
$$y \geq 0, y[p] = 0.$$

Now we illustrate the previous results concerning implicit places in the case of GSPNs representing closed cyclic queueing networks with BBS-SO blocking mechanisms.

Let us consider a closed cyclic queueing network with M nodes and BBS-SO blocking mechanisms, Figure 2 shows its GSPN representation.

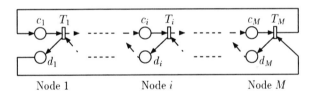

Fig. 2. The GSPN modeling a cyclic FC-QN with M BBS-SO nodes.

The incidence and the preconditions matrices, for this Petri net, are:

$$C = \begin{array}{c|ccccccc} & T_1 & \cdots & T_{i-1} & T_i & \cdots & T_{M-1} & T_M \\ \hline c_1 & -1 & \cdots & 0 & 0 & \cdots & 0 & 1 \\ d_1 & 1 & \cdots & 0 & 0 & \cdots & 0 & -1 \\ \vdots & \vdots & \vdots & \vdots & \vdots & \vdots & \vdots & \vdots \\ c_i & 0 & \cdots & 1 & -1 & \cdots & 0 & 0 \\ d_i & 0 & \cdots & -1 & 1 & \cdots & 0 & 0 \\ \vdots & \vdots & \vdots & \vdots & \vdots & \vdots & \vdots & \vdots \\ c_M & 0 & \cdots & 0 & 0 & \cdots & 1 & -1 \\ d_M & 0 & \cdots & 0 & 0 & \cdots & -1 & 1 \end{array}$$

$$Pre = \begin{array}{c|ccccccc} & T_1 & \cdots & T_{i-1} & T_i & \cdots & T_{M-1} & T_M \\ \hline c_1 & -1 & \cdots & 0 & 0 & \cdots & 0 & 0 \\ d_1 & 0 & \cdots & 0 & 0 & \cdots & 0 & -1 \\ \vdots & \vdots & \vdots & \vdots & \vdots & \vdots & \vdots & \vdots \\ c_i & 0 & \cdots & 0 & -1 & \cdots & 0 & 0 \\ d_i & 0 & \cdots & -1 & 0 & \cdots & 0 & 0 \\ \vdots & \vdots & \vdots & \vdots & \vdots & \vdots & \vdots & \vdots \\ c_M & 0 & \cdots & 0 & 0 & \cdots & 0 & -1 \\ d_M & 0 & \cdots & 0 & 0 & \cdots & -1 & 0 \end{array}$$

From the incidence matrix C we can observe that for any place c_i (with $1 \le i \le M$) $C[c_i, \cdot] = \sum\limits_{j=1,\ j \ne i}^{M} C[d_j, \cdot]$. It follows that any place c_i is structurally implicit and the corresponding vector y has the components equal to 1 in the positions corresponding to places d_j (with $j \ne i$) and all the others are equal to 0.

The initial marking of place c_i such that it becomes implicit can be computed using Theorem 3. We can see that from vectors y-s and from the structure of the GSPN the linear programming problem (2) has a simple interpretation.

The second inequality of (2), that is, $y \cdot C \le C[c_i, \cdot]$, derives from Theorem 2 and defines the vector y.

Furthermore, let be $T_i \in c_i^\bullet$, we have that $y \cdot Pre[\cdot, T_i] = Pre[d_{i+1}, T_i] = -1$, but also $Pre[c_i, T_i] = -1$, hence the third inequality of (2) becomes an equality when $h = 0$. In this case the initial marking of place c_i such that it becomes implicit has to satisfy the following inequality

$$m_0[c_i] \ge \sum_{j=1,\ j \ne i}^{M} m_0[d_j]. \tag{3}$$

The previous results can be interpreted in terms of the parameters of the FC-QN with BBS-SO nodes represented by the GSPN. We have to remember that the tokens in all the places c_i represent the customers circulating within the FC-QN, i. e., for any reachable marking m we have that $\sum_{i=1}^{M} m[c_i] = N$ (the set of places c_i is the support set of a minimal P-semiflow). The tokens in places d_i represent the available positions in the buffer of the i-th node. For any reachable marking m we have that $m[c_i] + m[d_i] = b_i$ $(i = 1, \ldots, M)$, where b_i is the size of the buffer of the i-th node. From this it follows that Inequality (3) can be rewritten as

$$m_0[c_i] \ge \sum_{j=1,\ j \ne i}^{M} b_j - m_0[c_j]$$

$$N \ge \sum_{j=1,\ j \ne i}^{M} b_j. \tag{4}$$

If Inequality (1) of Theorem 1 is satisfied then, for any $i = 1, \ldots, M$, we have that

$$N \ge \sum_{j=1,\ j \ne i}^{M} b_j.$$

Hence all the places c_i are implicit.

On the other hand, if all places c_i are implicit, Inequalities (4) are satisfied for any $1 \le i \le M$ and this implies that Inequality (1) holds. The previous results can be summarised with the following theorem that represent the GSPN interpretation of Theorem 1.

Theorem 4. *Let $\langle \mathcal{P}, \mathcal{T}, W, Q, \mathbf{m_0} \rangle$ be a GSPN modeling a closed cyclic queueing network with BBS-SO blocking mechanisms. The places of the GSPN representing the queues are implicit iff*

$$N \geq \sum_{i=1}^{M} b_i - \min_{j=1}^{M} b_j.$$

4.1 Implicit Places for Deriving New Product Form Results

Let us consider a closed cyclic queueing network with $M-1$ BBS-SO nodes, and one BBS-SNO node. Without loss of generality we assume that l is the index of the BBS-SNO node. Figure 3 shows the GSPN representation of a such FC-QN.

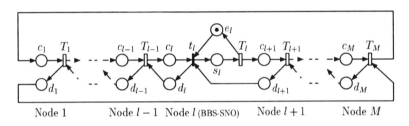

Fig. 3. The GSPN modeling a cyclic FC-QN with one BBS-SNO node and $M-1$ BBS-SO nodes.

The incidence and the preconditions matrices, for this Petri net, are:

$$C = \begin{array}{c} \\ c_1 \\ d_1 \\ \vdots \\ c_{l-1} \\ d_{l-1} \\ c_l \\ d_l \\ s_l \\ e_l \\ c_{l+1} \\ d_{l+1} \\ \vdots \\ c_M \\ d_M \end{array}
\begin{array}{|ccccccc|}
T_1 & \cdots & T_{l-1} & t_l & T_l & T_{l+1} & \cdots & T_M \\
\hline
-1 & \cdots & 0 & 0 & 0 & 0 & \cdots & 1 \\
1 & \cdots & 0 & 0 & 0 & 0 & \cdots & -1 \\
\vdots & \vdots & \vdots & \vdots & \vdots & \vdots & \vdots & \vdots \\
0 & \cdots & -1 & 0 & 0 & 0 & \cdots & 0 \\
0 & \cdots & 1 & 0 & 0 & 0 & \cdots & 0 \\
0 & \cdots & 1 & -1 & 0 & 0 & \cdots & 0 \\
0 & \cdots & -1 & 1 & 0 & 0 & \cdots & 0 \\
0 & \cdots & 0 & 1 & -1 & 0 & \cdots & 0 \\
0 & \cdots & 0 & -1 & 1 & 0 & \cdots & 0 \\
0 & \cdots & 0 & 0 & 1 & -1 & \cdots & 0 \\
0 & \cdots & 0 & -1 & 0 & 1 & \cdots & 0 \\
\vdots & \vdots & \vdots & \vdots & \vdots & \vdots & \vdots & \vdots \\
0 & \cdots & 0 & 0 & 0 & 0 & \cdots & -1 \\
0 & \cdots & 0 & 0 & 0 & 0 & \cdots & 1
\end{array}$$

$$\boldsymbol{Pre} = \begin{array}{c} \\ c_1 \\ d_1 \\ \vdots \\ c_{l-1} \\ d_{l-1} \\ c_l \\ d_l \\ s_l \\ e_l \\ c_{l+1} \\ d_{l+1} \\ \vdots \\ c_M \\ d_M \end{array}
\begin{array}{|ccccccc|}
T_1 & \cdots & T_{l-1} & t_l & T_l & T_{l+1} & \cdots & T_M \\
\hline
-1 & \cdots & 0 & 0 & 0 & 0 & \cdots & 0 \\
0 & \cdots & 0 & 0 & 0 & 0 & \cdots & -1 \\
\vdots & \vdots & \vdots & \vdots & \vdots & \vdots & \vdots & \vdots \\
0 & \cdots & -1 & 0 & 0 & 0 & \cdots & 0 \\
0 & \cdots & 0 & 0 & 0 & 0 & \cdots & 0 \\
0 & \cdots & 0 & -1 & 0 & 0 & \cdots & 0 \\
0 & \cdots & -1 & 0 & 0 & 0 & \cdots & 0 \\
0 & \cdots & 0 & 0 & -1 & 0 & \cdots & 0 \\
0 & \cdots & 0 & -1 & 0 & 0 & \cdots & 0 \\
0 & \cdots & 0 & 0 & 0 & -1 & \cdots & 0 \\
0 & \cdots & 0 & -1 & 0 & 0 & \cdots & 0 \\
\vdots & \vdots & \vdots & \vdots & \vdots & \vdots & \vdots & \vdots \\
0 & \cdots & 0 & 0 & 0 & 0 & \cdots & -1 \\
0 & \cdots & 0 & 0 & 0 & 0 & \cdots & 0
\end{array}$$

We can split the analysis of this FC-QN into three parts: identification of the implicit places, product form analysis, and computation of the analytical solution.

Identification of the Implicit Places. From the incidence matrix C we can observe that for any place c_i, with $i = 1, \ldots, M$, and $i \neq l+1$ (the place corresponding to the BBS-SO node that follows the BBS-SNO node) $C[c_i, \cdot] = \sum_{j=1, \ j \neq i}^{M} C[d_j, \cdot]$. For the place c_{l+1}, i. e., the node that immediately follows the unique BBS-SNO node, we have that $C[c_{l+1}, \cdot] = C[e_l, \cdot] + \sum_{j=1, \ j \neq l+1}^{M} C[d_j, \cdot]$.

From these equations it follows that all the places c_i (included places c_l and c_{l+1}) are structurally implicit. For each place c_i we identify the vector $\boldsymbol{y}$ involved in the LPP (2). To distinguish these vectors we denote by $\boldsymbol{y}^{(i)}$ the vector corresponding to place c_i. For any place c_i, with $i \neq l+1$ we have that $\boldsymbol{y}^{(i)}$ has the components equal to 1 in the positions corresponding to places d_j (with $j \neq i$) and all the other components are equal to 0. For place c_{l+1}, the vector $\boldsymbol{y}^{(l+1)}$ has the components equal to 1 in the positions corresponding to places d_j (with $j \neq l+1$), and in the one corresponding to place e_l, and all the other components are equal to 0.

Given the structure of the GSPN that models this FC-QN, and the form of vectors $\boldsymbol{y}^{(i)}$ (for $i = 1, \ldots, M$) we see that LPP (2) has a simple interpretation. Let us consider the following two cases: $i = l+1$, and $1 \leq i \leq M$ with $i \neq l+1$. In each one of these possible cases, if $t \in c_i^{\bullet}$ then the vector $\boldsymbol{y}^{(i)}$ has the entry corresponding to place c_i equal to 0 and the entry corresponding to place d_{i+1} equal to 1. From this it follows that $\boldsymbol{y}^{(i)} \cdot \boldsymbol{Pre}[\cdot, t] = \boldsymbol{Pre}[d_{i+1}, t] = -1$, but also $\boldsymbol{Pre}[c_i, t] = -1$. This implies that the third inequality of the LPP (2) becomes an equality when $h = 0$. To compute the initial marking of place c_i such that it becomes implicit we must take into account the different structures of the vector $\boldsymbol{y}^{(i)}$-s. In particular, for any $i = 1, \ldots, M$, the only non zero entries are those corresponding to places d_j, with $j = 1, \ldots, M$, and $j \neq i$. When $i = l+1$ we must consider that also the entry corresponding to place e_l is equal to 1. It follows that LLP (2), which gives the initial marking of c_i such that it becomes implicit, assumes the following form:

$$
\boldsymbol{m_0}[c_i] \geq \begin{cases} \sum_{j=1, \ j \neq i}^{M} \boldsymbol{m_0}[d_j] & \text{if } i \neq l+1 \\ \boldsymbol{m_0}[e_l] + \sum_{j=1, \ j \neq i}^{M} \boldsymbol{m_0}[d_j] & \text{if } i = l+1. \end{cases} \tag{5}
$$

Next step is the interpretation of the previous inequalities in terms of the parameters of the FC-QN. To this aim we need to know the structure of the P-semiflows of the GSPN of Figure 3. In this GSPN we have that $N = \sum_{i=1}^{M} \boldsymbol{m}[c_i] + \boldsymbol{m}[s_l]$, $b_i = \boldsymbol{m}[c_i] + \boldsymbol{m}[d_i]$ (with $i \neq l, i \neq l+1$), $b_l - 1 = \boldsymbol{m}[c_l] + \boldsymbol{m}[d_l]$, $b_{l+1} = \boldsymbol{m}[c_{l+1}] + \boldsymbol{m}[d_{l+1}] + \boldsymbol{m}[s_l]$, and $1 = \boldsymbol{m}[s_l] + \boldsymbol{m}[e_l]$. We split the analysis of Inequalities (5) into three cases:

Node i, with $i \neq l$ and $i \neq l+1$

$$m_0[c_i] \geq \sum_{\substack{j=1 \\ j \neq i, j \neq l, j \neq l+1}}^{M} m_0[d_j] + m_0[d_l] + m_0[d_{l+1}]$$

$$m_0[c_i] \geq \sum_{\substack{j=1 \\ j \neq i, j \neq l, j \neq l+1}}^{M} (b_j - m_0[c_j]) + b_l - 1 - m_0[c_l] + b_{l+1} - m_0[c_{l+1}] - m_0[s_l]$$

$$N \geq \sum_{\substack{j=1, \ j \neq i}}^{M} b_j - 1.$$

Node l

$$m_0[c_l] \geq \sum_{\substack{j=1 \\ j \neq l, j \neq l+1}}^{M} m_0[d_j] + m_0[d_{l+1}]$$

$$m_0[c_l] \geq \sum_{\substack{j=1 \\ j \neq l, j \neq l+1}}^{M} (b_j - m_0[c_j]) + b_{l+1} - m_0[c_{l+1}] - m_0[s_l]$$

$$N \geq \sum_{\substack{j=1, \ j \neq l}}^{M} b_j.$$

Node $l+1$

$$m_0[c_{l+1}] \geq \sum_{\substack{j=1 \\ j \neq l+1, j \neq l}}^{M} m_0[d_j] + m_0[d_l] + m[e_l]$$

$$m_0[c_{l+1}] \geq \sum_{\substack{j=1 \\ j \neq l+1, j \neq l}}^{M} (b_j - m_0[c_j]) + b_l - 1 - m_0[c_l] + m[e_l]$$

$$\sum_{j=1}^{M} m_0[c_j] \geq \sum_{\substack{j=1, \ j \neq l+1}}^{M} b_j - m[s_l]$$

$$N \geq \sum_{\substack{j=1, \ j \neq l+1}}^{M} b_j.$$

The previous inequalities are satisfied if

$$N \geq \sum_{i=1}^{M} b_i - \min_{j=1}^{M} b_j.$$

We summarise all the previous reasoning in the following lemma.

Lemma 1. *Given a cyclic queueing network with $M-1$ BBS-SO nodes and one BBS-SNO node, in the GSPN representation of this FC-QN, the places corresponding to the queues of the network are implicit if*

$$N \geq \sum_{i=1}^{M} b_i - \min_{j=1}^{M} b_j. \tag{6}$$

There is an interesting relation between Inequality (6) and the condition to ensure that the FC-QN is deadlock free. Deadlock prevention for some types of blocking mechanisms has been discussed in [9, 12, 14]. In these papers it is stated that a cyclic queueing network with $M-1$ BBS-SO nodes and one BBS-SNO node is deadlock free if the number of customers is

$$N < \sum_{i=1}^{M} b_i - 1. \tag{7}$$

If the minimum among the buffer capacities is equal to 1 then the value of N satisfying Inequality (6) implies that the network is deadlocked. To satisfy both Inequality (6) and Inequality (7) the minimum among the buffer capacities must be

$$\min_{j=1}^{M} b_j \geq 2.$$

Product Form Analysis. Figure 4 shows the GSPN of Figure 3 without the implicit places.

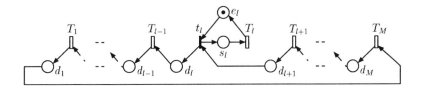

Fig. 4. The GSPN of Figure 3 without the implicit places.

In this GSPN the tokens in the places d_i represent the empty positions circulating within the FC-QN. If $N = \sum_{i=1}^{M} b_i - 1$, from Inequality (7), it follows that the GSPN of Figure 3 is deadlocked because for any node i of the network there is no available room in the destination node $i+1$ and hence all nodes are blocked. For the GSPN of Figure 4 the sum of the number of tokens in places d_i is zero. If $\min_{j=1}^{M} b_j \geq 2$ then $N = \sum_{i=1}^{M} b_i - 2$, satisfies Inequality (6) and Inequality (7). For this value of N the number of tokens in the places d_i is equal to 1. We show that, in this case, the model has a closed form expression for its steady state probability distribution, and that there exists a SPN having the same average

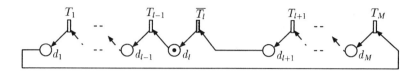

Fig. 5. The SPN with the same performance indices of the GSPN of Figure 4.

number of tokens in the places d_i (for $i = 1, \ldots, M$), and the same throughput of the transitions T_i of the GSPN of Figure 4. Figure 5 shows this SPN.

The SPN of Figure 5 represents a cyclic queueing network with M stations and only one customer. It is easy to see that the equilibrium distribution of this SPN is product form

$$\pi(\boldsymbol{m}) = \frac{1}{G} \left(\frac{1}{\overline{\mu_l}}\right)^{m_{l+1}} \cdot \prod_{\substack{i=1 \\ i \neq l+1}}^{M} \left(\frac{1}{\mu_{i-1}}\right)^{m_i}, \tag{8}$$

where G is a normalisation constant, μ_0 is the rate of transition T_M, and $\overline{\mu_l}$ is the rate of transition $\overline{T_l}$.

Now we derive the rate of $\overline{T_l}$ such that the models of Figure 4 and of Figure 5 have the same equilibrium distributions of the number of tokens in the places d_i (for $i = 1, \ldots, M$), the same average waiting time of the token in these places, and the same throughput of the transitions. Since all transitions T_i have the same throughput, we denote this measure by χ. We can write $\chi = 1/\left(\sum_{i=j}^{M} \overline{w_j}\right)$, where $\overline{w_j}$ is the average waiting time time spent by the token in place d_j. In the SPN of Figure 5 there is only one token circulating in the net and hence for any $j \neq l+1$ we have that $\overline{w_j} = 1/\mu_{j-1}$. For $j = 1$ we have that $\overline{w_1} = \frac{1}{\mu_M}$. The computation of the average waiting time spent by the token in place d_{l+1} requires a more complex analysis on the GSPN of Figure 4. We can compute $\overline{w_{l+1}}$ using this expression:

$$\overline{w_{l+1}} = P^a\{\text{the token arr. in } d_{l+1} \text{ finds } \#s_l > 0\} \cdot \frac{1}{\mu_l} + P^a\{\text{the token arr. in } d_{l+1} \text{ finds } \#e_l > 0\} \cdot 0,$$

where $P^a\{\text{the token arr. in } d_{l+1} \text{ finds } \#s_l > 0\}$ (resp. $P^a\{\text{the token arr. in } d_{l+1} \text{ finds } \#e_l > 0\}$) is the probability that the arriving token in place d_{l+1} finds place s_l marked (resp. the probability that the arriving token in place d_{l+1} finds place e_l marked).

The arrival-instant probabilities used in the previous equation can be expressed in terms of steady state solution of the model of Figure 4 as follows: $P^a\{\text{the token arr. in } d_{l+1} \text{ finds } \#s_l > 0\}$ is the ratio between the frequency of arrivals in d_{l+1} when s_l is marked and the frequency of arrivals in d_{l+1}, that is,

$$P^a\{\text{the token arr. in } d_{l+1} \text{ finds } \#s_l > 0\} = \frac{\pi(\{d_{l+2}, s_l\})\mu_{l+1}}{\chi},$$

where $\pi(\{d_{l+2}, s_l\})$ is the equilibrium probability of the state with one token in d_{l+2} and one in s_l, and χ is the frequency of arrivals in d_{l+1}, that is the throughput of T_{l+1}. Since all the service rates of the timed transitions are marking independent we can compute the throughput of T_{l+1} as $\chi = \pi(\{d_{l+2}\})\mu_{l+1}$, where $\pi(\{d_{l+2}\})$ is the equilibrium probability of the state with one token in d_{l+2}. It follows that we can write the previous arrival-instant probability in the following manner

$$P^a\{\text{the token arr. in } d_{l+1} \text{ finds } \#s_l > 0\} = \frac{\pi(\{d_{l+2}, s_l\})}{\pi(\{d_{l+2}\})}. \tag{9}$$

If we set the rate of transition $\overline{T_l}$, i. e. , $\overline{\mu_l}$ as $\overline{\mu_l} = 1/\overline{w_{l+1}}$, we obtain that the throughput of the transitions in the model of Figure 5 is the same as the one of the model Figure 4. This is the same for the average waiting time of the token in the places d_i (for $i = 1, \ldots, M$), and hence it follows from the Little law that also the number of tokens in these places is equal. Since there is only one token circulating in the net, the average number of tokens also give the marginal distributions of the tokens in these places.

Analytical Solution. Now we derive a method for the computation of the arrival-instant probability of Equation (9).

The GSPN of Figure 4 shows the GSPN representation of a FC-QN with $M - 1$ BBS-SO nodes and one BBS-SNO node without the implicit places. If we consider the model of Figure 4 we can see that this system (with only one token circulating in places d_i) is equivalent to the $M/H_{M-1}/1/2$ queueing system. The $M/H_{M-1}/1/2$ is a queueing system where the customers arrivals form a Poisson process with rate λ. The service times of customers are independent identically distributed random variables, the common distribution being $M - 1$ stages hypoexponential where ν_i, for $1 \leq i \leq M - 1$ is the rate of the i-th stage. The third parameter of the notation $M/H_{M-1}/1/2$ means single server queue, while the last parameter is maximum number of customers, that is, in the queueing system there can be up to 2 customers. For equivalence we mean that continuous time Markov chain of the GSPN of Figure 4 is equal to that one of the $M/H_{M-1}/1/2$ queueing system.

From this it follows that we can compute the arrival-instant probability of Equation (9) on the $M/H_{M-1}/1/2$ queueing system.

The arrival rate λ of the queueing system corresponds to the service rate of the BBS-SNO node (the one with index l). The rate of the first stage of the hypo-exponential distribution is equal to the service rate of the BBS-SO node with index $l - 1$, the rate of the second stage is equal to the service rate of the BBS-SO node with index $l - 2$, and so on up to the service rate of the last stage that is equal to the service rate of the BBS-SO node with index $l + 1$.

Table 1 shows the mapping between the states (markings) of the GSPN of Figure 4 and states of the $M/H_{M-1}/1/2$. In this table each state of the $M/H_{M-1}/1/2$ is denoted by a pair (n, s), where n represents the number of customers in the system and s is the stage of the customer currently in service. Each marking of the GSPN is represented by a list of the marked places. From the previous table we can see that the arrival-instant probability of Equation (9)

State of the $M/H_{M-1}/1/2$	Marking of the GSPN
$(0,0)$	$\{s_l, d_{l+1}\}$
$(1,1)$	$\{s_l, d_l\}$
$\vdots$	$\vdots$
$(1, M-1)$	$\{s_l, d_{l+2}\}$
$(2,1)$	$\{e_l, d_l\}$
$\vdots$	$\vdots$
$(2, M-1)$	$\{e_l, d_{l+2}\}$

Table 1. Mapping between states of the queueing system and markings of the GSPN of Figure 4

can be computed as

$$P^a\{\text{the token arr. in } d_{l+1} \text{ finds } \#s_l > 0\} = \frac{P\{(1, M-1)\}}{P\{(1, M-1)\} + P\{(2, M-1)\}}, \quad (10)$$

where $P\{(1, M-1)\}$ and $P\{(2, M-1)\}$ are the equilibrium probabilities of the states $(1, M-1)$ and $(2, M-1)$ of the $M/H_{M-1}/1/2$ queueing system. These equilibrium probabilities can be obtained using standard queueing techniques (see [11] for details). From Equation (10) we can derive that:

$$\begin{aligned}
\overline{\mu_l} &= \frac{1}{\overline{w_{l+1}}} \\
&= \frac{\mu_l}{P^a\{\text{the token arr. in } d_{l+1} \text{ finds } \#s_l > 0\}} \\
&= \frac{\mu_l \cdot (P\{(1, M-1)\} + P\{(2, M-1)\})}{P\{(1, M-1)\}}.
\end{aligned} \quad (11)$$

We summarise the previous derivations in the following lemma.

Lemma 2. *Given a cyclic queueing network with $M-1$ BBS-SO nodes and one BBS-SNO node. If the number of customers N circulating within the network is such that*

$$N = \sum_{i=1}^{M} b_i - 2, \quad (12)$$

with $\min_{j=1}^{M} b_j \geq 2$, then the queueing network has a closed form expression for the steady state probability distribution. Moreover there exists a product form solution model having the same performance measures of the cyclic queueing network. The product form model has M stations. The service rate of station i (for $i = 1, \ldots, M$, and $i \neq l$) is the same of the corresponding station of the FC-QN. The service rate of station l is $\overline{\mu_l}$ and it is obtained using Equation (11).

Using the product form equilibrium distribution (8) with the well known computational algorithms (for instance the normalisation constant algorithm [6], or the mean value analysis [16]) we can derive the performance measures for the SPN of Figure 5, in particular we can compute the average number of tokens in place d_i and the throughput of the transitions. From these indices we can derive the measures of the FC-QN represented by the GSPN of Figure 3. Let us denote with $\overline{n_i}$ the average number of customers in the node i and with $\overline{d_i}$ the average number of tokens in place d_i. For any node i, with $i = 1, \ldots, M$, and $i \neq l$, $i \neq l+1$, the average number of customers in the node $\overline{n_i}$ is given by $\overline{n_i} = b_i - \overline{d_i}$. For $i = l$ we have that $\overline{n_l} = b_l - 1 - \overline{d_l}$ gives the average number of customers queued at node l and does not take into account the position in front of the server (represented by place s_l). To derive the average number of tokens in place s_l we can use the following relation: let χ be the throughput of the transitions. Since the service rates are marking independent, we have that on the GSPN of Figure 4, $\chi = P\{\#s_l > 0\} \cdot \mu_l$, where $P\{\#s_l > 0\}$ is the probability that place s_l is marked. From the knowledge of χ we can derive $P\{\#s_l > 0\}$. Since place s_l can contain at most one token, we have that $\overline{s_l} = P\{\#s_l > 0\}$. In the GSPN of Figure 3 we can observe that places s_l, c_{l+1}, and d_{l+1} are covered by a minimal P-semiflow. From this we can compute the average number of customers at node $l + 1$ as follows: $\overline{n_{l+1}} = b_{l+1} - \overline{s_l} - \overline{d_{l+1}}$. In this manner from the performance measures of the SPN of Figure 5 we have derived the measures for the FC-QN represented by the GSPN of Figure 3.

Remarks. We must point out that the GSPN of Figure 4 does not have product form solution. However, we are claiming that the SPN of Figure 5 has product form equilibrium distribution and that the performance measures (average number of tokens in the places, average waiting times, throughput of the transitions) of this SPN are the same as those of the GSPN of Figure 4.

In other words, with the help of the implicit places we can compute the performance measures of a non-product form model (the GSPN of Figure 4) using a product form one (the SPN of Figure 5).

In principle we could derive the analytical form of the steady state probabilities for the GSPN of Figure 4 without using any product form analysis and without the help of the SPN of Figure 5. Since the GSPN of Figure 4 is equivalent to the $M/H_{M-1}/1/2$ queueing system, we can use the closed form for the equilibrium distribution of this system for deriving the steady state probabilities for the GSPN. Nevertheless we present the product form analysis because product form results can also be used to investigate models that do not have this nice property.

In the literature there are several proposals of this type of studies. One possible technique would be the derivation of Mean Value Analysis equations [16] for the product form case and then use these equations as a basis for developing approximate techniques similar to those proposed in [17]. Other examples of use of the product form as a basis for approximate techniques are described in [5]. In [19] the product form is the basis for developing bounding techniques.

Another issue that we have to point out is that unfortunately the product form result is valid only under very special circumstances: the total number of customers circulating within the queueing network must be equal to the sum of all buffer capacities minus 2, and this result can not be easily generalised. However, the availability of the product form can be used for the exploitation of approximate and bounding techniques for non-product form models.

As can be seen in [3, 14], the product form solution exists only for a limited class of queueing network with finite capacity, and the results of this paper represent an extension of this class.

4.2 Cyclic Networks with More Than One BBS-SNO Node

In principle, the previous method can be generalised to cases of FC-QNs with more than one BBS-SNO node. We illustrate this idea by means of the following example.

Example 1. Figure 6(a) shows a GSPN modeling a cyclic FC-QN with 4 BBS-SNO and one BBS-SO node.

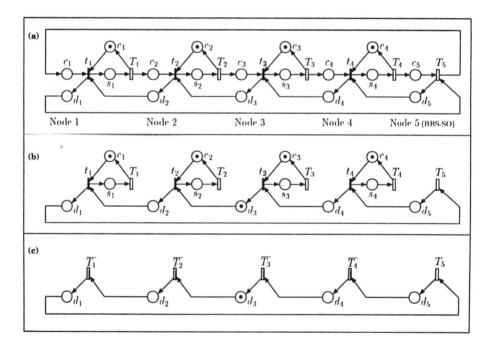

Fig. 6. The GSPN modeling a cyclic FC-QN with 4 BBS-SNO and one BBS-SO node (a), the same GSPN without the implicit places (b), the SPN with the same performance indices of the GSPN without the implicit places (c).

Using Theorem 2 we can prove that places c_1, c_2, c_3, c_4, and c_5 are structurally implicit. Theorem 3 allows us to compute the the initial marking such that these places become implicit. Let us assume that the initial marking is such that in the GSPN obtained by removing the implicit places there is only one token circulating within places d_i $(i = 1, \ldots, 5)$. In Figure 6(b) it is depicted a such GSPN. We can apply the same technique used in the case of a cyclic network with only one BBS-SNO node (arrival instant probabilities). We can build a product form solution model that has the same performance measures of the GSPN of Figure 6(b). Figure 6(c) shows this measure equivalent model. This SPN has product form solution:

$$\pi(\boldsymbol{m}) = \frac{1}{G} \left(\frac{1}{\mu_5} \right)^{m_1} \left(\frac{1}{\overline{\mu_1}} \right)^{m_2} \left(\frac{1}{\overline{\mu_2}} \right)^{m_3} \left(\frac{1}{\overline{\mu_3}} \right)^{m_4} \left(\frac{1}{\overline{\mu_4}} \right)^{m_5} \quad \forall \, \boldsymbol{m} \in RS,$$

where G is a normalisation constant, m_i (for $i = 1, \ldots, 5$) is the marking of place d_i, and $\overline{\mu_i}$ is the rate of transition $\overline{T_i}$ (for $i = 1, \ldots, 4$).

However, we must point out that, in this case, we do not have an auxiliary model (the $M/H_{M-1}/1/2$ queueing system) that allows to compute in a closed form the rates of the transitions $\overline{T_i}$ (the shadow transitions). The example only shows that there is a class of FC-QNs for which there exist equivalent models with product form solution and this equivalence can be found by using the technique based on the structural implicit places.

4.3 Another New Case of Product Form Solution

Let us consider a closed cyclic queueing network with $M - 1$ BBS-SO nodes, and one BAS node. Figure 7(a) shows the GSPN representation of a such FC-QN. Here, with respect to the representation of a BAS node presented in Figure 1(c), we have removed the inhibitor arc by using the complementary place e_l. We can

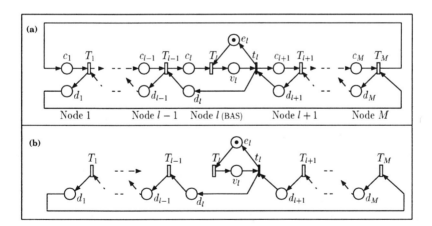

Fig. 7. The GSPN modeling a cyclic FC-QN with one BAS node and $M - 1$ BBS-SO nodes (a), the same GSPN witout the implicit places (b).

see that the GSPN representation of a such FC-QN is similar to that one of the case with only one BBS-SNO node. We can repeat the same reasoning used for that cyclic FC-QN. We can summarise the result in the following lemmas.

Lemma 3. *Given a cyclic queueing network with $M-1$ BBS-SO nodes and one BAS node in the GSPN representation of this FC-QN the places corresponding to the queues of the network are implicit if*

$$N - 1 \geq \sum_{i=1}^{M} b_i - \min_{j=1}^{M} b_j. \tag{13}$$

Figure 7(b) shows the GSPN without the implicit places.

Lemma 4. *Given a cyclic queueing network with $M-1$ BBS-SO nodes and one BAS node. If the number of customers N circulating within the network is such that*

$$N = \sum_{i=1}^{M} b_i - 1, \tag{14}$$

then we can build a product form solution model having the same performance measures of the cyclic queueing network. The product form model has M stations. For any $i = 1, \ldots, M$, with $i \neq l$, the service rate of station i is the same of the corresponding station of the FC-QN. The service rate of station l is $\overline{\mu_l}$ and it is obtained using Equation (11).

Please note the difference between the case of FC-QN with one BBS-SNO node and several BBS-SO nodes and the one with one BAS node and several BBS-SO nodes. In both cases there exist the measure equivalent PF models only when the sum of tokens in places d_i $(i = 1, \ldots, M)$ is equal to 1. For the case of one BAS node and several BBS-SO nodes this is obtained with $N = \sum_{i=1}^{M} b_i - 1$. The measure equivalent model is the same for both cases (SPN of Figure 5).

5 Conclusions

In this paper we have proposed an approach that allows to discover new quantitative results for queueing networks with blocking using structural Petri net properties. The studies are based on the representation of FC-QNs by means of GSPNs. We have used the notion of *implicit places* for studying product form equilibrium distributions of FC-QNs. In particular using this notion we have characterised a class of FC-QNs such that for each element of this class there exists a model with the same performance measures and with product form equilibrium distributions.

Future plans include the application of the described technique for deriving other new product form results. Another direction of future research could be the derivation of other Petri net driven techniques that allows to transform a GSPN representation of a non-product form FC-QN into a product form one.

Acknowledgements

This work has been supported in part by the 60% projects, and in part by the Esprit Human Capital and Mobility project MATCH.

References

1. M. Ajmone Marsan, G. Balbo, G. Conte, S. Donatelli, and G. Franceschinis. *Modelling with Generalized Stochastic Petri Nets*. John Wiley & Sons, 1995.
2. S. Balsamo and V. De Nitto-Personé. Closed queueing networks with finite capacities: Blocking types, product-form solution and performance indices. *Performance Evaluation*, 12:85–102, 1991.
3. S. Balsamo and V. De Nitto-Personé. A survey of product-form queueing networks with blocking and their equivalences. *Annals of Operation Research*, 48:31–61, 1994.
4. F. Baskett, K. M. Chandy, R. R. Muntz, and F. Palacios. Open, closed and mixed networks of queues with different classes of customers. *Journal of the ACM*, 22(2):248–260, April 1975.
5. B. Baynat and Y. Dallery. A ufified view of product-form approximation techniques for general closed queueing networks. *Performance Evaluation*, 18:205–224, 1993.
6. J. P. Buzen. Computational algorithms for closed queueing networks with exponential servers. *Communications of the ACM*, 16(9):527–531, September 1973.
7. J. M. Colom and M. Silva. Improving the linearly based characterization of P/T nets. In *Proc. 10th Intern. Conference on Application and Theory of Petri Nets*, pages 52–73, Bonn, Germany, June 1989.
8. W. J. Gordon and G. F. Newell. Cyclic queueing systems with restricted queues. *Operations Research*, 15:266–278, 1967.
9. M. Gribaudo and M. Sereno. GSPN semantics for queueing networks with blocking. In *Proc. 7th Intern. Workshop on Petri Nets and Performance Models*, Saint Malo, France, June 1997. IEEE-CS Press.
10. J. R. Jackson. Jobshop-like queueing systems. *Management Science*, 10(1):131–142, October 1963.
11. L. Kleinrock. *Queueing Systems Volume I: Theory*. Wiley, New York, NY, 1975.
12. S. Kundu and I. F. Akyldiz. Deadlock free buffer allocation in closed queueing networks. *Queueing Systems*, 4:47–56, 1989.
13. T. Murata. Petri nets: properties, analysis, and applications. *Proceedings of the IEEE*, 77(4):541–580, April 1989.
14. R. O. Onvural. Survey of closed queueing networks with blocking. *ACM Computing Surveys*, 22:83–121, 1990.
15. H. G. Perros. *Queueing Networks with Blocking*. Oxford, 1994.
16. M. Reiser and S. S. Lavenberg. Mean value analysis of closed multichain queueing networks. *Journal of the ACM*, 27(2):313–322, April 1980.
17. P. J. Schweitzer. A survey of mean value analysis, its generalizations, and applications, for networks of queues. Technical report, University of Rochester, Rochester, USA, Dec 1990.
18. M. Silva. *Las Redes de Petri en la Automatica y la Informatica*. Ed. AC, Madrid, Spain, 1985. In Spanish.
19. N. van Dijk. A simple bounding methodology for non-product-form queueing networks with blocking. In *Proc. First International Workshop on Queueing Networks with Finite Capacity*, Raleigh, North Carolina, USA, May 1988.

Deadlock Detection in the Face of Transaction and Data Dependencies

E. Bertino[1], G. Chiola[2], and L.V. Mancini[3]

[1] Dipartimento di Scienze dell'Informazione Università di Milano
Via Comelico 39, 20135 Milano, Italy
[2] Dipartimento di Informatica e Scienze dell'Informazione, Università di Genova
Via Dodecaneso 35, 16146 Genova, Italy
[3] Dipartimento di Scienze dell'Informazione, Università di Roma "La Sapienza"
Via Salaria 113, 00198 Roma, Italy [†]

Abstract. Deadlock detection, which is fairly well-understood for the traditional transaction model used for concurrency control to databases, needs to be revisited when dealing with advanced transaction models. This is because a transaction in these models is organized as a collection of tasks; specific decisions (such as commit or abort) about a task may be based on the outcome or status of other tasks in the same transaction. Although this gives flexibility to the application programmer, a set of concurrent transactions may contain two types of dependencies: data and transaction dependencies. Commit and abort dependencies specifying constraints on transaction termination order are well-known examples of transaction dependencies. Data dependencies arise when transactions concurrently access common data items under conflicting modes. In this paper, we show that in the face of these dependencies, deadlocks may arise that the conventional deadlock detection algorithms are not able to detect. We show that transaction waiting states are characterized by AND-OR graphs and propose an algorithm for detecting deadlocks in these graphs. This algorithm has a computational complexity linear in the number of nodes and edges of the AND-OR graphs. We prove the correctness of our algorithm by characterizing deadlocks in a subclass of Petri nets equivalent to AND-OR graphs.

1 Introduction

Transaction models are usually at the base of the design of a concurrency control mechanism for the access to a shared database. To overcome the limitations of the traditional transaction models, advanced transaction models have been developed with the goal of enhancing flexibility of the application programmers [1–3, 12]. The basic idea of these models is to provide transaction primitives and run-time environments so that users can define their own transaction models.

An advanced transaction is organized in various *tasks*, interrelated by *transaction dependencies*. The transaction dependency mechanism provides a form of

---

[†] Partially supported by the Italian M.U.R.S.T.

computation by which specific decisions (such as commit or abort) about a task in an advanced transaction may be taken during the transaction execution on the basis of the outcome or the status of other tasks in the same transaction. In addition to the transaction dependencies, concurrent execution of the various tasks is constrained by *data dependencies*. Data dependencies arise from conflicting accesses in read/write mode to the same data items when different tasks within the same advanced transaction need to exchange information.

Since data dependency is the traditional form of dependency among transactions, transaction processing issues related to it have been widely investigated by the research community. However, advanced transactions have several other types of dependencies, and the issues arising from the combination of them have yet to be deeply investigated. We refer the reader to [11] for an overview of advanced transaction models and related research issues.

In this paper, we show that the deadlock problem, which is fairly well-understood for conventional transaction models [6], needs to be revisited in the face of both data and transaction dependencies. When using a traditional transaction model, application programmers do not need to worry about concurrent execution of steps within the same transaction. This is no longer true for advanced transaction models because not only tasks in an advanced transaction may compete for the same data, but they may be interrelated by transaction dependencies also. Therefore, it is necessary that the programmer understand the effects of concurrent executions of tasks within a single advanced transaction.

To illustrate, consider the following simple example. Suppose that transactions T_i and T_j are tasks within the same advanced transaction. Suppose that a dependency is specified stating that if both T_i and T_j commit, the commit of T_i must precede the commit of T_j. Note that this dependency only constrains the commit order of the two transactions; therefore, T_i and T_j can execute in parallel. Suppose moreover that T_j acquires a write lock on a data item x and that later on T_i issues a read lock request for x. Obviously, T_j cannot release the lock until it commits; however, T_j must wait for T_i to commit. T_i, on the other hand, is waiting for T_j to release the lock on x.

Observe that conventional deadlock detection algorithms would not detect such deadlocks because they only consider transaction waiting states arising from data dependencies among transactions. For our example, the wait-for-graph will only show transaction T_i waiting for the lock on x to be released by T_j. One might argue that the data dependency in our example can be eliminated if transactions that belong to the same advanced transaction are allowed to share locks. The difficulty with this solution is that if we build a wait-for-graph where each node corresponds to an advanced transaction, then the graph would signal deadlocks even in situations in which the deadlocks do not really exist. An example of this is an advanced transaction that may complete even if one of its component transactions is waiting for locks.

A related deadlock problem occurs in the case of *nested transactions* [8]. One of the locking rules for nested transactions states that when a subtransaction waits for a lock, all its ancestors also wait for the lock (i.e., they cannot commit until the lock is granted). This rule introduces *indirect wait* conditions that must be taken into account to correctly detect deadlock situations. If two or more subtransactions belonging to a nested transaction need to access a common data item under conflicting modes, this nested transaction can deadlock with itself. We refer the reader to [8] for additional details. In [8] it is shown that the nested transaction relationship can be represented by conventional wait-for-graph and that deadlock situation can be detected by checking the wait-for relation (including indirect waits) for cycles when new wait-for edges are added.

The deadlock problem we treat here can be seen as a generalization of the problem addressed for nested transactions [8]. We consider a general form of transaction dependencies in which a transaction's commit or abort may depend on a set of other transactions in conjunctive modes, disjunctive modes, or any combination of these. The following is an example of a general commit dependency: $T \rightarrow T_i$ AND $(T_j$ OR $T_k)$. Intuitively, this dependency specifies that T can commit only after T_i and one among T_j and T_k terminate.[1],

Because of this general form of transaction dependencies, transactions and data dependencies among advanced transactions must be modeled as AND-OR graphs. AND-OR graphs have been used to model communication deadlocks and resource deadlocks [6], which arise when a process is allowed to simultaneously require multiple resources. The difference between a communication deadlock and a resource deadlock is that in the former the waiting process is unblocked when it is given *one* of the required resources, whereas in the latter the waiting process is unblocked only when it is given *all* the required resources.

Unfortunately, a cycle in the transaction AND-OR graph does not necessarily represent a deadlock. The classical graph theory does not provide a simple construct to describe a deadlock situation in an AND-OR graph. A known algorithm for deadlock detection in AND-OR graphs is presented in [5,6] and is an application of the technique of *diffusing computations*. The complexity of such algorithm is $O(N^2(N-1))$ where N is the number of nodes in the AND-OR graph. However, N can grow exponentially with the number of transactions since the graph used by the algorithm is a representation of the transactions AND-OR requests in a Disjunctive Normal Form. Therefore, there is a need for a more efficient algorithm.

The major contributions of our work are summarized as follows:

1. combine the conventional wait-for-graph and the interactions between data dependencies and transaction dependencies into a common formalism based on Petri Nets;
2. provide an efficient deadlock detection algorithm for AND-OR graphs;
3. avoid the exponential growth of the graph by directly representing the original AND-OR requests of the transactions;
4. prove the correctness of the deadlock detection algorithm by characterizing the deadlock situation in a subclass of Petri nets "equivalent" to AND-OR graphs from the deadlock point of view.

---

[1] Formal definitions of transaction dependencies are presented in the following section.

The remainder of this paper is organized as follows. We first introduce the preliminary definitions concerning advanced transactions and illustrate the deadlock problem. Then, we present our deadlock detection algorithm for AND-OR graphs together with a formal proof of its correctness based on Petri net properties [9]. The algorithm is also proven to be optimal in terms of complexity.

2   The Advanced Model

The following definitions establish a simple advanced transaction model that is used as the framework for discussing the deadlocks. It is based on commit and abort dependencies; we permit a transaction to depend on a set of transactions for commit or abort.

Definition 1. Pairwise dependency. Let T_i, T_j be transactions.

1. There is a *pairwise commit dependency* between T_i and T_j if T_i cannot commit until T_j commits. Note that this does not imply that if T_j aborts, then T_i should abort as well. This commit dependency is denoted by $T_i \rightarrow T_j$.
2. There is a *pairwise abort dependency* between T_i and T_j if T_i should abort whenever T_j aborts. Note that this does not imply that T_i should commit if T_j commits, nor that T_j should abort if T_i aborts. The above abort dependency is denoted by $T_i \rightsquigarrow T_j$.   □

Note that the enforcement of these dependencies requires that the commit of the transaction that appears on the left-hand side of the dependency (i.e., T_i in the above definition) wait for the termination of the transaction that appears on the right-hand side of the dependency (i.e., T_j in the above definition). Indeed, the outcome of T_j (abort vs. commit) may determine the outcome of T_i. For example, the pairwise abort dependency $T_i \rightsquigarrow T_j$ specifies that the abort of T_j is a sufficient condition for the abort of T_i. Of course, the abort of T_j is not a necessary condition for the abort of T_i. T_i may abort for other reasons, including abort dependencies with respect to other transactions. Therefore T_i must still wait for the outcome of T_j upon completing its normal execution.[2]

As indicated, we consider a more general form of dependencies and assume that dependencies can exist not only between two transactions but also between a transaction and a set of transactions. In addition, transaction dependencies can be combined using the AND/OR logical operators. Therefore, we assume that an expression obtained as a Boolean combination of transactions may appear on the right-hand side of a dependency. We also assume that logical expressions are given in some minimal form.

---

[2] In theory abort dependencies can be enforced also accepting the commit of T_i and enforcing the commit of T_j later. In practice it is not always possible to guarantee the commit of T_j, when failures are due to incorrectly programmed transactions, data entry errors or operator errors.

Definition 2. General dependency. Let $\mathcal{T}$ be a set of transactions and let T be a transaction in $\mathcal{T}$. Moreover, let $\mathcal{TD}$ be a subset of $\mathcal{T}$ not including T. A *Generalized Dependency* between T and transaction set $\mathcal{TD}$ is defined as a commit or abort dependency between T and elements of $\mathcal{TD}$ obeying the following syntax:

R1   <gendep>   ::= <cdep> <adep>
R2.1 <cdep>   ::= empty
R2.2 <cdep>   ::= $T \rightarrow$ <term>
R3.1 <adep>   ::= empty
R3.2 <adep>   ::= $T \rightsquigarrow$ <term>
R4.1 <term>   ::= $T' : T' \in \mathcal{TD}$
R4.2 <term>   ::= <andterm>
R4.3 <term>   ::= (<orterm>)
R5   <andterm> ::= $T' : T' \in \mathcal{TD}$ AND <term>
R6.1 <orterm> ::= $T' : T' \in \mathcal{TD}$ OR <orterm>
R6.2 <orterm> ::= $T' : T' \in \mathcal{TD}$ OR <term> □

As usual, we assume that the AND composition specified by rule R5 takes precedence over the OR composition specified by rule R6.2. The reverse precedence can be enforced by the use of parenthesized OR expression, as specified by rule R4.3.[3] The semantics of the above notation is the obvious one, defined in terms of the basic predicates:

$$Terminate(T) = \text{ true if } T \text{ commits or aborts, false otherwise;}$$
$$Abort(T) = \text{ true if } T \text{ aborts, false otherwise.}$$

A generalized commit dependency specifies that transaction T cannot commit until the right-hand side Boolean expression evaluates to true when each transaction T' is substituted by its corresponding $Terminate(T')$ predicate. Analogously, a generalized abort dependency forces the commit of transaction T to wait that the Boolean expression, specified by the right-hand side of the dependency, evaluates to true when each transaction T' is substituted by its corresponding $Terminate(T')$ predicate. At that point, transaction T is forced to abort if the Boolean expression specified by the right-hand side of the dependency evaluates to true when each transaction T' is substituted by its corresponding $Abort(T')$ predicate. Pairwise dependencies are thus obtained as a special case of our general notion of dependencies.

Definition 3. Advanced transaction. A *advanced transaction* is a triplet $< \mathcal{T}, R, \mathcal{D} >$ where:

- $\mathcal{T}$ is a set of transactions with a partial order R specifying the execution order. Transactions in $\mathcal{T}$ are called *component transactions*.

---

[3] The use of parenthesized expressions for OR and not for AND allows the treatment of data dependencies by manipulating only edges and not nodes of the AND-OR graph, as defined in Section 3.2.

- $\mathcal{D}$ is a set of generalized dependencies for transactions in $\mathcal{T}$ according to Definition 2. □

Figure 1 presents an example of an advanced transaction that specifies several commit and abort dependencies among its component transactions. It uses the language defined for the *multiform transaction model* given in [7]. In this language, an advanced transaction is specified as a sequence of coordination blocks; a *coordination block*, in turn, consists of a set of transactions together with the specification of their partial execution order and a *dependency clause*. The partial execution order is specified by stating which transactions can be executed in parallel and which ones need to be executed in sequence.

The example in Figure 1 illustrates an advanced transaction consisting of a single coordination block. According to this syntax, a *cobegin–coend* block denotes the parallel execution of all the transactions it contains. When a cobegin–coend block follows another cobegin–coend block, the transactions in the former are executed only after the transactions in the latter have completed their execution. Note that a transaction completes when it has executed all its code. A completed transaction terminates by moving either to the committed state or to the aborted state. The decision on abort or commit could have to wait for other transactions that might just start. In this respect a *completed* transaction is not the same as a *terminated* transaction.

The dependency clause specifies a set of dependencies among the transactions in the coordination block. As an example consider the second dependency in the dependency clause in Figure 1. It specifies that T_2 can commit only after one of the following is true: (i) transaction T_5 terminates, or (ii) transaction T_6 terminates, or (iii) both transactions T_3 and T_4 terminate.

```
void example_advanced ()
{     coordinate;
      cobegin
          begin_trans (T₁) ... end_trans (T₁);
          begin_trans (T₂) ⋯ end_trans (T₂);
          ⋯
          begin_trans (Tₙ) ⋯ end_trans (Tₙ);
      coend;
      using dependency {
              T₁ → T₂
              T₂ → (T₅ OR T₆ OR T₃ AND T₄)
              Tₙ⤳ T₅ AND (T₃ OR T₄)
              } }
```

Fig. 1. Example of commit and abort dependencies

3 Deadlock Detection Issues

We assume that two-phase locking is used as concurrency control when executing component transactions of an advanced transaction. As we discussed, two-phase locking can potentially cause deadlocks among not only concurrent advanced transactions, but component transactions of an advanced transaction also. However, deadlock detection within an advanced transaction poses additional problems. A component transaction T_i can wait for another component T_j within the same advanced transaction for two different reasons:

- there is a *data dependency* between T_i and T_j on a shared data item;
- there is a *transaction dependency* between T_i and T_j which occurs if the dependencies specified in the advanced transaction establish a particular order of commit or abort of T_i and T_j.

When both these dependencies occur within a set of concurrent transactions the conventional deadlock detection algorithms fail because they cannot cope with the interaction between data dependencies and transaction dependencies. We address the problem of deadlock detection when general dependencies are specified among transaction components and show how the conventional wait-for-graph can be extended to detect a deadlock. Before doing so, we illustrate the additional deadlock problem with some examples.

3.1 Illustrative examples

In this section, we give examples of two advanced transactions. The first one presents a deadlock. The second advanced transaction modifies the transaction dependency of the first example and, therefore, does not deadlock. The reason for giving these examples is to emphasize the point that it is more difficult to detect deadlocks when transaction dependencies are involved in addition to the ordinary data dependencies.

Consider an advanced transaction composed of three component transactions T_1, T_2 and T_3. Assume that the dependency $T_1 \rightarrow T_2$ AND T_3 holds; thus, T_1 cannot commit before T_2 and T_3 do. Suppose that T_1 writes a data item x whereas T_2 reads x. The following deadlock may arise:

1. T_1 acquires a write lock on x before T_2 and completes its execution; however T_1 is not committed, hence it does not release its locks.
2. T_2 waits for T_1 to release the write lock on x, before being able to proceed with its execution.
3. Even if T_3 commits, T_1 cannot commit and release its write lock on x as T_2 has not yet committed or aborted.

The example is reported in Figure 2. In particular, the coordination block shown specifies that T_1 must be executed first, followed by a parallel execution of T_2 and T_3.This transaction is always deadlocked. However, if the transaction dependency of this advanced transaction is modified as shown in Figure 3, the

```
void advanced_deadlock() {
        coordinate
            begin_trans (T₁)
                w[x];
            end_trans (T₁);
            cobegin
                begin_trans (T₂)
                r[x];
                end_trans (T₂);
                ...
            coend
        using dependency {
                T₁ → T₂ AND T₃
                }
}
```

Fig. 2. A deadlock-prone advanced transaction

deadlock no longer arises. Transaction T_1 can terminate after either T_2 or T_3 have committed.

Once a deadlock is detected the usual strategy to break it is to abort any one of the transactions involved. With transaction dependencies, a good strategy is to abort and restart the transaction which was supposed to commit last as this will allow the advanced transaction to terminate with success. The problem of how to select transactions as victims is not discussed here.

3.2 Extended wait-for-graph

To detect possible deadlocks within an advanced transaction, we extend the notion of a wait-for-graph to include transaction dependencies. Given an advanced transaction, the initial AND-OR graph is generated by a static analysis of the transaction dependencies according to the following definition:

Definition 4. AND-OR graph. Let $< \mathcal{T}, R, \mathcal{D} >$ be an advanced transaction. Its corresponding AND-OR graph is defined as follows:

- Each component transaction T_i corresponds to a node in the AND-OR graph.
- Each parenthesized OR term (as specified by rule R4.3 in our syntactic definition) in a generalized dependency expression is represented by an additional node of the AND-OR graph, called a *pseudo-node*.
- An abort dependency $T_i \rightsquigarrow T_j$ is represented as a commit dependency $T_i \rightarrow T_j$ in the wait-for-graph since both types of dependencies involve the same waiting condition for the termination of transaction T_i.
- Edges in the wait-for-graph are defined by the following algorithm that exploits the parse-tree of an expression according to the syntax in definition 2:
  R2.2, R3.2 : define parent_node= T, edge_type=AND_EDGE.

```
void no_deadlock() {
      coordinate
          begin_trans (T₁)
              w[x];
          end_trans (T₁);
          cobegin
              begin_trans (T₂)
                  r[x];
              end_trans (T₂);
                  . . .
          coend
      using dependency {
              T₁ → (T₂ OR T₃)
              }
}
```

Fig. 3. A deadlock-free advanced transaction

R4.1, R5, R6.1, R6.2 : add an edge of edge_type from parent_node to T'.
R4.2 : define edge_type=AND_EDGE.
R4.3 : new pseudo_node (add node corresponding to parenthesized term);
define parent_node=pseudo_node, edge_type=OR_EDGE.   □

The AND-OR graphs for the advanced transactions in Figures 2 and 3 are straightforward. For the example in Figure 2, there is a set of AND edges from T_1 to T_2 and T_3, while for the example in Figure 3, there is a set of OR edges from T_1 to T_2 and T_3. Figure 4 depicts the AND-OR graph for the advanced transaction presented in Figure 1. In the picture, a line connecting the edges denotes a set of AND edges, while a set of edges without a connecting line represents an OR set. Nodes T_{or1} and T_{or2} in Figure 4 are pseudo_nodes.

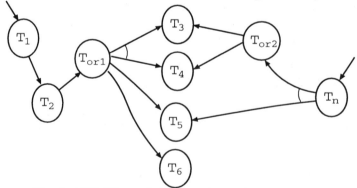

Fig. 4. AND-OR graph for the advanced transaction in Figure 1

Since data dependencies are run-time notions deduced from the lock/unlock requests, the initial AND-OR graph generated by a static analysis of the transaction dependencies is maintained by the Lock Manager. In particular, during the execution of an advanced transaction $< \mathcal{T}, R, \mathcal{D} >$, the initial AND-OR graph is modified by:

(i) adding/removing edges, due to lock/unlock requests and thus representing data dependencies;

(ii) removing edges representing transaction dependencies when the relevant transactions terminate.

Data dependency edges can be added/removed safely to/from the initial AND-OR graph since the syntax in Definition 2 and the translation algorithm in Definition 4 guarantee that only AND edges may depart from transaction nodes (OR terms imply the addition of pseudo-nodes). A high-level specification of the actions required for the maintenance of an AND-OR graph is presented in Figure 5.

---

1. An AND type data dependency edge from transaction T_i to transaction T_j is included in the AND-OR graph, if T_i is waiting for T_j to release a lock. When the lock is granted to T_i, this data dependency edge is removed from the graph.
2. When transaction T_j terminates, the node T_j is removed from the AND-OR graph together with the following edges:
    (a) if there is an OR edge from some T_i to T_j, then *all outgoing edges* of T_i are removed;
    (b) if there is an AND edge from T_i to T_j, then *only the edge* between T_i and T_j is removed.
3. When pseudo nodes corresponding to parenthesized terms become terminal due to previous node/edge eliminations, the AND-OR graph is recursively modified by removing the terminal pseudo nodes and their relevant edges.

Fig. 5. Maintenance of the AND-OR graph of an advanced transaction

Notice that a cycle in the transaction AND-OR graph does not necessarily represent a deadlock. Deadlocks in the AND-OR graph can be detected by the repeated application of the deadlock detection algorithm for an OR graph (i.e., a graph with only OR edges and no AND edges), exploiting the fact that the deadlock is a stable property.

4 Petri Net Characterization of Deadlock in AND-OR Graphs

We propose a more efficient algorithm to detect deadlocks in an AND-OR graph which is linear in the number of nodes and edges and which does not require a graph expansion. Our algorithm has been derived from Petri net techniques in a sequence of steps. First, the AND-OR graph is mapped into a Petri net model. Enabling a transition in the Petri net model of the AND-OR graph corresponds to the possibility of terminating a transaction. Second, the resulting Petri net model is shown to belong to a subclass of Free-choice nets for which liveness can be characterized in terms of the non-existence of a structure of type "syphon." [4] Third, a transition elimination algorithm is proposed to detect the existence of such syphon structures on the Petri net. Fourth, the transition elimination algorithm is re-stated in terms of the original AND-OR graph. We shall use an illustrative example and semi-formal reasoning rather than developing a complete formalism to support the proof for the sake of readability.

4.1 Mapping AND-OR graphs to Free-choice Petri nets

Consider the AND-OR graph depicted in Figure 6. This graph is translated into

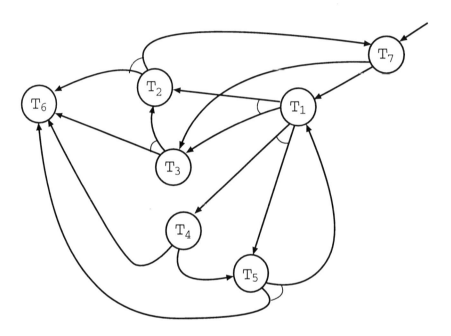

Fig. 6. An example of AND-OR graph.

the Petri net model depicted in Figure 7. The translation is performed according to the following schema: (1) define one Petri net transition associated with each node in the AND-OR graph; (2) define one place for each set of OR edges in the graph; (3) define one additional transition for each set of AND edges connected in OR with a node; (4) define one place for each edge of the AND-OR graph

---

[4] In the Petri net literature what we call "syphon structures" are usually called "deadlocks." In this paper we avoid the use of the "deadlock" term referring to Petri net structures in order to avoid confusion with the deadlock property of transactions that cannot terminate.

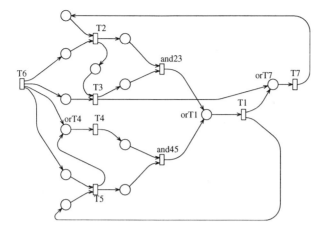

Fig. 7. Translation in structurally persistent, ordinary Petri net.

which is not in OR relation with other edges; (5) for each transition representing a node, connect an output arc to the place representing the precedence relation to any other node or AND term or OR term.

The rationale of this mapping can be understood by considering Definition 2 as specifying dependencies among $Terminate(T_i)$ predicates. Firing a transition "Ti" in the Petri net models the fact that the corresponding predicate evaluates to true. For example, transition "T6" in Figure 7 has no input arcs (since the termination of node T_6 does not depend on the termination of any other node) and four output arcs that enforce the precedence of node T_6 with respect to nodes T_2, T_3, T_4, and T_5. Node T_4 has an OR set of precedence edges, so that the input place "orT4" of transition "T4" has more than one input arc (one for each transition modeling a node that must precede T_4, namely the two transitions "T5" and "T6"). Transition "T2" (that models the completion of node T_2) has two input places, modeling the AND precedence constraint from nodes T_6 and T_7. Transitions "and23" and "and45" together with place "orT1" model the more complex precondition for the termination of node T_1, that results in a OR combination of two AND terms.

4.2 Structural deadlock detection for Petri nets

We call the class of Petri net models that are generated by the translation of AND-OR graphs outlined in the previous section *AND-OR Nets* (AO-Nets). By construction, AO-Nets are *ordinary* (i.e., with arcs valuated 1) and *structurally persistent* (since each place has exactly one output arc) and, hence, *free-choice* [9] (notice that they are not Marked Graphs because a place may be connected to more than one input arc).

Free-choice Petri nets (and, therefore, AO-Nets) have the nice property that their behavior in terms of presence/absence of deadlocks is completely characterized by their structure and their initial marking, as stated in the following theorem:

Theorem 1 (Commoner's Property). *A (unbounded) free-choice net is deadlock free if each "syphon" structure contains a "trap" structure that is marked in the initial marking M_0.* □

Syphons are defined as follows (we do not use traps) [9]:

Definition 5. syphon S:

$$S \subseteq P : \quad \forall t : \quad t^\bullet \cap S \neq \emptyset, \quad {}^\bullet t \cap S \neq \emptyset$$

Intuitively, the main characteristics of a syphon structure is that no transition exists that has output places belonging to the syphon without having input places belonging to the syphon itself. Hence, if all places in the syphon structure happen to have an empty marking, then there is no way mark them.

Lemma 1 (Empty syphons in AO-Nets). *For AO-Nets, Commoner's condition for absence of deadlock is satisfied if and only if no syphon structure exists. Moreover, the transitions with at least one input place contained in a syphon can never be enabled.* □

The Lemma is trivial to prove by considering that the initial marking is empty for all places, so that no trap structure, even if it exists, may be marked. Hence, by our translation semantics, a transaction may terminate iff the corresponding transition in the AO-Net has no input place contained in a syphon structure.

Property 1. If all transitions have at least one input arc, then the set of all places P is a syphon structure. □

Property 2. The definition of syphons is closed under the union operation so that the union of two or more syphons is a syphon itself. □

Definition 6. Maximal syphon. The union of all syphon structures of a Petri Net is a syphon called *maximal*. □

Since we are interested in finding whether at least one syphon structure exists (to prove the presence of a deadlock), we may look for the maximal syphon in an AO-Net: if this is empty, then no syphons exist in the net.

Theorem 2 (Deadlock characterization). *In an AO-Net, all transitions can fire at least once iff the maximal syphon is the empty set.* □

Proof Sketch: If the maximal syphon of the net is not empty then at least one place is contained in it. Since each place has exactly one output transition, the output transitions of all places belonging to the maximal syphon can never fire. On the other hand, if the maximal syphon is the empty set, the net is live by the Commoner's property, so that all transitions may fire (infinitely many times). Q.E.D.

Corollary 1. *A deadlock exists in the AND-OR graph iff a dead transition exists in the corresponding AND-OR Net that can never fire.* □

Proof sketch: Due to the particular construction rules for the Petri net model, if the input place of a transition representing an AND term is part of a syphon structure, one of the input places of the transition representing the node that is connected to that place must also belong to the same syphon, so that the transition representing the node is also dead. Q.E.D.

The last corollary is useful since dead transitions represent either individual AND terms or nodes, so that one could argue that only AND transitions, but no node transitions, are deadlocked.

4.3 An efficient algorithm for detecting the maximal syphon

An algorithm for the construction of the maximal syphon is outlined as follows:

1. Start with the set $S = P$ (all places of the net).
2. If no transition exist without input arcs, then S is a syphon (by Definition 5).
3. Otherwise, if some transitions exist without input arcs, delete these transitions from the net, together with all their output places.
4. When a place is deleted, all arcs connected to it are also deleted.

When steps 3 and 4 above are executed, a smaller Petri net $\mathcal{N}'$ is obtained to which the same algorithm is recursively applied, unless all places and transitions are eliminated, in which case no syphon structure existed in the original net $\mathcal{N}$.

In the example in Figure 7, transition "T6" qualifies for elimination, together with its four output places in the first step. In the second step, we examine the reduced net $\mathcal{N}'$ in which transition "T4" has no input (due to the elimination of place "orT4" from the original net). We can then delete "T4" together with its only output place (which is also input for transition "and45"). After this second step, no more transitions can be found without input arcs, so that all remaining places form the maximal syphon of the net. Because those places are empty in the initial marking, we have thus detected a deadlock in which no other transaction can terminate after the termination of T_6 and T_4.

Consider, as a further example, a small variation of the AND-OR graph depicted in Figure 6, in which the AND type edge from node T_5 to node T_1 is not present. By applying our translation procedure to the modified graph, we obtain the Petri net model depicted in Figure 8. This net can be shown to be deadlock-free, using our net reduction algorithm, as follows:

1. Initially, transition "T6" is the only one without input. Its elimination together with its four output places make "T4" and "T5" without input.
2. Deleting transitions "T4" and "T5" together with their output places makes "and45" without input.
3. The elimination of "and45" together with its output place "orT1" makes transition "T1" without input.
4. The elimination of "T1" together with its output place "orT7" makes "T7" without input.
5. The elimination of "T7" together with its output place makes "T2" without input.

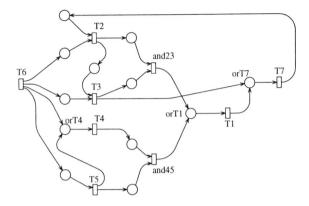

Fig. 8. Translation of the modified example

6. The elimination of "T2" together with its two output places makes "T3" without input.
7. The elimination of "T3" together with its output place (place "orT7" was already deleted in a previous step) makes "and23" without input.
8. The elimination of "and23" corresponds to the complete reduction of the net (no places or transitions are left), so that we can conclude that no syphon structure existed in the original model.

Clearly, the complete elimination of a net corresponds to the worst case in terms of number of steps performed by the algorithm before stopping. As we saw in our example, the complete elimination involves a computational complexity linear in the number of nodes and arcs of the Petri net model. This proves that our deadlock detection algorithm has linear complexity in the size of the problem. In particular, if we consider an AND-OR graph with n nodes and m dependency edges, the complexity of our algorithm is bounded by $O(n + m)$ (in the worst case of absence of deadlock).

In the next section, we show how such a maximal syphon search on the Petri net structure can be translated directly into a pruning algorithm for the original AND-OR graph structure.

5 Deadlock Detection Algorithm on AND-OR Graphs

An algorithm to detect deadlocks in an AND-OR graph which is linear in the number of nodes and edges is outlined. This is shown to be optimal in terms of worst case complexity. The algorithm presented in Figure 10 is a direct translation of the pruning technique developed in the previous section on the Petri net representation of the AND-OR graph.

The algorithm works as follows. Whenever the transaction manager suspects that any transaction is in deadlock, it invokes function DeadlockDetection(G),

```
┌─────────────────────────────────────────────────────────────────────────┐
│                                                                           │
│ Data Structures :                                                         │
│                                                                           │
│ outwardEdge :          is a matrix containing N rows, each one associated │
│                        with a node i of the graph. In particular the i-th │
│                        element of outwardEdge contains a vector of        │
│                        integers, the k-th element of this vector indicates│
│                        the outward degree for the k-th group of AND edges │
│                        having initial endpoint i.                         │
│ pruned :               is a vector of N boolean and when pruned[i] holds  │
│                        true the i-th node can be removed from the graph.  │
│ sinkNode :             this list contains all the nodes that have outward │
│                        degree equal to zero, that is the sink nodes of the│
│                        graph.                                             │
│ inwardEdge :           this data structure local to procedure Prune       │
│                        contains the list of inward edges of a given node. │
│                                                                           │
│ Procedures :                                                              │
│                                                                           │
│ BuildOutwardEdge(i,G) : this procedure fills the element of the matrix    │
│                         outwardEdge associated with node i.               │
│ Outward(i,G) :          returns the nodes j reachable by all edges of type│
│                         (i,j)                                             │
│ InEdge(j,G) :           returns the list of edges (i,j), inward edges of j,│
│                         such that i has not yet been pruned.              │
│ AndCounter(i,j) :       returns the element of outwardEdge[i] related to  │
│                         the group of AND edge that contains (i,j).        │
│ InsList(el,list) :      insert the element el at the beginning of list.   │
│ RemList(list) :         returns and removes from list the first element.  │
│                                                                           │
└─────────────────────────────────────────────────────────────────────────┘
```

Fig. 9. Data structures and procedures used by the deadlock detection algorithm

where G is the current AND-OR graph. The boolean value returned by the function represents the condition whether a deadlock was found or not.

The algorithm uses three major global data structures: a matrix called the outwardEdge, a vector called the pruned, and a list called the sinkNode. The matrix outwardEdge contains N rows, each row associated with a node i of the graph. The i-th element of the outwardEdge contains a vector of integers, and the k-th element of this vector indicates the outward degree for the k-th group of AND edges having the initial endpoint i. The vector pruned contains N elements of type Boolean. When pruned[i] holds the value true, the i-th node can be removed from the graph. Note that in the present algorithm the actual elimination of the node from the graph is not carried out: the knowledge that the node can be potentially removed is sufficient to detect a deadlock. Finally, the list sinkNode contains all the nodes that have outward degree equal to zero (i.e., the sink nodes of the graph). This list is particularly useful for improving the efficiency of the pruning algorithm; indeed during the execution of the algorithm it is crucial to determine in a constant time which of the inner nodes have lost all outward edges and are becoming sink nodes.

```
matrix outwardEdge[N][M] ; vector pruned[N] ; list sinkNode ;

bool DeadlockDetection (graph G) {
    Initialize(G) ; Prune(G) ; return CheckDeadlock(G.N) ;
}
void Initialize (graph G) {
    SetEmptyQueue(Q) ; Mark(G.root) ; Enqueue(G.root,Q) ;
    while (NOT Empty(Q)) {
        i = Dequeue(Q) ; BuildOutwardEdge(i,G) ;
        if (Empty(Outward(i,G))) {
            pruned[i] = TRUE ; insList(i,sinkNode) ;
        } else {
            pruned[i] = FALSE ;
            for each j in Outward(i,G)
                if (NOT Marked(j)) {
                    Mark(j) ; Enqueue(j,Q) ;
                }
        }
    }
}
void Prune (graph G) {
    while (NOT Empty(sinkNode)) {
        node = RemList(sinkNode) ; inwardEdge = InEdge(node,G) ;
        while (NOT Empty(inwardEdge)) {
            (i,node) = RemList(inwardEdge) ;
            if (NOT pruned[i]) {
                k = AndCounter(i,node);
                outwardEdge[i][k] = outwardEdge[i][k] -1;
                if (outwardEdge[i][k] == 0) {
                    pruned[i] = TRUE; InsList(i,sinkNode);
                }
            }
        }
    }
}
bool CheckDeadlock (integer N) {
    deadlock = FALSE ;
    for (i=0; i<N; i=i+1)
        deadlock = deadlock OR NOT pruned[i];
    return deadlock;
}
```

Fig. 10. The deadlock detection algorithm

The algorithm consists of three main procedures: `Initialize`, `Prune`, and `CheckDeadlock`.

Procedure `Initialize` executes a Breadth-First-Search of the graph. It visits each node and each edge of the graph just once. When visiting node i, this procedure initializes the three data structures for the node i. Hence the time complexity of procedure `Initialize` is $O(N + M)$, where N is the number of nodes and M is the number of edges of the AND-OR graph.

Procedure `Prune` scans the list `sinkNode`. For each sink node j the list of its inward edges (i, j) is constructed. For each one of such edges, the relevant entry of `outwardEdge[i]` is decremented to record that the edge (i, j) is pruned. If the relevant entry of `outwardEdge[i]` becomes zero then node i is pruned and inserted in the list `sinkNode`. Note that procedure `Prune` marks as pruned every node and every edge of the graph at most once, thus its time complexity is also $O(N + M)$.

Finally, procedure `CheckDeadlock` verifies whether all nodes have been pruned by scanning the vector `pruned`. If this vector contains all elements equal to `true` then there is no deadlock since all nodes have been removed. The time complexity of `CheckDeadlock` is $O(N)$.

Summarizing, the overall time complexity of the deadlock detection algorithm is $O(N + M)$ which is optimal. This is because the lower bound to solve the problem is $\Omega(N + M)$, since no deadlock detection algorithm could work against an "oracle" without considering at least all nodes and all edges of the AND-OR graph.

The correctness of the pruning algorithm derives from its relation to the maximal syphon search algorithm for the Petri net model. In particular, the data structure `outwardEdge` of the algorithm contains the number of input edges of Petri net transitions representing elementary AND terms (which may reduce to transitions representing nodes in case the dependency does not contain any OR combination). More precisely, value `outwardEdge[j][l]` corresponds to the number of input edges of the l-th input transition for the place "orTj" in case the dependency for T_j contains an OR; otherwise (if the dependency does not contain any OR) the only element `outwardEdge[j][l]` represents the number of input arcs of transition "Tj" in the Petri net. The value `outwardEdge[j][l]`=0 corresponds to a transition without input arcs in the Petri net model. Once at least one of the counters associated with T_j is equal to zero (i.e., if $\exists$ l such that `outwardEdge[j][l]`=0), then the l-th input transition becomes without input, and we can mark it to be deleted (together with place "orTj" and transition "Tj," if they exist); all dependency edges represented by the output places of "Tj" are also removed, thus implying a decrement of the counter for the corresponding AND transitions. Suppose that the k-th AND term transition for the i-th node had an input from one of the output places of "Tj"; then the counter `outwardEdge[i][k]` must be decremented by one to take the place removal into account.

The reader is urged to check how the elimination steps of the Petri net level algorithm outlined in the two examples in the previous section are mapped into steps of the algorithm depicted in Figure 10 in a natural way.

6 Conclusions

We have given an algorithm for detecting deadlocks when both data and transaction dependencies are present in advanced transactions. The proposed deadlock detection algorithm for the general case of AND-OR precedence graphs is optimal from several points of view.

From a theoretical point of view, its worst case complexity $O(m + n)$ is minimal because no deadlock detection algorithm could work against an "oracle" without considering at least all nodes and all edges of the AND-OR graph.

From a pragmatic point of view, our algorithm improves the previously known algorithms in at least two aspects. First, it does not necessarily require the use of a canonical form for the logical composition of precedence constraints. Second, it does not require any heuristics for the determination of a "starting point" for the construction of the set of deadlocked transactions: syphons structures are constructed by pruning the graph structure (elimination of nodes that are not deadlocked) rather than by incremental addition of nodes (which would require the hypothesis that a given starting node is deadlocked).

The particular cases of AND-only and OR-only graphs can of course be handled by (simplified versions of) our algorithm. For example, in the nested transactions model [8], the parent/child dependency can be represented by AND-only graph, where a parent develops a commit dependency on each one of its child transactions in a conjunctive mode and a child transaction establishes an abort dependency on its parent. The abort dependency guarantees the abort of an uncommitted child if its parent aborts, the commit dependency preserve the commit order among the nested transaction. Note that in nested transaction when a child transaction commits its effects are made visible only to its parent, and its parent inherits the commiting child's locks. The deadlock problem addressed for nested transactions in [8] can be detected by checking such an AND-only wait-for-graph for cycles when new data dependency edges are added.

If a transaction T which is waiting for the commit of another transaction happens to be part of a syphon structure and spontaneous aborts after procedure DeadlockDetection in Figure 10 is invoked but before it terminates, then a *false deadlock* [10] may be detected by the deadlock detection algorithm. (Procedure DeadlockDetection works on the initial snapshot of the wait-for-graph and T could be just the transaction that by aborting breaks the syphon detected by the procedure. Note that Definition 2 allows a transaction on the left-hand-side of a general dependency to abort without waiting the termination of the right-hand-side.) This false deadlock problem can be dealt with the help of a Lock Manager. Whenever a transaction T aborts while the deadlock detection is executing the Lock Manager inserts T in the list sinkNode used by procedure DeadlockDetection. In this way, the deadlock detector prunes T and all its

285

incoming edges from the AND-OR graph before terminating and hence avoids the signal of a false deadlock.

We conclude by remarking that we used a particular class of Petri nets to provide a structural characterization of the existence of a deadlock situation into a general AND-OR precedence graph. We translated the problem into the Petri net domain because no structural characterization was available for AND-OR graphs comparable to the usual (AND only) precedence graphs.

The structural characterization algorithm in terms of existence of a non-empty maximal syphon was then translated back to the AND-OR graph domain, so that no actual use of the Petri net formalism is required, once the algorithm has been proven correct. However, the idea and the technique of combining data dependencies and transaction dependencies into a common formal framework based on Petri Nets appear to be valuable. In this setting it is possible that other properties of transaction dependencies can be formally studied and optimal algorithms can be derived.

References

1. A. Biliris, S. Dar, N. Gehani, H. V. Jagadish, and K. Ramamritham. Asset: A system for supporting extended transactions. In *Proceedings of the ACM SIGMOD International Conference on Management of Data*, Minneapolis, Minnesota, May 1994.
2. S. Jajodia et al., editor. *Advanced Transaction Models and Architectures*. Kluwer Academic Publ., 1997.
3. D. Georgakopoulos, M.F. Hornick, and A.P. Sheth. An Overview of Workflow Management: from Process Modeling to Workflow Automation Infrastructure. *Distributed and Parallel Databases*, V.3, N.2, pp.119-153, April 1995.
4. J. Gray and A. Reuter. *Transaction Processing: Concepts and Techniques*. Morgan Kaufmann Publishers. San Mateo (Calif.), 1993.
5. T. Hermann, and K. Chandy. A distributed procedure to detect AND/OR deadlock. TR LCS-8301, Dept. of Computer Science, University of Texas, Austin, 1983.
6. E. Knapp. Deadlock Detection in Distributed Databases. *ACM Computing Surveys*, 19(4):303–328, December 1987.
7. L. Mancini, I. Ray, E. Bertino, and S. Jajodia. Flexible Commit Protocols for Advanced Transaction Processing. In *Advanced Transaction Models and Architectures*, S. Jajodia and L. Kerschberg, eds., Kluwer, 91–124, 1997.
8. J. Eliot B. Moss. *Nested Transactions: An Approach to Reliable Distributed Programming*. The MIT Press. Cambridge (Massachusetts), 1985.
9. T. Murata. Petri nets: properties, analysis, and applications. *Proceedings of the IEEE*, 77(4):541–580, April 1989.
10. R. Obermarck. Distributed Deadlock Detection Algorithm. *ACM Transactions on Database Systems*, 7(2):187-208, June 1982.
11. K. Ramamritham and P. K. Chrysanthis. A Taxonomy of Correctness Criteria in Database Applications. *The VLDB Journal*, 5(1):64–84, January 1996.
12. Aidong Zhang, Marian Nodine, Bharat Bhargava, and Omran Bukhres. Ensuring Relaxed Atomicity for Flexible Transactions in Multidatabase Systems. In *Proceedings of the ACM SIGMOD International Conference on Management of Data*, pages 67–78, May 1994.

Petri Net Based Certification of Event-Driven Process Chains

Peter Langner[1], Christoph Schneider[2] and Joachim Wehler[3]

[1] INNOBIS Unternehmensberatung und Software GmbH, Willhoop 7,
D-22453 Hamburg, P.Langner@innobis.de
[2] Christoph Schneider, cke-schneider.de dataservice, Paul Robeson Straße 40,
D-10439 Berlin, 100422.133@compuserve.com
[3] Softlab GmbH, Zamdorfer Straße 120, D-81677 München, wej@softlab.de

Abstract. One of the widespread methods for modeling business processes is the method of event-driven process chains (EPCs) (Ereignisgesteuerte Prozesskette [EPK]). The paper shows that EPCs can be translated into a simple class of colored Petri nets, which have a single color of type *Boole* and formulas from propositional logic as guards. The structure of the resulting Boolean net is a tree of bipolar synchronization (bp) graphs. This property simplifies considerably the behavioral analysis of EPCs, because Genrich and Thiagarajan proved, that well-formedness of bp schemes can be tested by a reduction algorithm. If the Boolean net resulting from the translation of an EPC is well-formed, it can be eventually translated into a free-choice net showing the same behavior. Therefore the translation of EPCs into Boolean Petri nets fixes the semantics of EPCs and allows a formal analysis of the EPC-method. In the domain of business process engineering only those EPCs, which have been certified as well-formed, can be recommended for further steps like simulation, activity based cost analysis or workflow.
Topics. System design and verification using nets, analysis and synthesis, structure and behavior of nets.

1 Introduction

In the wake of standard software systems like SAP/R3 or Baan IV different methods and tools for the modeling of business processes flourish on the market. Some of them use Petri nets, other do not. In Germany the method of *event-driven process chains* (EPCs) ([Sch1994]) is one of the most widespread methods used in commercial projects. In a continuously increasing variety of projects this method serves for different purposes: To model business processes, to document industrial reference models ([SAP1996a]) and also to design workflows ([SAP1996b])[1].

But in spite of their wide spreading and their acceptance by customers EPCs suffer from a serious drawback: Their lack of formal rigor, neither the syntax nor the semantics of an EPC is well defined. This fault will become manifest at least

---
[1] Baan IV uses a type of Petri nets, which are very similar to EPCs.

when there is real need to check EPCs for their consistency in order to control workflow systems.

Therefore we have set out to provide EPCs with an exact syntax and semantics, to define the concept of a *well-formed* EPC and to look out for an algorithm for the verification of well-formedness. We show in this paper, that all these goals can be reached by translating EPCs into Petri nets and applying Petri net theory[2].

Concerning their expressive power EPCs correspond to a rather simple class of Petri nets, which we call Boolean nets. A Boolean net is a colored Petri net, particularly well-suited for modeling the control flow of a system: The tokens of a Boolean net carry a single color with the two values *true* resp. *false*. They represent activation resp. explicit deactivation. Branching and alternatives of the control flow are modeled by using formulas from propositional logic as guards.

We consider Boolean nets an interesting net type due to the following reasons:

1. Boolean nets strengthen EPCs by Petri net theory. The benefits are: Boolean nets provide a formal syntax and semantics for the EPC-method, which grew up apart from theoretical computer science in the domain of business process engineering.
2. Boolean net systems, which result from the translation of EPCs, provide the computer scientist with examples of bipolar synchronization schemes (bp schemes) from the field of applications. The advantage of bp schemes: Their well-behavedness can be verified by a reduction algorithms without any need to consider the case graph. In addition, the synthesis problem has been solved for well-formed bp schemes by Genrich-Thiagarajan.
3. And finally a motivation for the management: Many projects, which aim at the improvement of business processes, use EPCs as a language for process specification. But the formal correctness of this specification is a precondition to execute simulations and to derive reasonable decisions from an activity based cost analysis. After translation of EPCs into Boolean nets the certification of EPCs is possible.

2 Translation of EPCs into Boolean Nets

EPCs model the flow of control using three different types of net elements: Events, functions and logical connectors. EPCs were invented by Keller, Nüttgens and Scheer ([KNS1991]), the method is characterized by Nüttgens ([Nüt1995]): *"The EPC-method is based on Petri net theory in the main and can be considered as a variant of the condition-event net enlarged by logical connectors. "*

Boolean nets are a simple class of colored Petri nets, but sufficient to model the control flow of a system. Like other colored nets they have an underlying

---

[2] Due to lack of space full proofs and the application of polynomial algebras over the field F_2 to the split resp. fusion of Boolean transitions will appear as technical report [LSW1997b].

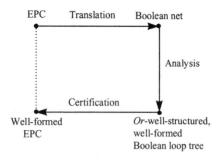

Fig. 1. Quality assurance for EPCs

p/t net, of which the Boolean structure is just an enrichment by some logical constructs, namely by

1. two kinds of tokens modeling *true* and *false*
2. formulas of propositional logic serving as guards of the transitions.

In this chapter we define Boolean nets and translate EPCs into Boolean nets.

Example 1 (Event-driven process chain). Throughout the whole paper we consider a fictitious model of the business process "Order Processing", which is represented as an event-driven process chain in Fig. 2.

Obviously the reader catches an intuitive understanding of the process. This is the great advantage of the EPC-method. It makes clear, why the method gained quick acceptance from consultants and customers in commercial projects and proves good in daily work.

On the other hand, a formal syntax for EPCs is lacking up to now. Therefore, we propose the following Definition 1, which we had to reconstruct from the original paper [KNS1991] as well as from examples in the literature.

Definition 1 (Event-driven process chain). *A connected directed graph $EPC = (N, A)$ is called* event-driven process chain *(EPC) iff it satisfies the following properties:*

1. *The set N of nodes is the union of three pairwise disjoint sets $E \neq \emptyset$ (events), $F \neq \emptyset$ (functions), K (connectors of type xor, or, and).*
2. *Every element from the set A of arcs selects an orientation between two nodes of different types.*
3. *Only nodes from K branch. All nodes in the preset of a connector belong to the same type and all nodes in the postset of a connector belong to the same type. The preset type is different from the postset type.*
4. *All nodes at the border of EPC belong to E, there exists at least one start event without input arcs and at least one final event without output arcs.*

289

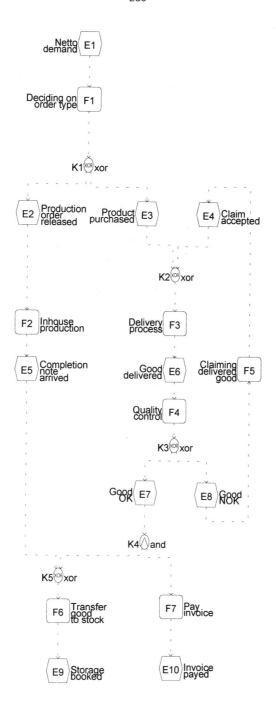

Fig. 2. EPC "Order Processing"

Remark 1 (Semantics of EPCs). Besides the lack of a formal syntax the semantics of an EPC is undefined, too. This shows up at the closing logical connectors. At a closing *and*-connector the process has to wait until all elements of the preset happen, but how to interpret closing *or*-connectors resp. *xor*-connectors?

1. Is the closing *or*-connector allowed to occur, when the first of its pre-events has happened, and to occur a second time for every following event? What does it mean in the model: the *first*?
2. Presumably the closing *xor*-connector shall be in deadlock, when more than one of its pre-events are activated at the same time. But what does it mean: at the *same* time?

EPCs do not model a global time or the concept of simultaneity, hence the transition rule for the closing *or*-connector and for the closing *xor*-connector is undefined.

Questions like the aforementioned have not been treated in the original sources about EPCs ([KNS1991]). In the meantime the semantics of a closing *or*- resp. *xor*-connector has been fixed in a pragmatic way by the implementation of EPCs in SIMPLE^{++}[3]. This simulation tool, which forms part of release 3.2 of ARIS-Toolset[4], uses a global time: The closing binary *xor*-connector is in deadlock if both events happen at the same time, while it occurs two times if they happen in sequence. Similarly the closing binary *or*-connector fires only once, if both events happen at the same time, whereas it occurs two times if they happen in sequence.

In the present paper we follow a different approach: We translate an EPC into a Petri net by a formal procedure and define the semantics of the EPC as the semantics of the resulting Petri net.

In [LSW1997a] we introduced a class of colored Petri nets — called *Boolean nets* — which are powerful enough to represent the functionality of EPCs. For Boolean nets we consider Boolean markings, which induce live and safe markings on the underlying p/t net, if we forget about the color of all Boolean tokens and the guards of all Boolean transitions. Because we require the resulting p/t system to be live and safe, any deadlock of a Boolean net system is due to the logic embodied in the guard formulas and the token values. It cannot originate from the underlying p/t system. Concerning the notation for colored nets cf. [Jen1992].

Definition 2 (Boolean net).

1. A Boolean net $BN = (N, x, g)$ *is a colored Petri net consisting of a p/t net* $N = (P, T, A)$ *annotated in the language* $BOOLE$ *of Boolean expressions. The annotation consists of*
   (a) an arc annotation

$$x : A \rightarrow variables(BOOLE)$$

   assigning a Boolean variable $x(a)$ *to every arc* $a \in A$,

---

[3] SIMPLE^{++} is a product of AESOP GmbH, Stuttgart
[4] ARIS-Toolset is a product of IDS Prof. Scheer GmbH, Saarbrücken

(b) and a transition annotation

$$g : T \to BOOLE, t \mapsto g_t,$$

assigning a Boolean expression g_t, the guard formula, to every transition $t \in T$. The variables that occur in the guard are the ones annotating the input and output arcs of t. A transition of N together with its guard formula is called Boolean transition *of BN. The net has a single color set $Boole = \{true, false\}$.*

2. *Depending on the structure of the underlying p/t net we define the subclasses of* Boolean free-choice nets, Boolean T-nets *resp.* Boolean P-nets.
3. *Markings of a Boolean net BN are considered as maps*

$$(M_0, M_1) : P \to \mathbb{N}^2,$$

where M_0 counts the tokens of color false and M_1 counts the tokens of color true. A marking $BM = (BM_0, BM_1)$ is called Boolean marking, *iff the induced marking M of the underlying p/t net N*

$$M : P \to N, M(p) := BM_0(p) + BM_1(p),$$

which counts the tokens independent from their color, is live and safe.

4. *A* Boolean net system *$BNS = (BN, BM)$ consists of a Boolean net BN provided with an initial Boolean marking BM. The behavior of BNS is determined by the firing rule of colored Petri nets.*

Procedure 1 (Translation of EPCs into Boolean nets). *In order to translate an EPC into a Boolean net we assume for the sake of simplicity that every connector of the EPC is*

1. *either* single-double, *i.e. it has a single input arc and two output arcs or vice versa,*
2. *or* double-double *and of type xor, i.e. it is of type xor with two input and two output arcs.*

The translation proceeds along the following four steps:

1. *If the EPC contains a circuit one has to check in the first step, if the circuit models a loop and if there is only one double-double xor-connector modeling begin and end of the loop. We call this connector the articulation point of the loop, cf. Definition 9.*
2. *The second step translates the resulting EPC according to the rules in the following Tab. 1.*
   The guards for Boolean transitions of type xor, or resp. and will be introduced in the next chapter, cf. Definition 4.
3. *During the third step one has to ensure that every Boolean transition is connected to places and that every articulation point is connected to transitions. I.e. after the translation of a single-double connector into a Boolean transition one has to add the necessary places. And after the translation of a double-double connector into a place one has to add the necessary transitions.*

4. In the final step one adds a distinguished place, called start/end *or* basepoint *to the resulting Boolean net, and connects every place, which corresponds to a start event of the original EPC, with the basepoint. If the given EPC has more than one start event one has to model carefully the different possible combinations of the start events of the EPC with the help of Boolean transitions. Similarly one connects to the basepoint every desired combination of the final events of the EPC.*

Table 1. Translation rules

EPC	Boolean net
event	place
function	transition
single-double connector of type *xor, or, and*	Boolean transition of the same type
double-double connector of type *xor*	place

Definition 3 (Boolean net of an EPC). *We call the Boolean net, which results from the translation of an EPC according to Procedure 1, the* Boolean net of the EPC.

Remark 2 (Heuristic of the translation). We consider loops with more than one begin resp. with more than one end as error. We demand, that the modeler uses his process know-how to correct this error. Similarly we consider it a mistake, to model loops with their begin different from their end. But the second kind of error can easily be corrected in a formal way, because every loop can be translated into a loop with exit test on top of the body. If necessary the body of the loop has to be duplicated and repeated before the articulation point.

The example in Fig. 2 contains a circuit, which models the complaint loop for those goods, which failed the quality test. This loop begins at the *xor*-connector K3 and ends at the *xor*-connector K2, hence it lacks a well-defined articulation point. We translate the loop into a loop with a single articulation point after having recognized the following two facts:

1. The body of the loop is formed by the sequence "E8, F5, E4, F3, E6, F4".
2. The sequence "F3, E6, F4" shall be executed before checking the loop condition for the first time.

We decided to translate the logical connectors of an EPC into Boolean transitions, in order to use the expressive power of the guard formulas to represent arbitrary logical formulas.

The occurrence rule of a Petri net requires *all* places in the preset of an activated transition to be marked. In particular, for the activation of a closing *xor*-connector exactly one place of the preset has to be marked with an activation token, while all other places in the preset carry tokens representing deactivation. Therefore we introduce two different types of tokens: The token color has two values *true* and *false*. Tokens with logical value *true* represent the current position of the control flow, while tokens with logical value *false* represent the "shadow" of the control flow.

While EPCs lack any net elements marking the current position of the control flow, the introduction of Boolean tokens resolves the indeterminacy in the semantics of the closing connectors. The closing *or*-connector and the closing *xor*-connector inherit their semantics from the occurrence rule of colored Petri nets: First one has to wait for complete information about the marking of all places in the preset, secondly the guard formula decides on the base of the collected information if the control flow is allowed to pass the connector or not. In any case, for a logical connector to occur a second time *all* places of the preset have to be marked a second time.

3 Boolean guards

The guard formulas of Boolean nets, which arise from the translation of EPCs, use only a subset of all formulas from propositional logic. They focus on the logical operators *xor, and* resp. *or*, an explicit negation operator is not part of the guard formulas. This expresses the fact, that an EPC does not model any spontaneous activation or deactivation of the control flow. To capture this property we introduce the concept of *faithfulness concerning activation*.

Definition 4 (Boolean transition of type xor, and, or). *The logical type of a Boolean transition is determined by its guard formula: A Boolean transition with input variables $x_i, i = 1, \ldots, n$, and output variables $y_j, j = 1, \ldots, m$ has logical type xor resp. or resp. and iff it has the guard formula,*

$$or(x_1, x_2, \ldots, x_n, y_1, y_2, \ldots, y_m) \Rightarrow [op(x_1, x_2, \ldots, x_n) and\ op(y_1, y_2, \ldots, y_m)],$$

where the Boolean operators

$$op : Boole^k \to Boole, op \in \{xor, or, and\},$$

are defined at $(b_1, b_2, \ldots, b_k) \in Boole^k$ as

$$\begin{cases} xor(b_1, b_2, \ldots, b_k) := true, \text{ iff } b_i = true \text{ for exactly one } i = 1, \ldots, k \\ or(b_1, b_2, \ldots, b_k) := true, \quad \text{iff } b_i = true \text{ for at least one } i = 1, \ldots, k \\ and(b_1, b_2, \ldots, b_k) := true, \text{ iff } b_i = true \text{ for all } i = 1, \ldots, k \end{cases}$$

Remark 3 (Bindings of a Boolean transition). Depending on its logical type a Boolean transition t with input variables $x_i, i = 1, \ldots, n$, and output variables $y_j, j = 1, \ldots, m$, has the bindings $b \in Boole^{n+m}$ as shown in Tab. 2.

We will use the algebraic value 1 as synonym for the logical value *true* resp. the algebraic value 0 for the logical value *false*.

Each of the logical types allows null-bindings, which are necessary to propagate the "shadow" of the control flow.

Table 2. Bindings of Boolean transitions

Logical type	Bindings
xor	1. $b = 0 := (0, \ldots, 0)$ "null-binding"
	2. $b = (b_{x_1}, \ldots, b_{x_n}, b_{y_1}, \ldots, b_{y_m})$ with $b_{x_i} = 1, b_{y_j} = 1$ for a unique $i = 1, \ldots, n$ and a unique $j = 1, \ldots, m$
and	1. $b = 0$
	2. $b = 1 := (1, \ldots, 1)$
or	1. $b = 0$
	2. $b = (b_{x_1}, \ldots, b_{x_n}, b_{y_1}, \ldots, b_{y_m})$ with $b_{x_i} = 1, b_{y_j} = 1$ for at least one $i = 1, \ldots, n$ and at least one $j = 1, \ldots, m$

Definition 5 (Elementary logical alternative).

1. *We call a Boolean transition with a single input arc an* opening transition *and use the notation* branch- *(resp.* fork- *resp.* branch/fork-*) transition for an opening transition of logical type xor (resp. and resp. or).*
    Analogously we call a Boolean transition with a single output arc a closing transition *and use the notation* merge- *resp.* join- *resp.* merge/join-*transition for a closing transition of logical type xor resp. and resp. or.*
2. *We call the Boolean net in Fig. 3 a n-ary elementary logical alternative of type xor resp. and resp. or iff the Boolean transitions (t_1, t_2) are of type (branch, merge) resp. (fork, join) resp. (branch/fork, merge/join).*

Definition 6 (Branch/fork resolution). *According to the logical formula*

$$x \text{ or } y \Leftrightarrow (x \text{ xor } y) \text{xor} (x \text{ and } y)$$

every binary elementary or-alternative can be resolved into a series of branch- and fork-alternatives, its branch/fork resolution, *according to Fig. 4.*

Definition 7 (Faithfulness concerning activation). *A Boolean net BN is called* faithful concerning activation *iff it has no spontaneous activations or deactivations, i.e. iff every binding b of a Boolean transition t of BN satisfies:*
If $b = (b_x, b_y) \in Boole^{n+m}$ with respect to the input variables $x = (x_1, \ldots, x_n)$ and the output variables $y = (y_1 \ldots, y_m)$ of t then

$$b_x = 0 \Leftrightarrow b_y = 0.$$

4 Boolean loop trees

The analysis of a Boolean net can be divided into different parts. In the present chapter we analyze the structure of the underlying p/t net. Due to Definition 2 the well-formedness of the underlying p/t net is equivalent to the existence of

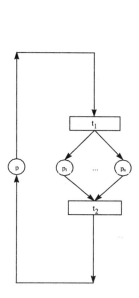

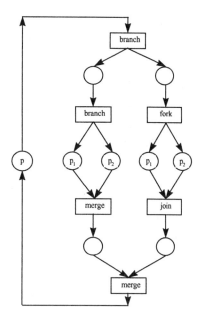

Fig. 3. *n*-ary elementary logical alternative

Fig. 4. Branch/fork resolution

a Boolean marking on a Boolean net. Those p/t nets, which result from the translation of well-structured EPCs, have a particular net structure: They form a tree of loops. We define a *loop tree* (Schleifenbaum) as a p/t net, which results from the successive adjunction of loops in a prescribed manner, and prove that loop trees are always well-formed.

Due to our translation of EPCs into Boolean nets from Procedure 1 the resulting net has a distinguished place, which we call its basepoint.

Definition 8 (Adjunction of pointed nets).

1. *A pointed net* (N, p) *is a net* N *with a distinguished place* p, *which is called its* basepoint.
2. *Let* $N_i, i = 0, 1$, *be two disjoint p/t nets and select two places* $l_1 \in N_0, p_1 \in N_1$. *We denote by*

$$N = N_0 \coprod_{(l_1, p_1)} N_1$$

the net N *resulting from the fusion of* N_0 *and* N_1 *at the places* l_1 *and* p_1. *In the case of pointed nets*

$$(N_i, p_i), i = 0, 1, \text{ and } l_1 \neq p_0$$

we call the pointed net (N, p) *with*

$$N = N_0 \coprod_{(l_1, p_1)} N_1 \text{ and basepoint } p = p_0$$

the adjunction *of* (N_1, p_1) *to* (N_0, p_0) *at the place* l_1. *We write*

$$(N,p) = (N_0, p_0) \coprod_{l_1} (N_1, p_1).$$

Definition 9 (Loop tree).

1. *A pointed T-net* $EL = (N,p)$ *is called* elementary loop *iff* N *is strongly connected and* $N \setminus p$ *is acyclic.*
2. *A pointed net* $LT = (N, p_0)$ *is called* loop tree *(Schleifenbaum) iff there exist*
   (a) elementary loops $EL_i = (N_i, p_i), i = 0, \ldots, n$, *pairwise disjoint, i.e.*

$$(N_i \setminus p_i) \cap (N_j \setminus p_j) = \emptyset \text{ for } i \neq j,$$

   (b) and pairwise disjoint places $l_i \neq p_0$ *of* N *with* ${}^\bullet(l_i^\bullet) = \{l_i\}, i = 1, \ldots, n$, *such that* $LT = LT_n$ *according to the inductive adjunction* $LT_0 := EL_0$ *and*

$$LT_i := LT_{i-1} \coprod_{l_i} EL_i, i = 1, \ldots, n.$$

3. *For a loop tree* LT *we call the subnets* $EL_i, i = 0, \ldots, n$, *the* loop components *of* LT, *the distinguished component* EL_0 *is called the* root component *and the fusion places* $l_i, i = 1, \ldots, n$, *are called* articulation points.

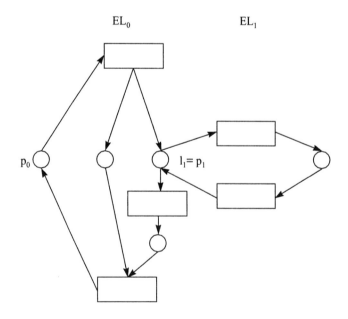

Fig. 5. Loop tree LT with two loop components

Remark 4 (Loop tree). Every loop tree is a tree: The loop components are the nodes and the loop component EL_j is a direct successor of EL_i iff the articulation point l_j, adjoining EL_j, belongs to EL_i.

Due to the condition about the neighborhood of its articulation points every loop tree is a free-choice net. The condition concerning the articulation point is respected by Procedure 1, step 3.

Proposition 1 (Siphons, traps and P-components). *Consider a loop tree LT with place set P and basepoint p_0.*

1. *For a subset $R \subset P$ of places we have the equivalence:*
   (a) R is a minimal siphon
   (b) R is a minimal trap
   (c) R is the set of places of a P-component.
   In all these cases $N(R, {}^\bullet R)$, the subnet of LT generated by R and ${}^\bullet R$, is covered by circuits.
2. *Every siphon in LT contains the basepoint p_0.*
3. *LT is covered by P-components.*

Theorem 1 (Well-formedness of a loop tree). *Every loop tree is well-formed: Marking the net with a single token at the basepoint is a live and safe marking.*

Proof. Denote by LT the given loop tree and by M_0 the distinguished marking.

1. By Commoner's theorem a free-choice system is live iff every minimal siphon contains an initially marked trap ([DE1995], Chap. 4.3.)
   This property is satisfied by (LT, M_0) due to Proposition 1, part 1 and part 2.
2. A live free-choice system is safe iff it is covered by P-components, which carry at most one token ([BD1990], Corollary 5.6):
   This property is satisfied by (LT, M_0) due to Proposition 1, part 3.

$\square$

Definition 10 (Boolean loop tree). *A Boolean net BN is called* Boolean loop tree *iff the underlying p/t net is a loop tree. Marking the basepoint of BN with a single token of value true defines the* base marking *of BN.*

Corollary 1. *The base marking of a Boolean loop tree is a Boolean marking.*

Definition 11 (Cyclization and decyclization).

1. *Denote by $EL = ((P, T, A), p_0)$ an elementary loop with basepoint p_0. Choose two new places p_i and p_f, which do not belong to P. The net N, which results from splitting p_0 into an initial place p_i and a terminal place p_t, is called the* decyclization *of EL, i.e.*

$$N := decyl(EL) = (P_N, T_N, A_N)$$

with places $P_N := (P \setminus p_0) \cup \{p_i, p_t\}$, transitions $T_N := T$ and arcs $A_N := (A \mid N \setminus p) \cup \{(p_i, p^\bullet), ({}^\bullet p, p_t)\}$.

2. *Denote by N an acyclic T-net with two uniquely determined places*

$$p_i = min(N) \ and \ p_t = max(N),$$

where min resp. max refer to the partial order defined by the precedence relation. The elementary loop EL with basepoint p_0, which results from the fusion of p_i and p_t to a new place p_0, is called the cyclization *of N. We write $EL = cyl(N)$.*

3. *For Boolean nets we define the concepts of cyclization and decyclization by the analogous concepts referring to the underlying p/t nets.*

5 Analysis of Boolean nets and EPCs

After the translation of EPCs into Boolean nets according to the procedure in Chapter 2 and due to the results about these nets in the Chapters 3 and 4 we are now ready to analyze EPCs by means of Petri net theory.

We distinguish between a structural net analysis and a behavioral analysis. EPCs, which pass the first one, are qualified as *well-structured*: They are structured as loop tree and have either none or always paired *or*-transitions, a condition, which restricts the unstructured use of *or*-transitions. In particular, exits from *or*-alternatives are forbidden. Those EPCs, which in addition pass the behavioral analysis, are called *well-formed*: Their Boolean loop tree is free of deadlocks and has only live transitions with respect to the base marking. We present a reduction algorithm for both types of analysis, which extends the Genrich-Thiagarajan reduction for well-formed bp schemes. Concerning the structure of EPCs we define:

Definition 12 (Well-structuredness of Boolean loop trees and EPCs).

1. *The set of elementary Boolean loops, which are or-well-structured, is the smallest set EL_{ows} with the following properties:*
   (a) *EL_{ows} contains every elementary Boolean loop without transitions of type or.*
   (b) *EL_{ows} contains every elementary or-alternative (cf. Definition 5).*
   (c) *For $B_1, B_2 \in EL_{ows}$ also the refinement of a place of B_1, which is different from the basepoint, by $decyl(B_2)$ belongs to EL_{ows}.*
2. *A Boolean loop tree is or-well-structured iff every loop component belongs to EL_{ows}.*
3. *An EPC is well-structured iff its Boolean net is an or-well-structured Boolean loop tree.*

Remark 5 (Or-well-structured elementary Boolean loops). Every *or*-transition of a logical alternative EL belongs to a pair (t_{bf}, t_{mj}) with a branch/fork transition t_{bf} and a merge/join transition t_{mj}. Setting $p_i := {}^\bullet t_{bf}$ and $p_t := t_{mj}^\bullet$ this pair has the following properties:

1. Both transitions t_{bf} and t_{mj} belong to the same loop component.
2. If we denote by $\Gamma(p_i, p_t)$ the set of directed simple paths within EL from p_i to p or from p to p_t, then every $\gamma \in \Gamma(p_i, p_t)$ covers both places, namely p_i as start and p_t as end.
3. $outdeg\ (t_{bf}) = indeg\ (t_{mj}) =: k$.
4. If we denote by $N(t_{bf}, t_{mj})$ the subnet of EL, which is generated by all directed simple paths within EL from p_i to p_t, then

$$N(t_{bf}, t_{mj}) \setminus \{t_{bf}, t_{mj}, p_i, p_t\}.$$

splits into k different connectedness components.

The pair (t_{bf}, t_{mj}) and its properties 1 – 4 do not change, neither when a place of EL, which is different from the base point, is refined by the decyclization of an element of EL_{ows}, nor when $decyl(EL)$ itself is substituted as place refinement into another element of EL_{ows}. Hence the above remark holds also for every elementary Boolean loop, which is *or*-well-structured.

In Definition 12, part 3 we require a separate condition about the *or*-connectors in order to qualify a given EPC as well-structured. Solely well-formedness of the corresponding Boolean loop tree would be too weak, to rule out some type of EPCs we consider to be ill-structured: E.g. a Boolean loop tree having only Boolean transitions of type *branch/fork* and *merge/join* is well-formed according to Theorem 1, nevertheless it can be ill-structured in our opinion: A lot of EPCs from the literature and from commercial projects in the field of business process engineering demonstrate that the unrestricted use of closing *or*-connectors does not model any real situation. Rather it reveals the failure of the modeler to synchronize in a correct way all alternatives he has created. A closing *or*-transition never generates any deadlock but often it has only been chosen to remedy a situation, which got out of control.

Concerning the behavior of EPCs we define:

Definition 13 (Well-formedness of Boolean loop trees and EPCs).

1. *A Boolean loop tree BLT, faithful concerning activation, is* well-formed *iff the Boolean net system (BLT, BM) is live concerning the base marking BM.*
2. *An EPC is* well-formed *iff it is well-structured and its Boolean loop tree is well-formed.*

Proposition 2 (Well-formed resp. or-well-structured Boolean loop trees).
Denote by BLT a Boolean loop tree, which is faithful concerning activation.

1. *BLT is well-formed iff the Boolean system (BLT, BM) is reversible and has no dead transitions, i.e. iff it satisfies the following two conditions:*
   (a) BM is a homespace (Reversibility)
   (b) For every Boolean transition t of BLT there exists a reachable marking

$$BM_{pre} \in [BM >$$

   activating a binding $b \neq 0$ of t (Non deadness).

2. *BLT is well-formed (resp. or-well-structured and well-formed) iff every of its loop components is well-formed (resp. or-well-structured and well-formed).*

Proposition 3 (Well-formedness with respect to place refinement). *Assume BN to be an elementary Boolean loop with an acyclic subnet N, which has two unique places $p_i = min(N)$ and $p_f = max(N)$ different from the basepoint of BN. Denote by BLT the Boolean loop tree, which results from BN by fusing both places p_i and p_f.*

1. *Then BLT has two loop components, the root component EL_0 and a second component $EL_1 = cycl(N)$.*
2. *We have the equivalence:*
   (a) BN is well-formed
   (b) BLT is well-formed
   (c) EL_0 and $cycl(N)$ are well-formed.

By Proposition 2, part 2, we have reduced the question, if a given Boolean loop tree is *or*-well-structured and well-formed, to the analogous question about an elementary Boolean loop. The following remark follows easily from Definition 12.

Remark 6 (Or-well-structured and well-formed elementary Boolean loops). The class of *or*-well-structured and well-formed elementary Boolean loops is the smallest set EL_{owf} with the following properties:

1. EL_{owf} contains every well-formed elementary Boolean loop without transitions of type *or*.
2. EL_{owf} contains every elementary *or*-alternative (cf. Definition 5).
3. For $B_1, B_2 \in EL_{owf}$ also the place refinement of B_1 by B_2 at a place different from the base point of B_1 belongs to EL_{owf}.

The question about well-formedness of elementary Boolean loops, which have only transitions of logical type *and* resp. *xor*, has already been answered by Genrich and Thiagarajan ([GT1984]). They introduced a class of net systems, called *bipolar synchronization schemes* (bp schemes), and solved the corresponding synthesis problem. Bp schemes turn out to be special Boolean net systems.

Remark 7 (Bp schemes). A Boolean net system $BNS = (BN, BM)$ is called *bipolar synchronization scheme* (bp scheme) iff BN is a Boolean T-net and all transitions have logical type *xor* resp. *and*.

For a bp scheme BNS the following facts hold:

1. *BNS* is live iff *BNS* is deadlockfree ([GT1984], Theorem 2.12)
2. The synthesis problem for live bp schemes has been solved: *BNS* is live iff it can be constructed from an elementary bp scheme by a kit of eight synthesis rules ([GT1984], Theorem 6.19)
3. There exists a terminating reduction algorithm ([GT1984], Chapter 6.5) using six reduction rules with the property: *BNS* is live iff it can be reduced to an elementary bp scheme.

Algorithm 1 (Or-well-structured and well-formed Boolean loop trees).

Input: *Boolean loop BLT having only Boolean transitions of logical type xor, or resp. and.*
Output: *Either successful termination "or-well-structured and well-formed", or termination with error "not or-well-structured or not well-formed".*
Begin: *Traverse the Boolean loop tree BLT post-order. For the current loop component (EL, p) of BLT do:*

1. *Step: (a) Denote by T_{bf} the set of branch/fork-transitions and by T_{mj} the set of merge/join-transitions of EL.*
2. *Step: (a) Find an element t_{bf} from T_{bf} with no successor transition from T_{bf}.*

   If $T_{bf} = \emptyset$:

   (a) Check that $T_{mj} = \emptyset$, otherwise stop with error.

   (b) Check that the bp scheme EL is well-formed, otherwise stop with error.

   (c) Fold EL to its basepoint.

   (d) Exit and terminate the processing of the current node.
3. *Step: (a) For t_{bf} determine the set of nearest successor transitions from T_{mj}.*

   (b) Check that there is exactly one such transition t_{mj}, if not stop with error.
4. *Step: (a) For t_{mj} determine the set of nearest ancestor transitions from $T_{bf} \cup T_{mj}$.*

   (b) Check that there is exactly one such transition, namely t_{bf}, if not stop with error.
5. *Step:*

   (a) Set $p_i := {}^{\bullet}t_{bf}$ and $p_t := t_{mj}^{\bullet}$ and denote by $\Gamma(p_i, p_t)$ the set of directed simple paths within EL from p_i to p or from p to p_t.

   (b) Check that every path $\gamma \in \Gamma(p_i, p_t)$ covers both places p_i and p_t, if not stop with error.
6. *Step: (a) Check that $outdeg(t_{bf}) = indeg(t_{mj})$, if not stop with error.*
7. *Step: (a) Denote by $N(p_i, p_t)$ the subnet of EL, which is generated by all directed simple paths within EL from p_i to p_t.*

   (b) Check that the net $N(p_i, p_t) \setminus \{t_{bf}, t_{mj}, p_i, p_t\}$ splits into $k := outdeg(t_{bf})$ different connectedness components N_j, $j = 1, \ldots, k$, if not stop with error.

   (c) Check that every bp scheme $cycl(N_j), j = 1, \ldots, k$, is well-formed, if not stop with error.
8. *Step: (a) Replace the net $N(p_i, p_t)$ by a single place, which results as the fusion of p_i and p_t.*

   (b) Denote by EL the resulting elementary loop.
9. *Step: (a) Repeat step 1.*

End.

The above algorithm proceeds by elimination of *or*-transitions, it reduces each *or*-well-structured *or*-alternative to a single place. Afterwards the elementary Boolean loop is a bp scheme and the Genrich-Thiagarajan reduction can be performed.

Remark 8 (Certification of EPCs as well-formed). At this point we have reached the final step of our net analysis. Looking back, the whole procedure to certify a given EPC as well-formed comprises the following steps in sequence:

1. Check the syntax of the EPC according to Definition 1.
2. Translate the EPC into a Boolean net according to Procedure 1.
3. Check by standard graph algorithms that the resulting net is a Boolean loop tree.
4. Apply Algorithm 1 to check, that the Boolean loop tree is *or*-well-structured and well-formed.

The EPC is well-formed iff it passes every step with success.

Example 2 (Well-formedness of the EPC "Order Processing"). Figure 6 shows the translation of the EPC "Order Processing" in Fig. 2 into a Boolean net according to Procedure 1. Before applying the procedure the EPC has been standarized as mentioned in Remark 2. The transitions K100 and K200 have been introduced in order to connect the basepoint "Start/End" with the boundary events of the EPC. Nodes without annotation have been introduced to conform to the syntax of a net as a bipartite graph. Obviously the EPC is well-structured, because the resulting Boolean net is a loop tree without any *or*-alternatives. Beside the root component with basepoint "Start/End" there exists a second loop component with articulation point K3.

Both loop components are bp schemes, the second — a linear sequence — is obviously well-formed. But the root component is not well-formed. The Genrich-Thiagarajan algorithm reduces the root component to the net in Fig. 8 and stops without further reduction to an elementary bp scheme. The problem which hinders well-formedness is the partial synchronization of the two threads, which originate at connector K1 and merge at connector K5. If connector K1 decides to send a 1-token to place E2 and a 0-token to place E3, then the closing *join*-transition K200 gets into deadlock. Even if we change transition K200 to a *merge*-transition, we can produce a similar deadlock by sending a 1-token to place E3 and a 0-token to place E2.

This problem shows that the attachment of the boundary events of the EPC to the additional place *start/end* requires a careful analysis of the possible combinations of the boundary events: In the present case the process always ends with event E9 and sometimes with event E10 in addition. In order to avoid the partial synchronization we first duplicate transition F6 and place E9, then join the purchasing alternative at connector K10 and finally synchronize both alternatives by the *merge*-transition K200, which corresponds to the *branch*-transition K1. The resulting net in Fig. 7 is reduced by the Genrich-Thiagarajan algorithm to the well-formed elementary bp scheme in Fig. 9.

Remark 9 (EPCs and free-choice systems). Every well formed bp scheme can be translated into a live and safe free-choice system ([GT1984], Theorem 3.13).

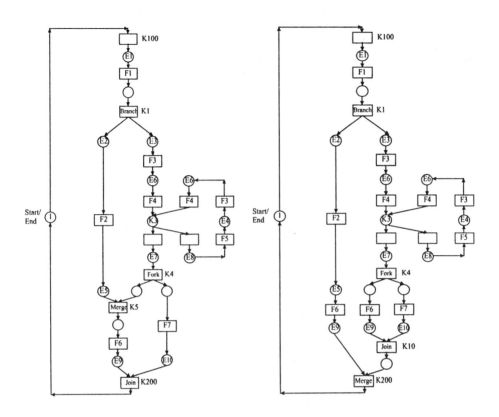

Fig. 6. Ill-formed Boolean net "Order Processing"

Fig. 7. Well-formed Boolean net "Order Processing"

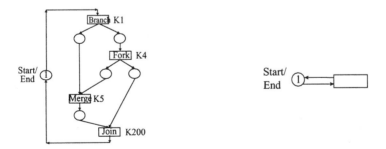

Fig. 8. Genrich-Thiagarajan reduction: Termination in the ill-structured case

Fig. 9. Genrich-Thiagarajan reduction: Termination in the well-structured case with an elementary bp scheme

Hereby one translates the Boolean transitions using the following standard sub-sitution: Branch/merge-transitions are replaced by a shared place, and all an-notations, all guard formulas and all tokens of logical value *false* are erased. Similarly one can translate the branch/fork-resolution of the Boolean loop tree belonging to a well formed EPC into a live and safe free-choice system. At the articulations points the free-choice property is guaranteed by their branching mode according to Definition 9.

6 Tool support and relation to other work

6.1 Tool-Support

According to our theoretical work a software-tool *Net-proof* [5] was built, which is used in consulting for business process reengineering. EPCs can be checked with respect to syntax, connectedness, inappropriate cycles and logic alternatives — in an interactive way. It is planned to support the complete process of quality assurance for EPCs according to Fig. 1.

6.2 Relation to other work

Scheer in joint work with Chen ([CS1994]), as well as other authors ([Brö1996], [LSW1997a], [Rod1997]) have proposed translations of EPCs into Petri nets. All these approaches as well as the resulting net classes differ. In addition to his own proposal Rodenhagen ([Rod1997]) compares and comments some of the differences. Our work differs from other approaches by the introduction of 0-tokens, which allow to analyze EPCs by means of bp schemes.

An other approach has been followed by van der Aalst ([Aal1997]). His aim is not the translation of EPCs but — more general — the identification of a class of Petri nets, which is suitable to model the procedures of a workflow. Van der Aalst introduces the class of *sound workflow nets*, which proves to be a subclass of well-formed p/t nets. Every loop tree is a sound workflow net. The main difference between the approach of van der Aalst and our approach seems to be the use of different net classes:

1. van der Aalst works within the class of p/t nets and introduces the class of workflow nets
2. our paper deals with colored nets and introduces the class of Boolean nets and its subclass of Boolean loop trees.

As noted in Remark 9 a Boolean net, which corresponds to a well-formed EPC, can be transformed into a well-formed free-choice net. The resulting free-choice nets form a proper subset of all sound workflow nets. On the other hand the net analysis of the corresponding EPCs can be made by a reduction algo-rithm, the problem of the case graph explosion does not appear for EPCs due to

[5] Net-proof is a product of cke-schneider.de dataservice, Berlin

the relation between well-formed EPCs and bp schemes. Moreover the solution of the synthesis problem by Genrich and Thiagarajan provides even a complete kit of construction rules for well-formed EPCs.

References

[Aal1997]   *Van der Aalst, Wil M.P.*: Verification of Workflow Nets. In: *Azéma, Pierre; Balbo, Gianfranco* (Eds.): Application and Theory of Petri Nets 1997. Lecture Notes in Computer Science 1248. Springer, Berlin et al. 1997, p. 62–81

[BD1990]   *Best, Eike; Desel, Jörg*: Partial order behavior and structure of Petri nets. Formal aspects of computing 2 (1990), p. 123–138

[Brö1996]   *Bröker, Axel*: Transformation ereignisgesteuerter Prozeßketten in Prädikat-Transitions-Netze sowie Vergleich der Modellierungstools ARIS-Toolset und INCOME. Diplomarbeit FH Pforzheim, Hochschule für Gestaltung, Technik und Wirtschaft. Pforzheim 1996

[CS1994]   *Chen, R.; Scheer, August-Wilhelm*: Modellierung von Prozeßketten mittels Petri-Netz Theorie. Veröffentlichungen des Instituts für Wirtschaftsinformatik, Heft 107, Saarbrücken 1994

[DE1995]   *Desel, Jörg; Esparza, Javier*: Free choice Petri nets. Cambridge University Press, Cambridge 1995

[GT1984]   *Genrich, Hartmann; Thiagarajan, Pazhamaneri*: A Theory of Bipolar Synchronization Schemes. Theoretical Computer Science 30 (1984), p. 241–318

[Jen1992]   *Jensen, Kurt*: Colored Petri Nets. Basis Concepts, Analysis Methods and Practical Use. Springer, Berlin et al. 1992

[KNS1991]   *Keller, Gerhard; Nüttgens, Markus; Scheer, August-Wilhelm*: Semantische Prozeßmodellierung auf der Grundlage "Ereignisgesteuerter Prozeßketten (EPK)". Veröffentlichungen des Instituts für Wirtschaftsinformatik, Heft 89, Saarbrücken 1991

[LSW1997a]   *Langner, Peter; Schneider, Christoph; Wehler, Joachim*: Ereignisgesteuerte Prozeßketten und Petri-Netze. Universität Hamburg, Fachbereich Informatik, Bericht Nr. 196, FBI-HH-B-196/97, 1997

[LSW1997b]   *Langner, Peter; Schneider, Christoph; Wehler, Joachim*: Relating Event-driven Process Chains to Boolean Petri Nets. Ludwig-Maximilians-Universität München, Institut für Informatik, Bericht 9707, 1997

[Nüt1995]   *Nüttgens, Markus*: Koordiniert-dezentrales Informationsmanagement: Rahmenkonzept - Koordinationsmodelle - Werkzeug-Shell. Gabler, Wiesbaden 1995

[Rod1997]   *Rodenhagen, Jörg*: Darstellung ereignisgesteuerter Prozeßketten (EPK) mit Hilfe von Petrinetzen. Diplomarbeit, Universität Hamburg, Fachbereich Informatik, Hamburg 1997

[SAP1996a]   *SAP*: CA R/3 Reference Model. R/3 System Release 3.0. (Product documentation), Walldorf 1996

[SAP1996b]   *SAP*: SAP Business Workflow. R/3 System Release 3.0. (Product documentation), Walldorf 1996

[Sch1994]   *Scheer, August-Wilhelm*: Business Processes Engineering. Reference Models for Industrial Enterprises. Springer, Berlin et al. 2nd 1994

M-net Calculus Based Semantics for Triggers

Véronique Benzaken[1], Nicolas Hugon[1,2], Hanna Klaudel[3], Elisabeth Pelz[3] and Robert-C. Riemann[2,3,4]

[1] Equipe d'Informatique, Université Paris I Panthéon-Sorbonne
[2] LRI, Université Paris-Sud
[3] Equipe d'Informatique, Université Paris XII Val de Marne, 61, Av. de Gaulle, F-94010 Créteil, France
[4] Institut für Informatik, Universität Hildesheim

Abstract. A formal semantics for the trigger concept in active data base systems is proposed. Such data base systems have the capability to react to the occurrence of some events, allowing to execute automatically some treatments. These capabilities to react are given by adding to the data base system a set of production rules, called *triggers*. During the last decade, a lot of works have been devoted to the design and implementation of triggers in data base systems leading to the generic field of active data bases. While the idea of using Petri nets to give a semantics for triggers has already been pointed out, the existing works either only suggest such a use and does not show how to do it, or capture only a very small part of the execution model. Also, they lack the use for high-level Petri nets only able to provide a concise net semantics. In this paper we propose to extensively make use of a specific kind of high level Petri nets: the M-nets. Such nets, allowing for compositionality appear particularly well-suited to give a formal semantics for the general *Event–Condition–Action* (ECA) model of triggers.

1 Introduction

M-nets, the coloured version of high level Box-Calculus, are widely accepted now to give semantics to concurrent or object-oriented programming languages, to protocols or algorithms, e.g. [4, 3, 5, 23, 24, 1, 11]. The most original aspect of M-nets with respect to other high level net classes is their full compositionality thanks to their interfaces and a set of various net-operations defined for them. In fact, M-nets constitute a net algebra. Their interest is augmented by the ability to use in practice an associated tool, PEP [19], which also offers various implemented methods for verification and analysis.

When we speak about the modeling of a system, this includes as well the specification of a system to be constructed and the description of an already existing one. Whenever the system to be modelled consists of various distinct conceptual parts, which need to be combined or coordinated in non trivial ways, a very modular and compositional proceeding is necessary to be able to control the correctness of modeling. M-nets just offer these features.

In this article, the complex systems we wish to deal with are Active Data Base Systems (ADBS). An ADBS is a Data Base System (DBS) having the capability to react to the occurrence of some events, allowing by that way to execute automatically several treatments. These capabilities to react are given to the DBS by adding a set of production rules, called *triggers*.

Usually, a trigger is viewed as a "data base predefined procedure". More precisely, a trigger consists in a production rule combining an *event* part, a *condition* part together with an *action* part. Triggers are fired in an automatic way. This means that their firing is event-driven: neither programmers nor applications are responsible for triggering them. Indeed, the action will be undertaken when the specific event arises provided that the condition is fulfilled. Each trigger is given with the specification of its execution mode, the so-called *coupling modes* of its parts.

In the active data base field, the importance of such a tool is crucial and has been widely admitted as it allows for the modeling of many tasks that have to be managed by the data base system. In particular, triggers allow for the definition and maintenance of so-called integrity constraints, for the modeling and control of data accesses, for automatic replication of data, for automatic view maintenance...

However, due to their expressive power, triggers should be used carefully. An ill-designed trigger could lead to chaotic behaviour of the data base. Moreover, as there does not exist a common, well understood and accepted formal semantics for them, the task of predicting their (expected) behaviour is a painstaking one. In this article, we propose to use the Mnet-calculus to provide a semantics for triggers. It is also the first time, the coupling modes of triggers are treated in a formal semantics giving in this way the observability of executions under several coupling modes.

We will associate to each conceptual unit of an ADBS its semantic counterpart in terms of an M-net: in particular, to each trigger rule, to each transaction, to those parts of the Data Base Management System (DBMS) concerning the execution modes of triggers, and so on. For the sake of brevity we assume that the M-net for a distributed data base system is given together with its interfaces. Thus we will deal here neither with the Data Base itself, nor with the temporary copies for each transaction, nor with the administration and control of concurrent access to the data. This part would be managed in a similar way as done in [28] with coloured Petri nets.

The compositionality of M-nets is used on three levels:

1. On the *external* level: We never have to construct explicitly the whole net of the ADBS. We only define separately all M-net representations of the various conceptual DB units, put them side by side (by parallel composition) and precise over which actions they should be synchronised.

2. On the *internal* level: Each M-net, for instance for a trigger rule, will be constructed compositionally. We first give a general scheme which has to be completed by the M-net counterpart of some concrete program using successive substitutions.

3. On the *event* level: The event part of a trigger rule is build from simple events using composition operations of some dedicated algebra. The definition of a corresponding M-net algebra expressing events was non trivial and constitutes certainly one of the most original contributions of this paper.

The rest of the paper is organised as follows. Section 2 introduces a generalised ECA model. The M-net Calculus is briefly described in section 4. The trigger semantics in the M-net Calculus is formally defined in section 5. Some concluding remarks are given at the end in section 6.

2 Generalised ECA Model

Triggers, i.e., a system of rules, in ADBS are in general defined in the ECA (Event–Condition–Action) model. Designers might use this mechanism to influence the behaviour of a DBMS in a structured and automated way. The model allows, on one side, to specify the syntax of the rules and on the other side to give an informal description of their intended behaviour.

However, up to now there is no common standard for the ECA model. There are several versions corresponding either to the implementation of a specific data base prototype or to the inclusion of triggers in some of the main commercial DBS. Thus we choose to generalise the model including all the possibilities offered by the different prototypes and/or commercial versions.

Rules in the ECA model are defined as a triple ⟨*Event, Condition, Action*⟩. The intuitive semantics of such a triple is as follows: when an occurrence of *Event* is detected and *Condition* is true, the part *Action* is executed [10, 13]. Their syntax can be given as follows:

> Define Rule ⟨ rule name ⟩
> On *Event*
> If *Condition* Do *Action*

The Event Part: We distinguish two kinds of events: simple (or basic) ones and composite ones.

The set of simple events includes internal ones, i.e., usual manipulation of the data base such as *insert*, *update*, *delete*, and *select*, (methods *call*, *create*, *update*, *destroy*, *attach*, ..., respectively in OODB) or the beginning *BOT* or end *EOT* of a transaction. They may also be temporal events, where we distinguish absolute ones (e.g., *at 17-11-97*), relatives ones (e.g., 30 days after ...), and periodic ones (e.g., each month). Finally they may be external, like the beginning and end of a program, signals from peripherics, ...

Composite events are built from simple ones by combining them arbitraryly by the following operators: $\wedge$, $\vee$, *Not*, ; (sequence), $ANY(n, e_1, \ldots, e_m)$ (n out of a list of m events), $TIMES(n, e)$ (n iterations of the same event e), $\star$ (arbitrary number of iterations), and $In[s - f]$ or $In[I]$ (in an interval of time).

So we define an *event algebra*, where the eight proposed operations are the collection of those found in [7, 14, 15, 25] separately.

Some prototypes (e.g., HIPAC, Samos and Sentinel) extend the event part such that the usage of parameters in the event expression becomes possible. These parameters are instantiated at the time of the occurrence of the event and are used in the parts *Condition* and *Action* (we say then, that the parts *Event-Condition-Action* are related by these variables). We choose this more general concept and handle events with parameters.

The condition part: is built by predicates on the data base built from a query language like SQL, OQL, method calls or logical formulas. They concern either the current state or the intermediate state via local tables (delta structure) or local variables (old, new, current).

The action part: Previously, in the SQL2 norm, this part consisted in aborting the current transaction. Nowadays, it may consist of arbitrary queries, some code written in a procedure language (PL, SQL, O_2C, ...), or a call of procedure or program. We use this very general concept. It includes the possibility for the action part to trigger some rules.

One of the most important feature of active data bases is to allow for defining several execution modes of triggers. Transactions which usually are considered as atomic are managed in such a way that all intermediate computations only change the temporary data base, and only at the end the result of a successful terminated transaction (i.e., no abort) is copied from *DBtemp* to *DB*.

Triggers may interrupt such executions or create new concurrent transactions. To this end, two *coupling modes* have to be precised: one between the event and the condition part (E-C) and one between the condition and action part (C-A). The E-C coupling mode can be *immediate* or *defered*. Immediate says that the transaction is temporarily interrupted until the end of the execution of the rule. Defered says that first the transaction will continue until its end and then, just before *TCommit*, the condition part of the rule starts.

The coupling mode of C-A can be *immediate* or *separated*. As before, immediate says that the action is executed immediately after the condition has been detected true while the rest of the transaction is waiting. Separated says that the action will be considered as a new transaction executed concurrently to the original one. We deal with all these coupling modes in our model ([20]). Due to space limitation we present only one combination: immediate E-C with seperated C-A coupling mode. We choose such combination in order the reader to grasp the underlying ideas.

Not only is it important to define the coupling mode of triggers but it is also of crucial importance to be able to specify whether the execution of a trigger is to be atomic or not and whether concurrent executions of triggers are allowed.

The problem of trigger atomicity raises when the action part of a rule may fire another trigger. At this point, it is necessary to know whether the rule which raises the triggering event will be suspended to execute the other triggers or whether the triggering event is to be delayed until the action part of the firing rule is completed. In the former case, the rule is said *interruptible*: its execution will be suspended until all recursively fired triggers terminate. In the latter case, the rule is said *atomic*: the execution of all other potentially triggered rules is delayed until the action part has completed.

Notice that an atomic policy for triggers imposes some kind of precedence with respect to coupling mode. In fact, if an atomic rule R triggers another rule R' whose event-condition mode is immediate then the evaluation of the condition part of R' will not be immediate anymore but will rather be performed at the end of R. The choice for atomicity is specified in an ad-hoc way when the trigger is actually defined.

In most ADBS, an event may fire several triggers. We are then faced with the following alternative: either forcing a sequential execution of rules or allowing a concurrent execution (provided that the data base run time system allows for such a concurrent execution). The first possibility is usually achieved by requiring the trigger designer to specify some kind of order among rules. As we think that imposing such an order is too arbitrary we place ourselves in the more general framework of concurrent execution of triggers.

3 Related Works

During the last decade, a lot of works have been devoted to the design and implementation of triggers in DBS leading to the generic field of active data bases. This research yielded many prototypes or products either relational [12, 29, 7, 10], object-oriented [14, 8] or deductive [22, 6].

All those systems define their own vision of the ECA model. Such differences are mainly due to the fact that there does not exist a clear and well understood semantics for such a model.

However, the need for defining such a semantics has been pointed out and in particular, the potential benefits expected with respect to trigger termination, observability and confluence has been one of the strongest motivations for several works.

In [30, 9] a denotational semantics has been proposed for the relational and object-oriented models respectively. Though such a formalism is well-suited, due to its flexibility, to give a semantics to triggers in most of current systems, it does not address operational aspects.

Meanwhile, attempts to give a deductive-based semantics for triggers have been followed [31, 18]. In general, those attempts are not able to take into account all specificities of triggers. Only a restricted class of triggers is considered and neither with the coupling mode is dealt with nor with atomicity or concurrency. In [27, 26], the idea of using Petri nets to give a semantics for triggers have been first pointed out. However, the first work only suggests such a use and never really shows how to do it. The second work constitutes a more in-depth application of Petri nets but again, only a very small part of the execution model is captured (the coupling modes are not taken into account). Both works lack the use for high-level Petri nets. In this paper we propose to extensively make use of a specific kind of Petri nets: the M-nets. Such nets, allowing for compositionality are particularly well-suited to give a semantics for the general

ECA model presented in section 2. A preliminary presentation of parts of this work can be found in [20].

4 The M-net Model

The main difference between M-nets and predicate/transition or coloured nets [17, 21] is that M-nets carry additional information in their place and transition inscriptions to support composition operations. In M-nets, besides the usual annotations on places (set of allowed tokens), arcs (multiset of variables) and transitions (occurrence condition), we have an additional label on places denoting their status (entry, exit or internal) and an additional label on transitions, denoting the communication and hierarchical interface. We give a comprehensive introduction to the M-net model. More detailed descriptions of the model and its algebraic properties can be found in [4, 3, 5, 11].

Let Val be a fixed but suitable large set of $values$, and Var a set of $variables$. We assume the existence of a fixed but sufficiently large set A of $actions$. Each action $A \in$ A is assumed to have an arity $ar(A) \in \mathbb{N}$ which gives the number of its parameters. The set A is, by definition, the carrier of a bijection: $: A \to A$, called $conjugation$, satisfying $\forall A \in A : \overline{A} \neq A \wedge \overline{\overline{A}} = A$. It is assumed that $\forall A \in A : ar(A) = ar(\overline{A})$. A construct $A(\tau_1, \ldots, \tau_{ar(A)})$, where A is an action and $\forall j : 1 \leq j \leq ar(A) : \tau_j \in Var \cup Val$, is a $parameterised\ action$.

We also assume the existence of a fixed but suitably large set X of $hierarchical$ $actions$. The latter will be the key to substitutions, and thus to any hierarchical presentation of a system, since they represent a kind of 'hole' to be later replaced by some corresponding M-net.

Definition 1. *An M-net is a triple* (S, T, ι) *such that S is a set of places, T is a set of transitions with $S \cap T = \emptyset$, and ι is an inscription function with domain $S \cup (S \times T) \cup (T \times S) \cup T$ such that:*

i) For every place $s \in S$, $\iota(s)$ is a pair $\lambda(s).\alpha(s)$, where $\alpha(s)$, the type of s, is a nonempty set of values from Val, and $\lambda(s) \subseteq \{e, i, x\}$, also nonempty, is called the label of s.

ii) For every transition $t \in T$, $\iota(t)$ is a pair $\lambda(t).\alpha(t)$, where $\lambda(t)$, the label of t, is a finite multiset of parameterised actions, or a hierarchical action symbol, i.e., $\lambda(t) \in X$; $\alpha(t)$, the guard of t, is a multiset of terms over Val, Var and a set of suitable operators.

iii) For every arc $(s, t) \in (S \times T)$ $\iota((s, t))$ is a finite multiset of variables from Var and values respecting the type of the adjacent place s, (analogous for arcs $(t, s) \in (T \times S)$).

The arc inscriptions specify the variables and constants by which tokens flow. An empty arc inscription means that no tokens may ever flow along that arc, i.e., there exists no effective connection along it.

Each type $\alpha(s)$ delimits the set of tokens allowed on s, and $\lambda(s)$ describes the $status$ (entry e, internal i or exit x) of a place s. It is for instance possible that an entry place plays the rôle of a run place, in this case, it is also internal, i.e., $\lambda(s) = \{\mathsf{e}, \mathsf{i}\}$. The label $\lambda(s)$ drives place-based composition operations. For instance, composing two M-nets sequentially means that the exit places of the first net are combined with the entry places of the second net and become internal places in the combined net [4, 3]. A typical place inscription is $\iota(s) = \{\mathsf{i}\}.\{0, 1\}$, in figures denoted i.$\{0, 1\}$, meaning that s is internal and may hold tokens 0 and 1.

The transition label $\lambda(t)$ drives transition based composition operations. For instance, as in CCS, transition synchronisation is driven by conjugate actions, in the labels of two transitions. A typical transition inscription is

$$\iota(t) = \{A(a, b), \overline{B}(b, c)\}.\{a = 1, b > 0\}.$$

For the enabling of t a binding σ has to be found, such that σ binds all variables in the inscription of t and in all its input and output arcs. The guard, $\alpha(t)$ plays the rôle of an *occurrence condition* in the sense that t may occur under a binding σ only if each member of $\alpha(t)$ is *true* for σ.

A *marking* of an M-net (S, T, ι) is a mapping $M : S \to \mathcal{M}_f(Val)$ which associates to each place $s \in S$ a finite multiset of values from $\alpha(s)$. A transition t is *enabled* at a marking M if there is a (enabling) binding σ of t such that the variables on its input arcs are bound by tokens from the corresponding input places and the guard $\alpha(t)$ is true. The effect of an occurrence of t is to remove all tokens used for the enabling binding σ of t from the input places and to add tokens according to σ to its output places.

In [4, 3] an algebra of M-nets was defined comprising operations like sequential composition (;), parallel composition ($\|$), iteration ([$*$ $*$]), choice ($\square$), synchronisation (**sy**) and restriction (**rs**). This algebra was applied in [5] for a semantics of a parallel block-oriented programming language B(PN)^2. In that work the main idea in describing a block was to juxtapose the M-net semantics for its declarations of variables and the semantics for its command, to synchronise over all matching (conjugate) actions of the data (declaration) part and the control (command) part, and then to restrict them in order to make local variables invisible outside the block. A similar scheme will be used in defining a compositional semantics for active data bases. The key operation will be here the synchronisation, so we will sketch briefly its definition.

The intuitive idea behind the synchronisation operation of an M-net consists of a conglomeration of certain basic synchronisations. The definition is splitted into two parts: general synchronisation scheme and basic synchronisation.

Definition 2. *(Synchronisation scheme) Let $N = (S, T, \iota)$ be an M-net and A an action. The net $N' = N$ **sy** $A = (S', T', \iota')$ is defined as the smallest M-net satisfying:*

(a) *The set of places of N and N' (and their inscriptions) are the same: $S = S'$.*
(b) *Every transition of N (and its set of surrounding arcs) is also in N', with the same inscriptions as in N.*

(c) If t_1 is a transition of N and t_2 a transition of N', such that one of them contains a parameterised action $A(.)$ in its label and the other one a parameterised action $\overline{A}(.)$, then any transition t arising through a basic synchronisation out of t_1 and t_2 over A (and its surrounding arcs) is also in N'.

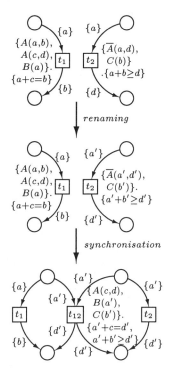

Fig. 1. Explanation of the basic synchronisation in creating N **sy** A.

To illustrate the above synchronisation scheme consider Fig. 1. The upper part of the figure shows two transitions, t_1 and t_2 which contain conjugate actions in their labels: t_1 contains $A(.,.)$ (twice) and t_2 contains $\overline{A}(.,.)$ (once). This implies, that t_1 and t_2 can be synchronised over A and yield two new transitions, depending on which of the action $A(.,.)$ is chosen from the label of t_1 to be matched with the action $\overline{A}(a,d)$ of the label of t_2.

Let us choose the first, i.e., $A(a,b)$. Matching $A(a,b)$ with $\overline{A}(a,d)$ creates a new transition t_{12} from t_1 and t_2 in two steps, which are depicted in Fig. 1. First, the variables in the areas of t_1 and t_2 are substituted in order to make $var(t_1)$ and $var(t_2)$ disjoint. This is necessary because by synchronisation, the two areas of t_1 and t_2 are combined to a new single area. Thus we consider two renamings ρ_1 (pertaining to t_1) and ρ_2 (pertaining to t_2). The variables in the area of t_1 are substituted through ρ_1 by themself. In the area of t_2 a is substituted through ρ_2 by a', b by b' and d by d'. The middle part of Fig. 1 shows the two transition after these renamings.

Next, we look for a unifier θ for the vectors (a,b) and (a',d') corresponding to the parameters of A and $\overline{A}$, respectively. We may take $\theta = (a/a', b/d')$. In the second step, a new transition t_{12} is created. The label of t_{12} is the multiset sum of the two constituent labels, substituted by θ, minus the matching pair of actions. The annotation of t_{12} is the union of the two constituent annotations (modulo θ). The same happens with the arcs around t_{12}. The lower part of Fig. 1 shows t_{12} with its full annotation, but, for brevity, the annotations of t_1 and t_2 have been omitted (they are the same as in the top row of the figure).

Had we initially chosen the action $A(c,d)$ to be synchronised with the action $\overline{A}(a,d)$ of t_2, then we would have different substitutions, and a different (not renaming equivalent) transition t'_{12} would have resulted. The transition t_{12} contains an action $A(.,.)$ and it can again be synchronised with transition t_2 which contains an action $\overline{A}(.,.)$ (this is what was meant by a conglomeration of the basic synchronisation).

Another important operation for our application is the M-net substitution (which can be seen as a very simple case of a refinement) allowing a stepwise construction of nets. The M-net substitution $N[X_i \leftarrow N_i \mid i \in I]$ is only allowed for hierarchical transitions t_i (labeled X_i) which have exactly one input and one output place. Moreover, the entry places of the substituting nets N_i have to have the same type as the input place of t_i, and similarly for the exit places of N_i and the output place of t_i. Under these restrictions the M-net substitution $N[X_i \leftarrow N_i \mid i \in I]$ can be applied and means 'N where all X_i-labeled transitions are replaced by a copy of N_i, for each i in the indexing set I'. The nets N_i simply replace hierarchical transitions t_i, their surrounding arcs and input and output places. The entry places of N_i inherit all input connections that the input place of t_i had, and similarly for the exit places of N_i.

5 An ECA Semantics in the M-net Calculus

5.1 Generic Boxes for the ECA Model

The great complexity of the execution model of triggers makes it difficult to develop a global representation of all its components and internal relationships. A formal description, direct and complete, of all the aspects of the ECA model is no longer feasible because of the number of relationships between various components of ADB. As a consequence, the only approach which seems reasonable would be to consider independently some basic parts of the model, establish their formal representations in order to make then links between them.

It turns out that the M-net Calculus offers the needed capability of a compositional design. M-nets are able to express in a compositional way the control structures (programs) as well as the manipulated data. It means that in order to obtain a global model providing a semantics for triggers, it is not necessary to give a direct representation of a complex system of ADB, but it would be enough to identify the principal conceptual units and compose the models obtained for each of them using composition operations given by the M-net formalism.

We have seen in the informal description of the ECA model that a semantics of triggers need to be expressed dynamically as a common execution of the data base with its rule system and a set of user-launched transactions. Then it clearly appears that the elements to take into account in establishing a formal semantics are on one hand the data: the permanent DB and its temporary copies, contained in what we call the Distributed Data Base, including also the management of concurrent access to the data. This part would be a less original work because already managed in a similar way in [28] with standard coloured Petri nets. As in this paper, we assume that the DB itself contains all basic data as tokens. Thus, we choose not to treat here this part of modeling, and an M-net for this data part will be considered as given. This net will play the rôle of the Data Boxes in the semantics of concurrent programs, cf. [5]. On the other hand we need to consider the transactions, the rules with their coupling modes and the management of all these parts. Here, we are really able to present an original study.

The M-nets associated to the transactions will play the rôle of the Control Boxes in concurrent programming. However, the expression of the rules is the most complicate one. It seems to be necessary to define a new family of M-nets providing a representation of the rule system, i.e., for the set of triggers in charge of the dynamic behaviour of the data base. This third family of M-nets, called Rule Boxes, does not really correspond to any other previously cited families of Boxes. In fact, Rule Boxes have the particularity to be similar to Control Boxes (because they concern a set of programs working on the data of the DB using operations of their Condition and Action parts), and to Data Boxes (because their event part is formed from conjugate actions representing events associated with the operation of a transaction, or operations from an action part of a rule or from actions belonging to the external environment).

So, the model will be based on two principal classes of Boxes: Transaction Boxes and Rule Boxes.

5.2 The Semantics of the Active Data Base

The semantics of triggers is given compositionally by basic Boxes and the operations on M-nets. We start with the global definition where we use several basic Boxes, which will be defined in the sequel. We obtain the entire M-net, Box_ADB, by instantiation (substitution) and composition of the different associated Boxes. All basic Boxes proposed here are M-nets which can be (and will be) composed by the operations of the M-net algebra. In order to observe the behaviour of the triggers, we need to model the dynamic ADB, i.e., Box_ADB, together with a certain number of user-launched transactions on this ADB. Thus, the entire M-net semantics is given by the following expression:

$[[Box\_ADB\|Box\_Transactions]$ **sy** $\{A\_Trans, A\_Abort\}]$ **rs** $\{A\_DBdyn\}$

with the following definitions for particular Boxes:

$Box\_ADB = [Box\_distrDB\|Box\_Triggers\|Box\_CreaTrans\|Box\_Def]$
　　　　　sy $\{A\_Start, A\_Def\}$, where

$Box\_Triggers = Box\_Rule_1\|\ldots\|Box\_Rule_n$, for some n and for $i \leq n$:

　$Box\_Rule_i = ((Box\_R_i[EVENT \longleftarrow Box\_E_i])[BODY \longleftarrow Box\_BodyR_i])$,

$Box\_Transactions = (Box\_Trans_1\|\ldots\|Box\_Trans_m)$,

　for some m and for $j \leq m$:

　$Box\_Trans_j = [Box\_T_j[BODY \longleftarrow Box\_BodyT_j]\|Box\_Abort_j]$ **sy** A_DB.

To complete, we use the following sets of action names in the Boxes, over which synchronisations and restrictions are defined above:

$A\_Start = \{Mount2, Unmount2\} \cup \{MountR_i, UnmountR_i \mid i \leq n\}$

$A\_Def = \{DeferedR_i \mid i \leq n\}$

$A\_DB = \{Bot, Eot, TBegin1, TCommit1, TAbort1, NewT\}$

$A\_Op = \{Insert, Update, Delete, Select\}$

$A\_Event = \{e_1, \ldots, e_k\}$ is the set of action names for simple events

$A\_Triggering = \{TriggeringRi, NonTriggeringRi, TriggeringDefRi,$
　　　　　　$EndRi, StartDef, EndDef \mid i \leq n\}$

$$\mathcal{A}\_Trans = \{TBegin0, TCommit0, TBegin2, TCommit2\} \cup \mathcal{A}\_Op \cup \mathcal{A}\_Event$$
$$\cup \mathcal{A}\_Triggering \cup \{TBeginRi, TCommitRi \mid i \leq n\}$$
$$\mathcal{A}\_Abort = \{TAbort, Abort, EmptyDef\} \cup \{EmptyRi \mid i \leq n\},$$
$$\mathcal{A}\_DBdyn = \mathcal{A}\_Start \cup \mathcal{A}\_Def \cup \mathcal{A}\_DB \cup \mathcal{A}\_Trans \cup \mathcal{A}\_Abort.$$

As indicated in the introduction and section 5.1, we assume that for the distributed DB kernel (the DB, the temporary copies of the DB, the management of concurrent access to the DB) an M-net is given. We call it $Box\_distrDB$. For each action $A \in \mathcal{A}\_DB \cup \mathcal{A}\_Op$, $\overline{A}$ appears in the communication interface of $Box\_distrDB$ (i.e., as a label of some of its transitions). As we only treat one combination of coupling modes, due to space limitation, we do not present here Box_Def which manages the defered triggering rules (and in which all action names containing Def appear). This Box_Def can be found in [20]. All the other basic Boxes will be defined explicitly in the following subsections.

5.3 Transaction Boxes

Transactions might be seen as small "programs" which are executed in parallel. Each of these programs starts always by the initialisation $TBegin$ and ends either by an validation via the command $TCommit$, by an explicit abort when the command $TAbort$ is executed, or as well by an implicit failure $(Abort)$ when it emerges from an external failure signal (from another rule or the system). The body of such a program consists of sequentially composed elementary operations of the data base, which can be Insert, Update, Delete, Select.

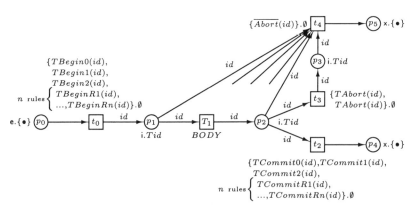

Fig. 2. Transaction Box: Box_T_i

We can associate to each transaction a "Transaction Box", called Box_T_i (See Fig. 2), which plays the rôle of a Control Box in the semantics of parallel programming languages. Such a Box provides the representation of the general structure for transactions. We distinguish between the initialisation and the termination, represented by transitions t_0 and t_2, t_3 and t_4, respectively. The body of the transaction is given by the hierarchical transition T_1. Transitions t_0, t_2, t_3 and t_4 are labeled by actions which allow a synchronisation with $Box\_distrBD$ for the temporary copy of the DB associated to the current transaction and with each rule Box, as well as with a certain number of other Boxes which are necessary for the dynamics of the system (cf. section 5.5). For instance, *TBeginRi(id)* provokes synchronisation with the corresponding action in the Box for rule i having as effect that the identifier *id* of the transaction being available in the Box for rule i.

The current body of a rule is obtained by refining the hierarchical transition T_1. The refining box, Box_BodyT_i, is defined accordingly to a construction rule which depends on the operations that have to be executed, their associated triggering and non triggering events as well as the coupling mode of the triggered rules.

Let us describe the construction of Box_BodyT_i in four steps:

First: Each elementary operation which act on the temporary data base for this transaction, is represented by a transition labeled by $\alpha.\beta$, where α is the correspondent parameterised action from A_Op and β the condition specified by the operation.

Second: These operations and the initialisation and termination commands of the transaction may generate simple events before and/or after their execution. Each of these simple events which may trigger one or several rules of our DBS gives also rise of a transition. This transition is labeled by a set of action names whose cardinality depends on the number k of rules which await this event. Furthermore, it is placed in the substituting box, just before the transition for the operation generating the event if it is a *BEFORE* event or just after it if it is an *AFTER* event. The latter one of these two transitions in sequence will receive k output places.

Third: For each one of these output places (i.e., for each possibly triggered rule) we add two alternating transitions, having this place as input. The first one being labeled *Non-triggering* and the other one labeled *Triggering*. If the E-C coupling mode is immediate, the latter one is followed by a transition *end of rule* which allows to suspend the current transaction. This part allows the synchronisation of the possible triggering of the rules with the current transaction. In fact, whenever an event is awaited by at least one rule this implies
- either the triggering of these rules if it is the only triggering event for the rules or if all other waiting events have already been executed in the desired order,
- or a non triggering if other events are necessary for the triggering of the rules or if the events did not occur in the wanted order.

Fourth: All these basic parts are composed together using sequence, choice, etc. according to the code of the transaction, as it is done for $B(PN)^2$ programs [5].

5.4 Rule Boxes

Triggers might as well be seen as small programs which are executed in parallel. These programs are activated by *Mount* when starting the system (cf. Fig. 7) and they are terminated by *Unmount* when ending the session. They have the particularity to be event-triggered: the event part of each rule describes some combination of simple events which need to appear in this combination for the rest of the program to be executed. The operations which have to be executed

then are a sequence of operations on the DB grouped in the Condition part (IF
...) and the Action part (DO ...).

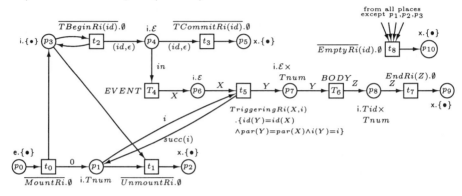

Fig. 3. Rule Box: Box_R_i

Fig. 3 shows the representation of a trigger: a Box Box_R_i $(i \leq n)$ is associated to
each one of the n rules. The Box is a scheme of the general structure of a trigger,
which consists of two parts: the *event part* and the *rule body*. The first specifies
the simple or composite event which will trigger the rule, the latter includes
the condition and action parts which give the access and updating operations
of the data base, as well as the execution strategy of the rule. The two parts
are represented by two hierarchical transitions T_4 and T_6 and are adjacent to
several other places and transitions. Each of these transitions corresponds to
a specific step in the process of triggering the trigger. We distinguish between
the actions for the activation and for the deactivation of the rule. The *Mount*
and *Unmount* commands of the DB are described by two transitions t_0 and
t_1 which put, respectively remove, the token of the run-place $p3$. In the same
way transitions t_2 and t_3 correspond to the actions of the initialisation and
validation of the transaction. They provide the identifiers which are necessary in
order to identify events. The triggering phase is started, when the event which
was awaited by the rule is detected. During this phase a number identifying the
triggering is added to the token which circulates in the M-net. This is done by
transition t_5 which represents as well the fact that *EVENT* was detected and
that *BODY* might be executed. The inscription of transition t_5 depends on the
coupling mode E-C. It wears the action name *Triggering* for immediate E-C of
the rule R_i (or *TriggeringDef* for defered E-C, not shown here). The end of the
triggering phase is indicated by transition t_7. It provides the necessary signal to
the current transaction or other rules which await the end of the execution of
the rule for their own resumption.

Event Part: The syntax of the event part in the generalised ECA model (see
section 2) is given by an event algebra built from simple events by the control
connectives $\wedge$, $\vee$, ;, $ANY(\ldots)$, $TIMES(\ldots)$, Not, $\star$, and $In[\ldots]$. Thus, the simple
or composite event is given by a term E_i of this algebra.

319

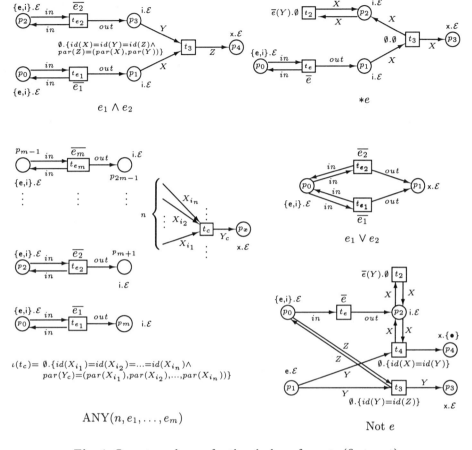

Fig. 4. Operator schemes for the algebra of events (first part)

The event part of Fig. 3 is obtained by a substitution of the hierarchical transition T_4. The substituting M-net needs to recognise the sequence of events described by the expression E_i between all generated events.

We associate to each simple event e a transition t_e, which is labeled with the action name of the event $\bar{e}$. It has one entry and one exit place which have the same type $\mathcal{E} = Tid \times Tpar*$ which can be marked with the identifiers of the current transaction together with a list of parameters. This list is initially empty (ϵ) in place p_4 in Fig. 3, and contains in the exit place the parameters *param* of the generated event. The precise label is $\iota(t_e) = \{\bar{e}(param)\}.\{id(in) = id(out) \wedge par(out) = par(in), param\}$, where *in* and *out* are the inscriptions of the incoming, respectively outgoing arc of t_e; in figures, however, we will only indicate the label by $\bar{e}$. The entry place is in fact a run place, since further occurrences of event e by the current transactions are possible; so its status is $\{e, i\}$.

320

For an internal event the firing is enabled by the event transition preceding or following the generating operation (see section 5.3). For temporary or external ones it is enabled because the transitions of their respective event generators are fired.

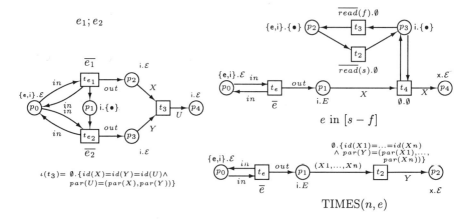

Fig. 5. Operator schemes for the algebra of events (second part)

Fig. 4 and Fig. 5 gives the schemes which are associated by the semantical function to each operator of the algebra of events.

The internal transitions of such a scheme which allow to check the necessary conditions for the construction of composite events (e.g., $id_{e1} = id_{e2}$ in the scheme of the $\wedge$ construct), corresponds to a non-triggering state of the rule. They are connected to internal places, also of type $\mathcal{E}$, which are marked with the transaction identifiers and the event parameters resulting from the concatenation of the parameters of each appeared simple event which enter in the connection.

Let us explain some of the schemes. In the net for $ANY(n, e_1, \ldots, e_m)$ we have for each choice c of n events $\{e_{i_1}, \ldots, e_{i_n}\}$ in $\{e_1, \ldots, e_m\}$ a transition t_c having $p_{i_1+m-1}, \ldots, p_{i_n+m-1}$ as entry places and p_x as output place; in particular p_x is the only exit place of the net. Concerning the net for e in $[s - f]$, notice that the place p_3 is a run place during the time interval $[s - f]$.

The operator schemes in Fig. 4 and Fig. 5 are slightly simplified, since there are in fact additional internal transitions, corresponding to non-triggering states, which specify complementary conditions to those necessary for the construction of the composite event, e.g., $id_{e1} \neq id_{e2}$ in the scheme of the $\wedge$ construct. Although, these transitions are necessary for a correct event detection, they do not change the current state of the concerned temporary data bases. Thus they are omitted in our presentation for the sake of simplicity.

Applied to an expression of the event algebra, the semantical scheme of the associated M-net algebra of Fig. 4 and Fig. 5 generates an M-net Box_E_i, which may refine the hierarchical transition T_4 of Fig. 3.

321

Body: The body of a rule comprises the condition and the action part of the trigger. It is obtained by substituting the hierarchical transition T_6 by the M-net Box_BodyR_i, depicted in Fig. 6. In general, Box_BodyR_i starts directly with the condition part.

The condition part itself starts with the hierarchical transition T_1 which insures the selection of the data necessary for the evaluation of the predicates. It is followed by two alternative transitions, one for the condition being true, t_2, and one for being false, t_3. More precisely, T_1 groups the set of operations for the selection in the temporary data base allowing to collect the necessary data for the verification of the condition. In its substituting net each selection operation is represented by a transition which is labeled with an instantiation of the data base operation *select*. Each of these transitions returns a set of values which describes the state of the data base at the associated instance. They are concatenated with the parameters which are already present in the token, so they can be used by the following operations and for the evaluation of the condition. Then, depending on the truth of the condition, one of the two transitions t_2 or t_3 is fired. The firing of t_2 leads to continue with the body of the rule, while firing of t_3 corresponds to an exit of the rule without executing the action part.

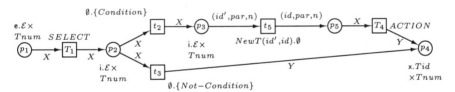

Fig. 6. Refinement of the hierarchical transition BODY: Box_BodyR_i

If the condition is satisfied, i.e., t_2 is fired, the action part of the rule (represented by the hierarchical transition T_4) will be executed. The substituting M-net contains usually an event generating data base operation which might itself trigger one or several rules. Therefore, it is constructed similarly to the transaction body. The differences concern the coupling mode C-A of the rule and the atomicity of the execution. The C-A coupling mode separated implies that the action part of the rule has to be executed in a new transaction concurrently to the others. Thus we have a transition t_5 labeled *NewT* which synchronises with $Box\_distrDB$ creating a new transaction with new identifier heriting in the temporary DB the state of the transaction having triggered the rule. Fig. 6 shows the M-net with E-C coupling mode immediate and C-A coupling mode separated.

Furthermore, this action part uses not only the construction rule of the M-net Box_BodyT_i but as well a part of that of Box_T_i (see Fig. 2). The second difference takes into account the choice of the atomicity of the rule, i.e., certain rules cannot be interrupted during their execution in order to execute those which were triggered. Therefore, the construction of Box_BodyT_i is modified such that the triggering and non triggering transitions are placed in parallel at the end of the body of the rule, instead of putting them right after the *event*

322

transition. The triggering of the rule is done as well at the end and the atomicity of the rules is taken into account.

Finally, it is necessary to allow an abortion of the transaction before starting with the set of rules being executed, see Fig. 3. Therefore, transition t_8 is introduced. It represents the reception of an abort signal (coming from the abort Box of the next section) for a transition with identifier *id*. The firing rule for this transition is slightly particular (i.e., not simulable by using the usual firing rule but implementable in an easy way): if transaction *id* sends an abort signal, t_8 empties explicitly each place of the Box which is marked with a token whose identifier is *id*. By doing so, each rule Box, where we removed the tokens for the aborted transaction, will be in a coherent state.

5.5 M-nets Necessary for the Dynamic Behaviour of the Model

M-net Generating the Transaction Identifiers As mentioned above, the representation of all conceptual units need an identifier *id*, which references one of (several possible) transactions occuring at the same time. This identifier appears at the initialisation of a transaction by the command $\overline{TBegin0}$, as well by all commands *TBeginRi* in all other parts (rules, ...) by synchronisation with Box_T_i from Fig. 2, and is preserved during the execution as a part of any token flowing through the M-nets for conceptual units, finally it is deleted by the command of the validation or the abort of the transaction.

The link between the identifier *id* and its corresponding transaction is made by the M-net, depicted in Fig. 7, called $Box\_CreaTrans$.

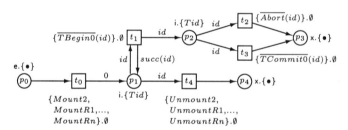

Fig. 7. Box for the generation of transaction identifiers: $Box\_CreaTrans$

Transitions t_0 and t_4 of this M-net are dedicated to the activation and the deactivation of the data base. In other words, they correspond to commands *MountRi* and *UnmountRi* (where each *Ri* refers to a trigger rule of the DB). These transitions synchronise with those of the rule Box $Box\_Triggers$. Their firing correspond on one hand to the start of the data base, and on the other hand its stop. Between these two stages, there are several transactions coming from users or from the system, which are all distinguishable by their identifiers. The identifiers come from the run place p_1 which is initialised during the activation of the data base. This place contains at each time the identifier available for the next transaction. It is connected to a transition t_1 labeled by the action of the initialisation of transactions $TBegin_0$, which synchronises with the corresponding transition in the transaction box. The place p_2 (output place of t_1) stores identifiers of transactions which are in progress. These identifiers are present in p_2 until the corresponding transactions are stopped by a validation ($TCommit0$) or an abort ($Abort$) performed in the Transaction Box (i.e., until the transition t_2 or t_3 is fired). This generation of transaction identifiers allows us to know at any time which transactions are in progress.

M-net for Aborting a Transaction The problem of aborting a transaction has already been mentioned in the previous sections. Thus, while each of these nets is able to take into account this aborting by eliminating corresponding tokens, they cannot communicate it to each other. In order to solve this problem, an M-net Box_Abort_i is introduced for aborting each transaction. It is in charge to communicate to all Boxes the necessity to begin their "empty" process for tokens of the aborted transaction.

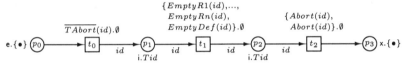

Fig. 8. Box for the abort of a transaction: Box_Abort_i

This Box begins with the transition t_0 labeled by the conjugate of the action $TAbort$. The firing of this transition occurs only in the case of an explicit abort of the transaction id, and it is followed by the firing of the transition t_1 labeled by the actions $EmptyR_i$ whose effect is to send the signal to abort the transaction id to each rule Box. The firing of t_1 activates the "empty" process in all concerned Boxes. When the tokens are eliminated, it is enough to suppress also the token with id from the transaction Box in order to correctly finish the action of aborting. This is done by transition t_2 labeled by the action $Abort$ which sends the necessary signal.

This finishes the presentation of the M-nets entering in the global semantics of the dynamic ADBS. These M-nets are put side by side as concurrent parts of the whole net. Their correct interaction is ensured by the synchronisations specified in section 5.2, followed by final restriction over the set of all action names.

6 Conclusion

We have provided the triggers in active data base systems with a high level Petri net semantics. We have extensively made use of the modularity features of the M-net Calculus and established thus a fully compositional model.

The central part of this work is the definition of the event algebra in the domain of M-nets. In our knowledge, no other (Petri net or other) framework possesses an equally large set of possibilities.

The integrated treatment of several coupling modes of triggers may be seen as an original aspect of our semantics. It is indeed the first attempt in this area. It makes possible the observability of executions under those modes by the study of the net behaviour. This is a well known area: by executing the M-net, i.e. by tracing the concurrent behaviour (its process or partial word semantics), respectively its interleaved behaviour (its firing sequences) all possible executions on the data base can be observed. Another motivation for formal modeling is to obtain proofs of properties such as termination or confluence, for a set of triggers of an active data base system. Termination corresponds to the reachability of the natural final marking of the whole M-net (all exit places need to be marked and only them). To prove such properties, surely we would like to use verification methods and tools like PEP [19] (which works on M-nets and the underlying low level Petri net model). Although, the work presented in this article seems to be a promising starting point in this direction, there is still some work to do. We intend to complete the modeling in the M-net model in such a way that an effective use of model checking techniques becomes soon possible. Nevertheless, defining a formal trigger semantics is an essential step towards the analysis of ADBS.

References

1. E. Best. A Memory Module Specification using Composable High Level Petri Nets. Formal Systems Specification, The RPC-Memory Specification Case Study, LNCS Vol. 1169, 109–160 (1996).
2. E. Best, R. Devillers, and J.G. Hall. The Box Calculus: a New Causal Algebra with Multilabel Communication. *Advances in Petri Nets 92.* LNCS Vol. 609, 21–69 (1992).
3. E. Best, H. Fleischhack, W. Fraczak, R.P. Hopkins, H. Klaudel, and E. Pelz. A Class of Composable High Level Petri Nets. *ICPN'95.* LNCS Vol. 935, 103–120 (1995).
4. E. Best, W. Fraczak, R.P. Hopkins, H. Klaudel, and E. Pelz. M-nets: An Algebra of High-level Petri Nets with an Application to the Semantics of Concurrent Programming Languages. To Appear in *Acta Informatica.*
5. E. Best, H. Fleischhack, W. Fraczak, R.P. Hopkins, H. Klaudel, and E. Pelz. An M-Net Semantics of $B(PN)^2$. *STRICT'95* Proceedings. Springer, 85–100 (1995).
6. S. Ceri and J. Widom. Deriving Production Rules for Constraint Maintenance. Proc. 16. Int. Conf. on Very Large Data Bases, 566–577, (1990).
7. S. Chakravarthy, V.K. E. Anwar, and A.K. Kim. Composite Events for Active Databases: Semantics, Contexts and Detection. *Proc. 20. Int. Conf. on Very Large Data Bases*, 606–617, (1994).
8. C. Collet, T. Coupaye and T. Svensen. NAOS - Efficient and modular reactive capabilities in an Object-Oriented Database System. *Proc. 20. Int. Conf. on Very Large Data Bases*, 132–143, (1994).
9. T. Coupaye and C. Collet. Denotational Semantics for Active Rule Execution Model. LNCS Vol. 985, 36–50, (1995).
10. U. Dayal, E. Hanson, and J. Widom. Active Database Systems. *Modern Database Systems*, 434–456, (1995).
11. R. Devillers, H. Klaudel and R.-C. Riemann. General Refinement for High Level Petri Nets. *FSTTCS'97*, LNCS Vol. 1346, 297–311, (1997).

12. K.P. Eswaran. Specifications, Implementations and Interactions of a Trigger Subsystem in an Integrated Database System. IBM Research Laboratory, Report RJ 1820, (1976).

13. P. Fraternali and L. Tanca. A Structured Approach for the Definition of the Semantics of Active Databases. *ACM Transactions on Database Systems*, 20(4):414–471, (1995).

14. S. Gatziu and K.R. Dittrich. Events in an Active Object-Oriented Database System. *Proc. 1. Int. Workshop on Rules in Database Systems*, 23–39, (1993).

15. S. Gatziu and K.R. Dittrich. Detecting Composite Events in Active Database Systems Using Petri Nets. *Proc. 4. Int. Workshop on Research Issues in Data Engineering*, 1–8, (1994).

16. N.H. Gehani, H.V. Jagadish, and O. Shmueli. Composite Event Specification in Active Databases: Model and Implementation. *Proc. 18. Int. Conf. on Very Large Data Bases*, 327–338, (1992).

17. H. Genrich. Predicate-Transition Nets. In *Petri Nets: Central Models and their Properties, Advances in Petri Nets 1986 Part I*. LNCS Vol. 254, 207–247 (1987).

18. G. Gottlob, G. Moerkotte, and V.S. Subrahmaniam. The PARK Semantics for Active Rules. LNCS Vol. 1057, 35–55, (1996).

19. B. Grahlmann and E. Best. PEP - More than a Petri Net Tool. TACAS'96, LNCS Vol. 1055, 397-401 (1996).

20. N. Hugon. Une Sémantique pour les Triggers. Memoire de DEA, Théorie et Ingénierie des Bases de Données, Universities Paris I and Paris-Sud, (1996).

21. K. Jensen *Coloured Petri Nets. Basic Concepts, Analysis Methods and Practical Use. EATCS Monographs on Theoretical Computer Science*, Vol. 1 Springer (1992).

22. J. Kiernan and C. de Maindreville and E. Simon. The Design and Implementation of an Extensible Deductive Database System. SIGMOD Records, (1989).

23. J. Lilius. OB(PN)^2: An Object Based Petri Net Programming Notation. Euro-Par'96, Parallel Processing, Second Int. Euro-Par Conference. LNCS Vol. 1123, 660–663 (1996). .

24. J. Lilius and E. Pelz. An M-net Semantics for B(PN)^2 with Procedures. Proc. 11. Int. Symposium on Computer and System Science, 365–374, (1996).

25. R. Meo, G. Psaila, and S. Ceri. Composite Events in Chimera. LNCS Vol. 1057, 56–76, (1996).

26. W. Naqvi and M.T. Ibrahim. REFLEX Active Database Model: Application of Petri-Nets. LNCS Vol. 720, 233–240, (1993).

27. S.B. Navathe, A.K. Tanaka, and S. Chakravarthy. Active Database Modeling and Design Tools: Issues, Approach, and Architecture. *IEEE Bulletin of the Technical Commite on Data Engineering*, 15(1–4):6–9, (1992).

28. K. Voss. Petri Nets for Information Systems Modelling. *ICPN'95*. LNCS Vol. 935, 23–24 (1995). Full Version as: Arbeitspapiere der GMD, Nr. 1004, June 1996.

29. J. Widom. The Starburst Rule System. IEEE Data Engineering Bulletin, 15:1-4, 15–18, (1992).

30. J. Widom. A Denotational Semantics for the Starburst Production Rule Language, SIGMOD Record, 21:3, pages 4–9, (1992).

31. C. Zaniolo. A Unified Semantics for Active and Deductive Databases. Proc. 1. Int. Workshop on Rules in Database Systems, 271–287, (1993).

SWN Analysis and Simulation
of Large Knockout ATM Switches

Rossano Gaeta[1] and Marco Ajmone Marsan[2]

[1] Dipartimento di Informatica, Università di Torino
Corso Svizzera 185, 10149, Torino, Italy
rossano@di.unito.it
[2] Dipartimento di Elettronica, Politecnico di Torino
Corso Duca degli Abruzzi 24, 10129, Torino, Italy
ajmone@polito.it

Abstract. This paper approaches the performance evaluation of large
ATM switches with Stochastic Well-formed Nets (SWN), a class of Colored Generalized Stochastic Petri Nets (CGSPN). The architecture of
the ATM switches under investigation derives from the Knockout switch
design, one of the most classical proposals for the implementation of
large and fast ATM switches. The GSPN and SWN approaches to ATM
network modeling are first discussed, then the Knockout architecture is
presented, and the SWN models are illustrated. Results in terms of the
state space complexity of the models and of the performance metrics
obtained with different Knockout switch configurations are presented to
prove the viability of the proposed approach.

1 Introduction

State space largeness is a common problem in the performance evaluation of
complex systems with both analytical and simulative techniques.

Actually, with few exceptions corresponding to the cases in which simple
closed form expressions (that are however difficult to apply in the study of complex systems) are known, probably it is even fair to say that state space largeness
is *the* problem in performance analysis of complex systems.

Petri Net (PN) based performance evaluation does not circumvent this difficulty, since the computation of performance metrics normally relies either on
the solution of systems of equations with a number of unknowns that equals
the cardinality of the state space of the underlying stochastic process or on the
execution of the PN model to generate a possible behavioral trajectory through
the state space.

Clever approaches to diminish the impact of state space largeness on the
cost of the analysis of PN-based performance models have been devised over the
years, trying to exploit either the symmetries or the compositionalities in the
system behavior.

The adoption of PN-based approaches in the performance analysis of ATM
networks was recently suggested by several authors [1–8], and results were ob-

tained to quantify the performance of ATM switch architectures as well as ATM LANs exploiting the ABR ATM service category.

Performance analysis of ATM switches with GSPNs (Generalized Stochastic Petri Nets) [9,10] was shown to be a viable approach for moderate size systems [4,5,7], but the analysis could be carried on just as far as permitted by the growth in the cardinality of the state space of the models.

Some preliminary attempts [7] indicated that the exploitation of symmetries through SWN (Stochastic Well-formed Net) models [11,12] could allow the investigation of the performance of ATM switches of much larger sizes.

In this paper we further proceed along this line, and show that SWN models can allow the performance evaluation of medium size ATM switches with analytical techniques, and that large ATM switches can be efficiently studied with a simulative approach based on SWN models. This achievement results from the possibility of exploiting the model symmetries through the concept of symbolic marking of SWNs, in both the analytical and the simulative computation of performance metrics.

The papers is organized as follows. Sections 2 and 3 concisely overview the GSPN and SWN approaches to ATM network modeling, and the Knockout switch architecture, respectively. Section 4 illustrates the GSPN and SWN models of the Knockout ATM switch architecture, and Section 5 discusses the state space reductions that can be achieved by exploiting symmetries with the symbolic markings of SWNs, with respect to the ordinary markings of GSPNs. Section 6 presents curves of the performance parameters that are typically used to assess the effectiveness of ATM switch architectures. Finally, Section 7 presents some concluding remarks and the possible future steps of this work.

2 The GSPN and SWN Approaches to ATM Network Modeling

It was recently shown in the literature [4–8], that it is possible to accurately analyze ATM networks with PN models in which all transitions are immediate, with just one exception: one transition is timed with a constant delay τ defining the time unit in the model. Note that this timed transition actually defines the clock of the model and thus always has concession. The stochastic process generated by the dynamic behavior of such a PN model is a semi-Markov process (SMP) with constant sojourn times, with an embedded discrete-time Markov chain (DTMC) whose evolution over the state space is isomorphic to the tangible marking process and whose transition probabilities are computed from the reachable markings and from the weights of the enabled immediate transitions.

However, the association of the only timed transition with either a constant or an exponentially distributed random delay makes no difference for the computation of a large quantity of interesting performance parameters. Indeed, while the PN model with the deterministic transition originates a DTMC, the PN model with the exponential transition originates a continuous-time Markov chain

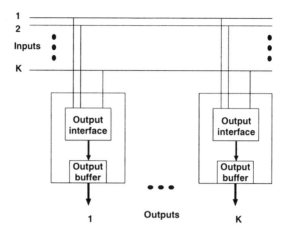

Fig. 1. Block diagram of ATM switch architectures with paths disjoint in space

(CTMC); the relation between the two MCs is very tight: the DTMC is the embedded MC of the CTMC. It is well-known that the steady-state probabilities $\pi_k^{(Y)}$ of an ergodic CTMC $Y(t)$ can be obtained from the stationary probabilities $\pi_k^{(Z)}$ of its embedded DTMC Z_n through the relation

$$\pi_k^{(Y)} = \frac{\pi_k^{(Z)} E[W_k]^{(Y)}}{\sum_{i \in S} \pi_i^{(Z)} E[W_i]^{(Y)}}$$

where S is the state space of the two MCs, and $E[W_i]^{(Y)}$ is the average sojourn time in state i for the CTMC $Y(t)$. Since $\forall k \in S : E[W_k]^{(Y)} = \tau$ (throughout the paper we shall assume $\tau = 1$), the steady-state probabilities $\pi_k^{(Y)}$ of the CTMC are identical to the stationary probabilities $\pi_k^{(Z)}$ of the embedded MC.

As a result, PN models of ATM networks can be built with a particular type of GSPNs that comprise just one (exponentially) timed transition, and a (large) number of immediate transitions.

Since SWNs are a special class of colored GSPNs, SWN models of ATM networks can be built exactly with the same approach, using a color formalism to concisely represent the similar behaviors of a number of network elements.

3 The Knockout ATM Switch

According to the terminology of [13], the Knockout switch is a disjoint-path based switch, with paths disjoint in space. This means that physically separate paths exist for cells arriving at different switch input ports to reach their intended switch output port. The block diagram representing this class of ATM switch architectures is depicted in Fig. 1.

The switch comprises a set of passive slotted busses (one for each input channel) that are used to broadcast incoming cells to the output channel interfaces. Each output interface filters cells in order to discard those that are not directed to the channel it controls, retaining only those that should be transmitted on that channel. Thus, the internal switching fabric is non-blocking, and cell queuing takes place only at the output port. This means that the number of cells that can arrive in the same slot at the output interface equals the number of busses, hence of input channels K. However, the output interfaces usually do not allow more than a fixed number $SU \leq K$ (SU stands for speed-up; this parameter is often denoted by L in the literature) of cells to be accepted simultaneously within the output queue due to speed limitations of the output interface.

The Knockout switch [14] is a very well-known disjoint-path architecture proposed for ATM switching, where the choice of the cells to be accepted within the output queue is performed at random, or equivalently, where the cells that have to be dropped (up to $K - SU$) are randomly selected.

The Knockout switch was a very important contribution to the field of ATM switch design, and its performances were deeply investigated in several configurations (see for example [15]).

4 GSPN and SWN Models of the Knockout ATM Switch

Since the Knockout ATM switch architecture is non-blocking with output queuing, we are able to develop a highly modular GSPN model that consists of different components:

- descriptions of the cell arrival processes at the different switch input ports (the *workload models*)
- a description of the internal switch operations to bring the cells from the input port interfaces to the output port interfaces (the *switching fabric model*)
- a description of the cell output queues and output interfaces (the *output models*)

We first present the GSPN descriptions of the workload and output models (Sects. 4.1 and 4.2, respectively), then the GSPN description of the switching fabric model (Section 4.3), and finally the GSPN and SWN models of the portion of the Knockout switch that refers to one output interface.

The model components comprise only immediate transitions, whose firing is driven by the only timed transition in the GSPN, that is named *clock*, and whose firing delay represents the time unit within the ATM switch (which normally is an integer divisor of the slot time on input and output channels); we can think of *clock* as being a deterministic transition in the model description, in order to better understand the model, but it will be considered an exponential transition in the model solution, as we explained. Transition *clock* always has concession, but it becomes enabled only when no (higher-priority) immediate transition is enabled. Thus, the evolution of the GSPN model alternately repeats two phases: the first phase comprises the enabling time of *clock* and the firing

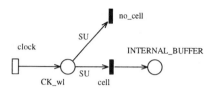

Fig. 2. Bernoulli workload model

of this transition; the second phase consumes no time, and comprises the firing of several immediate transitions, terminating only when no more immediate transitions are enabled. When *clock* fires, one token is deposited in the places named CK_wl, CK_sw, and CK_out in the following subsections. The presence of tokens in these places activates the GSPN model components.

It is worthwhile observing that the assignment of priorities to the different immediate transitions in the model is quite a delicate matter, since it defines the sequence of operations that are performed in zero time after the firing of *clock*. Only a careful setting of the priorities results in a correct model of the switch operations. Priorities in our model increase from the input interface section to the output interface section, since they must avoid that a cell that just entered the switch crosses the input interface, the switching fabric, and the output interface in zero time. Priorities will be discussed when presenting the complete GSPN model, rather than included in the description of the different GSPN model components.

4.1 Workload Models

Similarly to what happens in the majority of ATM products, where the input cell flows are synchronized before entering the switching fabric, we assume that the arrivals of cells at input ports are synchronized, and that the internal switch operations proceed at a rate that is a multiple of the cell arrival rate at the input interfaces according to the integer SU. Thus, the workload model is not activated at every firing of *clock*, but only once every SU firings, in order to determine whether new cells have arrived from the input channels.

Bernoulli Source Models. The GSPN model for one source producing a Bernoulli cell flow is depicted in Fig. 2. The accumulation of SU tokens in place CK_wl enables the two conflicting immediate transitions *cell* and *no_cell*. The firing of *no_cell* (whose weight is $1 - p$) indicates no cell arrival at the input port during the current time slot, whereas the firing of *cell* (whose weight is p) models the arrival of a cell. This cell is transferred to the internal buffer, modeled by place INTERNAL_BUFFER.

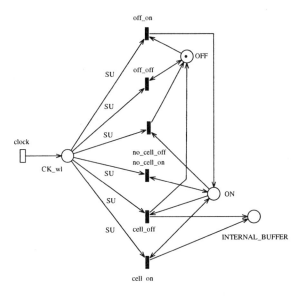

Fig. 3. MMBP workload model

MMBP and MMDP Source Models. Slightly more elaborate GSPN workload models can account for more complex cell arrival processes. For example, Markov-modulated source models can be simply described with GSPNs; this is a class of workload models that is commonly used when studying ATM networks, since it provides larger correlations in the cell arrival streams, thus better approximating the behavior of real users. In Fig. 3 we depict the workload model for one source generating a cell flow that is the discrete-time version of a Markov-modulated Poisson process (a Markov Modulated Bernoulli Process – MMBP).

In this case the arrival process can be either on (place ON is marked) or off (place OFF is marked). If the arrival process is on, the four transitions *cell_on*, *cell_off*, *no_cell_on*, and *no_cell_off* are enabled if SU tokens are in place CK_wl. The firing of one of the two transitions *cell_on* and *cell_off* models the arrival of a cell that is transferred to the internal buffer modeled by place INTERNAL_BUFFER. Transition *cell_on* (whose weight is $pP(on-on)$) leaves place ON marked, whereas transition *cell_off* (whose weight is $p[1-P(on-on)]$) removes the token from place ON and deposits a token in place OFF, thus modeling the state of the arrival process in the next slot. Similarly, the firing of one of the two transitions *no_cell_on* and *no_cell_off* (with weights $(1-p)P(on-on)$ and $(1-p)[1-P(on-on)]$, respectively) models the lack of a cell arrival during the current slot, and the state of the arrival process in the next slot.

If the arrival process is off, no cell can arrive: the two transitions *off_on*, and *off_off* (with weights $1-P(off-off)$ and $P(off-off)$, respectively) are

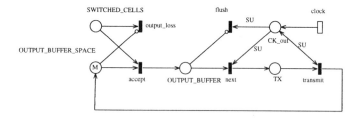

Fig. 4. Output interface model

enabled if SU tokens are in place CK_wl, and the firing of one of the two models the state of the arrival process in the next slot.

With this MMBP source model, the cell arrival process on and off periods are geometrically distributed random variables, whose averages are the inverses of the probabilities $1 - P(on - on)$ and $1 - P(off - off)$. The source *activity factor* (AF) is defined to be ratio between the average on period duration and the sum of the average on and off period durations; with trivial algebra we get:

$$AF = \frac{1 - P(off - off)}{[1 - P(on - on)] + [1 - P(off - off)]}$$

The *average load* generated by the MMBP source is $\rho = p\,AF$ and the *average burst size* is $BS = \rho/(1 - P(on - on))$. The cell inter-arrival times during the on periods are geometrically distributed random variables, with average $1/(1 - p)$.

A further minor modification of the GSPN workload model can lead to the representation of cell arrival streams following a Markov-modulated Deterministic Process (MMDP), which also is often used in the study of ATM systems. In the case of MMDP sources, the arrival process can be either on or off (like for MMBP sources), but, when the process is on, one cell surely arrives in each slot. The GSPN model for a MMDP source is obtained from that depicted in Fig. 3 simply by deleting the two transitions *no_cell_on* and *no_cell_off*.

4.2 The Output Model

In ATM switches with output queuing, the output port interface comprises one or more buffers for the storage of cells that await their turn for the transmission on the outgoing channel, and a transmitter that can load a cell onto every slot available on the output link; this slot duration is tantamount to SU slot times within the switch. Thus, also the output model, exactly as the workload model, is not activated at every firing of *clock*, but only once every SU firings.

The GSPN model of the output interface is shown in Fig. 4, assuming that just one buffer is present to store cells awaiting transmission.

Cells that arrive from the switching fabric are modeled by tokens in place SWITCHED_CELLS. When a cell arrives from the switching fabric, either one of the two transitions *output_loss* or *accept* can be enabled. The firing of *output_loss*

333

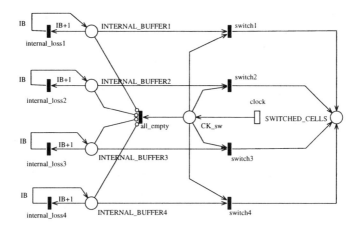

Fig. 5. Knockout switching fabric model

models the loss of a cell due to the lack of space in the output buffer (no token is present in OUTPUT_BUFFER_SPACE). The firing of *accept* instead models
the acceptance of the cell into the output buffer; one token is removed from
OUTPUT_BUFFER_SPACE, and one token is generated in OUTPUT_BUFFER. The
number of tokens in place OUTPUT_BUFFER_SPACE, initially set to the value M,
indicates the free space in the output buffer, whereas the number of tokens in
place OUTPUT_BUFFER indicates the number of cells awaiting transmission.

When the firing of *clock* results in the accumulation of SU tokens in place
CK_out, the boundary of the slot on the output channel is reached. If one cell was
being transmitted (one token was in place TX), the transmission is completed
through the firing of transition *transmit*, and one position in the output buffer
is freed. Then, if cells are waiting in the buffer, the first one is brought to the
transmitter through the firing of transition *next*. Otherwise, the SU tokens in
CK_out are discarded through the firing of *flush*.

4.3 The Switching Fabric Model

In Fig. 5 we show the GSPN model of the portion of a Knockout switching fabric
that refers to one output port, and that is thus necessary to investigate the cell
loss performance and the throughput at one of the output interfaces.

The model in Fig. 5 assumes that the considered output port receives cells
from only 4 input ports, that are called, with respect to the considered output
port, the *active* input ports. At every firing of *clock* one token is deposited into
place CK_sw and the operations of the switching fabric model are activated. If
all internal buffers are empty, transition *all_empty* is enabled, and the token
in CK_sw is eliminated. Otherwise, a random equally likely choice is performed
among those of the transitions $switch_i$ (with $i = 1, 2, 3, 4$) that are enabled due to
the presence of a token in INTERNAL_BUFFER$_i$ (note that the equally likely choice
disregards the possible unfairness that may result from the physical positions of

the input links in an implementation). Tokens corresponding to cells that are switched to the considered output port are generated in place SWITCHED_CELLS.

In our model, contrary to the models of the Knockout switch that appeared in the literature [15], the cells that have not been accepted within the output queue are not immediately dropped; instead, cells that are not moved from the internal buffers to the output buffer in one slot correspond to tokens remaining in places INTERNAL_BUFFER$_i$. These cells may be lost (knocked-out) because of a new arrival from the same active input port, if the capacity of the internal buffer (denoted as IB) is exceeded. This loss is modeled by the firing of transition $internal\_loss_i$. This can be a more accurate representation of the actual switch behavior, and results in a lower internal cell loss rate compared with the results presented in [15].

In order to obtain with our GSPN model exactly the same results that were analytically derived in [15], it is sufficient to set $IB = 0$, and to connect with a test arc with multiplicity SU each transition $internal\_loss_i$ to place CK_wl$_i$, so as to align the knock-out of the cells that could not be accepted within the output queue with the link slot boundaries. Note that whereas our model allows the results of [15] to be easily generated, the approach in [15] cannot cope with the presence of internal buffers of size $IB > 0$.

4.4 The Complete GSPN Model

The complete GSPN model for the Knockout switch, representing only the portion of the switch that refers to one output port, and assuming that only 4 inputs load the considered output port, is shown in Fig. 6. It can be obtained by composing 4 replicas of the sub-models presented in Section 4.1, the sub model of Section 4.2 and that of Section 4.3.

As we already noted, the fact that the Knockout switch is non-blocking allows each output port to be separately studied. Thus, the investigation of all the characteristics of a $K \times K$ Knockout switch requires the solution of K models similar to the one shown in Fig. 6. Each model comprises a workload description corresponding to the traffic directed to the output port under investigation. Thus, investigating unbalanced traffic patterns is not a problem.

The priorities of all transitions in the model are presented in Table 1.

Table 1. Immediate transitions priority for the Knockout GSPN model

Transition name	Priority value
$cell_i$, no_cell_i	1
$internal\_loss_i$	2
$next$, $flush$	3
$switch_i$, all_empty	4
$output\_loss$, $accept$	5
$transmit$	6

335

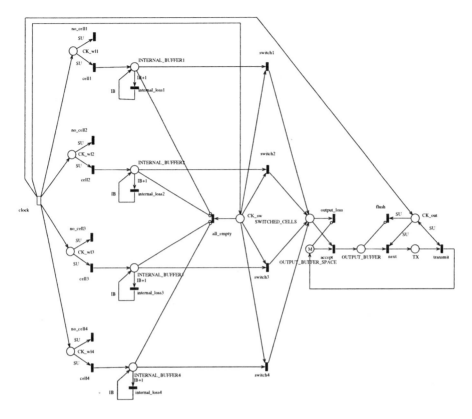

Fig. 6. The complete GSPN model for one output port of the 4 × 4 Knockout switch

It can be observed that, as we previously noted, priorities increase from the
input interface section to the output interface section, to avoid that a cell that
just entered the switch crosses the input interface, the switching fabric, and
the output interface in zero time. Assigning the highest priority to transitions
in the output interface model allows the management of the transmission side
first, before new cells cross the switch. The second set of operations (modeled
by intermediate priority transitions) moves cells through the switching fabric,
before accepting newly arrived cells. Finally, the last set of operations concerns
the input workload model, which comprises transitions at the lowest priority
levels. Note however that an exception to the general rule is that transitions
next and *flush* in the output model have lower priority than the transitions in
the switching fabric model (*switch$_i$*, *all_empty*).

4.5 Exploiting Symmetries with SWN

The intrinsic symmetry of the GSPN model presented in Fig. 6 naturally suggests the use of colored GSPNs for a compact representation of the system

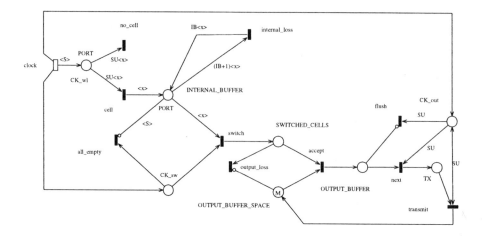

Fig. 7. The complete SWN model the Knockout switch

behavior. Among the different proposals of colored GSPNs available in the literature, SWNs [11] offer the advantage of an automatic detection of the model symmetries, and of their exploitation in the model solution, through the concept of *symbolic marking* [12].

The SWN model of the Knockout switch is depicted in Fig. 7. The system description in this SWN model is exactly equivalent to the one adopted in the GSPN model in Fig. 6. Only one output port is considered, but now the model is parametric in the number of active input ports.

The SWN model comprises a part without colors that corresponds to the only output buffer, and is identical to the GSPN model of this component, as well as a colored part that corresponds to N active input ports loaded by Bernoulli cell flows with identical parameter p (the weight of transition *cell* is p, while that of transition *no_cell* is $1 - p$), and to the switching part.

We describe next the colored part of the model. Only one basic *color class*, named $PORT$, is defined; it is used to identify the active input ports of the switch:

$$PORT = \{port_1, port_2, \ldots, port_N\}$$

CK_wl and INTERNAL_BUFFER are the only colored places; their *color domain* is $PORT$. All the remaining places are not colored (we also say that they have neutral color domain).

Each time the transition *clock* fires, it deposits N colored tokens in place CK_wl through the *arc function* $\langle S \rangle = \langle port_1 \rangle + \langle port_2 \rangle + \ldots + \langle port_N \rangle$; after SU firings of transition *clock*, the marking of place CK_wl is equal to

$$SU \cdot \langle port_1 \rangle + SU \cdot \langle port_2 \rangle + \ldots + SU \cdot \langle port_N \rangle$$

therefore colored transitions *cell* and *no_cell* are enabled by N *firing color instances*. For each firing color instance, transitions *cell* and *no_cell* are in conflict;

upon firing of transition *cell* for color instance $x \leftarrow port_i$ $(1 \leq i \leq N)$, *SU* colored tokens $\langle port_i \rangle$ are consumed from input place CK_wl, and one colored token $\langle port_i \rangle$ is deposited in place INTERNAL_BUFFER. On the contrary, upon firing of transition *no_cell*, *SU* colored tokens $\langle port_i \rangle$ are consumed from input place CK_wl and no tokens are deposited in place INTERNAL_BUFFER.

Colored transition *internal_loss* is enabled for firing color instance $x \leftarrow port_i$, $(1 \leq i \leq N)$ if and only if the marking of place INTERNAL_BUFFER contains at least $IB + 1$ tokens $\langle port_i \rangle$. When transition *internal_loss* fires for firing color instance $x \leftarrow port_i$, the multiplicity of colored token $\langle port_i \rangle$ in the marking of place INTERNAL_BUFFER is decreased by one. The firing of colored transition *internal_loss* models the loss of a cell that is knocked out by a new arrival on the same active input port.

Upon firing of colored transition *switch* for firing color instance $x \leftarrow port_i$, $(1 \leq i \leq N)$ one colored token $\langle port_i \rangle$ is withdrawn from place INTERNAL_BUFFER and one neutral token is deposited in place SWITCHED_CELLS, thus modeling the arrival of a cell at the output buffer. Like in the GSPN model, if space is available in the output buffer, the incoming cell is moved to the transmitter queue through the firing of transition *accept*, otherwise it is lost by the firing of neutral transition *output_loss*.

The SWN model of the Knockout switch depicted in Fig. 7, that we just described, is developed under the assumption that all input ports load in the same fashion the considered output port, so that a complete symmetry exists. If the output port load is not equal for all active input ports, but just for some of them, a SWN model can still be constructed to take advantage of the remaining system symmetry. If two groups of active input ports can be identified, and all ports within the same group load the output port in the same fashion, the basic color class *PORT* can be partitioned in two *static subclasses* named *LOAD1* and *LOAD2*, with

$$PORT = LOAD1 \ \cup \ LOAD2$$

$$LOAD1 = \{port_1, \ldots, port_J\}, \ \ LOAD2 = \{port_{J+1}, \ldots, port_N\}$$

with $1 \leq J < N$, and transitions *cell* and *no_cell* can be duplicated and augmented by a *transition predicate* to restrict their enabling only to those instances belonging to the corresponding static subclass. Moreover, the weights of immediate transitions $cell_1$ and $cell_2$ must be different in order to model Bernoulli processes with different parameters.

5 Largeness Results

The number of symbolic states generated by the SWN model, that have to be used in the computation of steady-state probabilities, is extraordinarily smaller than the number of states generated by the GSPN model. This induces drastic reductions of the computational complexity of the solution, and allows a much wider set of switch configurations to be studied.

338

Table 2. Number of states of the SWN and GSPN models of the Knockout switch for a variable number of active input ports N, with $IB = 1$, $SU = 8$, $M = 0$ under uniform Bernoulli load.

N	$|TSRG|$	$|VSRG|$	$|TRG|$	$|VRG|$
8	44	117	1,279	8,609
12	76	715	27,486	50,082,554
16	108	1,745	499,141	21,146,490,931
20	140	3,335	8,298,668	6.5942e + 12
24	172	5,613	133,956,619	1.9703e + 15
28	204	8,707	2,146,833,754	5.7646e + 17

Table 3. Number of states of the SWN and GSPN 'efficient' models of the Knockout switch for a variable number of active input ports N, with $IB = 1$, $SU = 8$, $M = 0$ under uniform Bernoulli load.

N	$|TSRG|$	$|VSRG|$	$|TRG|$	$|VRG|$
8	44	82	1,279	2,305
12	76	196	27,486	384,778
16	108	326	499,141	41,880,819

As an example, in Table 2 we report the number of states for the SWN and GSPN Knockout switch models for a variable number of active input ports N, with the following parameter values: $IB = 1$, $SU = 8$, $M = 0$, and uniform Bernoulli input load. The first column in the table gives the number of modeled active input ports N; other columns show the number of symbolic tangible SWN states (second column), the number of symbolic vanishing SWN states (third column), the number of ordinary tangible GSPN states (fourth column), and the number of ordinary vanishing GSPN states (fifth column). All numbers refer to the case $M = 0$, but the growth of M just induces a linear increase of the number of markings.

It is quite evident that the degree of aggregation (that we define as the ratio between the number of ordinary GSPN states and the number of symbolic SWN states) is very high: it ranges from 29 (for $N = 8$) to about 10^7 (for $N = 28$) for tangible states, and from 73 (for $N = 8$) to 10^{13} (for $N = 28$) for vanishing states.

It should be remarked that a reduction in the number of (ordinary and symbolic) vanishing markings is possible at the cost of some extra modeling effort. Indeed, by providing an aggregate representation of the modeled active input ports, in which $N + 1$ transitions represent the arrival of cells from $0, 1, 2, \cdots, N$ inputs, the number of vanishing markings to be visited is greatly reduced, as can be seen from Table 3. Nevertheless, the degree of aggregation provided by the use of SWN remains extremely large. The state space cardinalities that are

Table 4. Number of states of the SWN and GSPN models of the Knockout switch for variable speedup, with $N = 8$, $IB = 1$, $M = 250$ under uniform Bernoulli load.

SU	$|TSRG|$	$|VSRG|$	$|TRG|$	$|VRG|$
2	4, 261	21, 703	128, 008	2, 005, 478
3	6, 008	23, 405	189, 515	2, 070, 869
4	7, 502	24, 365	243, 833	2, 013, 600
5	8, 745	24, 590	284, 102	1, 746, 959
6	9, 739	24, 087	306, 990	1, 290, 490
7	10, 486	22, 863	316, 067	834, 299
8	10, 988	20, 925	318, 277	576, 188

Table 5. Number of states of the SWN and GSPN models of the Knockout switch for $N = 16$, $IB = 1$, $M = 0$ with active input ports partitioned in two subsets with different Bernoulli load parameters.

J	$|TSRG|$	$|VSRG|$	$|TRG|$	$|VRG|$
5	493	1, 563	499, 141	6, 509, 019
6	532	1, 687	499, 141	5, 015, 079
7	556	1, 764	499, 141	4, 244, 197
8	564	1, 980	499, 141	4, 516, 438

presented in the next tables always refer to this less natural but more efficient representation of the input cell flows.

The adoption of the SWN modeling paradigm allows the investigation of switch configurations where not only the number of active input ports is increased, but also other parameters take values that are more critical for the model solution, for example smaller speedup values: Table 4 shows the numbers of states generated by the GSPN and SWN models for variable values of the switch internal speed-up SU. In this case the Knockout switch models are characterized by the following parameter values: $N = 8$, $IB = 1$, $M = 250$ and uniform Bernoulli input load.

If the Knockout switch load is not uniform, but active input ports can be grouped in two classes, as described before, the gains resulting from the use of SWN models remain significant: Table 5 presents the numbers of states generated by the GSPN and SWN models for variable numbers of active input ports in one class. The Knockout switch models are now characterized by the following parameter values: $N = 16$, $SU = 8$, $IB = 1$, $M = 0$.

These results must be compared with those in the third row of Table 3, where all active input ports were identical. In that case we obtained a degree of symmetry equal to 4,621 for tangible states and 128,468 for vanishing states. Of course, the difference in the active input port characterization decreases the degree of symmetry that now goes from 1,012 (for $J = 5$) to 885 (for $J = 8$) for

Table 6. Number of states of the SWN and GSPN models of the Knockout switch for $SU = 8$, $IB = 1$, $M = 0$ with Bernoulli and MMBP active input ports

N_B	N_{MMBP}	$\|TSRG\|$	$\|VSRG\|$	$\|TRG\|$	$\|VRG\|$
4	4	248	488	2,558	4,899
8	4	560	1,488	54,972	258,007
4	2+2	896	1,848	5,116	10,295
8	2+2	2,704	7,738	165,328	788,934
4	8	560	1,440	54,972	183,839
8	8	1,128	3,592	998,282	7,233,329

tangible states, and from 4,164 (for $J = 5$) to 2,281 (for $J = 8$) for vanishing states.

Finally, SWN models also allow the investigation of the case in which some active input ports receive Bernoulli input traffic, while some others receive MMBP input traffic, In Table 6 we report the state space cardinalities for models with either 4 or 8 identical Bernoulli active input ports, and either 4 or 8 MMBP active input ports. The latter can either be identical, or divided into two groups of identical elements. All MMBP sources within a group (comprising 2, 4, or 8 elements) have the same parameters, and are driven by the same modulating process; this increases the correlation of the input cell flows, and significantly reduces the state space cardinalities.

6 Performance Results

As an example of the numerical results that can be obtained with the SWN model that we illustrated, we present some curves of the cell loss probability within the Knockout switch, first using a numerical approach for the solution of the Markov chain associated with the SWN models of medium size Knockout switches, then resorting to simulation for large switch configurations[1].

The discussion of numerical results aims at proving the viability of the proposed SWN modeling approach for switches of medium to large size, not at a complete characterization of the performance of the Knockout switch architecture, which is outside the scope of this paper.

All numerical results were obtained with the *GreatSPN* package [16].

In our SWN model, two types of immediate transitions model the loss of a cell: transition *internal_loss* models the loss of a cell at one of the input interfaces, and transition *output_loss* models the loss of a cell at the output interface. We can thus define two contributions to the cell loss probability, which is normally called cell loss ratio (CLR) in the ATM jargon.

---

[1] Note that simulation in this case is just an alternate approach for the derivation of numerical results from the SWN model, that becomes attractive when the modelled system is quite large, not an approach for the validation of the numerical results obtained from the SWN model.

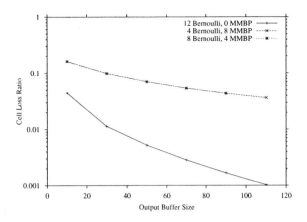

Fig. 8. CLR values for the Knockout switch

1. Output Cell Loss Ratio ($OCLR$) defined as

$$OCLR = \frac{X(output\_loss)}{X(cell_B) + X(cell_{MMBP})}$$

where $X(t)$ denotes the throughput of immediate transition t, i.e., $OCLR$ is the ratio between the steady-state throughput of transition $output\_loss$, and the total load of the output port $\rho = X(cell_B) + X(cell_{MMBP})$.

2. Internal Cell Loss Ratio ($ICLR$) defined as

$$ICLR = \frac{X(internal\_loss)}{X(cell_B) + X(cell_{MMBP})}$$

i.e., as the ratio between the the steady-state throughput of the transition modeling the loss of an incoming cell at the temporary internal buffers, and the total load of the output port.

The cell loss ratio is defined as $CLR = OCLR + ICLR$, and (obviously) it cannot exceed 1 (since tokens can be used to fire the loss transitions only after they are generated by the firing of input transitions).

Numerical results are presented in Fig. 8 as curves of CLR for increasing values of the output buffer size M, considering switches with the characteristics reported in Table 7.

In particular, we consider three different workload patterns: 12 active input ports are loaded with either 12 Bernoulli sources, or 8 Bernoulli and 4 MMBP, or 4 Bernoulli and 8 MMBP. The total load is fixed to 0.99; Bernoulli sources are characterized by a total load equal to 0.49 while MMBP sources have a total load equal to 0.5. In the case of 12 Bernoulli sources the total load is equal to 0.99.

Note that the considered load of the output link is quite high, higher than the average load of links in a well-designed network. However, it is clear that

Table 7. Parameters of the Knockout switch used in the derivation of numerical results

Parameter	Value
number of active input ports	$N = 12$
number of active Bernoulli input ports	$N = 12, 8, 4$
number of active MMBP input ports	$N = 0, 4, 8$
internal speed-up	$SU = 8$
internal buffer size	$IB = 1$
total load	$\rho = 0.99$
Bernoulli load	$\rho_B = 0.49$
MMBP load	$\rho_{MMBP} = 0.5$
MMBP load activity factor	$AF = 0.6$
MMBP load burst size	$BS = 64$

temporary link overloads are possible due to statistical traffic fluctuations, and that such overloads may drastically degrade performance. For these reasons the investigation of the system behavior very close to saturation is interesting.

Curves are plotted using a logarithmic scale for the vertical axis. Recall that CLR values refer to one of the switch output ports; we can thus investigate uniform as well as unbalanced traffic patterns. This is due to the independence of the behaviors of the different output ports, that results from the fact that the considered ATM switch is non-blocking with output queuing.

The observation of the numerical results leads to a number of remarks. As expected, the $OCLR$ curves tend to 0 as the output buffer size increases (this must be true at least until $\rho < 1$). The $ICLR$ term is obviously independent of the output buffer size M but in this setting its value is always less than 10^{-6} which is the accuracy we used for the numerical solution (this is not surprising since we have $SU = 8$ and some internal buffer capability but only 12 active ports). The high correlation in the input streams given by the MMBP sources yields a slower decrease of the CLR values compared to the case where only Bernoulli sources are considered.

As a final remark, the computational cost for the derivation of numerical results is quite small: the CPU time needed for the computation of the infinitesimal generator that is used to obtain one point on our curves varies from a few seconds for small values of M to about 20-30 minutes for the maximum values of M.

We also conducted discrete-event simulation of a large switch configuration. We modified the SWN model depicted in Fig. 7 by coloring the output model using an additional basic color class to distinguish the different output ports. The main idea is to speed the simulation of rare events (such as the loss of a cell in a large output buffer) by considering the aggregate state of different output ports performing the *symbolic simulation* [17] of the resulting SWN model. The performance index that can be estimated is thus the Cell Loss Ratio of the *whole* Knockout switch under a given workload pattern. We considered a 64x64 switch where each output port has an output buffer with $M = 512$. The switch speed-up value is $SU = 16$ and the internal buffering is $IB = 1$. The color class representing the output ports is partitioned in three static subclasses, named $DEST_1$, $DEST_2$ and $DEST_3$, whose cardinalities are 60, 2 and 2 respectively. The color class representing the input ports are also partitioned in three static subclasses named $LOAD_1$, $LOAD_2$, and $LOAD_3$: the first one comprises 60 ports, and each port is loaded by a MMBP which uniformly chooses a destination output port among the 64 different choices. The second subset is composed of three ports that are loaded by a MMDP that broadcasts a cell to each output port belonging to $DEST_2$. The third static subclass identifies one port loaded by a MMDP that broadcasts a cell to each output port in $DEST_2$ and $DEST_3$.

The symbolic simulation mechanism is much more efficient compared to the simulation that works on the ordinary representation of the SWN marking. For the model we described, the number of symbolic transition firings per second was 1,057 while the number of ordinary firings per second was just 147. Furthermore, even though convergence of the estimator for rare events remains a problem when considering high accuracy simulation (e.g., 10% accuracy, 95% confidence interval) of lightly loaded switches, we observed a faster convergence rate when performing the symbolic simulation w.r.t. the ordinary simulation.

7 Conclusions and Future Work

The adoption of the SWN modeling paradigm for the performance evaluation of medium to large size Knockout ATM switches with either numerical or simulative techniques was proposed and experimented, finding out that the development of SWN models of ATM network components with a significant degree of symmetry can be quite natural, and that the advantages gained in terms of the cost of the computation of the performance metrics of interest can in general be quite remarkable, and in some cases even exceptional.

The possibility of exploiting the SWN modeling approach, and its limited complexity in particular, for the development of models that consider not just one component of the ATM network, but a portion of the net, or even a whole network, are the natural next step of this work.

Acknowledgments

This work was supported in part by a research contract between Politecnico di Torino and CSELT, in part by the EC through the Copernicus project 1463 ATMIN, in part by the Esprit Human Capital and Mobility project MATCH, in part by the Italian Ministry for University and Research.

References

1. B.Haverkort, H.P.Idzenga, B.Kim: Performance Evaluation of Threshold-Based ATM Cell Scheduling Policies Under Markov-Modulated Poisson Traffic Using Stochastic Petri Nets. Performance Modelling and Evaluation of ATM Networks, Editor: D.D.Kouvatsos, Chapman & Hall, pp. 551-572, 1995.

2. H.P.Idzenga, B.R.Haverkort: Structural Decomposition and Serial Solution of Stochastic Petri Net Models of the Gauss Switch. PNPM 95, Durham, NC, USA, October 1995, poster paper.

3. L.Kant, W.H.Sanders: Loss Process Analysis of the Knockout Switch Using Stochastic Activity Networks. ICCCN '95, Las Vegas, NV, USA, September 1995.

4. M.Ajmone Marsan, R.Gaeta: GSPN Analysis of the Knockout ATM Switch. 4th IFIP Workshop on Performance Modelling and Evaluation of ATM Networks, Ilkley, UK, July 1996.

5. M.Ajmone Marsan, R.Gaeta: GSPN Models of ATM Switches. PNPM '97, Saint Malo, France, June 1997.

6. M.Ajmone Marsan, K.Begain, R.Gaeta, M.Telek: GSPN Analysis of ABR in ATM LANs. PNPM '97, Saint Malo, France, June 1997.

7. M.Ajmone Marsan, K.Begain, R.Gaeta: GSPN Models of ATM Networks. submitted for publication.

8. R.Gaeta, K.Begain, M.Ajmone Marsan: Stop & Go ABR in ATM LANs: Performance Analysis with GSPNs. submitted for publication.

9. M.Ajmone Marsan, G.Balbo, G.Conte: A Class of Generalized Stochastic Petri Nets for the Performance Evaluation of Multiprocessor Systems. ACM Transactions on Computer Systems, Vol. 2, n. 2, May 1984, pp. 93-122.

10. M.Ajmone Marsan, G.Balbo, G.Conte, S.Donatelli, G.Franceschinis: Modelling with Generalized Stochastic Petri Nets, John Wiley & Sons, 1995.

11. G.Chiola, C.Dutheillet, G.Franceschinis, and S.Haddad: On well-formed coloured nets and their symbolic reachability graph. 11th International Conference on Application and Theory of Petri Nets, Paris, France, June 1990. Reprinted in High-Level Petri Nets. Theory and Application, K. Jensen and G. Rozenberg (editors), Springer Verlag, 1991.

12. G.Chiola, C.Dutheillet, G.Franceschinis, and S.Haddad: Stochastic well-formed coloured nets for symmetric modelling applications. IEEE Transactions on Computers, Vol. 42, n. 11, November 1993, pp. 1343-1360.

13. R.Y.Awdeh, H.T.Mouftah: Survey of ATM Switch Architectures. Computer Networks and ISDN Systems, Vol. 27, n. 12, November 1995, pp. 1567-1613.

14. Y.S.Yeh, M.G.Hluchyi, A.S.Acampora: The Knockout Switch: A Simple, Modular Architecture for High-Performance Packet Switching. JSAC, Vol. 5, n. 8, 1987, pp. 1274-1283.

15. H.Yoon, M.T.Liu, K.Y.Lee, Y.M.Kim: The Knockout Switch Under Nonuniform Traffic. IEEE Transaction on Communications, Vol. 43, n. 6, June 1995, pp. 2149-2156.

16. G.Chiola, G.Franceschinis, R.Gaeta, M.Ribaudo: GreatSPN 1.7: GRaphical Editor and Analyzer for Timed and Stochastic Petri Nets. Performance Evaluation, Vol. 24, n. 1,2, November 1995, pp. 47-68.

17. R.Gaeta: Efficient Discrete-Event Simulation of Colored Petri Nets. IEEE Transaction on Software Engineering, Vol. 22, n. 9, September 1996, pp. 629-639.

Flexibility in Algebraic Nets

Ekkart Kindler and Hagen Völzer*

Humboldt-Universität zu Berlin, Institut für Informatik, D-10099 Berlin, Germany**

Abstract. *Algebraic Petri nets* as defined by Reisig [17] lack a feature for modelling distributed network algorithms, viz. *flexible arcs*. In this paper we equip algebraic Petri nets with flexible arcs and we call the resulting extension *algebraic system nets*. We demonstrate that algebraic system nets are better suited for modelling distributed algorithms.

Besides this practical motivation for introducing algebraic system nets there is a theoretical one. The concept of *place invariants* introduced along with algebraic Petri nets has a slight insufficiency: There may be place invariants of an unfolded algebraic Petri net which cannot be expressed as a place invariant of the algebraic Petri net itself. By introducing algebraic system nets along with a slightly more general concept of place invariants we also eliminate this insufficiency.

Moreover, we generalize the concept of place invariants which we call *simulations*. Many well-known concepts of Petri net theory such as *siphons*, *traps*, *modulo-invariants*, *sur-invariants* and *sub-invariants* are special cases of a simulation. Still, a simulation can be verified in the same style as classical place invariants of algebraic Petri nets.

Keywords: Algebraic Petri nets, place invariants, verification techniques.

1 Introduction

Algebraic Petri nets as proposed by Reisig [17] lack a feature which is important for modelling distributed network algorithms: Arcs with flexible throughput – *flexible arcs* for short – are not allowed. We will motivate the use and the necessity of flexible arcs by help of an example. Then, we formally introduce a generalized version of algebraic Petri nets which allows for flexible arcs. We call this version *algebraic system nets*.

Algebraic system nets will be equipped with a concept of *place invariants* which overcomes a problem of the version in [17]. There, the unfolded algebraic Petri net may have a (low-level) place invariant which has no corresponding (high-level) place invariant in the algebraic Petri net. We will give an example for such a place invariant.

For convenience, we do not use the traditional representation of a place invariant as a vector of weight functions [9] or a vector of terms [17]. Rather,

---
* supported by the DFG: Konsensalgorithmen
** Email: { kindler | voelzer }@informatik.hu-berlin.de

we represent a place invariant as a *multiset-valued linear expression* in which place names may occur as bag-valued variables. Though this difference is only syntactical, it allows a smoother transition between Petri net properties and temporal logic (cf. [18, 12, 24, 11]). Moreover, it gives rise to a generalization: We can use expressions which evaluate to an arbitrary *commutative monoid* equipped with some *affine preorder*. We call this generalization *simulation* — algebraically, a simulation is a homomorphism from the occurrence graph of the net to the preordered commutative monoid. The use of linear weight functions into more general domains has been proposed before (cf. [21, 5]); the use of affine preorders, however, is new. It turns out that well-known concepts like *siphons* (*deadlocks*) and *traps* [15, 16], *modulo-invariants* [5], and *sur-invariants* and *sub-invariants* [14] are special cases of *simulations*. Traps and siphons for algebraic Petri nets have been introduced by Schmidt [19]. Modulo-invariants and sub- and sur-invariants for algebraic nets are introduced in this paper as the canonical extension of the low-level versions. Moreover, we introduce *semi-place-invariants* and *stabilization expressions* as further instances of simulations.

The use of flexible arcs in algebraic Petri nets is not completely new. Billington [2, 3] proposed some extensions which allow a restricted kind of 'flexibility' and Reisig [17] indicated some possible extensions. Our definitions of algebraic system nets and their non-sequential processes have been introduced in [10] — without any results and without the concept of place invariants. Here, we present the above mentioned results about algebraic system nets and the definition and investigation of place invariants. The relation of *algebraic system nets* to the versions of *algebraic Petri nets* of Vautherin [22] and Reisig [17] will be discussed in the conclusion.

Algebraic system nets can be considered as a slightly more formalistic version of coloured Petri nets [8]. The reason for a more rigid syntax for the inscriptions of a net is that, in principle, the correct application of the verification techniques can be checked automatically (e.g. by automatic theorem provers). In this paper, however, we are sometimes less restrictive about syntactical issues in order to avoid unnecessary technical overhead.

2 An Example

Before formally introducing *algebraic system nets* we present an example, which models a simple distributed algorithm. The example motivates the need for flexible arcs and provides some intuitive understanding of algebraic system nets and the concept of place invariants.

2.1 A Minimum Distance Algorithm

The algorithm works on a network of *agents* where some distinguished agents are so-called *roots* of the network. The algorithm computes the minimal distance from a root for each agent of the network . This algorithm was inspired by a simple spanning tree algorithm [4]; the net model was already presented in [10] and verified in [11].

We denote the set of agents by A, the set of distinguished root-agents by $R \subseteq A$; the set of other so-called *inner agents* is denoted by $I = A \setminus R$. The underlying network is denoted by $N \subseteq A \times A$. The algebraic system net Σ_1 shown in Fig. 1 models the behaviour of each agent $x \in A$: Initially, a root-agent

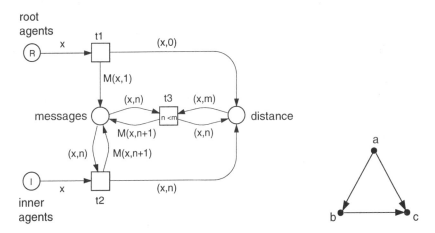

Fig. 1. A minimum distance algorithm Σ_1.   **Fig. 2.** A network of agents.

$x \in R$ sends a message to each of its *neighbours* in the network. In this message it informs its neighbours that they have distance 1 from a root (viz. from x itself). The agent $x \in R$ creates an entry for its own distance 0 from a root. The currently known distance n of an agent x from some root agent is represented as a pair (x, n) on place **distance**. So, an agent may be in exactly one of the three states **rootagent**, **inneragent** or it knows some **distance** from a root. The behaviour of a root agent is modelled by *transition* **t1** of Σ_1; a message m to an agent $y \in A$ is represented as a pair (y, m) on place **messages**. Suppose $y_1, \ldots, y_n$ are the neighbours of x in the network, then $M(x, 1)$ denotes the set of pairs[1] $[(y_1, 1), \ldots, (y_n, 1)]$, where each pair represents a message to one neighbour.

An *inner agent* $x \in I$ waits until it receives a message from some of its neighbours. When it receives a message it accepts the distance n from this message; in addition it sends a message $n + 1$ to each of its neighbours. This behaviour is modelled by transition **t2**.

When an agent $x \in A$ receives another message with a distance n which is shorter than the distance m which it already knows, it accepts the new distance n and sends the new distance $n + 1$ to each of its neighbours. This behaviour is modelled by transition **t3**, where the transition guard guarantees $n < m$. Altogether, this behaviour guarantees that eventually each agent knows its minimal

---

[1] The use of square brackets indicates that we actually use bags rather than sets.

distance to a root — if there is a path to some root at all. Note that for simplicity, the agents do not remove messages with higher distance information.

Let us consider how messages are sent out in Σ_1 in more detail: As we said above, a message to an agent x is modelled as a pair (x, n) on place messages where n represents the contents of the message — in our example a number. In order to get a simple and concise Petri net model of the algorithm we have modelled the sending of messages to all neighbours by a single transition; this is possible because $M(x, 1)$ resp. $M(x, n)$ represents a set of messages. Of course, the set denoted by $M(x, n)$ depends on the agent x and the underlying network N. Hence, the network topology is encoded in the function M. For the network shown in Fig. 2 we have: $M(a, n) = [(b, n), (c, n)]$, $M(b, n) = [(c, n)]$, and $M(c, n) = []$ for each $n \in \mathbb{N}$. For this network the number of pairs in $M(x, n)$ varies for the different agents. Therefore, the number of tokens 'flowing through' the arc from transition t_1 to place messages varies between 0 and 2. This is a typical example for a flexible arc. Therefore, Σ_1 is not a conventional algebraic Petri net as defined by Reisig [17] — even the extensions proposed by Billington and Reisig do not allow inscriptions such as $M(x, n + 1)$.

Of course, it is possible to model the above algorithm by a conventional algebraic Petri net. For example, one could send the messages to each neighbour one after the other. But, the resulting algebraic Petri net has more transitions and is more complicated than Σ_1; the simplicity of Σ_1 results from the use of flexible arcs. Moreover, sending messages to each neighbour in some order is a design decision, which is completely irrelevant for the correctness of the algorithm. In this sense the above model represents the algorithmic idea more concisely. Since sending messages to some neighbours is a primitive of network algorithms, it should be represented directly — without tricks.

2.2 Place Invariants as Linear Expressions

In our setting a *place invariant* of an algebraic system net is represented by a linear expression in which place names of the net may occur as variables (of the corresponding bag type). Such an expression is, for example, rootagents + inneragents + pr_1(distance). The function $pr_1 : A \times \mathbb{N} \to A$ is the projection of pairs to the first component, which is linearly extended to a function $pr_1 : \mathrm{BAG}(A \times \mathbb{N}) \to \mathrm{BAG}(A)$ in order to apply it to the bag distance.

Given a marking, the expression evaluates to some multiset. Each place name stands for the bag of tokens at that place at the given marking. The example expression evaluates to the multiset[2] $R + I = A$ in the initial marking. A linear expression is a place invariant, if for each occurrence of a transition the expression evaluates to the same value at the marking before and at the marking after this occurrence.

The expression rootagents + inneragents + pr_1(distance) is a place invariant of the above algebraic system net Σ_1. Since this expression evaluates to A in the initial marking, we can conclude that in each reachable marking of the system

---

[2] We treat sets as multisets by identifying them with their characteristic function.

the proposition rootagents + inneragents + pr_1(distance) = A holds. This property implies the previously mentioned observation that each agent is in exactly one of the three states rootagent, inneragent or distance.

For verifying that a linear expression is a place invariant of the system we have to check, for each transition, the validity of an equation. Let us consider transition t1 as an example. We construct the equation as follows: For the left-hand side of the equation we take the expression rootagents + inneragents + pr_1(distance) and substitute each place name by the inscription of the arc from that place to transition t1, and we substitute [] if no arc exists. This gives us $x + [] + pr_1([])$. For the right-hand side we substitute each place name by the inscription of the arc from t1 to that place; this gives us $[] + [] + pr_1((x,0))$. Obviously, the resulting equation $x + [] + pr_1([]) = [] + [] + pr_1((x,0))$ is valid.

The substitutions for the left-hand and right-hand side of the equation corresponding to a transition t will be denoted t^- and t^+ respectively. Then, a linear expression u is a place invariant of the algebraic system net, if for each transition t of the algebraic system net the equation $t^-(u) = t^+(u)$ holds true.

Usually, place invariants are characterized as follows: For each transition, $t^+ - t^-$ constitutes one column of the transposed incidence matrix N^T of the algebraic Petri net [17]. Then, a place invariant is a vector i of multiset terms satisfying $N^T \cdot i = \underline{0}$, where the multiplication is term substitution. Our approach is just a different view which is more convenient for correctness proofs because it allows a smoother transition from place invariant equations to temporal propositions. From an expression u which is a place invariant we can immediately deduce the invariant property $\Box u = A$ if u evaluates to A in the initial marking. Moreover, proofs in a temporal style are more coherent and better readable if place invariants are represented in the same style (see [12, 11, 24] for examples). Since place invariants of high-level nets cannot be computed by linear-algebraic techniques anyway, there is no reason to represent place invariants as vectors. The different representation of place invariants, however, is only a matter of convenience. Our concept of place invariants is more powerful because we allow 'flexible expressions' in place invariants — which will be demonstrated in Sect. 5. Note that this would also be possible in vector notation.

2.3 More Linear Expressions

A place invariant is a linear expression u of some multiset type. The verification condition for each transition is $t^-(u) = t^+(u)$. Now let u be a linear expression of any monoid type X, and let $\hookrightarrow \subseteq X \times X$ an affine[3] preorder in the monoid. Then we say u together with $\hookrightarrow$ simulates Σ if for each transition t we have $t^-(u) \hookrightarrow t^+(u)$. If u evaluates to u_0 in the initial marking then we have $u_0 \hookrightarrow u$ for each reachable marking which allows the inference of invariance propositions.

For example, if we choose the monoid $(2^A, \cup, \emptyset)$ and the preorder $\supseteq$ then $supp$ rootagents $\cup$ $supp$ inneragents is a linear expression which simulates Σ_1,

---

[3] A relation $\hookrightarrow$ is affine if for each $x \hookrightarrow y$ and each z we have also $x + z \hookrightarrow y + z$.

where *supp* denotes the support of a bag, i.e. the set of elements which occur at least once in the bag. We can conclude that for each reachable marking of Σ_1 holds $A \supseteq supp$ rootagents $\cup$ $supp$ inneragents.

Such an expression is called *(individual) siphon* of Σ: A transition adds a particular token to the siphon only if that token is also removed by that transition. Other verification techniques such as *traps* and *modulo-place-invariants* will be formalized similarly. Moreover, we introduce *semi-place-invariants* and *stabilization expressions* as further useful instances of simulations.

A stabilization expression simulates an algebraic system net together with a well-founded affine order. Therefore, transitions which strictly decrease the value of the expression can happen only finitely many times. A special case of stabilization is termination: A *termination expression* proves that in each run a deadlock is reached. Sometimes, in Petri net theory, *sur-place-invariants* and *sub-place-invariants* [14] are used to prove termination. They are closely related to termination expressions and they will also be defined as special simulations.

As all these verification techniques are instances of the same scheme they can be checked in the same way, by the simple local condition $t^-(u) \hookrightarrow t^+(u)$. This is the main benefit of this approach.

3 Algebraic System Nets

In this section we formalize algebraic system nets and their processes.

3.1 Basic Notations

First, we introduce some notations and basic concepts from algebraic specifications [6] and Petri nets [16]. The only new concept is the *bag-signature* together with a corresponding concept of a *bag-algebra*.

Sets, families, and functions. By $\mathbb{B}, \mathbb{N}, \mathbb{Z}$ we denote the set {true, false} of truth values, the set of natural numbers with 0, and the set of integers respectively. For a set A we denote the cardinality of A by $|A|$, we denote the set of all non-empty finite sequences over A by A^+, and we denote the set of all subsets of A by 2^A. A *family* of sets over some *index set* I is denoted by $(A_i)_{i \in I}$. The family $(A_i)_{i \in I}$ is *pairwise disjoint*, iff for each $i, j \in I$ with $i \neq j$ holds $A_i \cap A_j = \emptyset$. If $A = (A_i)_{i \in I}$ is a family of sets, then the set $\bigcup_{i \in I} A_i$ is often also denoted by A, for convenience. For two sets A and B we denote the set of all mappings from A to B by $B^A = \{f \mid f : A \to B\}$. If we have $f_1 : A \to B$ and $f_2 : C \to D$ such that A and C are disjoint then $(f_1 \uplus f_2) : A \cup C \to B \cup D$ denotes the union of both functions.

Monoids. A set A together with a commutative associative binary operation $+$ and a neutral element $0 \in A$ is called *commutative monoid*; if there is additionally a reflexive and transitive relation $\hookrightarrow \subseteq A \times A$, then we call $\mathcal{M} = (A, +, 0, \hookrightarrow)$

preordered commutative monoid iff $\hookrightarrow$ is *affine*, i.e. iff $\forall x, y, z \in A : x \hookrightarrow y \Rightarrow x + z \hookrightarrow y + z$.

Let $\mathcal{M} = (A, +, 0, \hookrightarrow)$ be a preordered commutative monoid and B be a set. By $\mathcal{L}_B(\mathcal{M}) = (A^B, +_l, 0_l, \hookrightarrow_l)$ we denote the *lifting* of $\mathcal{M}$ over B where $+_l, 0_l, \hookrightarrow_l$ are defined by $(f_1 +_l f_2)(x) = f_1(x) + f_2(x), 0_l(x) = 0$, and $f_1 \hookrightarrow_l f_2$ iff $\forall x \in B : f_1(x) \hookrightarrow f_2(x)$. We omit the index l where clear from the context.

Multisets and bags. A *multiset* over a fixed set A is a mapping $M : A \to \mathbb{Z}$. The set of all multisets over A is denoted by $\mathbb{Z}^A$. We write $M[a]$ instead of $M(a)$ for the *multiplicity* of an element a in M. We define addition $+$, the empty multiset $[]$, and inclusion $\leq$ of multisets by lifting $(\mathbb{Z}, +, 0, \leq)$ over A. The *support* of a multiset is defined by $supp\, M = \{x \in A \mid M[x] \neq 0\}$. M is *nonnegative* iff $M[x] \geq 0$ for all x in A, and M is *finite* iff $supp\, M$ is finite. We define the cardinality of a finite multiset M by $|M| = \sum_{x \in A} M[x]$.

A finite nonnegative multiset is also called *bag*. The set of all bags over A is denoted by $\mathrm{BAG}(A)$. We represent a bag by enumerating its elements in square brackets: $[a_1, \ldots, a_n]$ (according to the multiplicities).

Algebras and signatures. A *signature* $SIG = (S, OP)$ consists of a finite set S of *sort symbols* and a pairwise disjoint family $OP = (OP_a)_{a \in S+}$ of *operation symbols*. A *SIG-algebra* $A = ((A_s)_{s \in S}, (f_{op})_{op \in OP})$ consists of a family $A = (A_s)_{s \in S}$ of sets and a family $(f_{op})_{op \in OP}$ of total functions such that for $op \in OP_{s_1 \ldots s_n s_{n+1}}$ we have $f_{op} : A_{s_1} \times \ldots \times A_{s_n} \to A_{s_{n+1}}$. A set A_s of an algebra is called *domain* and a function f_{op} is called *operation* of the algebra.

In the following we assume that a signature SIG has a sort symbol $bool \in S$ and in each SIG-algebra the corresponding domain is $A_{bool} = \mathbb{B}$.

Variables and terms. For a signature $SIG = (S, OP)$ we call a pairwise disjoint family $X = (X_s)_{s \in S}$ with $X \cap OP = \emptyset$ a *sorted SIG-variable set*. A *term* is built up from variables and operation symbols. Each term is associated with a particular sort. Let $X = (X_s)_{s \in S}$ be a sorted SIG-variable set. The *set of SIG-terms over X of sort s* is denoted by $\mathbf{T}_s^{SIG}(X)$ and inductively defined by:

1. $x \in X_s$ implies $x \in \mathbf{T}_s^{SIG}(X)$.
2. $u_i \in \mathbf{T}_{s_i}^{SIG}(X)$ for $i = 1, \ldots, n$ and $op \in OP_{s_1 \ldots s_n s_{n+1}}$ implies $op(u_1, \ldots, u_n) \in \mathbf{T}_{s_{n+1}}^{SIG}(X)$

The set of all terms (of any sort) is denoted by $\mathbf{T}^{SIG}(X)$. A term without variables is called *ground term*. We denote the set of ground terms by $\mathbf{T}^{SIG} = \mathbf{T}^{SIG}(\emptyset)$ and the set of ground terms of sort s by $\mathbf{T}_s^{SIG} = \mathbf{T}_s^{SIG}(\emptyset)$.

Evaluation of terms. For a signature $SIG = (S, OP)$, a sorted SIG-variable set $X = (X_s)_{s \in S}$, and a SIG-algebra $A = ((A_s)_{s \in S}, (f_{op})_{op \in OP})$ a mapping $\beta : X \to A$ is an *assignment for X* iff for each $s \in S$ and $x \in X_s$ holds $\beta(x) \in A_s$. We canonically extend β to a mapping $\overline{\beta} : \mathbf{T}^{SIG}(X) \to A$ by:

1. $\overline{\beta}(x) = \beta(x)$ for $x \in X$.

2. $\overline{\beta}(op(u_1,\dots,u_n)) = f_{op}(\overline{\beta}(u_1),\dots,\overline{\beta}(u_n))$ for $op(u_1,\dots,u_n) \in \mathbf{T}^{SIG}(X)$.

The mapping $\overline{\beta}$ is called β-evaluation in $\mathcal{A}$. Let $\beta_\emptyset : \emptyset \to A$ be the unique assignment for the empty variable set. By eval $:= \overline{\beta_\emptyset}$ we denote the evaluation of ground terms.

Substitutions. Let X and Y be SIG-variable sets. A mapping $\sigma : X \to \mathbf{T}^{SIG}(Y)$ is called *substitution* iff $x \in X_s$ implies $\sigma(x) \in \mathbf{T}_s^{SIG}(Y)$. Analogously to evaluations, we also extend a substitution σ to a mapping $\overline{\sigma} : \mathbf{T}^{SIG}(X) \to \mathbf{T}^{SIG}(Y)$ in order to apply it to terms. In case of $Y = \emptyset$ we call σ *ground substitution*.

Bag-signatures and -algebras. We introduce bag-signatures as particular signatures. In a bag-signature we distinguish some *ground-sorts* and we assign a *bag-sort* to each ground-sort. In a bag-algebra the domain associated with a bag-sort must be a bag over the domain of the corresponding ground-sort.

Definition 1 (Bag-signature, $BSIG$-algebra). *Let $SIG = (S, OP)$ be a signature and $GS, BS \subseteq S$; $BSIG = (S, OP, bs)$ is a bag-signature iff $bs : GS \to BS$ is a bijective mapping. An element of GS is called* ground-sort*, an element of BS is called* bag-sort *of $BSIG$. A SIG-algebra $\mathcal{A}$ is a $BSIG$-algebra iff for each $s \in GS$ holds $A_{bs(s)} = \mathrm{BAG}(A_s)$, i.e., if for each* ground-domain *the corresponding* bag-domain *is actually the set of all bags over the ground-domain.*

A bag-signature $BSIG = (S, OP, bs)$ is a specialized signature $SIG = (S, OP)$ and by definition each $BSIG$-algebra is a SIG-algebra. Therefore, terms, assignments, evaluation, and substitutions are well-defined for bag-signatures, too.

3.2 Algebraic System Nets

Petri nets. A *Petri net* (*net* for short) $N = (P, T, F)$ consists of two disjoint sets P and T and a relation $F \subseteq (P \times T) \cup (T \times P)$. An element of P is called *place*, an element of T is called *transition*, and an element of F is called *arc* of the net. As usual, we graphically represent a place by a circle, a transition by a square, and an arc by an arrow between the corresponding elements. A net is finite iff both, P and T, are finite.

Definition 2 (Place/Transition system). *A place/transition system $\Sigma = (N, W, M_0)$ consists of*

1. *a net $N = (P, T, F)$,*
2. *a weight function $W : F \to \mathbb{N}$, and*
3. *a marking M_0, called* initial marking *of Σ, where a marking of a place/transition system is a mapping $M : P \to \mathbb{N}$.*

We extend W to $W : (P \cup T) \times (T \cup P) \to \mathbb{N}$ by $W(f) = 0$ if $f \notin F$.

Definition 3 (Algebraic system net). *Let $BSIG = (S, OP, bs)$ be a bag-signature with bag-sorts BS. An algebraic system net $\Sigma = (N, \mathcal{A}, X, i)$ over $BSIG$ consists of*

1. *a finite net $N = (P, T, F)$ where P is sorted over BS, i.e., $P = (P_s)_{s \in BS}$ is a bag-valued BSIG-variable set,*
2. *a BSIG-Algebra $\mathcal{A}$,*
3. *a sorted BSIG-variable set X disjoint from P,*
4. *a net inscription $i : P \cup T \cup F \to \mathbf{T}^{BSIG}(X)$ such that*
   (a) *for each $p \in P_s : i(p) \in \mathbf{T}_s^{BSIG}$, i.e., the restriction of i to P is a ground substitution for P,*
   (b) *for each $t \in T : i(t) \in \mathbf{T}_{bool}^{BSIG}(X)$, and*
   (c) *for each $t \in T$, and for each $p \in P_s$ with $f = (t, p) \in F$ or $f = (p, t) \in F$ holds $i(f) \in \mathbf{T}_s^{BSIG}(X)$.*

For a place $p \in P$ the inscription $i(p)$ is called symbolic initial marking *of p; for a transition $t \in T$ the term $i(t)$ is called* guard *of t.*

Note that we allow multiset-valued operations as well as multiset-valued variables in arc inscriptions.

Definition 4 (Pre- and post-substitution). *For each transition t of an algebraic system net Σ we define the two substitutions $t^-, t^+ : P \to \mathbf{T}^{BSIG}(X)$, called* pre- *and* post-substitution *respectively, by:*

$$t^-(p) = \begin{cases} i(p, t) & \text{if } (p, t) \in F \\ [] & \text{otherwise} \end{cases} \qquad t^+(p) = \begin{cases} i(t, p) & \text{if } (t, p) \in F \\ [] & \text{otherwise} \end{cases}$$

In a sense, Def. 3 gives the syntax of algebraic system nets. The algebra is still given semantically because we want to be flexible. In this paper, we are a little bit sloppy in the distinction of syntax and semantics. For convenience, we introduce new operations when needed; sometimes we do not distinguish between operation symbols and their meaning. This helps to avoid some technical overhead and does not cause any problems; in practice this problem can be tackled by a sufficiently rich language of predefined auxiliary functions for defining new operations.

The semantics, i.e. the processes of an algebraic system net, will be defined in Sect. 3.3. Here, we define *markings* and the *firing-rule* for algebraic system nets. A marking associates each place of an algebraic system net with a bag over the corresponding sort.

Definition 5 (Marking and initial marking). *Let BSIG be a bag-signature and Σ be an algebraic system net as in Def. 3. A marking M of Σ is an assignment for P. The marking M_0 with $M_0(p) = \text{eval}(i(p))$ for each $p \in P$ is called the* initial marking *of Σ. We define the addition and inclusion of markings by lifting bags over P.*

Transitions of algebraic system nets fire in *modes*. A *mode* of a transition associates each variable of X with some value of the algebra. In a particular mode, an arc-inscription evaluates to some bag. A transition t may fire in mode β, if all elements denoted by the inscriptions of the input arcs of t are present in the current marking and the guard of the transition evaluates to true. We formalize the firing-rule by associating each pair (t, β) with a marking t_β^- and a marking t_β^+. The marking t_β^- and the marking t_β^+ represent the elements which are removed and added respectively, when t fires in mode β.

Definition 6 (Firing rule and reachable markings). *Let Σ be an algebraic system net as in Def. 3. Let $t \in T$ and β be an assignment of X in $\mathcal{A}$. We define the two markings t_β^- and t_β^+ by $t_\beta^-(p) = \overline{\beta}(t^-(p))$ and $t_\beta^+(p) = \overline{\beta}(t^+(p))$.*

In a given marking M_1 a transition t is *enabled* in mode β, iff there exists a marking M such that $M_1 = M + t_\beta^-$ and $\overline{\beta}(i(t)) = \text{true}$. Then, transition t may fire in mode β, which results in the *successor marking* $M_2 = M + t_\beta^+$. We denote the firing of transition t in mode β by $M_1 \xrightarrow{t,\beta} M_2$. We say a marking M' is *reachable from* a marking M, denoted $M \xrightarrow{*} M'$, iff there exists a finite chain of markings $M_1, \ldots, M_n$ such that $M_1 = M$, $M_n = M'$, and for each i the marking M_{i+1} is a successor marking of M_i. We say that a marking M is a *reachable marking of Σ* iff M is reachable from M_0, i.e. the initial marking of Σ.

Remark 1. In the following we only consider algebraic system nets in which for each transition t and each mode β, the markings t_β^- and t_β^+ are nonempty. This helps to avoid some anomalies in the definition of processes (cf. also [1]).

3.3 Processes of Algebraic System Nets

Now we define non-sequential processes [7,1] for algebraic system nets. First we introduce some prerequisites, which mainly follow the lines of [1].

Definition 7. *Let $N = (P, T, F)$ be a net.*

1. *For an element $x \in P \cup T$ of N we define the* preset *of x by $^\bullet x = \{y \in P \cup T \mid (y, x) \in F\}$ and the* postset *of x by $x^\bullet = \{y \in P \cup T \mid (x, y) \in F\}$.*
2. *We define the* minimal elements *of N by $^\circ N = \{x \in P \cup T \mid {}^\bullet x = \emptyset\}$ and the* maximal elements *of N by $N^\circ = \{x \in P \cup T \mid x^\bullet = \emptyset\}$.*
3. *For $x \in P \cup T$ we define the set of predecessors by $\downarrow x = \{y \in P \cup T \mid (y, x) \in F^+\}$, where F^+ denotes the transitive closure[4] of the flow relation F.*

Processes are defined by help of *occurrence nets*. An *occurrence net* has two main features: The flow relation is acyclic and is not branching at places. Moreover, each element of an occurrence net has only finitely many predecessors. For a detailed motivation of all features we refer to [7,1].

Definition 8 (Occurrence net). *A net $K = (B, E, <)$ is an occurrence net if*

1. *$^\circ K \subseteq B$ and $K^\circ \subseteq B$,*
2. *$^\circ K$ is finite and for each $e \in E$ both $^\bullet e$ and $e^\bullet$ are finite,*
3. *for each $b \in B$ holds $|^\bullet b| \leq 1$ and $|b^\bullet| \leq 1$, and*
4. *for each $b \in B$ the set of predecessors $\downarrow b$ is finite and $b \notin \downarrow b$.*

For the sake of clarity, we use new symbols for places and transitions of an occurrence net. Moreover, we call a place of an occurrence net *condition* and a transition *event*. Next we define the *states* of an occurrence net.

---

[4] Note, that we do not use the transitive and reflexive closure of F. This way, we can express acyclicity of F by $p \notin \downarrow p$ for each place $p \in P$.

Definition 9 (States of an occurrence net). *Let $K = (B, E, <)$ be an occurrence net. For subsets of conditions $Q, Q' \subseteq B$ we define the occurrence relation $\rightarrow$ by: $Q \rightarrow Q'$ iff there exists an event $e \in E$ such that $^\bullet e \subseteq Q$ and $Q' = (Q \setminus {}^\bullet e) \cup e^\bullet$. The transitive and reflexive closure of $\rightarrow$ is denoted by $\overset{*}{\rightarrow}$. For $Q, Q' \subseteq B$ we say Q' is reachable from Q, if $Q \overset{*}{\rightarrow} Q'$.*

A subset of conditions $Q \subseteq B$ is a state *of K, if Q is reachable from $^\circ K$. The set $^\circ K$ is called the* initial state *of K.*

Processes of algebraic system nets. In a process each condition of the occurrence net is associated with some place of the algebraic system net along with an element of the corresponding domain. This is formalized as condition labelling.

Definition 10 (Condition labelling). *Let Σ be an algebraic system net over a bag-signature $BSIG$ as in Def. 3, and $K = (B, E, <)$ be an occurrence net. A mapping $r : B \rightarrow P \times A$ is a* condition labelling *of K, iff for each $b \in B$ with $r(b) = (p, a)$ it holds that $a \in A_s \Rightarrow p \in P_{bs(s)}$.*

For a given condition labelling r each finite subset $Q \subseteq B$ can be associated with a marking. We denote this marking by $r(Q)$ and define it by $r(Q) : P \rightarrow \mathrm{BAG}(A)$ with $r(Q)(p)[a] = |\{b \in Q \mid r(b) = (p, a)\}|$.

An occurrence net with labelled conditions is a *process* of an algebraic system net, if the initial state is labelled by the initial marking and each event corresponds to the firing of a transition in some mode.

Definition 11 (Process). *Let Σ be an algebraic system net, $K = (B, E, <)$ be an occurrence net, and r be a condition labelling of K. Then, (K, r) is a* process *of Σ, iff*

1. *$r(^\circ K) = M_0$, where M_0 is the initial marking of Σ, and*
2. *for each event $e \in E$ there exists a transition $t \in T$ and a mode β such that $\overline{\beta}(i(t)) = true$, $r(^\bullet e) = t_\beta^-$, and $r(e^\bullet) = t_\beta^+$.*

Def. 11 is the canonical extension of processes [1] to algebraic system nets (cf. Sect. 7), where we omit the labelling of events. The labelling of events by a pair of a transition and a mode would be somewhat awkward — in particular, when some variable does not occur at a transition. Actually, this omission of event-labels allows to define a mode as an assignment to all variables of the algebraic system net without any problems (if all domains are non-empty).

4 Place Invariants

In this section we will define and investigate place invariants for algebraic system nets. As already shown in the introduction we use linear expressions rather than vectors of terms for representing place invariants. In these expressions places are interpreted as variables of the corresponding bag sort.

Definition 12 (Place invariant). *Let BSIG be a bag-signature, Σ be an algebraic system net over BSIG with places P. Let $v \in \mathbf{T}^{BSIG}(P)$ be a multiset-valued expression with the place names of the net as variables. Given a marking M of Σ, i.e. an assignment for P, expression v can be evaluated to $v_M := \overline{M}(v)$; then, v is called* place invariant *of Σ iff*

1. *v is linear, i.e. for all M_1, M_2 it holds that $v_{M_1+M_2} = v_{M_1} + v_{M_2}$, and*
2. *for all transitions t the conditional equation $i(t) \Rightarrow t^-(v) = t^+(v)$ holds.*

Remark 2. Since $\mathbb{Z}^{\{\bullet\}}$ is isomorphic to $\mathbb{Z}$ we also take integer valued expressions into consideration for place invariants. We call such a place invariant *simple*.

Note that we defined linearity semantically. A syntactical characterization is straight-forward and can be found in [24]. As already stated, the evaluation of a place invariant is constant for all reachable markings:

Theorem 1. *If v is a place invariant of Σ and M_0 is its initial marking then all reachable markings M of Σ satisfy $v_M = v_{M_0}$.*

Proof. Consequence of the forthcoming Theorem 3.

Reisig [17] represents a place invariant by a P-vector of multiset terms: To each place $p \in P$ a non-flexible multiset term is assigned, which represents a function f_p. Here non-flexibility means: For all markings M_1, M_2 we have $|M_1(p)| = |M_2(p)|$ implies $|f_p(M_1(p))| = |f_p(M_2(p))|$. An immediate consequence of this is the following: For f_p there exists a number n_p such that $|f_p(p)| = n_p \cdot |p|$. The vector notation of [17] translates to the linear expression $f_{p_1}(p_1) + f_{p_2}(p_2) + \cdots + f_{p_n}(p_n)$.

In Section 6 we redefine place invariants where we allow also additional variables in the expression (Such variables are also allowed in the terms f_p of [17]). Such variables do not increase the expressivity of place invariants, but the use of them is sometimes convenient.

5 Unfoldings

In Sect. 3.3 we have defined the semantics of an algebraic system net in terms of processes. An alternative approach is to define the semantics of an algebraic system net by *unfolding* it to a place/transition system (e.g. [20]). Here, we will define the unfolding of an algebraic system net. The main reason, however, for defining unfoldings is that we want to relate the place invariants of an algebraic system net with the place invariants of its unfolding.

First, we will present the definition of an unfolding. Subsequently, we give an example of an algebraic Petri net [17] which has a place invariant in the unfolding but no corresponding place invariant (according to the definition of [17]) in the algebraic Petri net itself. Last we will show that this does no longer hold for our version of place invariants: According to our definition each place invariant of the unfolding has a corresponding place invariant in the algebraic system net itself.

5.1 Definition of the Unfolding

The unfolding of an algebraic system net is a place/transition-system. The main idea of the unfolding is the following: Each transition of the unfolding corresponds to a transition of the algebraic system net in a particular mode. Each place corresponds to a place of the algebraic system net projected to a particular element on that place. Technically, a transition of the unfolding is a pair of a transition t of the algebraic system net and a mode β; a place of the unfolding is a pair of a place of the algebraic system net and an element a of the corresponding domain. Arcs and the arc-inscriptions carry over accordingly.

Definition 13 (Unfolding). *Let $\Sigma = (N, \mathcal{A}, X, i)$ be an algebraic system net over $BSIG = (S, OP, bs)$ with net $N = (P, T, F)$, ground sorts GS, and initial marking M_0. We define*

1. $\widehat{P} = \bigcup_{s \in GS} \bigcup_{p \in P_{bs(s)}} \{(p, a) \mid a \in A_s\}$
2. $\widehat{T} = \bigcup_{t \in T} \{(t, \beta) \mid \overline{\beta}(i(t)) = true\}$
3. $\widehat{F} \subseteq (\widehat{P} \times \widehat{T}) \cup (\widehat{T} \times \widehat{P})$ by
   $\widehat{F} = \{((p, a), (t, \beta)) \mid (p, a) \in \widehat{P}, (t, \beta) \in \widehat{T}, \overline{\beta}(i(p, t))[a] \geq 1\} \cup$
   $\{((t, \beta), (p, a)) \mid (p, a) \in \widehat{P}, (t, \beta) \in \widehat{T}, \overline{\beta}(i(t, p))[a] \geq 1\}$
4. $\widehat{W} : \widehat{F} \to \mathbb{N}$ by $\widehat{W}((p, a), (t, \beta)) = \overline{\beta}(i(p, t))[a]$ resp. $\widehat{W}((t, \beta), (p, a)) = \overline{\beta}(i(t, p))[a]$ for $(p, a) \in \widehat{P}, (t, \beta) \in \widehat{T}$.
5. $\widehat{M_0} : \widehat{P} \to \mathbb{N}$ by $\widehat{M_0}((p, a)) = M_0(p)[a]$ for $(p, a) \in \widehat{P}$.

$\widehat{\Sigma} = ((\widehat{P}, \widehat{T}, \widehat{F}), \widehat{W}, \widehat{M_0})$ *is a place/transition-system called the* unfolding *of Σ.*

An example of an algebraic system net Σ_2 and its unfolding $\widehat{\Sigma_2}$ can be found in Fig. 3 and 4, where we assume that the domain of both places is $BAG(\{a, b\})$ and the set of variables is empty. This is a very simple example since each transition has exactly one mode (there are no variables).

5.2 Place Invariants of Unfoldings

In this section we will show that each place invariant of the unfolding can be represented as a place invariant of the original algebraic system net. Though, this is a desirable property and seems to be obvious, this does not hold for place invariants of Reisig [17]; this will be demonstrated by a simple example. Vice versa, each place invariant of the algebraic system net represents a set of place invariants in the low-level system. First, we present the classical definition of place invariants of a place/transition-system.

Definition 14 (Place invariants of place/transition-systems).
Let (N, W, M_0) be a place/transition-system with $N = (P, T, F)$. A mapping (often called vector in this context) $j : P \to \mathbb{Z}$ is a place invariant of the place/transition-system, if for each transition $t \in T$ the following equation holds:
$$\sum_{p \in P} j(p) \cdot W(p, t) = \sum_{p \in P} j(p) \cdot W(t, p).$$

The main idea of a place invariant j is that it can be interpreted as a valuation of markings by $j(M) = \sum_{p \in P} j(p) \cdot M(p)$. Then, we have for each two markings with $M \longrightarrow M'$: $j(M) = j(M')$.

A counter-example. First of all, we demonstrate that in the formalism of Reisig [17] there exists a place invariant of an unfolded algebraic Petri net which has no corresponding place invariant in the algebraic Petri net itself. Consider the algebraic Petri net Σ_2 of Fig. 3, where a and b are two different constants of the same sort. Figure 4 shows the unfolding $\widehat{\Sigma_2}$ of this algebraic system net. Obviously, $j = (p_1, a) + (p_2, a)$ is a place invariant of $\widehat{\Sigma_2}$. Now, we will show that Σ_2 has no place invariant which corresponds to j, when we restrict to non-flexible expressions. Actually, we show that Σ_2 has only a trivial non-flexible place invariant. Assume that a non-flexible expression u is a place invariant of Σ_2. Then, u can be represented by $f_1(p_1) + f_2(p_2)$. It follows that $|f_1(p_1) + f_2(p_2)|$ is also a place invariant of Σ_2 which can equivalently be rewritten to $|f_1(p_1)| + |f_2(p_2)|$. Since the invariant u was non-flexible, we know that there exist integer values n_1 and n_2 such that $|f_1(p_1)| + |f_2(p_2)| = n_1 \cdot |p_1| + n_2 \cdot |p_2|$. By definition this expression is a place invariant if and only if the following two equations hold true: $n_1 \cdot |[a]| + n_2 \cdot |[]| = n_1 \cdot |[]| + n_2 \cdot |[a]|$ and $n_1 \cdot |[a]| + n_2 \cdot |[]| = n_1 \cdot |[]| + n_2 \cdot |[a] + [b]|$. These equations can be simplified to $n_1 = n_2$ and $n_1 = 2 \cdot n_2$. This implies $n_1 = n_2 = 0$. Therefore, u is a place invariant which evaluates to 0 for each marking; i.e. u is a trivial place invariant.

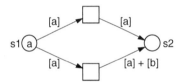

Fig. 3. An algebraic system net Σ_2.   **Fig. 4.** The Unfolding $\widehat{\Sigma_2}$.

The reason why there are only trivial place invariants of Σ_2 in the approach of Reisig [17] is that each token on a place is mapped to a multiset of the same cardinality. In order to express the invariant j of the unfolding, it is necessary to map a token a on places p_1 and p_2 to a singleton multiset (e.g. by $[a]$) and a token b to the empty multiset $[]$. The invariant of $\widehat{\Sigma_2}$ from Fig. 4 can be formulated as a place invariant of Σ_2 by the expression $p1 + f_a(p2)$ where f_a is a linear function defined by $f_a([a]) = [a]$ and $f_a([b]) = []$, where f_a is not a legal function in the approach of [17].

Correspondence of place invariants. Next, we will see that flexibility in arcs as well as in place invariants gives an exact correspondence of place invariants of an algebraic system net with the place invariants of its unfolding. Of course, this correspondence depends on the expressiveness of the underlying algebra. In order to formalize this result, we must formalize when a place invariant of an algebraic system net corresponds to a place invariant of the unfolding.

Since a place invariant j of the unfolding $\widehat{\Sigma}$ evaluates to $\mathbb{Z}$, we actually have a simple place invariant of the algebraic system net Σ corresponding to j

(cf. Remark 2). Therefore, we only define *correspondence of place invariants* for simple place invariants.

Definition 15 (Correspondence of place invariants). *Let Σ be an algebraic system net with places P and $u \in \mathbf{T}^{BSIG}(P)$ be a simple place invariant of Σ, and j be a place invariant of $\widehat{\Sigma}$. We say u corresponds to j, if for each marking M of Σ holds $u_M = \sum_{\hat{p} \in \widehat{P}} \widehat{M}(\hat{p}) \cdot j(\hat{p})$.*

Now, we fix an arbitrary place invariant j of the unfolding $\widehat{\Sigma}$. We define for each place $p \in P_s$ of Σ the operation $f_p^j : A_s \to \mathbb{Z}$ as linear extension of $f_p^j([a]) = j(p, a)$ for each $a \in A_s$. Then, $f_{p_1}^j(p_1) + \ldots + f_{p_n}^j(p_n)$ is a simple place invariant of Σ corresponding to j, where we assume that $P = \{p_1, \ldots, p_n\}$ are the places of Σ.

Theorem 2. *Let Σ be an algebraic system net with finitely many places and j be a place invariant of the unfolding $\widehat{\Sigma}$. Then there exists a simple place invariant u of Σ which corresponds to j.*

Proof. We choose $u = f_{p_1}^j(p_1) + \ldots + f_{p_n}^j(p_n)$. Obviously, u and j correspond to each other. It remains to be shown that u is a place invariant of Σ. We prove the contraposition. Let us assume that u is not a place invariant of Σ; now, we show that j is not a place invariant of $\widehat{\Sigma}$.

Since u is not a place invariant of Σ there exists a transition such that the implication $i(t) \Rightarrow t^-(u) = t^+(u)$ is not valid. Therefore, there exists an assignment β such that $\overline{\beta}(i(t)) = \text{true}$ and $\overline{\beta}(t^-(u)) \neq \overline{\beta}(t^+(u))$. By definition of $\widehat{\Sigma}$ there exists a transition $\hat{t} = (t, \beta) \in \widehat{T}$ in the unfolding $\widehat{\Sigma}$. Then, we have

$$
\begin{aligned}
&\overline{\beta}(t^-(u)) = && \text{def. of } u \text{ and } t^- \\
&\overline{\beta}(f_{p_1}^j(i(t, p_1)) + \ldots + f_{p_n}^j(i(t, p_n))) = && \text{def. of } \overline{\beta} \\
&f_{p_1}^j(\overline{\beta}(i(t, p_1))) + \ldots + f_{p_n}^j(\overline{\beta}(i(t, p_n))) = && \text{equiv. multiset-represent.} \\
&f_{p_1}^j(\sum_{a \in A} \overline{\beta}(i(t, p_1))[a] \cdot [a]) + \ldots + \\
&\quad f_{p_n}^j(\sum_{a \in A} \overline{\beta}(i(t, p_n))[a] \cdot [a]) = && \text{linearity of functions } f_p^j \\
&\sum_{a \in A} \overline{\beta}(i(t, p_1))[a] \cdot f_{p_1}^j([a]) + \ldots + \\
&\quad \sum_{a \in A} \overline{\beta}(i(t, p_n))[a] \cdot f_{p_n}^j([a]) = \\
&\sum_{a \in A} \sum_{p \in P} \overline{\beta}(i(t, p))[a] \cdot f_p^j([a]) = && \text{def. of } W \text{ and } f_p^j \\
&\sum_{a \in A} \sum_{p \in P} W((t, \beta), (p, a)) \cdot j(p, a) = && \text{def. of } \widehat{P} \\
&\sum_{\hat{p} \in \widehat{P}} W(\hat{t}, \hat{p}) \cdot j(\hat{p})
\end{aligned}
$$

By the same arguments we get $\overline{\beta}(t^+(u)) = \sum_{\hat{p} \in \widehat{P}} W(\hat{p}, \hat{t}) \cdot j(\hat{p})$. Then it follows from $\overline{\beta}(t^-(u)) \neq \overline{\beta}(t^+(p))$ that $\sum_{\hat{p} \in \widehat{P}} W(\hat{t}, \hat{p}) \cdot j(\hat{p}) \neq \sum_{\hat{p} \in \widehat{P}} W(\hat{p}, \hat{t}) \cdot j(\hat{p})$, which implies that j is not a place invariant of $\widehat{\Sigma}$.

Now we consider the reverse direction. A place invariant u of domain $\mathbb{Z}^B$ represents a family of simple place invariants $(u[b])_{b \in B}$. Each simple place invariant can be easily translated to a place invariant of the unfolding. Therefore, a place invariant u of Σ corresponds to a family of place invariants of $\widehat{\Sigma}$.

6 More Linear Verification Techniques

Now we define linear expressions - the basic notion of this section. Subsequently we define several known and some new linear verification techniques as special linear expressions.

Definition 16 (Expressions, linear expressions). *Let BSIG be a bag-signature with sorts S and let Σ be an algebraic system net over BSIG with places P and variables X. Furthermore let Y be a variable set disjoint from P and X. A Σ-expression $(u : \mathcal{M})$ consists of a term $u \in \mathbf{T}_s^{BSIG}(Y \cup P)$ and a preordered commutative monoid $\mathcal{M} = (A_s, +, 0, \hookrightarrow)$, called the* type *of the Σ-expression.*

Given an assignment γ for Y and an assignment M for P (i.e. a marking), the term u evaluates to $u_M^{\gamma} := \overline{\gamma \uplus M}(u)$. A Σ-expression $(u : \mathcal{M})$ is linear iff:

$$\forall \gamma : \forall M_1, M_2 : u_{M_1+M_2}^{\gamma} = u_{M_1}^{\gamma} + u_{M_2}^{\gamma} \tag{1}$$

We say $(u : \mathcal{M})$ simulates Σ (is a simulation of Σ) iff for each transition t of Σ the following condition is satisfied:

$$i(t) \Rightarrow \overline{t^-}(u) \hookrightarrow \overline{t^+}(u) \tag{2}$$

The following theorem is the basis for deriving invariance properties from simulations.

Theorem 3. *Let Σ be an algebraic system net with initial state M_0, $(u : \mathcal{M})$ a linear Σ-expression which simulates Σ. Then, for each assignment γ and for each reachable marking M of Σ we have $u_{M_0}^{\gamma} \hookrightarrow u_M^{\gamma}$.*

Proof. Let γ be an arbitrary assignment. First we show that $M \overset{t,\beta}{\to} M'$ implies $u_M^{\gamma} + u_{M'}^{\gamma}$ for all markings M, M' of Σ: If we have $M \overset{t,\beta}{\to} M'$ then we have $\overline{\beta}(i(t)) =$ true and it exists a marking $\widetilde{M}$ such that $M = \widetilde{M} + t_{\beta}^-$ and $M' = \widetilde{M} + t_{\beta}^+$. By (2) we get $\overline{\beta \uplus \gamma}(t^-(u)) \hookrightarrow \overline{\beta \uplus \gamma}(t^+(u))$ and therefore $u_{t_{\beta}^-}^{\gamma} \hookrightarrow u_{t_{\beta}^+}^{\gamma}$. By affinity of $\hookrightarrow$ also $u_{\widetilde{M}}^{\gamma} + u_{t_{\beta}^-}^{\gamma} \hookrightarrow u_{\widetilde{M}}^{\gamma} + u_{t_{\beta}^+}^{\gamma}$ holds. This yields $u_{\widetilde{M}+t_{\beta}^-}^{\gamma} \hookrightarrow u_{\widetilde{M}+t_{\beta}^+}^{\gamma}$ by linearity (1) which is what we wanted to show.

Now, by reflexivity and transitivity of $\hookrightarrow$ we get $u_{M_0}^{\gamma} \hookrightarrow u_M^{\gamma}$ for each reachable marking M of Σ.

We now derive traditional notions as special cases of simulations.

Definition 17 (Invariant expression, monotonic expression). *Let Σ be an algebraic system net, $\mathcal{M} = (B, +, 0, \hookrightarrow)$ a preordered commutative monoid and $(u : \mathcal{M})$ a linear Σ-expression which simulates Σ. Then, $(u : \mathcal{M})$ is called*

1. invariant expression *of Σ iff $\hookrightarrow$ is an equivalence.*
2. monotonic expression *of Σ iff $\hookrightarrow$ is an order.*

Definition 18 (Place invariant, modulo-place-invariant). *Let B be a set. An invariant expression $(u : \mathcal{M})$ of Σ is called*

1. place invariant *iff* $\mathcal{M} = \mathcal{L}_B(\mathbb{Z}, +, 0, =)$.
2. modulo-k-place-invariant *iff* $\mathcal{M} = \mathcal{L}_B(\mathbb{Z}, +, 0, \equiv_{\mathrm{mod}\ k})$, *where* $\equiv_{\mathrm{mod}\ k}$ *denotes the remainder class equivalence for some* $k > 0$.

The expressiveness of invariant expressions is quite restricted. They only imply invariant properties which are preserved under reverse firing. If a desired invariant property is not derivable from an invariant expression, a monotonic expression might help.

Definition 19 (Trap, siphon, semi-place-invariant). *Let* B *be a set. A monotonic expression* $(u : \mathcal{M})$ *of* Σ *is called*

1. (individual) trap *iff* $\mathcal{M} = (2^B, \cup, \emptyset, \subseteq)$.
2. (individual) siphon *iff* $\mathcal{M} = (2^B, \cup, \emptyset, \supseteq)$.
3. increasing semi-place-invariant *iff* $\mathcal{M} = \mathcal{L}_B(\mathbb{Z}, +, 0, \leq)$.
4. decreasing semi-place-invariant *iff* $\mathcal{M} = \mathcal{L}_B(\mathbb{Z}, +, 0, \geq)$.

In Σ_1 we have, for example, the trap $supp\ pr_1$(messages + distance): Once there is a token with x as its first component at messages or distance it remains so forever. Another trap of Σ_1 is F(distance) where F is defined by $F(x, n) = \{(x, m) \mid m \geq n\}$. Treating $F(x, n)$ as a multiset, F(distance) is even an increasing semi-place-invariant.

From a trap we may only conclude that there is a particular token at one of the corresponding places. An increasing semi-place-invariant, however, has more potential: If it contains negative terms we may directly infer implications such as: If there is a particular token at place p then there is some other token at place q (for an example see the full version of this paper [13]). Next we investigate some verification techniques for special liveness properties of an algebraic system net.

Definition 20 (Stabilization expression, termination expression). *Let* $\mathcal{M} = (B, +, 0, \succeq)$ *be a* regular *preordered commutative monoid, i.e. the monoid satisfies the following property:*

$$\forall x, y, z \in B : x + z = y + z \Rightarrow x = y \tag{3}$$

Furthermore let $(u : \mathcal{M})$ *be a monotonic expression of* Σ.

1. *A transition* t *of* Σ *is called* strict *with respect to* $(u : \mathcal{M})$ *iff*

$$i(t) \Rightarrow \overline{t^-}(u) \neq \overline{t^+}(u) \tag{4}$$

2. $(u : \mathcal{M})$ *is called* stabilization expression *iff* $\succeq$ *is well-founded[5].*
3. *A stabilization expression is called* termination expression *iff all transitions of* Σ *are strict with respect to it.*

Theorem 4. *Let* Σ *be an algebraic system net and* $(u : \mathcal{M})$ *a stabilization expression of* Σ. *Then, each process of* Σ *contains only finitely many occurrences of transitions which are strict w.r.t.* $(u : \mathcal{M})$.

---

[5] An order $\succeq$ is well-founded iff there is no infinite strictly decreasing chain $x_0 \succ x_1 \succ x_2 \succ \dots$.

Proof. Since $(u : \mathcal{M})$ is a simulation for each $M \overset{t,\beta}{\to} M'$ holds $u_M \succeq u_{M'}$ (see proof of Theorem 3). Moreover we can show in the same manner that $u_M \neq u_{M'}$ when t is strict w.r.t. $(u : \mathcal{M})$. This is because the contraposition of (3) is affinity of $\neq$. Since $\succeq$ is well-founded, we know that the value of u can be strictly decreased only finitely many times. Therefore, there can be only finitely many occurrences of strict transitions in a process.

As a corollary we get: If there is a termination expression of Σ then every process of Σ is finite. If we consider Σ_1 and choose the monoid $\mathbb{N} \times \mathbb{N}$ together with the lexicographic order then $(|\text{rootagents}+\text{inneragents}|, SUM(pr_2(\text{distance})))$ is a termination expression, where $SUM : \text{BAG}(\mathbb{N}) \to \mathbb{N}$ denotes the sum of all elements of a bag.

Definition 21 (Sur-place-invariant, sub-place-invariant).
1. *An increasing semi-place-invariant is called* sur-place-invariant *iff all transitions are strict with respect to it.*
2. *A decreasing semi-place-invariant is called* sub-place-invariant *iff all transitions are strict with respect to it.*

If we have in addition to a sur-place-invariant (sub-place-invariant) also a higher (lower) bound for the expression then we know that the system always terminates. Proving termination this way is sometimes more convenient than proving it by a termination expression as it allows negative terms, i.e. the use of the difference, in the expression.

7   Processes and Unfoldings

In Sect. 3.3 we have defined the semantics of an algebraic system net in terms of its processes. In Sect. 5 we have defined the unfolding to a place/transition-system as an alternative semantics. Now, there is a standard concept of processes for place/transition-systems [1]. Therefore, we have two different versions of processes of an algebraic system net: the processes of the direct definition and the processes of the unfolding. In this last section, we will demonstrate that both definitions coincide. To this end, we rephrase the definition of a process of a place/transition system, which mainly follows the lines of [1].

Definition 22. *Let* $((P,T,F),W,m)$ *be a place/transition system. Furthermore, let* $K = (B,E,F)$ *be an occurrence net and let* $r : B \to P$ *be a mapping. The pair* (K,r) *is a process of the place/transition-system, iff*
1. *for each place* $p \in P$ *holds* $|\{b \in {}^\circ K \mid r(b) = p\}| = m(p)$ *and*
2. *for each event* $e \in E$ *there exists a* $t \in T$ *such that for each* $p \in P$ $|\{b \in {}^\bullet e \mid r(b) = p)\}| = W(p,t)$ *and* $|\{b \in e^\bullet \mid r(b) = p)\}| = W(t,p)$ *holds.*

Finally we observe that each process of an algebraic system net is a process of its unfolding and vice versa.

Theorem 5. *Let* Σ *be an algebraic system net, K be an occurrence net. Then, (K,r) is a process of Σ, if and only if (K,r) it is a process of the unfolding $\widehat{\Sigma}$.*

The proof is purely technical and can be found in [13].

8 Conclusion

In this paper we have defined algebraic system nets along with a corresponding concept of place invariants. The main motivation was a net formalism for modelling distributed network algorithms. For the same reason, we have introduced a different syntactical representation of place invariants, viz. linear expressions, and their generalization to simulations. In particular, traps, stabilization expressions, and termination expressions turned out to be useful in the verification of distributed algorithms [12, 24, 23].

Algebraic system nets are a generalization of algebraic Petri nets which overcomes some insufficiencies of the place invariant concept. Though inspired by the work of Vautherin [22] and Reisig [17], algebraic system nets as proposed in this paper show some fundamental differences:

1. There are no flexible arcs in [22, 17].
2. Reisig [17] uses algebraic specifications [6] for representing the involved algebra. Here, we do not focus on that aspect; rather, we are free to use any appropriate formalism for representing the used algebra.
3. Reisig [17] represents a place invariant as a vector of terms. For convenience we represent a place invariant as a *linear expression* in which places may occur as variables. This representation was inspired by verification techniques for algebraic system nets, since linear expressions allow a smooth transition form Petri net concepts such as place invariants to temporal properties (cf. [18, 12, 24, 11]).
4. Reisig [17] introduces a firing rule as semantics for algebraic nets, only. In this paper we also introduce the non-sequential behaviour for algebraic system nets, which we call *processes* of the algebraic system net. This is justified, since we have shown that the set of processes of an algebraic system net exactly corresponds to the processes [1] of the unfolding.

Acknowledgements We thank Wolfgang Reisig and Karsten Schmidt for helpful suggestions and comments.

References

1. E. Best and C. Fernández. *Nonsequential Processes*. Springer, 1988.
2. J. Billington. Extending coloured Petri nets. Technical Report 148, University of Cambridge, Computer Laboratory, Oct. 1988.
3. J. Billington. *Extensions to Coloured Petri Nets and their Application to Protocols*. Technical Report 222, University of Cambridge, May 1991.
4. M. Broy. On the design and verification of a simple distributed spanning tree algorithm. SFB-Bericht 342/24/90 A, Technische Universität München, Dec. 1990.
5. J. Desel, K.-P. Neuendorf, and M.-D. Radola. Proving nonreachability by modulo-invariants. *Theoretical Computer Science*, 153:49–64, 1996.
6. H. Ehrig and B. Mahr. *Fundamentals of Algebraic Specifications 1, Equations and Initial Semantics*, Springer, 1985.

364

7. U. Goltz and W. Reisig. The non-sequential behaviour of Petri nets. *Information and Control*, 57:125–147, 1983.
8. K. Jensen. *Coloured Petri Nets, Volume 1: Basic Concepts.* Springer, 1992.
9. K. Jensen. *Coloured Petri Nets. Volume 2: Analysis Methods.* Springer, 1995.
10. E. Kindler and W. Reisig. Algebraic system nets for modelling distributed algorithms. *Petri Net Newsletter*, 51:16–31, Dec. 1996.
11. E. Kindler and W. Reisig. Verification of distributed algorithms with algebraic Petri nets. In C. Freksa, M. Jantzen, and R. Valk, editors, *Foundations of Computer Science: Potential – Theory – Cognition, LNCS* 1337, pp. 261–270. Springer 1997.
12. E. Kindler, W. Reisig, H. Völzer, and R. Walter. Petri net based verification of distributed algorithms: An example. *Formal Aspects of Computing*, 9:409–424, 1997.
13. E. Kindler and H. Völzer. Flexibility in algebraic nets. Informatik-Bericht 89, Humboldt-Universität zu Berlin, Institut für Informatik, 1997. Available at http://www.informatik.hu-berlin.de/˜ kindler/papers.html
14. G. Memmi and G. Roucairol. Linear algebra in net theory. In W. Braucr, cditor, *Net Theory and Applications, LNCS* 84, pp. 213–223. Springer, Oct. 1979.
15. J. L. Peterson. *Petri Net Theory And The Modeling of Systems.* Prentice-Hall 1981.
16. W. Reisig. *Petri Nets*, Springer, 1985.
17. W. Reisig. Petri nets and algebraic specifications. *Theoretical Computer Science*, 80:1–34, May 1991.
18. W. Reisig. Petri net models of distributed algorithms. In J. van Leeuwen, editor, *Computer Science Today: Recent Trends and Developments, LNCS* 1000, pp. 441–454. Springer, 1995.
19. K. Schmidt. Verification of siphons and traps for algebraic Petri nets. In P. Azéma and G. Balbo, editors, *Application and Theory of Petri Nets 1997, International Conference, Proceedings, LNCS* 1248, pp. 427–446. Springer, June 1997.
20. E. Smith and W. Reisig. The semantics of a net is a net, an exercise in general net theory. In K. Voss, H. Genrich, and G. Rozenberg, editors, *Concurrency and Nets.* Springer, 1987.
21. R. Valk. Bridging the gap between place- and Floyd-invariants with applications to preemptive scheduling. In M. A. Marsan (ed), *Application and Theory of Petri Nets 1993, International Conference, Proceedings, LNCS* 691, pp. 431–452. Springer, June 1993.
22. J. Vautherin. Parallel systems specifications with coloured Petri nets and algebraic specifications. In G. Rozenberg, editor, *Advances in Petri Nets, LNCS* 266, pp. 293–308. Springer, 1987.
23. H. Völzer. Verifying fault tolerance of distributed algorithms formally: An example. In *CSD98, 'International Conference on Application of Concurrency to System Design'*, Aizu-Wakamatsu City, Japan, Mar. 1998. IEEE Computer Society Press.
24. M. Weber, R. Walter, H. Völzer, T. Vesper, W. Reisig, S. Peuker, E. Kindler, J. Freiheit, and J. Desel. DAWN: Petrinetzmodelle zur Verifikation Verteilter Algorithmen. Informatik-Bericht 88, Humboldt-Universität zu Berlin, Dec. 1997.

ESTL: A Temporal Logic for Events and States*

Ekkart Kindler, Tobias Vesper

Humboldt-Universität zu Berlin, Institut für Informatik, Unter den Linden 6,
D-10099 Berlin**

Abstract. In some phases of system development *state-based* methods
are adequate; in others *event-based* methods are adequate. Petri nets
provide a system model which supports both methods and thus allow a
smooth transition between the different phases of system development.
Most temporal logics for Petri nets, however, do not support both methods.
In this paper we introduce a temporal logic for Petri nets which allows
to argue about states as well as to argue about events. This way, specifications in the early phases can be event-based and verification in later
phases can be state-based within a single formalism.

Keywords: Temporal logic; events; states; Petri nets; system development; specification; verification.

Introduction

Most *formal methods* employed for the specification and development of distributed systems are either *event-based* or *state-based*. The event-based methods
highlight the events and their relation; the state-based methods emphasize the
states and the state changes. Both approaches have their pros and cons which
should not be played off against each other.

For system development both views seem to be equally important [1]. For
example, in the case study HDMS of the KORSO project [3] the informal requirements are event-based. In the later phases properties are given state-based
and are verified in a state-based temporal logic [4]. More generally, we believe
that in the early phases of systems development event-based methods are often
more suitable than state-based methods (e.g. SADT [16,9]); in contrast to later
phases where often state-based methods seem to be more suitable. The reason is
that — in the field of business processes — users describe their business in terms
of activities and events which trigger these activities; in order to communicate
with the users in the early design phases, event-based description techniques are
necessary. In later phases the use of state-based techniques is more suitable since
implementation languages are often state-based. Therefore, a formal method (or
a set of collated methods) should cover both, event-based and state-based views
and should provide a smooth transition between these views.

---

* supported by the DFG within the research group "Petri Net Technology"
** e-mail: {kindler,vesper}@informatik.hu-berlin.de

Petri nets are a formal model which is equally well suited for both views; *places* correspond to the state-based view and *transitions* correspond to the event-based view. Maybe, one of the main features of Petri nets is the perfect balance between both views. Therefore, formal methods based on Petri nets allow a smooth transition between the event-based view and the state-based view.

Most temporal logics introduced for Petri nets do not support both views — these logics are either state-based or event-based (cf. [17]). In this paper we introduce a temporal logic which supports both views. This logic is an extension of a set of related state-based temporal logics for Petri nets [13,18,14], which have been developed for the verification of distributed algorithms and are called *Distributed Algorithms' Working Notation (DAWN)*. We call the extension *Event-and-State-based Temporal Logic (ESTL)*. ESTL can be used in the early design phases for formalizing informal event-based requirements as well as in the later phases to verify state-based properties. Actually, ESTL was inspired by informal requirements of the case study HDMS [3], where many informal requirements are event-based.

The emphasis of this paper is on the introduction of ESTL and the interpretation of its temporal operators on Petri nets. The basic idea is much clearer for low-level Petri nets than for high-level Petri nets. Therefore, we start with the definition of ESTL for Place/Transition-systems[1]. In a second step we present the extension of ESTL to *algebraic system nets* [6].

One feature of ESTL is that state-based formulas of DAWN preserve their meaning; this way proof rules of DAWN [7,18] are still valid. The new rules presented in this paper only provide a flavour of ESTL rules; they are by no means complete. A set of adequate proof rules for this new logic is still under development.

The paper is organized as follows. First, we demonstrate by means of an example that sometimes an event-based notation allows a more faithful formalization of informal requirements. Then, the basic definitions of nets and their runs will be introduced in Sect. 2. In Sect. 3 we introduce ESTL for Place/Transition-systems. In Sect. 4 we present some simple verification techniques which are applied to the example. Then, we turn to high-level nets. We introduce algebraic system nets and their runs in Sect. 5. At last, we extend ESTL to algebraic system nets in Sect. 6.

1 A Simple Example

In order to demonstrate the benefits of an event-based logic, we present a simple example. The example shown in Fig. 1(a) models the usual procedure to enter a foreign country. First, you take your passport and obtain a visa from the consulate of the foreign country. Only with this visa (e.g. stamped into your passport) you are allowed to enter the country. After some time you leave the

---

[1] This part of our work was already presented at PNSE '97 [8].

country. Note that we neglect the fact that a visa is usually valid only for a limited period of time.

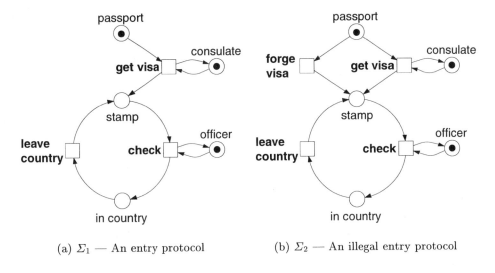

(a) Σ_1 — An entry protocol   (b) Σ_2 — An illegal entry protocol

Fig. 1. Two examples

Now, the required property of this procedure is that you may only enter the country if you have been at the consulate before and received your visa. Often, this property is implicitly formalized[2] in a state-based way by

$$\Sigma_1 \models \Box \text{ (in country } \rightarrow \Diamond \text{stamp)} \qquad (1)$$

Precisely, this formula means: Whenever (i.e. 'always' when) someone is in the country he must ('once') have had a stamp in his passport. This implicit formalization has a slight flaw. For example, consider the net model shown in Fig. 1(b); this system satisfies the state-based formal requirement, but does not satisfy the informal requirement — no country wants a forger to enter the country. So, in contrast to the informal requirement the formalization "permits" forgery because the temporal formula is valid for the net with the additional transition forge visa, too.

Therefore, we would like to have a notation which allows to explicitly express that someone who passes the control has got a legitimate visa before. To this end, we use an event-based temporal logic:

$$\Sigma_1 \models \Box \text{ (check } \rightarrow \Diamondtwo \text{ get visa)} \qquad (2)$$

---

[2] The temporal operators $\Box$ and $\Diamond$ read 'always' and 'once'; they will be formally introduced in Sect. 3.

In addition to the state-based logic, we also allow transitions in the expressions; moreover, we use different but related temporal operators.

In this paper we formally define the meaning of these formulas and show how the state-based logics of [13, 18] smoothly extend to an event-based logic. Note that we use different symbols for the 'same' temporal operators in the event-based version and the state-based version because we want to integrate both views in a single temporal logic. The use of different operators allows nesting of event-based and state-based temporal formulas. Moreover, purely state-based formulas have the same meaning as before.

Before formalizing this logic, let us consider the above example again. Why does the state-based formalization not capture the informal representation? The reason is that in the informal specification the activities are taken for granted and transitions inscribed by these activities (e.g. by get visa) are considered to be faithful. In contrast, the inscription of a place (e.g. stamp) is not faithful because it could be forged. If we would allow to inscribe the forge transition by get visa the event-based specification would turn out to be as useless as the state-based formalization! This shows that there is no absolute argument in favour of event-based approaches; actually below each event-based view you can find a state-based view again (on a lower level of abstraction) and vice versa. This shows that there is no lowest level of abstraction which is event-based or state-based. Fortunately, we are not looking for the lowest level of abstraction but for the most adequate level of abstraction. We argue that often an event-based view is adequate to start with.

2 Basic Definitions

In this section we introduce the prerequisites for a formal definition of the logic. We describe *Place/Transition-systems* (*P/T-systems*) and their non-sequential *runs*. The definitions mainly follow the lines of [11, 2]. Section 2.1 introduces P/T-systems along with some standard Petri net notations. Section 2.2 formalizes the runs of a Petri net and some related concepts.

2.1 Place/Transition-Systems

Readers familiar with Place/Transition-Systems can skim this section; the only restrictions imposed to the standard definition are that all arcs are (implicitly) inscribed by 1, the initial marking is finite, and all transitions have non-empty and finite presets and postsets.

Definition 1 (Net, P/T-system). *Let P and T be two disjoint sets and F be a relation, such that $F \subseteq (P \times T) \cup (T \times P)$. A triple $N = (P, T, F)$ is a net. The elements of P, T and F are called* places, transitions *and* arcs, *respectively.*

A net N is T-restricted *iff for each transition $t \in T$ there exist places $p, q \in P$, such that $(p, t) \in F$ and $(t, q) \in F$ hold. A net is* finitely-branching *iff for each transition $t \in T$ the set $\{p \in P : (p, t) \in F$ or $(t, p) \in F\}$ is finite.*

A function $M : P \to \mathbb{N}$ *is a* marking *of* N. *A pair* (N, M_0) *is a* P/T-system *iff* N *is a T-restricted and finitely-branching net and* M_0 *is a finite marking of* N.

As usual, places, transitions and arcs are graphically represented by circles, squares, and arrows, respectively. A marking is graphically represented by the corresponding number of black dots (so-called *tokens*) in a place.

Notation 1 *Let* $N = (P, T, F)$ *be a net. For short, we write* $x \in N$ *for* $x \in P \cup T$. *For* $x \in N$ *the* preset $^\bullet x$ *and the* postset $x^\bullet$ *are defined by* $^\bullet x = \{y \in N : (y, x) \in F\}$ *and* $x^\bullet = \{y \in N : (x, y) \in F\}$.

The minimal elements $^\circ N$ *and the* maximal elements N° *of a net* N *are defined by* $^\circ N = \{x \in N : {^\bullet x} = \emptyset\}$ *and* $N^\circ = \{x \in N : x^\bullet = \emptyset\}$.

A marking M_1 *is* included in *a marking* M_2, *denoted by* $M_1 \leqslant M_2$, *iff for each* $p \in P$ *holds* $M_1(p) \leq M_2(p)$. *Let* M_1 *and* M_2 *be markings of a net* N. *We define the* addition $M_1 + M_2$ *and, if* $M_2 \leqslant M_1$, *the* subtraction $M_1 - M_2$ *of markings elementwise.*

Where clear from the context, a set of places $Q \subseteq P$ also stands for the marking represented by the characteristic function of Q. This convention is used in the following definition for the preset $^\bullet t$ and the postset $t^\bullet$ of a transition t for defining the firing rule.

Definition 2 (Occurrence Rule). *Let* $N = (P, T, F)$ *be a net and* M *be a marking of* N. *A transition* $t \in T$ *is* enabled at M *iff* $^\bullet t \leqslant M$. *A transition* $t \in T$ *which is enabled at* M *may* occur, *leading to the* successor marking M', *which is defined by* $M' = (M - {^\bullet t}) + t^\bullet$. *A marking* M' *is* reachable *from a marking* M *iff there exists a finite (possibly empty) sequence of occurrences of transitions leading from* M *to* M'. *A marking* M *is a* reachable marking *of a P/T-system* (N, M_0) *iff it is reachable from* M_0.

2.2   Runs of P/T-systems

Up to now, we have defined the system model. Next, we will define the behaviour of a system in terms of its runs. We use non-sequential runs of P/T-systems as defined by Goltz and Reisig [5] for two reasons: First, non-sequential runs faithfully model concurrency. Second, in these runs the occurrence of both, places and transitions are represented in a natural way. Therefore, we can easily define a logic for events and states based on these runs.

We start with an example: Figure 2 shows a run of Σ_1. Informally, a run is an unwinding of the P/T-system, where conflicts are resolved. Technically, a run is an *occurrence net* (i.e. an acyclic and conflict-free net) equipped with a labelling which establishes the correspondence between the P/T-system and the occurrence net. For a detailed motivation of the technical definitions of a run we refer to [5, 2].

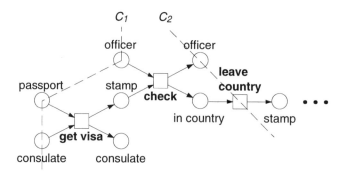

Fig. 2. R_1 — A run of Σ_1

Definition 3 (Occurrence Net). *A net $K = (B, E, \lessdot)$ is an* occurrence net *iff*

1. *for each $b \in B$ holds $|{}^\bullet b| \leq 1$ and $|b^\bullet| \leq 1$,*
2. *the transitive closure of $\lessdot$ (denoted by $<$ in the following) is acyclic, and*
3. *for each $x \in K$ the set of all predecessors of x (i.e. $\{y \in K : y < x\}$) is finite.*

A run of a P/T-system is an occurrence net together with a labelling function:

Definition 4 (Run). *Let $\Sigma = (N, M_0)$ be a P/T system with $N = (P, T, F)$. Moreover, let $K = (B, E, \lessdot)$ be an occurrence net and $\varrho : B \cup E \to P \cup T$ be a labelling function. For a set $X \subseteq B \cup E$ we denote the set $\{\varrho(x) : x \in X\}$ by $\varrho(X)$. The pair (K, ϱ) is a* run *of Σ iff*

1. *$\varrho(B) \subseteq P$ and $\varrho(E) \subseteq T$,*
2. *for each $p \in P$ holds $M_0(p) = |\{b \in {}^\circ K : \varrho(b) = p\}|$,*
3. *for each $e \in E$ the restrictions of ϱ to ${}^\bullet e$ and to $e^\bullet$ are injective; moreover we require ${}^\bullet \varrho(e) = \varrho({}^\bullet e)$ and $\varrho(e)^\bullet = \varrho(e^\bullet)$, and*
4. *for each $t \in T$ the condition ${}^\bullet t \subseteq \varrho(K^\circ)$ does not hold.*

A *cut* of a run (K, ϱ) is a maximal set of elements of K which are not ordered by $<$. In the example of Fig. 2, C_1 is the so-called *initial cut*. Since it consists of places only, we call it *state-cut*. The cut C_2 is no state-cut, since it contains the transition labelled by leave country.

Definition 5 (Cut, State-cut). *Let $K = (B, E, \lessdot)$ be an occurrence net. A set $Q \subseteq K$ is a* co-set *of K iff for each $q, r \in Q$ neither $q < r$ nor $r < q$ holds. A co-set Q is a* cut *of K iff Q is maximal, i.e. there exists no co-set $Q' \neq Q$ with $Q \subseteq Q'$. A cut Q is a* state-cut *iff $Q \subseteq B$. The set ${}^\circ K$ is the* initial cut *of K.*

Let C and C' be finite cuts of an occurrence net K. C' is reachable *from C, denoted by $C \preceq C'$, iff for each $c \in C$ there exists a $c' \in C'$, such that $c < c'$ or $c = c'$ holds.*

Note that the reachability $C \preceq C'$ of finite state-cuts in a run of a system corresponds to the reachability of the corresponding markings in the P/T-system. This can be easily seen; the proof, however, requires some technical effort (cf. [2]).

3 Properties of P/T-systems

Now, we will formalize the temporal operators which are already known from the introduction. The operators $\Box$, $\Diamond$, $\boxminus$, and $\Diamondminus$ are used in the usual meaning [10] and are read *always, eventually, so far,* and *once,* respectively. But, we interpret them on (non-sequential) runs as suggested in [13]. These operators refer to state-cuts only. In order to formalize event-based properties, we introduce a corresponding set of temporal operators $\boxdot$, $\Diamonddot$, $\boxdotminus$, and $\Diamonddotminus$, which are interpreted on arbitrary cuts. These operators read *every-time, sometime, every-time in the past,* and *sometime in the past,* respectively. One benefit of introducing two versions of temporal operators is that purely state-based formulas keep their original meaning.

3.1 Syntax

In the formal definition of the syntax, we only introduce the operators $\Diamond$, $\Diamondminus$, $\Diamonddot$, and $\Diamonddotminus$ because the other operators can be defined as dual versions. The atoms from which a system property can be built are the places and transitions of the P/T-system. A place in a system property indicates that the corresponding place occurs in the considered cut; a transition indicates that the transition occurs in the cut.

Definition 6 (System Property). *Let* $\Sigma = ((P, T, F), M_0)$ *be a P/T-system. The set of system properties* SP *is inductively defined by:*

1. *for each* $p \in P$ *holds* $p \in SP$,
2. *for each* $t \in T$ *holds* $t \in SP$,
3. *if* $\varphi \in SP$ *then* $\neg\varphi \in SP$,
4. *if* $\varphi, \psi \in SP$ *then* $(\varphi \vee \psi) \in SP$,
5. *if* $\varphi \in SP$ *then* $\Diamond\varphi \in SP$,
6. *if* $\varphi \in SP$ *then* $\Diamondminus\varphi \in SP$,
7. *if* $\varphi \in SP$ *then* $\Diamonddot\varphi \in SP$,
8. *if* $\varphi \in SP$ *then* $\Diamonddotminus\varphi \in SP$.

Notation 2 *The operators* $\wedge$ *and* $\rightarrow$ *are the usual abbreviations. The operators* $\Box\,\varphi$, $\boxdot\,\varphi$, $\boxminus\,\varphi$, *and* $\boxdotminus\,\varphi$ *are abbreviations (dual versions) for* $\neg\Diamond\neg\varphi$, $\neg\Diamonddot\neg\varphi$, $\neg\Diamondminus\neg\varphi$, *and* $\neg\Diamonddotminus\neg\varphi$, *respectively.*

3.2 Semantics

Now, we define the semantics of a *system property.* To this end, we define when a *system property* holds in a finite cut of a run. A P/T-system satisfies a system property, if the property holds in the *initial cut* of each run of the system.

Definition 7 (Validity of a System Property). *Let* $\Sigma = ((P, T, F), M_0)$ *be a P/T-system,* $R = (K, \varrho)$ *be a run of* Σ, *and* C *be a finite cut of* R. *We define the* validity of a system property *inductively as follows:*

1. $C \models p$ *iff* $p \in \varrho(C)$,
2. $C \models t$ *iff* $t \in \varrho(C)$,
3. $C \models \neg\varphi$ *iff* $C \models \varphi$ *does not hold,*
4. $C \models (\varphi \vee \psi)$ *iff* $C \models \varphi$ *or* $C \models \psi$ *holds,*
5. $C \models \Diamond\varphi$ *iff there exists a finite state-cut* C', *such that* $C \preceq C'$ *and* $C' \models \varphi$ *holds,*
6. $C \models \Diamond\hspace{-0.5em}\raise0.3ex\hbox{}\varphi$ *iff there exists a finite state-cut* C', *such that* $C' \preceq C$ *and* $C' \models \varphi$ *holds,*
7. $C \models \Diamond\hspace{-1.1em}\diamond\,\varphi$ *iff there exists a finite cut* C', *such that* $C \preceq C'$ *and* $C' \models \varphi$ *holds,*
8. $C \models \Diamond\hspace{-1.1em}\diamond\,\varphi$ *iff there exists a finite cut* C', *such that* $C' \preceq C$ *and* $C' \models \varphi$ *holds.*

A system property $\varphi \in SP$ *is* valid in run R *(denoted by* $R \models \varphi$*) iff* $^\circ K \models \varphi$ *holds, it is* valid in Σ *(denoted by* $\Sigma \models \varphi$*) iff* φ *is valid in all runs of* Σ.

Let us consider some examples of system properties:

$$\square \ (\textsf{passport} \ \vee \ \textsf{stamp} \ \vee \ \textsf{in country})$$

$$\boxdot \ (\textsf{passport} \ \vee \ \textsf{stamp} \ \vee \ \textsf{in country})$$

$$\boxdot \ (\textsf{passport} \ \vee \ \textsf{get visa} \ \vee \ \textsf{stamp} \ \vee \ \textsf{check} \ \vee \ \textsf{in country} \ \vee \ \textsf{leave country})$$

The first one and the third one are valid in R_1 and Σ_1 (see Fig. 2 and 1(a)), the second one is not valid in R_1 and Σ_1 because in R_1 there exists a cut (e. g. C_2) where no element is labelled by passport, stamp, or in country. Note that this is not a contradiction to the validity of the first property because the violating cut is no state-cut. So, the first and the second example show the essential difference between the operators $\square$ and $\boxdot$.

In the state-based logic the first property can be easily proven by help of a *place invariant* (e.g. [11]). This technique also works for the purely state-based formulas of the extended logic. The third property shows a generalization of the concept of place invariants; we add transitions to the formula which may occur 'between' two states.

The above definitions immediately imply the following rules:

Lemma 1. *Let* Σ *be a P/T-system and* $\varphi \in SP$ *a system property. Then we have:*

1. *If* $\Sigma \models \Diamond\varphi$ *then* $\Sigma \models \Diamond\hspace{-1.1em}\diamond\,\varphi$,
2. *If* $\Sigma \models \Diamond\hspace{-0.5em}\raise0.3ex\hbox{}\varphi$ *then* $\Sigma \models \Diamond\hspace{-1.1em}\diamond\,\varphi$,
3. *If* $\Sigma \models \square\varphi$ *then* $\Sigma \models \boxdot\varphi$,
4. *If* $\Sigma \models \boxdot\varphi$ *then* $\Sigma \models \boxdot\varphi$.

So far, the atoms of the temporal logic are quite simple; the only legal atoms are places and transitions. For more sophisticated applications more complex atoms are necessary. For example, we would like to write $p_1 + p_2 + p_3 = 1$ for places p_1, p_2, and p_3. It is straightforward to extend the language of legal atoms. We will introduce a suitable extension in Sect. 6 in the context of high-level nets. Here, we concentrated on the temporal operators.

4   Proof Rules

In this section we will provide some proof rules for system properties. Since the state-based fragment of the temporal logic is semantically equivalent to the purely state-based logic (cf. [10, 13, 18]) the corresponding rules are still valid. Therefore, we concentrate on rules for event-based properties and rules which relate both views. Still, we can only give some selected rules which are sufficient for our example.

The first proof rule is based on a simple observation: If a transition t occurs then its preset was marked before.

Proposition 1. *Let* $\Sigma = ((P, T, F), M_0)$ *be a P/T-system and* $t \in T$ *be a transition of* Σ. *Then we have*

$$\Sigma \models \square \left(t \to \diamondsuit \bigwedge_{p \in {}^\bullet t} p \right)$$

We can apply this rule to our introductory example (see Fig. 1(a)), with $t =$ check :

$$\Sigma_1 \models \square \left(\text{check} \to \diamondsuit (\text{officer} \wedge \text{stamp}) \right) \tag{3}$$

The second rule is based on the following observation: If we know that a currently marked place has been initially unmarked then a transition in its preset must have occurred before.

Proposition 2. *Let* $\Sigma = ((P, T, F), M_0)$ *be a P/T-system and* $p \in P$ *such that* $M_0(p) = 0$. *Then we have*

$$\Sigma \models \square \left(p \to \diamondsuit \bigvee_{t \in {}^\bullet p} t \right)$$

Now we will apply this rule to our example. We know that initially the place stamp is not marked. The application of rule 2 gives us:

$$\Sigma_1 \models \square \left(\text{stamp} \to \diamondsuit (\text{get visa} \vee \text{leave country}) \right) \tag{4}$$

From (3) and the standard weakening rule follows:

$$\Sigma_1 \models \square \left(\text{check} \to \diamondsuit \text{stamp} \right) \tag{5}$$

In combination with (4), Lemma 1.2, and a $\diamondsuit$-transitivity rule (e.g. [10], p. 265) follows:

$$\Sigma_1 \models \square \left(\text{check} \to \diamondsuit (\text{leave country} \vee \text{get visa}) \right) \tag{6}$$

An analogous application of rule 1 and rule 2 leads to the following property of Σ_1:

$$\Sigma_1 \models \square \left(\text{leave country} \rightarrow \lozenge \, \text{check} \right) \tag{7}$$

Let us consider properties (6) and (7) together. We know from Def. 3.3 that each occurrence of transition check has a finite history. Property (6) ensures that in the past there exists an event labelled by leave country or an event labelled by get visa. In the first case there exists another event labelled by check in its past (7). Because of the finite history there also exists an event labelled by get visa in its past. The following proof rule formalizes this observation. Note that this proof rule holds in a purely state-based proof system as well.

Proposition 3. *Let* $\Sigma = ((P,T,F), M_0)$ *be a P/T-system. Let* $\varphi, \psi, \chi \in SP$ *be system properties of* Σ. *If the conditions* $\Sigma \models \square \left(\varphi \rightarrow \lozenge \, (\psi \vee \chi) \right)$, $\Sigma \models \square \left(\chi \rightarrow \lozenge \, \varphi \right)$, *and* $\Sigma \models \square \neg (\varphi \wedge \chi)$ *hold, then the following holds, too:*

$$\Sigma \models \square \left(\varphi \rightarrow \lozenge \, \psi \right)$$

We can apply this proof rule to Σ_1: Let $\varphi = \text{check}$, $\chi = \text{leave country}$, and $\psi = \text{get visa}$. Properties (6) and (7) ensure the validity of the first two assumptions of rule 3. It remains to show

$$\Sigma_1 \models \square \neg (\text{check} \wedge \text{leave country}) \tag{8}$$

which can be proven by a generalization of place invariants, where also transitions are taken into account[3]. Now we can apply rule 3 which finishes the proof:

$$\Sigma_1 \models \square \left(\text{check} \rightarrow \lozenge \, \text{get visa} \right) \tag{9}$$

Though these rules are very restricted, they are sufficient to prove a slightly extended example. Consider the P/T-system Σ_3 in Fig. 3. Structurally, it would be possible for a criminal to forge a visa. Fortunately, there is no criminal. Therefore, the runs of Σ_1 and Σ_3 are the same. This means that the same system properties hold for Σ_1 and Σ_3, which is in particular true for property (2).

But how about a proof? Following analogous proof steps we obtain:

$$\Sigma_3 \models \square \left(\text{check} \rightarrow \lozenge \, (\text{get visa} \vee \text{forge visa}) \right) \tag{10}$$

---

[3] The generalization would read $\square$ (passport + get visa + stamp + check + in country + leave country = 1); but as we did not introduce these atoms, we do not formalize this rule either.

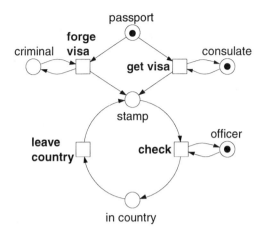

Fig. 3. Σ_3 — Another entry protocol

Furthermore, we can pick up the following property easily[4]:

$$\Sigma_3 \models \Box\ \neg\text{forge visa} \tag{11}$$

By the standard weakening rule we get:

$$\Sigma_3 \models \Box\ \left(\text{forge visa}\ \rightarrow \Diamond\!\!\!\!\Diamond\ \text{check}\right) \tag{12}$$

Together with (10) we can apply rule 3 again and we obtain (2).

The proof rules 1 and 2 allow verification of typical safety properties which occur in many case studies. Analogous proof rules for *leads-to* properties exist as well. Leads-to properties are particular liveness properties which are well suited for the specification of distributed algorithms ([14, 15, 18]). In terms of our temporal logic, leads-to properties are system properties of the form: $\Box\ \left(\varphi \rightarrow \Diamond\!\!\!\!\Diamond\ \psi\right)$. Here we show that a simple form of the *progress rule* from [13] can be decomposed into two even simpler rules: The first rule says that an enabled transition will either eventually occur or a transition in conflict will occur. The second rule says, whenever a transition occurs its postset will eventually be marked.

Proposition 4. *Let $\Sigma = ((P, T, F), M_0)$ be a P/T-system and $t \in T$. Then, the following holds:*

$$\Sigma \models \Box\ \left(\bigwedge_{p \in {}^\bullet t} p \rightarrow \Diamond\!\!\!\!\Diamond \bigvee_{t' \in ({}^\bullet t)^\bullet} t'\right) \qquad \Sigma \models \Box\ \left(t \rightarrow \Diamond \bigwedge_{p \in t^\bullet} p\right)$$

---

[4] Again, this follows from the generalized place invariant $\Box$ (criminal + forge visa = 0).

The two parts of this proposition resemble the *progress property* which guarantees that an activated transition either eventually occurs itself or it eventually becomes disabled by the occurrence of a conflicting transition.

5 Labelled Algebraic System Nets and Their Runs

Up to now, we have presented the essential ideas of ESTL. For clarity we used Place/Transition-systems and their runs. For real-world applications we need to deal with data. Therefore, we extend ESTL to high-level nets. We use algebraic system nets [6] and their runs, which will be defined in this section.

In the logic we do not only refer to different tokens on places, but to different occurrence modes of transitions. An explicit representation of modes in formulas, however, would require a syntactical representation of modes. We have chosen a different approach: We equip each transition with a term, which evaluates to some value in any mode. In the formulas we only refer to this value. We formalize this idea by labelled algebraic system nets, which will be defined in Sect. 5.2. Then, in Sect. 6 we will present ESTL and its interpretation on labelled algebraic system nets.

5.1 Prerequisites

We start with an informal introduction of some basic algebraic notions. A formal definition of these notions can be found in [6]. Readers familiar with algebraic specifications and algebraic Petri nets may skim this section; the concepts and notations are taken from [12, 6].

Bags In contrast to sets in *bags* multiple occurrences of elements are possible. For a set A we denote the *set of all bags over A* by $\mathbb{N}^A$. For an element a we denote the *number of occurrences of a* in a bag m by $m[a]$. If $m[a] = 0$ for all $a \in A$, then m is called *empty bag* and is denoted by $[\,]$.

Signatures and algebras A *signature* represents the syntactic structure of a class of algebras. Technically, a signature consists of a finite set of sort symbols and a family of operation symbols. For a signature SIG = (S, OP) a SIG-*algebra* $\mathcal{A} = ((A_s)_{s \in S}, (f_o)_{o \in OP})$ consists of a family of sets (domains) corresponding to the sort symbols and an operation for each operation symbol. A special sort symbol *bool* is assumed to be included in each signature. The corresponding domain in the algebra is $A_{bool} = \{true, false\}$.

Bag-algebras For the definition of our system model, from now on we only consider *bag-algebras*. Their corresponding *bag-signature* BSIG = $(S, OP, bs : S' \to S)$ is a signature, which contains for a certain set $S' \subseteq S$ of *ground-sorts* a set of *bag-sorts*. Furthermore there is a mapping bs, which assigns to each ground sort its corresponding bag-sort. For a signature SIG = (S, OP) and a bag-signature BSIG $= (S, OP, bs : S' \to S)$ a SIG-algebra is a BSIG-algebra, if for each $s \in S'$ holds $A_{bs(s)} = \mathbb{N}^{A_s}$; i.e. for each *ground domain* A_s the corresponding *bag domain* is actually a bag over A_s.

Variables and terms For a given bag-signature BSIG with sorts S a pairwise disjoint family $X = (X_s)_{s \in S}$ is called *variables* for BSIG. From these variables and the operation symbols of BSIG we can inductively build *terms* in the usual way. We denote the set of BSIG-terms with variables X and sort s by $\mathbf{T}_s^{\mathrm{BSIG}}(X)$. The set of all terms (of any sort) is denoted by $\mathbf{T}^{\mathrm{BSIG}}(X)$.

Assignments and evaluations Let $\mathcal{A}$ be an BSIG-algebra with a domain $A = (A_s)_{s \in S}$. Values from the corresponding domain can be assigned to variables. Formally, an *assignment* $\beta : X \to A$ is a mapping, such that the sort of each variable corresponds to the domain of the value. The *set of all possible assignments* is denoted by $\mathrm{ASS}(X, A)$. For a given assignment, a term can be evaluated to a value of the domain of the algebra. Remember, that this value can be a bag as described above. An *evaluation* is defined inductively over the structure of a term in the usual way. Formally, for an assignment β an evaluation $\overline{\beta}$ is a mapping $\overline{\beta} : \mathbf{T}^{\mathrm{BSIG}}(X) \to A$. Note that there exists only one evaluation if the set X is empty: By this uniquely defined evaluation each ground term is assigned a value of the algebra. We denote this evaluation by *eval*.

5.2 Algebraic system nets

Before we formally define algebraic system nets let us give an example: Consider the labelled algebraic system net Σ_4 in Fig. 4.

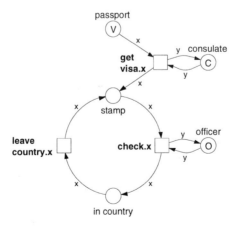

Fig. 4. Σ_4 — a labelled algebraic system net

The system models the procedure to enter a foreign country which was already described in Sect. 1. The main difference is that here we model the behaviour of a set of persons V (voyagers). Moreover, we have a set of different consulates C, e.g. at different locations. Finally, we also have a certain set of officers O at the border of the country.[5]

In Sect. 1 we have already formulated the property that someone who enters a country has got a visa before. When formalizing this property for Σ_4 we take advantage of the fact that the transitions of Σ_4 are *labelled*. This allows us to abstract from certain *modes* in which a transition may occur: For instance, in our system we are interested in the passport of the person who enters a foreign country but not in the officer who checks the visa. The person who enters the country is assigned to the variable x in each occurrence of transition check. The actual officer assigned to the variable y is not important for the correctness of the protocol. We denote this by the transition labelling check.x.

The desired property now reads as follows:

$$\Sigma_4 \models \square \, (\text{check}.x \to \diamondsuit \, \text{get visa}.x) \tag{13}$$

In order to make this more precise, we define *algebraic system nets* and their *runs*.

Definition 8 (Algebraic System Net). *Let* $\text{BSIG} = (S, OP, bs)$ *be a bag-signature with ground-sorts* S'. *Let* $\mathcal{A}$ *be a* BSIG*-algebra. Let* X *be a set of* BSIG*-variables. Let* $N = (P, T, F)$ *be a net. Let* $d : P \to S'$ *and* $g : T \to \mathbf{T}^{\text{BSIG}}_{bool}(X)$ *be mappings. Let* $\omega : F \to \mathbf{T}^{\text{BSIG}}(X)$ *be a mapping, such that for each* $f \in F$ *with* $f = (p, t)$ *or* $f = (t, p)$ *holds* $\omega(f) \in \mathbf{T}^{\text{BSIG}}_{bs(d(p))}(X)$. *Furthermore, let* $m_0 : P \to$ $\mathbf{T}^{\text{BSIG}}(\emptyset)$ *be a mapping, such that for each* $p \in P$ *holds* $m_0(p) \in \mathbf{T}^{\text{BSIG}}_{bs(d(p))}$.

Then, $\Sigma = (N, \mathcal{A}, X, d, \omega, g; m_0)$ *is an* algebraic system net.

In the above definition the mapping d denotes the sorts of places and the mapping g denotes the transition guards. If for a transition t the transition guard $g(t)$ is not given explicitly, we assume $g(t) = true$. The mapping ω denotes the arc inscriptions and m_0 is the symbolic initial marking.

A *marking* assigns to each place of an algebraic system net a bag of the corresponding domain of the algebra:

Definition 9 (Marking of an Algebraic System Net). *Let* Σ *be an algebraic system net as in Def. 8. A* marking $M : P \to \mathbb{N}^A$ *is a mapping such that for each place* $p \in P$ *holds* $M(p) \in \mathbb{N}^{A_{d(p)}}$. *The marking* M_0 *with* $M_0(p) = eval(m_0(p))$ *is called the* initial marking *of* Σ.

In order to formalize the tokens consumed and produced by a transition in some mode we define the following markings. For each transition t *and each*

---

[5] Note that here we still model one (not further specified) country.

assignment β we define $^-t_\beta$ and t_β^+ by:

$$^-t_\beta(p) = \begin{cases} \overline{\beta}(\omega(p,t)) & \text{for } (p,t) \in F \\ [\,] & \text{for } (p,t) \notin F \end{cases} \qquad t_\beta^+(p) = \begin{cases} \overline{\beta}(\omega(t,p)) & \text{for } (t,p) \in F \\ [\,] & \text{for } (t,p) \notin F \end{cases}$$

for each $p \in P$. Then, $^-t_\beta$ denotes the tokens consumed by transition t in mode β and t_β^+ denotes the tokens produced by t in mode β.

5.3 Labelled algebraic system nets

In labelled algebraic system nets we assign a label to each transition. This allows to argue about certain aspects of occurrence modes of transitions, as described in the previous example.

Definition 10 (Labelled Algebraic System Net). *Let Σ be an algebraic system net over a bag-signature BSIG. Let L be some fixed set of labels. Let $l : T \to L \times \mathbf{T}^{\mathrm{BSIG}}(X)$ be a mapping. Then, (Σ, l) is a labelled algebraic system net.*

Figure 4 shows a labelled algebraic system net. Note that we omit the transition names in the graphical representation of a labelled algebraic system net; we just give the labels of the transitions. Furthermore, we write $u.a$ for a transition mapping $l(t) = (u, a)$. In our example the set of labels and the set of transitions of the net are the same. But, there are situations when different transitions should have the same label. In examples we write Σ instead of (Σ, l), if the labelling is clear from the graphical representation.

5.4 Runs of labelled algebraic system nets

In a run of an algebraic system net each place of the underlying occurrence net is associated with a place of the algebraic system net together with an element of the corresponding domain. Each transition of the underlying occurrence net is associated with a transition of the algebraic system net together with a corresponding occurrence mode.

Definition 11 (Σ-inscription). *Let Σ be an algebraic system net over a bag-signature BSIG. Let $K = (B, E, \lessdot)$ be an occurrence net. Let $r_B : B \to P \times A$ be a mapping, such that for each $b \in B$ with $r_B(b) = (p, a)$ holds $a \in A_{d(p)}$.*

For a given mapping r_B each subset $Q \subseteq B$ can be associated with a marking. We denote this marking by $r_B(Q)$. We define it by $r_B(Q) : P \to \mathbb{N}^A$ with[6] $r_B(Q)(p)[a] = |\{b \in Q : r_B(b) = (p, a)\}|$.

Let $r_E : E \to T \times \mathrm{ASS}(X, A)$ be a mapping. The pair $r = (r_B, r_E)$ is called a Σ-inscription of K.

---

[6] $|A|$ denotes the cardinality of a set A.

In the graphical representation of a Σ-inscribed occurrence net we omit the inscriptions of the transitions. The inscription (p, a) of a place will be written $p.a$.

An occurrence net together with a Σ-inscription and a transition labelling is a *run of a labelled algebraic system net*, if the initial state of the occurrence net corresponds to the initial marking of the algebraic system net and the labelling of the transitions of the occurrence net corresponds to the labelling of the transitions in the algebraic system net.

Definition 12 (Runs of Labelled Algebraic System Nets). *Let (Σ, l) be a labelled algebraic system net, $K = (B, E, <)$ be an occurrence net, and $r = (r_B, r_E)$ be a Σ-inscription of K.*

Let $l' : E \to L \times A$ be a mapping, such that

1. $r_B(^\circ K) = M_0$
2. *for each $e \in E$ with $r_E(e) = (t, \beta)$ and $l(t) = (c, u)$ holds $\overline{\beta}(g(t)) = true$, $r_B(^\bullet t) = {}^- t_\beta$, $r_B(t^\bullet) = t_\beta^+$, and $l'(c) = (c, \overline{\beta}(u))$.*

Then (K, r, l') is a run of the labelled algebraic system net (Σ, l).

Figure 5 shows a run of Σ_4 for a concrete algebra where the sets V, C, and O are given by $\{v1, v2\}$, $\{c1, c2\}$, and $\{o1\}$, respectively.

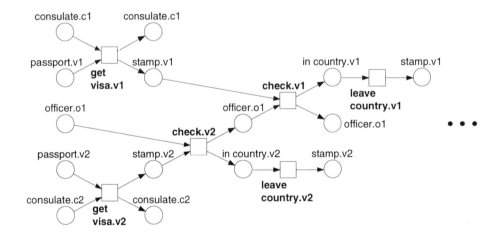

Fig. 5. R_2 — a run of Σ_4

The introduction of labels in algebraic system nets seems to break the duality of places and transitions. The run of Fig. 5, however, shows that actually the labels of transitions re-establish the duality — in a run places and transitions are both inscribed by a pair, where the second component of this pair is some element of the algebra. Without labels, transitions would be inscribed by some mode.

6 Properties of Labelled Algebraic System Nets

Now, we show how to express properties of algebraic system nets. First, we introduce some basic expressions, which correspond to the names of places and transitions in the specification of the properties of P/T-systems. Next, we extend the set of *algebraic system properties* by some logical and temporal operators. Most of them are already known from Sect. 3. Additionally, we have the quantifiers ∀ and ∃.

From now on, we extend every algebra A implicitly by the following operators. $.[.] : \mathbb{N}^A \times A \to \mathbb{N}$ denotes the multiplicity of an element in a bag. $. + . : \mathbb{N}^A \times \mathbb{N}^A \to \mathbb{N}^A$ denotes the (elementwise) addition of two bags. We also include the operators $. \geq . : \mathbb{N}^A \times \mathbb{N}^A \to bool$ and $. = . : \mathbb{N}^A \times \mathbb{N}^A \to bool$, which compare elementwise two bags in the usual way. Next, we extend every algebra by $\mathbb{N}$ together with the usual operations on $\mathbb{N}$. At last, we extend our set of variables. From now on, a place $p \in P$ is a variable of sort $bs(d(p))$. This way, we have $p[a] \geq 1 \in \mathbf{T}_{bool}^{\mathrm{BSIG}}(X \cup P)$ for $p \in P$ and $a \in A_{d(p)}$.

Definition 13 (ESTL for Algebraic System Nets). *Let (Σ, l) be a labelled algebraic system net over a bag-signature BSIG. Let P, L, and X be the set of places, labels, and variables of (Σ, l), respectively. The set of* algebraic system properties *ASP is inductively defined as follows:*

1. $\mathbf{T}_{bool}^{\mathrm{BSIG}}(X \cup P) \subseteq ASP$,
2. *if* $\mathsf{v} \in L$ *and* $o \in \mathbf{T}^{\mathrm{BSIG}}(X)$ *then* $\mathsf{v}.o \in ASP$,
3. *if* $\varphi \in ASP$ *then* $\neg\varphi \in ASP$,
4. *if* $\varphi, \psi \in ASP$ *then* $(\varphi \vee \psi) \in ASP$,
5. *if* $\varphi \in ASP$ *and* $x \in X$ *then* $(\exists x : \varphi) \in ASP$,
6. *if* $\varphi \in ASP$ *then* $\Diamond\varphi \in ASP$,
7. *if* $\varphi \in ASP$ *then* $\diamondsuit\varphi \in ASP$,
8. *if* $\varphi \in ASP$ *then* $\diamondsuit\varphi \in ASP$,
9. *if* $\varphi \in ASP$ *then* $\diamondsuit\varphi \in ASP$.

Notation 3 *We use the same abbreviations as in Not. 2. Furthermore, we write $p(o)$ for $p[o] \geq 1$ and we write $(\forall x : \varphi)$ for $\neg(\exists x : \neg\varphi)$.*

Now, we show some examples of properties for Σ_4: $\square \left(\mathsf{check}.x \to \diamondsuit \mathsf{get\ visa}.x \right)$ describes the property that someone who enters a country has got a visa before. The property $\square \left(\mathsf{officer}(o1) \vee (\exists x : \mathsf{check}.x) \right)$ describes the behaviour of officer $o1$ in our protocol: He is either in his ground state or there exists some person who is entering the country. The property $\square (\mathsf{passport} + \mathsf{stamp} + \mathsf{in\ country} = V)$ is an example for a place invariant.

For defining the meaning of the above formulas, we first extend the definition of an evaluation in a way that we can interpret place-variables.

382

Definition 14 (Assignment of Place-variables). *Let $\beta \in \mathrm{ASS}(X,A)$ be an assignment. Let $M : P \to A$ be a marking. We define an assignment $\beta_M : X \cup P \to A$ as follows:*

1. *For each $x \in X$ holds $\beta_M(x) = \beta(x)$,*
2. *For each $p \in P$ holds $\beta_M(p) = M(p)$.*

As mentioned before, β_M extends to an evaluation $\overline{\beta}_M : \mathbf{T}^{\mathrm{BSIG}}(X \cup P) \to A$ canonically over the structure of the terms.

Now we define the semantics of algebraic system properties:

Definition 15 (Semantics of ESTL). *Let (Σ, l) be a labelled algebraic system net over a bag-signature BSIG. Let $R = (K, r, l')$ with $K = (B, E, <)$ be a run of (Σ, l) and C be a finite cut of R. The validity of an algebraic system property under an assignment $\beta \in \mathrm{ASS}(X,A)$ is inductively defined as follows:*

1. *for each $u \in \mathbf{T}^{\mathrm{BSIG}}_{bool}(X \cup P)$ holds $(C,\beta) \models u$ iff $\overline{\beta}_{r(B \cap C)}(u) = true$,*
2. *$(C,\beta) \models \mathsf{v}.o$ iff there exists an $e \in E \cap C$, such that $l'(e) = \left(\mathsf{v}, \overline{\beta}(o)\right)$,*
3. *$(C,\beta) \models \neg\varphi$ iff $(C,\beta) \models \varphi$ does not hold,*
4. *$(C,\beta) \models (\varphi \vee \psi)$ iff $(C,\beta) \models \varphi$ or $(C,\beta) \models \psi$ holds,*
5. *$(C,\beta) \models (\exists x : \varphi)$ iff there exists an assignment $\beta' \in \mathrm{ASS}(X,A)$, such that $(C,\beta') \models \varphi$ holds and for all $y \in X \setminus \{x\}$ holds $\beta'(y) = \beta(y)$,*
6. *$(C,\beta) \models \Diamond\varphi$ iff there exists a finite state-cut C', such that $C \preceq C'$ and $(C',\beta) \models \varphi$ holds,*
7. *$(C,\beta) \models \Diamond\!\!\!\!\!-\,\varphi$ iff there exists a finite state-cut C', such that $C' \preceq C$ and $(C',\beta) \models \varphi$ holds,*
8. *$(C,\beta) \models \lozenge\!\!\!\!\diamond\,\varphi$ iff there exists a finite cut C', such that $C \preceq C'$ and $(C',\beta) \models \varphi$ holds,*
9. *$(C,\beta) \models \lozenge\!\!\!\!\diamond\,\varphi$ iff there exists a finite cut C', such that $C' \preceq C$ and $(C',\beta) \models \varphi$ holds.*

An algebraic system property $\varphi \in ASP$ is valid in a finite cut C, denoted by $C \models \varphi$ iff for each $\beta \in \mathrm{ASS}(X,A)$ holds $(C,\beta) \models \varphi$, it is valid in the run R iff $^{\circ}K \models \varphi$ holds, and it is valid in the labelled algebraic system net (Σ, l) iff it is valid in all runs of (Σ, l).

The previous examples hold in Σ_4:

$$\Sigma_4 \models \Box \left(\mathsf{check}.x \to \lozenge\!\!\!\!\diamond\,\mathsf{get\ visa}.x\right)$$

$$\Sigma_4 \models \Box \left(\mathsf{officer}(o1) \vee (\exists x : \mathsf{check}.x)\right)$$

$$\Sigma_4 \models \Box\,(\mathsf{passport} + \mathsf{stamp} + \mathsf{in\ country} = V)$$

In this paper, we have introduced two versions of ESTL; one for P/T-systems and one for algebraic system nets. A P/T-system, however, can be considered as a special algebraic system net, where the domain of each place is the set $\{\bullet\}$ and the arc-inscriptions are [•]. Similarly, we can consider the ESTL-formulas for P/T-systems as abbreviations: A place symbol p is an abbreviation for $p(\bullet)$ and a transition symbol t is an abbreviation for $t.\bullet$. This way, there is no need for P/T-systems and a P/T-version of ESTL. The reason for introducing ESTL for P/T-systems, first, was its clearness. We did not want to obscure the essential ideas of ESTL by technical details of the high-level approach.

Proof rules for algebraic system nets. Now, we have extended ESTL to algebraic system nets. But, we have not presented any proof rules. However, Lemma 1 and Proposition 3 immediately hold for ESTL on algebraic system nets, too. Since all temporal formulas of DAWN keep their meaning in ESTL, all rules of DAWN (e.g. [7, 18]) are also valid for ESTL. Nevertheless, a set of rules particularly designed for ESTL is still missing; this is subject of further research.

7 Conclusion

In this paper we have extended DAWN, a state-based temporal logic for Petri nets, by events which we call ESTL. ESTL enjoys almost the same balance between events and states as Petri nets themselves. Therefore, ESTL is equally well suited for formalizing requirements from both, the state-based view and the event-based view, and provides a smooth transition between them. This feature allows a smooth transition between different system development phases.

The need for a temporal logic which covers both, event-based and state-based properties, occurred in a practical application. The main contribution of this paper is an adequate definition of such a logic. Adequacy is justified by two facts: first, by the immediate translation of informal event-based requirements into formal ones; second, by the smooth integration into an existing state-based temporal logic, which allows to use a bunch of already known verification techniques.

The proof rules presented in this paper can only give a flavour of possible rules. A complete set of proof rules is subject to further research. More case studies must demonstrate its usefulness and that ESTL can actually cover all phases of system development.

References

1. Wil van der Aalst. Three good reasons for using a Petri-net-based workflow management system. In S. Navathe and T. Wakayama, editors, *Proceedings of the International Working Conference on Information and Process Integration in Enterprises*, pages 179–201, Cambridge, Massachusetts, 1996.
2. Eike Best and César Fernández. *Nonsequential Processes, EATCS Monographs on Theoretical Computer Science* 13. Springer-Verlag, 1988.

3. Felix Cornelius, Heinrich Hußmann, and Michael Löwe. The KORSO case study for software engineering with formal methods: A medical information system. In M. Broy and S. Jähnichen, editors, *KORSO: Methods, Languages, and Tools for the Construction of Correct Software, LNCS* 1009, pages 417–445. Springer-Verlag, 1995.

4. Claudia Ermel, Magdalena Gajewsky, Tobias Vesper, and Michael Weber. Verifikation strukturierter Netze. In H. Weber, H. Ehrig, and W. Reisig, editors, *Move-On-Workshop, DFG-Forschergruppe Petri Net Technology.* Technical University Berlin, 1997.

5. Ursula Goltz and Wolfgang Reisig. The non-sequential behaviour of Petri nets. *Information and Control,* 57:125–147, 1983.

6. Ekkart Kindler and Wolfgang Reisig. Algebraic system nets for modelling distributed algorithms. *Petri Net Newsletter,* 51:16–31, 1996.

7. Ekkart Kindler, Wolfgang Reisig, Hagen Völzer, and Rolf Walter. Petri net based verification of distributed algorithms: An example. *Formal Aspects of Computing,* 9:409–424, 1997.

8. Ekkart Kindler and Tobias Vesper. A temporal logic for events and states in Petri nets. In B. Farwer, D. Moldt, and M.-O. Stehr, editors, *Petri Nets in System Engineering,* pages 101–110, Hamburg, 1997.

9. David A. Marca and Clement L. McGowan. *SADT: Structured Analysis and Design Technique.* McGraw-Hill, 1988.

10. Zohar Manna and Amir Pnueli. *The Temporal Logic of Reactive and Concurrent Systems. Specification.* Springer-Verlag, 1992.

11. Wolfgang Reisig. *Petri Nets, EATCS Monographs on Theoretical Computer Science* 4. Springer-Verlag, 1985.

12. Wolfgang Reisig. Petri nets and algebraic specifications. *Theoretical Computer Science,* 80:1–34, 1991.

13. Wolfgang Reisig. Petri net models of distributed algorithms. In J. van Leeuven, editor, *Computer Science Today: Recent Trends and Developments, LNCS* 1000, pages 441–454. Springer-Verlag, Berlin, 1995.

14. Wolfgang Reisig. Interleaved progress, concurrent progress, and local progress. In D.A. Peled, V.R. Pratt, and G.J. Holzmann, editors, *Partial Order Methods in Verification, DIMACS Series in Discrete Mathematics and Theoretical Computer Science* 29, pages 99–115. AMS, 1997.

15. Wolfgang Reisig. *Elements of Distributed Algorithms. Modeling and Analysis with Petri Nets.* In preparation, Springer-Verlag, 1998.

16. Douglas T. Ross. Structured Analysis (SA): A language for communicating ideas. *IEEE Software Engineering Transactions,* 3(1):16–37, January 1977.

17. Antonia Sinachopoulos. Temporal logics of elementary net systems. Arbeitspapiere der GMD 353, 1988.

18. Michael Weber, Rolf Walter, Hagen Völzer, Tobias Vesper, Wolfgang Reisig, Sibylle Peuker, Ekkart Kindler, Jörn Freiheit, and Jörg Desel. DAWN: Petrinetzmodelle zur Verifikation Verteilter Algorithmen. Informatik-Bericht 88, Humboldt-University Berlin, December 1997.

Author Index

Springer
and the
environment

At Springer we firmly believe that an international science publisher has a special obligation to the environment, and our corporate policies consistently reflect this conviction.

We also expect our business partners – paper mills, printers, packaging manufacturers, etc. – to commit themselves to using materials and production processes that do not harm the environment. The paper in this book is made from low- or no-chlorine pulp and is acid free, in conformance with international standards for paper permanency.

Lecture Notes in Computer Science

For information about Vols. 1–1348

please contact your bookseller or Springer-Verlag